DATE DUE

Cold War

Cold War

THE ESSENTIAL REFERENCE GUIDE

James R. Arnold and Roberta Wiener, Editors

ABC-CLIO

Santa Barbara, California • Denver, Colorado • Oxford, England

Copyright 2012 by ABC-CLIO, LLC

Library of Congress Cataloging-in-Publication Data

Cold War : the essential reference guide / James R. Arnold and Roberta Wiener, editors.
    p. cm.
  Includes index.
  ISBN 978-1-61069-003-4 (hardcopy : alk. paper) — ISBN 978-1-61069-004-1 (ebook)
1. Cold War—Encyclopedias. 2. World politics—1945–1989—
Encyclopedias. I. Arnold, James R., 1952– II. Wiener, Roberta, 1952–
  D840.C645   2012
  909.82'503—dc23   2011028418

ISBN: 978-1-61069-003-4
EISBN: 978-1-61069-004-1

16   15   14   13   12   1   2   3   4   5

This book is also available on the World Wide Web as an eBook.
Visit www.abc-clio.com for details.

ABC-CLIO, LLC
130 Cremona Drive, P.O. Box 1911
Santa Barbara, California 93116-1911

This book is printed on acid-free paper ∞

Manufactured in the United States of America

Contents

PRIMARY SOURCE DOCUMENTS

Overview of the Cold War

The Cold War was as much an ideological battle as it was a military struggle. Although the origins of the conflict can be traced as far back as the November 1917 Russian Revolution, the Cold War began to take form in late 1945. It did not formally end until December 1991. Simply put, the Cold War can be defined as a state of mutual hostility, distrust, and rivalry between the United States and the Soviet Union. This contest soon pitted the capitalist West—and its allies around the world—against the communist-controlled East and its allies throughout the world. A large part of the Cold War "battle" involved competing political and economic ideologies. The capitalist West generally represented popularly elected, multiparty governments that supported individual rights and a free-market economy in which government control was limited. The emphasis was on individual initiative, personal and collective rights, and private property. Though some pro-Western governments were in reality not very democratic, they usually subscribed to some form of capitalism. The communist East advocated vastly different governmental and economic systems. Nearly all communist regimes were controlled by a single political party, which exercised strict control over individual rights and political participation. Communist economies were tightly regulated by the central government, and most private property was

forbidden. The idea of individual initiative was alien. Instead, the emphasis was on collective collaboration among the population. Thus, the Cold War symbolized two completely different ways of life.

Hot Wars within the Cold War

Although the Soviet Union and United States never engaged in direct military action against one another, the Cold War was marked by a series of both small and large wars. These conflicts were fought in almost every corner of the world. In most cases, the West backed one side while the East supported the other. In addition to the many small wars, the Cold War featured three major and prolonged conflicts: the Korean War (1950–1953), the Vietnam War (1946–1975), and the war in Afghanistan (1979–1989). The Cold War was also a period that witnessed a massive arms race and the rise of permanent and powerful defense industries. Many historians have pointed out that the Cold War "militarized" everyday life in both the East and the West. The world's major powers spent trillions of dollars on large standing armies and advanced weaponry. And unlike more conventional conflicts, which have fairly distinct beginning and end points, the Cold War endured for more than four decades. Each side was therefore obliged to arm itself to fight a large-scale, worldwide war for a seemingly indefinite period of time. Perpetual military readiness became a Cold War watchword.

Both national and international politics were affected by the Cold War. In many industrialized Western nations, the politics of anticommunism resulted in periodic civil liberty violations and overzealous attempts to suppress or outlaw communist or leftist organizations. As such, political freedom was sometimes diminished. Oftentimes, Western nations—particularly the United States—supported repressive and undemocratic governments abroad so long as they were anticommunist. This was especially the case in the developing world (particularly Latin America, Africa, and Asia). In the communist nations, the insistence on

a singular political-economic philosophy brought with it periodic crackdowns against those who dared to think or act differently. Sometimes this manifested itself as internal repression, as was the case during the Cultural Revolution in the People's Republic of China (PRC) in the late 1960s. At other times it brought external repression, as was the case when the Soviet Union crushed the 1956 Hungarian Revolution and the Prague Spring of 1968. Finally, the process of decolonization was profoundly influenced by Cold War politics. Conflicting ideologies forced many newly independent countries to choose one system or the other—capitalism or communism. Doing so could cause political instability, economic crisis, and even civil war in these fledgling nations.

Hungarians gather around the fallen statue of communist leader Josef Stalin in front of the National Theater in Budapest on October 24, 1956. The statue, pulled down the previous day by anticommunist demonstrators, was later smashed to pieces. The short-lived revolt against Soviet rule ended by November 4, 1956. (AP/Wide World Photos)

Causes of the Cold War

Immediate Causes

Because ideology was part of an all-encompassing zero-sum game, conflict and competition touched virtually every issue in the immediate post–World War II period. The Cold War was as much a fight over ideas and principles as it was a military confrontation. Long-standing mutual suspicions between East and West were made worse by the advent of the nuclear age in 1945, which greatly complicated superpower relations. Both the Americans and the Soviets sought to exploit the power vacuums that resulted from World War II. This occurred not only in Europe, but in Asia, Africa, and the Middle East as well. They also took advantage of severe economic dislocations to convince various populations to embrace their particular politico-economic systems. Finally, individual personalities and differing leadership styles must be factored into any study of Cold War developments. The "human factor" cannot be ignored in historical analysis.

Opposing Ideologies

During World War II, the United States, Soviet Union, Great Britain, and the other Allied nations put aside their considerable ideological differences and temporarily united to defeat the Axis nations. When the war ended in 1945, however, conflict among the Allies flared because the common enemy had been defeated. The Soviets sought to introduce their brand of communism to nations and territories that they occupied as a result of the war. They also hoped to strengthen communist parties in various Western nations—in Italy, Greece, and France for example—and perhaps even "convert" populations there to communist political and economic ideology. In short, the Soviet Union envisioned spreading its system of authoritarian, one-party rule and government-controlled economy to any nation in which it had influence. Furthermore, communist ideology regarded capitalism as the enemy, a grave peril that was to be countered vigorously. Believing that capitalism's primary goal was to expand, the Soviets saw in their opponents both ideological and physical threats.

The United States and the other Western European nations viewed communism and one-party rule in a very negative light. They were turned off by its undemocratic political system and its emphasis on a government-run economy in which personal initiative and property were forbidden. In addition, they perceived communist ideology that called for a worldwide revolution against capitalism as a direct threat to individual freedom and democracy. Instead, the West believed the future belonged to multiparty, democratic capitalism and, like the Soviets, tried to export that ideology wherever it could. This struggle between two opposing ways of life contributed significantly to the development of the Cold War. As long as East and West conceived of their rivalry in such stark and ideological ways, conflict was virtually guaranteed.

East–West ideological differences soon manifested themselves in Germany, which was split into western and eastern occupation zones in 1945. Soviet leader Josef Stalin hoped to unite Germany under a pro-Soviet government that would be loyal to communist ideals and serve as a buffer zone between East and West. He also demanded a harsh and punitive peace with the Germans. Among other things, Stalin sought huge war reparation payments and the dismantlement of German industry, which would be reassembled in the Soviet Union. The Americans, British, and French wanted a free and democratic Germany that would be reintegrated into the capitalist West. They opposed large reparations and Germany's deindustrialization, fearing that this would permanently cripple Germany and even reignite militarism there. The clash over Germany became irreconcilable, and the country was soon divided between East and West, a division that lasted until 1990.

The Atomic Bomb

In 1945, the United States was the only nation in the world to possess atomic bombs. Efforts by the British and Americans to develop such weapons had specifically excluded the Soviet Union. The Soviets certainly knew about the atomic bomb program (known as the Manhattan Project) through espionage activities and were upset that their allies had tried to keep the technology a secret. Beginning in 1944, the British and American governments cracked the Soviets' encrypted top-secret messages in Project

VENONA. Soon thereafter, the West became aware of an extensive Soviet spy ring. Clearly, the Soviets had channeled their espionage activities toward gathering information on the atomic bomb. By 1950, the arrests of Klaus Fuchs, Alger Hiss, and Julius and Ethel Rosenberg in both Britain and the United States offered clear evidence of Soviet infiltration of the Manhattan Project and subsequent nuclear weapons programs.

Soviet leaders were understandably suspicious of Western motives. They concluded that the American atomic monopoly might be used to force them to make concessions against their will or even compel them to cede control in areas over which they already had charge. They were especially worried that the United States might use its atomic might to push them out of Eastern Europe, creating a serious security problem along their western border. Furthermore, periodic right-wing political rhetoric in the United States gave the Soviets a reason to fear the atomic monopoly on a personal security level. A few hawkish lawmakers in Congress publicly advocated using atomic bombs against the Soviet Union in a preemptive war that would, they argued, get rid of the communist menace for good.

Strategic Imperatives and Power Vacuums

The power vacuums that resulted from World War II ensured that both East and West would rush in to fill the void. As a result of Allied war strategy during World War II, Soviet troops occupied all of Eastern Europe by 1945. Almost immediately, the Americans and Soviets were sharply divided over what type of governments would rule in Eastern Europe, particularly in Poland and Germany. The Soviets established pro-Soviet communist regimes in much of the region, to the dismay of American leaders. In the February

1945 Allied Declaration on Liberated Europe, the Americans, British, and Soviets had pledged to support free elections and self-rule throughout Eastern Europe. When the war ended, however, American policymakers quickly asserted that the Soviets had broken this agreement. But there was little they could do to change the situation because a huge contingent of Soviet troops had already secured much of the region. Indeed, they occupied all of Poland and Czechoslovakia and much of Austria, Hungary, Romania, Bulgaria, and Yugoslavia.

In Germany itself, East and West differed dramatically over how to treat the defeated enemy. The Soviets controlled eastern Germany and were already in a strategic position to dictate its future. The Soviets fortified the Communist Party in eastern Germany with the help of German communists trained in the Soviet Union under Moscow's careful guidance. In the end, Germany would be permanently divided during the Cold War, as West Germany was integrated into the Western orbit and East Germany fell into the Soviet orbit.

Power vacuums in other areas of the world meant that the Soviets and Americans would also try to impose their influence in vanquished territories. In Asia, for example, the United States insisted on complete control over Japan. The Soviet Union, on the other hand, wielded influence in nearby northern Korea and supported communist forces in China. World War II loosened French, British, and other colonial powers' ties to their overseas possessions. Thus, large swaths of Africa and Southeast Asia became Cold War battlegrounds. And as decolonization progressed throughout Africa, Asia, and the Middle East, both sides sought to achieve a strategic edge by gaining a foothold in newly independent countries. They even supported anticolonial movements in regions where they sought strategic dominance.

Economics

World War II wrought widespread devastation throughout Europe. This war—more than any other in history—visited unprecedented hardship on civilians and their property. Millions of Europeans were susceptible to indoctrination by both the Soviets and Americans, who offered very different prescriptions for postwar reconstruction. By 1945, many economies had been destroyed or badly crippled, and food, clothing, housing, and medical care shortages were rampant. The Soviets held out the promise that communism would bring an end to economic deprivation and inequality. The United States had emerged virtually undamaged from the war, so it used its immense economic power and wealth—not to mention promises of foreign aid—to convince war-weary Europeans that democratic capitalism offered the only acceptable way of achieving economic success and freedom. This tug-of-war further entrenched the U.S.–Soviet rivalry.

Leadership and Personalities

In April 1945, just a month before the defeat of Germany, President Franklin D. Roosevelt died, and Vice President Harry S. Truman became the new leader of the United States. Truman, who had been vice president for just three months, had little foreign policy experience and was largely ignorant of the content of Roosevelt's discussions with Stalin. Roosevelt's style of wartime diplomacy with Stalin had been very personal and informal. Being well-seasoned in foreign affairs, he did all he could to keep the Soviets in the war to stop them from seeking a separate peace with Germany, as they had done during World War I. Roosevelt sought compromise and therefore postponed making difficult postwar decisions. And the decisions he did reach with Stalin tended to be vague.

Truman's leadership style was far more forceful and direct than was Roosevelt's. This difference, combined with Truman's and Stalin's mutual unwillingness to compromise, especially after Germany's May 1945 defeat, led to significant U.S.–Soviet tensions in the immediate postwar period. These tensions were most pronounced when it came to the postwar order in Eastern Europe. Roosevelt had committed to imprecise and unenforceable agreements with the Soviets regarding the postwar settlement, especially at the February 1945 Yalta Conference. When Truman took over, he lacked both the experience and charm of his predecessor. Armed only with the knowledge of the immediate situation and not knowing exactly what Roosevelt had agreed to, Truman decided to take a hard line toward the Soviets. For his part, Britain's Prime Minister Winston Churchill tended to share Truman's distrust and suspicion of Soviet motives. The change in U.S. leadership played a central role in how the Cold War unfolded after April 1945.

U.S. president Harry Truman (center) shakes the hands of British prime minister Winston Churchill (left) and Soviet premier Josef Stalin (right) on the opening day of the Potsdam Conference in Berlin, Germany, July 17–August 2, 1945. (Harry S. Truman Presidential Library)

Intermediate Causes

Friction between East and West certainly predates World War II and the ensuing Cold War. In fact, if one is to comprehend the Cold War's origins, it is crucial to understand how 1930s foreign policy contributed to both World War II and the distrust among the Allies during and after the conflict. The way in which World War II was fought—the strategies involved—can help explain why so much disharmony existed once the war was over. The Soviets believed that they had been forced to endure too much of the burden in the war against Germany. Their losses were horrific and far worse than those suffered by the British and Americans, and they believed that their sacrifice empowered them to exercise influence over the areas that they

had liberated. Here we see repeated examples of how shortsighted policies designed to meet immediate needs can cause unforeseen and unwanted consequences in the longer term.

Foreign Policies of the 1930s

Two significant prewar foreign policy developments shaped the uneasy alliance formed among the Soviet Union, Great Britain, and the United States to defeat the Axis nations. They also contributed to mutual suspicions that turned into open hostility once World War II ended in 1945.

During the mid-to-late 1930s, Nazi Germany's Adolf Hitler made clear his intention to dominate all of Central and Eastern Europe. His Anschluss Osterreichs policy, which brought about the forceful annexation of Austria in March 1938, began a worrisome trend. Fearing more Nazi annexations, the French, British, and Soviets entered into negotiations to form an alliance or mutual defense pact. In doing so, they hoped to prevent a German offensive against Western Europe or the Soviet Union. However, these negotiations broke down by mid-1939 because of mutual suspicions and misunderstandings. The French and British feared that the Soviets would use any such agreement as a pretext to control Eastern Europe. The Soviets, in turn, were fearful of the West's continuing appeasement of Hitler. They also believed that the West was leaving them alone to face German aggression. This was especially so after the infamous September 1938 Munich Agreement, in which France and Britain ceded German-speaking portions of Czechoslovakia to Hitler. Josef Stalin was incensed by the Munich Agreement and was insulted that he had not been consulted, much less included, in the deliberations. Ultimately, these mutual fears and suspicions led the Soviets and West Europeans to pursue policies that proved quite damaging to each other. To make matters worse, the Americans displayed a "hands-off" policy toward the gathering storm in Europe. Isolationism and the continuing economic depression at home prevented President Franklin D. Roosevelt from playing a meaningful role in European affairs. In general, however, Roosevelt tacitly supported appeasement.

Just as the Munich Agreement angered the Soviets, the August 1939 Nazi-Soviet Non-Aggression Pact outraged the West. The pact was signed on August 23, 1939, just one week before Germany invaded Poland, marking the beginning of World War II. Thus, the Soviets stayed out of the war until they were attacked by Germany in June 1941. In a significant way, Western appeasement policies and unwillingness to fully engage the Soviets prior to 1939 left Stalin with little choice but to enter into the pact with Hitler. The Soviets viewed the pact as necessary for their survival. The Western powers, however, saw it as a great betrayal. Obviously, then, the World War II alliance cobbled together after June 1941 was based not on long-term trust or even long-term mutual interests. It was based only on the will to defeat a common enemy. Once the war was over, each side—East and West—recalled these prewar policies, and mutual suspicion replaced mutual cooperation.

Allied Conduct of World War II

The way in which the Allies conducted World War II also contributed to Cold War antagonism. Because the United States was tied down in the Pacific against Japan, it was unable to devote its full military resources to the war in Europe. As an example, in December 1943 U.S. troop deployments were evenly divided between the European and Pacific theaters. Each had received 1.8 million personnel. The fact that American troop strength in Europe represented just 50 percent of its total strength meant that the British and Soviets bore the brunt of the Nazi war machine in Europe. But the Soviet Union paid a much higher price than Britain because Hitler's ground forces had launched a massive invasion of Soviet territory. Much of the war in Europe, in fact, was fought on Soviet soil.

To make matters worse, British prime minister Winston Churchill continued to postpone the opening of the second front in Western Europe. Creating a second front would have necessarily relieved the Soviets. Roosevelt was initially anxious to open a second front to divert the Germans and accommodate the Soviets. As early as 1942, he had promised Stalin that the front would be opened before the end of the year. Churchill, however, argued that Britain was not ready for such a large undertaking. His nation would be used as the main staging area for an attack across the English Channel against German forces in northern France. Roosevelt reluctantly went along with Churchill. In July 1942 Roosevelt agreed to dispatch American troops to North Africa to fight along with the British against Nazi forces.

In 1943 the Americans and British further forestalled a cross-channel invasion of France. In spring 1943, with the North African campaign against the Nazis virtually won, Churchill convinced Roosevelt to launch an invasion of Italy, beginning in Sicily and moving north. Though this offensive forced the Germans to divert forces to Italy, it also meant that a full-scale invasion of France would not be possible before 1944, and the Italian offensive alone was not enough to bring the Soviets any significant relief. Instead, the Soviets fought fiercely against the Germans, who had laid siege to Stalingrad beginning in August 1942. By February 1943, the Soviets had turned the tide of the war and had the Germans retreating westward. But the failure to open the second front until June 1944 contributed to the wholesale devastation of the Soviet Union. It also greatly agitated the Soviets and compelled them to conclude that their British and American allies were not to be entirely trusted. They also believed that American and British decisions to postpone the second front contributed to their astronomically high World War II casualties.

War Damage and the Soviet Union

Among all of the World War II combatants, the Soviets suffered—by far—more damage than any other nation. Estimates now put Soviet war deaths at 27–28 million, including 7–8 million military dead and 19–20 million

civilian dead. The Soviets claimed that 1,700 towns and some 70,000 villages were destroyed, while major cities such as Stalingrad, Odessa, Kiev, and Leningrad suffered catastrophic damage. An estimated 25 million Soviets were homeless at war's end, and estimates hold that at least 25 percent of the total national wealth of the country had been wiped out. Stalin and his successors believed that their country would have suffered much less damage and far fewer deaths had its allies dedicated more resources to the World War II effort in Europe. They were similarly convinced that the postponement of the second front prolonged their struggle against the German Army. The Soviets' shocking war-damage figures go a long way in explaining why the Soviets felt so put upon at the end of the war. And they certainly explain why mutual distrust soon replaced mutual cooperation after the Axis nations were defeated.

Another by-product of Soviet war damage was that Stalin felt entitled to control Eastern Europe at war's end. He believed that the great suffering and sacrifices made by his citizenry had earned him the right to establish pro-Soviet regimes from Yugoslavia all the way to the Polish-Soviet border. He sought dominance there for ideological as well as security reasons.

Long-term Causes

An understanding of long-term historical trends is necessary to comprehend how and why the Cold War developed as it did. By examining the full sweep of history, we can see that individual events, decisions, policies, and consequences build on one another to shape the future in a particular way. History is not just an endless list of unconnected events. Rather, it is a dynamic, always-evolving process that fits together like the pieces of a puzzle. In this case, how the Soviets were perceived and treated when they first came to power in 1917 greatly affected how they reacted to events both internally and externally. These early experiences with the West "conditioned" the Soviets to act and react in a certain manner. Russian history—going back hundreds of years—also shaped Soviet Cold War policies. The West was similarly conditioned to view the Soviets in a specific way. Josef Stalin's internal policies of the 1920s and 1930s directly influenced Western views of the Soviet Union after 1945.

Soviet Security Concerns

Russian history is punctuated by invasions from outside forces. Its long experience of repeated invasions dates at least to the 13th century, when the Mongols (also referred to as Tatars) invaded much of Russia and brutally ruled there for almost 250 years. In the 14th century, Belarus and Ukraine, once controlled by the Russians, were annexed by Lithuania. In more modern times, Russia was subjected to three attacks from the West in less than 130 years. Napoleon Bonaparte invaded Russia in 1812. His armies caused considerable damage, and before his campaign bogged down in winter weather, he had managed to capture Moscow. Much of the city was burned during the siege. In August 1914, as World War I broke out, Germany declared war on Russia and swept into Russian territories shortly thereafter. Germany broke its 1939 nonaggression pact with the Soviets and again attacked Russia in June 1941. Given this history, Stalin was most concerned about securing his nation against attack once World War II ended. Especially worried about a resurgent Germany and a possible fourth invasion, he sought to establish a "security zone" along the Soviet Union's western border. This meant controlling much of Eastern Europe.

Also influencing Soviet actions in the region was the desire to "isolate" Soviet citizens from Western cultural and economic influences. Soviet leaders feared that such influences would undermine the Communist Party's uncontested grip on power. Thus, they viewed the construction of a "defensive" perimeter in the west as the best way to keep capitalist pressures at bay. Stalin's desire to establish a defensive perimeter in Eastern Europe contributed to the eventual clash with the West, which believed Eastern Europe should control its own destiny.

Western Interference in the Russian/ Bolshevik Revolution (1918–1921)

In January–February 1918, Great Britain, the United States, and France decided to intervene in the Russian Revolution of November 1917. The revolution led ultimately to a civil war. This struggle pitted the Bolsheviks (the "Reds"), who wished to bring communism to Russia, against anticommunist forces, sometimes referred to as the "White Russians." Bolshevik leaders Vladimir Lenin and Leon Trotsky alarmed the West by trying to export the revolution to neighboring countries. In fact, civil war was narrowly averted in Germany during 1918–1919, when leftist workers' councils tried to impose a communist system there. In nearby Hungary, the Hungarian Soviet Republic established itself for a brief time under the leadership of Béla Kun during March–August 1919. Kun's government was easily overthrown by the Romanian Army. Nevertheless, these developments led Western nations to conclude that unchecked Bolshevik communism would be permanently imposed in Russia and might well spread farther westward.

Britain, America, France, Japan, and several other Western nations sent troops to Russia to stop the Bolsheviks. The first troop deployments landed in Russia in the spring of 1918; by the end of the year, there were 180,000 foreign troops on Russian soil.

Among them were 10,000 U.S. troops. The European Allies had also imposed a naval blockade on Russia in an attempt to "starve" the Bolsheviks into submission. Neither the ground intervention nor the blockade worked as planned. By 1921, the Bolsheviks had consolidated their power and the West ended its intervention and blockade.

The Soviets (as they now called themselves) deeply resented the West's intervention in what was clearly an internal affair. Not only would they never forget that British and American troops were on their soil, they also realized that the West was to be their principle ideological and military adversary. This history weighed heavily on East–West relations. Thus, it is little wonder that the Cold War developed so quickly after the World War II alliance against the Axis had dissolved. Indeed, during one of Soviet leader Nikita Khrushchev's famous public tirades against the West in the early 1960s, he made reference to the fact that American and Western troops had "violated" Russian sovereignty in the past. This was a clear reference to the 1918–1921 intervention in the Russian Civil War. It also demonstrated just how deep Soviet indignation ran concerning Western hostility toward the November 1917 Russian Revolution.

Interwar Politics

After the West's failed attempt to reverse the communist revolution in Russia, relations between the Soviets and the major Western powers were practically nonexistent until the late 1930s. The West attempted to isolate the Soviet Union diplomatically and economically, to seal it off from the rest of Europe to prevent the spread of communism. The British did not recognize the Soviet government until 1924. The United States did not do so until 1933. Without the benefit of regular and formal diplomatic relations, each side

was compelled to guess the other's motives, which only increased mutual misapprehensions. This lack of understanding became far more problematic when the United States and Soviet Union became the world's two leading powers after World War II.

Stalin's dictatorial rule and ruthless politics during the 1920s and 1930s also played a part in the East–West conflict. Stalin's forced collectivization of agriculture in the 1920s and early 1930s is estimated to have caused nearly 5 million Soviet deaths. Many died because they opposed Stalin's policies and were eliminated by the state. Many more died as a result of a severe famine during 1932–1933. Stalin also suppressed his political opponents and "enemies of the state" by ordering their imprisonment or murder. Between 1935 and 1938, Stalin's purges may have resulted in as many as one million deaths. These horrendous human rights abuses did not go unnoticed by the West. Furthermore, they convinced Western leaders that Soviet communism posed both ideological and physical dangers and was antithetical to democracy. The West later turned a blind eye to Stalin's abuses during World War II for the sake of the alliance. However, they again became a major issue of contention as soon as the conflict had ended.

The Soviets were more than just shunned by the West after World War I. They were purposefully excluded from international politics. Failing to include the Russians in the 1919 Paris Peace negotiations after World War I, or the League of Nations, was a major miscalculation on the part of the West. By excluding the Soviets from such international venues, the West added another dimension of paranoia to Soviet rule. It also ensured that Soviet leaders would pursue internationalist policies only when absolutely necessary (as in World War II). They had little experience or incentive to do otherwise. Their national self-interest often trumped international cooperation, a situation that ensured conflict with the West after 1945.

Propaganda and the Red Scare

Soviet government propaganda during the 1920s and 1930s added yet another element of conflict between East and West. The Soviets portrayed Western democracies as depraved, greed-driven societies bent on world domination. This line of thinking helped solidify the Communist Party's power. But it also meant that the Soviet leadership would be dominated by doctrinaire ideologues who were sometimes unwilling or unable to seek and sustain compromise with the West. In the West, preconceived notions of communism were equally damaging. Seeking accommodation with the Soviets was futile, it was believed, because they were irrational and cared only about converting the world to communism. In the United States, the first anticommunist "Red Scare" during 1918–1921 resulted in serious civil liberty violations. U.S. attorney general A. Mitchell Palmer embarked on a zealous anticommunist crusade that employed crude propaganda and communist caricatures to stamp out the "red menace" in the United States. Although the Red Scare died out after Palmer left office in 1921, its lingering effects included irrational fears of communism and a fundamental misunderstanding of Soviet motivations. Thus, propaganda and the politics of anticommunism also informed the eventual East–West conflict.

Paul G. Pierpaoli Jr.

Consequences of the Cold War

Immediate Consequences

The long-standing mutual distrust and misunderstanding between East and West only intensified after World War II. In the first five years of the Cold War (roughly 1945–1950), much of the foundation of the Cold War was laid. Disputes over the future of Eastern Europe and Germany added immeasurably to Cold War tensions. Thus, each side was compelled to pursue policies that would solidify their power within their spheres of influence. The Americans began constructing an expansive foreign policy and military apparatus designed to contain the Soviets and the spread of communism. The Soviets likewise walled off Eastern Europe to protect it from Western influences. They also resorted to brutal and repressive measures to stamp out political opposition. The year 1949 was a critical one in the development of the Cold War. That year saw the end of the Berlin Blockade, the beginning of the North Atlantic Treaty Organization (NATO), and the end of the American atomic monopoly. It also witnessed the "loss" of China to the communists, and the permanent division of Germany.

Communist Containment, the Truman Doctrine, and the Marshall Plan

In February 1946, U.S. diplomat George F. Kennan sent an 8,000-word telegram (the "Long Telegram") from the U.S. embassy in Moscow to the State Department in Washington, D.C. In it he warned policymakers of the Soviets' tendency toward secretiveness, paranoia, and insecurity. He also cautioned that the Soviets were driven by communist ideology that viewed capitalism as an enemy and that called for world domination. He concluded that the current Soviet leadership could neither be trusted nor reasoned with. He urged a hard-line foreign policy toward the Soviet Union to counter Soviet aggression. Kennan's telegram had an immediate and substantial impact on U.S. policymakers. They began to talk about a containment policy that would resist Soviet military advances and prevent the spread of communism.

In response to communist pressures in Turkey and a civil war in Greece, where communists threatened to take control, President Harry S. Truman announced the Truman Doctrine on March 12, 1947. With Kennan's top-secret Long Telegram in mind, Truman proclaimed that the United States would commit itself to support any nation struggling against "armed minorities or outside pressures." U.S. foreign policy thereby formally adopted Kennan's containment policy. In the same speech, Truman asked Congress for $400 million to stop communist movements in Greece and Turkey. Congress readily agreed. In July 1947, Kennan anonymously published an article in *Foreign Affairs* in which he restated his Long Telegram positions. By publicly and explicitly stating the principles of containment, the United States put the Soviets on notice and reinforced the Truman Doctrine. The containment policy became a key component of U.S. foreign policy throughout the Cold War.

In June 1947, U.S. secretary of state George C. Marshall announced a U.S.-sponsored economic aid program (the Marshall Plan) to help European nations recover from World War II. Although the United States did not specifically exclude aid to them, the Soviets nonetheless refused to accept Marshall Plan aid. Josef Stalin viewed the program as a threat, a way for the Americans to control Soviet internal affairs and dictate policies in Eastern Europe. The Americans saw the plan as a potent weapon for their containment policy. By strengthening West European economies, the threat of communism taking hold in the region was diminished. The Marshall Plan was an overwhelming success. During 1947–1952, $13.5 billion went to Western Europe. Economic catastrophe was averted, containment efforts were bolstered, and the Soviets were put on the defensive.

The Soviets Consolidate Power: Internal Repression, Eastern Europe, the Cominform, and Comecon

By the beginning of 1948, the Soviets were reeling from the quick succession of U.S. foreign policy initiatives the previous year. Stalin was compelled to react, and in so doing essentially completed the partitioning of Europe into two rival camps. At home, Stalin tried to restore the Communist Party's supremacy by cracking down on dissidents, real and imagined. Thousands of World War II prisoners of war (POWs) returned home

to the Soviet Union only to be imprisoned in bleak labor camps (known as gulags) out of fear that they had been poisoned by capitalist ideology. Soviet officials launched a nationwide campaign in 1946 to force writers, artists, intellectuals, and even musicians to strictly adhere to Stalinist ideals. And in 1949, Stalin initiated a major purge of Communist Party officials in Leningrad because of their alleged betrayal of Stalinist policies. Many of those involved were either executed or imprisoned. By 1949, Stalin had consolidated his power and that of the party he controlled, creating a terribly repressive environment.

In Eastern Europe, the Soviet Union moved to strengthen its control, in a way mimicking the U.S. containment policy by walling off Eastern Europe from Western influence. During 1945–1949 it systematically imposed its political, economic, and cultural values throughout the region. Local communist parties, often with the backing of Moscow, began establishing socialist economic policies in East European nations as soon as World War II ended. Albania and Yugoslavia set up communist governments on their own by 1946. In Poland, the Soviets forced several million Poles, Germans, and Ukrainians to relocate as they redrew the nation's borders and established a pro-Soviet regime there. Bulgaria declared itself a communist republic in September 1946. By 1948 Romania had a communist government in place. During 1947–1948, Soviet-sponsored coups ensured that both Hungary and Czechoslovakia had installed communist regimes. In Soviet-controlled eastern Germany, Stalin was creating a puppet regime. After the 1948 Soviet–Yugoslav split, Stalin embarked on a merciless campaign to purge "revisionist elements" from communist governments throughout Eastern Europe. By doing so, he further tightened his grip over the area.

In response to the Truman Doctrine and the Marshall Plan, which the Soviets saw as a concerted effort to encircle them, Stalin organized the Informational Bureau of Communist Parties (Cominform) in September 1947. This was an effort to unify communist parties around the world and to put up a united front against capitalist aggression. In January 1949, the Soviets organized the Council for Mutual Economic Assistance (Comecon), a Russian version of the Marshall Plan designed to aid Eastern Europe in postwar reconstruction. It was also used to bind together the economies of the Soviet bloc, all under Moscow's strict supervision. By 1949, Europe was sharply divided into two rival political and economic systems.

Cold War Turning Points: The Berlin Blockade and NATO

In June 1948 the Soviets blockaded Berlin, located in the Soviets' eastern occupation zone. By doing so, they hoped to force the Western Allies to abandon the western half of the city. They also sought to stop the creation of an independent West Germany. Many historians view the Berlin Blockade as the first serious confrontation of the Cold War. From June 1948 to May 1949, when Stalin called off the blockade, the Allies supplied West Berliners with 500,000 tons of food and 1.5 million tons of coal via a huge airlift operation that at its peak employed 400 planes flying 24 hours a day. The Soviets' Berlin Blockade backfired, and they were forced to admit defeat. The blockade antagonized the West and increased the likelihood of a major war. It also accelerated the division of Germany. On May 3, 1949, The Federal Republic of Germany (FRG, West Germany) was founded as an independent state. In eastern Germany, the communist-led German Democratic Republic (GDR, East Germany) became a sovereign nation

on October 7, 1949. Germany was now formally divided.

The Western Allies had feared that the Berlin Blockade was a precursor to a Soviet invasion of Western Europe. Their response was the formation of NATO on April 4, 1949. This bound the United States, Canada, and West European nations together in a defensive military pact aimed at containing the Soviet Union. For the first time since the American Revolution, the United States entered into a permanent politico-military alliance. NATO forced the Soviets to respond in kind. In 1955 they founded the Warsaw Pact, a military and mutual defense pact between the Soviet Union and Eastern Europe.

The Soviet Atomic Bomb

The Western Allies' successes of early 1949 were short-lived. On August 29, 1949, the Soviets exploded their first atomic bomb, ending the American monopoly. This caused near-panic in the United States and dangerously increased the stakes in the growing Cold War. Many Americans now feared a Soviet nuclear attack. Many more concluded that the Soviets had suddenly changed the global balance of power. The Soviet atomic bomb also marked the beginning of a huge and costly nuclear arms race. The United States tested its first hydrogen (or thermonuclear) bomb in October 1952; the Soviet Union followed suit in November 1955.

The "Loss" of China

In October 1949, communist forces engaged in the long-running Chinese Civil War triumphed and proclaimed the creation of the People's Republic of China (PRC). Chinese Nationalist (anticommunist) forces were forced to seek refuge on Taiwan, off the southern coast of China. The Chinese communists, led by Mao Zedong, had been helped by the Soviets. And their

1949 victory precipitated great dismay in the West. The world's most populous nation had now been "lost" to the communists, and in Western eyes it seemed as if the communists had gained the upper hand in the Cold War. The Soviets immediately recognized the new PRC and began supplying it with economic and military aid. Just as the Soviets believed they had been "encircled" by the Truman Doctrine and Marshall Plan, the West believed the loss of China was part of a larger conspiracy to encircle capitalism. This development further polarized East–West relations and would lead to a serious escalation of Cold War tensions in the coming years. Indeed, the communist victory in China introduced the Cold War to Asia.

Intermediate Consequences

The evolving Cold War in Asia precipitated the Korean War (1950–1953). This conflict carried with it grave consequences. As the first "shooting war" of the Cold War, it not only escalated tensions between the superpowers, but as many historians argue, it came close to igniting World War III. The war also introduced unprecedented war strategies and made use of new technologies. During the 1950s and 1960s, Cold War pressures changed the political landscape in individual nations as well as at the regional and international levels. This period also witnessed a series of Cold War crises, the worst of which was arguably the 1962 Cuban Missile Crisis, which threatened to engulf the world in a nuclear war.

The Korean War

As a result of the Cold War, the Korean Peninsula was permanently divided by 1948. North of the 38th Parallel, Kim Il Sung presided over the communist, pro-Soviet Democratic People's Republic of Korea (DPRK, North Korea). In the south, Syngman Rhee led the anticommunist, pro-Western Republic of Korea (ROK, South Korea). Both leaders wished to unite Korea under their respective regimes. During 1948–1949, North and South Korea began engaging in a series of border clashes along the 38th Parallel. By then, the DPRK had built a formidable army using Soviet arms left over from World War II. The Soviets had also begun to train North Korean troops and were providing significant armaments to North Korea in the spring of 1950. Kim, after receiving promises of support from both Josef Stalin and Mao Zedong, prepared to invade the south, crush South Korean forces, and reunite Korea under his leadership.

On June 25, 1950, North Korea attacked South Korea. South Korean forces, badly outnumbered and outgunned, were caught off guard and began retreating southward. Seoul, the South Korean capital, fell in a matter of days. The war also took the United States by surprise. However, President Harry S. Truman acted quickly, taking the issue to the United Nations (UN) and sending U.S. troops to help South Korean forces. By mid-July, a 17-nation military coalition fighting under a U.S.-led UN Command was engaged in fierce fighting against advancing North Korean troops. And so began a bloody and costly three-year war. In late December 1950, China intervened in the war when UN forces were about to defeat North Korean forces. This move prolonged the war and made a wider war a distinct possibility. It also marked the only time that Western forces directly battled against a major communist power. The war ended in July 1953 in an armistice. No peace treaty was signed, and North and South Korea remain technically at war to this very day. The war resulted in several million casualties among the Chinese and North and South Koreans. The United States lost 33,686 soldiers, a rate that was significantly higher than that of the Vietnam War, in relative terms.

The Korean War was a great Cold War turning point. It introduced the concept of limited war as a way to prevent an escalation to a nuclear war. It forced both the United States and the Soviet Union to engage in a massive military buildup. It put U.S.–Chinese relations on ice for more than 20 years, and convinced the Americans to become involved in the Indochina War being fought between French and Vietnamese nationalist forces. The Korean War was also famous for witnessing the first jet fighter battle in history, using helicopters in combat, and employing Mobile Army Surgical Hospital (MASH) units to reduce war casualties. Additionally, it was the first major "test" of the UN and the first military operation undertaken by that body.

Political Realignments

In the United States, the Korean War and evolving Cold War had far-reaching effects. Among the most noteworthy was the change in U.S. politics. Korea fueled the politics of anticommunism and sustained McCarthyism. In February 1950, Sen. Joseph R. McCarthy (R-Wis.) charged that the U.S. State Department was riddled with communists. Although unproven and untrue, the allegation struck a chord among many Americans who feared communist subversion as the Cold War deepened. But it was the Korean War that made McCarthy—and McCarthyism—household words. McCarthy used the Korean conflict for personal political gain and to "prove" to the public that the Soviets and Chinese were bent on conquering the world. McCarthyism, an anticommunist witch hunt that lasted until 1954, resulted in serious civil liberty violations and a divisive political atmosphere. It ruined the careers of hundreds of writers, actors, and teachers who

were accused of being communists during McCarthy's many public hearings. By 1952, when McCarthyism was at its height, a sizable number of Americans believed that the nation was threatened by internal communist subversion and further believed that the Democratic Party was largely to blame.

Republicans, even those who disavowed McCarthy's baseless accusations, capitalized on McCarthyism. During the 1952 presidential elections, they used anticommunism and public disaffection with the Korean War as potent political weapons. The end result was quite dramatic. In November 1952, Dwight D. Eisenhower won the presidency, the first Republican to do so since 1928. Republicans also won control of both houses of Congress, a feat not seen since 1930. For the first time since the U.S. Civil War, the Republican Party "cracked" the so-called Solid South. Until then, the South had voted as a bloc, invariably for Democratic candidates. In the years to come, the primacy of the Democratic Party gradually diminished, politics took a turn toward the Right, and the Republicans steadily gained ground in the South. By the 1980s, in fact, the Republicans had become more powerful in the South than in any other region. These developments caused a fundamental realignment of political power in the United States. Except for a brief time in the mid-1960s, politics in the nation drifted to the Right, and Southern states increased their political clout.

In Western Europe, Cold War considerations prompted a movement toward economic and political integration in the 1950s and 1960s. The European Integration Movement was initially designed as a tool to counter Soviet domination in Eastern Europe and to equitably distribute defense burdens among many nations. As a result, Western Europe came together to control atomic energy, foster increased intra-European trade, encourage multinational industrial collaboration, and even to rearm West Germany. By the mid-1960s, increased political integration in Western Europe was also used as a device to counter the United States' economic and military dominance. It also allowed Western Europe greater freedom of action in foreign policy. Perhaps the most important benefit of European integration was that it ensured the full reintegration of West Germany into the Western alliance. This prevented a resurgence of German militarism and made war on the European continent far less likely by binding Western Europe together. When nations share common goals and economic interests, the likelihood of a war erupting among them is diminished significantly.

The Cold War also brought political turmoil to the communist bloc. In February 1956, Soviet leader Nikita Khrushchev stunned his communist colleagues at the Soviet Twentieth Party Congress by denouncing Josef Stalin and making public the true cruelty of his rule. Seeking to ease Cold War tensions and appear more accommodating to the West, Khrushchev embarked on a de-Stalinization campaign to rid his country and Eastern Europe of Stalinist political and economic influences. He also advocated peaceful coexistence with the capitalist West and admitted that communism need not be imposed forcefully. Furthermore, he promised that the Soviet Union would not attempt to incite revolution abroad. Khrushchev's radical pronouncements had dazzling consequences. Nations such as Poland and Hungary especially welcomed de-Stalinization. In Hungary, a significant democratization movement blossomed. But it soon became apparent that Khrushchev's new policies had a limit. When Hungary attempted to back away from the communist bloc and withdraw from the Warsaw Pact, Soviet forces invaded the country and crushed the revolution in

November 1956. There were obviously limits to de-Stalinization efforts, but in general they did bring about a bit more autonomy in Eastern Europe and made international communism a less monolithic movement.

In China, Khrushchev's new policies did not go over well. Mao Zedong disagreed with de-Stalinization and peaceful co-existence with the West. He viewed these efforts as a sell-out and argued that the Soviet Union had abdicated its right to lead the worldwide communist movement. In 1960, the Soviets and Chinese, once allies, broke off relations. The resulting Sino-Soviet split led to several border clashes between the two nations and forced the Chinese to pursue their own foreign policy objectives. They now directly competed with the Soviets, especially in the developing world. The Chinese thus broke the solidarity of communism and embarked on a concerted effort to become a predominant regional and international player. In 1964, China exploded its first atomic bomb, which further destabilized the communist bloc. Ironically, perhaps, the Sino-Soviet Split would lead to vastly improved Sino-American relations by the 1970s.

Cuba and the 1962 Missile Crisis

Despite Khrushchev's desire for peaceful coexistence, Cold War tensions flared dangerously in the late 1950s and early 1960s. First came the Soviets' 1958 ultimatum that the Western Allies vacate West Berlin. The West refused, and during 1958–1961 the fate of Berlin threatened to ignite a war between the superpowers. Only the Soviets' 1961 construction of the Berlin Wall put an end to the crisis. The 1959 Cuban Revolution, however, sparked the most dangerous confrontation of the entire Cold War. Fidel Castro, who seized control of Cuba in 1959, soon made it known that he had communist inclinations and would ally himself with the Soviet Union. The

Americans did all they could to destabilize and topple the Castro regime. In April 1961, the United States even sponsored a failed invasion of Cuba designed to oust Castro from power (the Bay of Pigs Invasion).

After that, the Soviets vowed to protect Cuba from U.S. intervention. Beginning in late summer 1962, the Soviets began secretly installing nuclear-capable missiles in Cuba. The John F. Kennedy administration, made aware of the situation through aerial reconnaissance, publicly confronted the Soviets and demanded that the missiles be removed. The Americans argued that the missiles posed a serious threat to their national security and destabilized the world balance of power. Kennedy forced a showdown with the Soviet Union by ordering a naval blockade of Cuba while insisting that the missiles be withdrawn. During October 21–28, 1962, the United States and Soviet Union stood at the brink of nuclear annihilation, the closest they would ever come to a full-fledged war. Both Kennedy and Khrushchev showed willingness to compromise, but it was ultimately Khrushchev's decision to remove the missiles that ended the crisis and averted nuclear war.

Long-term Consequences

The Cold War was perhaps unlike any other conflict in history. It touched the lives of people around the world in unprecedented

The SSBN *George Washington*, the first nuclear-powered submarine designed to launch Polaris ballistic missiles while submerged, on its launching at Groton, Connecticut, on June 9, 1959. The *George Washington* was built quickly by cutting an attack submarine in half and adding a missile compartment. (United States Naval Institute)

ways. And its reach went far beyond that of a traditional war or military conflict. The idea of national defense was transformed into national security, which meant that entire societies were kept perpetually mobilized. Because a full-blown war between East and West would have resulted in a global holocaust, the Cold War saw a series of proxy wars fought mainly in the developing world. The Vietnam War engulfed the United States in a "crusade" that brought with it great upheaval at home and embarrassment abroad. The Soviets experienced their own version of Vietnam in Afghanistan during 1979–1989. Finally, the Cold War resulted in a superpower arms race, space race, and technology race. On one hand this revolutionized modern life; on the other hand it brought with it the constant threat of instantaneous annihilation and environmental degradation.

The National Security State and Perpetual Mobilization

The Cold War necessitated both perpetual military mobilization and ideological motivation. Even in the democratic West, national security became a far-ranging effort that greatly increased the power of the central government. In 1947, the U.S. Congress passed the National Security Act (NSA). Among other things, the NSA created the Department of Defense, Central Intelligence Agency (CIA), and the National Security Council (NSC). The CIA was a powerful, centralized intelligence operation designed to oversee all aspects of espionage and counterespionage. The NSC worked directly with the president—often in secret—to assess foreign military threats and formulate national security strategies. The NSC and CIA, especially, marked a distinct departure in U.S. government operations. Policymaking became more secretive, more centralized, and more inaccessible to the average citizen. The government began spending hundreds

of millions of dollars a year on long-term spy operations, something quite unthinkable prior to the Cold War. Over the course of the Cold War, the CIA engaged in activities that sometimes undermined the United States' democratic ideals. CIA operations in Iran (1953), Guatemala (1954), and Chile (1973) ousted popularly elected governments thought to be communistic in nature. During 1984–1986, the CIA's illegal involvement in the Iran-Contra Affair tarnished the Ronald Reagan administration.

The Soviet bloc engaged in its own subversive activities. The Soviet Union's powerful KGB not only conducted espionage against the West, but was involved in inspiring revolutions in Asia and Africa and supporting national liberation movements, particularly in Angola and Mozambique. During the 1960s and 1970s, the KGB was also involved in activities at home, clamping down on dissidents who criticized the Soviet system. The same pattern emerged in Eastern Europe. In the late 1940s, for example, communist officials in East Germany set up the Ministry for State Security ("Stasi"). It became infamous for its repression and involvement in both internal and external covert activities.

In September 1950, the West was convinced that the Korean War was the beginning of the communist bloc's plan to systematically attack democratic capitalism. As a response, President Harry S. Truman approved the recommendations of a top-secret NSC memorandum known as NSC-68. The NSC recommended a massive rearmament program that would keep the United States partially—and permanently—mobilized. Between 1950 and 1953, the U.S. defense budget quadrupled from $13.5 billion to $52 billion. From that point on, defense budgets remained at levels inconceivable prior to the Cold War. Several million Americans worked in defense industries beginning in the 1950s. The aerospace industry, which exploded during the Cold War, turned Southern California into a major industrial defense region. By the late 1950s, a new defense economy, sometimes called the military-industrial complex, was transforming the country. Americans began leaving the older industrial areas of the Midwest and Northeast to seek employment in defense and hi-tech industries located in the South and Southwest. This demographic realignment shifted political and economic power to these regions. Cities in the North experienced population and tax losses that plunged them into a long and steep economic recession.

In the East, the Soviets embarked on a major military expansion of their own, spending billions on developing more powerful nuclear weapons and intercontinental ballistic missiles (ICBMs) to carry them. Briefly, beginning in 1959, Khrushchev de-emphasized heavy industrial and defense-related production through his Seven Year Plan. His goal was to increase agricultural and consumer goods production. However, after the 1962 Cuban Missile Crisis, the plan was abandoned and much emphasis was again placed on defense output. Doing so created periodic food and basic consumer goods shortages throughout the 1970s and 1980s. As a result, dissatisfaction with the Soviet system grew, which in turn weakened the power and prestige of the Communist Party. In China, Mao Zedong implemented the 1958 Great Leap Forward campaign to increase iron and steel output and promote heavy industry. This was to serve as a counterbalance to Soviet power and increase self-sufficiency. Mao's campaign increased Chinese output but also permitted much waste and increased bureaucratization and corruption to take place. In 1978 China launched another initiative to modernize its industries, to include defense. These periodic programs contributed to China's economic growth but, as in the United

States, also carried with them demographic and political dislocations.

Proxy Wars

Proxy wars were fought throughout the developing world as a way for the superpowers to retain—or expand—their control in a given region. During 1961–1973, the United States gradually escalated its involvement in the Vietnam War. During 1961–1963, the number of U.S. military personnel in South Vietnam increased from roughly 1,200 to 16,000. President Lyndon B. Johnson engaged in a steady escalation of the conflict there so that by 1968 550,000 U.S. troops were fighting the Vietnam War. The war had stunning effects on the United States. It demoralized and discredited the U.S. armed forces, especially the army, derailed social welfare programs, brought about inflation and economic stagnation, ended Johnson's political career, and helped the Republican Party's ascendancy. It also deeply polarized the American home front, which became home to sometimes violent confrontations between antiwar protesters and the government. Worse still, millions of Vietnamese were killed, Vietnam suffered severe environmental damage, and the United States lost 58,220 soldiers before the U.S. withdrawal in 1973.

In other parts of the world, but most notably in Africa, post–World War II decolonization movements witnessed both the Americans and Soviets competing for influence. This superpower rivalry either precipitated regional or civil wars or greatly prolonged conflicts already in progress. Such was the case in Congo (Zaire), Nigeria, Angola, Mozambique, Ethiopia, Somalia, and Kenya, among other African states. Untold millions died in these wars through government-sponsored genocide, forced relocations, and starvation, not to mention armed conflict itself.

During 1979–1989, the Soviet Union engaged in a war in Afghanistan not unlike the

U.S. war in Vietnam. For 10 years the Soviets fought to maintain control of the unstable nation, intervening in what began as a civil war in the fall of 1979. By 1980, 50,000 Soviet troops were engaged in guerrilla-style warfare against a determined enemy. Opposing the Soviets were the mujahideen, aided indirectly by the United States and other Western nations. By 1988, when the Soviets were forced to admit defeat, 115,000 Russian troops were stationed in Afghanistan. The war was a disaster for the Soviet Union. It ended détente and led to a reinvigorated Cold War with the United States. The war tarnished the reputation of the Red Army, badly weakened the Soviet system, and practically bankrupted the Kremlin. Russian casualties reached 50,000. Afghanistan suffered greatly, too. The nation's infrastructure was ruined, five million Afghanis became refugees, and perhaps one million civilians were killed. This conflict had a direct impact on the collapse of the Soviet Union and the end of the Cold War in 1991.

The Space and Technology Race

The nuclear arms race that began in earnest immediately after World War II spawned a concurrent space and technology race between East and West. The nuclear arms competition soon included Britain, France, and China; between 1953 and 1964 all three became nuclear powers. By the late 1970s, India, Pakistan, and Israel had also joined the nuclear club. In November 1957, the Soviet Union surprised the world and shocked many Americans when it launched *Sputnik 1*, the first manmade orbiting satellite. *Sputnik 2* was launched shortly after. The *Sputnik* launches not only set off the space race but also demonstrated Soviet rocket technology, which was adapted to ICBMs. ICBMs quickened the pace of the nuclear arms race and drastically altered nuclear strategy. Not to be outdone, in 1958 the U.S. Congress created the National Aeronautics and Space Administration (NASA). The United States launched its first rocket-propelled satellite in January 1958. In the coming years, the superpowers competed to achieve superiority in space. The Soviets claimed the first manned space flight in April 1961. The United States sent its first man into space via NASA's Mercury Program in May 1961. Mercury was followed by the Gemini Program and, finally, the Apollo Program that put the first man on the moon on July 20, 1969.

The space race bred the technology race between East and West that produced everything from computers to microcircuitry to global positioning satellites (GPS). Space technology was applied to advanced weapons systems that produced breakthroughs such as the cruise missile and smart bombs, first used in the 1991 Persian Gulf War. It is not possible to list even a fraction of the advances made during the space and technology races that began during the Cold War. This competition revolutionized human existence in the span of less than 25 years. Communications, transportation, health care, and education all were radically transformed by the technologies first used in military and space applications. And as technologies progressed—particularly in the computer field—the rate of change picked up even greater speed beginning in the mid-1980s. Indeed, the lifestyle you lead today and the technologies you use day-in and day-out would have seemed like science fiction when your parents were your age just a few decades ago. Never in human history has technology so rapidly changed and transformed everyday life in so short a span of time.

Paul G. Pierpaoli Jr.

A

Acheson, Dean Gooderham (1893–1971)

Dean Acheson was the chief architect of U.S. foreign policy in the formative years of the Cold War. Born on April 11, 1893, in Middletown, Connecticut, to British parents, Acheson attended the prestigious Groton School and graduated from Yale University in 1915. He earned a degree from Harvard Law School in 1918 and went on to serve as private secretary to Supreme Court Justice Louis Brandeis from 1919 to 1921. After his Supreme Court stint, Acheson joined a Washington, D.C., law firm. He entered public life in 1933 when President Franklin D. Roosevelt named him undersecretary of the treasury. Acheson resigned soon thereafter, however, over a disagreement concerning gold and currency policies. In 1940 he authored a key legal opinion that led to the Lend-Lease program. He became assistant secretary of state in 1941 and then undersecretary of state in 1945.

The possessor of a brilliant legal mind, a regal bearing, and a biting wit, Acheson initially favored a policy of postwar cooperation with the Soviet Union. But he quickly reversed his view and, along with George F. Kennan, became one of the chief proponents of the Cold War containment policy. Though Kennan believed that the contest with the Soviet Union was primarily political in nature, Acheson stressed the military dimension. Sobered by the failure of democratic nations to halt the Axis powers in the 1930s, Acheson advocated a policy of developing military strength before negotiating with the Soviet Union. After the USSR detonated its first atomic bomb in September 1949, Acheson played a leading role in persuading President Harry S. Truman to move ahead with the development of the hydrogen bomb.

Acheson also played a critical role in implementing major Cold War initiatives in Europe. When the British informed the United States in early 1947 that they no longer possessed the financial means to support Greece and Turkey, Acheson pushed the Truman administration to take quick action, warning that if the United States did not supplant British power in the eastern Mediterranean, the result would likely be Soviet control of the region. Truman subsequently announced his Greco-Turkish aid package and enunciated the Truman Doctrine to augment the containment policy. Acheson aggressively promoted the 1947 Marshall Plan to aid West European recovery efforts and to resist pressures that might lead to communist regimes there. Despite his role in creating the United Nations (UN), Acheson did not believe that it could prevent Soviet aggression or the spread of militant communism. Instead, he trusted military power and saw the North Atlantic Treaty Organization (NATO) as the best means of defending the West from the Soviets. NATO had the added benefits of strengthening U.S. ties with Europe, quelling internal unrest, and binding West Germany to the alliance.

When Acheson was sworn in as secretary of state on January 21, 1949, he was already recognized as the key architect of postwar foreign policy. Truman, a great admirer of Acheson, gave him wide latitude in foreign policy matters. During his tenure in office, Acheson pushed through the implementation of NSC-68 and won Senate approval for continued stationing of American troops in Europe and for extensive military aid to the NATO allies. He failed, however, to secure European approval for German rearmament, stymied by French opposition.

Acheson's tendency to view international affairs largely from a European perspective hampered his efforts to deal with rising nationalism in the developing world. His attachment to a world united by imperial prosperity and order created unnecessary problems for the Western Allies as well as for emerging nations. Asia, possessing no significant industrial base outside of Japan, ranked low among Acheson's priorities. He based American policy on the tenuous—and as it turned out faulty—premise that communist China was the puppet of the Soviet Union. He sided with the French regarding Indochina, advising Truman to make what proved to be a fateful commitment of American assistance to anti–Viet Minh forces in 1950. Acheson all but ignored Africa and Latin America, mainly because neither region was as yet on the front lines of the Cold War. Like those who preceded him, Acheson viewed Britain as an indispensable American ally and partner.

A primary target of Republican Senator Joseph McCarthy's anticommunist witch hunt, Acheson was lambasted for being friendly with alleged spy Alger Hiss, "losing" China to communism, and being unable to end the Korean War, which Acheson's enemies wrongly believed he provoked by publicly excluding it from America's "defense perimeter" in a January 1950 speech. Acheson also provided fodder for other Republicans, namely Richard M. Nixon, who in 1952 derided Democratic presidential nominee Adlai Stevenson for having graduated from "Dean Acheson's College of Cowardly Communist Containment."

Acheson retired from public life in 1953 but was not disengaged from public policy. He soon became the main Democratic critic of President Dwight D. Eisenhower's foreign policy. Acheson regarded NSC-68, which advocated the strengthening of conventional military forces to provide options other than nuclear war, as the foreign policy bible for the Cold War era. When the Eisenhower administration committed itself to a policy of massive retaliation that emphasized nuclear responses over conventional responses to crises, the former secretary of state reacted with utter disbelief to what he termed "defense on the cheap."

In the 1960s, Acheson returned to public life as the head of NATO task forces, special envoy, diplomatic trouble-shooter, and foreign policy advisor for Presidents John F. Kennedy and Lyndon B. Johnson. Acheson was noted for his hawkish advice to Kennedy during the Cuban Missile Crisis of 1962. Acheson died of a heart attack on October 12, 1971, in Sandy Spring, Maryland.

Caryn E. Neumann

Further Reading

Acheson, Dean. *Present at the Creation: My Years at the State Department*. New York: Norton, 1969.

Brinkley, Douglas. *Dean Acheson: The Cold War Years, 1953–71*. New Haven, CT: Yale University Press, 1992.

Chace, James. *Acheson: The Secretary of State Who Created the American World*. New York: Simon and Schuster, 1998.

McNay, John T. *Acheson and Empire: The British Accent in American Foreign Policy*. Columbia: University of Missouri Press, 2001.

Afghanistan War (1979–1989)

The Soviet–Afghan War represented the culmination of events dating to April 1978, when Afghan communists, supported by left-wing army leaders, overthrew the unpopular, authoritarian government of Mohammad Daoud and proclaimed the People's Democratic Republic of Afghanistan. Although the extent of Soviet involvement in the coup remains unclear, Moscow certainly welcomed it and quickly established close relations with the new regime headed by Nur Mohammad Taraki, who was committed to bringing socialism to Afghanistan.

With the ambitious, extremely militant foreign minister Hafizullah Amin as its driving force, the Taraki regime quickly alienated much of Afghanistan's population by conducting a terror campaign against its opponents and introducing a series of social and economic reforms at odds with the religious and cultural norms of the country's highly conservative, Muslim, tribal society. Afghanistan's Muslim leaders soon declared a jihad against "godless communism," and by August 1978 the Taraki regime faced an open revolt, a situation made especially dangerous by the defection of a portion of the army to the rebel cause.

As Afghanistan descended into civil war, Moscow grew increasingly concerned. Committed to preventing the overthrow of a friendly, neighboring communist government and fearful of the effects that a potential Islamic fundamentalist regime might have on the Muslim population of Soviet Central Asia, specifically those in the republics bordering Afghanistan, the Soviets moved toward military intervention. During the last months of 1979, the Leonid Brezhnev government dispatched approximately 4,500 combat advisors to assist the Afghan communist regime while simultaneously allowing Soviet aircraft to conduct bombing raids against rebel positions. Although Soviet Deputy Defense Minster Ivan G. Pavlovskii, who had played an important role in the 1968 Soviet invasion of Czechoslovakia, counseled against full-scale intervention in Afghanistan, his superior, Defense Minister Dmitry Ustinov, convinced Brezhnev to undertake an invasion, arguing that only such action could preserve the Afghan communist regime. He also promised that the Soviet presence there would be short.

Brezhnev ultimately decided in favor of war, the pivotal factor arguably being the September 1979 seizure of power by Hafizullah Amin, who had ordered Taraki arrested and murdered. Apparently shocked by Amin's act of supreme betrayal and inclined to believe that only a massive intervention could save the situation, Brezhnev gave approval for the invasion. Beginning in late November 1979 and continuing during the first weeks of December, the Soviet military concentrated the Fortieth Army, composed primarily of Central Asian troops, along the Afghan border. On December 24, Soviet forces crossed the frontier, while Moscow claimed that the Afghan government had requested help against an unnamed outside threat.

Relying on mechanized tactics and close air support, Soviet units quickly seized the Afghan capital of Kabul. In the process, a special assault force stormed the presidential palace and killed Amin, replacing him with the more moderate Barak Kemal, who attempted, unsuccessfully, to win popular support by portraying himself as a devoted Muslim and Afghan nationalist. Soviet forces, numbering at least 50,000 men by the end of January 1980, went on to occupy the other major Afghan cities and secured major highways. In response, rebel mujahideen

Soviet soldiers and a BMD-1 airborne combat vehicle in Kabul, Afghanistan, in March 1986. (Department of Defense)

forces resorted to guerrilla warfare, their primary goal being to avoid defeat in the hopes of outlasting Soviet intervention.

Moscow's invasion of Afghanistan had immediate and adverse international consequences, effectively wrecking détente, already in dire straits by December 1979 thanks to recent increases in missile deployments in Europe. Having devoted much effort to improving relations with Moscow, U.S. president Jimmy Carter believed that he had been betrayed. He reacted swiftly and strongly to the Afghan invasion.

On December 28, 1979, Carter publicly denounced the Soviet action as a "blatant violation of accepted international rules of behavior." Three days later, he accused Moscow of lying about its motives for intervening, and declared that the invasion had dramatically altered his view of the Soviet Union's foreign policy goals. On January 3, 1980, the president asked the U.S. Senate to

delay consideration of SALT II. Finally, on January 23, in his State of the Union Address, Carter warned that the Soviet action in Afghanistan posed a potentially serious threat to world peace because control of Afghanistan would put Moscow in a position to dominate the strategic Persian Gulf and thus interdict at will the flow of Middle East oil.

The president followed these pronouncements by enunciating what soon became known as the Carter Doctrine, declaring that any effort to dominate the Persian Gulf would be interpreted as an attack on American interests that would be rebuffed by force if necessary. Carter also announced his intention to limit the sale of technology and agricultural products to the USSR, and imposed restrictions on Soviet fishing privileges in U.S. waters. In addition, he notified the International Olympic Committee that in light of the Soviet invasion of

Afghanistan, neither he nor the American public would support sending a U.S. team to the 1980 Moscow Summer Games. The president called upon America's allies to follow suit.

Carter also asked Congress to support increased defense spending and registration for the draft, pushed for the creation of a Rapid Deployment Force that could intervene in the Persian Gulf or other areas threatened by Soviet expansionism, offered increased military aid to Pakistan, moved to enhance ties with the People's Republic of China (PRC), approved covert CIA assistance to the mujahideen, and signed a presidential directive on July 25, 1980, providing for increased targeting of Soviet nuclear forces.

Carter's sharp response was undercut to a certain extent by several developments. First, key U.S. allies rejected both economic sanctions and an Olympic boycott. Second, Argentina and several other states actually increased their grain sales to Moscow. Third, a somewhat jaded American public tended to doubt the president's assertions about Soviet motives and believed that he had needlessly reenergized the Cold War.

Ronald Reagan, who defeated Carter in the November 1980 presidential election, took an even harder stand against the Soviets. Describing the Soviet Union as an "evil empire" that had used détente for its own nefarious purposes, the Reagan administration poured vast sums of money into a massive military buildup that even saw the president push the development of the Strategic Defense Initiative (SDI) (labeled "Star Wars" by its critics, this was a missile defense system dependent on satellites to destroy enemy missiles with lasers or particle beams before armed warheads separated and headed for their targets). The Soviet response was to build additional missiles and warheads.

Meanwhile, confronted with guerrilla warfare in Afghanistan, the USSR remained committed to waging a limited war and found itself drawn, inexorably, into an ever-deeper bloody quagmire against a determined opponent whose confidence and morale grew with each passing month. To make matters worse for Moscow, domestic criticism of the war by prominent dissidents such as Andrei Sakharov appeared early on, while foreign assistance in the form of food, transport vehicles, and weaponry (especially the Stinger antiaircraft missile launchers) from the United States began reaching the mujahideen as the fighting dragged on.

Neither the commitment of more troops, nor the use of chemical weapons, nor the replacement of the unpopular Kemal could bring Moscow any closer to victory. Accordingly, by 1986 the Soviet leadership, now headed by the reformist General Secretary Mikhail Gorbachev, began contemplating ways of extricating itself from what many observers characterized as the "Soviet Union's Vietnam."

In April 1988, Gorbachev agreed to a United Nations mediation proposal providing for the withdrawal of Soviet troops over a 10-month period. One month later the departure of Soviet military forces, which had grown to an estimated 115,000 troops, commenced—a process that was finally completed in February 1989.

Although the Soviets left Afghanistan with a procommunist regime, a team of military advisors, and substantial quantities of equipment, the nine years' war had exacted a high toll, costing the Soviets an estimated 50,000 casualties. It seriously damaged the Red Army's military reputation, further undermining the legitimacy of the Soviet system, and nearly bankrupted the Kremlin. For the Afghans, the war proved equally costly. An estimated one million civilians were dead, and another five million were refugees. Much of the country was devastated.

Bruce J. DeHart

Further Reading

Hauner, Milan. *The Soviet War in Afghanistan: Patterns of Russian Imperialism.* Lanham, MD: University Press of America, 1991.

Judge, Edward, and John W. Langdon, eds. *The Cold War: A History through Documents.* Upper Saddle River, NJ: Prentice Hall, 1999.

MacKenzie, David. *From Messianism to Collapse: Soviet Foreign Policy, 1917–1991.* Fort Worth, TX: Harcourt Brace, 1994.

Russian General Staff. *The Soviet-Afghan War: How a Superpower Fought and Lost.* Lawrence: University of Kansas Press, 2002.

Africa

The Cold War in Africa commenced with the end of the colonial era, continued through Africa's independence movements, and finally ended in the postcolonial period. The Soviet Union linked African national liberation movements to its own Marxist-Leninist ideology in order to gain a foothold in the continent. The United States, on the other hand, responded fitfully and belatedly to African decolonization.

Individual African states—and regions—were an important component in the geopolitical chess match between the United States and the USSR, but not until later in the Cold War. From the late 1950s to the late 1970s, the United States purposely played a secondary role to that of the Europeans in Africa. During President Dwight D. Eisenhower's second term (1957–1961), the U.S. National Security Council proposed a "division of labor" for the developing world: the Europeans would be responsible for Africa, while

the United States would play the dominant role in Latin America. The White House, in particular, expected France to police francophone Africa, and Great Britain to take the lead in southern Africa. Nonetheless, the Eisenhower administration created the Bureau of African Affairs within the U.S. Department of State. In 1957, Senator John F. Kennedy presciently warned of growing communist influence in Africa. As the Cold War advanced, African countries became labeled as either pro-Soviet or pro-American. A shorthand for this dichotomy was membership in either the relatively radical Casablanca Group, led by Ghana's president Kwame Nkrumah, or membership in the more pro-West Monrovia Group.

From 1981 to 1988, U.S. military aid to sub-Saharan Africa amounted to about $1 billion. During the latter days of the Cold War, American aid became indistinguishable from U.S. geopolitical aims. Pro-Western governments such as the one in Senegal under President Abdou Diouf received aid, for instance, while Marxist governments such as President Didier Ratsiraka's of Madagascar did not. The United States routinely tied its aid to African nations to their geopolitical importance.

Generally speaking, America's Cold War geopolitical interests in sub-Saharan Africa were narrow in scope, but where the commitment existed it ran deep and often manifested itself in covert activity. Three regions deserve special mention: the Horn of Africa (Ethiopia and Somalia), where an intense superpower rivalry played out; Zaire (Democratic Republic of the Congo), one of the earliest battlegrounds of Cold War rivalry; and southern Africa, where the superpowers fought a proxy war in Angola and where they were directly or indirectly involved in an intricately latticed struggle for independence

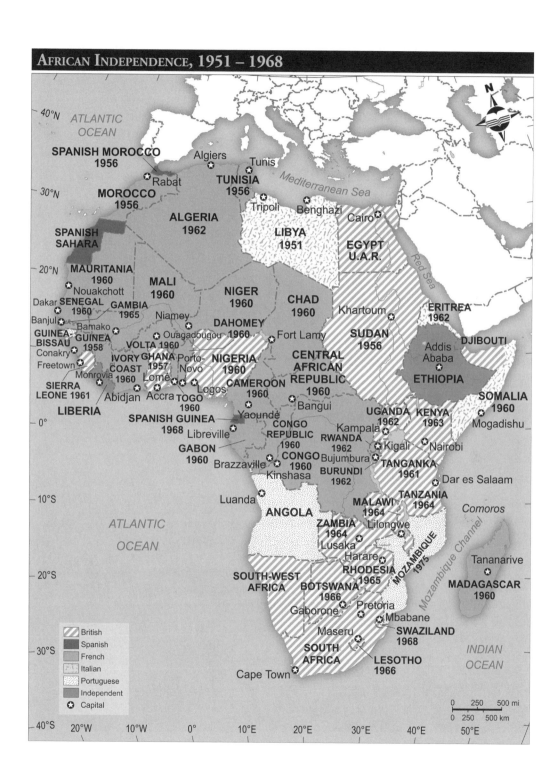

African Independence, 1951 – 1968

and freedom in Mozambique, Namibia, Rhodesia (Zimbabwe), and South Africa.

The Horn of Africa is composed of Ethiopia, Somalia, and Djibouti. Because it adjoins the Middle East and the Indian Ocean, flanks the oil-rich states of Arabia, controls the Bab el Mandeb Straits (an important choke point for oil), and overlooks the passages where the Red Sea, the Gulf of Aden, and the Indian Ocean converge, it was a very important piece in the Cold War geopolitical chess game. The competition between the United States and the Soviet Union in the Horn was intense, and their policies were analogous, if obviously in direct competition. American policy there was grounded on four principles: the economic security of the West (i.e., oil), stability and security in the Middle East and in the Horn, the ability

to block Soviet attempts to choke Western oil lanes, and keeping the Red Sea and the Indian Ocean open for Israeli and Israel-bound shipping. The Soviet strategy in the Horn was predicated upon strategic deterrence, naval presence, sea denial or sea control, and projection of power. The geopolitical competition between the United States and the USSR revolved around the Ethiopian–Somalian conflict.

America's foothold in the Horn was Ethiopia, where it had maintained a presence since 1953. The Soviet Union initially had a strong presence in Somalia. Between 1953 and 1974, when Ethiopian ruler Haile Selassie was overthrown, the United States supplied more than $200 million in military aid to Ethiopia, which in 1970 comprised almost half of all aid to sub-Saharan Africa.

African heads of state attend a meeting of the Organization of African Unity (OAU), November 9, 1966, in Addis Ababa, Ethiopia. OAU was created in May 1963 and is based in Addis Ababa. (AFP/Getty Images)

In 1953, an American military base opened at Kagnew Station in Asmara, Ethiopia, for, among other purposes, tracking space satellites and relaying military communications. More than 3,200 U.S. military personnel were stationed there. The United States also supported counter-insurgency teams fighting the Eritrean Liberation Movement. American support of Ethiopia was largely a response to the regional machinations of the Soviet Union. General Barre, the head of the Supreme Revolutionary Council of Somalia (an overtly socialist organization), had by 1977 received more than $250 million in military aid from the Soviets. The Soviet Union also helped construct port facilities at Berbera, overlooking the Red Sea, as well as communication facilities. This base was strategically situated almost directly opposite the Soviet naval facilities in South Yemen's port of Aden.

The strategic equation in the Horn took a strange twist beginning in the mid-1970s. With the weakening and then the collapse of Selassie's regime in Ethiopia, the United States was forced to abandon its base in Asmara and move its base of operations to the island of Diego Garcia (1,500 miles off the African coast in the Indian Ocean). Colonel Mengistu Haile Mariam, the leader of the Derg military junta, ruled Ethiopia under a Marxist-Leninist dictatorship from 1974 until 1991. This provided a window of opportunity that the Soviets could not resist, but they had to be careful not to alienate their Somali allies.

The Soviets responded to the new Ethiopian government's request for assistance (which the United States was no longer willing to provide) just as the Eritreans and Somalis were enjoying more success in Ethiopia. In September 1977, the Soviet Union began the delivery of approximately $385 million in arms, including 48 MiG jet fighters, 200 T-54 and T-55 tanks, and SAM-3 and SAM-7 antiaircraft missiles. The Soviet Union had gambled that its new relationship with Ethiopia would not affect its relationship with Somalia, a bet that it lost. The Soviet Union was expelled from Somalia in 1977. It also failed to achieve its aims in Ethiopia, for after seven years of civil war the Tigrean People's Liberation Front (TPLF) from far southern Ethiopia entered Addis Ababa in May 1991, overthrowing the Marxist regime. Meanwhile, the United States had become the major patron of Somalia, supported Barre throughout the 1980s, and inherited the strategic base in Berbera once held by the Soviets.

During the 1960s, Washington ordered a series of covert actions in the Democratic Republic of the Congo (DRC, Zaire). The DRC was a flashpoint in the Cold War almost from its inception. Three central events in its history punctuate the role it played in the U.S.–USSR geopolitical competition in sub-Saharan Africa: the defeat of Prime Minister Patrice Lumumba and the rise of Mobutu Sese Seko, the first secessionist crisis in Katanga (renamed Shaba in 1971) in 1960, and the second secessionist crisis in Shaba in 1978.

The first and most significant result of such actions was the assassination of Lumumba and the subsequent rise of the pro-Western Mobutu. Mobutu, who ran what became commonly known as a kleptocracy, received approximately $1.5 billion in economic and military aid over the course of nearly 25 years. The United States considered Mobutu a vital cog in its global anticommunist network, as well as a supplier of important strategic minerals (cobalt, copper, diamonds, gold, cadmium, and uranium).

In June 1960, the Belgian Congo gained independence and was renamed the Republic of Congo, with Joseph Kasavubu as its first president and Lumumba as its first prime minister. Lumumba, a leftist, almost immediately faced a secessionist crisis in the mineral-rich Katanga province. At the request of the Congolese government, United Nations (UN) troops were sent in to restore order. The United States opposed Lumumba's nationalist and nonaligned policies and his implicit support of the Soviet Union. In September 1960 President Kasavubu, along with the army, dismissed Lumumba and in January 1961 delivered him to the secessionists in Katanga province, who executed him.

From 1961 until 1964 (when Belgian paratroopers finally restored order), there was fighting between rival secessionist groups. American-educated Moise Tshombe then emerged as the leader of the Katanga secessionists. After a short period of exile, Tshombe was named the premier of the Government of Reconciliation by Kasavubu in 1964. Two years later Tshombe was dismissed and accused of treason and again went into exile. He was kidnapped and imprisoned in Algeria, where he died in prison in 1969. President Kasavubu was ousted in a second Mobutu-led coup in November 1965. By 1967, the pro-Lumumbist elements had been effectively defeated. Zaire then became a staging area for neighboring Cold War struggles.

Mobutu's involvement in neighboring Angola's civil war resulted in the Front for the National Liberation of the Congo (FLNC) invasion of Zaire's Shaba region in March 1977, known as the Shaba I Crisis. Included in the invading force was a small remnant of the Katangan rebels. The FLNC quickly captured several towns and gained control of the railroad to about 19 miles (30 km) from the copper mining town of Kolwezi. The dissidents aimed to take over the entire country and depose Mobutu. Their advance and the threat to Kolwezi forced Mobutu to appeal

for international assistance. Thus, Belgium, France, and the United States responded to Mobutu's request by immediately airlifting military supplies to Zaire. Other African states, namely Egypt and Morocco, also supported Zaire during the crisis. By the end of May, the joint force had regained control of Shaba. The FLNC then withdrew to Angola and Zambia.

Government reprisals after Shaba I drove 50,000–70,000 refugees into Angola. Also, Zaire's continued support for Angolan dissident groups ensured continued Angolan government support for the FLNC. The Shaba II Crisis was triggered in May 1978 when the FLNC launched its second invasion of Zaire in a little over a year. During early May 1978, 10 FLNC battalions entered Shaba through northern Zambia, a sparsely populated area inhabited by the same ethnic groups (Lunda and Ndembu) that made up the FLNC. A small group went toward Mutshatsha, about 60 miles west of Kolwezi, to block the path of Zairian reinforcements that threatened to move into the area. During the night of May 11–12, 1978, the remainder of the force moved to Kolwezi, where it joined with the rebels who had earlier infiltrated the town. The town of Kolwezi was lightly defended, and the rebels quickly gained a foothold in the mineral-rich Shaba (formerly Katanga) province, thereby controlling about 75 percent of the country's export earnings. The French and Belgian governments requested U.S. help in putting down the rebellion.

The administration of President Jimmy Carter viewed Shaba II as an instance of Soviet expansionism. Subsequently, U.S. planes transported roughly 2,500 French and Belgian troops and supporting equipment to the region. The American commitment to Mobutu and Zaire was consistent with its long-standing support of Mobutu and with the U.S. concern over Soviet/Cuban influence in neighboring

Angola. President Carter, in fact, rebuked Cuban leader Fidel Castro for supporting the FLNC attack launched from Angolan territory. Carter's national security advisor, Zbigniew Brzezinski, claimed that the invasion was launched with Moscow's blessing. The Carter administration believed that it had to respond to aggressive Soviet/Cuban penetration of Africa (15,000 Cuban troops and Soviet advisors were already in Ethiopia). By the end of May 1978, the second Shaba invasion was all but over. Belgian forces began to withdraw, leaving a battalion in Kamina, and the French Foreign Legion departed.

Southern Africa was the third African hot spot during the Cold War. The epicenter of American–Soviet conflict was Angola, but Namibia, Mozambique, Zimbabwe, and South Africa also featured prominently in the latter years of the Cold War. Each of these countries, with the notable exception of South Africa, was seen as aligned with the Soviet Union. Namibia, under tight South African control, was linked to the Angolan civil war. Mozambique, which gained independence on June 25, 1974, was a self-designated Marxist-Leninist regime led by Samora Machel, chairman of the Frente Libertação de Moçambique (Frelimo) and president of the People's Republic of Mozambique, and joined the Soviet-led Council of Mutual Economic Assistance. In turn, Frelimo, with the backing of the Soviet Union and other communist states, supported Robert Mugabe's Zimbabwe African National Union (ZANU) and its armed wing, the Zimbabwe African National Liberation Army (ZANLA), in the Rhodesia/Zimbabwe national liberation struggle against the settler regime of Ian Smith, leader of the Rhodesian Front (RF).

The RF had declared Rhodesia's independence from Great Britain in 1965, triggering a 15-year-long civil war. A second insurgency group in Rhodesia/Zimbabwe,

led by Joshua Nkoma's Zimbabwe African Peoples Union (ZAPU) along with its armed wing, the Zimbabwe People's Revolutionary Army (ZIPRA), was supported by the Soviet-aligned Popular Movement for the Liberation of Angola (MPLA). In an important subplot during the era, the United States was almost completely dependent on southern Africa for its uranium supply and was willing to go to great lengths to secure the critical fuel for its nuclear arsenal.

In March 1975, a civil war broke out in Angola. The United States initially supported the National Front for the Liberation of Angola (FNLA) as a counter to the Marxist MPLA. After the FNLA fell apart, America switched its support to the National Union for the Total Independence of Angola (UNITA). The United States refused to support the de jure MPLA government, and what followed was a quarter century of civil war. The Soviets and Cubans intervened in Angola in support of the Marxist MPLA regime, which subsequently developed close military ties with the South West Africa People's Organization (SWAPO, Namibia) and the socialist regime in Mozambique as well as with Zambia and the African National Congress in South Africa. American involvement in Angola was seriously inhibited by the U.S. Congress's Clark Amendment of 1975, which banned military aid to any Angolan party. For a decade, direct U.S. involvement in southern Africa was minimal. The election of President Ronald Reagan, however, changed that.

In July 1985, Congress repealed the Clark Amendment. Thus, the leader of UNITA, Jonas Savimbi, became a primary recipient of U.S. paramilitary aid under the Reagan Doctrine, which argued that the USSR should not only be contained but that its influence and gains abroad (such as in Angola) should be rolled back. Zaire was a major conduit (along with South Africa) for U.S. covert assistance. At the peak of America's clandestine operations, Reagan labeled Savimbi a "combatant for liberty."

In 1981, under the stewardship of Chester Crocker, assistant secretary of state for African affairs, the United States announced a policy of constructive engagement for southern Africa. This was the endgame for U.S.–Soviet competition in the region. Crocker linked the independence of Namibia (from South Africa) to the withdrawal of Cuban troops from Angola. This entailed a quasi-alliance with South Africa's apartheid government but not support for the regime in Pretoria per se. To some, this disinterred what was called the Tar Baby Option, President Richard Nixon's secret policy of rapprochement with Smith's white minority regime in Rhodesia/Zimbabwe embodied in Option Two of the National Security Study Memorandum 39, a review of U.S. African policy ordered by National Security Advisor Henry Kissinger. The United States became one of three UN members (along with Portugal and South Africa) that allowed trade with Rhodesia from 1971 to 1977 under the Byrd Amendment, which circumvented UN sanctions against Rhodesia by permitting importation of Rhodesian chrome.

Nevertheless, following eight long years of negotiations, constructive engagement led to the 1998 New York Accords and the subsequent exit from Angola of Cuban and South African forces aligned, respectively, with the MPLA and UNITA. The Cold War in southern Africa was over.

James J. Hentz

Further Reading

Borstelmann, Thomas. *Apartheid's Reluctant Uncle: The United States and Southern Africa in the Early Cold War.* New York: Oxford University Press. 1993.

Copson, Raymond. *Africa's War and Prospects for Peace.* Armonk, NY: Sharpe, 1994.

Crocker, Chester A. *High Noon in Southern Africa: Making Peace in a Rough Neighborhood.* New York: Norton, 1992.

Fatton, Robert. "The Reagan Foreign Policy toward South Africa: The Ideology of the New Cold War." *African Studies Review* 27, no. 1 (1984): 57–82.

Howe, Herbert. *Military Forces in African States: Ambiguous Order.* Boulder, CO: Lynne Rienner, 2001.

Lake, Anthony. *The "Tar Baby" Option: American Policy towards Southern Rhodesia.* New York: Columbia University Press, 1976.

Lyman, Princeton. *Partner to History: The U.S. Role in South Africa's Transition to Democracy.* Washington, DC: United States Institute of Peace Press, 2002.

Schraeder, Peter. *African Politics and Society: A Mosaic in Transformation.* New York: St. Martin's, 2000.

Schraeder, Peter. *United States Foreign Policy toward Africa: Incrementalism, Crisis and Change.* Cambridge: Cambridge University Press, 1994.

Arab Nationalism

Arab nationalism rose as a response to European imperialism after World War II and stressed unity of purpose among the Arab countries of the Middle East. Though respectful of Islam, Arab nationalist movements were mainly secular in tone and drew heavily on socialist economic principles and anti-imperialist rhetoric. While the socialist, anti-Western character of Arab nationalism attracted Soviet political and military support and increased Soviet influence in the Middle East, Arab leaders avoided domination by the Soviet Union and found common cause with the nonaligned nations of the third world. Political and military opposition to the State of Israel served as a focal point of Arab nationalist movements, although repeated Arab military defeats contributed to the decline of such movements.

Arab nationalism has its roots in the late 19th century, when European ideas of nationalism affected the Ottoman Empire. After World War I, as the British and French acquired mandate authority over various Arab territories of the former Ottoman Empire, Arab nationalist sentiment was divided between unifying notions of Pan-Arabism and individual independence movements. Such thinking contributed to the formation of the Arab League on the one hand and the growth of numerous regional nationalist groups such as the Society of the Muslim Brothers in Egypt and the Étoile Nord-Africaine in Algeria on the other. These and similar groups combined nationalism with strong Islamic identity in their drive for independence from Britain and France.

In the years following World War II, most Arab states gained their independence, yet were ruled by governments sympathetic to the interests of the European powers. Political crises in the late 1940s and 1950s, including the Arab defeat in the first war with Israel (1948), resulted in the overthrow of many of these governments and the establishment of new regimes willing to challenge the West, particularly in Egypt, Syria, and Iraq. These nations lay at the heart of the Arab nationalist movement during the Cold War. Ongoing conflict with Israel would play a major role in the growth of Arab unity. The common Israeli enemy provided the Arab states with a greater cause that overshadowed their individual differences.

Opposition to Israel and support for Palestinian refugees also served to link the resources of the newly wealthy oil states of the Persian Gulf to the larger Arab cause.

Finally, the conflict with Israel, combined with the importance of petroleum resources, made the Middle East a region of great strategic interest to the United States and the Soviet Union, and the two superpowers would have a substantial effect on the development and destiny of Arab nationalism.

Arab nationalism during the period of the Cold War stressed Arab unity, but not necessarily in the form of a single Arab state; different states could act in concert to achieve goals that would benefit the entire Arab world. In addition, Arab nationalist movements fit into a broader picture of postcolonial political ideologies popular in the developing world. Such ideologies stressed national or cultural identity, along with Marxist or socialist ideas, as a counter to Western influence. Promoted by the Soviets, socialism served as a reaction among developing nations to their former experiences with European imperialism.

The two most important Arab nationalist movements that took root were Baathism and Nasserism. The Baath (or Resurrection) Party became prominent in Syria after World War II. One of its founders, Michel 'Aflaq, a Syrian Christian, conceived of a single Arab nation embracing all the Arab states and recapturing the glory of the Arabian past. Though the movement was respectful of Islamic tenets, its rhetoric and agenda were largely secular and socialist. This socialism grew partly as a response to Western imperialism and partly as a result of increasing Soviet political and military support of Baathist Arab states. The Baath Party increased in influence in Syria and Iraq throughout the late 1950s and early 1960s. In Syria, it came to dominate the country's turbulent politics by the early 1960s and continued to do so throughout the regime of Hafez al-Assad (1971–2001). In Iraq, the party rose to power in 1963 and remained the predominant political force until the overthrow of Saddam Hussein in 2003.

Nasserism reflected the agenda and the political prowess of Gamal Abdel Nasser, Egypt's leader during 1952–1970. Raised amid British domination in Egypt, Nasser combined his rejection of imperialist influence with socialist principles and progressive Islam. Although he used religious rhetoric to appeal to the Egyptian people, his outlook, like that of the Baathists, was primarily secular. Nasser stressed modernization, state ownership of industry, and Egypt's role as the "natural" leader of the Arab world. His suspicion of the West, socialist economic prescriptions, and acceptance of Soviet military aid after 1955 drew him toward the Soviet sphere, but he avoided subservience to Moscow and supported the Non-Aligned Movement among developing nations. Nasser actively sought the leadership of a unified Arab world. The temporary union of Egypt and Syria in the United Arab Republic (1958–1961) illustrated his nationalist vision and the overlap of Nasserist and Baathist ideologies.

Israel served as a focal point for Nasser's brand of Arab nationalism; he viewed the defeat of Israel (never achieved) as an expression of Arab unity and a rejection of imperialist interference in the Middle East. In addition, Egyptian leadership in the struggle with Israel contributed to his stature in the Arab world as a whole. Nasser's position in Egypt and among Arab nations was further enhanced by the 1956 Suez Crisis. However, Egypt's attempted military intervention in Yemen (1962–1967) brought Nasser's vision of Arab nationalism into conflict with the royalist, Islamic views of Saudi Arabia and demonstrated the limits of his influence. Further, Egypt's disastrous defeat in the Six-Day War with Israel in June 1967 dealt a crippling blow to his power and prestige. Nasser's authority survived the 1967 War, and the overwhelming popular rejection of his resignation testified to the scope of his popular appeal, but the 1967 defeat ultimately signaled the end of the Nasserist vision of Arab unity. From that point onward, Baathism remained as the strongest single force of Arab nationalism.

Robert S. Kiely

Further Reading

Dawisha, Adeed. *Arab Nationalism in the 20th Century*. Princeton, NJ: Princeton University Press, 2003.

Hourani, Albert. *A History of the Arab Peoples*. Cambridge, MA: Harvard University Press, 1991.

Oren, Michael. *The Six Day War*. Novato, CA: Presidio, 2002.

B

Bay of Pigs (April 17, 1961)

In the spring of 1960, President Dwight Eisenhower approved a covert operation to send small groups of American-trained Cuban exiles to work in the Cuban underground as insurgents to overthrow Castro. President Eisenhower had soured on Castro after the latter nationalized a number of Cuban companies and began leaning toward the Soviet orbit of influence. There were also rumors of Cuban involvement in attempts to invade Panama, Guatemala, and the Dominican Republic. In 1960, the United States turned down Castro's request for economic aid and broke off diplomatic relations with Cuba. After the American rejection, Castro met with Soviet foreign minister Anastas Mikoyan to secure a $100 million loan from the Soviet Union. U.S. policymakers thus decided that Castro was becoming too close to the Soviets and should be overthrown.

By the fall, the plan, called Operation Pluto, had evolved into a full-fledged invasion by exiled Cubans, and included U.S. air support. The rebels of Brigade 2506, as they were called, deployed to Guatemala to train for the operation, under the leadership of the Central Intelligence Agency (CIA) with arms supplied by the U.S. government.

When President John F. Kennedy assumed office in January 1961, he could have called off the invasion but chose not to do so. During the 1960 presidential campaign, Kennedy had criticized Eisenhower's handling of the Cuban situation and so did not find it politically expedient to back down from the invasion. Kennedy was also anxious to prove

his hawkish stance toward the Soviets during a period of heightened Cold War tensions. But the new president was not well served by the CIA or its director, Allen W. Dulles, whom he inherited from the Eisenhower administration. The agency grossly underestimated the effectiveness of Castro's forces and overplayed the extent to which Cubans would rally behind the invasion force.

On April 17, 1961, an armed force of approximately 1,500 Cuban exiles landed in the Bahia de Cochinos (Bay of Pigs) on the southern coast of Cuba, although the invasion had technically commenced two days earlier when American B-26 medium bombers with Cuban markings bombed four Cuban airfields. The invasion began at 2:00 a.m. when a team of frogmen went ashore with orders to set up landing lights to guide the main landing force. Between 2:30 and 3:00 a.m., two battalions of exiles armed with American weapons came ashore at Playa Giron, while another battalion landed at Playa Largas. They hoped to find support from the local population, intending to cross the island to attack Havana. Cuban forces reacted quickly, and Castro ordered his air force to halt the invaders. Cuban aircraft promptly sank the invading force command-and-control ship and another supply vessel carrying an additional battalion. Two other ships loaded with supplies, weapons, and heavy equipment foundered just offshore. In the air, Cuban T-33 jets shot down 10 of the 12 slow-moving B-26 bombers that were supporting the invaders. President Kennedy, on the recommendation of Secretary of State Dean Rusk and other advisors, decided against providing the faltering invasion with official U.S. air support.

Lacking supplies or effective air cover, the invaders were hammered by Cuban artillery and tank fire. Within 72 hours, the invading force had been pushed back to its landing area at Playa Giron, where the troops were soon surrounded by Castro's forces. A total of 114 exiles were killed, and the remainder of the invasion force either escaped into the countryside or was taken captive. In all, 1,189 captured exiles were tried in televised trials and sentenced to prison.

Cuban exile leader José Miro Cardona, president of the U.S.-backed National Revolutionary Council, blamed the failure on the CIA and Kennedy's refusal to authorize air support for the invasion. In December 1962, Castro released 1,113 captured rebels in exchange for $53 million in food and medicine raised by private donations in the United States.

The Bay of Pigs invasion provoked anti-American demonstrations throughout Latin America and Europe and further embittered U.S.–Cuban relations. The poorly planned and executed invasion greatly embarrassed President Kennedy and subjected him to heavy criticism at home. More important, it led directly to increased tensions between the United States and the Soviet Union. During the invasion, Kennedy and Soviet Premier Nikita Khrushchev exchanged messages regarding the events in Cuba. Khrushchev accused America of being complicit in the invasion and warned Kennedy that the Soviets would help defend Cuba if necessary. Kennedy replied with an equally strong warning against any Soviet involvement in Cuba. Although the crisis quickly passed, it set the stage for increased Soviet military aid to Cuba, which led ultimately to the Cuban Missile Crisis in October 1962.

The failure of the invasion led to the resignation of Dulles and opened the way for closer scrutiny of U.S. intelligence gathering.

James H. Willbanks

Further Reading

Higgins, Trumbull. *The Perfect Failure: Kennedy, Eisenhower, and the CIA at the Bay of Pigs*. New York: Norton, 1989.

Kornbluh, Peter. *Bay of Pigs Declassified: The Secret CIA Report on the Invasion of Cuba*. New York: New Press, 1998.

Meyer, Karl E., and Tad Szulc. *The Cuban Invasion: The Chronicle of a Disaster*. New York: Praeger, 1968.

Rusk, Dean. *As I Saw It*. New York: Norton, 1990.

Wyden, Peter. *The Bay of Pigs: The Untold Story*. New York: Vintage/Ebury, 1979.

Berlin Blockade and Airlift (1948–1949)

As part of the Potsdam Agreements, Germany and Berlin were divided into occupation zones by the victorious World War II Allies (the United States, the Soviet Union, France, and Great Britain), reaffirming principles laid out earlier at the Yalta Conference. Although the provisions of the agreement allocated occupation sectors of Berlin to the other three Allies, no formal arrangements had been made for access to Berlin via the Soviet zone.

After the war, the relationship between the Soviet Union and the West deteriorated steadily, as demonstrated by disputes in the United Nations, Winston Churchill's March 1946 "Sinews of Peace" speech (also known as the "Iron Curtain" speech), U.S. emphasis on Soviet containment, Soviet hostility toward the Marshall Plan, and a growing Western commitment to consolidating occupation zones in western Germany to form a single, independent state. The Soviets, who had been invaded by Germany twice in the first half of the 20th century, were alarmed at the prospect of a reunited, independent Germany.

In late 1947, discussions on the fate of Germany broke down over Soviet charges that its former Allies were violating the Potsdam Agreements. After the decision of the Western powers to introduce a new currency in their zones, on March 20, 1948, the Soviets withdrew from the Four-Power Allied Control Council, which controlled Berlin. Ten days later, guards on the eastern German border began slowing the entry of Western troop trains bound for Berlin. On June 7, the Western powers announced

their intention to proceed with the creation of a West German state. On June 15, the Soviets declared the Autobahn entering Berlin from West Germany closed for repairs. Three days later all road traffic from the west was halted, and on June 21 barge traffic was prohibited from entering the city. On June 24, the Soviets stopped all surface traffic between West Germany and Berlin, arguing that if Germany were to be partitioned, Berlin could no longer be the German capital.

From the start of the Cold War, West Berlin had been a Western outpost deep (110 miles) within the Soviet occupation zone, a hotbed of intelligence operations by both sides, and the best available escape route

Berliners watch a U.S. Douglas C-54 transport land at Tempelhof Airport during the Berlin Airlift, a massive transfer of essential supplies into Berlin by the Western Allies during the Soviet-imposed Berlin Blockade, 1948–1949. (Library of Congress)

for East Germans fleeing communism and Soviet control. U.S. president Harry Truman was convinced that abandoning Berlin would jeopardize control of all of Germany. He further believed that the Soviets were determined to push the Western powers out of Berlin, thereby discrediting repeated American assurances to its allies and the rest of Europe that it would not allow Berlin to fall.

A military response to the blockade was initially considered, but rejected, as the Western powers lacked the manpower to counter the massive Red Army's numerical advantage. Thus the United States, working with its European allies, undertook to supply West Berlin via air corridors left open to them in a postwar agreement. The Berlin Airlift began on June 24, 1948, and continued uninterrupted for the next 324 days. Western fliers, under the leadership of U.S. Air Force Lieutenant General Curtis LeMay, made a total of 272,000 flights into West Berlin, delivering thousands of tons of supplies every day.

The airlift was at first meant to be a short-term measure, as Allied officials did not believe that the airlift could support the whole of Berlin for any length of time. The situation in the summer and fall of 1948 became very tense as Soviet planes buzzed U.S. transport planes in the air corridors over East Germany, but the Allies only increased their efforts to resupply the German city once it became apparent that no resolution was in sight. The Soviets never attempted to shoot down any of the Western aircraft involved in the airlift, no doubt because such a provocation might well have resulted in war.

Hundreds of aircraft were used to fly in a wide variety of cargo items, including more than 1.5 million tons of coal. By the fall, the airlift, called by the Americans "Operation Vittles," was transporting an average of 5,000 tons of supplies a day. At the height of the operation on April 16, 1949, an aircraft landed in Berlin every minute around the clock.

The airlift was an international effort; airplanes were supplied by the United States, the United Kingdom, and France, but there were also flight crews from Australia, Canada, South Africa, and New Zealand. The three main Berlin airfields involved in the effort were Tempelhof in the American sector, Gatow in the British zone, and Tegel in the French sector. The British even landed seaplanes on the Havel River.

The airlift gained widespread public and international admiration, and on May 12, 1949, the Soviets, concluding that the blockade had failed, reopened the borders in return for a meeting of the Council of Foreign Ministers, perhaps believing that they could have some influence on the Western Allies' proposed plans for the future of Germany. Even though the Soviets lifted the blockade in May, the airlift did not end until September 30 because the allies sought to build up sufficient amounts of reserve supplies in West Berlin in case the Soviets blockaded it again. In all, the United States, Britain, and France flew 278,118 flights transporting more than 2.3 million short tons of cargo. Thirty-one Americans and 39 British citizens, most of them military personnel, died in the airlift.

In the end, the blockade not only was completely ineffective but also backfired. The blockade provoked genuine fears of the Soviets in the West and introduced even greater tension into the Cold War. Instead of preventing an independent West Germany, it actually accelerated Allied plans to set up the state. It also hastened the creation of the North Atlantic Treaty Organization (NATO), an American–West European military alliance.

James H. Willbanks

Further Reading

Clay, Lucius D. *Decision in Germany*. Garden City, NY: Doubleday, 1950.

Collins, Richard. *Bridge across the Sky: The Berlin Blockade and Airlift, 1948–1949*. New York: Pan Macmillan, 1978.

Haydock, Michael D. *City under Siege: The Berlin Blockade and Airlift, 1948–1949*. London: Brassey's, 1999.

Schlain, Avi. *The United States and the Berlin Blockade, 1948–1949: A Study in Decision-Making*. Berkeley: University of California Press, 1983.

Tusa, Ann. *The Last Division: A History of Berlin, 1945–1989*. Reading, MA: Addison-Wesley, 1997.

Berlin Crises (1958–1961)

Continual disagreement between the Soviet bloc and the Western Allies over the control of Berlin had begun in earnest in the late 1940s, culminating in the Berlin Blockade (1948–1949). Renewed Cold War tensions transformed the city into one of the world's potential flash points during 1958–1961.

With Soviet prestige dramatically boosted by the launch of *Sputnik 1* in 1957, Soviet Premier Nikita Khrushchev decided to revive the issue of Berlin. On November 10, 1958, he sought to end the joint-occupation agreement in the city by demanding that Great Britain, France, and the United States withdraw their 10,000 troops from West Berlin. He also declared that the Soviet Union would unilaterally transfer its occupation authority in Berlin to the German Democratic Republic (GDR, East Germany) if a peace treaty were not signed with both East and the Federal Republic of Germany (FRG, West Germany) within six months. West Berlin would then become a free city. Khrushchev couched his demands by portraying West Berlin's proposed free-city

status as a concession because it lay in East German territory and therefore properly belonged to the GDR. None of the Western powers, however, formally recognized East Germany, viewing it as a mere subsidiary of the Soviet Union.

The United States flatly rejected Khrushchev's demands, although other Western powers initially tried to placate the Soviet leaders by proposing an interim Berlin agreement that placed a limit on Western forces and curtailed some propagandistic West Berlin activities, such as radio broadcasts that targeted East German audiences. These Allied proposals would have given the Soviets and East Germans some measure of power in West Berlin, a concession that many West Berliners viewed as a highly dangerous step toward neutralization and, ultimately, abandonment. In December 1958, the Allies issued a North Atlantic Treaty Organization (NATO) declaration rejecting Soviet demands and insisting that no state had the right to withdraw unilaterally from an international agreement.

Khrushchev gradually retreated from his hard-line stance on Berlin. American U-2 overflights of the Soviet Union indicated that the West had an accurate count of the comparatively small number of Soviet nuclear missiles, and the Soviet leader obviously feared starting a war that he could not win. The Soviets now envisioned a gradual crowding out of the Western powers without bloodshed. In the meantime, the economic situation in East Germany continued to deteriorate, with vast numbers of refugees fleeing to the West.

In 1961 the newly elected U.S. president John F. Kennedy abandoned the demand for German unification that had been part of U.S. policy since the 1940s. His foreign policy team had drawn the conclusion that such a policy was not only impractical but might

Russian and American tanks face off at the tense Friedrichstrasse checkpoint on the East–West Berlin border October 28, 1961. Seventeen hours after the confrontation began, Russian tanks pulled away from the border and moved up a side street in East Berlin, ending the crisis. (AP/Wide World Photos)

actually provoke a U.S.–Soviet war. Kennedy and his advisors decided that only three interests were worth the risk of nuclear war: the continued Allied presence in West Berlin, Allied access to West Berlin by land and by air, and the continued autonomous freedom of West Berlin. Realizing that a rather inconsequential event and a sequence of mutually threatening and unnecessary mobilizations had led to World War I in 1914, Kennedy worried constantly that a relatively minor incident in Germany could escalate into World War III.

Meanwhile, GDR leader Walter Ulbricht decided to close the East Berlin borders in an attempt to exercise control over all traffic to and from Berlin, including Allied military as well as German civilian travelers. On August 13, 1961, East German authorities began the construction of the Berlin Wall, essentially sealing off East Berlin from West Berlin. Ulbricht sought to control not only what went into East Berlin but also what came out, including thousands of East Germans who sought refuge in West Berlin. The Soviets and the East Germans had wagered that the West would not react to the construction of the Wall. Kennedy, in accordance with his policy, offered little resistance. Emboldened, Ulbricht began to take further measures to assert control over Berlin.

Ten days after closing the border, the GDR allowed tourists, diplomats, and Western military personnel to enter East Berlin only via the crossing point at Berlin Friedrichstrasse. The only other two checkpoints into East Germany were Helmstedt at the West German–East German border and Dreilinden at the West Berlin–East Germany border. According to the military's phonetic alphabet, the Helmstedt checkpoint became Alpha, Dreilinden was nicknamed Checkpoint Bravo, and the checkpoint at Friedrichstrasse was famously dubbed Charlie. Checkpoint Charlie would soon become one of the best-known symbols of the Cold War.

At all of the East German checkpoints tourists were fully screened, but the postwar occupation agreement prevented East German authorities from checking any members of the Allied military forces. On October 22, 1961, Allan Lightner, chief of the U.S. Mission in Berlin, attempted to pass through Checkpoint Charlie to attend the opera in East Berlin. East German police stopped Lightner and asked him for identification. Lightner, following long-standing instructions, stated that he was a member of the U.S. occupation authority as shown by his U.S. Mission license plate and that he therefore did not have to provide identification. The East German police refused to let Lightner pass. General Lucius D. Clay, the hero of the Berlin Airlift and now President Kennedy's personal representative in West Berlin, immediately dispatched a squad of U.S. soldiers to the site. With that, Lightner's car went through the checkpoint, backed up, and went through it again and again to make the point that U.S. officials were going to move freely. Although Kennedy was reluctant to precipitate a crisis over a somewhat trivial affair, Clay nonetheless ordered tanks to the checkpoint, while the Soviet military brought in its own tanks to oppose them.

The 1961 Checkpoint Charlie incident thus proved that the Soviets, not the East Germans, were actually in charge of East Germany. The photos of American and Soviet tanks facing each other at the checkpoint on October 25 became one of the most memorable images of the Cold War. The confrontation boosted the morale of West Berliners because it clearly showed that the Allies, particularly the United States, would not yield to East German or Soviet pressure tactics. It also unmasked the charade of an independent and autonomous GDR that could deal on an equal basis with the Western powers.

Caryn E. Neumann

Further Reading

Harrison, Hope M. *Driving the Soviets up the Wall: Soviet-East German Relations, 1953–1961*. Princeton, NJ: Princeton University Press, 2003.

Murphy, David E., Sergei A. Kondrashev, and George Bailey. *Battleground Berlin: CIA vs. KGB in the Cold War*. New Haven, CT: Yale University Press, 1997.

Smyser, W. R. *From Yalta to Berlin: The Cold War Struggle over Germany*. New York: St. Martin's, 1999.

Berlin Wall (August 13, 1961– November 9, 1989)

Officially known in East Germany as the "Antifascist Bulwark," the Berlin Wall was constructed in August 1961 to stop the flood of East German citizens seeking asylum in the Federal Republic of Germany (FRG, West Germany). *Republikflucht* (flight from the Republic) created tremendous economic strains.

Most of the people fleeing the German Democratic Republic (GDR, East Germany) were young skilled workers. Between 1949, when the GDR was created, and 1952, when the border was sealed off everywhere but in Berlin, almost 200,000 people left for West Germany each year. After the East Berlin Uprising in 1953, the number of refugees doubled, with more than 400,000 people leaving the GDR that year. Although flight from the GDR dropped to normal levels again for 1954, a mild economic crisis in 1956 led to another exodus.

Walter Ulbricht, the leader of the Socialist Unity Party (SED) that controlled the GDR, proposed to Soviet leader Nikita Khrushchev that the border in Berlin be sealed in early 1961. This was a risky move, as Berlin was still theoretically an open city under the control of all four Allied powers. Despite Soviet misgivings, GDR army, police, and volunteer (*Kampfgruppen*) units began the construction of the barrier on the night of August 12–13, 1961. The Brandenburg Gate was closed to traffic the following day, and by August 26 all crossing points into West Berlin had been sealed off. Eventually,

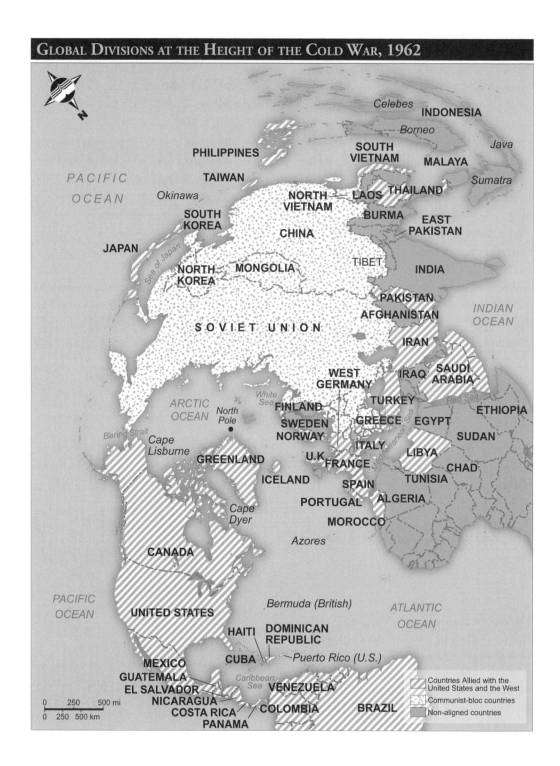

GLOBAL DIVISIONS AT THE HEIGHT OF THE COLD WAR, 1962

Celebes
INDONESIA
Borneo
Java
PHILIPPINES
SOUTH VIETNAM
MALAYA
TAIWAN
Sumatra
PACIFIC OCEAN
Okinawa
NORTH VIETNAM
LAOS
THAILAND
SOUTH KOREA
BURMA
EAST PAKISTAN
CHINA
JAPAN
TIBET
INDIA
Sea of Japan
NORTH KOREA
MONGOLIA
PAKISTAN
AFGHANISTAN
INDIAN OCEAN
SOVIET UNION
IRAN
SAUDI ARABIA
WEST GERMANY
IRAQ
ARCTIC OCEAN
North Pole
White Sea
FINLAND
TURKEY
Red Sea
ETHIOPIA
Bering Strait
SWEDEN
GREECE
EGYPT
Cape Lisburne
NORWAY
SUDAN
GREENLAND
U.K.
ITALY
LIBYA
FRANCE
CHAD
ICELAND
SPAIN
TUNISIA
Cape Dyer
PORTUGAL
ALGERIA
MOROCCO
Azores
CANADA
PACIFIC OCEAN
Bermuda (British)
ATLANTIC OCEAN
UNITED STATES
HAITI
DOMINICAN REPUBLIC
MEXICO
CUBA
Puerto Rico (U.S.)
GUATEMALA
Caribbean Sea
VENEZUELA
EL SALVADOR
NICARAGUA
COSTA RICA
COLOMBIA
BRAZIL
PANAMA

0   250   500 mi
0 250 500 km

Countries Allied with the United States and the West
Communist-bloc countries
Non-aligned countries

12 checkpoints were established to regulate traffic between the GDR and West Berlin. The most famous, in the center of Berlin, was called Checkpoint Charlie.

The Berlin Wall went through four generations of architecture. Far more than the symbolic barricade that cut through the center of Berlin and was so often photographed by tourists, the wall encircled the western half of the city. Until 1971, when a connecting road was constructed, two western exclaves existed behind the wall and were supplied solely by the American and British military. There were obstacles in canals, sewer lines, and communications and transportation tunnels that formed part of the Berlin Wall system. It stretched for 106 miles (155 km) and by 1989 contained 92 watchtowers, 20 bunkers, anti-vehicle trenches, and other advanced defensive systems.

The first two versions of the Berlin Wall consisted of concrete blocks and barbed wire. These were replaced in 1965 with a system of concrete slabs and steel girders topped by a sewage pipe to make scaling the wall more difficult. In 1975, this structure gave way to one made entirely of reinforced concrete some 12 feet high, not including the tube element on top. Behind this was the so-called death strip secured by dogs, tanks, trip-wire machine guns, and guards.

Though these measures prevented the flood of refugees in numbers like the late 1950s, they did not stop people from trying to escape from the GDR to the West. In the early days of the Berlin Wall, people jumped from buildings, used ladders to climb over the wall, or dug tunnels under it. As the system evolved, attempts became more dangerous and more complex. At least 171 people

An unidentified West Berliner swings a sledgehammer, trying to destroy the Berlin Wall near Potsdamer Platz, on November 12, 1989, where a new passage was opened nearby. (AP/Wide World Photos)

were killed trying to leave the GDR between August 13, 1961, and November 9, 1989, when the wall came down. More than 5,000 East Germans, including 574 GDR border guards, successfully crossed the wall.

East Germans were not the only victims of the Berlin Wall, however. Because the wall was actually built a few yards back from the border, in the early years of the wall West German citizens who strayed too close could be and were sometimes arrested by GDR border patrols. The restricted supplies and claustrophobic atmosphere of West Berlin caused a drop in population of some 340,000 people between 1963 and 1983. To keep the city alive, the FRG encouraged foreign immigration and granted special privileges to West Berliners.

The western half of the city became a symbol of freedom, recognized most famously in the phrase "*Ich bin ein Berliner*" (I am a resident of Berlin) in John F. Kennedy's 1963 speech. A later American president, Ronald Reagan, also recognized the symbolism of the Berlin Wall when he challenged Soviet leader Mikhail Gorbachev to "tear down this Wall" to prove his sincerity about reform. Soviet pressure for reform in fact did play a part in the fall of the Berlin Wall.

During the transitional crisis of late 1989, the new East Berlin regime lifted travel restrictions to West Berlin. Günter Schabowski, head of the SED's Berlin organization, announced on television on November 9, 1989, that the lifting of restrictions would be effective immediately. East Germans went, cautiously, to test this at the Berlin Wall; lacking specific instructions, border guards let them through. Within hours, Germans from both sides of the wall were sitting atop it, drinking champagne and celebrating the end of the divided city.

Today, the only reminder of the Berlin Wall is a strip of bricks that follows its former path. Most sections of concrete are in museums, many in foreign countries. While it existed, however, the Berlin Wall was one of the most infamous and powerful symbols of the Cold War.

Timothy C. Dowling

Further Reading

Bessel, Richard, and Ralph Jessen, eds. *Die Grenzen der Diktatur: Staat und Gesellschaft in der DDR*. Göttingen: Vanderhoeck and Ruprecht, 1996.

Buckley, William F. *The Fall of the Berlin Wall*. New York: Wiley, 2004.

Fulbrook, Mary. *Anatomy of a Dictatorship: Inside the GDR, 1949–1989*. Oxford: Oxford University Press, 1995.

Harrison, Hope M. *Driving the Soviets up the Wall: Soviet-East German Relations, 1953–1961*. Princeton, NJ: Princeton University Press, 2003.

Ladd, Brian. *The Ghosts of Berlin: Confronting German History in the Urban Landscape*. Chicago: University of Chicago Press, 1997.

Large, David Clay. *Berlin: A Modern History*. New York: Basic Books, 2000.

Brandt, Willy (1913–1992)

Born Hubert Ernst Karl Frahm in the town of Lübeck on December 16, 1913, Willy Brandt became the most charismatic German politician of the Cold War era. He joined the youth section of the German Socialist Workers' Party (SAP) in 1929 and then briefly became a member of the German Social Democratic Party (SPD) in 1930 before returning to the more radical SAP in 1931. He adopted the name Willy Brandt in 1933, when the rise of the National Socialists in Germany forced him to flee to Norway.

Brandt spent the war years as a journalist and organizer. He returned surreptitiously to

President John F. Kennedy and Mayor Willy Brandt of Berlin at the White House, March 13, 1961. (Library of Congress)

Berlin in 1936 to reorganize the SAP resistance, then went to Spain as an observer reporting from the republican side of the civil war there. The Nazi government stripped him of German citizenship in 1938. When World War II ended, Brandt returned to Germany; among his first jobs was covering the Nuremberg trials for the Scandinavian press.

Brandt became involved in politics again once his citizenship was restored in 1948. As a pragmatic socialist who was also an anticommunist, he was elected to the German parliament in 1949 as a member of the SPD. He served as president of the senate for the City of Berlin during 1955–1957 and, in 1957, won election as mayor of Berlin. Brandt proved his mettle during the crises of 1958–1962 and especially during the construction of the Berlin Wall in August 1961.

The SPD subsequently put Brandt forward as its candidate for chancellor in 1961 and again in 1965. Although both campaigns were unsuccessful, Brandt became foreign minister and vice chancellor in the SPD-Christian Democratic Union (CDU) Grand Coalition government that emerged in 1966. In 1969, when the SPD led a coalition with the Free Democratic Party, Brandt became chancellor.

He quickly set about implementing the policy that would become his legacy: *Ostpolitik*, or eastern politics. Brandt believed that the path to German success and unity lay in reconciliation with the Soviets and with Eastern Europe. He was particularly concerned with establishing normal relations with the German Democratic Republic (GDR, East Germany), a direct contravention of the previous regime's Hallstein Doctrine. Whereas Konrad Adenauer and the CDU had claimed to be the sole legitimate representatives of the German nation, Brandt was willing to accommodate "two states in one nation." In the wake of the Prague Spring of 1968, moreover, he had openly renounced violence in favor of mediation. To that end, he became the first chancellor of the FRG to visit the GDR when he went to Erfurt in March 1970 as part of an exchange of visits with Willi Stoph, chairman of the Council of Ministers for the GDR.

By all accounts, Brandt was received "like a rock star" in East Germany, and he moved quickly to consolidate his position. In August 1970, the FRG concluded a treaty of nonaggression with the Soviet Union, the so-called Moscow Treaty. The FRG recognized the borders of Poland and of the GDR and agreed to make no territorial claims. The Soviets, for their part, recognized that the FRG's position on unification remained unchanged but agreed to work for the normalization of the situation in Berlin. The Four-Power Agreement that realized that goal was signed in September 1971.

With the groundwork for normal relations with East Germany in place, Brandt signed a similar agreement with the Poles. In the Warsaw Treaty of December 1970, the FRG gave assurances that West Germany would accept the borders established in 1945, but Brandt's performance during the concluding visit was even more spectacular. At a ceremony commemorating the victims of the Warsaw Ghetto Uprising, Brandt dropped to his knees before a memorial to Jews victimized by the SS in 1943 and bowed his head in a gesture that demonstrated to many people that Germany had turned over a new leaf. In addition to being named *Time* magazine's Man of the Year for 1970, Brandt won a Nobel Peace Prize in 1971.

Brandt's achievements were not always readily accepted in the FRG. However, a constructive no-confidence vote forced the issue in April 1972. Brandt and the SPD were returned the following November with 45 percent of the vote, and they forged ahead. In June 1973, Brandt became the first German chancellor to visit Israel, where he offered words of consolation and apology for Germany's actions during World War II. Three months later, he became the first German chancellor to address the General Assembly of the United Nations.

Brandt's term as chancellor came to an end in 1974, when his loyalty to Gunter Guillaume, an aide who was revealed to be an East German spy, caused a scandal that brought down the government. Brandt continued in politics outside of Germany following his resignation. He was involved in negotiations for peace in the Middle East at several points and worked on nonproliferation issues in a number of capacities. Brandt died in Unkel am Rhein, near Bonn, on October 8, 1992.

Timothy C. Dowling

Further Reading

Brandt, Willy. *My Life in Politics*. London: Hamish Hamilton, 1992.

Marshall, Barbara. *Willy Brandt: A Political Biography*. New York: Palgrave Macmillan, 1997.

Pulzer, Peter G. J. *German Politics, 1945–1995*. Oxford: Oxford University Press, 1995.

Sarotte, M. E. *Dealing with the Devil: East Germany, Detente, and Ostpolitik, 1969– 1973.* Chapel Hill: University of North Carolina Press, 2001.

Brezhnev, Leonid (1906–1982)

Leonid Ilyich Brezhnev was born in the Ukrainian town of Dneprodzerzhinsk, then called Kamenskoye, on December 19, 1906. The son of a steelworker, he graduated as an engineer in 1935 from the Kamenskoye Metallurgical Institute and worked in the iron and steel industries of the eastern Ukraine. In 1939 he became CPSU secretary in Dnepropetrovsk in charge of the city's important defense industries.

Brezhnev matured as an unquestioning follower of Soviet dictator Josef Stalin and gained rapid promotion within the Communist Party hierarchy, especially after the political purges of the late 1930s opened up many positions. Following the German invasion of the Soviet Union in June 1941, Brezhnev was soon drafted into the Red Army as a political commissar. By the end of the war he was in charge of the Political Administration of the 4th Ukrainian Front.

After the war, Brezhnev's party career gained momentum. During 1946–1955 he served as party first secretary in Zaporozhe, Dnepropetrovsk, and then in the republics of Moldavia and Kazakhstan. In 1952 he was also appointed a member of the CPSU Central Committee. In 1957 he joined the Politburo.

Brezhnev's meteoric rise was due in large measure to the power of his new patron, Nikita Khrushchev. Nevertheless, Brezhnev, together with Alexei Kosygin, unseated Khrushchev during a 1964 CPSU power struggle. In the division of power that followed, on October 15, 1964, Brezhnev became first secretary of the CPSU, while Kosygin became prime minister. In 1966 Brezhnev named himself general secretary of the CPSU and began to dominate the collective leadership. In 1975 he was appointed an army general; in 1976 he became marshal of the Soviet Union (the highest military rank); and in 1977 he replaced Nikolai Podgorny as head of state.

During the Khrushchev years, Brezhnev had supported the leader's denunciations of Stalin's arbitrary rule and the liberalization of Soviet intellectual policies. But as soon as he had ousted Khrushchev, Brezhnev began to reverse this process. The 1966 trials of Soviet writers Yuri Daniel and Andrei Sinyavsky marked the reversion to a more repressive policy. The Komitet Gosudarstvennoi Bezopasnosti (KGB, Committee for State Security) regained much of the power it had enjoyed under Stalin, although there was no recurrence of the political purges of the 1930s and 1940s.

In August 1968 Brezhnev brought communist reforms in Eastern Europe to a halt by ordering the invasion of Czechoslovakia, where the Prague Spring had threatened to dissolve that country's political and military solidarity with Moscow and the Warsaw Pact. This military intervention was afterward justified by the Brezhnev Doctrine, which claimed for the Soviet Union the right to interfere in its client states' affairs in order to safeguard socialism and maintain the unity of the Warsaw Pact.

During Brezhnev's tenure, a nonaggression pact with the Federal Republic of Germany (FRG, West Germany) was concluded in 1970, marking the beginning of détente with the West. On a global level, Brezhnev carried out negotiations on arms control with the United States and signed the 1968 Anti-Ballistic Missile Treaty and the 1972 Strategic Arms Limitation Talks Treaty. On the whole, during the 1970s Brezhnev advocated a relaxation of Cold War tensions, which he also demonstrated by signing the 1975 Helsinki Final Act. This recognized the postwar frontiers of Central and Eastern Europe and in effect legitimized Soviet hegemony over the region. In exchange, the Soviet Union agreed to respect human rights and fundamental freedoms.

Relaxation abroad was not matched by liberalization at home. On the contrary, Brezhnev tried to neutralize the effects of détente by expanding the Soviet security apparatus and government control over society. His regime also became synonymous with corruption and the severe repression of dissidents. Urbanization had given rise to an ever-larger number of Soviet citizens, especially from the young and educated groups, hoping to live a Western lifestyle with access to Western culture and a Western middle-class standard of living.

The Soviet invasion of Afghanistan in 1979 signaled an end to détente. The Afghanistan War soon deteriorated into a debacle and contributed to the steady decline of the communist regime. Although the Soviet Union was awash in oil dollars, this money was of little help to the civilian economy because the regime frittered its wealth away on construction projects, corruption, and handouts to brother regimes and pumped it into military industries and the Afghan quagmire.

Parallel to the deterioration of the economic and political system, Brezhnev's physical health and mental awareness steadily declined in the late 1970s. The geriatric Politburo, however, with an average age of 70, feared change and thus kept him in power well beyond his time. Brezhnev died in Moscow on November 10, 1982, after several years of failing health, and was succeeded by KGB head Yuri Andropov.

Beatrice de Graaf

Further Reading

Bacon, Edwin, and Mark Sandle. *Brezhnev Reconsidered*. Basingstoke, UK: Palgrave Macmillan, 2002.

Kozlov, V. A., and Elaine McClarnand Mackinnon. *Mass Uprisings in the USSR: Urban Unrest under Khrushchev and Brezhnev, 1953–82*. Armonk, NY: Sharpe, 2002.

Navazelskis, Ina L. *Leonid Brezhnev*. Langhorne, PA: Chelsea House, 1987.

C

Central Intelligence Agency

Congress established the Central Intelligence Agency (CIA) in July 1947 to centralize and coordinate intelligence and espionage activities in reaction to the deepening Cold War. The CIA was to focus on the Soviet Union and its satellites. The CIA's primary function was to advise the National Security Council (NSC) on intelligence matters and make recommendations for coordination of intelligence activities. To accomplish these goals, the CIA was to correlate, evaluate, and disseminate intelligence and perform other services in accordance with NSC directives. President Harry S. Truman appointed legendary spymaster William "Wild Bill" Donovan to serve as the first CIA director.

The CIA assumed primary responsibility not only for intelligence collection and analysis but also for covert actions. Because Congress was vague in defining the CIA's mission, broad interpretation of the act provided justification for subsequent covert operations, although the original intent was only to authorize espionage. The CIA director was responsible for reporting on intelligence activities to Congress and the president. No CIA director ever exerted central control over the other 12 government entities in the U.S. intelligence community.

Known to insiders as "The Agency" or "The Company," the CIA consisted of four directorates. The Directorate of Operations (DO) supervised official and nonofficial agents in conducting human intelligence collection, covert operations, and counterintelligence. The DO was divided into geographic units and also contained the Center for Counterterrorism. The Directorate of Administration managed the CIA's daily administrative affairs and housed the Office of Security (OS). Created in 1952, the Directorate of Intelligence conducted research in intelligence sources and analysis of the results.

It produced the "President's Daily Brief" and worked with the National Intelligence Council in preparing estimates and studies. The Directorate of Science and Technology, created in 1963, was responsible for development and operation of reconnaissance aircraft and satellites, operation and funding of ground stations to intercept Soviet missile telemetry, and analysis of foreign nuclear and space programs. It also operated the Foreign Broadcast Information Service (FBIS), which monitored and analyzed all foreign media outlets.

During its first years, the CIA had difficulty prevailing in bureaucratic battles over authority and funding. For example, the State Department required CIA personnel abroad to operate under a U.S. ambassador. Walter Bedell Smith, who replaced Donovan in 1950, was an effective director, but the CIA's power increased greatly after Allen W. Dulles, brother of Secretary of State John Foster Dulles, became director in 1953. An 80 percent increase in the agency's budget led to the hiring of 50 percent more agents and a major expansion of covert operations.

The CIA played a key role in the overthrow of allegedly radical governments in Iran in 1953 and Guatemala in 1954. With the advice of CIA operative Edward G. Lansdale, Philippine Secretary of National Defense Ramon

Magsaysay crushed the Hukbalahap uprising in his country during 1950–1954. CIA agents in South Vietnam infiltrated the Michigan State University Advisory Group that trained police and administrators during 1955–1962 as a basis for nation building. In Laos, the CIA operated Air America and supported rightist politicians, while Donovan, who became U.S. ambassador to Thailand, organized Thai paramilitary units to fight communist forces in neighboring countries.

President John F. Kennedy lost confidence in the CIA after the disastrous Bay of Pigs invasion, which failed to oust Cuba's Fidel Castro in 1961. The CIA nonetheless continued to devise imaginative but somewhat improbable schemes to assassinate or discredit Castro, efforts suspended during the Cuban Missile Crisis. In 1961, however, a Soviet military intelligence (GRU) officer began providing the CIA with information on Soviet strategic capabilities, nuclear targeting policies, and medium-range ballistic missiles that would prove critical in the 1962 Cuban Missile Crisis. The CIA also penetrated the Soviet Foreign Ministry, the Defense Ministry and General Staff, the GRU, and the Komitet Gosudarstvennoi Bezopasnosti (KGB). But its covert activities—especially its operations to kill Castro and its involvement in the murders of South Vietnam's Ngo Dinh Diem and later the Congo's Patrice Lumumba—soon caused much of the world community to view the agency as a sinister force.

As direct American military action in Indochina grew, covert operations became less important, but by 1968 they witnessed a resurgence in the Phoenix Program that called for assassination of communist operatives. Debate continues over CIA involvement in the 1970 coup in Cambodia but not on its role in ousting Chile's Salvador Allende in 1973.

In 1975 public revelations of CIA assassination plots and an illegal operation to spy on American citizens protesting the Vietnam War led to the creation of the President's Intelligence Oversight Board as well as an Intelligence Committee in each house of Congress. In 1977 President Jimmy Carter increased oversight of the CIA and reduced its budget, but he reversed course after the 1979 Soviet invasion of Afghanistan.

During the presidency of Ronald Reagan, the CIA used its renewed power and clout to undermine communist regimes worldwide, providing support for Afghan rebel forces that included Osama bin Laden. Ignoring statutory limits, the CIA also participated in the secret sale of arms to Iran and used the proceeds to fund covert actions against Nicaragua's leftist government. In 1991 Congress passed a new oversight law to prevent another Iran-Contra Affair.

In 1991 the CIA correctly forecast a coup against Soviet leader Mikhail Gorbachev. But the sudden collapse of the Soviet Union beginning in August 1991 came as a complete surprise. Two-and-a-half years later, in February 1994, the arrest of agent Aldrich H. Ames for selling secrets for many years to the Soviets and compromising operatives provided critics with more evidence to back their controversial charges that the CIA had prolonged rather than helped to win the Cold War.

James I. Matray

Further Reading

Colby, William, with Peter Forbath. *Honorable Men: My Life in the CIA*. New York: Simon and Schuster, 1978.

Jeffreys-Jones, Rhodri. *The CIA and American Democracy*. 2nd ed. New Haven, CT: Yale University Press, 1998.

Prados, John. *Presidents' Secret Wars: CIA and Pentagon Covert Operations from*

World War II through the Persian Gulf. Chicago. IL: Ivan R. Dee, 1996.

Ranelagh, John. *The Agency: The Rise and Decline of the CIA, from Wild Bill Donovan to William Casey.* New York: Simon and Schuster, 1986.

Woodward, Bob. *Veil: The Secret Wars of the CIA, 1981–1987.* New York: Simon and Schuster, 1987.

Churchill, Winston (1874–1965)

Winston Churchill was born at Blenheim Palace, Oxfordshire, on November 30, 1874, the eldest son of Lord Randolph Churchill. His father was a rising Conservative politician, his mother, Jennie Jerome, an American heiress. From 1895 to 1899 he held a commission in the British Army, seeing active service in India, on the Afghan frontier, and in the Sudan, where he took part in the Battle of Omdurman. Captured by South African forces in 1899 while reporting on the Boer War as a journalist, he won popular fame after escaping.

Churchill entered politics in 1900 as a Unionist member of Parliament. In 1904 his party's partial conversion to protectionism caused him to join the Liberals, who made him president of the Board of Trade (1908–1910) and home secretary (1910–1911) after they returned to power. As first lord of the Admiralty (1911–1915), Churchill sought to modernize the Royal Navy, convert it to oil, and improve its administration. He championed the 1915 Dardanelles expedition against Turkey, the failure of which prompted his resignation. He spent the next six months to May 1916 on active service on the Western Front but regained high office in July 1917, when Prime Minister David Lloyd George made him minister of munitions. In December 1918 Churchill moved to the War Office, where he unsuccessfully

advocated forceful Allied action against Russia to eliminate that country's new communist government. In late 1920 he became colonial secretary. In 1924 he returned to the Conservatives, who in November 1924 made him chancellor of the exchequer, a post he held for five years.

By 1928 Churchill believed that the postwar peace settlement represented only a truce between wars, a view set forth in his book *The Aftermath* (1928). When Labour won the 1929 election Churchill lost office but soon began campaigning vigorously for major British rearmament, especially of the Royal Air Force (RAF). From 1932 onward he sounded this theme eloquently in Parliament, but Conservative leaders remained unsympathetic, and throughout the 1930s Churchill held no cabinet position. Churchill also became the most visible and vocal critic of the appeasement policies of the successive governments of Prime Ministers Stanley Baldwin and Neville Chamberlain, who effectively acquiesced in German rearmament and Chancellor Adolf Hitler's deliberate contravention of the provisions of the Treaty of Versailles.

When Britain declared war on Germany in September 1939, Churchill resumed his old position as first lord of the Admiralty. On May 10, 1940, the day Germany launched an invasion of France and the Low Countries, Churchill succeeded Chamberlain as prime minister. After the fall of France, and with Britain remaining as Germany's sole major military opponent, Churchill responded vigorously. An outstanding war leader, he delivered a series of rousing and eloquent speeches, affirming Britain's determination to continue the fight and his conviction of ultimate triumph. He also established a close relationship with U.S. president Franklin D. Roosevelt and persuaded U.S. policymakers to furnish substantial assistance. Churchill welcomed

British prime minister Winston Churchill (left), U.S. president Franklin D. Roosevelt (center), and Soviet leader Josef Stalin (right) at the Yalta Conference. The "Big Three" met in Yalta, Crimea (in what is now the Ukraine) on February 4–11, 1945, to discuss military and political strategy for ending the Second World War. (Library of Congress)

Japan's December 1941 attack on Pearl Harbor and the subsequent German declaration of war on the United States, believing that U.S. participation in the war guaranteed an Allied victory. Britain and the United States now worked closely together, establishing a Joint Chiefs of Staff and agreeing to pool technology.

After Germany invaded Soviet Russia in June 1941, Churchill also welcomed the Soviet Union as an ally, although his relations with Soviet Premier Josef Stalin were never as close as with Roosevelt. Churchill made repeated visits to the United States and met Roosevelt at other venues; all three leaders met at major international summit conferences in 1943 and 1945, and Churchill also met Stalin separately on several occasions. Stalin resented the Anglo-American failure to open a second front in Europe until June 1944, a decision due in considerable part to Churchill's fear that if Britain and the United States launched an invasion of Western Europe too soon, the campaign would degenerate into bloody trench warfare resembling that of World War I.

As the war proceeded and Soviet forces began to push back German troops in the eastern region, Churchill feared that the Soviet Union would dominate postwar Eastern Europe. Soviet support for communist guerrillas in occupied countries and for Soviet-backed governments-in-exile, as well as Moscow's failure to aid the uprising of Polish forces in Warsaw in August 1944, reinforced his apprehensions.

In October 1944 Churchill and Stalin negotiated the informal Percentages Agreement, whereby the two leaders delineated their countries' respective spheres of influence. At the February 1945 Yalta Conference, Churchill and Roosevelt both acquiesced in Soviet domination of most of Eastern Europe, Churchill most reluctantly. In April 1945 Churchill unavailingly urged American military commanders to disregard their existing understandings with Soviet forces and take Berlin.

From early in the war the Allies had committed themselves to the creation of a postwar international organization to maintain peace, which led to the United Nations (UN) in May 1945. Churchill, however, hoped that close Anglo-American understanding would be the bedrock of the international world order, a perspective intensified by his continuing fears of Germany.

In August 1945 the British electorate voted Churchill out of office, replacing his administration with a reformist Labour government. He was still, however, honored as "the greatest living Englishman" and the war's most towering figure. Churchill's six best-selling volumes of *The Second World War* depicted a rosy view of unclouded and harmonious Anglo-American wartime cooperation, carefully designed to promote the continuing alliance between the two countries, which had become his most cherished objective.

Churchill deliberately used his prestige to rally American elite and public opinion in favor of taking a stronger line against Soviet expansionism in Europe and elsewhere, a position he advanced to enormous publicity in his famous March 1946 "Sinews of Peace" speech (also known as the "Iron Curtain" speech) at Fulton, Missouri. Although the speech was cleared in advance with both British prime minister Clement Attlee and U.S. president Harry S. Truman, at the time many Americans criticized the address as unduly bellicose. One year later, however, the president's Truman Doctrine endorsed this position, and by the end of the 1940s the United States had launched the Marshall Plan to facilitate West European recovery and had joined the North Atlantic Treaty Organization (NATO).

From 1951 to 1955 Churchill served again as Conservative prime minister. Growing Soviet–American tensions and the awesome destructive power of nuclear weapons led him to urge U.S. president Dwight D. Eisenhower to negotiate an understanding with the Soviet Union to limit and perhaps reduce stocks of such bombs. Churchill also gave early support and encouragement to the movement for European integration, regarding this as the only means whereby the continent would be able to defend itself against the Soviet Union, become a credible international military and economic force, and avoid future destructive internecine conflicts.

Declining health eventually forced Churchill to resign from office. In retirement, he urged Prime Minister Harold Macmillan to repair Anglo-American relations after the damaging 1956 Suez Crisis, on the grounds that Britain could not afford lasting estrangement from its most vital ally, and offered his assistance in this endeavor. A House of Commons man to the core, Churchill consistently refused the peerage to which his services entitled him. He died at his London home on January 24, 1965, an occasion that for many marked the symbolic final passing of Great Britain's imperial age. An idiosyncratic political maverick whose pre-1939 record was at best mixed, Churchill rose to the occasion to become the greatest British war leader since the 18th-century Earl of Chatham. The prestige that Churchill won in this capacity enabled him to have a major impact on the development of the Cold War.

Priscilla Roberts

Further Reading

Boyle, Peter G., ed. *The Churchill-Eisenhower Correspondence, 1953–1955.* Chapel Hill: University of North Carolina Press, 1990.

Gilbert, Martin S. *Winston S. Churchill.* 8 vols. New York: Random House, 1966–1988.

Jenkins, Roy. *Churchill.* London: Macmillan, 2001.

Kimball, Warren F., ed. *Churchill and Roosevelt: The Complete Correspondence.* Princeton, NJ: Princeton University Press, 1984.

Larres, Klaus. *Churchill's Cold War: The Politics of Personal Diplomacy.* New Haven, CT: Yale University Press, 2002.

Lukacs, John. *Churchill: Visionary, Statesman, Historian.* New Haven, CT: Yale University Press, 2002.

Ramsden, John. *Man of the Century: Churchill and His Legend since 1945.* New York: Columbia University Press, 2002.

Seldon, Anthony. *Churchill's Indian Summer: The Conservative Government, 1951–55.* London: Hodder and Stoughton, 1981.

Civil Defense

Civil defense refers to programs and preventive measures to help defend civilian populations from military attack. During the Cold War, such efforts were directed mainly at protecting civilians during a nuclear attack. The civil defense programs of the Soviet Union and the United States can be regarded as standardized systems. These nations exported their civil defense organizations to their allies.

Soviet civil defense consisted of a system of state-sponsored measures designed to secure the population and national economy in time of war and to manage rescue and recovery efforts with the purpose of minimizing casualties. The Soviet civil defense apparatus was well organized, thought to be reliable, and based on two primary principles. First, civil defense was organized on a territorial-industrial basis to protect the entire nation. Citizens underwent continuous training in civil defense measures, and high emphasis was placed on fallout shelters, which were designed to safeguard the population from the effects of nuclear detonations. Second, civil defense called on the mobilization of material and human resources of the nation as a whole.

The Soviet government approached civil defense with four major premises. The first was that a well-trained populace would be less prone to injury or death and less susceptible to panic in the event of a war. Second, adequate training would help the population to deal with dangers contingent on an enemy attack. Third, people trained in civil defense would be capable of providing aid to the injured and could be mobilized to begin recovery efforts as soon as possible. Fourth, civil defense training would reinforce the defensive capabilities of the country. During the Cold War, some 30 million Soviet citizens and 70 percent of the industrial workforce were directly involved in civil defense programs. It is estimated that the Soviet Union spent $1 billion per year on civil defense measures.

Two organizations oversaw the Soviets' civil defense program. The Local Civil Defense (MPVO) system was organized in individual municipalities. The objective of the MPVO was to protect local citizens against enemy attacks of various kinds. In charge of the Municipal Executive Committee of the

Council of Workers' Deputies (ECCWD) was the municipal chief. The committee chief exercised the exclusive right to issue direct orders and make decisions in the best interest of the locality. Such committees were responsible for providing a diverse range of services by order of the Soviet government in order to maximize civil defense measures during an attack.

The second civil defense organization was the Volunteer Society for Assistance to the Army, Air Force, and Navy (DOSAAF). The objective of DOSAAF was to train people in the basics of military warfare. DOSAAF provided training to the civilian population, especially youth, to develop basic skills in firing weapons, skiing, driving, parachuting, piloting aircraft, and radio communications. In the process, DOSAAF also promoted various sports. DOSAAF fell under the aegis of the National Defense Ministry and worked closely with MPVO units.

In the event of enemy attack, one of nine warning signals would be transmitted to cities and towns by means of siren alarms, loudspeakers, whistles, and radio. The majority of fallout shelters were public; in fact, the construction of family or individual shelters was not encouraged, as the common perception was that an enemy attack would focus on public places such as industrial centers, factories, and motorways. Soviet shelters were classified in part by their sophistication, including blast shelters with high-level, industrially manufactured air filtering equipment; blast shelters with simplified filtering equipment; nuclear shelters equipped to handle peacetime accidents (such as nuclear reactor accidents); and simple nuclear shelters fabricated from readily available materials to offer refuge from nuclear attack. Fallout shelters were also classified according to capacity: small-scale (accommodating up to 150 persons),

medium (150–450 persons), and large-scale (450 or more persons).

In the event that people could not reach fallout shelters in time, Soviet citizens were trained to wear protective clothing. Usually, they wore suits of rubber or plastic equipped with a breathing apparatus and gas mask, protective gloves, and footwear. Respirators were issued to high-ranking officials and civil defense chiefs. Families and individuals had to obtain protective gear at their own expense.

In the United States, civil defense was not nearly as well organized. Civil defense measures were left primarily to local and state authorities, with the federal government playing a relatively minor role, mainly coordinating and disseminating information. American civil defense emphasized individual self-help, privatization, voluntarism, and decentralization. Unlike Soviet citizens, Americans were routinely prompted to construct their own individual fallout shelters, and many did, particularly in the 1950s.

The first national Cold War civil defense agency was created in January 1951 as a response to the Soviets' first atom bomb detonation in 1949 and to the Korean War (1950–1953). This agency, the Federal Civil Defense Administration (FCDA), had a narrow mission, which was chiefly geared to educating the populace on appropriate civil defense measures to take in the event of a nuclear attack. Although the FCDA recommended the construction of fallout shelters as part of a comprehensive civil defense apparatus, the federal government never allowed for the construction of adequate public shelter protection, and no cohesive national civil defense policies were ever implemented. The emphasis remained on regional and local programs.

The U.S. government did, however, develop a civil defense plan aimed at protecting

A volunteer in Battle Creek, Michigan, stands beside the 14-day emergency food supply for two persons that she purchased in a 1961 test of how much the food would cost, how much it would weigh, and how much space it would take to store it. Her particular supply consisted of 113 articles of 67 foods, cost just under $28 to buy, and weighed 118 pounds. Such a food supply was recommended by the Office of Civil Defense of the Defense Department. (National Archives)

America's industrial base. In August 1951 President Harry S. Truman announced the National Industrial Dispersion Policy, a program designed to decentralize American manufacturing, thereby making it less vulnerable to a concentrated Soviet air attack. The dispersion program itself, however, was highly decentralized, and the onus of implementation was placed on individual localities. Thus, almost no federal funds were allotted to the endeavor, and the policy had little impact on the protection of America's industrial sector. By the late 1950s, with the proliferation of highly destructive hydrogen bombs and Intercontinental Ballistic Missiles

(ICBMs), the National Industrial Dispersion Policy was rendered largely moot and faded into obscurity.

The closest the United States ever came to duplicating the more ambitious Soviet civil defense efforts was the National Security Resources Board (NSRB), created in 1947 to mobilize national resources and industrial production in time of war. It did not play a large role in more traditional civil defense preparations. In December 1950, in response to the reversal of fortunes in the Korean War, the Truman administration established the Office of Defense Mobilization (ODM), whose task was to coordinate all military and defense production—much like the War Production Board of World War II. But again, the ODM played almost no role in civil defense procedures. In 1953 President Dwight D. Eisenhower combined the NSRB and the ODM into one agency, although its mission did not change. In 1958, U.S. officials decided to merge mobilization and civil defense readiness into one agency when they consolidated the FCDA and the ODM into one unit: the Office of Civil and Defense Mobilization (OCDM). The OCDM went through several permutations over the years and became more of a disaster relief agency than a civil defense apparatus, especially after nearly all military and civilian defense operations were consolidated into the Federal Emergency Management Agency (FEMA) in 1978.

Most U.S. communities developed their own emergency plans and tasked local civil defense officers with specific functions. Additionally, civil defense volunteers underwent training to complement regular officers. The responsibility of alerting the public of an impending nuclear attack rested with the national, state, and local civil defense offices. These agencies arranged training courses for volunteers who had to be ready to assist authorities in managing existing shelters, decontamination procedures, fire fighting, first aid administration, and recovery efforts.

Adequate advance warning depends on the detection of approaching aircraft or missiles as far from the nation's borders as possible. To this end, the National Warning System (NAWAS) was established in 1957. It worked with local warning systems to form the Civil Defense Warning System. Telephones, radios, teletype, and other communication systems were used to transmit

Ground Zero Cincinnati. (AP/Wide World Photos)

urgent civil defense information. Public sirens were also used for early warning. To provide early warning, the North American Air Defense Command (NORAD) still maintains a sophisticated surveillance network including ground radar and radar-equipped aircraft deployed across the entire North American continent. Detection first begins at the Distant Early Warning Line, a radar wall extending some 4,000 miles across the Arctic through the Bering Sea and into the North Pacific.

The United States possessed two civil defense alert warning signals. The first was a steady, three- to five-minute siren that indicated an advanced-warning alert signal. This was used if enough time remained for people to seek protection in public or family fallout shelters. The second, a series of short siren blasts for five minutes, meant that immediate cover should be taken, indicating an imminent attack within minutes.

Local alert transmission systems differed from locale to locale. Two main alarm transmission systems were in place: a National Emergency Alarm Repeater (NEAR) system and a Control of Electromagnetic Radiations (CONELRAD) system. NEAR was designed to provide for almost instantaneous warning of an impending attack for the indoor public. NEAR had the capability of reaching 96 percent of the population in homes, offices, factories, schools, and other indoor public places. This system was especially valuable in that it was capable of transmitting alarm signals to rural areas, where installation of outdoor alarm systems would be costly. Meanwhile, CONELRAD was invented to assure radio communications in a national emergency and to prevent enemy aircraft from using radio signals in search of targets. CONELRAD's importance decreased as the potential of attack via ballistic missiles increased, but it is still used to ensure more efficient communications between public officials and civilians.

Cold War fallout shelters in the United States were classified on the basis of their protection factor (100 meant the radiation level outside a shelter could be 100 times as high as that inside a shelter). During and after the Cuban Missile Crisis of 1962, relaxed civil defense qualifications yielded 110 million shelter spaces, of which more than 70 million had a protection factor of 100 or greater, and an additional 35 million shelters with a protection factor between 49 and 99. The shelters with a protection factor of 100-plus were concentrated in the larger cities of the United States. Only shelters with protection factors of 100 or greater were stocked with food and survival supplies.

Jaroslav Dvorak and Paul G. Pierpaoli Jr.

Further Reading

Gouré, Leon. *War Survival in Soviet Strategy: USSR Civil Defense.* 1976. Reprint, Westport, CT: Greenwood, 1986.

McEnaney, Laura. *Civil Defense Begins at Home: Militarization Meets Everyday Life in the Fifties.* Princeton, NJ: Princeton University Press, 2000.

Rose, Kenneth. *One Nation Underground: The Fallout Shelter in American Culture.* New York: New York University Press, 2001.

Vale, Lawrence J. *The Limits of Civil Defense in the USA: Switzerland, Britain, and the Soviet Union; The Evolution of Policies since 1945.* New York: St. Martin's, 1987.

Yegorov, Pavel Timofaevich. *Civil Defense: A Soviet View.* Honolulu: University Press of the Pacific, 2002.

Committee on the Present Danger

Committee on the Present Danger was a bipartisan group of senior U.S. government officials, academics, and opinion leaders first organized in 1950, subsequently revived in 1976, to convince the U.S. public and policymakers of the dangers posed by the Soviet Union's military and foreign policies. The success of this organization in the 1950s spurred the creation of a similar body that bore the same name and had similar goals 25 years later.

The first Committee on the Present Danger was founded shortly after the Korean War began, to campaign for the permanent expansion of U.S. military forces, capabilities, and commitments, especially the deployment of far more substantial U.S. troop contingents in Western Europe to strengthen the infant North Atlantic Treaty Organization (NATO). Similar prescriptions had been made earlier that year in the National Security Council Report 68 (NSC-68), a paper prepared by the Policy Planning Staff (PPS) and largely authored by the second PPS director, Paul H. Nitze. President Harry S. Truman initially rejected its recommendations, which effectively called for a major militarization of the existing policies of containment of the Soviet Union, but accepted most of them once the Korean War erupted in June 1950. Even before the war began, several State and Defense Department officials and consultants who supported NSC-68 hoped to establish a citizens committee to press for major increases in American defense budgets and commitments.

Headed by James B. Conant, president of Harvard University, and largely run by former army undersecretary Tracy S. Voorhees, the committee, although formally a private organization, received strong backing and assistance from leading Truman administration officials, including Secretary of State Dean Acheson and Undersecretary of Defense Robert A. Lovett as well as Nitze. Established in December 1950 after extensive preliminary discussions with administration officials, the committee compared the Soviet menace to the Nazi threat a decade earlier and pressed for the restoration of the military draft, doubling the size of the existing U.S. military, and the deployment of several additional divisions to Western Europe. The committee quickly attracted an array of prominent members, including several college presidents, lawyers, media figures— among them Edward R. Murrow of CBS, Julius Ochs Adler of the *New York Times*, and Screen Actors Guild president Ronald Reagan—and William J. Donovan, former director of the Office of Strategic Services.

The committee worked closely with Central Intelligence Agency (CIA) officials and with the Psychological Strategy Board (PSB) established by Truman in the spring of 1951 to coordinate efforts to win the loyalties of peoples in Soviet-controlled states, especially in Eastern Europe. Committee members campaigned energetically for the policies they favored, speaking and writing extensively, sponsoring films, disseminating cartoons and other publicity, briefing journalists, lobbying congressmen, and writing detailed policy recommendations and briefs for sympathetic administration officials.

The committee's efforts contributed significantly to the Great Debate of 1951 on U.S. foreign policy, the outcome of which decisively oriented the country away from isolationism and toward a militarily assertive position of high defense expenditures, large armed forces, and major overseas alliance commitments. Leading committee officials, including Voorhees, successfully urged the sympathetic General Dwight D. Eisenhower to seek the Republican Party nomination for president in 1952, in the hope that this would check the influence of Republican isolationists and wed that party, like the Democrats, to the militarized internationalism that the committee favored. After Eisenhower's election victory in November 1952 and the Korean War armistice the following summer, the committee members felt that the committee's mission had been accomplished, and by late 1953 it had effectively faded away.

The first committee subsequently served as a model for the second Committee on the Present Danger, founded in the mid-1970s by foreign policy experts—including academics, former officials, and opinion makers—who argued that an expansionist Soviet Union was increasing the size, composition, and capabilities of its military arsenal in spite of arms control agreements and a general warming of superpower relations, known as détente. Committee members feared that the Soviets were preparing to wage—and prevail in—a nuclear exchange with the United States, thus giving the Soviet Union enormous leverage in any future confrontation with America or its allies. The committee favored the development of new American weapons and opposed arms control agreements, which it believed bolstered Soviet military dominance. In 1981, when Reagan (an early member of the committee) became president, many of the committee's positions became official government policy.

Veteran U.S. foreign policy advisor and NSC-68 drafter Nitze and Yale Law School Dean Eugene V. Rostow, formerly an undersecretary of state for President Lyndon B. Johnson, conceptualized the organization in late 1975. While they were finalizing plans the following year, Nitze and several other like-minded foreign policy experts were asked to scrutinize the government's recent assessment of the Soviet Union. They ultimately concluded that the United States was systematically underestimating Soviet military capabilities. These findings further spurred the committee's organizational efforts. Eventually, political scientist and future United Nations (UN) ambassador Jeane Kirkpatrick, congressional aide Max Kampelman, labor leader Lane Kirkland, and novelist Saul Bellow joined Rostow, Nitze, and 142 others as founding members of the second Committee on the Present Danger.

Although the foreign and defense policies of Republican president Gerald R. Ford and Secretary of State Henry A. Kissinger were the committee's main focus during its formative stages, organizers believed that their efforts were necessary regardless of who won the 1976 national election. Thus, two days after Ford was defeated by Democrat Jimmy Carter, the committee formally announced its establishment. Over the next several years, the group undertook a high-profile campaign, including disseminating analytical studies, conducting public opinion polling, and offering congressional testimony in support of new nuclear weapons and greater skepticism of détente. The committee vigorously opposed Carter's effort to conclude a Strategic Arms Limitation Treaty with the Soviet Union.

Critics of the committee believed that it was misreading Soviet military developments and foreign policy goals. To these observers, changes in the Soviets' arsenal could be explained benignly as defensive in nature or dismissed as a logical reaction to American actions. They believed that the committee's antagonism toward the Soviet Union and advocacy of new weapons reflected discredited past approaches and only increased the likelihood of a dangerous superpower confrontation. The committee's critique of American policy did not waver, however, and many of its suggestions were implemented by the Reagan administration, particularly during 1981–1985.

Christopher John Bright
and Priscilla Roberts

Further Reading

Cahn, Anne Hessing. *Killing Detente: The Right Attacks the CIA*. University Park: Pennsylvania State University Press, 1998.

Hershberg, James G. *James B. Conant: Harvard to Hiroshima and the Making of the Nuclear Age*. New York: Knopf, 1993.

Sanders, Jerry Wayne. *Peddlers of Crisis: The Committee on the Present Danger and the Politics of Containment*. Boston: South End Press, 1983.

Tyroler, Charles, II. *Alerting America: The Papers of the Committee on the Present Danger*. Washington, DC: Pergamon-Brassey's, 1984.

Communist Revolutionary Warfare

Communist revolutionary warfare in the Cold War context is usually associated with the Chinese communist theoretician Mao Zedong and Vietnamese General Vo Nguyen Giap. Based on his experiences in the Chinese Civil War and against the Japanese in World War II, Mao argued that in predominantly rural countries such as China, the revolution of the masses did not have to be led by the proletariat, as Vladimir Lenin had taught. Rather, the peasantry would be in the vanguard. Giap subsequently showed during the Indochina War against the French that Mao's approach could be adapted to more densely populated regions and that it applied as well when the principal enemy was a colonial power. But Giap's chief contribution to revolutionary warfare came in his assessment of the political and psychological difficulties that confront a democracy in waging a protracted war. Giap believed that public opinion would at some point demand an end to the bloodshed and that political leaders would find themselves forced to promise an early end to the fighting.

Communist revolutionary warfare required that certain conditions develop, which were clearly evident in the wake of World War II. These included a peasantry dissatisfied with the status quo, the discrediting of colonial regimes, and the rise of nationalism. Mao's views received a further boost following the final Chinese Communist victory over the Nationalists in October 1949. Communist revolutionary warfare was also an appealing strategy during the Cold War because it provided a means by which the major communist powers—the Soviet Union and the People's Republic of China (PRC)—could support surrogate movements around the world while minimizing the potential for nuclear confrontation with the United States and its allies. Finally, the strategy relied on guerrilla warfare, so it reduced the advantages that a government and its supporting states might have in terms of firepower and technology and placed the conflict in a venue in which that government was less comfortable.

In its orthodox form, Mao's approach set forth a three-stage progressive process by which the Communist Party would ultimately achieve victory. The transition to a higher stage required that certain conditions be met, but reversion to a lower stage could also occur if a change in the situation so warranted. In the first stage, subversion, the party established and publicized a basic cause for the insurgency and highlighted the government's contradictions—that is, its weaknesses and inability to meet the needs of the people. It built cells and arms stores, organized and trained guerrilla units, carried out acts of sabotage and terrorism, and generally attempted to reduce public confidence in the regime's ability to both handle the situation and govern the country.

Once insurgency leaders believed that the party had become strong enough to confront the government directly, the second, or guerrilla, stage began. Starting in remote areas where government control was weakest, the party focused on building up its base areas—a communist underground in the villages—while guerrillas conducted operations, designed to prevent government interference with this process, in the surrounding areas. As success was achieved, the areas under insurgent control expanded, and the costs to the government increased. When these costs began to be unacceptable to the existing government, the insurgents seized the initiative and gained momentum. If the government was unable to reverse the situation, its defeat became inevitable.

Concurrently during the second stage, the insurgents built and trained main force units for commitment during the third stage, the war of movement. When the party leadership believed that the government was on the verge of collapse, the transition to the final stage occurred. Fresh main force units were committed in a general offensive in the expectation that a mass uprising would occur and the government would be overthrown. In sum, communist revolutionary warfare employed the elements of time, space, and cost in protracted warfare to destroy the will and ability of the government to resist. Everything, including military operations, was subordinate to political considerations.

The methodical, elastic, and relatively low-cost nature of communist revolutionary warfare provided the insurgents with advantages in dealing with a weak government, particularly if that government was unable to develop the proper counterstrategy. The insurgents were not without challenges of their own, however, and a failure to address these satisfactorily could have fatal consequences. Gaining popular support early on was critical. This required identifying a basic cause that generated widespread appeal and

exploiting inequities in the country that could be blamed on the government, even if they were not the government's fault. Selecting the right cause was important because it had to promote national unity, even among those who might not be receptive to the communist message. Successful communist insurgent movements, such as those in Vietnam, solved this potential problem by creating fronts such as the Viet Minh, composed of all political groups, and then controlling the fronts from behind the scenes.

The Republic of Vietnam (RVN, South Vietnam) during the latter half of the 1950s provides a classic situation in which this relationship was ripe for exploitation. President Ngo Dinh Diem's rejection of the elections scheduled under provisions of the 1954 Geneva Conference that ended the Indochina War—a course that had the full support of Washington—led to a resumption of fighting. Diem's actions reinforced the impression that his government could not win the election because it was corrupt and oppressive, was uninterested in correcting long-standing inequities such as land ownership, and was unable to address the growing insurgent threat.

Conversely, the effect of a weak-cause contradictions message can be seen in the Malayan insurgency. There, the Malayan Communist Party (MCP) attempted to unite the Malayan people behind an anticolonialist/nationalist banner as well. However, this failed to resonate because the MCP was 93 percent Chinese in an ethnically diverse society. In addition, the contradictions of the colonial government were offset by the sustained British effort to prepare Malaya for independence and by an effective British counterinsurgency campaign.

Guerrilla success required strong leadership and organization. The presence of a charismatic leader such as Ho Chi Minh in Vietnam was highly beneficial. In addition, the movement had to be well organized and well disciplined, not only to show that it could support a national effort but also to be able to administer territory that came under its control and to demonstrate that it provided a credible alternative to the government. Again, the Malayan communists suffered in this regard because the government's declaration of a state of emergency in the summer of 1948 forced the party to enter the guerrilla stage before it was fully prepared to do so.

The strength of an insurgent movement could be further bolstered if it received outside support. Generally this took the form of political or moral support, infiltration of material and personnel assistance, or access to cross-border sanctuaries. The value of such support depended on the insurgents' ability to use it to exploit government weaknesses. Geography could also have a bearing on the potential success of an insurgency. The presence of difficult terrain such as mountains and jungles, for instance, was beneficial because it provided the insurgents with space in which to work and was more difficult for the government to access, especially if its administrative infrastructure and communications systems were deficient.

Unless a government took immediate action to develop and implement the correct counterstrategy, the situation would progressively deteriorate and inevitably lead to an insurgent victory. The most comprehensive counterstrategy to deal with communist revolutionary warfare was the so-called oil spot theory. This theory, promoted by British strategists in Malaya, maintained that an effective counterstrategy had to have a clear aim and had to be comprehensive and based on the rule of law in order to reinforce the government's legitimacy. This legitimacy differentiated it from the insurgents, who employed terror and other extralegal means. As a first step, the government had to secure its own base areas, particularly population, economic, and communications centers. Once this had been accomplished, the government could expand its control progressively, first to the immediate outlying areas that were less infiltrated by the insurgents and then into the more heavily infiltrated regions that lay beyond. In doing so it had to place priority on destroying the subversion, the communist underground, and not on the guerrillas, whose purpose was to protect the underground and to disrupt pacification—the government's effort to establish its control over the area. In this view, it was essential that the government counterstrategy be closely coordinated as a single effort: its primary aim was both offensive and constructive, that of nation building; its secondary, defensive aim was destruction of the guerrillas; and the two were joined by pacification.

The high point of communist revolutionary warfare coincided with the era of post–World War II decolonization and nation building. However, it was neither the only form of protracted war pursued by insurgents during the Cold War, as illustrated by revolutionary movements such as those in Algeria and Mozambique, nor the only one employed by communists, as demonstrated in Greece and Cuba. Although its proponents frequently tried to surround it with an aura of invincibility, the record shows that communist revolutionary warfare enjoyed only mixed success. Its most notable victories occurred in the Chinese Civil War and in Indochina, but it was defeated in Malaya, the Philippines (Hukbalahap), Thailand, and Peru (Shining Path).

George M. Brooke III

Further Reading

Chaliand, Gérard, ed. *Guerrilla Strategies.* Berkeley: University of California Press, 1982.

Mao Zedong. "On Protracted War." In *Selected Military Writings,* 187–267. Beijing: Foreign Languages Press, 1967.

O'Neill, Bard E. "Insurgency: A Framework for Analysis." In *Insurgency in the Modern World,* edited by Bard E. O'Neill, William R. Heaton, and Donald J. Alberts, 1–42. Boulder, CO: Westview, 1980.

Tanham, George K. *Communist Revolutionary Warfare: The Vietminh in Indochina.* Santa Monica, CA: RAND Corporation, 1961.

Thompson, Robert. *Defeating Communist Insurgency: The Lessons of Malaya and Vietnam.* New York: Praeger, 1966.

Thompson, Robert. *Revolutionary War in World Strategy.* London: Secker and Warburg, 1970.

Vo Nguyen Giap. *People's War, People's Army.* New York: Praeger, 1962.

Congo Civil War (1960–1965)

The involvement of the United States and the Soviet Union with opposing factions in the Congo Civil War transformed a nationalist struggle for control in the newly independent country into a Cold War battleground. The conflict began in July 1960 and comprised three main phases. The first was the secession of the Katanga and South Kasai provinces and the ensuing struggle to restore them to the nation. The second phase was the battle for control between the opposition governments of Joseph Kasavubu and Patrice Lamumba, and the third was the fight for power between Kasavubu and Moise Tshombe. Throughout the five-year conflict, the United States supported Kasavubu, while the communist bloc provided assistance to his main opponents. The interlocking conflicts were finally resolved when army chief of staff General Joseph Désiré Mobutu (Mobutu Sese Seko) seized power, with American support, on November 24, 1965, presenting the Americans with a perceived victory.

Hopes of an orderly transfer of power from Belgian colonial rule ended when dissatisfaction throughout the Congo turned violent. An army mutiny on July 5, 1960, was followed by the secession of two provinces: Katanga (Shaba) on July 11 and South Kasai on August 8. As rioting spread, Belgium sent in troops to protect the lives and property of its citizens. Faced with the disintegration of their country and an unauthorized foreign intervention, President Kasavubu and Prime Minister Lumumba appealed to the United Nations (UN). On July 14, 1960, a UN resolution called for the withdrawal of Belgian troops and organized a UN military force to restore order. Although the United States supported the UN action, there was increasing concern that Lumumba's leftist political orientation might provide an opportunity for communist infiltration. Thus, President Dwight D. Eisenhower authorized covert action to oust Lumumba and cultivate pro-Western leaders, such as Kasavubu and Mobutu.

On September 5, 1960, Kasavubu dismissed Lumumba as prime minister, initiating the next phase of the war. Asserting that this action exceeded Kasavubu's constitutional authority, Lumumba, in return, dismissed the president. As conflict loomed, Mobutu took control and ordered Lumumba's arrest. In response, Antoine Gizenga, as leader of the Lumumbists, established an alternative government at Stanleyville (Kisangani) in November. By the end of 1960, the Congo was divided into four warring regions: Katanga under Tshombe's leadership, South Kasai led by Albert Kalonji, the western Congo under Mobutu's control, and the eastern regions under Gizenga.

When the world learned in February 1961 of Lumumba's death while in government custody, protests erupted against Mobutu's regime. The USSR formally recognized Gizenga's government, while the United States declared its support for Mobutu's government in Leopoldville (Kinshasa). By the summer of 1961, with direct UN action and indirect U.S. action, Mobutu defeated Gizenga's rebel regime and ended the Kasai secession. Civilian control returned in July when an agreement was reached for the formation of a coalition government containing representatives from all three factions. Kasavubu resumed the presidency, with Cyrille Adoula as prime minister.

Tshombe, however, refused to join the coalition government, continuing to assert Katanga's independence. His recalcitrance encouraged the Lamumbists, and the coalition began to collapse. Gizenga left the government, joined forces with Tshombe, and by November 1962 directly threatened Adoula's rule. When the Soviets offered Adoula military aid, the United States urged the UN to act. On December 28, 1962, Belgian troops supplied and financed by the Americans led the UN operation to restore Katanga to the Congo. On January 21, 1963, Tshombe, realizing defeat was inevitable, surrendered, ending the Katanga secession.

Gizenga, however, continued to oppose the Kasavubu-Adoula regime with support from the communist bloc and by the summer of 1964 controlled more than half of the Congo's territory. Fearing that Kasavubu was not strong enough to withstand the Lamumbist advance, the United States stabilized the government by pressuring Kasavubu to accept Tshombe, a staunch anticommunist, as prime minister while persuading Belgium to provide military support for the Congolese Army, enabling it to defeat the Lumumbist insurgency.

Although 1965 began with a seemingly unified Congo, a power struggle developed between Kasavubu and Tshombe, both of whom wanted executive control. When they attempted to oust each other, civil war again threatened. But on November 24, 1965, Mobutu, allegedly with U.S. support, dismissed all the politicians and assumed power, thereby ending the Congo Civil War.

Donna R. Jackson

Further Reading

Bender, Gerald, James Coleman, and Richard Sklar, eds. *African Crisis Areas and United States Foreign Policy*. Berkeley: University of California Press, 1985.

Meditz, Sandra, and Tim Merrill. *Zaire: A Country Study*. Washington, DC: Federal Research Division, Library of Congress, 1994.

Schraeder, Peter J. *United States Foreign Policy toward Africa: Incrementalism, Crisis and Change*. Cambridge: Cambridge University Press, 1994.

Cuba

The largest and westernmost island of the West Indies chain, Cuba is in the Caribbean Sea, west of Hispaniola and 90 miles south of Key West, Florida. Cuba became a politically independent state on May 20, 1902. For the first half of the 20th century, the United States set the standards to which the Cuban population aspired.

General Fulgencio Batista's military coup on March 10, 1952, occurred only two months before an election in which nationalist forces were within reach of the presidency. The destruction of the Cuban democracy by Batista's rightist junta did not generate significant opposition in Washington. Indeed, the United States backed Batista as an ally in the Cold War. For its part, the Cuban authoritarian right manipulated the West by presenting itself as a bulwark against communism. In practice, the Batista government was actually undermining democracy with its repressive policies. And Batista's regime did little to improve living standards for poor Cubans, while the middle class and elites enjoyed a close and lucrative relationship with American businesses.

A potent popular insurrection against Batista's regime had grown in the eastern and central parts of Cuba by 1958. The leaders of the revolution, Fidel Castro and Ernesto "Che" Guevara, questioned Cuban dependence on the United States as well as market economy principles. They perceived their movement as part of a developing-world rebellion against the West and as a natural ally of the communist bloc.

The United States was not prepared to deal with the charismatic and doctrinaire Castro. After his takeover, the United States underestimated the profound grievances provoked by American support for the Batista regime. Some of Castro's early measures, such as land reform, the prosecution of Batista's cronies (with no guarantee of due process), and the nationalization of industries, were overwhelmingly popular, but at the same time they met stiff U.S. resistance.

Against this backdrop, Castro approached the Soviet Union for support, and in February 1960 a Soviet delegation led by Vice Premier Anastas Mikoyan visited Cuba and signed a trade agreement with Castro's government. The Soviets then began to replace the United States as Cuba's main trade and political partner. Soviet leader Nikita Khrushchev soon promised Cuba new machinery, oil, consumer goods, and a market for Cuban products now subject to American sanctions.

In April 1961, U.S.–Cuban relations collapsed completely, thanks to the abortive Bay of Pigs fiasco sponsored by the U.S. Central Intelligence Agency (CIA). The assault was condemned to failure, given Castro's popularity and the lack of U.S. air support for the rebel force. The botched attack only encouraged closer relations between the Soviet Union and Cuba. Khrushchev subsequently proposed installing nuclear-tipped missiles in Cuba to ensure a better bargaining position with the United States and as a means of offering protection to Cuba. Castro was elated. Khrushchev naively assumed that the missiles could be installed without U.S. detection. U.S. intelligence quickly discovered the activity, however, leading to the Cuban Missile Crisis, the most dangerous confrontation between the two superpowers of the Cold War. President John F. Kennedy declared a naval quarantine against the island in October 1962. For nearly two weeks the world stood at the edge of a nuclear abyss. In the end, Kennedy and Khrushchev worked out an agreement in which the Soviets withdrew the missiles in return for U.S. promises not to invade Cuba and to withdraw Jupiter missiles from Turkey.

The end of Kennedy's quarantine did not conclude the strife between Cuba and the United States, however. In addition to an embargo that continues to this day, the United States launched additional covert operations against Castro's government. The most important one, Operation Mongoose, included 14 CIA attempts to assassinate Castro. American hostility was reinforced by the Cuban revolution's transformation from a nationalist rebellion against authoritarianism to a totalitarian state aligned with the Soviet Union, with serious shortcomings in civil and political liberties.

The solution to the Cuban Missile Crisis also created serious strains between Havana and Moscow. Cuba's foreign policy was made in Havana, and therefore Castro refused to accept Moscow's or Beijing's directives. In 1968 he cracked down on a group of Cuban communists, accusing them of working with Soviet agents in Havana. In the end, he used the 1968 Soviet intervention in Czechoslovakia against the Prague Spring to broker a compromise by which Cuba preserved its autonomy but promised not to criticize the USSR publicly. Cuba thus became a Comecon member and received significant additional economic aid from the communist bloc.

In Latin America, the Cuban government actively supported revolutionary movements with leftist or nationalist agendas, especially those that challenged American hegemony in the region. But the 1960s witnessed successive failed Cuban attempts to export revolution to other countries. Guevara's 1967 murder in Bolivia concluded a series of subversive projects encouraged by Havana. Cuban revolutionary attempts were part of Cubans' core revolutionary beliefs and also a response to the rupture of diplomatic relations with Havana by all the Latin American countries except Mexico.

From the 1970s to 1990, as part of the Cold War conflict, Cuba played a major role in the international context. A high point of Castro's foreign policy came at the 1979 Sixth Summit of the Non-Aligned Movement in Havana. Cuba became a major conduit of alliance between the developing world and the communist bloc. Havana's diplomatic success and military involvement were accompanied by a massive civilian involvement in aid programs to African, Latin American, and Asian countries in the areas of health and education.

Cuba adopted a foreign policy suited to a medium-sized power. Castro sent 40,000 troops to Angola to support the pro-Soviet Popular Movement for the Liberation of Angola (MPLA) government in its struggle against the National Union for the Total Independence of Angola (UNITA) forces backed by South Africa and the United States. Cuba also dispatched troops to aid the pro-Soviet government of Ethiopia. In all, Cuba deployed more than 300,000 troops or military advisors to Angola, Ethiopia, the Congo, Guinea Bissau, Algeria, Mozambique, Syria, and South Yemen. The fight in southern Africa was ended through a skillfully designed tripartite agreement signed by Cuba, Angola, and South Africa and mediated by President Ronald Reagan's administration. This agreement led to the independence of Namibia.

Paradoxically, due in part to these Cold War commitments, Cuba missed its best chance to solve its conflict with the United States. During 1970–1980 the Americans sought serious negotiations with Cuba. This began under Richard Nixon's presidency and saw the most promise during Jimmy Carter's presidency (1977–1981). Carter demonstrated that he was serious in his desire to improve relations among the nations of the hemisphere and promote human rights. In 1977 Carter went so far as so say that the United States did not consider a Cuban retreat from Angola a precondition for beginning negotiations. Castro, however, insisted on continuing what he defined as "revolutionary solidarity" and "proletarian internationalism."

The Cuban government was interested in negotiations with the Americans but insisted on a radical leftist solution to problems. Castro took significant steps in releasing political prisoners and allowing visits to the island by Cuban exiles as goodwill gestures to the United States. In the international arena, Cuba informed the Americans about the Katanga rebellion in Zaire. Nevertheless, Cuba gave priority to its relations with other revolutionary movements, especially in Africa. In 1977 Castro sent 17,000 Cuban troops to Ethiopia to support dictator Mengistu Haile Mariam in his territorial conflict with Somalia. This development, despite the progress in several bilateral issues, represented a major blow to the prospect of improved Cuban–U.S. relations, as did Castro's support for the Sandinista government of Nicaragua in the 1980s.

A new development came in 1976 when Ricardo Boffill, Elizardo Sanchez, and Gustavo Arcos founded the first human rights group in Cuba since 1959. A new generation of opposition groups based on strategies of civil disobedience slowly emerged, gaining strength in the 1990s. During the 1970s Cuban civil society also began to emerge from totalitarian ostracism that had reduced its religious communities to a minimum. This evolution continued, and at the end of the 1980s the religious groups were growing at a fast pace.

The collapse of the communist bloc beginning in 1989 was a major catastrophe for Castro's government, as Cuba lost its major benefactors. At the same time, the international community, particularly Latin America and the former communist countries, adopted general norms of democratic governance opposed to the goals and behavior of the Cuban leadership. Without Soviet backing, Cuba adjusted its economy and foreign policy to survive in a world that was no longer safe for revolution. In 1988 Castro withdrew Cuban troops from Angola and reduced the Cuban military presence in the Horn of Africa.

Cuba's gross domestic product fell by almost one-third between 1989 and 1993. The collapse of the Cuban economy was particularly hard on imports, which fell from 8.6 billion pesos in 1989 to about 2 billion pesos in 1993. In response to the economic collapse, Castro permitted limited private enterprise, allowed Cubans to have foreign currencies, and pushed for foreign investment, particularly in tourism. His reforms, however, did little to stop the economic hemorrhaging.

In addition, Cuban troops were withdrawn from wherever they were posted. More than 15 years after the Cold War wound down, Castro remains one of the last leaders of the old-style communist order.

Arturo Lopez-Levy

Further Reading

Dominguez, Jorge I. *To Make a World Safe for Revolution: Cuba's Foreign Policy.* Cambridge, MA: Harvard University Press, 1989.

Gleijeses, Piero. *Conflicting Missions: Havana, Washington, and Africa, 1959–1976.* Chapel Hill: University of North Carolina Press, 2002.

Pastor, Robert. *The Carter Administration and Latin America.* Occasional Paper Series, Vol. 2, No. 3. Atlanta, GA: Carter Center of Emory University, 1992.

Smith, Wayne. *The Closest of Enemies: A Personal and Diplomatic History of the Castro Years.* New York: Norton, 1987.

Cuban Missile Crisis (October 1962)

The Cuban Missile Crisis was the closest the two Cold War superpowers, the United States and the Soviet Union, came to full-scale nuclear war. In 1958 an indigenous revolutionary movement led by Fidel Castro seized power from Fulgencio Batista, a U.S. client who since 1933 had been dictator of the Caribbean island of Cuba, less than a hundred miles from the American coast. Although Castro initially declared that he was not a communist, in the spring of 1959 he covertly sought Soviet aid and military protection. American economic pressure and boycotts quickly gave him an excuse to move openly into the Soviet camp. In response, the Central Intelligence Agency (CIA) planned to assist Cuban exiles to attack the island and overthrow Castro. Initiated under President Dwight D. Eisenhower and inherited by his successor John F. Kennedy, the April 1961 Bay of Pigs invasion attempt proved a humiliating fiasco for the United States. Kennedy and Secretary of Defense Robert S. McNamara continued to develop plans for a second invasion, and their advisors also devised various ingenious and often far-fetched schemes to overthrow or assassinate Castro. Castro, in turn, sought further Soviet aid.

In mid-1961, as the concurrent Berlin Crisis intensified and culminated in the building of the Berlin Wall, military hard-liners in the Kremlin, frustrated for several years, succeeded in implementing a 34 percent increase in spending on conventional forces. Both the Bay of Pigs and Kennedy's bellicose inauguration rhetoric that his country would "pay any price, bear any burden, meet any hardship, support any friend, oppose any foe, in order to assure the survival

and the success of liberty," may have energized them. Despite claims of a missile gap between the Soviet Union and the United States, in practice the strategic missile imbalance greatly favored the United States, which had at least eight times as many nuclear warheads as its rival. Even American leaders were unaware of just how lopsidedly the nuclear situation favored them, believing the ratio to be only about three to one. The then recent U.S. deployment of 15 intermediate-range missiles in Turkey, directly threatening Soviet territory, further angered Nikita Khrushchev, the Soviet Communist Party's general secretary, making him eager to redress the balance. It seems that he also hoped to pressure the United States into making concessions on Berlin while he rebutted communist Chinese charges that the Soviets were only paper tigers who were unwilling to take concrete action to advance the cause of international

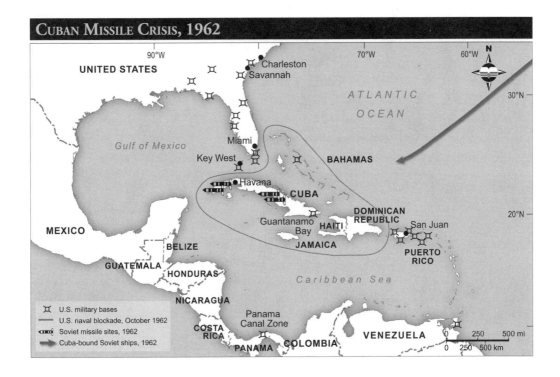

CUBAN MISSILE CRISIS, 1962

revolution. In addition, Khrushchev apparently felt a romantic sense of solidarity with the new Cuban state, which reassured him and other old communists that their cause still possessed international vitality.

Early in 1962, Khrushchev offered Soviet nuclear missiles, under the control of Soviet technicians and troops, to Castro, who accepted and oversaw their secret installation. Khrushchev apparently believed that these would deter American plans to invade Cuba. Rather optimistically, he calculated that Kennedy and his advisors would find the prospect of nuclear war over the Cuban missiles so horrifying that, despite their chagrin, once the missiles were in place they would accept their presence in Cuba.

The Bay of Pigs fiasco followed by Khrushchev's June 1961 summit meeting with Kennedy at Vienna apparently convinced the Soviet leader that Kennedy was weak and would be easily intimidated. So confident was Khrushchev that when Kennedy administration officials warned in July and August 1962 that the United States would respond strongly should the Soviets deploy nuclear or other significant weaponry in Cuba, he implicitly denied any intention of doing so. Admittedly, by this time the missiles had already been secretly dispatched, and their installation was at least a partial fait accompli. At this stage of his career, moreover, Khrushchev's behavior tended to be erratic. In any case, he miscalculated. Instead of treating

Aerial view of the San Cristobal medium range ballistic missile launch site number two, Cuba, November 1, 1962. (U.S. Air Force)

the Cuban missiles as deterrent weapons, the Kennedy administration regarded them as evidence of Soviet aggressiveness and refused to accept their presence.

In October 1962, U-2 reconnaissance planes provided Kennedy with photographic evidence that Soviet officials had installed intermediate-range missiles in Cuba. When the president learned on October 16, 1962, of the presence of the missiles, he summoned a secret Executive Committee of 18 top advisors, among them chairman of the Joint Chiefs of Staff Maxwell D. Taylor, CIA director John McCone, Secretary of State Dean Rusk, Secretary of Defense Robert S. McNamara, National Security Advisor McGeorge Bundy, Vice President Lyndon B. Johnson, and the president's brother and closest advisor, Attorney General Robert F. Kennedy, to decide on the American response. President Kennedy also included senior members of the broader foreign policy establishment, including former secretary of defense Robert A. Lovett and former secretary of state Dean Acheson.

Whatever the logical justification for Khrushchev's behavior, politically it would have been almost impossible for any American president to accept the situation. The American military calculated that the missiles would increase Soviet nuclear striking force against the continental United States by 50 percent. In reality, U.S. officials underestimated missile numbers, and they actually would have doubled or even tripled Soviet striking capabilities, reducing the existing American numerical advantage to a ratio of merely two or three to one. Kennedy, however, viewed the missiles less as a genuine military threat than as a test of his credibility and leadership. Taylor, speaking for the U.S. military, initially favored launching air strikes to destroy the missile installations, a course of action that would almost certainly

have killed substantial numbers of Soviet troops, was unlikely to eliminate all the missiles, and might well have provoked full-scale nuclear war. Another option, invasion by U.S. ground forces, also risked nuclear war. Discussions continued for several days. Eventually, on October 22, Kennedy publicly announced the presence of the missiles in Cuba, demanded that the Soviet Union remove them, and announced the imposition of a naval blockade around the island.

Several tense days ensued, in the course of which, on October 27, Soviet antiaircraft batteries on Cuba shot down—apparently without specific authorization from Kremlin leaders, whom this episode greatly alarmed—a U.S. U-2 reconnaissance aircraft. Seeking to avoid further escalation of the crisis, Kennedy refused to follow Taylor's advice to retaliate militarily and deliberately refrained from action. After some hesitation, Khrushchev acquiesced in the removal of the missiles, once his ambassador in Washington, Anatoly Dobrynin, secretly obtained an unpublicized pledge from Robert Kennedy that his brother would shortly remove the missiles in Turkey. Provided that the Soviet missiles were removed and not replaced, the United States also promised not to mount another invasion of Cuba.

Recently released tapes of conversations among President Kennedy and his advisors reveal that to avoid nuclear war, he was prepared to make even greater concessions to the Soviets, including taking the issue to the United Nations and openly trading Turkish missiles for those in Cuba. In so doing, he parted company with some of his more hardline advisors. Showing considerable statesmanship, Kennedy deliberately refrained from emphasizing Khrushchev's humiliation, although other administration officials were less diplomatic and celebrated their victory to the press.

Newly opened Soviet documentary evidence has demonstrated that the Cuban situation was even more dire than most involved then realized. Forty-two thousand well-equipped Soviet troops were already on the island, far more than the 10,000 troops that American officials had estimated. Moreover, although Kennedy's advisors believed that some of the missiles might already be armed, they failed to realize that no less than 158 short- and intermediate-range warheads on the island, whose use Castro urged should the United States invade, were already operational and that 42 of these could have reached American territory. A bellicose Castro was also hoping to shoot down additional U-2 planes and provoke a major confrontation. The potential for a trigger-happy military officer to set off a full-scale nuclear war certainly existed.

The Cuban Missile Crisis had a sobering impact on its protagonists. Humiliation at American hands was among the factors that compelled Soviet leaders to undertake an expensive major nuclear buildup to achieve parity with the United States, reaching this in 1970. Khrushchev's fall from power in 1964 was probably at least partly due to the missile crisis. Soviet officials also felt that they had come dangerously close to losing control of the actual employment of nuclear weapons in Cuba, either to their own military commanders on the ground or even potentially to Castro's forces. Even though the settlement effectively ensured his regime's survival, Castro felt humiliated that the Soviets and Americans had settled matters between them without regard for him. Before Khrushchev's fall from power, the two men were reconciled, and Soviet–Cuban relations remained close until the end of the Cold War. To the chagrin of successive U.S. presidents, however, Castro remained in power into the 21st century, eventually becoming the doyen among world political leaders.

The Cuban Missile Crisis tested and perhaps weakened the Western alliance. West European political leaders, including Harold Macmillan of Britain, Konrad Adenauer of the Federal Republic of Germany (FRG, West Germany), and most notably Charles de Gaulle of France, felt some discomfort that although Kennedy dispatched Acheson to brief them on the crisis, American officials had not consulted them on decisions of great importance to their own countries' survival. This may have been one factor impelling de Gaulle to follow a highly independent foreign policy line in subsequent years.

The crisis exerted a certain salutary, maturing effect on Kennedy, making the once-brash young president a strong advocate of disarmament in the final months before his untimely death in November 1963. His stance compelled the Soviet leadership to establish a hotline between Moscow and Washington to facilitate communications and ease tensions during international crises. The two powers also finally reached agreement in 1963 on the Partial Test Ban Treaty (PTBT), which halted nuclear testing in the atmosphere, under water, and in space. From then on both superpowers exercised great caution in dealing with each other, and on no subsequent occasion did they come so close to outright nuclear war.

Priscilla Roberts

Further Reading

Allison, Graham, and Philip Zelikow. *Essence of Decision: Explaining the Cuban Missile Crisis*. 2nd ed. New York: Longman, 1999.

Ausland, John C. *Kennedy, Khrushchev, and the Berlin-Cuba Crisis, 1961–1964*. Oslo: Scandinavian University Press, 1996.

Beschloss, Michael R. *The Crisis Years: Kennedy and Khrushchev, 1960–1963.* New York: HarperCollins, 1991.

Blight, James, and David Welch, eds. *Intelligence and the Cuban Missile Crisis.* London: Frank Cass, 1998.

Blight, James, and David Welch. *On the Brink: Americans and Soviets Reexamine the Cuban Missile Crisis.* New York: Hill and Wang, 1989.

Brune, Lester H. *The Cuba-Caribbean Missile Crisis of October 1962: A Review of Issues and References.* Claremont, CA: Regina Books, 1996.

Frankel, Max. *High Noon in the Cold War: Kennedy, Khrushchev, and the Cuban Missile Crisis.* New York: Ballantine, 2004.

Freedman, Lawrence. *Kennedy's Wars: Berlin, Cuba, Laos, and Vietnam.* New York: Oxford University Press, 2000.

Fursenko, Aleksandr, and Timothy Naftali. *"One Hell of a Gamble": Khrushchev, Castro, and Kennedy, 1958–1964.* New York: Norton, 1997.

Gaddis, John Lewis. *We Now Know: Rethinking Cold War History.* New York: Oxford University Press, 1997.

Hilsman, Roger. *The Cuban Missile Crisis: The Struggle over Policy.* Westport, CT: Praeger, 1996.

Kennedy, Robert F. *Thirteen Days: A Memoir of the Cuban Missile Crisis.* New York: Norton, 1999.

May, Ernest R., and Philip D. Zelikow, eds. *The Kennedy Tapes: Inside the White House during the Cuban Missile Crisis.* Cambridge, MA: Harvard University Press, 1997.

Nathan, James A. *Anatomy of the Cuban Missile Crisis.* Westport, CT: Greenwood, 2001.

Stern, Sheldon. *Averting "The Final Failure": John F. Kennedy and the Secret Cuban Missile Crisis Meetings.* Stanford, CA: Stanford University Press, 2003.

Taubman, William S. *Khrushchev: The Man and His Era.* New York: Norton, 2003.

Thompson, Robert Smith. *The Missiles of October: The Declassified Story of John F. Kennedy and the Cuban Missile Crisis.* New York: Simon and Schuster, 1992.

White, Mark J. *The Kennedys and Cuba: The Declassified Documentary History.* Chicago: Ivan R. Dee, 1999.

D

Dominican Republic, U.S. Interventions in

Occupying the eastern two-thirds of the island of Hispaniola, the Dominican Republic has witnessed two large-scale U.S. military interventions. The first occurred during 1916–1924 and the second in 1965. The first American intervention, when U.S. president Woodrow Wilson sent U.S. Marines to the island nation in 1916, was justified as being necessary to terminate lawlessness and Dominicans' failure to meet their financial obligations to the United States. As early as 1905, the Americans had taken over the receivership of the Dominican Republic's customs, which lasted until 1940.

Though the military occupation improved the island republic's infrastructure to some degree, nationalist opposition to U.S. rule was especially focused on the U.S.-established National Guard, which oftentimes acted with considerable brutality. When the United States withdrew its forces from the country, it left power in the hands of the National Guard, led by Rafael Trujillo. Trujillo ruled the Dominican Republic for more than three decades, from 1930 until his assassination in May 1961.

Trujillo ruled with considerable savagery, using the National Guard and his feared secret police force to suppress and eliminate any political dissent. Meanwhile, he treated the Dominican Republic as his personal fiefdom. Until the late 1950s, Trujillo enjoyed the uncritical support of the United States. He also quickly learned how to exploit Cold War fears of communism in the Caribbean to secure favors from Washington.

The removal of Trujillo in May 1961 was partly assisted by the growth of inter-American and U.S. opposition to his brutal rule and a decision by the John F. Kennedy administration to reduce American support and impose economic sanctions. The period between Trujillo's assassination and the 1965 U.S. military intervention was marked by a complicated history of attempts to create a stable political climate in which Trujillo's cronies and relatives tried, unsuccessfully, to continue the dictator's rule.

In national elections in 1962, the first democratic elections in nearly four decades, a nationalist-reformist coalition, the Dominican Revolutionary Party (PRD), came to power with the support of middle-class sectors and some populist movements. The new government was headed by the Dominican novelist Juan Bosch. After an initial honeymoon period in which the Kennedy administration responded warmly to the new government, relations with Washington began to deteriorate, especially when Bosch made clear his intentions to recognize the Cuban government of Fidel Castro. Bosch's economic reforms, which included modest land reform and the nationalization of several major enterprises, further aroused anti-communist fear within the Dominican Republic and in the United States.

With signs of U.S. approval, in September 1963 elements of the nation's armed forces led by archconservative General Elias Wessin y Wessin overthrew Bosch, who went into exile in Puerto Rico. The coup installed a military triumvirate headed by businessman Donald Reid Cabral.

The leaders of the new regime abolished the constitution, but nearly two years of corruption and brutal internal repression produced a popular uprising on April 24, 1965, which restored Bosch and his Constitutionalist movement to power. For four days the Constitutionalists and their military and civilian supporters, led by Colonel Francisco Caamaño, fought to prevent a counterattack led by Wessin y Wessin.

The fighting in Santo Domingo soon took on the characteristics of a popular insurrection and began to spread to other regions of the country. Despite their use of tank assaults and aerial bombing, the Wessin-led forces were on the verge of defeat. The impending collapse of the Wessin forces and faulty intelligence supplied by U.S. ambassador William Tapley, who reported to the U.S. State Department that the lives of American citizens were imperiled by communist-led hordes, set the scene for a full-scale U.S. intervention.

On April 28, 1965, a clearly panicked President Lyndon B. Johnson ordered 20,000 U.S. troops into the Dominican Republic. The Americans' official rationale was that the action was needed to prevent a communist takeover of the country and the emergence of a "second Cuba." Evidence of communist influence within the insurrection was, however, very thin. The Communist Party's small number of militants and the members of the Castroite June 14 Movement certainly played a role in the Constitutionalist resistance, but the popular insurrection was overwhelmingly made up of the urban poor of Santo Domingo. The American intervention in practice seemed designed to prevent a return to Constitutional government by Bosch and to block radical social and economic change in the island republic.

U.S. intervention forces were soon aided by an Organization of American States (OAS) intervention peace force. The OAS force was the result of vigorous U.S. lobbying and was in violation of inter-American prohibitions on foreign military intervention in the affairs of the region. American and OAS forces took a month to defeat the Constitutionalist insurrection and impose an interim administration before new elections were convened. In the elections of June 1966, a large majority of voters elected Joaquín Balaguer, a former Trujillo loyalist, and his Reformist Party. Balaguer remained in power for most of the next 28 years. Systematic police terror, an astronomical increase in political corruption, and the transformation of the Dominican Republic into a secure location for foreign investors were the main legacies of the U.S. intervention.

Barry Carr

Further Reading

Black, Jan Knippers. *The Dominican Republic: Politics and Development in an Unsovereign State*. Boston: Allen and Unwin, 1986.

Gleijeses, Piero. *The Dominican Crisis: The 1965 Constitutionalist Revolt and American Intervention*. Baltimore: Johns Hopkins University Press, 1978.

Moreno, José. *Barrios in Arms: Revolution in Santo Domingo*. Pittsburgh, PA: University of Pittsburgh Press, 1970.

Dulles, John Foster (1888–1959)

Born in Washington, D.C., on February 25, 1888, John Foster Dulles studied under Woodrow Wilson at Princeton University and at the Sorbonne, earned a law degree from George Washington University, and in 1911 joined the prestigious Wall Street law firm of Sullivan and Cromwell. Appointed to the U.S. delegation at the 1919 Paris Peace

Conference, Dulles unsuccessfully sought to restrain Allied reparations demands on Germany.

Active between the wars in internationalist organizations, Dulles initially opposed American intervention in World War II. Once American belligerency seemed probable, however, he focused intensely on postwar planning. A prominent Presbyterian, in 1941 he became chairman of the Commission to Study the Bases of a Just and Durable Peace, established by the Federal Council of Churches of Christ in America, representing 25 million American Protestants. Its blueprint for international reform, finished in 1943, urged the creation of international organizations to facilitate peaceful resolution of disputes among states, economic integration, arms control, and religious, intellectual, and political freedom, objectives all consonant with the 1941 Atlantic Charter.

Dulles also became prominent in Republican politics, advising presidential candidate Governor Thomas E. Dewey on international affairs. Seeking to secure bipartisan political support for his foreign policy, President Harry S. Truman included Dulles in virtually all major international meetings, beginning with the 1945 San Francisco Conference that drafted the final United Nations Charter. Briefly appointed Republican senator for New York in 1948–1949, Dulles strongly supported creation of the North Atlantic Security Organization (NATO). He also supported European integration as a means of strengthening the continent's economies and militaries.

By the late 1940s Dulles had become a dedicated anticommunist. When Chinese communists won control of the mainland in 1949, he advocated American backing for Jiang Jieshi's Guomindang (Nationalist) regime on Taiwan. In June 1950, when the Democratic People's Republic of Korea (DPRK, North Korea) invaded the Republic of Korea (ROK, South Korea), Dulles urged U.S. intervention and the extension of protection to Taiwan. As a foreign affairs advisor to the Republican presidential campaign in 1952, Dulles argued that the Truman administration had been timorous in merely containing Soviet communism when it should have moved to roll back Soviet influence in Eastern Europe.

Named secretary of state by President Dwight D. Eisenhower in 1953, Dulles deferred to the president's leadership, although the two men were very different in style. A supporter of Eisenhower's New Look defense policy of heavy reliance on nuclear weapons, Dulles rhetorically threatened to wreak "massive retaliation" against American enemies, a tactic nicknamed "brinkmanship." In practice, however, he was often more cautious. Although Dulles's bellicose anticommunist rhetoric alarmed many European leaders, his policies proved pragmatic, effectively respecting established Soviet interests in Europe. When discontented East Berlin workers triggered an uprising in the German Democratic Republic (GDR, East Germany) in 1953 and again when Hungarians rebelled against Soviet rule in 1956, Dulles and Eisenhower welcomed refugees but offered no other support.

Dulles and Eisenhower ended the Korean War in 1953, pressuring both sides to accept an armistice, and established a series of alliances around Asia, supplementing the 1951 United States–Japan Security Treaty and Australia, New Zealand, United States Security Treaty (ANZUS) Pact with bilateral security treaties with South Korea and Taiwan and with the Southeast Asia Treaty Organization (SEATO). When possible, Eisenhower avoided direct major military interventions, preferring to rely on covert operations orchestrated by the Central Intelligence Agency (CIA), headed by Dulles's younger brother Allen. The CIA played key roles in coups that overthrew Left-leaning governments in Iran in 1953 and Guatemala in 1954.

In Indochina in 1954, Dulles and Eisenhower withstood pressure from U.S. military leaders and, after Britain had declined to assist, refused to authorize air strikes to rescue French troops surrounded by insurgent Viet Minh forces at Dien Bien Phu. Dulles attended the 1954 Geneva Conference but would not sign the resulting accords that partitioned Vietnam, instead calling for countrywide elections within two years, a contest that Viet Minh leader Ho Chi Minh was widely expected to win. Instead, Dulles and Eisenhower broke the accords and provided economic aid to the noncommunist Republic of Vietnam (RVN, South Vietnam), seeking to build it up to ensure its independence.

Dulles and Eisenhower considered strengthening America's West European allies as their first priority. In March 1953, Soviet dictator Josef Stalin died, and new Soviet leaders advanced suggestions for German reunification and neutralization. Distrust on both sides made such proposals ultimately fruitless, although the former World War II allies agreed on a peace treaty with Austria that left that state neutral throughout the Cold War. Seeking to reinforce NATO, Eisenhower and Dulles backed proposals for a multinational European Defense Community (EDC), a plan that France vetoed in 1954.

Dulles's relations with Britain and France, whose imperialism he deplored, reached their nadir in 1956. In 1953 Egyptian nationalist Gamal Abdel Nasser came to power. Initially, he sought military and economic aid from the United States, but the Israeli lobby prevented such aid. He then obtained arms from the Soviet bloc. This, in turn, led Dulles in 1956 to rescind an earlier American pledge to provide Nasser with funding for his Aswan Dam project, whereupon Nasser nationalized the Suez Canal, co-owned by the British and French governments. While openly joining Dulles in negotiations with Egypt, Britain and France covertly agreed with Israel on war against Egypt to regain the canal, mounting an invasion in early November 1956 just before the U.S. presidential election. Dulles and Eisenhower strenuously pressured all three powers to withdraw, which they eventually did, but the episode soured Anglo-American relations. Although Dulles hoped to align the United States with nationalist forces around the world, the open growth of Soviet interest in the Middle East brought the announcement the following spring of the Eisenhower Doctrine, whereby the United States claimed the right to intervene militarily against indigenous or external communist threats in the region. This provoked significant anti-Americanism throughout the world.

The emergence of Nikita Khrushchev as top Soviet leader in the mid-1950s seemed to promise a relaxation of Soviet–American tensions, as Khrushchev openly repudiated Stalinist tactics and called for peaceful coexistence between communist and noncommunist nations. Eisenhower hoped to conclude substantive disarmament agreements with Khrushchev. In practice, however, Khrushchev was often far from accommodating. The USSR's success in launching the first space satellite (*Sputnik*) in 1957, Soviet possession of nuclear and thermonuclear weapons, and Khrushchev's seeming readiness from late 1958 onward to provoke an international crisis over Berlin all alarmed American leaders, including the ailing Dulles (diagnosed in 1957 with cancer).

Although American nation-building efforts in both Taiwan and South Vietnam enjoyed apparent success, during the Second Taiwan Strait Crisis (1958) Dulles was notably more cautious about gratuitously challenging either communist China or possibly, by extension, the Soviets. When his cancer worsened, he resigned as secretary on April 15, 1959. Dulles died in Washington, D.C., on May 24, 1959.

Priscilla Roberts

Further Reading

Guhin, Michael A. *John Foster Dulles: A Statesman and His Times*. New York: Columbia University Press, 1972.

Hoopes, Townsend. *The Devil and John Foster Dulles*. Boston: Little, Brown, 1973.

Immerman, Richard H. *John Foster Dulles: Piety, Pragmatism, and Power in U.S. Foreign Policy*. Wilmington, DE: Scholarly Resources, 1999.

Marks, Frederick W., III. *Power and Peace: The Diplomacy of John Foster Dulles*. Westport, CT: Praeger, 1993.

Toulouse, Mark G. *The Transformation of John Foster Dulles: From Prophet of Realism to Priest of Nationalism*. Macon, GA: Mercer University Press, 1985.

E

Eisenhower, Dwight David (1890–1969)

Born in Denison, Texas, on October 14, 1890, Dwight Eisenhower grew up in Abilene, Kansas, and graduated from the U.S. Military Academy, West Point, in 1915. Posted to France during World War I, he arrived only after the end of combat operations. In 1939 Eisenhower became chief of staff to the new Third Army. Transferred to the War Department in Washington following the Japanese attack on Pearl Harbor, he held increasingly responsible staff jobs, working in the War Plans Division, where he helped to plan the Europe First strategy before his summer 1942 transfer to London as commander of American and Allied forces in Britain. In November 1942 he organized the North African campaign and in late 1943 launched the invasion of Italy. In December 1943 he was named to command the Allied forces scheduled to invade Western Europe in 1944, and in spring 1945 he was promoted to general of the army.

From 1945 to 1948 Eisenhower served as chief of staff of the army. He was president of Columbia University from 1948 to 1952. During this time he was actively involved with the Council on Foreign Relations and spent time in Washington, informally chairing the Joint Chiefs of Staff during Admiral of the Fleet William D. Leahy's illness. Eisenhower strongly endorsed President Harry S. Truman's developing Cold War policies, including intervention in Korea. Eisenhower's focus, however, remained the European situation and Soviet–American rivalry. In January 1951 he took leave from Columbia to serve as supreme commander of the armed forces of the North Atlantic Treaty Organization (NATO).

In 1952 the Republican Party, desperate to choose a candidate who would be assured of victory, turned to Eisenhower. As a candidate, he promised to end the Korean War but otherwise continued Truman's Cold War policies. Eisenhower won the November elections, defeating Democrat Adlai Stevenson.

Under Eisenhower, U.S. defense commitments around the world solidified into a network of bilateral and multilateral alliances. While maintaining its existing commitments to NATO, the Rio Pact, Japan, and the ANZUS South Pacific alliance, the United States established the Southeast Asia Treaty Organization (SEATO) in 1954, associated itself with the Middle Eastern Baghdad Pact in 1959, and signed bilateral security treaties with South Korea and the Republic of China on Taiwan.

A fiscal conservative uncomfortable with high defense budgets, Eisenhower introduced the New Look strategy of relying heavily on nuclear weapons rather than on conventional forces. Critics of the New Look defense strategy complained that it left the United States unprepared to fight limited wars.

In March 1953 Soviet dictator Josef Stalin died, to be replaced first by a triumvirate of Soviet officials headed by Georgy Malenkov and then in 1955 by Nikita Khrushchev. Stalin's death may well have facilitated efforts to end the Korean War, although Soviet

General of the Army, Dwight D. Eisenhower commanded the Western Allied forces in the invasion of Europe and the defeat of Germany in World War II and was the first supreme commander of North Atlantic Treaty Organization (NATO) forces (1950–1952). Eisenhower served two terms as president of the United States during 1953–1961. (Library of Congress)

proposals in 1953 to neutralize and reunite all Germany proved fruitless. As president, Eisenhower fulfilled his campaign pledge to end the Korean War, seemingly threatening to employ nuclear weapons unless an armistice agreement was concluded.

Alarmed by the increasing destructiveness of nuclear armaments, Eisenhower was the first president to attempt, albeit rather unsuccessfully, to reach arms control agreements with the Soviet Union. British prime minister Winston Churchill, in office when Eisenhower first became president, strongly urged him to reach such understandings. Eisenhower's efforts began with his "Atoms for Peace" speech of December 1953, developed into his Open Skies Proposal at the 1955 Geneva Conference, and evolved into lengthy negotiations for a treaty to restrict atmospheric nuclear testing, which by the time the Geneva Conference was held in 1959 seemed likely to be successful.

In February 1956 Khrushchev repudiated much of Stalin's legacy, including his personality cult and his use of terror against political opponents, a move suggesting that the potential existed for a Soviet–American rapprochement. Soon afterward, Khrushchev expressed his faith that it might be possible for the East and West to attain a state of peaceful coexistence with each other. Progress toward this end was patchy, however. From 1958 until 1961, Khrushchev made repeated attempts to coerce and intimidate the Western powers into abandoning control of West Berlin.

In September 1959, after a protracted Geneva conference on disarmament, Khrushchev visited the United States, a trip that included an address to the United Nations, an apparently fruitful meeting at Camp David, a stay on Eisenhower's Maryland farm, and a presidential tour of the nearby Gettysburg battlefield. The much-vaunted Spirit of Camp David, however, soon evaporated. In May 1960, a long-planned summit meeting between Eisenhower and Khrushchev ended in fiasco after Russian artillery shot down an American U-2 spy plane over Soviet territory on May 5, shortly before the meeting began. Eisenhower took full responsibility for this event but refused to yield to Khrushchev's demands that the United States apologize and cease all such overflights. In response, Khrushchev angrily canceled the summit.

As the Bandung Non-Aligned Movement gained strength around the developing world, especially in decolonizing Asia, Africa, and the Middle East, where nationalist sentiments frequently ran high, Eisenhower sought to entice Third World nations into the U.S. camp. In July 1956 the United States rescinded an earlier offer to grant Gamal Abdel Nasser, Egypt's new and fiercely nationalist president, a loan for the Aswan Dam project, leading Nasser to seize the Suez Canal from France and Great Britain. Eisenhower refused to endorse the subsequent invasion of Egypt by those two nations, in conjunction with Israel, in late October 1956, and instead put heavy, and effective, pressure on them to pull their forces back.

Shortly afterward, the Soviet Union issued a statement threatening to intervene should there be any further Western threats to Middle Eastern countries. The United States, suspicious of any Soviet initiative that might jeopardize Western control of Middle Eastern oil, responded promptly in January 1957 with the Eisenhower Doctrine, pledging American military and economic assistance to any Middle Eastern country that sought to resist communism. Except for Lebanon and Iraq, few nations welcomed this doctrine, because most countries in the region believed that they had more to fear from Western imperialism than from Soviet expansionism. In 1958 Egypt and Syria encouraged Pan-Arab sentiment by their brief union in the United Arab Republic. Civil war broke out in Lebanon as Muslims sought to replace the predominantly Christian government with an Arab state. Eisenhower responded by landing U.S. Marines on Beirut's beaches to restore order.

As president, Eisenhower was generally cautious in risking American troops in overseas interventions. He boasted proudly that during his presidency no American soldier lost his life in combat duty. Despite Republican claims during the 1952 presidential campaign that they would roll back communism across Eastern Europe, when workers rose against Soviet rule in East Berlin in June 1953 and again when Hungarians attempted to expel Soviet troops in the autumn of 1956, Eisenhower refused to intervene. Although he would not recognize the People's Republic of China (PRC), he reacted cautiously in the successive Taiwan Straits crises of 1954–1955 and 1958, leaving ambiguous the likely U.S. reaction to a Chinese attack on the Guomindang-held offshore Jinmen (Quemoy) and Mazu islands.

In 1954 Eisenhower declined to commit American forces in Indochina after French troops were defeated at Dien Bien Phu. When the 1954 Geneva Accords were announced ending the First Indochinese War and temporarily partitioning Vietnam until countrywide elections could be held, Eisenhower refused to recognize them. His administration encouraged the government of the southern Republic of Vietnam (RVN, South Vietnam) in its refusal to hold the elections mandated for 1956, and provided military and economic assistance to bolster its independence. Eisenhower justified these actions by citing the domino theory—that if the United States permitted one noncommunist area to become communist, the infection would inevitably spread to its neighbors.

Eisenhower also relied heavily on covert activities, authorizing the Central Intelligence Agency (CIA) to back coups in both Iran and Guatemala in 1953 and 1954 and encouraging it to undertake numerous other secret operations. These included plans for an ill-fated coup attempt against Cuba's communist leader, Fidel Castro.

Rather ironically, in his Farewell Address of January 1961 Eisenhower warned that Cold War policies tended to undercut the democratic values that the United States claimed to defend. He also expressed his concern that high levels of defense spending had created a military-industrial complex with a vested interest in the continuation of international tensions. Nevertheless, Eisenhower himself contributed to its development by engaging the United States in the Space Race and mounting a major educational and industrial drive to enable the United States to surpass Soviet scientific achievements.

After leaving office in 1961, Eisenhower backed American intervention in Vietnam, an area that he specifically warned his successor John F. Kennedy not to abandon. In retirement Eisenhower wrote two volumes of presidential memoirs. He died in Washington, D.C., on March 28, 1969.

Priscilla Roberts

Further Reading

Ambrose, Stephen E. *Eisenhower: The President*. 2 vols. New York: Simon and Schuster, 1984.

Ambrose, Stephen E., and Richard H. Immerman. *Ike's Spies: Eisenhower and the Espionage Establishment*. Garden City, NY: Doubleday, 1981.

Bowie, Robert R., and Richard H. Immerman. *Waging Peace: How Eisenhower Shaped an Enduring Cold War Strategy*. New York: Oxford University Press, 1998.

Brands, H. W., Jr. *Cold Warriors: Eisenhower's Generation and American Foreign Policy*. New York: Columbia University Press, 1988.

Chandler, Alfred D., Jr., and Louis Galambos, eds. *The Papers of Dwight D. Eisenhower*. 21 vols. to date. Baltimore: Johns Hopkins University Press, 1970–.

Clarfield, Gerard H. *Dwight D. Eisenhower and the Shaping of the American Military Establishment*. Westport, CT: Praeger, 1999.

Craig, Campbell. *Destroying the Village: Eisenhower and Thermonuclear War*. New York: Columbia University Press, 1998.

Dockrill, Saki. *Eisenhower's New Look: National Security Policy, 1953–1961*. New York: St. Martin's, 1996.

Perret, Geoffrey. *Eisenhower*. New York: Random House, 1999.

G

Geneva Conference (1954)

The Geneva Conference on the Far East opened in that Swiss city on April 26, 1954, with negotiations concentrating on transforming the previous year's armistice in Korea into a permanent peace. Negotiations on that issue produced no results. Separate negotiations over the ongoing war in Indochina began on May 8, one day after the fall of the French bastion of Dien Bien Phu in northwest Vietnam to the Viet Minh. The Indochina talks involved representatives of France, the Democratic Republic of Vietnam (DRV, North Vietnam), the United States, the Soviet Union, the People's Republic of China (PRC), Britain, Laos, Cambodia, and the State of Vietnam (later the Republic of Vietnam).

The Viet Minh capture of Dien Bien Phu seemed to offer a perfect opportunity to resolve the long Indochina War. The Western powers were able to resist a demand by the communist powers that the "resistance governments" of Laos and Cambodia (the Pathet Lao and the Free Khmer, respectively) be represented at the talks. On June 17 longtime critic of the Indochina War Pierre Mendès-France became French premier and foreign minister. On June 20 he imposed a 30-day timetable for an agreement, promising to resign if one was not reached. The Geneva Accords were signed on the last day of the deadline, July 20, but only because the clocks were stopped; it was actually early on July 21.

The leading personalities at Geneva were Mendès-France, PRC foreign minister Zhou Enlai (Chou Enlai), Soviet foreign minister Vyacheslav Molotov, British foreign minister Anthony Eden, U.S. secretary of state John Foster Dulles, DRV premier Pham Van Dong, and State of Vietnam foreign minister Nguyen Quoc Dinh. Dulles left the conference after only a few days. He saw no likelihood of an agreement on Indochina that Washington could approve, and he disliked the idea of negotiating with Zhou (the United States had yet to recognize the PRC), whom he deliberately snubbed. Dulles ordered the U.S. delegation not to participate in the discussions and to act only as observers.

The Geneva Conference produced separate armistice agreements for Vietnam, Cambodia, and Laos. But Pham Van Dong found himself pressured by Zhou and Molotov into an agreement that gave the Viet Minh far less than it had won on the battlefield. Pending unification of Vietnam, there was to be a temporary dividing line ("provisional demarcation line") at the 17th Parallel. A demilitarized zone would extend 3 miles (5 km) on either side of the line in order to prevent incidents that might lead to a breach of the armistice. The final text provided that "the military demarcation line is provisional and should not in any way be interpreted as constituting a political or territorial boundary." Vietnam's future was to be determined "on the basis of respect for the principles of independence, unity, and territorial integrity" with "national and general elections" to be held in July 1956. Troops on both sides would have up to 300 days to be regrouped north or south; civilians could also move in either direction if they so desired. An international supervisory and control commission (ISCC) composed of representatives from Canada, Poland, and India (a Western state, a communist state, and a nonaligned state) would oversee implementation of the agreements.

Pham was bitterly disappointed that nationwide elections were put off for two years. Eager to take advantage of the Viet Minh's military successes, he had initially sought a delay of only six months after conclusion of a cease-fire. The DRV accepted the arrangements only under heavy pressure from the PRC and USSR and because it was confident that it could control southern Vietnam. There is every reason to believe that the Chinese leadership was willing to sabotage their ally in order to prevent the formation of a strong regional power on their southern border.

As it worked out, in 1956 the new government of the Republic of Vietnam (RVN, South Vietnam) headed by Ngo Dinh Diem claimed that it was not a party to the Geneva Agreements and was thus not bound by them. Supported by the Eisenhower administration in this stand, Ngo refused to authorize the previously agreed-upon elections to reunify Vietnam. This decision led to a resumption of the war, with the Americans taking the place of the French.

Spencer C. Tucker

Further Reading

Arnold, James R. *The First Domino: Eisenhower, the Military, and America's Intervention in Vietnam.* New York: William Morrow, 1991.

Devillers, Philippe, and Jean Lacouture. *End of a War: Indochina, 1954.* Translated by Alexander Liven and Adam Roberts. New York: Praeger, 1969.

Randle, Robert F. *Geneva 1954: The Settlement of the Indochinese War.* Princeton, NJ: Princeton University Press, 1969.

Gorbachev, Mikhail (1931–)

Born on March 2, 1931, in Privolnoye, Stavropol Province, Russia, to a peasant family, Mikhail Sergeyevich Gorbachev joined the Komsomol (Communist Union of the Young) in 1946 and in the same year began driving a harvester for an agricultural cooperative. In 1951 he entered the Law Faculty of Moscow State University, where he earned a law degree in 1955.

Returning to Stavropol following his studies in Moscow, Gorbachev enjoyed a remarkably rapid rise within the ranks of the CPSU, first through various posts in the Komsomol and then in the party apparatus in Stavropol in the second half of the 1950s and the first half of the 1960s. Gorbachev became a member of the CPSU Central Committee in 1971, a candidate member of the Politburo in 1979, a full member in 1980, and general secretary of the CPSU Central Committee in March 1985. A keen politician, Gorbachev's political ascendancy was further promoted by Mikhail Suslov and particularly by Yuri Andropov.

Once in power, Gorbachev consolidated his position within the party and proceeded to move forward with internal reforms. He termed his reform agenda *perestroika* (restructuring) and *glasnost* (openness). What soon became called the "politics of perestroika" was a process of cumulative reforms, ultimately leading to results that were neither intended nor necessarily desired.

Perestroika had three distinctive phases. The first phase was aimed mainly at the acceleration of economic development and the revitalization of socialism. The second phase was marked by the notion of glasnost. During this period, Gorbachev emphasized the need for political and social restructuring as well as the necessity of dealing openly with the past. Media freedoms were enhanced considerably as part of this process. In the economic arena, limited market-oriented elements were introduced, and greater latitude was given to state-owned enterprises. The third and final phase of perestroika was aimed at democratizing the Soviet political process. Reformers created a new bicameral parliament, and new procedures allowed for the direct election of two-thirds of the members of the Congress of People's Deputies. In March 1990, the Congress abolished the CPSU's political monopoly, paving the way for the legalization of other political parties.

Perestroika's third phase was also marked by some incongruous paradoxes. While the power of the CPSU was waning, Gorbachev's power was on the increase. In October 1988, he replaced Andrey Gromyko as head of the Presidium of the Supreme Soviet. Seven months later, Gorbachev became chairman of the new Supreme Soviet. Finally, in March 1990, the Congress elected him president of the USSR, a newly established post with potent executive powers. At the same time, Gorbachev's economic reforms were yielding little fruit. Perestroika was already being overshadowed by civil unrest, interethnic strife, and national and regional independence movements, particularly in the Baltic and Caucasus regions.

Gorbachev enjoyed his most remarkable successes in foreign policy. He quickly eased tensions with the West. Two summits with U.S. president Ronald Reagan (Geneva in 1985 and Reykjavík in 1986) paved the way for historic breakthroughs in Soviet–U.S. relations and nuclear arms reductions. On December 8, 1987, the Intermediate-Range Nuclear Forces (INF) Treaty was signed by both nations, the first agreement in history that eliminated an entire class of nuclear weapons. In the succeeding years, Gorbachev's international stature continued to grow. In 1988,

he ordered the withdrawal of Soviet troops from Afghanistan, ending his nation's disastrous decade-long struggle there. He also promised publicly to refrain from military intervention in Eastern Europe. In fact, Gorbachev embraced the new democratically elected leadership in the region. Especially significant was his agreement to the reunification of Germany and the inclusion of the new united Federal Republic of Germany (FRG, West Germany) in the North Atlantic Treaty Organization (NATO). Awarded the Nobel Peace Prize in 1990, Gorbachev is generally considered a driving force behind the end of the Cold War.

While Gorbachev's foreign policy was being hailed abroad, problems within the Soviet Union continued unabated. Old-line communists considered Gorbachev's policies as heresy, and economic dislocations multiplied. In 1990, several Soviet-controlled republics, including Russia, declared their independence. Gorbachev tried to stem this tide but was unsuccessful. Talks between Soviet authorities and the breakaway republics resulted in the creation of a new Russian federation (or confederation), slated to become law in August 1991.

Many of Gorbachev's reforms were tainted by an attempted coup of reactionary opponents of perestroika in August 1991. Led by high-ranking officials, among them the chief of the Komitet Gosudarstvennoi Bezopasnosti (KGB), the defense minister, the prime minister, and the vice president, Gorbachev was put under house arrest in his home in Foros after rejecting any negotiations with the putsch leaders. With the courageous intervention of the Russian Republic leader Boris Yeltsin, the coup collapsed after two days. Gorbachev returned to Moscow but was now dependent on Yeltsin, who banned the CPSU from the Russian Republic. On August 24, 1991, Gorbachev resigned as CPSU general secretary. On December 7, 1991, the presidents of Russia, Ukraine, and Belarus created a loose confederation called the Community of Independent States (CIS). Soon afterward, eight other republics joined, and the CIS treaty was concluded on December 21. Gorbachev resigned as Soviet president on December 25, and the Soviet Union became extinct on December 31, 1991.

Magarditsch Hatschikjan

Further Reading

Brown, Archibald Haworth. *The Gorbachev Factor*. Oxford: Oxford University Press, 1996.

D'Agostino, Anthony. *Gorbachev's Revolution*. New York: New York University Press, 1998.

Gorbachev, Mikhail. *Memoirs*. Translated by Georges Peronansky and Tatjana Varsavsky. New York: Doubleday, 1996.

Matlock, Jack F. *Reagan and Gorbachev: How the Cold War Ended*. New York: Random House, 2004.

Greek Civil War (1946–1949)

Greece's civil war was rooted in age-old divisions within Greek society and was complicated by the rivalry between the Soviet Union and the United States. The nationalists were strongly supported by Britain and the United States. The war was one of the earliest Cold War tests of will between East and West and claimed the lives of an estimated 80,000 Greeks, a fatality rate that surpassed the suffering of that nation in World War II. Both sides committed atrocities and tried to settle old scores under the guise of conflicting ideologies. The conflict's greatest legacy was the Truman Doctrine, which committed the United States and its allies to come to the aid of any nation threatened by communist takeover. This set the stage for President Harry S. Truman's containment policy.

In the early years of the 20th century, conservative and liberal parties in Greece struggled for power, engaging in a series

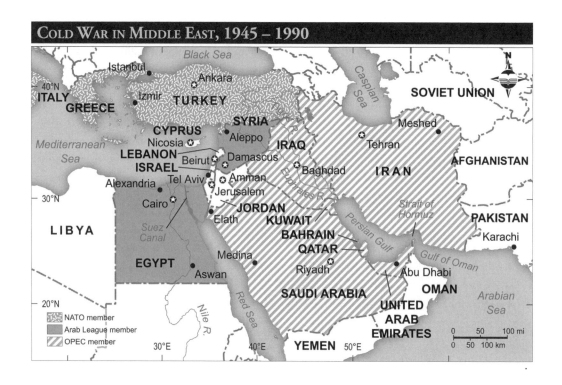

COLD WAR IN MIDDLE EAST, 1945 – 1990

of bloodless purges that heightened political instability and created great anger and bitterness. This atmosphere provided fertile ground for authoritarianism, and in 1936 General Ioannis Metaxas established a fascist-style dictatorship, further polarizing the country.

Metaxas's death in 1941 and the flight of the Greek government to Egypt after the German invasion left Greece in virtual chaos. The Greek Communist Party (KKE) persecuted under Metaxas, stepped into the power vacuum by creating the National Liberation Front (EAM), dedicated to the liberation of Greece. By 1944 the EAM boasted nearly two million members, and its military arm, the National Liberation Army (ELAS), had enlisted 50,000 fighters.

In October 1944, British prime minister Winston Churchill, fearful of a communist takeover in Greece and the loss of control over the eastern Mediterranean, met with Soviet Premier Josef Stalin in Moscow and struck a deal over control of the Balkans. In return for Soviet dominance in Bulgaria, Romania, and Poland, Stalin ceded Greece to Great Britain and vowed not to directly support the KKE after the war.

Relations between the British-backed Greek monarchy and the EAM quickly soured as the communists suppressed dissent and tried to assert control over the country. In retaliation, the British rehabilitated the collaborationist police, returned monarchist military units to the nation, and demanded that the ELAS disarm. On December 2, 1944, collaborationist police fired on antigovernment demonstrators, triggering the Battle for Athens. It resulted in a victory for the nationalists and the disarming of the ELAS. The EAM splintered as moderates and socialists abandoned it, while KKE membership plummeted from its peak of more than 400,000 to only 50,000. KKE leader Nikos Zachariades

attempted to impose tighter party discipline but was stymied by the strength of the nationalist forces.

In an attempt to maintain order, the British strengthened the Greek National Guard and turned a blind eye as security forces conducted a campaign of repression against the communists. In the Greek parliamentary elections of March 1946, the rightist candidates won a landslide victory. The allegedly rigged elections prompted the KKE to declare a state of civil war and reorganize ELAS units as the Democratic Army of Greece (DSE). The DSE won notable gains in the first year of fighting due in part to support from the communist governments of Yugoslavia and Albania.

Fearing that the nationalists might indeed lose the war against the DSE, the British appealed for help from the United States. Previous British requests for American assistance in Greece had been rebuffed, but by 1947 American attitudes had begun to change. President Truman's growing antipathy toward the Soviets and their tightening of control in Eastern Europe hardened his stance. On March 12, 1947, he addressed a joint session of Congress, enunciating the Truman Doctrine and requesting a $300 million aid package to support the Greek nationalists and anticommunists in nearby Turkey.

The KKE did not take the Truman Doctrine seriously, believing that the nationalists would capitulate even with U.S. support. By 1948, however, it was becoming clear that the DSE was in dire straits as the American-backed nationalist army grew exponentially. In January 1949, KKE leaders foolishly declared that the goal of the civil war was no longer the restoration of parliamentary democracy, as they had previously stated, but rather the establishment of a proletarian dictatorship. The DSE then shifted from a mobile war of attrition to a campaign to defend territory, a tactical miscalculation that played into the hands of the revitalized nationalist army.

In the spring of 1949, the nationalist army cleared the communist rebels out of southern Greece and launched a two-pronged offensive designed to drive them completely out of the country. As the fighting reached its climax, Yugoslavia closed its border and ended arms shipments that had kept the DSE insurgency viable. After sustaining more than 2,000 casualties in the summer of 1949, DSE fighters withdrew into Albania during the night of August 29, 1949, effectively ending the civil war. Although sporadic DSE raids continued into 1950, the victory of the nationalist forces was by then complete.

Vernon L. Pedersen

Further Reading

Clogg, Richard. *A Concise History of Greece.* 2nd ed. Cambridge: Cambridge University Press, 2002.

Close, David H. *The Greek Civil War, 1943–1950: Studies of Polarization.* London: Routledge, 1993.

Close, David H. *The Origins of the Greek Civil War.* New York: Longman, 1995.

Gerolymatos, Andre. *Red Acropolis, Black Terror: The Greek Civil War and the Origins of Soviet-American Rivalry.* New York: Basic Books, 2004.

Iatrides, John O. *Greece in the 1940s: A Nation in Crisis.* Hanover, NH: University Press of New England, 1981.

Gromyko, Andrey (1909–1989)

Born on July 18, 1909, to a peasant family in Starye Gromyki, Belorussia, Andrey Andreyevich Gromyko studied agricultural economics at the Minsk School of Agricultural Technology, earning a degree in 1936. He also became active as a Komsomol (Communist Youth) official. After working as a research associate and economist at the Soviet Academy of Sciences in Moscow, he entered the Foreign Affairs Ministry, where he was named chief of the U.S. division of the People's Commissariat of Foreign Affairs in 1939. That same year he began working at the Soviet embassy in Washington, D.C. In 1943 Soviet leader Josef Stalin appointed Gromyko as Moscow's youngest-ever ambassador to the United States.

Gromyko played an important role in coordinating the wartime alliance between the Americans and Soviets and played a fairly prominent role at diplomatic events such as the February 1945 Yalta Conference and the July–August 1945 Potsdam Conference. He also attended the conference establishing the United Nations (UN) in October 1945 and became Moscow's UN representative in 1946. He served briefly as the ambassador to the United Kingdom during 1952–1953 and then returned to the Soviet Union.

In 1956 Gromyko attained full membership on the Central Committee of the Communist Party of the Soviet Union (CPSU). In 1957 he began his 28-year tenure as foreign minister. In 1973 he ascended to the Politburo.

During his long career, Gromyko became known as an expert and cunning negotiator. In the West he was dubbed "Mr. Nyet" (Mr. No) because of his hard bargaining and staunch communist views. At home, he exhibited a great talent for adjusting to the ruling leaders. Thus, he did not develop a characteristic line of politics of his own. Under Soviet Premier Nikita Khrushchev, Gromyko readily adapted to the leader's erratic whims and played a key role in the Berlin and Cuban Missile crises. Under Soviet leader Leonid Brezhnev, Gromyko reached the apogee of his powers. Brezhnev believed in a system of loyalty combined with freedom to rule one's own destiny. Therefore, he gave Gromyko virtual free rein in setting Soviet foreign policy.

During 1973–1975 Gromyko negotiated on behalf of the Soviet Union during the Conference on Security and Cooperation in Europe, which led to the landmark 1975 Helsinki Final Act. This act recognized Europe's postwar borders and set a political template for further negotiations concerning human rights, science, economics, and cultural exchanges. The Helsinki Final Act marked the full flowering of East–West détente, but because it did not match expectations about liberalization in the Soviet Union and Eastern Europe, it precipitated mounting dissent at home and protest abroad.

In 1985 Soviet leader Mikhail Gorbachev appointed his own protégé, Eduard Shevardnadze, as foreign minister and named Gromyko president of the Presidium of the Supreme Soviet of the USSR, by then a purely symbolic position. He remained in this post until 1988. Gromyko died on July 2, 1989, in Moscow.

Beatrice de Graaf

Further Reading

Gromyko, Anatoli. *Andrey Gromyko: In the Kremlin's Labyrinth.* Moscow: Avtor, 1997.

Gromyko, Anatoli. *Memories.* New York: Arrow Books, 1989.

Gulags

The term *gulag* arose from the Russian acronym for Glavnoye Upravleniye Lagerey (State Director of Camps), an agency of the Soviet secret police that administered the Soviet system of forced labor camps where political dissenters, dissidents, and other alleged enemies of the state were sent.

The first gulags were established in tsarist Russia and in the early Soviet era under Vladimir Lenin. The gulags reached their zenith in the period of Josef Stalin's rule. Unlike other labor camps before and after, people were imprisoned not just for what they had done but also for who they were in terms of class, religion, nationality, and race. The gulag was one of the means of implementing Stalin's political purges, which cleansed the Soviet Union of real and imagined enemies.

The first gulag victims were hundreds of thousands of people caught in the collectivization campaigns in the early 1930s. After the Red Army's invasion of the Baltic states and Poland in June 1941, the secret police incarcerated potential resistors. When Adolf Hitler sent German armies into the Soviet Union in June 1941, people of German ancestry in Eastern Europe were incarcerated as well. Following the German defeat at Stalingrad, the Red Army advanced west, capturing and imprisoning enemy soldiers. Stalin also incarcerated partisan groups from all over Eastern Europe.

Following World War II, the Allies agreed that all Russian citizens should be returned to the Soviet Union. This naturally included Soviet prisoners of war held by the Germans. The Western Allies also forced anti-Soviet émigrés, many of whom had fought with Hitler, to return to the Soviet Union. The vast majority of these were either shot or simply disappeared into a gulag. In March 1946, the Soviet secret police began incarcerating ethnic minorities, Soviet Jews, and youth groups, as well as people who were viewed as a hindrance to Sovietization campaigns in Eastern Europe, for allegedly anti-Stalinist conspiracies.

The juridical process for sentencing people to a gulag comprised a three-person panel, which could both try and sentence the accused or simply rely on Article 58 of the

Barbed wire surrounds the Soviet penal colony at Minsk in the USSR, February 16, 1958. (Bettmann/ Corbis)

Soviet Criminal Code. Article 58 deprived Soviet citizens suspected of illegal activity of any rights and permitted the authorities to send anyone to the camps for any reason, justified or not. The gulag served as an institution to punish people but also was meant to fulfill an economic function, for Stalin sought to deploy workers in remote parts of Russia that had brutal climates but were rich with natural resources.

In the early 1950s, gulag authorities issued reports revealing that the camp system was unprofitable. Stalin, however, commanded further construction projects such as railways, canals, power stations, and tunnels. Thus, thousands of prisoners died, and maintenance costs skyrocketed. To an extent, the situation changed in the gulags after the war because the inmates had changed. These new politicals were well-organized

and experienced fighters who often banded together and dominated the camps. Slowly, authorities lost control.

Immediately following Stalin's death in March 1953, Lavrenty Beria briefly took charge, reorganized the gulags, and abandoned most of Stalin's construction projects. Beria granted amnesty to all prisoners sentenced to five years or less, pregnant women, and women with children under age 18. He also secretly abolished the use of physical force against detainees. In June 1953, he announced his decision to liquidate the gulags altogether. However, he was subsequently arrested and executed. The new Soviet leadership under Nikita Khrushchev reversed most of Beria's reforms, although it did not revoke the amnesties.

Because neither Beria nor Khrushchev rehabilitated the political prisoners, they began to fight back with their new and well-organized groups. They killed informers, staged strikes, and fomented rebellions. The biggest of these occurred in Steplag, Kazakhstan, and lasted from spring until late summer 1954. Inmates seized control, but Soviet authorities brutally quashed the revolt.

In the aftermath of the Steplag rebellion, the secret police relaxed gulag regulations, implemented an eight-hour workday, and gradually began to reexamine individual cases. This process was accelerated by Khrushchev's condemnation of Stalin's rule in February 1956. In the so-called Thaw Era, the gulags were officially dissolved, and the two biggest camp complexes in Norilsk and Dalstroi were dismantled. Despite the Thaw, certain politicals were still incarcerated.

Under Leonid Brezhnev, politicals were renamed "dissidents." In the wake of the Hungarian Revolution in October 1956, the Komitet Gosudarstvennoi Bezopasnosti (KGB) used two camps in Moldovia and Perm to incarcerate dissidents. In contrast to former prisoners, these detainees consciously criticized the government and purposely invited incarceration to gain the attention of Western media. By 1966 Brezhnev, and later Yuri Andropov, then chairman of the KGB, declared these dissidents "insane" and imprisoned them in psychiatric hospitals. When Mikhail Gorbachev took power in 1985 and embarked on reform, perestroika brought a final end to the gulags in 1987, and glasnost allowed limited access to information about their history.

It is impossible to determine just how many people were imprisoned and how many died in the gulags. Conservative estimates hold that 28.7 million forced laborers passed through the gulag system. There were never more than two million people at a time in the system, although perhaps as many as three million people died in the camps during the Stalin era.

Frank Beyersdorf

Further Reading

Applebaum, Anne. *Gulag: A History*. New York: Broadway Books, 2003.

Ginzburg, Evgeniia. *Journey into the Whirlwind*. Translated by Paul Stevenson and Max Hayward. New York: Harcourt Brace and World, 1967.

Ivanova, Galina Mikhailovna, with Donald J. Raleigh. *Labor Camp Socialism: The Gulag in the Soviet Totalitarian System*. Translated from the Russian by Carol Fath. Armonk, NY: Sharpe, 2000.

Khevniuk, Oleg. *History of the Gulag*. New Haven, CT: Yale University Press, 2003.

Solzhenitsyn, Aleksandr. *The Gulag Archipelago, 1918–1956: An Experiment in Literary Investigation*. 3 vols. New York: Harper and Row, 1974–1978.

H

Helsinki Final Act (1975)

The Helsinki Final Act was signed by representatives of 35 European and North American states on August 1, 1975, in Helsinki, Finland, and was the summation agreement of the Security and Cooperation in Europe Conference (CSCE). The act bridged significant differences between Western and Eastern Europe through far-reaching concurrences on political borders, trade and, most notably, human rights. The accord is often described as the high point of détente and was a key diplomatic turning point in the Cold War.

The Helsinki Final Act was not a formal treaty. It was an international agreement to which countries were bound politically but not legally. The act was the result of years of negotiations, first proposed by the Soviets in Geneva in 1954. Discussions commenced in earnest with the Helsinki Consultations of November 22, 1972, and the formal opening of the CSCE on July 3, 1973. The Consultations and talks that followed focused on four baskets of issues. The first dealt with 10 principles guiding relations in Europe, including the inviolability of frontiers, the territorial integrity of states, and the peaceful settlement of disputes. The first basket also incorporated confidence-building measures such as advanced notification of military troop maneuvers. The second basket addressed economic, scientific, and technological cooperation among CSCE states, and the third basket concentrated on such humanitarian issues as the reunification of families, improved working conditions for journalists, and increased cultural exchanges. The fourth basket focused on follow-up procedures.

The signing of the Helsinki Final Act was initially unpopular in many Western countries because it conceded Soviet domination of Eastern Europe and formally recognized the Soviet Union's annexation of Estonia, Latvia, and Lithuania. Yet the publication of the Helsinki Final Act in Eastern Europe spurred the formation of Helsinki Monitoring Groups, the most prominent of which was founded in Moscow by Yuri Orlov, Yelena Bonner, and nine other Soviet human rights activists. These monitoring groups called upon Eastern bloc nations to uphold their Helsinki commitments and drew international attention to their reports of human rights abuses. These groups became part of a larger political and social movement that ultimately prefigured the end of the Cold War.

The Helsinki Final Act marked the beginning of an ongoing process, known as the Helsinki Process, in which CSCE states convened periodically to review the implementation of the act and initiate further efforts to decrease East--West tensions. In 1989, as the Berlin Wall came down and the Czechoslovakian Velvet Revolution moved into high gear, many East European reformers, including Czechoslovakia's Václav Havel, cited the Helsinki Process as a key part of their success in throwing off the yoke of communist totalitarianism.

Sarah B. Snyder

Further Reading

Hanhimaki, Jussi. " 'They Can Write it in Swahili': Kissinger, The Soviets, and the

Helsinki Accords, 1973–1975." *Journal of Transatlantic Studies* 1, no. 1 (2003): 37–58.

Maresca, John J. *To Helsinki: The Conference on Security and Cooperation in Europe, 1973–1975*. Durham, NC: Duke University Press, 1985.

Hiss, Alger (1904–1996)

Born on November 11, 1904, in Baltimore, Maryland, Alger Hiss was educated at Johns Hopkins and Harvard universities. He joined the U.S. State Department in 1936. Among several important assignments, he was private secretary to U.S. Supreme Court Justice Oliver Wendell Holmes, secretary to the Dumbarton Oaks Conference (1944), and among the U.S. delegation to the 1945 Yalta Conference. Hiss also served as secretary-general of the United Nations' (UN) organizing conference in San Francisco (1945–1946). In February 1947, with support from John Foster Dulles, Hiss became head of the Carnegie Endowment for International Peace.

In August 1948 Whittaker Chambers, a self-confessed ex-communist, accused Hiss of having been a member of the Communist Party in the 1930s and of having betrayed State Department secrets to the Soviets. Hiss strenuously denied the charges under oath. He was subsequently indicted by a grand jury for perjury, as the statute of limitations for treason had expired, and was bound over for trial, which resulted in a hung jury in July 1949. Then, in a highly publicized retrial in January 1950, Hiss was found guilty and served 44 months in the Lewisburg Federal Penitentiary. He continued to assert his innocence and so too did a large and influential body of supporters, which precipitated one of the most intense and enigmatic debates of the entire Cold War.

Archival revelations in the 1990s, including those from Russian sources, vindicated neither Hiss nor his defenders. Historical evidence now seems to suggest that Hiss was indeed guilty of treason. The strange case of Alger Hiss was a defining episode not only in the Cold War but also in modern American politics. It rallied conservatives, gave birth to the excesses of McCarthyism, and spotlighted Hiss's nemesis, the little-known California congressman Richard M. Nixon, who would later go on to become a U.S. senator, vice president, and president. Hiss died on November 15, 1996, in New York City.

Phillip Deery

Further Reading

Lowenthal, John. "Venona and Alger Hiss." *Intelligence and National Security* 15, no. 3 (2000): 98–130.

Weinstein, Allen. *Perjury: The Hiss-Chambers Case*. New York: Knopf, 1978.

White, G. Edward. *Alger Hiss's Looking-Glass Wars: The Covert Life of a Soviet Spy*. Oxford: Oxford University Press, 2004.

Ho Chi Minh (1890–1969)

Born Nguyen Sinh Cung on May 19, 1890, in Kimlien, Annam, Vietnam, his father was a Confucian scholar who had served in the Vietnamese imperial bureaucracy but resigned to protest the French occupation of his country. Nguyen received his secondary education at the prestigious National Academy, a French-style lycée in Hue. In 1911 he hired on as a merchant ship cook, traveling to the United States, Africa, and Europe. He then became first a photography assistant and then an assistant pastry chef in London. With the beginning of World War I, Nguyen moved to Paris, where he became active in the French Socialist Party. Changing his name to Nguyen Ai Quoc (Nguyen the Patriot), he became a leader in the large Indo-Chinese community in France. After the war, he helped draft a petition to the Allied leaders at the Paris Peace Conference demanding self-determination for colonial peoples; the petition was ignored.

When the Socialist Party split in 1920, Nguyen became one of the founders of the new French Communist Party. He spent the early 1920s in Moscow at the headquarters of the Communist International (Comintern). In 1924 he went to Guangzhou (Canton), China, and during the next two years worked to form a Marxist-Leninist revolutionary organization in French Indochina. In 1925 he organized the Vietnamese Revolutionary Youth League as a training ground for the future Vietnamese Communist Party. In 1929 he presided over a meeting in Hong Kong that brought several communist factions together, forming a single Vietnamese Communist Party, later renamed the Indochinese Communist Party (ICP).

By the early 1940s Nguyen had taken the name Ho Chi Minh (Bearer of Light). He left Hong Kong and returned to Vietnam in early 1941, where he formed a broad nationalist alliance, the League for the Independence of Vietnam (Viet Minh), to combat both the French and Japanese occupations. The Viet Minh generally downplayed orthodox communist ideology and emphasized anti-imperialism and land reform, although it was dominated by the ICP.

During World War II Ho shuttled between Vietnam and China to build support for his movement. He was held in detention for a year in China by the anticommunist Chinese Guomindang (GMD, Nationalists), who released him in 1944. He had also worked with the U.S. Office of Strategic Services (OSS). When Japan surrendered in August 1945, the Viet Minh occupied Hanoi, and Ho established the Democratic Republic of Vietnam (DRV, North Vietnam). He became president of the newly formed nation on March 2, 1946. Ho sought to avoid hostilities with France, but differences between the Viet Minh nationalists and the French, who steadfastly refused to give up their hold on Vietnam, led to fighting and the beginning of the Indochina War in December 1946.

During the eight-year conflict against the French, Ho played an active part in policy formulation, while Viet Minh General Vo Nguyen Giap was chief military strategist. Following the defeat of the French at the Battle of Dien Bien Phu in 1954, Vietnam was

Pictured here in 1954, Vietnamese communist and nationalist Ho Chi Minh founded the Indochina Communist Party in 1930 and was president of the Democratic Republic of Vietnam from 1945 to 1969. (Library of Congress)

divided along the 17th Parallel, with elections in North Vietnam and the Republic of Vietnam (RVN, South Vietnam) scheduled for 1956. When South Vietnamese president Ngo Dinh Diem refused to accede to the elections, with the blessing of U.S. president Dwight D. Eisenhower's administration, fighting resumed in the south and in 1960 Ho and the North Vietnamese leadership decided to support it. Although Ho was certainly a staunch communist, he was first and foremost a Vietnamese nationalist, determined to see his nation unified no matter the cost.

During the subsequent long war with the United States, Ho remained an important symbol of nationalist resistance and played an active part in formulating North Vietnamese policy. He was primarily responsible for North Vietnamese dealings with both the Soviet Union and the People's Republic of China (PRC). Ho did not live to see his dream of a united Vietnam realized. He died in Hanoi on September 3, 1969. In 1975, when North Vietnamese troops were victorious, the South Vietnamese capital of Saigon was renamed Ho Chi Minh City in his honor. Today, Ho's body is on public display in a mausoleum in Hanoi.

James H. Willbanks

Further Reading

Duiker, William J. *Ho Chi Minh: A Life*. New York: Hyperion, 2000.

Duiker, William J. *The Rise of Nationalism in Vietnam, 1900–1941*. Ithaca, NY: Cornell University Press, 1976.

Herring, George C. *America's Longest War: The United States and Vietnam, 1950–1975*. 4th ed. New York: McGraw-Hill, 2001.

Ho Chi Minh. *Ho Chi Minh on Revolution: Selected Writings, 1920–1966*. New York: Signet, 1967.

Tucker, Spencer C. *Vietnam*. Lexington: University Press of Kentucky, 1999.

Hoover, John Edgar (1895–1972)

Born on January 1, 1895, in Washington, D.C., J. Edgar Hoover studied law at George Washington University and earned an LLB in 1916 and a master of law degree the next year. He went to work for the Department of Justice in 1917.

Beginning in 1919, Hoover spent two years as a special assistant to Attorney General A. Mitchell Palmer. Hoover's anticommunist crusade began under Palmer when he assisted in the arrests of more than 4,000 suspected radicals and resident aliens, a number of whom were deported. Following this First Red Scare, the Palmer Raids, and the financial scandals of President Warren Harding's administration, on May 10, 1924, Hoover was appointed director of the Bureau of Investigation (soon to become known as the Federal Bureau of Investigation). He turned his attention to reforming the agency, increasing its professionalism, and, above all, crafting an image of himself as a tough, progressive, and scientific crime fighter.

By the late 1930s Hoover was convinced that communism threatened social values and posed a significant threat to the United States. This attitude hardened in the postwar period when the FBI liaison to the highly secret Venona project, an army intelligence effort to decode thousands of Soviet diplomatic cables, reported the discovery of a Soviet spy ring within the U.S. government.

Hoover's fear that the hidden apparatus of the Communist Party had permeated American liberal organizations set much of the domestic tone of the early Cold War in the United States. His belief that President Harry S. Truman's loyalty program had not gone far enough to stanch the communist threat prompted his testimony in 1947 before the House Un-American Activities Committee

(HUAC). Hoover also elaborated on the dangers posed by communism in such books as *Masters of Deceit* (1958) and *A Study of Communism* (1962). Under his direction, the FBI arrested the leaders of the Communist Party of the United States of America (CPUSA), utilizing provisions of the anticommunist Smith Act; tracked down secret communists in government, such as Alger Hiss, a former State Department official accused of espionage; and arrested and interrogated Julius and Ethel Rosenberg, who were accused of betraying the secret of the atom bomb to the Soviet Union.

The 1950s perhaps marked the height of Hoover's influence, as he enjoyed the trust of President Dwight D. Eisenhower and lived a privileged life that included the company of millionaires and Hollywood celebrities. By the end of the decade the FBI had broken the back of the CPUSA, which forced the Soviet Union to replace its network of ideologically motivated spies with professionals and paid informants. Hoover nonetheless refused to acknowledge his anticommunist successes and continued to devote FBI resources to fighting the CPUSA and other radical groups, often at the expense of emerging hot-button issues such as growing violence against civil rights workers in the South and the continued rise of organized crime.

Hoover had a strained relationship with President John F. Kennedy, but President Lyndon B. Johnson understood Hoover's clout and used the FBI much as President Franklin Roosevelt had, as a tool to advance his political agenda. Johnson pushed Hoover to destroy the network of violent Ku Klux Klan organizations in the South through use of the FBI's counterintelligence program (COINTELPRO). It combined wiretapping with the use of informants and disinformation campaigns designed to disrupt target groups. However, the presence of former and current Communist Party members in civil rights and antiwar groups inspired Hoover to direct COINTELPRO operations against civil rights leader Reverend Martin Luther King Jr., the Black Panthers, the tiny Socialist Workers' Party, and many others groups and individuals who attracted the FBI's attention.

Hoover, the longest-serving FBI director in history, died of a heart attack on May 2, 1972, in Washington, D.C. Although still respected at the time of his death, revelations about the extent of his domestic spying and the FBI's illegal activities as well as about the details of his personal life greatly tarnished his reputation.

Vernon L. Pedersen

Further Reading

DeLoach, Cartha D. "Deke." In *Hoover's FBI: The Inside Story by Hoover's Trusted Lieutenant*. Washington, DC: Regnery, 1995.

Gentry, Curt. *J. Edgar Hoover: The Man and the Secrets*. New York: Norton, 1991.

Powers, Richard Gid. *Secrecy and Power: The Life of J. Edgar Hoover*. New York: Free Press, 1988.

Theoharis, Athan G., and John Stuart Cox. *The Boss: J. Edgar Hoover and the Great American Inquisition*. Philadelphia: Temple University Press, 1988.

Human Rights

Rights are rule-governed powers of some people to activate duties that others owe them but cannot extinguish unilaterally. Duties may be to act or refrain from acting. For example, the right to free speech confers the duty on people to refrain from interfering with each other's expression of opinion according to rules that exclude, say, speech that constitutes a clear and present danger.

Some philosophers posit that rights must protect legitimate interests and create an inviolable, morally justified cordon around a person. For example, each person has a legitimate interest in receiving due process; it is morally justified. The right to due process creates a protective cordon around each one of us. By contrast, an effort to silence all people who happen to disagree with a particular person is illegitimate. It is not morally justified, and so there is no protective cordon around that person.

Human rights are those rights that each person possesses by virtue of his or her humanity; for example, the right to life or free expression. By contrast, civil rights are those that some people retain by virtue of being citizens; for example, the right to vote freely in an election. Special rights are ones that we enjoy because of our particular situation in the world; for example, a right to inherit from our particular parents or wear the specific shirt we bought.

The idea of universal human rights that are equally applicable to all human beings without distinction of citizenship, culture, geographical location, or historical context has been philosophically and politically controversial. The Westphalian Order that ended the Thirty Years' War in Europe in 1648 gave extensive powers to sovereign rulers, most notably to determine the state's religion. Modern state sovereignty resolved the religious conflicts in Europe but also removed the legal grounds for the intervention of one state in the internal affairs of another, particularly in the case of human rights abuses.

The Anglo-American tradition of political philosophy connects the legitimacy of the sovereign state with its duty to guarantee rights. Thomas Hobbes suggested that the state is based on a social contract wherein the sovereign state guarantees to its subjects a right to life in return for all their other native natural rights. John Locke assigned to the state the duty of guaranteeing the rights of its citizens. When the American colonists set out to justify their claim for independence, they formulated their arguments in Lockean terms as a reaction to the king's violation of their rights, the same rights that he was supposed to guarantee. Shortly thereafter, the French Revolution codified human rights for the first time in a political document, the *Declaration of the Rights of Man and Citizen* (1793). However, this declaration was issued during the Reign of Terror (1793–1794), which witnessed the worst excesses of the French Revolution. For the next century and a half, the concept of human rights hardly played a role in international politics, with the possible exception of certain aspects of the struggle against slavery and the slave trade. Still, the democratic emphasis on rights within the context of the Cold War was a natural development of tradition that did not quite exist in Eastern Europe.

World War II brought human rights to the forefront of international politics. On the one hand, the unique wickedness of Nazism made the war against it a moral one rather than just a clash of nations and their interests. The positive content of that moral struggle was couched, especially by Americans, in terms of universal human rights. On the other hand, the tentative and ideologically awkward alliance between Western democracies and the Soviet Union required some positive common denominator— good versus evil—that transcended a common enemy. These two trends were further strengthened after the war, when the true scale of Nazi atrocities and the Holocaust became apparent and World War II acquired its established character as a war of good against evil. This good was interpreted by many as human rights. The Nuremberg War

Crimes Tribunals of 1945–1946, presided over by American, British, French, and Soviet judges, introduced the concept of crimes against humanity into international law. Although formulated and applied after the fact, the construct of crimes against humanity set standards of human rights according to which Nazi leaders could be tried and punished not just for atrocities committed in occupied territories but also for those against German citizens on German territory.

The United Nations (UN) went even further to promote the rhetoric, if not the practice, of human rights in its founding Charter and in the December 1948 Convention on the Prevention and Punishment of the Crime of Genocide and the Universal Declaration of Human Rights. The significance of these documents was declarative rather than normative, because no enforcement mechanisms with appropriate powers were created following these declarations. As noted above, there are no rights for some without duties for others. For humans to have rights, some institution must be entrusted with enforcing them; otherwise, declarations remain just that. Since the Universal Declaration of Human Rights was a compromise between communist and democratic representatives, it included economic rights clauses that clearly make no normative sense in a universal context; for example, the right of every human to enjoy a paid vacation.

The onset of the Cold War stifled attempts to enforce a universal regime of human rights because communist totalitarianism was inherently founded on the state's right to violate any right of its subjects, while Western democracies protected communist client states that abused human rights in the developing world, from Iran to Haiti to Latin America. The so-called realist approach to international relations promoted by Henry Kissinger, for example, dictates nonintervention in the internal human rights policies of other countries and the determination of U.S. foreign policy based exclusively on its geopolitical interests. For example, in 1973 the United States supported the Chilean military in deposing leftist president Salvador Allende and instituting a regime that exhibited worse human rights violations than its predecessor. For political expediency, it also engaged in an alliance with Maoist China, although China's Cultural Revolution violated human rights on a scale far greater than in the Soviet Union.

A variety of UN-sponsored human rights covenants and agreements from the 1960s further broadened the rhetorical connotations of human rights to encompass social, economic, and ethnic issues but also deepened the divide between the public rhetoric and actual practices of signatory nations to these covenants. Both sides in the Cold War used human rights rhetoric as a tool in their ideological war. The West lambasted communist states for allegedly violating the liberties of their subjects, while the communists harped on the alleged violation of the right to work of the unemployed in free market economies.

The policing of human rights became more effective by the mid-1970s through the introduction of various new methods for enforcement. The United States attempted to use its economic might to pressure human rights violators. In 1973, the U.S. Congress linked foreign aid to the human rights record of recipient countries. The Jackson-Vanik Amendment to the U.S. Trade Act of 1974 attempted to use the Soviets' reliance upon American wheat to pressure the Soviet Union to increase Jewish, Baltic, and Baptist emigration by linking free emigration with a most-favored nation (MFN) trade status. However, the generally low volume of trade between the two blocs limited the effectiveness of this kind of leverage. The Soviets reacted by linking emigration to the state of their negotiations with the United States over disarmament and other political issues.

The 1975 Helsinki Final Act Covenant on Human Rights was probably viewed by the Soviet leadership as yet another declarative statement of little lasting effect. It included safety clauses that precluded intervention in the internal affairs of Soviet-bloc countries. Yet its ratification by Soviet-bloc nations provided international legal grounds for East European dissidents to assist their governments in its implementation. The Helsinki Process provided a legal basis for the resurrection of civil society in Eastern Europe, especially through the Charter 77 dissident movement in Czechoslovakia and the Soviet Human Rights Committee of Andrei Sakharov and Sergei Kovaljov. Dissident groups were able to pressure their governments to respect human rights through exposure of their violations in the Western media, which were then broadcast back beyond the Iron Curtain via Radio Liberty. Dissidents pressed on to assert their rights to express their opinions in samizdat publications (typed carbon copies that circulated among friends) and in informal gatherings where banned music and theater could be performed and critical lectures could be delivered. The dissidents were supported most effectively by nongovernmental organizations (NGOs) in the West, which put greater pressure on the Soviet regimes than governments ever could.

A somewhat parallel development took place west of the Iron Curtain, where NGOs such as Amnesty International became significant in enforcing human rights through monitoring and reporting and by embarrassing the perpetrating governments in the forum of world public opinion. When U.S. president Jimmy Carter took office in 1977,

he refocused his nation's foreign policy to promote global human rights, although he continued to support some traditional U.S. allies, such as Shah Mohammad Reza Pahlavi of Iran, despite their dismal human rights records. Still, the idealistic shift in policy persisted through the presidency of Ronald Reagan. The Reagan administration attempted to improve the human rights situation in nations in Latin America, Indonesia, and East Asia, albeit through private channels rather than public diplomacy and sometimes by utilizing illegal means. In 1985, human rights were one of four items on the agenda of Soviet and American negotiators as the Cold War began to wind down.

In 1987 the Soviet Union moved to improve its human rights record by releasing political prisoners and granting freedom of speech, the press, assembly, and travel, which ultimately led to political freedom and, after 1991, to national self-determination. Soviet leader Mikhail Gorbachev's perestroika and glasnost policies were in large measure responsible for these momentous turns of events. The problem then, as now, has been the lack of institutional guarantees of human rights in the former Soviet states that would systematically enforce rights.

Gorbachev's attempt to reform communism proved that totalitarian communist regimes could not easily introduce human rights into their system. Totalitarianism is, in essence, an all-or-nothing proposition. Once it allows its people to possess rudimentary human rights, it loses its claim to power; the people demand greater distribution of rights from the rulers to the ruled, and totalitarianism ends. This process had already been predicted by Czech dissident Václav Benda in his 1978 essay "A Parallel Polis."

In the closing years of the Cold War, as international tensions subsided, the U.S. interest in supporting regimes that violated human rights for the sake of political expediency waned. Consequently, a wave of democratization swept Latin America and South Africa. Yet the end of the Cold War also exposed the inability of the international community to enforce human rights even in the most extreme cases of genocide, such as in Rwanda, the Sudan, and the former Yugoslavia.

Aviezer Tucker

Further Reading

Donnelly, Jack. *International Human Rights.* Boulder, CO: Westview, 1993.

Falk, Barbara J. *The Dilemmas of Dissidence in East-Central Europe: Citizen Intellectuals and Philosopher Kings.* Budapest: Central European University Press, 2003.

Falk, Richard. *Human Rights and State Sovereignty.* New York: Holmes and Meier, 1981.

Forsythe, David P. *Human Rights and World Politics.* Lincoln: University of Nebraska Press, 1983.

Liang-Fenton, Debra, ed. *Implementing U.S. Human Rights Policy: Agendas, Policies, and Practices.* Washington, DC: United States Institute of Peace Press, 2004.

Müllerson, Rein. *Human Rights Diplomacy.* New York: Routledge, 1997.

Tucker, Aviezer. *The Philosophy and Politics of Czech Dissidence from Patočka to Havel.* Pittsburgh, PA: Pittsburgh University Press, 2000.

Hydrogen Bomb

Hydrogen bombs (also known as H-bombs) rely on the fusion of hydrogen isotopes, unlike an atom bomb, which relies on the fission (or splitting) of radioactive isotopes. Fusion occurs when neutrons collide with an unstable hydrogen isotope, causing two lighter isotopes to join together to make a heavier element. During the fusion process, some of the mass of the original isotopes is released as energy, resulting in a powerful explosion. Because of the loss of mass, the end product, or element, weighs less than the total of the original isotopes. H-bombs are referred to as thermonuclear devices because temperatures of 400 million degrees Celsius are required for the fusion process to begin. In order to produce these temperatures, an H-bomb has an atomic bomb at its core. The explosion of the atomic device and the fission process in turn leads to the fusion process in hydrogen isotopes that surround the atomic core.

An H-bomb, depending on its size, can produce an explosion powerful enough to devastate an area of approximately 150 square miles, while the searing heat and toxic radioactive fallout from such devices can impact an area of more than 800 square miles. The explosion of an atomic bomb by the Soviet Union in September 1949 ended the U.S. atomic monopoly and led to a nuclear arms race. The development of more powerful weapons such as the H-bomb and of new methods of delivering nuclear bombs, such as ballistic missiles, were primarily a result of the Cold War conflict and concomitant arms race.

In 1946 the U.S. Atomic Energy Act created the Atomic Energy Commission (USAEC). The USAEC was responsible for the development and control of the U.S. atomic energy program after World War II. The commission consisted of five members appointed by the president. A civilian advisory committee was also created, and Robert Oppenheimer, scientific head of the atomic bomb project, served as its chairman. The USAEC also worked with a military liaison with whom it consulted on all atomic energy issues that had military applications. By 1949, the year the Soviets exploded their first atomic bomb, Cold War tensions were running high. Nuclear physicist Edward Teller, USAEC Commissioner Lewis Strauss, and other scientists formed a coalition together with military officials to urge President Harry Truman to initiate a program to construct a superweapon, or H-bomb. This new weapon would be measured in megatons instead of kilotons and could yield an explosion equivalent to millions of tons of TNT. Despite opposition from Oppenheimer and several other nuclear scientists, Truman, under siege for being soft on communism, authorized an H-bomb program in January 1950.

It took the combined efforts of a number of scientists as well as Stanislaw Ulam, a mathematician, to solve the theoretical and technical problems related to building a hydrogen weapon. They carried out their work at Los Alamos, New Mexico, the same facility that had helped produce the atomic bomb. The prototype H-bomb was first detonated on November 1, 1952, on Enewetak Atoll in the South Pacific. The explosion virtually obliterated the island, creating a crater a mile wide and 175 feet deep. After the detonation of the prototype, scientists constructed an H-bomb that could be dropped by aircraft. That weapon was tested successfully in 1954.

Hydrogen bomb test IVY MIKE. This photo was taken at the height of approximately 12,000 feet and 50 miles from the detonation site. Two minutes after Zero Hour, the cloud rose to 40,000 feet. Ten minutes later, as it neared its maximum, the cloud stem had pushed upward about 25 miles, deep into the stratosphere. The mushroom portion went up to 10 miles and spread for 100 miles, October 31, 1952 (November 1, 1952, local time). (U.S. Air Force)

The Soviet Union tested its own H-bomb on August 12, 1953. The British also developed a hydrogen weapon, which they tested on May 15, 1957.

Unable to maintain a monopoly on nuclear weapons or to force the Soviet Union to alter its policies through either deterrence or the threat represented by nuclear arms, the United States instead found itself engaged in a nuclear arms race. Despite collective security agreements and pacts such as the North Atlantic Treaty Organization (NATO), the United States maintained that only nuclear superiority would guarantee the security of the United States and its allies. The launching of the first satellite to orbit Earth, the Soviet-built *Sputnik 1* in 1957, represented a dual threat to the West. It seemed to suggest that Soviet scientists had pulled ahead of their American counterparts. More critically, it also posed the high probability of delivering nuclear weapons with missiles rather than by planes. As a result, the United States increased funding for its space program and redoubled its efforts to fully develop and deploy intercontinental ballistic missiles (ICBMs) and, later, submarine-launched ballistic missiles (SLBMs).

The rapid proliferation of nuclear weapons, of course, increased the threat of nuclear war, whether by accident or by choice. With the advent of H-bombs and ballistic missile systems that could hurl bombs at an adversary in a matter of minutes, most civil defense preparations became exercises in futility. The Soviet Union's installation of long-range missiles in Cuba led to the Cuban Missile Crisis of October 1962. President John F. Kennedy imposed a naval quarantine around Cuba and refused to allow Soviet ships through the blockade. Faced with the real possibility of a catastrophic thermonuclear war, both sides engaged in a flurry of diplomacy. The Soviets backed down, dismantling the missiles by the end of the year. The Cuban Missile Crisis, one of the few direct confrontations between the Americans and Soviets, showed the potential peril of the nuclear arms race. After the crisis passed, both U.S. and Soviet officials sought new ways to avoid the unthinkable consequences of a nuclear exchange. In 1963, the Partial Test Ban Treaty had been agreed to by both sides, the first small step toward eventual nuclear arms reductions. The threat posed by nuclear weapons did not end with the collapse of the Soviet Union in 1991, although reduced tensions have lessened the potential for a full-scale nuclear conflict.

Melissa Jordine

Further Reading

Kaplan, Fred. *The Wizards of Armageddon: Strategists of the Nuclear Age*. New York: Simon and Schuster, 1983.

Millett, Allan R., and Peter Maslowski. *For the Common Defense: A Military History of the United States of America*. New York: Free Press, 1994.

Rhodes, Richard. *Dark Sun: The Making of the Hydrogen Bomb*. New York: Simon and Schuster, 1995.

I

Indochina War (1946–1954)

The French had established themselves in Indochina in the 1840s, and by 1887 they had formed French Indochina, made up of the three divisions of Vietnam (Tonkin, Annam, and Cochin China) and the kingdoms of Cambodia and Laos. The cause of the Indochina War was the French refusal to recognize that the days of colonialism were over. In the aftermath of World War II, a weakened France was determined to hold on to its richest colony

In 1941 veteran Vietnamese communist leader Ho Chi Minh had formed the Viet Minh to fight the Japanese, then in military occupation of Vietnam, and the French. A fusion of communists and nationalists, the Viet Minh had by 1944 liberated most of the northern provinces of Vietnam. The defeat of Japan in August 1945 created a power vacuum into which Ho moved. At the end of August 1945, Ho established in Hanoi the provisional government of the Democratic Republic of Vietnam (DRV, North Vietnam), and on September 2, 1945 he proclaimed Vietnamese independence.

With no support from either the Soviet Union or the United States, Ho was forced to deal with France. He and French diplomat Jean Sainteny concluded an agreement in March 1946 to allow 15,000 French troops into North Vietnam, with the understanding that 3,000 would leave each year and all would be gone by the end of 1951. In return, France recognized North Vietnam as a free state within the French Union. France also promised to abide by the results of a referendum in Cochin China to determine if it would be reunited with Annam and Tonkin.

The Ho-Sainteny Agreement fell apart with the failure of the Fontainebleau Conference in the summer of 1946 to resolve outstanding substantive issues and with the decision of new French governor-general of Indochina Admiral Georges Thierry d'Argenlieu to proclaim on his own initiative the independence of a republic of Cochin China. Paris officials were not worried. They believed that the Vietnamese nationalists would not go to war against France and that if they did they would be easily crushed. Violence broke out in Hanoi in November 1946, whereupon d'Argenlieu ordered the shelling of the port of Haiphong, and the war was on.

The French motives were primarily political and psychological. Perhaps only with its empire could France be counted as a great power. Colonial advocates also argued that concessions in Indochina would adversely impact other French overseas possessions, especially in North Africa, and that further losses would surely follow.

The North Vietnamese leadership planned for a protracted struggle. Former history teacher Vo Nguyen Giap commanded the military forces, formed in May 1945 into the People's Army of Vietnam (PAVN). Giap modeled his strategy on that of Chinese communist leader Mao Zedong. Giap's chief contribution came in his recognition of the political and psychological difficulties for a democracy waging a protracted and inconclusive war. He believed that French public opinion would at some point demand an end to the bloodshed. In the

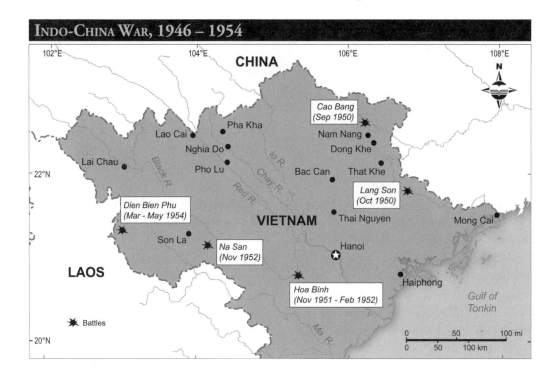

INDO-CHINA WAR, 1946 – 1954

populous rice-producing areas, the Viet Minh would employ guerrilla tactics and ambushes. In the less populated mountain and jungle regions, the Viet Minh would engage in large-scale operations.

For eight years the French fought unsuccessfully to defeat the Viet Minh, with a steady succession of French generals directing operations. One French tactical innovation was the riverine division composed of naval and army forces, the Divisions Navales D'assaut, abbreviated as Dinassaut. By 1950 the French had six permanent Dinassauts in Indochina. The French also developed commando formations, the Groupement des Commandos Mixtes Aéroportés (GCMA, Composite Airborne Commando Groups), later known as the Groupement Mixte d'Intervention (GMI). Essentially guerrilla formations of about 400 men each, these operated behind enemy lines, sometimes in conjunction with friendly Montagnard

tribesmen or Vietnamese. By mid-1954 the French had 15,000 men in such formations, but they placed a heavy strain on the badly stretched French airlift capacity.

Sometimes the French cut deeply into Viet Minh–controlled areas, but as soon as the French regrouped to attack elsewhere the Viet Minh reasserted its authority. With their superior firepower the French held the cities and the majority of the towns, while the Viet Minh managed to dominate most of the countryside, more of it as the years went by. French commanders never did have sufficient manpower to carry out effective pacification. The war was increasingly unpopular in France, and no conscripts were ever sent there, although a quarter of all of France's officers and more than 40 percent of its noncommissioned officers were in Indochina.

With Ho and the Viet Minh registering increasing success, Paris tried to appease nationalist sentiment by setting up a pliable indigenous Vietnamese regime as a competitor to the Viet Minh. In the March 1949 Elysée Agreements, Paris worked out an arrangement with former emperor Bao Dai to create the State of Vietnam (SV). Incorporating Cochin China, Annam, and Tonkin, it was to be independent within the French Union. France never did give the SV genuine independence, however. Paris retained actual control of its foreign relations and armed forces. The result was that it was never able to attract meaningful nationalist support. There were in effect but two alternatives: the Viet Minh, now labeled by the French as communists, or the French.

Meanwhile, the military situation continued to deteriorate for the French. PAVN forces achieved their successes with arms inferior in both quantity and quality to those of the French. Disparities in military equipment were offset by the Viet Minh's popular backing.

Until the end of 1949, the United States showed little interest in Indochina, apart from urging Paris to take concrete steps toward granting independence. The U.S. government did not press too much on this issue, however, fearful that it might adversely affect France's attitude toward cooperation in the formation of the North Atlantic Treaty Organization (NATO) and the European Defense Community (EDC). France was then virtually the only armed continental West European power left to stand against the Soviet Union. In effect, Washington supported France's Indochina policy in order to ensure French support in containing the Soviet Union in Europe. The United States underwrote the French military effort in Vietnam indirectly, but leaders in Washington expressed confidence based on assurances from Paris that France was granting Vietnam its independence.

The U.S. policy of indirect aid to the French effort in Indochina changed after October 1949 and the communist victory in China. This and the beginning of the Korean War in June 1950 shifted U.S. interest to the containment of communism in Asia. Paris convinced Washington that the war in Indochina was a major element in the worldwide containment of communism. Zealous anticommunism now drove U.S. policy and Washington now saw the French effort no longer as a case of colonialism versus nationalism but rather as a free world stand against communist expansionism. With the communist victory in China, in effect the war was lost for the French. China had a long common frontier with Tonkin, and the Viet Minh could now receive large shipments of modern weapons, including artillery captured by the Chinese communists from the nationalists. In 1950, in a series of costly defeats, the French were forced to abandon a string of fortresses in far northern Tonkin along Route Coloniale 4. In these battles, the Viet Minh captured French arms sufficient to equip an entire division. Then in 1951 Giap launched a series of attacks in the Red River Delta area that turned into hard-fought and costly battles during 1951–1952. In these, Giap tried but failed to capture Hanoi and end the war. But as the French concentrated resources in the north of the country, the Viet Minh registered impressive gains in central and southern Vietnam.

In January 1950 both the People's Republic of China (PRC) and the Soviet Union recognized the North Vietnamese government. The next month, the United States extended diplomatic recognition to the SV. U.S. military aid to the French in Indochina now grew dramatically, from approximately $150 million in 1950 to more than $1 billion in 1954. By 1954, the United States was also paying 80 percent of the cost of the war. The French insisted that all aid to Bao Dai's government be channeled through them, frustrating American hopes of bolstering Bao Dai's independence. Even though a Vietnamese National Army was established in 1951, it remained effectively under French control. Meanwhile, the administrations of both President Harry S. Truman and President Dwight D. Eisenhower assured the American public that actual authority in Vietnam had been transferred to Bao Dai.

By mid-1953, despite substantial aid from the United States, France had lost authority over all but a minor portion of the country. In September, with strong American encouragement, France entered into one final and disastrous effort to achieve a position of strength from which to negotiate with the Viet Minh. Under Lieutenant General Henri Navarre, the new commander in Indochina, France now had 517,000 men, 360,000 of whom were Indochinese.

The Battle of Dien Bien Phu from April to May 1954 was the culminating and most dramatic battle of the war. At this remote location in northwestern Tonkin, the French constructed a complex of supporting fortresses, defended by artillery. Navarre's strategy was to entice the Viet Minh to attack this supposedly impregnable position and there destroy them. At best he expected one or two Viet Minh divisions. Giap accepted the challenge but committed four divisions. The French mistakenly assumed that the Viet Minh could not get artillery to this remote location, but eventually the Viet Minh outgunned the French. French air assets also proved insufficient. The surrender of Dien Bien Phu on May 7 enabled the French politicians to shift the blame to the army and withdraw France from the war.

Not coincidental to the battle, a conference had already opened in Geneva to discuss Asian problems. It now took up the issue of Indochina. The April 26–July 21 Geneva Conference provided for independence for Cambodia, Laos, and North Vietnam. Vietnam was to be temporarily divided at the 17th Parallel, pending national elections in 1956. In the meantime, Viet Minh forces were to withdraw north of that line and French forces south of it.

In the war, the French and their allies sustained 172,708 casualties: 94,581 dead or missing and 78,127 wounded. These break down as 140,992 French Union casualties (75,867 dead or missing and 65,125 wounded) with the allied Indochina states losing 31,716 (18,714 dead or missing and 13,002 wounded). French dead or missing numbered some 20,000; Legionnaires, 11,000; Africans, 15,000; and Indo-Chinese, 46,000. The war took a particularly heavy toll among the officers, 1,900 of whom died. Viet Minh losses were probably three times those of the French and their allies, and perhaps 150,000 Vietnamese civilians also perished. One major issue was that of prisoners, both soldiers and civilians, held by the Viet Minh in barbarous conditions. Only 10,754 of the 36,979 reported missing during the war returned, and some were not released until years afterward.

The Indochina War had been three wars in one. Begun as a conflict between Vietnamese nationalists and France, it became a civil war between Vietnamese, and it was also part of the larger Cold War. As it turned out, in 1954 the civil war and the East–West conflict were only suspended. Ten years later a new war broke out in which the Americans replaced the French.

Spencer C. Tucker

References

Currey, Cecil B. *Victory at Any Cost: The Genius of Viet Nam's Gen. Vo Nguyen Giap.* Washington, DC: Brassey's, 1997.

Dalloz, Jacques. *The War in Indo-China, 1945–54*. Translated by Josephine Bacon. New York: Barnes and Noble, 1990.

Gras, Yves. *Histoire de la guerre d'Indochine*. Paris: Editions Denoël, 1992.

Spector, Ronald H. *United States Army in Vietnam: Advice and Support; The Early Years, 1941–1960*. Washington, DC: Center of Military History, U.S. Army, 1985.

Tucker, Spencer C. *Vietnam*. Lexington: University Press of Kentucky, 1999.

Israel

Modern Israel dates from the end of World War I and the resulting defeat of the Ottoman Empire. The secret wartime Sykes-Picot Agreement between Britain and France to partition Turkish Middle Eastern territory gave control of Lebanon and Syria to France, with Britain receiving Palestine and Iraq. Following the Allied victory, the Paris Peace Conference awarded these areas as mandates under the new League of Nations, envisioning their ultimate independence.

The war also prompted the Zionist movement of Jews seeking a nation-state in Palestine. In order to enlist the support of international Jewry during the war effort, the British government issued the Balfour Declaration in 1917. The declaration announced London's support for the creation of a "national home for the Jewish people" in Palestine. The parameters of this home were not spelled out. In 1922 Britain split Palestine into Transjordan east of the Jordan River and Palestine to the west. The Jewish homeland would be in Palestine. There were several schemes for achieving this while balancing the interests of the Arab population with those of the Jewish minority and the goals of the Zionist movement. Contradictory British assurances to both sides failed to satisfy either the Zionists or the Arabs,

however. Meanwhile, increasing numbers of European Jews arrived in Palestine and purchased land there, leading to Arab-Jewish rioting that the British authorities were not always able to control.

Events immediately before and during World War II accelerated the Jewish migration to Palestine. Adolf Hitler's persecution of the Jews in Germany as well as anti-Semitism in Poland and elsewhere led to increasing Jewish migration and interest in a Jewish state. Once the war began, Hitler embarked on a conscientious effort to exterminate world Jewry. During the Nazi-inspired Holocaust an estimated six million Jews perished. Late in the war and afterward, many of the survivors sought to immigrate to Israel. The great lesson of World War II for Jews was that they could not rely on other nations; they would require their own independent state. The Holocaust also created in the West a sense of moral obligation for the creation of such a state. At the same time, however, the Arabs of Palestine were adamantly opposed to the implantation of a large foreign population in their midst.

After World War II, Jewish refugees and displaced persons streamed into Palestine, many of them only to be turned away by British naval ships patrolling Palestine's Mediterranean coast just for this purpose. At the same time, the British authorities wrestled with partitioning Palestine into Arab and Jewish states. Jews and Arabs proved intransigent, and in February 1947 after both rejected a final proposal for partition, Britain turned the problem over to the United Nations (UN). In November the UN General Assembly passed its own resolution to partition Palestine, with Jerusalem to be under a UN trusteeship. While the Jews accepted this arrangement, the Arabs rejected it.

In December 1945 the Arab League council announced that it would halt the creation of a Jewish state by force. The Arabs then began raids against Jewish communities in Palestine. The United States, with the world's largest and wealthiest Jewish population, became the chief champion and most reliable ally of the Jews. This position would, however, cost the United States dearly in its relations with the Arab world and would also influence Cold War geopolitics.

In January 1948 London announced its intention to withdraw from Palestine. This precipitous British policy led to war. The British completed the pullout on May 14, 1948, and that same day David Ben-Gurion, executive chairman and defense minister of the Jewish Agency, declared the existence of the independent Jewish state of Israel. Ben-Gurion became the first prime minister, a post he held during 1948–1953 and 1955–1963.

At first, the interests of the United States and those of the Soviet Union regarding the Jewish state converged. U.S. recognition of Israel came only shortly before that of the Soviet Union. Officials in Moscow found common ground with the Jews in their suffering at the hands of the Nazis in the war and also identified with the socialism espoused by the early Jewish settlers in Palestine as well as with their anti-British stance. The Cold War, the reemergence of official anti-Semitism in the Soviet Union, and Moscow's desire to court the Arab states by supporting Arab nationalism against the West would soon change all that.

The Israeli independence proclamation led immediately to fighting. In the first Arab-Israeli War of 1948–1949, hard-pressed Israeli forces managed to stave off the far more numerous and better-equipped but poorly organized and inadequately trained Arab forces. In the process, many Palestinians living in Israel either fled or were forced out of the territory.

Soviet military support for Egypt and Syria led to increased U.S. military support for Israel. The rise of Egypt's president Gamal Abdel Nasser only exacerbated the situation. Trumpeting Arab nationalism, Nasser blockaded Israeli ships in the Gulf of Aqaba and Israel's access to the Indian Ocean. Egypt also supported cross-border raids into Israeli territory by *fedayeen*, or guerrilla fighters. Nasser's turn to the Soviet Union for arms led to the withdrawal of U.S. support for his pet project of constructing a high dam at Aswan on the Nile. This led him to nationalize the Suez Canal. British prime minister Anthony Eden was determined to topple Nasser, and a coalition of Britain, France, and Israel then formed. Leaders of the three states developed secret plans whereby Israel would invade Egypt's Sinai Peninsula and move to the canal. Britain and France would then use this as an excuse to introduce military forces into the canal zone.

At the end of October 1956, Israeli forces swept into the Sinai, easily destroying Egyptian forces there. When Nasser's response to French and British demands proved unsatisfactory, their forces also invaded Egypt from Cyprus. Although the Soviet Union threatened to send volunteers, it was the strong opposition of the United States and heavy economic pressure brought to bear on Britain that proved decisive. All three powers subsequently withdrew their forces, greatly strengthening Nasser despite the abysmal showing of his armed forces. Israel was one of the chief winners of the 1956 war. It had cleaned out the *fedayeen* bases and secured a buffer of UN observers in the Sinai. It also ended the blockade of the Gulf of Aqaba.

The Soviet Union made good on Egyptian material losses from the war and, over the next decade, sent considerable quantities of additional arms to the Arab states, including Egypt, Syria, and Iraq. In May 1967, Nasser

Israeli forces in Galilee near the Arab village of Sassa, during the Israeli War for Independence, January 1, 1948. (Government Press Office)

moved Egyptian troops into the Sinai and ordered out the UN observers who served as a buffer with Israel. Believing that they would soon be attacked, Israeli leaders ordered a preemptive strike. On June 5, 1967, the Israeli Air Force wiped out most of the Egyptian Air Force on the ground and then struck the Syrians. Although Israel made a bid for Jordan to stay out of the war, that country joined the fighting against Israel and paid a heavy price for it. The Israelis won the so-called Six-Day War and, in the process, seized the Sinai Peninsula from Egypt, the West Bank of the Jordan River along with Jerusalem from Jordan, and the Golan Heights from Syria.

On October 6, 1973, at the start of the Jewish holy days of Yom Kippur, Egypt, now led by Anwar Sadat, launched a surprise attack on Israel. Joined by Syrian forces, the Egyptians caught the Israeli government of Prime Minister Golda Meier (1969–1974) by surprise and crossed over the Suez Canal, then took up defensive positions to destroy much of the counterattacking Israeli armor with Soviet-supplied antitank missiles. Ultimately, however, the Israelis beat back the Arab attacks. Having recrossed the canal, the Israelis were in position to drive on to Cairo. Both sides then agreed to a cease-fire.

Israel appeared menaced on all flanks except the Mediterranean. But Sadat, dismayed by the inability of the United States to pressure Israel into concessions, took the unprecedented step of traveling to Israel in November 1977, eventually leading to the Camp David Agreement of September 1978 and a peace settlement between Egypt and Israel. Begun in 1979, Israel completed a withdrawal of the Sinai Peninsula in 1982. Syria, meanwhile, had moved closer to the

Israeli troops withdrawing from the Suez Canal area of Egypt in 1974 in accordance with an agreement reached by the United Nations Disengagement Observer Force. (Corel)

Soviet Union, and the Syrians then moved into Lebanon in support of Palestinians there and the Lebanese Muslims. This produced civil war in Lebanon, and following the shelling of Israeli settlements from southern Lebanon, Israeli forces invaded Lebanon in 1982. In September 1983, Israeli forces withdrew to the Awali River. During 1987–1991, Israeli security forces had to deal with a wide-scale uprising by Palestinians known as the Intifada within Israeli-occupied territory in the West Bank and Gaza. The end of the Cold War brought a large influx of hundreds of thousands of Jews from the Soviet Union. Despite peace between Egypt and Israel, at the end of the Cold War a general Middle Eastern peace agreement remained illusive.

Daniel E. Spector and Spencer C. Tucker

Further Reading

Flapan, Simha. *The Birth of Israel: Myths and Realities*. New York: Pantheon, 1987.

Quandt, William B. *Peace Process: American Diplomacy and the Arab-Israeli Conflict since 1967*. Washington, DC: Brookings Institution and University of California Press, 1993.

Sachar, Abram L. *The Redemption of the Unwanted: From the Liberation of the Death Camps to the Founding of Israel*. New York: St. Martin's, 1983.

Sachar, Howard M. *A History of Israel: From the Rise of Zionism to Our Time*. New York: Knopf, 1976.

Schoenbaum, David. *The United States and the State of Israel*. New York: Oxford University Press, 1993.

Stafran, Nadav. *Israel, The Embattled Ally*. Cambridge: Harvard University Press, 1978.

J

Johnson, Lyndon Baines (1908–1973)

Lyndon Johnson was born in Stonewall, Texas, in a farmhouse on the Pedernales River on August 27, 1908. His early life was touched by rural poverty, which would later make him a champion of the poor and underprivileged. In 1931 Johnson became active in Democratic Party politics and that same year went to Washington, D.C., to serve as secretary to a Texas congressman.

A shrewd, brilliant, and sometimes overbearing politician, Johnson honed his political skills for the next two decades. In 1948 Johnson won election to the Senate and in 1953 became its youngest majority leader in history. As majority leader, he worked with President Dwight D. Eisenhower's administration to maintain a bipartisan foreign policy. Johnson was instrumental in defeating the proposed Bricker Amendment, which would have prohibited executive agreements with foreign powers, and also supported the Formosa Resolution and the Eisenhower Doctrine.

In 1960 Johnson was elected vice president on the Democratic ticket with President John F. Kennedy. Riding in the Dallas motorcade on November 22, 1963, during which Kennedy was assassinated, Johnson was sworn in as president that same day. Taking advantage of the outpouring of grief immediately following the assassination, Johnson mustered his pitch-perfect political skills to ensure congressional passage of the landmark 1964 Civil Rights Act, which forbade discrimination in all public places and in hiring practices based on race, religion, sex, or national origin. Hugely popular, Johnson won the presidency in his own right in the November 1964 election, handily defeating his conservative Republican opponent, Barry Goldwater.

Despite the lengthening shadows cast by the Vietnam War, Johnson took full advantage of his electoral mandate by ushering in some of the most far-reaching domestic reforms since the New Deal. Johnson soon became overwhelmed by the course of events in Vietnam. Ultimately, many of his Great Society programs languished as the war consumed additional resources and more public attention.

Upon becoming president, Johnson had informed the South Vietnamese government that he would stay the course and help it secure victory over the communist insurgency. He approved OPLAN 34A, a U.S.-supported series of raids by the South Vietnamese along the Democratic Republic of Vietnam's (DRV, North Vietnam) coast. A raid on July 31, 1964, coupled with a signals intelligence–gathering desoto patrol by the destroyer *Maddox*, helped precipitate the Gulf of Tonkin incidents and led to the subsequent Tonkin Gulf Resolution, giving the president carte blanche to deploy U.S. forces in Southeast Asia. He used the resolution as legal justification to escalate the Vietnam War.

After the 1964 election, Johnson felt obliged to reverse the deteriorating military and political situation in the Republic of Vietnam (RVN, South Vietnam). With the support of most of his civilian and military advisors, he pursued a policy of gradual escalation beginning in 1965. In February 1965 he ordered a sustained bombing campaign against North Vietnam, code-named Operation Rolling Thunder. In March, he deployed the Marines to protect U.S. airbases. U.S. Army troops followed, and Johnson announced an open-ended commitment to South Vietnam in late July. By the end of 1965, he had dispatched 180,000 American troops to Vietnam. He defended his decision to escalate the war as a "political necessity" that he believed was essential to secure passage of Great Society legislation.

Other foreign policy issues came to the fore, including the 1965 American intervention in the Dominican Republic. Johnson dispatched Marines there on April 28, 1965, to protect American lives and prevent a potential communist takeover of the government. In June 1967, Johnson met with Soviet Premier Alexei Kosygin for two days in Glassboro, New Jersey, to discuss Vietnam, the impact of the Six-Day War in the Middle East, and the potential for arms control talks and nuclear nonproliferation.

In the end, Vietnam overshadowed everything else. During 1966–1967, American troop strength in Vietnam sharply escalated, bombing increased, casualties mounted, and yet the war ground on without resolution. Johnson grew increasingly frustrated by critics of his Vietnam policies, some of which were from his own party. Public disaffection with the war also increased. Large antiwar demonstrations became commonplace by 1967, some resulting in violence and rioting. Meanwhile, as the war siphoned resources away from domestic programs, racial tensions increased dramatically, widespread urban riots and arson plagued the nation, and college campuses became hotbeds of political radicalism and antiwar activism. Johnson, who once seemed politically invin-

cible, appeared incapable of dealing with the mounting crises.

In late January 1968, after the administration had assured the American public that the war was being won, North Vietnamese and Viet Cong forces launched the Tet Offensive, a nationwide military operation that destroyed the credibility of the Johnson administration. Although a tactical victory for the Americans and South Vietnamese, Tet 1968 permanently undermined American support for the war and the president who escalated it. With 500,000 U.S. troops in Vietnam and growing violence and radicalism on the home front, Johnson took the nation by surprise on March 31, 1968, following a setback in the Democratic primary in New Hampshire, by announcing that he would not seek another presidential term. He then authorized exploratory truce talks with the North Vietnamese, which almost immediately stalled as the fighting continued. Johnson left office a broken man, both physically and mentally. He was immensely unpopular by 1968 and would always be associated with America's failure in Vietnam. In retirement, he wrote his memoirs. Johnson died on January 22, 1973, at his ranch in Johnson City, Texas.

Richard M. Filipink Jr.

Further Reading

Beschloss, Michael, ed. *Taking Charge: The Johnson White House Tapes, 1963–1964.* New York: Simon and Schuster, 1997.

Brands, H. W. *The Wages of Globalism: Lyndon Johnson and the Limits of American Power.* New York: Oxford University Press, 1995.

Caro, Robert. *Master of the Senate: The Years of Lyndon Johnson.* New York: Knopf, 2002.

Dallek, Robert. *Flawed Giant.* New York: Oxford University Press, 2003.

Dumbrell, John. *President Lyndon Johnson and Soviet Communism.* Manchester, UK: Manchester University Press, 2004.

Gardner, Lloyd. *Pay Any Price: Lyndon Johnson and the Wars for Vietnam.* Chicago: Ivan R. Dee, 1995.

Goodwin, Doris Kearns. *Lyndon Johnson and the American Dream.* New York: St. Martin's, 1976.

Johnson, Lyndon B. *The Vantage Point: Perspectives of the Presidency 1963–1969.* New York: Holt, Rinehart and Winston, 1971.

K

Kennan, George Frost (1904–2005)

Born in Milwaukee, Wisconsin, on February 16, 1904, George Kennan attended Princeton University and joined the U.S. Foreign Service in 1926, undergoing intensive, specialized Russian training at Berlin University and Riga.

As one of the State Department's small coterie of Russian experts, Kennan spent five years in the American embassy in Moscow, returning there in 1944 as minister-counselor. Despite his distaste for the Soviet regime, as World War II ended he recommended reassigning control of Eastern Europe to the Soviets. His influential February 1946 "Long Telegram" argued that the internal dynamics of Russian communism made genuine Soviet–Western understanding unattainable. The "Long Telegram" proved immensely influential.

From 1947 to 1949 Kennan headed the State Department's Policy Planning Staff, exercising his greatest impact on American foreign policy by enunciating the containment doctrine that became the basis of U.S. Cold War strategy toward the Soviet Union. However, Kennan soon found himself increasingly out of sync with the evolving Cold War policies. In the late 1940s and again during the 1950s, he called for the neutralization and unification of Germany, and he opposed the creation of the North Atlantic Treaty Organization (NATO) in 1949. Kennan initially supported U.S. intervention in the Korean War but regretted the decision to carry the war into the Democratic People's Republic of Korea (DPRK, North Korea). In 1951 he took part in unofficial negotiations with Soviet diplomats that led to the opening of armistice talks. In 1952 he was briefly ambassador to the Soviet Union, but his criticism of Josef Stalin's regime resulted in expulsion. Kennan then began a lengthy career as a historian and political commentator.

Keen to encourage polycentrism within the communist world, Kennan welcomed his 1961 appointment as ambassador to Yugoslavia, where he remained until 1963. He applauded the manner in which President John F. Kennedy and Soviet leader Nikita Khrushchev handled the Cuban Missile Crisis and the Limited Nuclear Test Ban Treaty. Kennan believed that American preoccupation with Vietnam distracted officials from pursuing détente with the Soviets. He applauded French president Charles de Gaulle's initiatives toward détente and called for Western recognition of the German Democratic Republic (GDR, East Germany). Initially outraged by the 1968 Soviet invasion of Czechoslovakia, Kennan demanded massive American troop reinforcements in Western Europe but soon endorsed Federal Republic of Germany (FRG, West Germany) chancellor Willy Brandt's Ostpolitik.

Kennan initially showed little interest in Vietnam. In 1950 he had urged American attempts to encourage noncommunist, nationalist "third forces" in Indochina but by 1955 had grown pessimistic that such endeavors would succeed. Despite misgivings, he endorsed President Lyndon B. Johnson's 1964 Tonkin Gulf Resolution. Johnson's subsequent escalation of the war convinced

U.S. diplomat and historian George F. Kennan was an energetic proponent of a containment policy against communist expansion. He is among the most influential foreign policy makers of the post–World War II era. (Library of Congress)

Kennan that the United States was too heavily involved in a country of relatively slight strategic significance. He suggested that the United States restrict itself to defending strategic enclaves and supporting the Republic of Vietnam (RVN, South Vietnam) government. During widely publicized congressional hearings in 1967, he argued that employing the force levels needed to ensure victory in Vietnam would likely trigger Chinese intervention and full-scale, probably nuclear, Sino-American war. By November 1969 he publicly advocated American military withdrawal, notwithstanding the probability that the communists would then take over South Vietnam.

In 1967 and 1972 Kennan published two volumes of best-selling confessional memoirs. He continued to write well into his 90s, frequently warning against the American tendency to intervene in nations and conflicts of little direct strategic interest and suggesting that wider concerns, particularly the environment, population growth, and arms control, were of far greater importance. Kennan died in Princeton, New Jersey, on March 17, 2005.

Priscilla Roberts

Further Reading

Bucklin, Steven J. *Realism and American Foreign Policy: Wilsonians and the*

Kennan-Morgenthau Thesis. Westport, CT: Praeger, 2001.

Gellman, Barton D. *Contending with Kennan: Toward a Philosophy of American Power*. New York: Praeger, 1984.

Hixson, Walter L. *George F. Kennan: Cold War Iconoclast*. New York: Columbia University Press, 1989.

Kennan, George F. *Around the Cragged Hill: A Personal and Political Philosophy*. New York: Norton, 1994.

Kennan, George F. *Sketches from a Life*. New York: Pantheon, 1990.

Mayers, David. *George Kennan and the Dilemmas of US Foreign Policy*. New York: Oxford University Press, 1988.

Miscamble, Wilson D. *George F. Kennan and the Making of American Foreign Policy, 1947–1950*. Princeton, NJ: Princeton University Press, 1992.

Stephanson, Anders. *Kennan and the Art of Foreign Policy*. Cambridge: Harvard University Press, 1989.

Kennedy, John Fitzgerald (1917–1963)

John F. Kennedy was born in Brookline, Massachusetts, on May 29, 1917, into a large and wealthy Irish Catholic family. His father, Joseph P. Kennedy, was a multimillionaire with presidential aspirations, and his mother, Rose Fitzgerald, came from a prominent and politically active Boston family. After attending the elite Choate Preparatory School in Wallingford, Connecticut, Kennedy earned his bachelor's degree from Harvard University in 1940. He also spent six months of his junior year working in the U.S. London embassy while his father was U.S. ambassador to Great Britain. His observations during this time inspired his senior honors thesis on British foreign policies, which was published the year he graduated under the title *Why England Slept*. During World War II Kennedy served four years in the U.S. Navy. He was awarded the Navy and Marine Corps Medals and the Purple Heart for action as commander of *PT-109*, which was rammed and sunk by a Japanese destroyer in the South Pacific.

Kennedy worked for a brief time as a newspaper correspondent before entering national politics at the age of 29, winning election as Democratic congressman from Massachusetts in 1946. In Congress, he backed social legislation that benefited his largely working-class constituents and criticized what he considered to be President Harry Truman's "weak stand" against communist China. Throughout his career, in fact, Kennedy was known for his vehement anti-communist sentiments.

Kennedy won election to the U.S. Senate in 1952. In 1953 he wed the New York socialite Jacqueline Bouvier. Kennedy had a relatively undistinguished Senate career. Never a well man, he suffered from several serious health problems, including a back operation in 1955 that nearly killed him. While he recuperated from his back surgery, he wrote his second book, *Profiles in Courage*, for which he won the 1957 Pulitzer Prize in history.

Despite his fragile health and lackluster performance in the Senate, Kennedy nonetheless was reelected in 1958 after losing a close contest for the vice presidential nomination at the Democratic National Convention in 1956. He now set his sights on the presidency. Four years later, he won the Democratic nomination for president on the first ballot. As a northerner and Roman Catholic, he recognized his weakness in the South and shrewdly chose Senator Lyndon Baines Johnson of Texas as his running mate. As a candidate, Kennedy promised more aggressive defense policies, health care reform, and

U.S. president John F. Kennedy and Soviet premier Nikita Khrushchev meet in Vienna, Austria, for their summit on June 3–4, 1961. (John F. Kennedy Presidential Library)

housing and civil rights programs. He also proposed his New Frontier agenda, designed to revitalize the flagging U.S. economy and to bring young people into government and humanitarian service. Winning by the narrowest of margins, he became the nation's first Roman Catholic president. Only 43 years old, he was also the youngest man ever to be elected to that office.

In his inaugural address, Kennedy spoke of the need for Americans to be active citizens and to sacrifice for the common good. His address, which in some respects was a rather bellicose call to arms, ended with the now-famous exhortation "ask not what your country can do for you—ask what you can do for your country." As president, Kennedy

set out to fulfill his campaign pledges. Once in office, he was forced to respond to the ever-more-urgent demands of civil rights advocates, although he did so rather reluctantly and tardily. By establishing both the Alliance for Progress and the Peace Corps, Kennedy delivered American idealism and goodwill to aid developing countries.

Despite Kennedy's idealism, no amount of enthusiasm could blunt the growing tension of the U.S.–Soviet Cold War rivalry. One of his first attempts to stanch the perceived communist threat was to authorize a band of American-supported Cuban exiles to invade the communist island in an attempt to overthrow Fidel Castro in April 1961. The Bay of Pigs invasion, which turned into an embarrassing debacle for the president, had been planned by the Central Intelligence Agency (CIA) under the Dwight Eisenhower administration. Although Kennedy harbored reservations about the operation, he nonetheless approved it. The failure heightened already-high Cold War tensions with the Soviets and ultimately set the stage for the Cuban Missile Crisis of 1962.

Cold War confrontation was not limited to Cuba. In the spring of 1961, the Soviet Union renewed its campaign to control West Berlin. Kennedy spent two days in Vienna in June 1961 discussing the hot-button issue with Soviet Premier Nikita Khrushchev. In the months that followed, the crisis over Berlin was further intensified by the construction of the Berlin Wall, which prevented East Berliners from escaping to the West. Kennedy responded to the provocation by reinforcing troops in the Federal Republic of Germany (FRG, West Germany) and increasing the nation's military strength. The Berlin Wall, unwittingly perhaps, eased tensions in Central Europe that had nearly resulted in a superpower conflagration. In the meantime, Kennedy had begun deploying what would be some 16,000 U.S. military "advisors" to prop up Ngo Dinh Diem's regime in the Republic of Vietnam (RVN, South Vietnam). In so doing, Kennedy had put the United States on the slippery slope of full-scale military intervention in Vietnam.

With the focus directed away from Europe, the Soviets began to construct missile-launching sites clandestinely in Cuba. On October 14, 1962, U.S. spy planes photographed the potential placement of nuclear missiles only 90 miles from America's shores and thus began a new threat to destabilize the Western Hemisphere and undermine the uneasy Cold War nuclear deterrent. Kennedy imposed a naval quarantine

on Cuba, designed to interdict any offensive weapons bound for the island. The world held its collective breath as the two Cold War superpowers appeared perched on the abyss of thermonuclear war, but after 13 harrowing days of fear and nuclear threat, the Soviet Union agreed to remove the missiles. In return, the United States pledged not to preemptively invade Cuba and to remove secretly its obsolete nuclear missiles from Turkey.

Both Kennedy and Khrushchev had been sobered by the Cuban Missile Crisis, realizing that the world had come as close as it ever had to a full-scale nuclear war. Cold War tensions were diminished when the Soviets, British, and Americans signed the Limited Nuclear Test Ban Treaty on August 5, 1963, forbidding atmospheric testing of nuclear weapons. In October 1963, the same three nations agreed to refrain from placing nuclear weapons in outer space. To avoid potential misunderstandings and miscalculations in a future crisis, a hotline was installed that directly linked the Oval Office with the Kremlin.

Following the nerve-wracking Cuban Missile Crisis, Kennedy looked toward 1963 with considerable enthusiasm. In November 1963 Kennedy embarked on a whirlwind tour of Texas. On November 22 in Dallas, Texas, just as Kennedy's motorcade neared the end of its course and as onlookers cheered, shots rang out. Kennedy, riding in an open car, was fatally wounded by an assassin's bullet. In the hours immediately after the murder, Lee Harvey Oswald was arrested for the assassination of the president. Two days later, as the president's body lay in state at the U.S. Capitol, Jack Ruby fatally shot Oswald in the basement of the Dallas police station as millions of Americans watched the latest bizarre event on television in dazed horror. In a great national outpouring of grief, Kennedy was laid to rest in Arlington National Cemetery on November 25, 1963.

Lacie A. Ballinger

Further Reading

Beschloss, Michael R. *The Crisis Years: Kennedy and Khrushchev, 1960–1963.* New York: HarperCollins, 1991.

Bradlee, Benjamin C. *Conversations with Kennedy.* New York: Norton, 1975.

Dallek, Robert. *An Unfinished Life: John F. Kennedy, 1917–1963.* Boston: Little, Brown, 2003.

Freedman, Lawrence. *Kennedy's Wars: Berlin, Cuba, Laos, and Vietnam.* New York: Oxford University Press, 2000.

Kennedy, Robert F. *Thirteen Days: A Memoir of the Cuban Missile Crisis.* New York: Norton, 1999.

Schlesinger, Arthur M. *A Thousand Days: John F. Kennedy in the White House.* New York: Houghton Mifflin, 1965.

Sidey, Hugh. *John F. Kennedy, President.* New York: Atheneum, 1964.

Khrushchev, Nikita (1894–1971)

Born on April 17, 1894, in Kalinovka, Kursk Province, to a peasant family, Nikita Sergeyevich Khrushchev worked beginning at age 15 as a pipe fitter in various mines near his home. His factory work exempted him from wartime service. In 1918 he joined the Russian Communist Party.

In 1919 Khrushchev became a political commissar in the Red Army, accompanying troops fighting both the Poles and Lithuanians. In 1922 he returned to school and completed his education. In 1925 he became Communist Party secretary of the Petrovosko-Mariinsk District. Recognizing the importance of Communist Party secretary Josef Stalin, Khrushchev nurtured a friendship with Stalin's associate and party

secretary in Ukraine, Lars Kaganovich, who helped him secure a full-time party post in the Moscow city party apparatus in 1931.

By 1935 Khrushchev was secretary-general of the Moscow Communist Party, in effect mayor of the capital. In 1938 he became a candidate (nonvoting member) of the Politburo, and in 1939 he was a full member. He was one of only a few senior party officials to survive Stalin's Great Purges. After the German invasion of the Soviet Union in June 1941, Khrushchev was made a lieutenant general and placed in charge of resistance in Ukraine and relocating heavy industry eastward.

With the Red Army's liberation of Ukraine, Khrushchev took charge of that region. This led to his first clash with Stalin. With Ukraine suffering major food shortages in 1946, Khrushchev concentrated on efforts to increase agricultural production, while Stalin wanted emphasis to be on heavy industry. As a consequence, Stalin demoted Khrushchev. By 1949, however, Khrushchev was back in favor in his previous post as head of the Communist Party machinery in Moscow. In 1952, at the 19th Party Congress, Khrushchev received the assignment of drawing up a new party structure, which led to the replacement of the old Politburo by the Presidium of the Central Committee. Khrushchev benefited from this change as one of the powerful committee secretaries.

Following Stalin's death on March 5, 1953, a brief power struggle ensued, with no one person on the 10-member Presidium dominating. Khrushchev did not appear to be a likely choice for supreme power, but on March 14, when Georgy Malenkov suddenly resigned as secretary of the Central Committee, Khrushchev succeeded him. Malenkov, however, retained his post as head of the party. Shortly thereafter, another Khrushchev rival, Lavrenty Beria, was removed from authority and executed. Over the next four years, Malenkov and Khrushchev struggled over who would dominate the Soviet state. Khrushchev had taken responsibility for Soviet agriculture, and by 1953 he registered considerable successes in that vital sector of the economy. His Virgin Lands program the next year opened new agricultural lands in Kazakhstan and western Siberia. Early successes in that region assisted his rise to power, although they proved temporary. Unpredictable climatic conditions and overuse of chemical fertilizers undermined the program, but not until he was already in power.

Meanwhile, Malenkov advocated increases in consumer goods to benefit the Soviet people. Hard-liners in the party leadership and military opposed this and sought continued concentration in heavy industry and increases in defense spending. Khrushchev took the tactical decision to side with the hard-liners, and in February 1955 Malenkov was defeated in a party plenum called on this issue, and resigned as party chairman. On Khrushchev's recommendation, Nikolai Bulganin succeeded Malenkov. For a time it appeared as if both Bulganin and Khrushchev were running the Soviet state, although Khrushchev wielded actual power through his control of the party machinery.

Malenkov remained a member of the Presidium, where he continued to intrigue against Khrushchev. In June 1957 Khrushchev took full authority when an attempt by Malenkov, Kaganovich, and Vyacheslav Molotov to unseat Khrushchev miscarried and they themselves were purged. It speaks volumes about the change in the Soviet state under Khrushchev, however, that the three men were not executed.

Indeed, Khrushchev's greatest—and perhaps most risky—achievement as leader of the Soviet Union was the unmasking of Stalin's legacy and his attempt to de-Stalinize Soviet society. The most powerful blow to the Stalinists came during Khrushchev's famous speech at a closed session of the 20th Party Congress on February 25, 1956, in which he documented just some of the crimes and purges of the Stalinist period. In fact, the Soviet Union became gradually more liberal under Khrushchev, and it never did return to the kind of oppressive barbarism for which Stalin was known.

Nevertheless, the overall thrust of Khrushchev's policies tended to be ambivalent and was overshadowed by surprising shifts, inconsistencies, and poorly conceptualized initiatives. Success during the 1950s in economic policy, industrial production, and the space program, in which he took special interest, compelled Khrushchev to proclaim that, by 1970, the Soviet Union would surpass the United States in per capita production. In 1980, he predicted, America would embrace communism.

In reality, severe economic problems persisted in the Soviet Union, particularly with respect to consumption and agriculture, where the early initiative to develop the Virgin Lands ended poorly. During Khrushchev's reign, the ideological and political atmosphere often changed. To some extent, his orientation in this regard depended on his standing within the Soviet leadership and the international communist movement. In 1957 he forbade the publication of Boris Pasternak's *Doctor Zhivago*, whereas in 1962 he allowed the publication of Aleksandr Solzhenitsyn's (much more critical) novel *One Day in the Life of Ivan Denisovich*.

In foreign policy, Khrushchev generally attempted to ease tensions with the West, particularly with the United States. He rejected Stalin's thesis that wars between capitalist and socialist countries were inevitable and instead sought peaceful coexistence. On the whole, up until 1960, Soviet–American relations improved. Khrushchev's 1959 visit to the United States was a remarkable success. His talks with President Dwight D. Eisenhower produced, at least for a brief time, what came to be called the Spirit of Camp David. Another highlight of improved East–West relations was the July 25, 1963, signing of a Nuclear Test Ban Treaty.

But Khrushchev engaged in some rather dubious and dangerous foreign policy initiatives as well. He initiated the 1958 Berlin Crisis, authorized the construction of the Berlin Wall in 1961, and used the U-2 Crisis in 1960 to provoke a showdown with Eisenhower and torpedo the May 1960 Paris Conference.

Most disturbing of all, in 1962 Khrushchev decided to install intermediate-range ballistic missiles in communist Cuba. After a brief but extremely tense confrontation with President John F. Kennedy's administration in October 1962, during which the superpowers were poised on the abyss of thermonuclear war, Khrushchev decided to remove the weapons. The Cuban Missile Crisis was by far Khrushchev's worst foreign policy mistake. Although he did exact a few concessions from the Americans in return for the missiles' removal, the crisis was clearly a humiliating loss of face for the Soviets and for the Soviet leader personally. Ultimately, it became an important factor in his fall from power less than two years later.

Khrushchev's policy toward other socialist states was equally ambivalent. He restored Soviet relations with Yugoslavia in 1955, after the Tito-Stalin break of 1948. He promoted de-Stalinization programs in Eastern bloc states and allowed a certain extent of limited autonomy for communist parties abroad. However, Khrushchev was not above cracking down on dissent when it was in his best interest. When his secret 1956 speech

on Stalin and the ensuing de-Stalinization campaign led to revolts in Poland and Hungary, he intervened in both cases. In fact, he ordered the 1956 Hungarian Revolution crushed by brute force. He was unable to head off crises in Soviet-Albanian and Sino-Soviet relations when Albanian and Chinese officials criticized his de-Stalinization policies and rapprochement with the West. Both crises became quite serious by the early 1960s and led to permanent schisms. Particularly noteworthy was the Sino-Soviet split, for which Khrushchev was largely blamed.

Because of the failure of Khrushchev's agricultural policies, the Sino-Soviet split, the debacle of the Cuban Missile Crisis, and the leader's increasingly unpredictable and unstable leadership, he was ousted by the party's Central Committee on October 14, 1964, and relieved of all his positions. He then wrote his memoirs, which were published in the West beginning in 1970. Khrushchev died in Moscow on September 11, 1971, following a massive heart attack.

Magarditsch Hatschikjan

Further Reading

Beschloss, Michael R. *The Crisis Years: Kennedy and Khrushchev, 1960–1963*. New York: HarperCollins, 1991.

Khrushchev, Nikita S. *Khrushchev Remembers*. Introduction and commentary by Edward Crankshaw. Translated by Strobe Talbott. Boston: Little, Brown 1970.

Khrushchev, Nikita S. *Khrushchev Remembers: The Glasnost Tapes*. Translated and edited by Jerrold L. Schecter with Vyacheslav V. Luchkov. Boston: Little, Brown, 1990.

Khrushchev, Nikita S. *Khrushchev Remembers: The Last Testament*. Translated and edited by Strobe Talbott. Boston: Little, Brown, 1974.

Khrushchev, Nikita S. *Memoirs of Nikita Khrushchev*. Edited by Sergei Khrushchev and translated by George Shriver. University Park: Pennsylvania State University Press, 2004.

Linden, Carl. *Khrushchev and the Soviet Leadership, 1957–1964*. Baltimore: Johns Hopkins University Press, 1966.

Medvedev, Roi A. *Khrushchev*. Translated by Brian Pearce. Oxford, UK: Blackwell, 1982.

Taubman, William. *Khrushchev: The Man and His Era*. New York: Norton, 2003.

Kissinger, Henry (1923–)

Of German-Jewish extraction, Henry Alfred Kissinger was born on May 27, 1923, in Fürth, Germany. He left Adolf Hitler's Germany for New York in 1938 and became an American citizen five years later. After serving in the U.S. Army, Kissinger became a professor of government at Harvard University, publishing his doctoral dissertation, *A World Restored* (1955), which focused particularly on the Austrian Prince von Metternich, whom Kissinger admired and in some ways modeled himself on. He also published a study of U.S. atomic policy for the prestigious Council on Foreign Relations.

Although his intellectual capabilities were highly respected, Kissinger's real ambitions lay in the practice, not the study, of international relations. He used his Harvard position to meet major political figures and served as an advisor to leading Republicans, including Governor Nelson A. Rockefeller of New York and former vice president Nixon. Kissinger's efforts won him only minor assignments under President John F. Kennedy, but when Nixon became president he appointed Kissinger as his national security advisor. Kissinger greatly overshadowed William P. Rogers, nominal secretary of state until August 1973, when Kissinger succeeded him, taking virtual control of U.S. foreign policy.

Kissinger's undoubted abilities included an immense capacity for hard work, a talent for grand designs and broad conceptualization, and the imagination to reformulate the international system to accommodate the relative weakness of the United States, de-emphasizing ideology in favor of a balance of power and the pursuit of closer relations with communist People's Republic of China (PRC) and détente with the Soviet Union. This resulted in the 1972 Strategic Arms Limitation Treaty (SALT) I and the Anti-Ballistic Missile Treaty that imposed limits on Soviet and American nuclear arsenals and delivery systems; the 1975 Helsinki Accords that normalized relations between Eastern and Western Europe and created the permanent Conference on Security and Cooperation in Europe (CSCE); and a rapprochement between communist China and the United States that Kissinger pioneered with a secret 1971 personal visit to Beijing. He also proved himself to be an excellent negotiator in complicated and protracted shuttle diplomacy designed to resolve long-standing Arab–Israeli tensions and disputes after the October 1973 Yom Kippur War.

Kissinger's weaknesses included a penchant for secrecy and intrigue, enormous vanity, and overweening personal ambition, all of which sometimes impelled him to decidedly unscrupulous behavior; an overriding concern to maintain international stability that often led him to endorse brutal right- or left-wing regimes; and a focus on realism in foreign policy to the near exclusion of all considerations of morality. The latter was apparent in his involvement in the secret bombing of Cambodia in the early 1970s, an operation that Congress halted when it became public in 1973, and the 1970–1971 invasion of that country despite Nixon's promise when he took office to end the Vietnam War as soon as possible; acquiescence in a 1973 military coup that brought the death of left-wing president Salvador Allende of Chile; endorsement of Indonesia's military takeover of Portuguese East Timor in December 1975 and the brutal suppression of indigenous resistance there; and readiness to authorize wiretapping against American bureaucrats suspected of leaking official information to the press. These aspects of Kissinger and his failure, constant negotiations notwithstanding, to end the Vietnam War—a conflict that his Cambodian policies effectively broadened—until 1973 made him the bête noire of many American liberals.

Likewise, conservative Republicans found much to dislike in Kissinger's willingness to accommodate the communist Soviet Union and the PRC and, if Sino-American rapprochement required, to jettison the Republic of China (ROC, Taiwan), a longtime U.S. ally. Under Nixon's successor, Gerald R. Ford, who became president in August 1974 when the Watergate scandal forced Nixon's resignation, both SALT I and the Helsinki Accords on Europe that Kissinger helped to negotiate with the Soviets became targets for attack by such conservatives as California governor and presidential hopeful Ronald W. Reagan, who assailed the Soviet human rights record. The fall of Vietnam to communist forces in April 1975, little more than two years after Kissinger had negotiated the Paris Peace Accords supposedly ending the war, also damaged his credibility. On November 3, 1975, Ford replaced Kissinger as national security advisor, although Kissinger remained secretary of state until Ford left office in January 1977.

Upon leaving government, Kissinger established an influential business consultancy firm. He continued to provide unofficial advice to successive administrations, wrote and spoke extensively on international affairs, and published three weighty volumes

of memoirs. He remains a perennially controversial figure.

Priscilla Roberts

Further Reading

Burr, Willliam, ed. *The Kissinger Transcripts: The Top-Secret Talks with Beijing and Moscow.* New York: New Press, 1998.

Hanhimäki, Jussi. *The Flawed Architect: Henry Kissinger and American Foreign Policy.* New York: Oxford University Press, 2004.

Hersh, Seymour. *The Price of Power: Kissinger in the Nixon White House.* New York: Simon and Schuster, 1983.

Isaacson, Walter. *Kissinger: A Biography.* New York: Simon and Schuster, 1992.

Kissinger, Henry A. *The White House Years.* Boston: Little, Brown, 1979.

Kissinger, Henry A. *Years of Renewal.* New York: Simon and Schuster, 1999.

Kissinger, Henry A. *Years of Upheaval.* Boston: Little, Brown, 1982.

Schulzinger, Robert D. *Henry Kissinger: Doctor of Diplomacy.* New York: Columbia University Press, 1989.

Korean War (1950–1953)

The Korean War was a watershed conflict within the Cold War. The first shooting war of the Cold War, it was also the first limited war of the nuclear age. Korea was long the scene of confrontation among China, Japan, and Russia. Controlled by either China or Japan for most of its modern history, Korea was divided in half after World War II. Wartime agreements called for the United States to temporarily occupy southern Korea up to the 38th Parallel, while the Soviet Union did the same north of that line. The Cold War brought the permanent division of Korea into two states.

Efforts to establish a unified Korea failed, and in September 1947 the United States

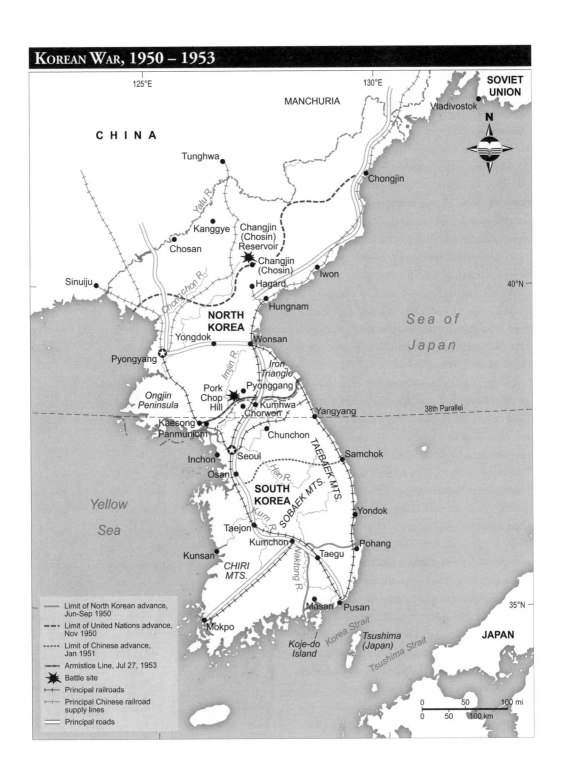

KOREAN WAR, 1950 – 1953

SOVIET UNION

MANCHURIA

Vladivostok

CHINA

N

Tunghwa

Chongjin

Kanggye

Changjin (Chosin) Reservoir

Chosan

Changjin (Chosin)

Iwon

Sinuiju

Hagard

40°N

Hungnam

NORTH KOREA

Sea of Japan

Yongdok

Wonsan

Pyongyang

Iron Triangle

Ongjin Peninsula

Pork Chop Hill

Pyonggang

38th Parallel

Kumhwa

Chorwon

Yangyang

Kaesong

Panmunjom

Chunchon

Inchon

Seoul

Samchok

Osan

SOUTH KOREA

Yondok

Taejon

Kumchon

Pohang

Kunsan

Taegu

CHIRI MTS.

35°N

Masan

Pusan

Mokpo

JAPAN

Koje-do Island

Tsushima (Japan)

Yellow Sea

TAEBAEK MTS.

SOBAEK MTS.

Han R.

Kum R.

Naktong R.

Imjin R.

Chongchon R.

Yalu R.

Korea Strait

Tsushima Strait

—— Limit of North Korean advance, Jun-Sep 1950

- - - Limit of United Nations advance, Nov 1950

····· Limit of Chinese advance, Jan 1951

—— Armistice Line, Jul 27, 1953

✸ Battle site

╂─╂ Principal railroads

╂─╂ Principal Chinese railroad supply lines

—— Principal roads

0   50   100 mi

0   50   100 km

referred the issue to the United Nations (UN), which called for a unified Korean government and the withdrawal of occupation forces. In January 1948 Soviet authorities refused to permit a UN commission to oversee elections in northern Korea, but elections for an assembly proceeded in southern Korea that spring. By August 1948 the Republic of Korea (ROK, South Korea) had officially formed, with its capital at Seoul and headed by 70-year-old Syngman Rhee, a staunch conservative. Washington then terminated its military government and agreed to train South Korea's armed forces.

In September 1948 the communists formed the Democratic People's Republic of Korea (DPRK, North Korea), with its capital at Pyongyang and led by veteran communist Kim Il Sung. Kim had fought the Japanese occupation and ended World War II as a major in the Soviet Army.

Both Korean governments claimed authority over the entire peninsula, but in December 1948 the UN General Assembly endorsed the ROK as the only lawfully elected government. That same month the USSR announced that it had withdrawn its forces from North Korea. The United States withdrew all its troops from South Korea by June 1949.

Beginning in May 1948, sporadic fighting began along the 38th Parallel. Fearful that it might be drawn into a civil war, the United States purposely distanced itself from these clashes. President Harry S. Truman announced that fighting in Korea would not automatically lead to U.S. military intervention. In January 1950 Secretary of State Dean Acheson excluded Korea from the U.S. strategic Asian defensive perimeter. The Joint Chiefs of Staff (JCS) agreed with this, as did U.S. Far Eastern commander General of the Army Douglas MacArthur. Such pronouncements undoubtedly encouraged Kim

to believe that the United States would not fight for Korea.

For many years North Korea, the USSR, and the People's Republic of China (PRC) maintained that the Korean War began with a South Korean attack on North Korea. This was propaganda. Beginning in late 1949 North Korea prepared for full-scale war. Its Korean Peoples Army (KPA) was well armed with Soviet weapons, including such modern offensive arms as heavy artillery, T-34 tanks, trucks, automatic weapons, and about 180 new aircraft. The KPA numbered about 135,000 men in 10 divisions.

South Korea's military situation was far different. The Republic of Korea Army (ROKA) lacked equipment and trained leaders because of Washington's unwillingness to fight in Korea and because the meager

North Korean propaganda poster of August 1950 urging citizens to work for victory over United Nations forces. (National Archives)

U.S. defense budget would not allow it. ROKA training was incomplete and lacked heavy artillery, tanks, and antitank weapons. South Korea had no air force apart from trainers and liaison aircraft. The South Korean military numbered 95,000 men in eight divisions, only four of which were at full strength.

Washington was aware of the North Korean military buildup but believed that the communist powers would not risk war. Limited war was still a foreign concept to U.S. planners. The U.S. military was also woefully unprepared and ill-equipped. The army numbered only nine divisions and 630,000 men.

Kim planned to use his military superiority to invade and quickly conquer South Korea. Twice he consulted Soviet leader Josef Stalin, promising him victory in a matter of weeks, assuring him that there would be a communist revolution in South Korea, and insisting that Washington would not intervene. Moscow and Beijing were actively preparing for the invasion as early as the spring of 1949, and Russian military advisors assisted in its planning. Stalin concluded that even if the United States decided to intervene, it would come too late.

Stalin pledged military assistance but not direct Soviet military involvement. He also insisted that Kim meet with PRC leader Mao Zedong and secure his assent to the plans. In late 1949, Mao released the People's Liberation Army (PLA) 164th and 166th Divisions of Korean volunteers who had fought against the Japanese and in the Chinese Civil War, providing North Korea with 30,000–40,000 seasoned troops.

On June 25, 1950, KPA forces invaded South Korea. The UN Security Council called for an immediate cease-fire and the withdrawal of North Korean forces, a resolution that went unchallenged because of a Soviet UN boycott. On June 27 the Security Council asked UN member states to furnish assistance to South Korea. President Harry S. Truman also extended U.S. air and naval operations to include North Korea and authorized U.S. Army troops to protect the port of Pusan. On General MacArthur's recommendation, President Truman committed U.S. Far Eastern ground forces to Korea on June 30.

The invasion caught both MacArthur and Washington by surprise. Yet U.S. intervention was almost certain, given the Truman Doctrine, domestic political fallout from the communist victory in China in 1949, and the belief that success in Korea would embolden the communists elsewhere. During the three-year conflict, no war was ever formally declared; Truman labeled it a "police action."

At the time of the invasion the United States had four poorly trained and equipped divisions in Japan. By cannibalizing his 7th Infantry Division, MacArthur was able to dispatch the 24th and 25th Infantry Divisions and the 1st Cavalry Division to Korea within two weeks. Meanwhile, Seoul fell on June 28. Most of South Korea's equipment was lost when the bridges spanning the Han River were prematurely blown.

On July 5 the first American units battled the KPA at Osan, 50 miles south of Seoul. Expected to stop a KPA division, Task Force Smith consisted of only 540 men in two rifle companies and an artillery battery. The KPA, spearheaded by T-34 tanks, easily swept it aside.

At the request of the UN Security Council, the UN set up a military command in Korea. Washington insisted on a U.S. commander, and on July 10 Truman appointed MacArthur to head the UN Command (UNC). Seventeen nations contributed military assistance, and at peak strength UNC forces numbered about 400,000 South Korean troops, 250,000

U.S. troops, and 35,000 troops from other nations. Two British and Canadians units formed the 1st Commonwealth Division. Turkey provided a brigade, and there were troops from Australia, Thailand, the Philippines, Colombia, Ethiopia, France, Greece, Belgium, Luxembourg, the Netherlands, and New Zealand. Other nations provided medical units.

U.S. forces were unprepared for the fighting. Difficult terrain, primitive logistics, poor communication, and refugees did as much to delay the North Korean offensive as did the defenders. In the chaotic atmosphere of the UNC retreat, both sides committed atrocities. The South Koreans executed some 2,000 political prisoners. U.S. and UNC troops shot a number of innocent civilians as the KPA infiltrated throngs of refugees and used them as human shields. North Korea committed far greater atrocities during its occupation of South Korea, however, slaying an estimated 26,000 political opponents. The KPA also executed American prisoners of war (POWs) in the fall of 1950.

By mid-July UNC troops had been pushed back into the so-called Pusan Perimeter, an area of 30–50 miles around the vital port of Pusan on the southeastern coast of Korea. Here U.S. and ROK forces bought valuable time and ultimately held. This success was attributable to UNC artillery, control of the skies, and Eighth Army (EUSAK, Eighth U.S. Army in Korea) commander Lieutenant General Walton Walker's brilliant mobile defense. The KPA also failed to employ its early manpower advantage to mount simultaneous attacks along the entire perimeter.

Even as the battle for the Pusan Perimeter raged, MacArthur was planning an amphibious assault behind enemy lines. Confident that he could hold Pusan, MacArthur deliberately weakened EUSAK to build up an invasion force. He selected Inchon as the invasion site. As Korea's second largest port and only 15 miles from Seoul, Inchon was close to the KPA's main supply line south. Seizing it would cut off KPA troops to the south. MacArthur also knew that he could deal North Korea a major political blow if Seoul were promptly recaptured.

The Inchon landing was a risky venture, and few besides MacArthur favored it. Inchon posed the daunting problems of a 32-foot tidal range that allowed only 6 hours in 24 for sea resupply, a narrow winding channel, and high seawalls. On September 15, Major General Edward Almond's X Corps of the 1st Marine Division and the 7th Infantry Division commenced the invasion. Supported by naval gunfire and air attacks, the Marines secured Inchon with relatively few casualties. UNC forces reentered Seoul on September 24.

At the same time, EUSAK broke out of the Pusan Perimeter and drove north, linking up with X Corps on September 26. Only one-quarter to one-third of the KPA escaped north of the 38th Parallel. Pyongyang ignored MacArthur's call for surrender, and on October 1 South Korean troops crossed into North Korea. On October 7 the UN General Assembly passed a resolution calling for a unified, independent, and democratic Korea, and two days later MacArthur ordered U.S. forces across the 38th Parallel. Pyongyang fell on October 19 as stunned KPA forces fled north.

MacArthur then divided his forces for the drive to the Yalu River. He ordered X Corps transported by sea around the Korean Peninsula to the east coast port of Wonsan. Almond would then clear northeastern Korea. EUSAK would remain on the west coast and drive into northwest Korea. The two commands would be separated by a gap of between 20 and 50 miles. MacArthur believed, falsely as it turned out, that the north-south

United States Marines of the 1st Division scale a sea wall during the Inchon invasion on September 15, 1950. The Inchon landing was a brilliant strategic coup that turned the tide of the war against North Korea. (National Archives)

Taebaek Mountain range would obviate large-scale communist operations there. The Eighth Army crossed the Chongchon River at Sinanju, and by November 1 elements of the 24th Division were only 18 miles from the Yalu. Several days earlier a South Korean unit reached the Yalu, the only UNC unit to get there.

China now entered the war—unofficially. Alarmed over possible U.S. bases adjacent to Manchuria, Mao had issued warnings about potential Chinese military intervention. He believed that the United States would be unable to counter the Chinese numerical advantage and viewed American troops as soft and unused to night fighting. On October 2 Mao informed Stalin that China would enter the war.

Stalin agreed to move Soviet MiG-15 fighters already in China to the Korean border. In this position they could cover the Chinese military buildup and prevent U.S. air attacks on Manchuria. Soviet pilots began flying missions against UNC forces on November 1 and bore the brunt of the communists' air war. Stalin also ordered other Soviet air units to deploy to China, train Chinese pilots, and then turn over aircraft to them.

Although Russian and Chinese sources disagree on what the Soviet leader promised Mao, Stalin clearly had no intention of using his air units for anything other than defensive purposes. China later claimed that Stalin had promised complete air support for their ground forces, but this never materialized.

On October 25 Chinese troops entered the fighting in northwestern Korea, and Walker wisely brought the bulk of EUSAK back behind the Chongchon River. Positions then stabilized, and the Chinese offensive slackened. The Chinese also attacked in northeastern Korea before halting operations and breaking contact. On November 8 the first jet battle in history occurred when an American F-80 shot down a MiG-15 over Sinanju.

The initial Chinese incursion ended on November 7. In a meeting with President Truman at Wake Island on October 15, General MacArthur had assured the president that the war was all but won but that if the Chinese were to intervene, their forces would be slaughtered. UNC airpower, he believed, would nullify any Chinese threat. Yet from November 1, 1950, to October 1951, MiGs so dominated the Yalu River area that U.S. B-29 bombers had to cease daylight operations.

The initial Chinese intervention had consisted of 18 divisions. In early November they moved an additional 12 divisions into Korea, totaling some 300,000 men. MacArthur responded by ordering the air force to destroy the bridges over the Yalu. Washington revoked the order, but MacArthur complained that this threatened his command. Washington gave in. On November 8, 79 B-29s and 300 fighter-bombers struck bridges and towns on either side of the Yalu. The bombing had little effect. At the time most of the Chinese were in North Korea, and the Yalu was soon frozen.

Meanwhile, Washington debated how to proceed. The political leadership and the JCS under the chairmanship of General Omar Bradley believed that Europe was the top priority. Washington decided that Manchuria would remain off-limits, but MacArthur could take other military steps that he deemed advisable, including resumption of the offensive. The Democrats were reluctant to show weakness in Korea, and the Republicans had gained seats in the November 1950 congressional elections.

While much was being made in the United States about the prohibitions of strikes on Manchuria, the communist side also exercised restraint. With the exception of a few ancient biplanes that sometimes bombed UNC positions at night, communist airpower was restricted to north of Pyongyang. No effort was made to strike Pusan, and UNC convoys traveled without fear of air attack. Nor did communist forces attempt to disrupt Allied sea communications.

MacArthur had made X Corps dependent logistically on EUSAK instead of Japan, and Walker insisted on delaying resumption of the offensive until he could build up supplies. Weather also played a factor, with temperatures already below zero. Finally, Walker agreed to resume the offensive on November 24. To the east, X Corps was widely dispersed.

MacArthur seemed oblivious to any problems, seeing the advance as an occupation rather than an offensive. It went well on the first day, but on the night of November 25–26 the Chinese attacked the Eighth Army in force. The Americans held, but on December 26 the South Korean II Corps disintegrated, exposing EUSAK's right flank. The Chinese poured 18 divisions into the gap, endangering the whole Eighth Army. In a brilliant delaying action at Kunuri, the U.S. 2nd Division bought time for the other EUSAK divisions to recross the Chongchon. MacArthur now ordered a retirement just below the 38th Parallel to protect Seoul.

Washington directed MacArthur to pull X Corps out of northeastern Korea to prevent it from being flanked. Under heavy Chinese attack, X Corps withdrew to the east coast for sea borne evacuation along with the South

Korean I Corps. The retreat of the 1st Marine Division and some army elements from the Chanjin Reservoir to the coast was one of the most masterly withdrawals in military history. X Corps was redeployed to Pusan by sea. On December 10, Wonsan was evacuated. At Hungnam through December 24, 105,000 officers and men were taken off, along with about 91,000 Korean refugees who did not want to remain in North Korea.

The Korean War had entered a new phase: in effect, the UNC was now fighting China. MacArthur refused to accept a limited war and publicized his views to his supporters in the United States, making reference to "inhibitions" placed on his conduct of the war. UNC morale plummeted, especially with General Walker's death in a jeep accident on December 22. Not until Lieutenant General Matthew Ridgway arrived to replace Walker did the situation improve. In the United States, Truman found himself under heavy pressure from Republicans to pursue the war vigorously. But the administration reduced its goal in Korea to restoring the status quo ante bellum.

UNC forces again had to retreat when the Chinese launched a New Year's offensive, retaking Seoul on January 4. But the Chinese outran their supply lines, and Ridgway took the offensive. His methodical, limited advance was designed to inflict maximum punishment rather than to secure territory. Nonetheless, by the end of March UNC forces recaptured Seoul, and by the end of April they were again north of the 38th Parallel.

On April 11, 1951, President Truman relieved MacArthur of command, appointing Ridgway in his stead. Lieutenant General James Van Fleet took over EUSAK. Although widely unpopular at the time, MacArthur's removal was fully supported by the JCS, as MacArthur had publicly expressed

his disdain of limited war. He returned home to a hero's welcome, but much to his dismay, political support for him promptly faded.

On April 22 the Chinese counterattacked in Korea. Rather than expend his troops in a defensive stand, Van Fleet ordered a methodical withdrawal with maximum artillery and air strikes against communist forces. The Chinese pushed the UNC south of the 38th Parallel, but the offensive was halted by May.

UNC forces then counterpunched, and by the end of May the front stabilized just above the 38th Parallel. The JCS generally limited EUSAK to that line, allowing only small local advances to gain more favorable terrain.

The war was now stalemated, and a diplomatic settlement seemed expedient. On June 23, 1951, Soviet UN representative Jacob Malik proposed a cease-fire. With the Chinese expressing interest, Truman authorized Ridgway to negotiate. Meetings began on July 10 at Kaesong, although hostilities would continue until an armistice was signed.

UNC operations from this point were essentially designed to minimize friendly casualties. Each side had built deep defensive lines that would be costly to break through. In August armistice talks broke down, and later that month the Battle of Bloody Ridge began, developing into the Battle of Heartbreak Ridge and lasting until mid-October. In late October negotiations resumed, this time at Panmunjom, although the fighting continued. Half of the war's casualties occurred during the period of armistice negotiations.

On November 12, 1951, Ridgway ordered Van Fleet to cease offensive operations. Fighting now devolved into raids, local attacks, patrols, and artillery fire. In February 1953 Van Fleet was succeeded as EUSAK commander by Lieutenant General Maxwell

D. Taylor. Meanwhile, UNC air operations intensified to choke off communist supply lines and reduce the likelihood of communist offensives.

In November 1952 General Dwight Eisenhower was elected president of the United States on a mandate to end the war. With U.S. casualties running 2,500 a month, the war had become a political liability. Eisenhower instructed the JCS to draw up plans to end the war militarily including the possible use of nuclear weapons, and made the plans known to the communist side. More important in ending the conflict, however, was Stalin's death on March 5, 1953. As the armistice negotiations entered their final phase in May, the Chinese stepped up military action, initiating attacks in June and July to remove bulges in the line. UNC forces gave up some ground but inflicted heavy casualties.

The chief stumbling block to peace was the repatriation of POWs. The North Koreans had forced into their army many South Korean soldiers and civilians, and thousands of them had subsequently been captured by the UNC. If all KPA prisoners were repatriated, many South Koreans would be sent to North Korea. Also, many Chinese POWs sought refuge on Taiwan (Formosa) instead of returning to the PRC. Truman was determined that no prisoner be repatriated against his will. This stance prolonged the war, but some U.S. officials saw a moral and propaganda victory in the Chinese and North Korean defections. The communist side rejected the UNC position out of hand.

Following intense UNC air strikes on North Korean hydroelectric facilities and the capital of Pyongyang, the communists accepted a face-saving formula whereby a neutral commission would deal with prisoner repatriation. On July 27 an armistice was signed at Panmunjom, and the guns finally fell silent.

Of 132,000 North Korean and Chinese military POWs, fewer than 90,000 chose to return home. Twenty-two Americans held by the communists also elected not to return home. Of 10,218 Americans captured by the communists, only 3,746 returned. The remainder were murdered or died in captivity. American losses were 142,091, of whom 33,686 were killed in action. South Korea sustained 300,000 casualties, of whom 70,000 were killed in action. Other UNC casualties came to 17,260, of whom 3,194 were killed in action. North Korean casualties are estimated at 523,400 and Chinese losses at more than a million. Perhaps 3 million Korean civilians also died during the war.

The war devastated Korea and hardened the divisions between North and South. It was also a sobering experience for the United States. After the war, the U.S. military establishment remained strong. For America, the Korean War institutionalized the Cold War national security state. It also accelerated the racial integration of the armed forces, which in turn encouraged a much wider U.S. civil rights movement.

China gained greatly from the war in that it came to be regarded as the preponderant military power in Asia. This is ironic, because the Chinese Army in Korea was in many respects a primitive and inefficient force. Nonetheless, throughout the following decades exaggeration of Chinese military strength was woven into the fabric of American foreign policy, influencing subsequent U.S. policy in Vietnam.

The Korean War effectively militarized the containment policy. Before the war, Marshall Plan aid had been almost entirely nonmilitary. U.S. aid now shifted heavily toward military rearmament. The war also marked a sustained militarization of American foreign policy, with the Vietnam War a logical consequence.

Additionally, the Korean War solidified the role of the United States as the world's policeman and strengthened the country's relationship with its West European allies and the North Atlantic Treaty Organization (NATO). The war facilitated the rearmament of the Federal Republic of Germany (FRG, West Germany). It also impacted Japan and was a major factor fueling that nation's economy.

No formal peace has ever been concluded in Korea. Technically, the two Koreas remain at war, and the 38th Parallel remains one of the Cold War's lone outposts.

Spencer C. Tucker

Further Reading

Blair, Clay. *The Forgotten War: America in Korea, 1950–1953*. New York: Times Books, 1987.

Crane, Conrad C. *American Airpower Strategy in Korea, 1950–1953*. Lawrence: University Press of Kansas, 2000.

Ent, Uzal. *Fighting on the Brink: Defense of the Pusan Perimeter*. Paducah, KY: Turner Publishing, 1996.

Field, James A. *History of United States Naval Operations: Korea*. Washington, DC: Naval History Division, 1962.

Korea Institute of Military History. *The Korean War*. 3 vols. Seoul: Korea Institute of Military History, 1997.

Pierpaoli, Paul G., Jr. *Truman and Korea: The Political Culture of the Early Cold War*. Columbia: University of Missouri Press, 1999.

L

Laos

Comprising 91,428 square miles, about twice the size of the U.S. state of Pennsylvania, Laos is a landlocked nation bordering Vietnam to the east, Cambodia to the south, Thailand to the west, and Burma and China to the north. It had a 1945 population of some 1.7 million people. During the Cold War, Laos was consumed by revolution and war. Landlocked by larger neighbors and the buffer between ancient empires, after World War II Laos found itself at the intersection of French colonialism, Indochinese nationalism, communist expansionism, and U.S. containment policies.

Once an ancient Thai kingdom, in 1893 Laos was incorporated into French Indochina. Lao nationalism developed rapidly upon Japan's conquest of Indochina during World War II. Lao King Sisavangvong proclaimed Lao independence in March 1945. But with Japan's defeat shortly thereafter, he renounced the declaration and instead endorsed a French protectorate. His prime minister, Prince Phetsarath, did not agree with this decision and in September 1945 proclaimed Lao independence. The king dismissed him, and Phetsarath joined the dissident Lao Issara (Free Lao) movement.

The Lao Issara was intertwined with the communist-led Viet Minh in neighboring Vietnam. Many Lao nationalists, such as Prince Souvannaphong, were linked to Vietnam by ethnicity or marriage. In March 1946 Lao and Vietnamese guerrillas fought together against French rule. The French prevailed, and the Lao Issara fled in disarray

to Thailand. Laos was then reabsorbed into French Indochina. Badly weakened by World War II and conflict with the Viet Minh that included the latter's invasion of Laos, in 1953 France granted the Royal Lao Government (RLG) nominal independence. The independence of Laos was confirmed in the July 1954 Geneva Accords.

The United States began economic and social programs to develop Laos. However, aid created a dependency on the United States that eventually spawned considerable resentment. Prince Souvannaphong and others joined the communist Pathet Lao (Country of Lao), which opposed Western imperialism, including aid from the West. Fearing a civil war, a neutralist solution emerged in the mid-1950s, centered on Prince Souvanna Phouma. Intelligent and mild-mannered, Souvanna was well respected by most Lao. However, U.S. officials saw him as a communist dupe. Souvanna believed that Laos could survive the Cold War only through neutrality. He also tried to bridge divisions by building coalition governments. In 1956 Souvannaphong and other leftists representing the Neo Lao Hak Xat (NLHX, Lao Patriotic Front) joined Souvanna's coalition.

The success of the NLHX in the 1958 elections alarmed the Americans, leading to the withdrawal of U.S. aid. This action destabilized Souvanna's government and gave rise to Phoui Sananikhone, a pro-American rightist. He became prime minister in August 1958 and brought members of the Royal Lao Army (RLA) into government, notably Colonel Phoumi Nosavan. Phoumi led the RLA against North Vietnamese forces using

Lao territory for what would become the Ho Chi Minh Trail into the Republic of Vietnam (RVN, South Vietnam). When Phoui challenged this, Phoumi took control of the government in a December 1959 coup.

Phoumi was related to Thai strongman Sarit Thanarat and developed links through him to the U.S. military in Thailand. This alienated some Lao, even within the RLA, who resented foreign domination. In August 1960, RLA soldiers led by Captain Kong Le launched a coup of their own to restore Souvanna's neutralist government. Humiliated, Phoumi withdrew to secret bases in northern Thailand. U.S. president Dwight Eisenhower's administration decided to reestablish aid programs to Souvanna and restrain Phoumi, but Thailand refused to lift its blockades of the Lao border. Souvanna appealed to the Soviet Union, which airlifted supplies to Vientiane. In December 1960, Phoumi's forces drove Souvanna out of Vientiane. Kong Le's men retreated to the Vietnamese border, where they linked up with the Pathet Lao. Phoumi installed yet another government under Prince Boun Oum.

The Democratic Republic of Vietnam (DRV, North Vietnam) now feared that Phoumi would shut down the Ho Chi Minh Trail and allow American air bases in Laos. American strategy was to deny communist access through Laos to insurgencies in South Vietnam and northern Thailand, and Laos thus became an important litmus test of America's anticommunist resolve. Washington backed Phoumi and increased aid to Thailand, which became the base for many operations throughout Indochina.

U.S. president John F. Kennedy's administration continued these policies but by 1962 decided to abandon the volatile Phoumi. Instead, Kennedy reluctantly put his faith in Souvanna. After months of negotiations, in June 1963 an international agreement was reached barring foreign military advisors and establishing a neutralist, coalition government in Laos. Souvanna returned as prime minister, with both Souvannaphong and Phoumi serving in his cabinet.

The agreement did not last. North Vietnamese soldiers remained in eastern Laos, while American and Thai operations continued in other parts of the country. Infighting paralyzed the Lao government with assassinations and ceaseless power struggles. Finally, Souvanna abandoned neutralism, convinced that Hanoi controlled the Pathet Lao. In December 1964 he authorized U.S. military operations against communists in the country, drawing Laos ever closer to the war next door in Vietnam.

In Operation Barrel Roll, the United States routinely bombed the Ho Chi Minh Trail in eastern Laos, and by 1968 there were between 200 and 300 U.S. air strikes in the country daily. Laos soon became the most heavily bombed country in the history of warfare. As a result, untold thousands of Lao people were killed, with ethnic minorities, comprising 50 percent of the population, caught in the middle. Many minority Hmong, Yao, Akha, and other peoples became refugees. Some joined anticommunist irregular forces under the command of Hmong RLA officer Vang Pao, who was trained and supplied by the Thais and Americans to fight the so-called Secret War in Laos.

By 1970 the communists controlled much of Laos. The Americans responded with more bombing, expanded covert operations, and then a South Vietnamese invasion aimed at cutting the Ho Chi Minh Trail. All failed. RLG losses were very high, and by 1970 a large number of Vang Pao's men were in fact Thais secretly reassigned to Laos. Facing defeat, in 1973 the RLG secured a ceasefire upon the Paris Peace Accords between North Vietnam and the United States. A new coalition government emerged, dominated by the NLHX.

Communist victories in Cambodia and South Vietnam did not immediately spread to Laos. Pathet Lao success came from Vietnamese backing and did not translate into wide popular support. Many still favored Souvanna and Lao King Savana Vatthana. Gradually, the NLHX eliminated its rivals. Finally, in December 1975, the communists forced Souvanna and the king to resign their offices. The NLHX took power with Souvannaphong as president and banned all other political parties.

There was, however, no peace for Laos. Armed resistance continued, particularly among the Hmong. Many Lao people died or disappeared in communist reeducation camps, including the royal family. Border clashes with Thailand flared throughout the 1980s, and innumerable economic problems made Laos one of the world's poorest countries. Laos became even more dependent on Vietnam, which itself was isolated from the world community because of its Cambodian occupation. Only very recently has Laos opened up and begun to address the long, painful process of rebuilding.

Arne Kislenko

Further Reading

Castle, Timothy N. *At War in the Shadow of Vietnam: U.S. Military Aid to the Royal Lao Government, 1955–1975.* New York: Columbia University Press, 1993.

Evans, Grant. *A Short History of Laos: The Land in Between.* Crows Nest, Australia: Allen and Unwin, 2002.

Hamilton-Merritt, Jane. *Tragic Mountains: The Hmong, the Americans, and the Secret Wars for Laos, 1942–1992.* Bloomington: Indiana University Press, 1993.

McMahon, Robert J. *The Limits of Empire: The United States and Southeast Asia since World War II.* New York: Columbia University Press, 1999.

Stuart-Fox, Martin. *A History of Laos.* Cambridge: Cambridge University Press, 1997.

Latin America, Popular Liberation Movements in

The Cold War contest between the United States and the Soviet Union affected people everywhere. In Latin America, Fidel Castro's successful consolidation of the revolutionary state in Cuba after 1959 encouraged the mobilization of popular resistance movements. These liberation movements generally had two targets: standing governments that repressed popular political ambitions and aspirations, and the international order that, according to the theoretical assertions of the organizers of the liberation movements, held Latin America in a subordinate position.

The Cuban Revolution did not in itself spark liberation movements in other countries. In fact, efforts by Ernesto "Che" Guevara to sponsor other revolutions through the creation of organizational *focos* failed.

Foco meant literally a focal point of organizational activity, associated with *foquismo*, whereby the term was blown up into a theory of revolution. Guevara and his followers asserted that a small group of committed revolutionaries could, given the circumstances of Latin America's general exploitation and widespread poverty, move into any isolated or impoverished area and generate a community of resistance by providing an example of sacrifice, organization, and ideological commitment. This theory had been extrapolated from the Cuban revolutionary experience in the Sierra Maestra, the highlands of central Cuba, where a small band of committed revolutionaries galvanized popular support for the movement to overthrow Fulgencio Batista. Guevara and his later supporters built up their experience into a general plan for revolutionary struggle and change. Their assertions were particularly influential for rebel efforts in Central America and Chiapas in southern Mexico. In 1967 Guevara himself was captured and executed in Bolivia during such an attempt.

The atmosphere that produced the spread of popular liberation movements was more complex. First, the Cold War fostered the rise of powerful dictatorships in much of Latin America. During the 1940s and 1950s, governments in Argentina, Brazil, Colombia, Guatemala, Peru, and Venezuela that had mobilized popular sectors with promises of economic and social reform had been forced from power by military coups (often sponsored by the United States), foreign invasion, or interparty strife. By the start of the 1960s, the power of the regimes that had come into being earlier in the Cold War had weakened substantially, and in turn frustration over the lack of substantive reform had grown.

A variety of examples had appeared in and beyond Latin America that helped inspire organized challenges to state power. The defeat of the French in Indochina in 1954 helped demonstrate the potential success of a guerrilla insurgency against a stronger foe. Algerian resistance to French control beginning in November 1954 generated important theoretical and practical lessons. The brief success of the Bolivian Revolution in 1952 and the ability of Castro and his communist rebels to challenge one of Latin America's most entrenched dictatorships demonstrated that a social base for revolution existed within the region.

In the 1960s, two distinct intellectual streams inspired the development of revolutionary organizations. The Marxist tradition,

central to the Cuban Revolution, enjoyed broad support among intellectuals, students, and organizations linked to industrial workers. Although communist parties, in existence for decades in almost every Latin American country, remained largely isolated from the popular mobilization under way, in universities, large cities, and within unions clandestine radical groups formed and began to organize for revolution. Groups that defined themselves as Marxist and dedicated themselves to the revolutionary struggle appeared in almost every Latin American country before 1965.

Coincidentally, within organizations associated with the Roman Catholic Church, a second revolutionary front took shape. Responding to calls from the Church hierarchy to make the Church more responsive to the needs of the poor and oppressed, lay organizers and clergy alike began reaching out to communities in new and important ways. The worker-priest movement in Argentina and the Comunidades Eclesiales de Base (CEBs, Ecclesial Base Communities) in Brazil and elsewhere are notable examples of this trend. As this push for social and political engagement peaked in response to the instructions that Vatican Council II (1962–1965) provided, many of the clergy became radicalized by the experience. Discouraged by the Catholic Church's conservatism, individuals resigned their positions and became political activists.

The spread of revolutionary organizations did not result in many successful challenges to established regimes in the 1960s, however. Urban revolutionary cells in Mexico, Nicaragua, and Venezuela appeared and quickly collapsed. In Guatemala, efforts to organize a peasant revolt collapsed under pressure from military campaigns that the United States helped coordinate and support.

The few successful organizations relied on a community or institutional base. Radical Marxist groups in Peru took shape in Andean universities. In Argentina, the Ejército Revolucionario del Pueblo (ERP, Revolutionary Army of the People) and the Montoneros emerged from groups that had splintered off from the Perónist political movement. Other groups, such as the Fuerza Armada Revolucionaria Colombiana (FARC, Colombian Revolutionary Armed Forces), the M-19 in Colombia, and the Frente Sandinista de Liberación Nacional (FSLN, Sandinista National Liberation Front) in Nicaragua, survived and expanded by shifting from urban to rural bases.

The Catholic Church unintentionally contributed to the survival and spread of popular liberation movements in much of Latin America. Church officials eventually backed away from the political engagement that Vatican II had dictated, but local parishes provided space and protection for community groups that initially focused on community needs and concerns. The meeting places and community base allowed leaders to shift these groups into more radical directions. This trend, which took place in the late 1960s and early 1970s, came at times in reaction to attempts at repression or came as a result of links to other radical cells that effectively recruited locals to their broader causes.

In the 1970s, incompetent or incomplete efforts to destroy guerrilla groups and protest organizations helped galvanize liberation movements in some cases. Most notably in Nicaragua, the clumsy and brutal actions of the Anastasio Somoza dictatorship helped win sympathy and support for the FSLN. By 1979, united with opposition political parties, reform groups, and other dissenters, the FSLN overthrew the dictatorship and moved to establish a new Marxist revolutionary regime.

By the end of the 1970s, applying the lessons learned from the Vietnam War and motivated by the challenge that the Sandinista government represented to its authority in the region, the United States became more directly involved in a military reaction to popular liberation movements. U.S. intervention in El Salvador helped transform the conflict there into a bloody stalemate. Aid and advice to the Guatemalan military sustained its struggle against peasant-based resistance groups. Military governments in Argentina and Uruguay effectively neutralized urban guerrilla movements. But in other contexts, government actions helped maintain the strength of liberation movements into the 1980s and beyond.

Daniel Lewis

Further Reading

Eckstein, Susan, ed. *Power and Popular Protest: Latin American Social Movements.* Berkeley: University of California Press, 2001.

McClintock, Cynthia. *Revolutionary Movements in Latin America.* Washington, DC: United States Institute of Peace Press, 1998.

Literature

The Cold War was fought on the literary as well as the diplomatic and political fronts. Although it did not provide such immediately absorbing subject matter for writers as did the two world wars of the 20th century, it created a tense, competitive environment in which all thoughtful writers operated. Sometimes openly, but often by parable or indirection, serious writers confronted the social, political, and philosophical issues raised by the conflict, which eventually split the world into two opposing ideological camps. During the McCarthy era of the early 1950s, a significant number of American writers found their careers threatened should they express sympathy for communism. Their often-coerced testimonies before the House Un-American Activities Committee (HUAC) and Senator Joseph McCarthy's Senate subcommittee were invariably dramatic and sometimes life-altering. Always mindful of the feared blacklist, writers learned to proceed with caution. Those who did not conform resorted to the use of pen names. At the same time, the interest generated by Senate hearings and Cold War intrigues provided the more openly commercial writers, those who produced entertainment that titillated casual readers, a superabundance of plot possibilities.

Decades before the Cold War began, numerous men and women of letters had found socialist and Marxist ideas attractive. Some had flirted with communism and had looked toward the Soviet Union as a noble experiment. Naturalism, the literary movement that dominated serious European and American fiction in the first half of the 20th century, had actually encouraged many writers in this direction. Since the time of Émile Zola in late 19th-century France, practitioners of literary naturalism had prided themselves on their ability to rouse the public and mitigate miserable living conditions by highlighting social abuses in fiction. Because these writers knew the social problems of Western Europe and the United States best and juxtaposed this reality to the rosy propaganda that was emanating from the Soviet Union, it was not uncommon for them to respond positively to features of the communist message.

As the HUAC hearings got under way, writers who had worked in Hollywood were particularly vulnerable to the committee's scrutiny. Lillian Hellman (1905–1984) was perhaps the most highly publicized writer to confront HUAC directly. A major American dramatist and woman of letters, she had earned her reputation with such plays as *The Children's Hour* (1934), one of the first Broadway dramas to treat lesbianism, and *Watch on the Rhine* (1941), an antifascist play. Although born in New Orleans to an affluent family, she had become involved in radical politics under the influence of her companion, Dashiell Hammett (1894–1961).

Hellman became an eager student of Marxist texts and briefly joined the Communist Party for humanitarian and idealistic reasons. In the early years of World War II, she had carefully followed the party line, first urging the United States to stay out of the conflict, during the Nazi-Soviet Pact, and later advocating involvement when Germany violated its treaties by invading the Soviet Union in 1941. By the time she was called to testify before HUAC, her days with the party were over. By skillful management of public relations, she was able to avoid tattling on former associates without going to prison herself.

Hammett was not so fortunate. Although a dedicated Marxist who had supported radical movements in the United States, he claimed that he had never actually joined the Communist Party. Nevertheless, he refused to cooperate with HUAC, invoking the Fifth Amendment 80 times during his testimony. Refusing to identify communist sympathizers he had known, he was sentenced to six months in federal prison, was blacklisted in Hollywood, and was hounded by the Internal Revenue Service (IRS) for the rest of his life. His writings, identified as subversive by Senator McCarthy and McCarthy's sidekick Roy Cohn, were removed from many libraries. This was a considerable disappointment to Hammett's many readers, who regarded him as a creator of the American hard-boiled school of detective fiction with his Sam Spade and Thin Man stories. His best-known works, such as *Red Harvest* (1927) and *The Maltese Falcon* (1930), are still regarded as classics of the genre.

Other writers with strong Hollywood connections caught up in the HUAC net included Clifford Odets (1906–1963), Ring Lardner Jr. (1915–1983), and Arthur Miller (1915–2005). Odets emerged as one of the sadder figures of the McCarthy era. A leading playwright of the 1930s and 1940s and the author of *Waiting for Lefty* (1935) and *Golden Boy* (1937), Odets was a member of the Marxist League of American writers, which had included the great American novelist Theodore Dreiser (1871–1945). Odets joined the party itself around 1935. According to his later testimony, he resigned six or eight months later in disappointment. The communist publications *The Daily Worker* and *The New Masses* had unfavorably reviewed his plays, labeling him a "hack writer" who did not properly promote proletarian themes. When he later testified before HUAC, Odets attempted to downplay leftist influence in Hollywood, claiming that the collaborative system that produced Hollywood films made it next to impossible for a writer to inject Marxist ideas into scripts. Because of his conciliatory approach to the committee, many of his colleagues accused him of collusion with the enemy, and the experience left him disheartened.

Lardner was the son of a popular American humorist and had been an Academy Award–winning screenwriter in 1942. He was the youngest of the group of motion picture screenwriters and directors accused of communist sympathies, designated as the Hollywood Ten. In the 1930s he had visited the Soviet Union to judge the Marxist experiment firsthand. At that time he had truly believed it his duty to try to communicate Marxist ideas through film. HUAC regarded him as an important witness, but his failure to answer the committee's questions resulted in a citation for contempt, a year's prison sentence, a $1,000 fine, and the Hollywood blacklist. For two years he was forced to make his living anonymously. His novel *The Ecstasy of Owen Muir* appeared in England in the 1960s but could not be published in the United States. He was finally able to return to Hollywood in the 1960s, where he earned a second Academy Award for his work on the screenplay of *M*A*S*H* (1970).

Miller, like Hellman, was a major 20th-century American playwright whose drama *Death of a Salesman* (1949) redefined tragedy for the modern theater. A liberal activist from youth, Miller had still never been willing to put himself under the discipline of the Communist Party. He rejected its doctrine that all artists should employ their talents to further the party line. Yet he believed that the Communist Party should be able to function legally in the United States, and he condemned HUAC as a pack of witch-hunters. Though Miller was willing to be forthright with HUAC about his own beliefs and actions, he firmly refused to testify against others. On several occasions in later years, Miller publicly expressed his conviction that the very existence of civilization depended on trust and loyalty. Although his career survived and he became a media celebrity upon his marriage to Hollywood actress Marilyn Monroe, Miller did not escape unscathed. He was even refused a passport by the State Department.

Two later Miller plays powerfully reflect his reactions to HUAC and the anticommunist hysteria that damaged the careers of people close to him. *The Crucible* (1953), ostensibly about the Salem witch trials of early American colonial history, was generally understood to be a parable of McCarthyism. *After the Fall* (1964) was a more direct depiction of Miller's personal experiences as a harassed artist and husband of a neurotic film star.

To those who were seized by the Red hysteria, it often seemed that all American letters had turned leftist. There were, however, significant counterbalances. During the early years of the Cold War, Ernest Hemingway (1899–1961) and William Faulkner (1897–1962) were among the most admired American writers. Hemingway believed that a writer betrayed his art if he used it to promulgate an ideology. The extreme subjectivity of Hemingway and the social conservatism of Faulkner made them unlikely heroes of the Left.

Nineteen Eighty-Four (1947), a horrific piece of political satiric fiction by the English writer George Orwell (1903–1950), circulated throughout the United States and was widely interpreted as a vision of what the West would become if dominated by the Soviet Union. In the society of Oceania, as described in the book, the omnipresent television set indoctrinates folk in the Big Lie, the government's interpretation of everything. All speech, action, and even thought are controlled by Big Brother.

Another book that profoundly influenced American thought appeared in 1949. *The God That Failed* was a collection of essays by important novelists, poets, and journalists whose earlier ideals had been betrayed by the reality of what the Soviet Union had become. They had all initially believed communism to be the best hope for the oppressed masses of the world. The participants in *The God That Failed* were Arthur Koestler, a Hungarian novelist; Louis Fischer, an American journalist; André Gide, a French essayist and novelist; Richard Wright, a major African American novelist; Ignazio Silone, an Italian journalist and novelist; and the British poet Stephen Spender.

Especially moving was Richard Wright's narrative of his emergence from Mississippi plantation life to a writing career in Chicago.

The Communist Party had promised equality for all, with particular concern for the plight of the African American in the years before the successes of the civil rights movement. Wright's eventual discovery of the tyranny and duplicity of the party was a painful epiphany.

Equally powerful was Gide's account of his visit to the Soviet Union in June 1936 as a guest of the Soviet Society of Authors. He had approached his visit with the conviction that the Russian experiment was the wave of the future. Although he was shown every courtesy and provided the finest accommodations the country had to offer, his eyes and ears were open. He was unable to deny that the vast masses of Soviet citizens still lived in abject poverty. While the rest of the world was bombarded with rosy visions of an ideal state by the party's propaganda machine, Russian workers continued to suffer under deplorable tyranny that rivaled that of the czars.

Perhaps the most outspoken and abrasive literary opponent of communism in the United States during the Cold War was Ayn Rand (1905–1982), a native of Russia who had experienced communism firsthand and passionately hated it and all its works. Her novels, which sometimes became bestsellers and always attracted a cult following, were rarely more than fictional embodiments of her ideas and prejudices. *We, the Living* (1936), *The Fountainhead* (1943), and *Atlas Shrugged* (1957) extolled the virtues of self-interest, the fulfillment of individual potential, and the value of capitalism as the system best designed to favor self-fulfillment. As a friendly witness before HUAC in October 1947, Rand attacked early Hollywood portrayals of life in the Soviet Union as an idealized lie. She testified that the Soviet Union was in fact a prison from which many were risking their lives to escape. Her claim that

Russians smiled only "privately and accidentally" was widely quoted and was ridiculed by Hellman and others.

In the English language, it was genre fiction that most directly exploited the Cold War. Spy thrillers became a staple, expertly penned by Graham Greene (1904–1991), Ian Fleming (1908–1964), John le Carré (1931–), Tom Clancy (1947–), and others. Greene was a major British writer who rarely concealed his hostility toward American policies. He divided his literary output into two clear categories: his serious fiction, which explored religious and philosophical themes, and his entertainments, often set against worldwide political conflicts. *The Third Man* (1948) unfolded in postwar Vienna with a leading character who bore a remarkable resemblance to Soviet mole Kim Philby, a man for whom Greene had once worked. *The Quiet American* (1955) used Vietnam as a backdrop, at the beginning of the American involvement in the turmoil generated by the French and by nationalist and communist factions. *Our Man in Havana* (1958) revealed a cloak-and-dagger world of espionage more ridiculous than awesome.

Fleming, another British writer, created the character of James Bond, perhaps the most popular of all fictional Cold War spies, certainly so after the cinema discovered him. Bond's most notable Cold War adventures erupted in *From Russia with Love* (1957) in which Bond romped with buxom Soviet female agents as he battled SMERSH, the Soviet organ of vengeance, interrogation, torture, and death; in *For Your Eyes Only* (1960), in which SHAPE headquarters, a Russian hideout near Paris, is destroyed; and in *Octopussy* (1966), which found Bond snaring a top Soviet agent found bidding for a Fabergé egg in a Sotheby auction. The Bond stories were splendid camp, and their exaggerations made many feel that the Soviets were more buffoons than threats.

Le Carré, a third British spy novelist, made good use of his personal experiences in the British Foreign Service as background for his novels. Among his best-known thrillers are *The Spy Who Came in from the Cold* (1963) and *Tinker, Tailor, Soldier, Spy* (1974). These narratives suggest a grim, lonely espionage underworld in which values are often blurred and loyalties sometimes ambiguous.

Clancy, an American, wrote thrillers rivaling the appeal of the leading British spy novelists. Books with special Cold War relevance included *The Hunt for Red October* (1984), *Red Storm Rising* (1986), *Patriot Games* (1987), and *Cardinal of the Kremlin* (1988). He wrote a fast-paced adventure narrative, more real-world than were the James Bond adventures, yet he avoided the moral ambiguities that intrigued Greene and le Carré.

Science fiction became the most popular literary category during the Cold War, particularly after paperbacks became widely distributed. This genre at its best provided an even more provocative attack on communism than had the spy stories. Hundreds of paperbacks were published each year, some predicting dystopian futures in which tyranny would prevail. Others painted a horrifying panorama of a planet devastated by a Cold War turned hot in a thermonuclear disaster. These narratives generally refrained from siding with either East or West in the conflict. The destructive potential, they seemed to say, is spread about equally throughout the human race. The bomb had become the new Frankenstein monster, the golem through which the suicidal impulses of humanity would find expression.

Two of these apocalyptic novels attracted special attention. Nevil Shute (1899–1960) was a British writer living in Australia when he published *On the Beach* (1957). He envisioned a near future where nuclear war has wiped out all life in the Northern Hemisphere. Australians alone survive, but only for a few days, with full awareness that global winds will soon bring radioactive contamination to them.

Three years after the appearance of *On the Beach*, Walter M. Miller Jr. (1922–1996) published his hauntingly poetic *A Canticle for Leibowitz*, one of the few science fiction books that has crossed over literary categories to become recognized as a significant work of 20th-century American fiction. In this unusual science fiction story, after the nuclear holocaust the tiny Catholic Order of Leibowitz undertakes the task of preserving some memory of previous civilization.

Although writers in the English language have most notably confronted the Cold War in their fiction, European literature has also been strongly conditioned by the events of the period, often struggling with Cold War issues on a philosophical or religious plane. In Italy, France, and elsewhere on the European continent, atheistic views, strongly influenced by the dialectal materialism of Karl Marx and Friedrich Engels, have battled Christianity in the minds and hearts of serious writers.

In France, Jean-Paul Sartre (1905–1980), highly sympathetic to Marxism although frequently critical of the Soviet Union, best represented the atheistic position. In 1945 Sartre founded a political and literary magazine, *Les Temps Modernes*, which reflected his position as an independent socialist addressing Cold War issues. His novels, such as *The Age of Reason* (1945) and *Troubled Sleep* (1949), gave fictional embodiment to his social and philosophical ideas. A more mellow atheistic French voice was that of Albert Camus, a fellow existentialist who

had actually once been a Communist Party member. His novel *The Plague* (1947) has been variously interpreted as a parable of Resistance fighters in Paris revolting against Nazi domination and as a protest against all revolutionary movements that justify the use of any methods to achieve their ends.

Espousing Christianity even in a France often labeled "post-Christian" were writers such as Georges Bernanos (1888–1948), François Mauriac (1885–1970), and Julian Green (1900–1998), an American citizen who spent most of his life in France and wrote almost exclusively in the French language. Much of the career of Bernanos was devoted to writings that promoted his liberal views, which included his denunciations of French bourgeois values and Spanish dictator Francisco Franco's exploits. As a frequent essayist, Bernanos took positions with which both communists and ultra-rightists could occasionally agree.

Mauriac, who was awarded the Nobel Prize for literature in 1952, affirmed Christian values with novels that were more concerned with personal and family relationships than social movements. His message in numerous novels was that beneath prosperous exteriors, regardless of the political system, human beings are torn by uneasy emotions in disordered lives of their own making.

Green likewise concentrated on the wars within the human personality in books that reflected his personal dilemmas, his conversion from Protestantism to Catholicism, and his acknowledgment of his homosexuality. These introspective works included *Moira* (1950) and *Each in His Own Darkness* (1960).

In Italy, Alberto Moravia (1907–1990), an influential intellectual tormented by the plight of the poor, skeptical of Christian solutions, and alert to the appeal that the Communist Party made to postwar Italians, became the best known of his country's novelists throughout Europe and the United States. From the beginning, the socially alienated were his choice subjects, while his style was sparse and realistic. *A Woman of Rome* (1947), about a Roman prostitute, and *Time of Desecration* (1978), a political allegory, were among his most penetrating works.

While the intellectuals were debating the social reality portrayed by Moravia and examining his implied solutions, masses of people were devouring the Don Camillo stories of Giovannino Guareschi (1908–1968). These were simple tales somewhat reminiscent of medieval legends of St. Francis, about a village priest in the Po Valley who converses with the crucifix above his altar and verbally spars with his old friend, Pepponi, the communist mayor of his village. The books made the simple plea for Christian virtues above the vapid promises of communism.

On the other side of the Iron Curtain, Russian writers faced very different problems than their Western counterparts, who often had a bewildering assortment of philosophical options from which to choose. Instead of castigating their opponents, Soviet writers had to concern themselves with pleasing their government and following the party line or else circulating their manuscripts through a flourishing Russian underground. Writing guilds in the Soviet Union operated under clearly defined precepts of socialist realism, which an individual author violated only with considerable courage. In Soviet Russia under Josef Stalin, there was to be no art for art's sake. All writings were to serve the proletarian revolution. Crude propaganda novels flooded the Russian market, celebrating women who chose to forgo singing in the Moscow opera in order to increase their egg production on collective farms or men allowed to marry their intended only after factory quotas had been surpassed.

Ilya Ehrenburg (1891–1967) was one of the best-known writers of genuine talent to faithfully follow the party line. He was, not surprisingly, awarded two Stalin Prizes for *The Fall of Paris* (1941), a fictional account of French societal decay from 1935 through 1940, and *The Storm* (1948), a war novel with Tolstoyan pretensions. Vera Panova (1905–1973) was another loyal Soviet novelist who, nevertheless, managed to convey in her writing the compassion and humanistic vision that had been the identifying feature of the great 19th-century Russian novelists. She received the Stalin Prize in 1947 for *The Train*. Although she did not fail to tackle social issues according to the cannons of socialist realism, she is best remembered for her loving portraits of children, such as *Evodokiia* (1959).

Mikhail Sholokhov (1905–1984), who became the Nobel laureate of 1965, was acclaimed by his government as an obedient communist as well as a powerful writer. His most loved work was *And Quiet Flows the Don*, written between 1928 and 1940. It presented a vast panorama of the revolutionary period in a way that did not displease the authorities.

Two serious Russian writers came into open conflict with their government when they were awarded Nobel Prizes. During the Cold War the prize itself, still the most prestigious in the world for literary achievement, became politicized. In 1958, Boris Pasternak (1890–1960) was coerced by his government into refusing the prize, which was awarded to him not only for a distinguished body of poetry but also for his masterpiece *Doctor Zhivago*, completed in 1956 but not published in his native land until 1988. *Doctor Zhivago*'s theme was the aspirations of the individual pitted against the demands of doctrinaire systems.

In 1970 Aleksandr Solzhenitsyn (1918–2008) was awarded the Nobel Prize. His writings—fictionalizations of personal experiences—had exposed the underside of Soviet life, the ruthlessness of the prison camps, and the injustice of the courts. *First Circle* (1968) was based on the years that he spent in a prison research institute, while *Cancer Ward* (1968) resulted from his hospitalization and treatment for cancer during a forced exile in Kazakhstan in the 1950s. *The Gulag Archipelago*, which began publication in Paris in 1973, was considered his most thorough exposé of the notorious Soviet prison and labor camps. Living under almost constant harassment, Solzhenitsyn did not bend to the Soviet authorities but remained a thorn in their flesh until he finally was expelled from the country in 1974. Equally unhappy in the West, despite the acclaim he received both for his writing and his political courage, he returned to Russia in 1994.

On both sides of the Iron Curtain, the Cold War conditioned both serious and popular literature. The unsettled quality of life and the fears generated by the reality of mutual assured destruction (MAD) may be easily discerned in the novels of several decades, although the conflict failed to call forth the epic writing that has always resulted from the world's great armed conflicts.

Allene Phy-Olsen

Further Reading

Brown, Edward J. *Russian Literature since the Revolution*. New York: Collier-Macmillan, 1963.

Feldman, Burton. *The Nobel Prize: A History of Genius, Controversy, and Prestige*. New York: Arcade Publishing, 2000.

Lipschutz, Ronnie D. *Cold War Fantasies: Film, Fiction, and Foreign Policy*. New York: Rowman and Littlefield, 2001.

Schaub, Thomas Hill. *American Fiction in the Cold War*. Madison: University of Wisconsin Press, 1991.

M

Malayan Emergency (1948–1960)

The Malayan Emergency was a 12-year guerrilla war that began on June 18, 1948. The conflict was an indigenous attempt by the Malayan Communist Party (MCP) to overthrow British colonial rule. Expected to last no more than a few months, the insurgency continued until July 31, 1960, three years after Malaya had gained its independence. The Malayan Emergency was Britain's longest colonial conflict and turned out to be far more costly in human and material terms than anyone could have foreseen.

The war's immediate catalyst was the murder of three rubber plantation managers in Perak, Malaya, on June 16, 1948. The MCP guerrillas in the mobile corps committed the murders three months after the party had called for an armed insurrection against British rule. Two days later the British high commissioner, Sir Edward Gent, declared a state of emergency. The conflict was called an "emergency" for economic reasons, as London insurance companies would cover property losses to Malayan rubber and tin estates during riot or commotion in an emergency, but not in an armed insurrection or civil war.

The Malayan Emergency was rooted primarily in postwar economic and political dislocations in Malaya. Despite the importance of these local factors, however, the predominant explanation for both the origins of the insurgency and the British determination to defeat it was the Cold War paradigm of communist containment. The inaugural conference of the Cominform in September 1947 and the Calcutta conference of the Indian Communist Party in February 1948, which adopted Andrei Zhdanov's two-camps thesis, were presumed to be linked to the armed rebellions against colonial rule in Burma, Indonesia, Malaya, and the Philippines.

Britain treasured its role in Southeast Asia, as it relied on the region for both economic and strategic reasons. Britain's massive military commitment to defeat the insurgency (by October 1950 nearly 50,000 British troops were deployed) at a time of severe postwar fiscal austerity had a significant economic dimension. After the Japanese defeat in 1945, the British were determined to return to Malaya, and Malaya's dollar-earning potential made British control over its colonial possession absolutely essential. In dollar terms, rubber sales exceeded in total value all other domestic exports from Great Britain to the United States. Interruption of that supply would inflict significant damage on the British economy. When the insurgency commenced, Britain was struggling to maintain the value of its currency. This made earnings from the Sterling Area, of which Malaya was the linchpin, all the more vital. Crushing the insurgency would ensure the maintenance of British economic interests.

But the insurrection was not easy to quell. Initially, the British response was fitful, uncertain, and inept. Not until 1950, when Lieutenant-General Sir Harold Briggs became director of operations, did the British initiate a more systematic and coordinated approach to the crisis. Britain's new program, in which the insurgents were detached from their supply sources and their support bases, provided a key breakthrough in the rebellion. Through a major relocation process, which prefigured the American policy of strategic hamlets in the Republic of Vietnam (RVN, South Vietnam), more than half a million Chinese squatters living near guerrilla areas were moved into 450 so-called New Villages. The villages hampered MCP operations and increased their vulnerability to the military operations of British-controlled security forces.

This population control, initiated by Briggs, was harsh but effective. It was prosecuted even more vigorously by General Sir Gerald Templer, appointed high commissioner in early 1952, with full powers over the military, police, and civilian authorities. Templer also fought the counterinsurgency on other fronts. He developed an efficient, synchronized, and expanded intelligence apparatus; implemented the so-called hearts and minds approach meant to address popular aspirations; enlarged the intelligence budget so that informers could be paid; and coordinated the use of sophisticated black propaganda and psyops by MI6 personnel.

Aerial warfare was refined as well. Safe conduct passes accompanied by promises of monetary rewards were airdropped to encourage or accelerate defections. Aerial drops of millions of strategic leaflets, such as handwritten letters and photographs from surrendered guerrillas, were used in conjunction with voice aircraft to personalize propaganda. British aircraft also dropped 1,000-pound bombs, chemical defoliants, and napalm on MCP jungle camps.

By 1954, when Templer departed, these measures had transformed the conflict. The insurgents had been forced back into the jungle, where they struggled to sustain themselves. In 1955 the MCP offered, in vain, to negotiate a settlement. In 1957, upon Malaya's independence, the insurgency lost its

motive as a war of colonial liberation. In 1958, after mass defections, the MCP demobilized, and by 1960 the movement was limited to a small nucleus hiding on the Malayan-Thai border, from which it conducted hit-and-run raids along the northern Malay Peninsula for the next 25 years. A final peace settlement was signed on December 2, 1989.

The Malayan Emergency cast a long shadow over the new nation. Its mythology has come to dominate the modern history of Malaya, and it became a benchmark of the Cold War in Southeast Asia. For Americans embarking on military involvement in Vietnam and wishing to apply successful British strategies, the Malayan Emergency became the quintessential counterinsurgency primer.

Phillip Deery

Further Reading

Harper, T. N. *The End of Empire and the Making of Malaya*. Cambridge: Cambridge University Press, 1999.

Peng, Chin. *Alias Chin Peng: My Side of History*. Singapore: Media Masters, 2003.

Ramakrishna, Kumar. *Emergency Propaganda: The Winning of Malayan Hearts and Minds, 1948–1958*. London: Curzon, 2002.

Mao Zedong (1893–1976)

Born in Shaoshan, Hunan Province, on November 19, 1893, Mao Zedong graduated from the Hunan First Normal School in 1918. He then went to Beijing to work in the Beijing University Library, where he learned Marxist ideology and developed his revolutionary plan to save China. Mao helped found the Chinese Communist Party (CCP) in Shanghai in 1921. In 1924, following the Comintern's instructions, Mao joined the Guomindang (GMD, Nationalist) party, forming the first United Front aimed at Chinese national unification. In so doing, he bought time for the infant CCP to grow under the GMD shield. However, the United Front broke down in mid-1927 when GMD leader Jiang Jieshi decided to purge the Chinese communists, thereby beginning the CCP–GMD power struggle that lasted for two decades.

Following the breakdown of the United Front, Mao and other frustrated Chinese communists worked on their own to develop a unique Chinese path to carry out the socialist revolution. In January 1935 Mao became

Mao Zedong (old spelling Mao Tse-tung) led the Communists in the civil war against the Nationalists in China and was the leader of the People's Republic of China from 1949 to 1976. Although remembered as one of the great Chinese leaders who made China a major player on the world stage, he was also responsible for the disastrous Great Leap Forward and the Cultural Revolution. (The Illustrated London News Picture Library)

the CCP chairman, a post he held until his death. His ascension to power is attributed to his ideological and tactical pragmatism, which rejected the rigid application of Soviet orthodox thinking and instead emphasized the uniqueness of Chinese history and culture. After expelling Jiang's GMD government from the mainland, Mao proclaimed the establishment of the PRC on October 1, 1949, officially ending the Chinese Civil War. Mao's reign can be divided into three periods: 1949–1957, 1958–1965, and 1966–1976.

The first period was characterized by imitation of the Soviet model in reconstructing China and consolidating the CCP's power. On foreign policy matters, Mao coined the three principles of make another stove, clean the house and then invite the guests, and lean to one side. According to the first two principles, Mao was determined to start anew by pursuing an anticolonial and anti-imperialist policy to eliminate China's century-old semicolonial status, imposed by imperial powers since the mid-19th century. Because the PRC's birth coincided with the Cold War, Mao's policy of lean to one side signaled a pro-Soviet and anti-American stance. His first foreign policy initiative was a visit to Moscow in December 1949, culminating in the Sino-Soviet Treaty of February 1950.

The PRC's anti-American stance was vividly showcased over the question of Taiwan, where Jiang's GMD government still retained power, as well as in the Korean War, the Geneva Conference, the first and second Taiwan Strait crises, and the Bandung Conference, at which Mao attacked America for its "imperialist" designs in the Taiwan Strait.

Domestically, Mao selectively transplanted the Soviet model. Politically, he preferred a democratic dictatorship, along the principles of democratic centralism and coexistence with other revolutionary parties and noncommunist classes, to the Soviets' proletarian dictatorship. Mao wished to avoid the Soviet political purges of the 1930s. Yet he ensured that real power and leadership rested in the hands of the CCP, as the terms "dictatorship" and "centralism" suggested.

In economic matters, Mao strictly adhered to the Soviet model, with Soviet technical and material assistance. In early 1950, he ushered in land reform, which involved government confiscation and the redistribution of agrarian land to peasants. This stage was completed in late 1953 and was succeeded by collectivization aimed at boosting agricultural production. In 1953, Mao launched the First Five-Year Plan, which strove to develop heavy industries and was completed a year ahead of schedule.

To consolidate his control over the country, Mao adopted mass socialization. The government encouraged the formation of numerous mass organizations in the early 1950s to mobilize the population to participate in such movements as the Resist-America Aid-Korea Campaign, the Three-Anti Movement to combat corruption and wasteful bureaucracy, and the Five-Anti Movement against bribery, tax evasion, fraud, theft of government property, and leakage of state economic secrets.

The second period of Mao's rule demonstrated his determination to establish a unique brand of Chinese socialism, designed to wean China from Soviet aid. The year 1958 began with the Second Five-Year Plan, which was much more ambitious than the first. To accelerate China's industrialization, Mao launched the three-year Great Leap Forward program at year's end, a radical measure designed to catch up with and surpass British industrial output. To this end, he ordered the establishment of nationwide People's Communes, which was also an essential step in facilitating the socialist transformation of China.

The Great Leap Forward, however, was doomed to failure, as the PRC was not ready for such a radical transformation. The results were measured in massive manpower and property losses. Another adverse impact was the growing division within the PRC leadership. Realizing his miscalculation and hoping to avoid becoming the scapegoat for further losses, Mao gave up his PRC chairmanship to Liu Shaoqi in April 1959 while retaining the chairmanship of the CCP. In September 1959, Mao relieved Peng Dehuai of his post as defense minister because of his opposition to the Great Leap Forward. The failure of the Great Leap Forward convinced moderate leaders such as Deng Xiaoping and Zhou Enlai that socialization should be slowed down, a view that made both men targets of the Cultural Revolution in later years. To compensate for the economic dislocation and destruction of the Great Leap Forward, Mao reluctantly agreed to relax economic socialization by dismantling the communes and using material incentives to revive the Chinese economy, cures proposed by Liu and Deng. By the mid-1960s, China's economy had been restored to its 1957 level.

Mao's drive for independence also resulted in the collapse of the Sino-Soviet alliance. His insistence on proceeding with the radical Great Leap Forward alarmed Soviet leader Nikita Khrushchev, who decided to stop assisting the PRC's national reconstruction in 1958. This forced Mao to pursue a lone course in implementing both the Second Five-Year Plan and the Great Leap Forward.

Mao's unilateral initiation of the Second Taiwan Strait Crisis in September 1958 prompted Khrushchev to withhold nuclear information. The Sino-Soviet split became official after Mao passed the chairmanship to Liu, who intensified the ideological attack against Soviet revisionism and Khrushchev's advocacy of de-Stalinization and peaceful coexistence with the West. By

1963, Sino-Soviet unity had all but disappeared. To compensate for the loss of Soviet aid, Mao promoted closer PRC ties with Asian and African countries. His success in this enabled the PRC to become an influential leader in the developing world, transforming the bipolar Cold War world into a tripolar one.

The decade-long Cultural Revolution constituted the third period of Mao's era, during which the PRC experienced violent chaos and disorder. Determined to reassert his personal authority and monolithic leadership over the country, Mao launched the Cultural Revolution in 1966 through his wife Jiang Qing. In reviving the class struggle and Marxist-Leninist teachings, he purged all potential opponents, including old comrades, from both the government and the CCP. To ensure his personal control, Mao packed the party and the government with his supporters, such as his wife and Hua Guofeng, both of whom were made Politburo members. Outside the government, Mao incited the Red Guards, radical youths indoctrinated with Maoism, to criticize old customs and practices by employing violence and mass rallies. The Red Guards were also sent into the countryside to encourage the so-called cult of Mao. This 10-year period constituted the darkest days of the PRC's history, characterized by a reign of red terror that badly bruised Mao's revolutionary legacy.

The Cultural Revolution also had a direct bearing on the PRC's foreign policy. On the one hand, the revolution aroused grave hostility and suspicion from the PRC's allies, who either severed diplomatic relations with the PRC or recalled their foreign service delegations. Combined with the Sino-Soviet split, the Cultural Revolution almost completely isolated the PRC within the international community. On the other hand, the Cultural Revolution made possible the normalization of U.S.–Chinese relations because of their mutual desire to enhance each other's bargaining position vis-à-vis the Soviet Union. In February 1972, Mao received U.S. president Richard M. Nixon in Beijing, which culminated in American diplomatic recognition of the PRC in 1979. This rapprochement marked the end of China's diplomatic isolation.

Mao died in Beijing on September 9, 1976. Shortly after his death, in October 1976, Hua, now the premier, seized power and ended the Maoist era by officially terminating the Cultural Revolution.

Law Yuk-fun

Further Reading

Chang Jung and Jon Halliday. *Mao: The Unknown Story*. New York: Knopf, 2005.

Chen, Jian. *Mao's China and the Cold War*. Chapel Hill: University of North Carolina Press, 2001.

Karnow, Stanley. *Mao and China: A Legacy of Turmoil*. New York: Penguin, 1990.

Lynch, Michael J. *Mao*. London: Routledge, 2004.

Lyons, Thomas P. *Economic Integration and Planning in Maoist China*. New York: Columbia University Press, 1987.

Mao Zedong. *Selected Works of Mao Zedong*. Beijing: Foreign Languages Press, 1966–1977.

Marshall Plan

In the wake of World War II, Europe experienced a severe economic crisis because of the crippling effects of nearly six years of war. The United States had attempted to promote European recovery through limited reconstruction loans, relief assistance, German war reparation transfers, and new multilateral currency and trade arrangements. By the winter of 1947, however, it was apparent that these piecemeal stabilization efforts were not working. Millions of West Europeans were unemployed, inflation and shortages were rampant, and malnutrition had become a widespread concern.

The central problem facing Europe was low industrial productivity. Industrial and agricultural production lagged behind prewar levels, as the wartime destruction or disruption of factories and equipment had led to dramatically decreased industrial output. Adequate funds were not available for reconstruction and replacement, and none of the nations involved had the wherewithal to raise large amounts of capital. To make matters worse, basic building-block industrial materials such as steel and coal were scarce.

The growing economic troubles fed frustration, hopelessness, and despair. And many Europeans had begun to seek out political solutions to their troubles. Alienated from capitalism, some began turning to communism as an alternative. In France, Italy, and Germany, the crisis had eroded government support and lent credence to communist promises of economic stability. In Great Britain, serious financial woes forced policymakers to reduce international agreements that had helped resist the spread of communism. Only by eliminating the economic conditions that encouraged political extremism could European governments withstand the influence of communism, and nobody seemed to understand that better than the Americans.

U.S. policymakers believed that rejuvenated West European economies would provide a strong demand for American goods and help maintain the United States as the world's leading economic power. They also envisioned Western Europe as an integral part of a multilateral economic system of free world trade crucial to the liberal-capitalist world order that Washington had in mind for itself and its allies. Clearly, unity and prosperity in Western Europe would create

A worker shovels rubble during the rebuilding of West Berlin in front of a building adorned with a sign supporting the Marshall Plan. This massive United States financial aid program greatly assisted in the rebuilding of Western Europe after World War II. (National Archives)

an economy able to generate high productivity, decent living standards, and political stability.

The European Recovery Program, which came to be known as the Marshall Plan in honor of Secretary of State George C. Marshall, would serve to strengthen shaky pro-American governments and ward off the inroads being made by domestic communist parties and other left-wing organizations sympathetic to the Soviet Union. U.S. undersecretary of state Dean G. Acheson, who helped formulate the plan, argued that American foreign policy had to harness American economic and financial resources to preserve democratic institutions and to expand capitalism abroad. He also saw the Marshall Plan as necessary for long-term national security. Thus, the plan emerged as an all-embracing effort to revive the economies of Western Europe. The plan was unprecedented in terms of the massive commitment of American dollars, resources, and international involvement.

First formally proposed by Secretary of State Marshall on June 5, 1947, in a speech at Harvard University, the plan applied to all of Europe. Aid was not directed against communism specifically, but directed toward the elimination of dangerous economic conditions across all of Europe. Accordingly, the United States controversially planned to reconstruct Germany as an industrial power. Marshall had concluded that German resources, manpower, expertise, and production were absolutely essential to European recovery. For success, the plan had to allow full German participation but at the same time prevent German industrial power from becoming a future threat to peace.

Additionally complicating matters was Marshall's belief that the objective of the Soviet Union was to delay European economic recovery and therefore exploit the consequent misery and political instability. Yet Marshall did not want his nation to assume the responsibility for permanently dividing Europe. Thus, to avoid having the plan viewed as anti-Soviet, he invited the Soviet Union and its East European satellite states to participate in implementation of the plan. Nations eligible to receive economic assistance would be defined by those countries that were willing to cooperate fully with the American proposal. All the while, U.S. policymakers fully counted on Moscow's rejection.

President Harry S. Truman believed that the United States should not unilaterally devise a plan for recovery and force it on the Europeans. Instead, the particular aid initiatives came from the Europeans and represented not a series of individual requests but rather a joint undertaking by all of the countries in need of American assistance. In other words, the Americans wanted a lasting

cure for Europe's problem rather than a mere quick fix. America's role would be to assist in the drafting of a program and to support that program with American resources.

The Soviet Union together with Poland, Czechoslovakia, France, Great Britain, and 12 other European nations gathered at the first planning conference, convened in Paris on June 27, 1947. Soviet foreign minister Vyacheslav Molotov demanded that each country be allowed to fashion its own plan and present it to the United States. Georges Bidault and Ernest Bevin, the foreign ministers of France and Britain, respectively, opposed Molotov. Bidault and Bevin, in line with American wishes, stressed that the Marshall Plan had to be a continent-wide program in order to take advantage of the economies of the continent as a whole, or, seen in another light, to take advantage of the economies of scale rendered only through a jointly administered effort. As the United States had predicted, the Soviets quickly withdrew, denouncing the plan as an imperialist, anti-Soviet tool. Molotov warned that if Germany were to be revived, then the continent would be divided. Poland, Czechoslovakia, Hungary, and Romania still expressed interest in the Marshall Plan, but the Soviet Union pressured them into withdrawing.

The Soviets left Paris chiefly because participation in the plan would have required the disclosure of extensive statistical information about the Soviet Union's financial condition and also would have given the Americans some control over Russia's internal budget. Additionally, George Kennan, father of the U.S. containment policy and director of the State Department's policy planning staff, had earlier made it clear that aid would not be advanced to nations that refused to open their economies to U.S. exports. These requirements were unacceptable to the Soviets, as Kennan realized.

The Soviets kept their finances a well-guarded secret and set about weakening the Marshall Plan. They formed the Cominform on July 6, 1947, to help coordinate international propaganda aimed at torpedoing the plan. On July 12, 1947, the Soviet Union negotiated trade agreements with its communist satellites that diverted a substantial amount of trade from Western Europe to Eastern Europe. Finally, later that year, the Soviets proposed the Molotov Plan for East European recovery as an alternative to the Marshall Plan.

Lengthy negotiations thus ensued without the Soviets or their client states. Participating nations laid the groundwork for the recovery plans and requested $28 billion to be spent over the course of four years. On March 15, 1948, the U.S. Senate endorsed the plan by a 69–17 vote after the House had approved it by a 329–74 margin, but only allocated $17 billion in aid. The Marshall Plan passed despite growing conservative objections to international agreements. The communist-led overthrow of the Czechoslovakian government and the Soviet Union's badgering of Finland for military bases had apparently convinced U.S. legislators of the seriousness of the Soviet threat.

When the plans were finalized, the United States created the Economic Cooperation Administration (ECA) and named Paul Hoffman as its head. The ECA made the ultimate determination of specific aid and projects to be undertaken. The fundamental way in which the Marshall Plan contributed to increased European productivity was by furnishing capital, food, raw materials, and machinery that would have been unavailable without American help. The ECA made U.S. funds available to foreign governments to buy goods that were primarily obtained from their own private agricultural and industrial producers. The ECA also authorized purchases in other countries, especially Canada

and Latin America. These policies also helped to reduce excessive demand on raw materials in the United States, thereby protecting the U.S. economy from inflationary pressures. The plan additionally benefited non-European countries and contributed to the development of multilateral trade. Recipients of the largest amounts of aid were Britain, France, Italy, the Federal Republic of Germany (FRG, West Germany), and the Netherlands.

Participating European governments sold American-financed goods to their own people. The payments received were placed in special funds that were employed where they could best serve economic recovery and ensure financial stability. Italy used its funds for public works projects, such as replacing bombed-out bridges. The British reduced government debt to check inflation.

During 1948–1952, approximately $13.5 billion in Marshall Plan aid went to the revitalization of Western Europe and guided it onto the path of long-term economic growth and integration. By 1950, industrial production in Marshall Plan countries was 25 percent higher than 1938 levels, while agricultural output had risen 14 percent from the prewar level. The volume of intra-European trade among Marshall Plan beneficiaries increased dramatically, while the balance-of-payments gap dropped significantly. Britain had sufficiently recovered by January 1951 so that Marshall Plan aid was suspended at that time, a full year and a half before the scheduled termination of the program. It should be noted, however, that the onset of the Korean War in June 1950 and the autumn 1950 decision to deploy American troops to Western Europe to bolster North Atlantic Treaty Organization (NATO) defenses also contributed to increased European productivity.

The Marshall Plan also advanced European unification and integration. The Americans sought a single large market in which quantitative restrictions on the movement of goods, monetary barriers, and trade tariffs had been largely eliminated. The creation of an integrated free market modeled after the United States would encourage the growth of consumer demand and large-scale industry. It would also permit more efficient use of materials and labor while stimulating competition. The West Europeans removed a number of economic barriers and established subregional agreements such as the European Coal and Steel Community (ECSC). The success of the Marshall Plan ultimately paved the way for the establishment of the Common Market in 1958.

The Marshall Plan did not cure all of Europe's problems. Productivity advanced considerably but leveled off by 1952, the last year of the plan. Europe's dollar gap had also begun to widen. The Korean War and concomitant rearmament program diverted resources and manpower to defense production, thereby creating scarcities of certain commodities. As a result, inflation became problematic.

The intensification of the Cold War and the onset of the Korean War hastened the end of the Marshall Plan. The Mutual Security Act of 1951, signed in the wake of the Korean War, provided a new strategy for European recovery that largely superseded the Marshall Plan. The act made military security rather than economic self-reliance the major objective of American policy in Western Europe. Aid recipients had to sign new agreements assuring the fulfillment of military obligations and promising to maintain European defensive strength. The ECA was abolished in favor of a Mutual Security Agency that was responsible for supervising and coordinating all foreign aid programs— military, technical, and economic.

Caryn E. Neumann

Further Reading

Gimbel, John. *The Origins of the Marshall Plan*. Stanford, CA: Stanford University Press, 1976.

Hoffmann, Stanley, and Charles Maier, eds. *The Marshall Plan: A Retrospective*. Boulder, CO: Westview, 1984.

Hogan, Michael J. *The Marshall Plan: America, Britain, and the Reconstruction of Western Europe, 1948–1952*. New York: Cambridge University Press, 1987.

Mayne, Richard. *The Recovery of Europe: From Devastation to Unity*. London: Weidenfeld and Nicolson, 1970.

Milward, Alan S. *The Reconstruction of Western Europe, 1945–51*. Berkeley: University of California Press, 1984.

McCarthyism

McCarthyism refers to an era of intense anticommunist sentiment, sometimes referred to as the Second Red Scare, that dominated American politics and society, resulting in civil liberty encroachments and widespread paranoia. As the Cold War settled in during the late 1940s, Americans became increasingly concerned with the perceived communist threat at home. President Harry Truman initiated his Loyalty Program in 1947, aimed at rooting out communists from the federal government. Politicians in both major parties began vying with one another in an attempt to prove their patriotism and anticommunist mettle. Senator Joseph R. McCarthy, a Wisconsin Republican looking for a political opportunity and instant fame, seized the moment and turned the politics of anticommunism into a high art form, in the process becoming one of the nation's most notorious demagogues. McCarthy did not begin the Second Red Scare, but his name became synonymous with it, and his actions coarsened political discourse, cheapened basic constitutional freedoms, and ruined the careers of many innocent individuals. McCarthyism began in earnest in 1950 and ended in 1954, when McCarthy was finally censured for his reckless activities.

McCarthy, who won election to national office in 1946, had experienced a most uninspiring career in the Senate. Facing the potential prospect of losing his seat in the 1952 elections, he decided to take advantage of the anticommunist atmosphere. Thus, during a February 1950 speech in Wheeling, West Virginia, he claimed—quite dramatically—that he held in his hand a list of 205 communists working in the State Department. This captured the immediate attention of the American press, which gave McCarthy wide coverage, and he soon became a household name.

By employing what one historian has termed "multiple untruths," McCarthy's mostly bogus claims went largely unquestioned by the press and even by his own political colleagues. He gained the most notoriety through his myriad hearings, during which he accused hundreds of writers, actors, teachers, scholars, and others of having communist sympathies. The outbreak of the Korean War in June 1950 added immense fuel to the fires of McCarthyism. Indeed, it is difficult to imagine McCarthy's enormous popularity had the war not occurred. His antics created a supercharged atmosphere of paranoia and hysteria seldom seen in American society.

For a time, McCarthy was so powerful and so feared that few people seriously scrutinized his allegations or the corrosive results of his hearings, some of which were conducted through the House Un-American Activities Committee (HUAC), although the vast majority were conducted on his own via a Senate subcommittee. By bombarding witnesses with vast amounts of conflicting, unsubstantiated, and ever-changing information, McCarthy evaded serious challenges to his credibility. His clever use of "multiple untruths" combined with his courtship of the American press made it nearly impossible to pin him down on any particular allegation, although in retrospect it may be said that almost none of his charges resulted in the discovery of the "vast communist conspiracy" that he claimed resided in the top echelons of government. McCarthy's accusations resulted in the blacklisting of a host of Hollywood actors and screenwriters, as most studios feared the repercussions of the senator's indictments. In 1952, McCarthyism had become so entrenched that when the senator implied that General George C. Marshall, chief of staff of the U.S. Army in World War II and an icon of that conflict, had ties to communism, nobody, including General Dwight D. Eisenhower, publicly rebuked McCarthy for such a patently absurd accusation.

The age of McCarthyism had serious ramifications and enormous reach. For example, when a group of teachers in New York came under fire for their alleged "communist leanings," the U.S. Supreme Court upheld the McCarthyites' attacks in *Adler et al. v. Board of Education of the City of New York*. Reviewing the case in 1952, the Court ruled that schoolteachers did not have the right to work on their own terms and that past and present associations were relevant because of teachers' responsibility for shaping the minds of their students. McCarthyism also had a devastating impact on the State Department. McCarthy's accusations against the department's Asian experts left a void in the department's ability to correctly analyze developments in East and Southeast Asia.

In 1954, during the nationally televised Army-McCarthy Hearings in which the Wisconsin demagogue tried to claim communist subversion in the U.S. Army, the subterfuge of McCarthyism was finally laid bare. McCarthy's bizarre allegations, bullying

Wisconsin senator Joseph McCarthy delivers a televised speech in 1953. (Library of Congress)

of witnesses, and generally boorish behavior shocked many Americans. The national press finally undermined the senator's credibility, while the reputation and gravitas of the U.S. Senate was seriously undermined. After the hearings were suspended, McCarthy was formally censured by his Senate colleagues and stripped of his committee assignments. The fall of McCarthy in 1954 was as spectacular as his rise, but the long shadows of McCarthyism would not be soon forgotten. Many of McCarthy's victims never did revive their ruined careers, and the McCarthy era serves as a cautionary tale of how intolerance mixed with fear-mongering can chisel away at the most basic of constitutional rights.

Valerie Adams and Paul G. Pierpaoli Jr.

Further Reading

Fried, Richard M. *Nightmare in Red: The McCarthy Era in Perspective.* New York: Oxford University Press, 1990.

Reeves, Thomas C. *The Life and Times of Joe McCarthy.* 1980. Reprint, Lanham, MD: Madison Books, 1997.

Schrecker, Ellen. *Many Are the Crimes: McCarthyism in America.* Princeton, NJ: Princeton University Press, 1998.

Missiles, Intercontinental Ballistic

The intercontinental ballistic missiles (ICBMs) deployed by the United States and the Soviet Union during the Cold War, along with the manned bomber and submarine-launched ballistic missiles (SLBMs), made up the strategic nuclear triad of these two superpowers. China later also developed ICBMs.

The land-based ICBMs offered survivability and quick delivery of nuclear weapons over long distances. Throughout the Cold War, the accuracy, reliability, and flexibility of ICBM systems continuously improved. At the peak of the Cold War in 1984, the United States maintained 1,054 ICBMs deployed in underground silos, while the Soviets possessed 1,398 ICBMs deployed in silos and in rail and road-mobile systems.

Development of the ICBM began shortly after the end of World War II. ICBMs are normally defined as long-range missiles that can attack targets located great distances from their launch sites. In 1966, the Air University Aerospace Glossary defined ICBMs as those missiles with a range of 5,000 miles or more. Other sources have defined the ICBM as a missile with a range of 1,500–2,000 miles. The ICBMs deployed during the Cold War were configured with nuclear warheads.

Initial missile programs, especially in the United States, focused more on air-breathing, jet-powered cruise missiles than on ballistic systems. By the late 1940s, however, both the United States and the Soviet Union had determined that ballistic missiles were better for long-range attack missions because flight times, survivability, and accuracy were much better than they were for slower, aerodynamic vehicles. By 1953, the development of smaller, lighter thermonuclear weapons made it possible to construct long-range missiles capable of delivering nuclear payloads. The earliest systems were complicated liquid-fueled missiles that employed liquid oxygen and kerosene or storable hypergolic chemicals (fuel and oxidizer that ignited and burned when mixed without a separate igniter) as propellants. The first versions were deployed on soft, above-ground launchers that required anywhere from 15 minutes to several hours to prepare for launch. They were guided by ground-based radio guidance systems that limited the number of missiles that could be launched at a single time. The first U.S. operational ICBM system, the Atlas D, was a 75-foot-long missile weighing more than 250,000 pounds. It was housed in either above-ground gantries or ground-level concrete structures, known as coffins, with three missiles and one guidance system at each complex. The first American ICBM attained nuclear alert (ready) status in October 1959.

Inertial guidance systems replaced the radio systems early in the life of ICBMs, with only the Atlas D and Titan I deployed with radio guidance. The inertial system was

Launch of an Atlas missile from the U.S. Air Force Missile Test Center, Cape Canaveral, Florida on February 20, 1958. (U.S. Air Force)

more accurate and reliable than radio guidance and allowed missiles to be based individually, providing a higher survivability scenario during a nuclear exchange. The early U.S. liquid-fueled cryogenic missiles were expensive to maintain, had low reliability, and were not exceptionally accurate. These systems, the Atlas and Titan I, carried single four-megaton nuclear warheads. The United States was quick to replace these missiles with the solid-fueled Minuteman missile, and by 1965 all Atlas and Titan I missiles were removed from service, to be replaced by the Minuteman and the hypergolic-fueled Titan II.

These new systems were easier to maintain and required far fewer missile combat crew members and maintenance personnel to keep them on alert. They were also much more survivable, with hardened silos scattered over wide areas, and were accurate to within a few hundred feet of the target. The United States maintained a force of 54 Titan II missiles, each with a nine-megaton warhead, on alert from the early 1960s to the mid-1980s. The Minuteman, which was developed in three versions (I, II, and III), first came on alert in 1962.

By 1967, 1,000 Minuteman missiles were on alert at six U.S. bases. The Minuteman I and II had single warheads of about 1.1 megatons, while the Minuteman III featured a multiple independently targeted reentry vehicle (MIRV) system equipped with up to three warheads of either 170 or 340 kilotons of yield. The entire force of Minuteman and Titan II missiles could be launched in a matter of minutes after the decision to execute was made. In the late 1980s, 50 Minuteman missiles at F.E. Warren Air Force Base, Wyoming, were replaced by 50 Peacekeeper missiles, a larger system that could carry up to 10 300-kiloton warheads capable of hitting 10 different targets.

The Soviets developed more varieties of missiles than did the Americans, early on relying on both cryogenic and hypergolic storable propellant systems. As with the United States, the Soviet Union quickly realized that the cryogenic systems were slow to launch and hard to maintain, but, unlike the United States, Russia concentrated on ICBM designs in the 1960s through the 1980s that featured storable liquid-fueled systems, with missiles deployed both in underground silos and in mobile launchers. The first Soviet ICBM, the SS-7 (known to the Soviets as R-16), employed storable propellants and was first put on alert on November 1, 1961.

The Soviets were slower to adopt solid-fueled ICBMs but eventually replaced their second- and third-generation liquid-fueled missiles with systems similar to the Minuteman and Peacekeeper systems. Soviet warheads were generally in the 1-megaton range, but two Soviet ICBMs (the SS-9 and SS-18) carried enormous 25-megaton warheads. In 1984, at the peak of the Cold War, the Soviets had 1,398 ICBMs deployed, including 520 SS-11s, 60 SS-13s, 150 SS-17s, 308 SS-18s, and 360 SS-19s.

China tested its first missile in 1960 but did not complete development and testing of an ICBM until 1980. China's first ICBM was liquid-fueled. China did not develop a solid-fueled ICBM until the early 1990s. Compared to the United States and the Soviet Union, the Chinese have maintained a very small ICBM force, with most of the emphasis on countering the threat posed by the Soviet Union rather than any threat by the United States.

Strategic arms limitation and reduction agreements between the United States and Russia resulted in a significant reduction in the number of ICBMs. The United States reduced its force to only 500 Minuteman III missiles, which will eventually have only one warhead apiece. All Minuteman II missiles were removed and the silos destroyed at three bases between 1994 and 1998, and Peacekeeper missiles were removed between 2002 and 2007. At the end of 2002, the Russians maintained a force of 709 ICBMs, a mix of SS-18, SS-19, SS-24, SS-25, and SS-27 liquid- and solid-fueled missiles in silos or mobile launchers.

Charles G. Simpson

Further Reading

Gibson, James N. *Nuclear Weapons of the United States: An Illustrated History.* Atglen, PA: Schiffer, 1996.

Levi, Barbara G., et al., eds. *The Future of Land Based Ballistic Missiles.* New York: American Institute of Physics, 1989.

Neufeld, Jacob. *The Development of Ballistic Missiles in the United States Air Force, 1945–1960.* Washington, DC: Office of Air Force History, 1989.

Moscow Meeting, Brezhnev and Nixon (May 22–30, 1972)

The summit meeting between U.S. president Richard Nixon and Soviet leader Leonid Brezhnev, May 22–30, 1972, marked a historic turning point in U.S.–Soviet relations. It was the first presidential visit to the Soviet Union since the presidency of Franklin D. Roosevelt. Nixon's nine-day summit meeting with Brezhnev solidified the superpower détente, underway since the late 1960s. Among the numerous agreements signed during the summit, the most important were the Treaty on the Limitation of Anti-Ballistic Missile Systems (ABM Treaty) and the accompanying Interim Agreement on Certain Measures with Respect to the Limitation of Strategic Offensive Weapons (Strategic Arms Limitation Agreement, SALT I Interim Agreement).

These agreements completed the first stages of the larger SALT discussions.

Crucial to understanding the nature of the Moscow summit is the international situation in which it occurred. In the early 1970s, relations between the United States and the Soviet Union improved dramatically because of the relaxation of tensions in Europe in the aftermath of the Soviet suppression of the 1968 Prague Spring in Czechoslovakia. In the spirit of détente, the Nixon administration embarked on a policy of multilateral disarmament agreements, such as the 1971 signing of the Seabed Treaty. Détente ultimately served not only U.S. interests but also Soviet security interests. Despite relaxed tensions in Europe, Asian events might have had a damaging effect on American–Soviet relations. The 1971 India-Pakistan War and the Vietnam War were additional irritants. To the Soviets, détente outweighed these concerns, and a secret trip to Moscow by Nixon's national security advisor, Henry Kissinger, in April 1972 finalized the summit plans.

In addition to the fruitful Moscow discussions and daily signatures of agreements between the conferees, Nixon made trips to Leningrad and Kiev and gave a live radio-television address to the Soviet people. His address highlighted the shared historical struggles of the two nations and reiterated their mutual responsibilities as global superpowers. During the summit, Nixon and Brezhnev discussed the status of the international community and a plethora of bilateral issues in hopes of continuing and furthering détente despite the differing ideologies of the two superpowers. The two leaders agreed that smaller third-party states should not interfere with maintaining détente. Bilateral negotiations included the limitation of strategic armaments; commercial and economic agreements; cooperation in health issues; environmental cooperation; scientific, educational, and cultural cooperation and exchanges; and cooperation in space exploration. The results of these negotiations provided the necessary framework for a joint space venture in 1975, large U.S. grain sales to the Soviets, and, most importantly, the SALT agreements.

The majority of the summit concentrated on the SALT agreements. The Nixon administration had inherited a legacy of outdated doctrines pertaining to U.S. nuclear strategy. The antiquated policy of maintaining nuclear superiority over the USSR was no longer practical. Through détente it was now possible to conduct negotiations limiting the growth of the superpower nuclear arsenals. In a first step toward the realization of SALT, on May 26 Nixon and Brezhnev signed the ABM Treaty and Interim Agreement. The ABM Treaty limited the deployment of antiballistic missiles for each nation to two sites. The SALT Interim Agreement froze the number of intercontinental ballistic missiles (ICBMs) possessed by each country.

In a move to reaffirm both American and Soviet commitments to détente, the two powers signed the Basic Principles of Mutual Relations between the United States of America and the Union of Soviet Socialist Republics. This document contained 12 principles and served to encapsulate the

General Secretary Leonid Brezhnev of the Soviet Union (left) and President Richard Nixon (right) shake hands in Moscow during talks regarding the Anti-Ballistic Missile Treaty of 1972. The treaty was the first significant arms limitation treaty between the United States and the Soviet Union. (National Archives)

spirit of the Moscow summit and the evolving superpower détente. Some of the more important principles included the notion of peaceful coexistence and the promise of future summit meetings.

Jonathan H. L'Hommedieu

Further Reading

Loth, Wilfried. *Overcoming the Cold War: A History of Détente, 1950–1991.* Translated by Robert F. Hogg. New York: Palgrave, 2002.

Stebbins, Richard B., and Elaine P. Adams, eds. *American Foreign Relations 1972: A Documentary Record.* New York: New York University Press, 1976.

Stevenson, Richard William. *The Rise and Fall of Détente: Relaxations of Tensions in US-Soviet Relations, 1953–1984.* Urbana: University of Illinois Press, 1985.

Mutual Assured Destruction

The doctrine of mutual assured destruction (MAD) was an important part of the Cold War beginning in the 1960s, and is cited as one of the main reasons that there was no direct military confrontation between the United States and the Soviet Union. The doctrine was founded on nuclear deterrence and based on the premise that both superpowers had enough nuclear weapons to destroy each other many times over. Thus, if one superpower launched a nuclear first strike, the other would launch a massive counterstrike, resulting in the total devastation of both nations.

President Dwight D. Eisenhower's administration in the mid-1950s warned that if the United States were attacked first it would

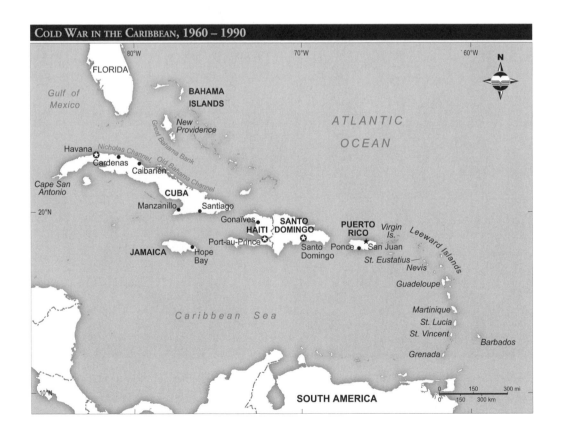

COLD WAR IN THE CARIBBEAN, 1960 – 1990

unleash massive retaliation. Thus, the MAD doctrine was born in the 1950s but did not reach fruition until the 1960s, when the Soviets achieved rough nuclear parity with the United States. Through the years, technological advances were constantly molding the doctrine. The U.S. deployment of submarine-launched ballistic missiles (SLBMs) in the early 1960s ensured a second-strike capability, thus further deterring the likelihood of a first strike.

The doctrine propagated the notion that each side had equal nuclear firepower and that if an attack occurred, retaliation would be equal to or greater than the initial attack. It followed that neither nation would launch a first strike because its adversary could guarantee an immediate, automatic, and overwhelming response consisting of a launch on warning, also known as a fail deadly. The final result would be the destruction of both sides. The end reasoning of MAD was that it contributed to a relatively stable peace.

The MAD doctrine survived into the 1970s and ironically contributed to the nuclear arms race. Each side tried to outwit and out produce the other, as the example of the introduction of multiple independently targeted reentry vehicles (MIRVs) demonstrates. MIRVs came on-line in the early 1970s and upped the ante of nuclear deterrence by placing multiple warheads on a single missile. The justification for this and other technological enhancements was that the more missiles produced, the less chance there would be of an intentional nuclear attack.

The MAD doctrine became essentially obsolete on July 25, 1980, when President Jimmy Carter adopted the so-called countervailing strategy by reorienting U.S. policy to win a nuclear war. This was to be achieved by attacking and destroying the Soviet leadership and its military installations. It was

A time exposure of eight Peacekeeper (LGM-118A) intercontinental ballistic missile reentry vehicles passing through clouds while approaching an open-ocean impact zone during a flight test, December 20, 1983. (Department of Defense)

assumed that such an attack would precipitate a Soviet surrender, thereby preventing the total destruction of the United States and the Soviet Union. This policy was taken even further by President Ronald Reagan, who proposed the Strategic Defense Initiative (SDI) in 1983. This was a system that would purportedly form a protective umbrella over the United States by destroying incoming nuclear missiles before they reached their targets. SDI has yet to be implemented, however, and many of its critics argue that there is no current technology available to make it a safe and reliable nuclear deterrent.

Regardless of the variety of opinions about MAD, the potential of nuclear holocaust tremendously influenced political leaders and their military advisers during the Cold War.

Dewi I. Ball

Further Reading

Glaser, Charles L. *Analyzing Strategic Nuclear Policy*. Princeton, NJ: Princeton University Press, 1990.

Lebow, Richard N., and Janice G. Stein. *We All Lost the Cold War*. Princeton, NJ: Princeton University Press, 1994.

Partos, Gabriel. *The World That Came in from the Cold: Perspectives from East and West on the Cold War*. London: Royal Institute of International Affairs, BBC World Service, 1993.

N

National Security Act
(July 26, 1947)

The National Security Act, signed into law on July 26, 1947, was a critical step in preparing America to wage the deepening Cold War. Its legislation made sweeping organizational changes in U.S. military and foreign policy establishments. Specifically, the act created the National Security Council (NSC), National Security Resources Board (NSRB), Central Intelligence Agency (CIA), Department of Defense (DOD), Joint Chiefs of Staff (JCS), and U.S. Air Force (the third branch of the U.S. armed forces). Congress amended the act in 1949 to provide the secretary of defense with more power over the individual armed services and their secretaries.

Soon after World War II ended, the uneasy alliance between the United States and the Soviet Union began to degenerate, and a long-standing ideological and military confrontation between the two superpowers quickly set in. By late 1946, the Truman administration had adopted a defense policy that became known as *containment*. This policy sought to contain Soviet influence and the spread of communism throughout the world. It was this mind-set that prompted passage of the National Security Act.

By the end of 1947, the containment policy had elicited both the enunciation of the Truman Doctrine and the implementation of the Marshall Plan. The National Security Act was an effort to add a domestic component to containment and to help coordinate U.S. diplomatic and military commitments to meet the challenges of the Cold War. The act was designed to centralize the military services under the single banner of the DOD (directed by the secretary of defense, a new cabinet-level position) to provide one main intelligence apparatus in the new CIA, and to provide foreign policy advice directly to the president via the NSC, which resided within the Executive Office of the president. The JCS, composed of a representative from each of the armed services, was to act as a military advisory group to the president and his civilian advisors.

The CIA emerged from the World War II Office of Strategic Services (OSS) and smaller postwar intelligence operations. Its first director was Rear Admiral Roscoe Hillenkoetter. The existing War and Navy Departments were folded into the DOD, whose first secretary was James V. Forrestal. The new U.S. Air Force, which became a free-standing entity, was built from the existing U.S. Army Air Corps. The NSC's chief role was to coordinate and prioritize information it received from other agencies and to advise the president on national security issues based on analysis of that information. At the time, there was no provision made for a national security advisor, a post that came into being under President Dwight D. Eisenhower in 1953. Taken in its totality, the National Security Act provided for a powerful, well-coordinated system that linked national security with foreign policy and military decision making.

Bevan Sewell

Further Reading

Hogan, Michael J. *A Cross of Iron: Harry S. Truman and the Origins of the National*

Security State, 1945–1954. New York: Cambridge University Press, 1998.

Leffler, Melvyn P. *A Preponderance of Power: National Security, the Truman Administration, and the Cold War*. Stanford, CA: Stanford University Press, 1992.

U.S. Department of State. *Foreign Relations of the United States, 1945–1950: Emergence of the Intelligence Establishment*. Washington, DC: U.S. Government Printing Office, 1996.

National Security Agency

The National Security Agency (NSA) is the highly secretive component of the U.S. intelligence community that specializes in cryptography and signals intelligence (SIGINT). Established on November 4, 1952, by President Harry S. Truman in the wake of a series of intelligence lapses regarding the Korean War, the NSA served as the U.S. government's primary technical intelligence-collection organization throughout the Cold War.

The United States was renowned for its success in the realm of SIGINT (the gathering and analysis of intercepted voice communications intelligence, or COMINT) and electromagnetic radiation (electronic intelligence, or ELINT) during World War II. Yet the Americans entered the early years of the Cold War with a disorganized SIGINT apparatus loosely coordinated among the independent and oftentimes redundant cryptologic agencies of the Army, Navy, and Air Force. In line with the centralizing theme of the 1947 National Security Act, Secretary of Defense Louis A. Johnson established the Armed Forces Security Agency (AFSA) in 1949 to streamline SIGINT collection. Plagued by the weaknesses of limited jurisdiction and ill-defined authority, however, deficiencies in AFSA's relationship with the service agencies were made readily apparent prior to and during the outbreak of the Korean War in June 1950.

At the urging of President Truman, Secretary of State Dean Acheson appointed New York attorney George Abbott Brownell to head a probe investigating AFSA's failings. The resultant "Brownell Committee Report" advocated replacing AFSA with a centralized national agency capable of unifying all U.S. SIGINT efforts. Fully agreeing with this recommendation, within months President Truman dissolved the AFSA and quietly signed into law the NSA.

Throughout the 1950s and early 1960s, the NSA established itself as a key intelligence player in virtually all major Cold War political and military conflicts. In 1953 the NSA began overflights of Soviet airspace using converted B-47 Stratojets equipped with various receivers capable of intercepting Soviet air defense radar signals. By intentionally triggering the activation of the Soviet air defense radar system, the B-47s could pinpoint and map the locations of Soviet systems on the ground, providing crucial information for U.S. pilots. By the late 1950s, the Stratojets had been replaced by the high-flying U-2 reconnaissance jet, and overflights to collect Soviet SIGINT data continued, focusing on radar emissions and telemetry information related to intercontinental ballistic missile (ICBM) launches. The overflight program ended suddenly amid an international crisis when, on May 1, 1960, U-2 pilot Francis Gary Powers was shot down over the central Soviet city of Sverdlovsk. Initially disavowing any knowledge of the overflight program, the Eisenhower administration was forced to concede that it had ordered the flights when faced with irrefutable evidence presented by Soviet Premier Nikita Khrushchev.

Although direct flights over Soviet airspace were terminated in the wake of the

Powers controversy, the NSA maintained a robust collection effort utilizing ground, air, sea, and space-based antennas and sensors to monitor the transmissions of the Eastern bloc as well as nonaligned and allied nations. In an often contentious relationship with the U.S. Navy, NSA listening posts were established on both adapted warships such as the *Liberty* and on smaller dedicated collection platforms such as the *Pueblo,* which loitered in international waters collecting transmissions, while NSA-directed submarines tapped into undersea communication cables. Ground stations concentrating on intercepting shortwave and very high frequency (VHF) emissions were established in strategically important locations around the globe, ranging from Ellesmere Island in the upper reaches of the Arctic Circle to Ayios Nikolaos in Cyprus, to Field Station Berlin in West Berlin, to Misawa Air Force Base in Japan. After the undisclosed launch of the first SIGINT satellite in June 1960, the NSA also began to establish an array of ground-based relay centers in remote locations on the periphery of the Soviet Union.

By the late 1970s the NSA was enjoying great success in decoding the encrypted Soviet messages that had previously eluded the U.S. intelligence community. As the NSA's mission grew, its budget increased exponentially. Exact budgetary figures from the Cold War period continue to be withheld as classified information, but during that time the NSA established itself as the largest U.S. intelligence agency in terms of both manpower and financial resources.

Robert G. Berschinski

Further Reading

Bamford, James. *Body of Secrets: Anatomy of the Ultra-Secret National Security Agency.* New York: Anchor, 2002.

Bamford, James. *The Puzzle Palace: A Report on America's Most Secret Agency.* New York: Penguin, 1983.

Bowie, Robert R., and Richard H. Immerman. *Waging Peace: How Eisenhower Shaped an Enduring Cold War Strategy.* New York: Oxford University Press, 1998.

Johnson, Chalmers. *The Sorrows of Empire: Militarism, Secrecy, and the End of the Republic.* New York: Metropolitan Books, 2004.

Nixon, Richard Milhous (1913–1994)

Born in Yorba Linda, California, on January 9, 1913, Richard Nixon graduated from Duke Law School and then practiced law in Whittier, California, until 1942. During World War II he spent four years in the U.S. Navy, serving in the South Pacific and becoming a lieutenant commander. After demobilization in 1946 he ran successfully for Congress as a Republican and in 1950 for a California Senate seat, races notable for his use of anticommunist smear tactics against his Democratic opponents. In 1952 Dwight D. Eisenhower selected Nixon as his running mate for the presidency, and Nixon spent eight years as vice president, demonstrating particular interest in foreign affairs and traveling extensively. In 1960 he narrowly lost the presidential race to John F. Kennedy. Eight years later Nixon was elected president on the Republican ticket.

As president, Nixon belied his earlier reputation as an uncompromising anticommunist, restructuring the international pattern of U.S. alliances by playing the China card and moving toward recognition of the communist People's Republic of China (PRC) while using the new Sino-American rapprochement to extract concessions on détente and arms control from the Soviet Union. In doing

Richard M. Nixon realized his dream of becoming president in 1969. A strong proponent of opening relations with the People's Republic of China and of détente with the Soviet Union, Nixon was forced to resign the office in August 1974 as a result of the Watergate Scandal. (National Archives)

so, Nixon worked closely with his energetic national security advisor, Henry A. Kissinger, restricting Secretary of State William P. Rogers largely to routine diplomatic business. Kissinger finally replaced Rogers in August 1973.

In 1968 the inability of the United States to achieve victory in the controversial Vietnam War, despite increasingly high deployments of troops, dominated the political agenda. Nixon, promising that he had a plan to end the war expeditiously, won the presidency. He accelerated the program of Vietnamization begun under President Lyndon B. Johnson, gradually withdrawing American troops while providing Republic of Vietnam (RVN, South Vietnam) forces with massive amounts of war supplies intended to enable them to defend themselves. In August 1969 Kissinger embarked on protracted negotiations with the Democratic Republic of Vietnam (DRV, North Vietnam). To win time for Vietnamization, Nixon ordered the secret bombing of Cambodia as well as a ground invasion of that country that helped bring the communist Khmer Rouge to power there later. At Christmas 1972 Nixon ordered a massive bombing campaign against North Vietnam to pressure its leaders to accept a settlement. Some assailed him for winning a peace settlement that effectively assured South Vietnam only a decent interval before a North Vietnam takeover two years later.

American withdrawal from Vietnam was only part of the broader strategic realignment that Nixon and Kissinger termed their Grand Design. The Nixon Doctrine, announced in July 1969, called on American allies to bear the primary burden of their own defense, looking to the United States only for supplementary conventional and, when necessary, nuclear assistance.

Conscious that their country no longer enjoyed the undisputed supremacy of the immediate post–World War II period and that growing economic difficulties mandated cuts in defense budgets, Nixon and Kissinger hoped to negotiate arms limitations agreements with the Soviet Union. To pressure the Soviets, whose relations with communist China had become deeply antagonistic by the early 1960s, Nixon began the process of reopening American relations with China, visiting Beijing in 1972, where he had extended talks with Chinese communist Chairman Mao Zedong and Premier Zhou Enlai, and preparing to de-emphasize the longstanding U.S. commitment to the Republic of China (ROC) on Taiwan and recognize the communist People's Republic of China (PRC) in its stead.

These tactics alarmed Soviet leaders and facilitated a relaxation of Soviet–American tensions, broadly termed détente. At a May 1972 Moscow summit meeting, Nixon and Soviet leader Leonid Brezhnev signed two arms limitations treaties, jointly known as SALT I, that took effect the following October. The Anti-Ballistic Missile (ABM) Treaty limited antiballistic missile defense sites in each country to two, with neither hosting more than a hundred ABMs. The Interim Agreement froze the number of nuclear warheads possessed by each side for five years. Détente did not mean the end of Soviet-American rivalry, however.

After winning a second presidential victory in 1972, Nixon hoped to move toward full recognition of the PRC and further arms control agreements. The outbreak of the Yom Kippur War in October 1973, however, diverted his administration's attention from these plans. The war precipitated an Arab oil embargo on Western states that followed pro-Israeli policies, contributing to an international spiral of skyrocketing inflation and high unemployment that afflicted the United States and Western Europe throughout the 1970s.

Presidential summit meetings with Brezhnev at Moscow and Yalta in June–July 1974 brought no immediate results, in large part due to Nixon's own calamitous domestic problems, even though they set the stage for the Helsinki Accords and additional arms control agreements under Nixon's successor, Gerald Ford. The Watergate political scandal, which led to Nixon's resignation in August 1974, aborted all his ambitions for further progress in overseas affairs.

Nixon devoted his final two decades to writing his memoirs and numerous other books and essays on international affairs, part of a broader and reasonably successful campaign to engineer his political rehabilitation and to win respect from contemporaries and a place in history for his presidential achievements and foreign policy expertise. In Nixon's final years, several presidents, including Ronald Reagan, George H. W. Bush, and William Jefferson Clinton, sought his insights on various international subjects, especially relations with the PRC and the Soviet Union. Nixon died in New York City on April 22, 1994.

Priscilla Roberts

Further Reading

Bundy, William. *A Tangled Web: The Making of Foreign Policy in the Nixon Presidency.* New York: Hill and Wang, 1998.

Burr, Willliam, ed. *The Kissinger Transcripts: The Top-Secret Talks with Beijing and Moscow.* New York: New Press, 1998.

Garthoff, Raymond L. *Détente and Confrontation: American-Soviet Relations from Nixon to Reagan.* Rev. ed. Washington, DC: Brookings Institution Press, 1994.

Greene, John Robert. *The Limits of Power: The Nixon and Ford Administrations.* Bloomington: Indiana University Press, 1992.

Hoff, Joan. *Nixon Reconsidered.* New York: Basic Books, 1994.

Kimball, Jeffrey. *Nixon's Vietnam War.* Lawrence: University Press of Kansas, 1998.

Litwak, Robert S. *Détente and the Nixon Doctrine: American Foreign Policy and the Pursuit of Stability, 1969–1976.* Cambridge: Cambridge University Press, 1984.

Nixon, Richard. *RN: The Memoirs of Richard Nixon.* New York: Grosset and Dunlap, 1978.

Non-Aligned Movement

The Non-Aligned Movement (NAM) was a loose association of nations opposed to Cold

War entanglements, which sought to create a third force between the Communist bloc and the Western bloc. It originally comprised 24 Afro-Asian countries plus Yugoslavia. It held its first summit in Belgrade in September 1961. From the outset, NAM embraced issues theoretically unrelated to the Cold War, including anticolonialism, antiracism, economic development, and, under the Arab states' influence, anti-Zionism. To date there have been 13 summits at approximately three-year intervals. In 2003, the movement had 116 members. Mutual interests in protecting state sovereignty and promoting development account for its expanding membership and durability.

Before NAM's foundation, Indonesian leader Sukarno's Asian-African Conference at Bandung in April 1955 demonstrated the value of small-state collaboration. Indian prime minister Jawaharlal Nehru's vaguely worded *Panch Sheel* (five principles of peace), which formed the basis for Sino-Indian relations and was popularized at Bandung, anticipated NAM principles by stressing mutual respect, preservation of state sovereignty, and peaceful coexistence. In the five years before the Belgrade conference, the founding countries—India, Yugoslavia, and Egypt—took exception to Great Power interference in weaker countries' affairs and to the superpowers' unwillingness to reduce nuclear tensions.

The simultaneous Suez Crisis and Hungarian Revolution of 1956 drew together Nehru, Yugoslavian marshal Josip Broz Tito, and Egyptian president Gamal Abdel Nasser. Although their politics were dissimilar, they shared concerns about the Cold War, decolonization, and national independence. The emergence of 16 African states in 1960, the intensification of South African apartheid, the worsening U.S.–Soviet relations, the Congo Intervention, the U.S.-sponsored Bay of Pigs incursion (1961), and the Second Berlin Crisis furnished the first summit's historical context.

The NAM's organizational meeting, which took place in Cairo in June 1961, confined membership to countries that rejected participation in what were termed "Great Power conflicts" or signaled their intention of eventually departing from them. Countries that did not fully meet these criteria could nevertheless be invited as observers. The Algerian provisional government's invitation as a full member, one year before that country's independence, underscored NAM's commitment to anticolonialism. Subsequent summits conferred diplomatic recognition on the Angolan provisional government, the Palestine Liberation Organization (PLO), the Zimbabwe African National Union/Zimbabwe African People's Union, the African National Congress (ANC) in South Africa, and the Southwest African People's Organization (SAPO) in Namibia. Members reached agreement by consensus rather than by ballot, a procedure that led to criticism from the United States at later summits.

Forty-seven countries attended the 1964 Cairo summit. NAM invited all members of the new Organization of African Unity (OAU) because its 1963 charter adopted nonalignment. Under Nasser, NAM called for a Palestinian homeland three years before the PLO's foundation. Cairo was also significant for what was ignored: in October and November 1962, the PRC invaded India. At Cairo, the Chinese invasion was not mentioned because many members wished to cultivate good relations with the PRC. The selective treatment of security issues where members' national interests were at stake typified this and subsequent meetings

Unlike the Afro-Asian People's Solidarity Organization (AAPSO), NAM was not an adjunct of Soviet foreign policy. Certain members, such as Saudi Arabia, had close U.S. ties, whereas others, such as Yugoslavia, feared Soviet interference. The movement nevertheless supported certain Soviet initiatives, such as the call for two special UN disarmament sessions and the establishment of nuclear-free zones. Quick to condemn Western countries' actions deemed to be violating developing-world countries' sovereignty, such as the continuing U.S. naval presence at Guantánamo Bay, Cuba, NAM did not apply this standard to Soviet interventions in Czechoslovakia and Afghanistan.

Although U.S. policymakers in the 1950s decried neutralism as aiding the Soviets, successive U.S. administrations retained strong relations with many uncommitted countries. Presidents Lyndon Johnson and Ronald Reagan issued reminders to the 1964 Cairo and 1983 New Delhi summits that Soviet expansion constituted another form of imperialism. The Soviets anticipated that NAM would facilitate their goal of frustrating Western–developing world alliances and of becoming eventual adherents to the Soviet bloc. A split over North–South issues in the 1970s demonstrated that Soviet and NAM interests were not identical, however.

The Non-Aligned Movement has repeatedly lobbied for economic aid to the developing world. A special NAM meeting in Cairo in 1962 called on the UN to facilitate development, which led in early 1964 to the first UN Conference on Trade and Development (UNCTAD) in Geneva, at which the Group of 77, then the world's poorest countries and including many NAM members, was formed. At the 1973 Algiers conference and afterward, NAM called for a special UN General Assembly session on development. In 1974, the UN passed the New International Economic Order (NIEO), an agenda

that sought increased technical, financial, and agricultural aid for nations in the developing world, to which the Soviets, partly for ideological reasons, showed little sympathy.

Joseph Robert White

Further Reading

Allison, Roy. *The Soviet Union and the Strategy of Non-Alignment in the Third World.* Cambridge: Cambridge University Press, 1988.

Brands, H. W. *The Specter of Neutralism: The United States and the Emergence of the Third World, 1947–1960.* New York: Columbia University Press, 1989.

Kumar, Satish. "Nonalignment: International Goals and National Interests." *Asian Survey* 23, no. 4 (April 1983): 445–62.

Singham, A. W., and Shirley Hune. *Non-Alignment in an Age of Alignments.* Westport, CT: Lawrence Hill, 1986.

Willetts, Peter. *The Non-Aligned Movement: The Origins of a Third World Alliance.* New York: Nichols, 1978.

North American Aerospace Defense Command

The North American Air Defense Command (NORAD) had its origins in the cooperation of the United States and Canada during World War II and a formal agreement on defense collaboration signed in 1947. In 1954, the two countries began developing the Distant Early Warning (DEW) Line across northern Canada and Alaska to provide advanced warning of a Soviet bomber attack across the polar region.

As the DEW Line became operational in August 1957, the United States and Canada reached agreement to create an integrated operational control system for the air defense forces of the two countries. NORAD was thus established in September. Its headquarters was located at Ent Air Force Base in Colorado Springs, while an operations center was constructed in a deep, hardened bunker inside nearby Cheyenne Mountain. Initial operations began in April 1966. The NORAD commander was a U.S. general who also commanded the U.S. Continental Air Defense (CONAD) Command and the U.S. Air Force component, the Air Defense Command (ADC). The deputy commander was a Canadian flag officer.

The NORAD command and control system integrated the full range of air defense capabilities. The early warning system included the northern DEW Line, the Mid-Canada Line, the Pinetree Line, coastal radar sites, Texas Tower radar sites at sea, U.S. Navy picket ships, and U.S. Air Force airborne radar platforms. NORAD directed its active defenses through a series of computerized operations centers that controlled air defense assets for designated regions of the two countries. The system controlled American and Canadian interceptor aircraft and U.S. Army and Air Force surface-to-air missiles (SAMs) dedicated to strategic defense as well as other available resources such as fighter aircraft that could be assigned to air defense in an emergency. As the missile threat evolved, NORAD also became responsible for the Ballistic Missile Early Warning System (BMEWS) and a range of space-tracking systems. Although CONAD was responsible for operational antiballistic missile (ABM) capabilities (the Safeguard system was briefly operational in 1975–1976), the Canadian government declined to become involved in ABM activities.

During the 1970s, the air defense forces assigned to NORAD were significantly reduced, and subordinate command structures were revised, reflecting the increased threat from ballistic missiles and changing national strategies. The strategic SAM sites

The Command Post of the North American Air Defense Command (NORAD) Cheyenne Mountain Complex in April 1984. (Department of Defense)

were phased out, dedicated interceptor units were substantially reduced, and the multiservice CONAD was disbanded, replaced by the Aerospace Defense Command. The Canadian component changed from the Canadian Forces Air Defence Command to the Air Defence Group. The role of NORAD shifted to emphasize warning and attack assessment as well as space surveillance and supporting nuclear deterrence by ensuring that a surprise attack would not destroy U.S. retaliatory forces. In 1979, a major U.S. Air Force reorganization resulted in most ADC operational capabilities being dispersed to the Tactical Air Command and Strategic Air Command (SAC), with the ADC being inactivated in 1981.

The increased role of space in NORAD operations was recognized when the name was changed to the North American Aerospace Defense Command in 1981. As the Cold War ended, NORAD's functions continued to provide the warning and space surveillance missions.

Jerome V. Martin

Further Reading

Collins, John M. *U.S.-Soviet Military Balance: Concepts and Capabilities, 1960–1980.* New York: McGraw-Hill, 1980.

Jockel, Joseph T. *No Boundaries Upstairs: Canada, the United States, and the Origins of North American Air Defense, 1945–1958.* Vancouver: University of British Columbia Press, 1987.

Jockel, Joseph T., and Joel J. Sokolsky, eds. *Fifty Years of Canada-United States Defense Cooperation: The Road from Ogdensburg.* Lewiston, NY: Edwin Mellen, 1992.

Schaffel, Kenneth. *The Emerging Shield: The Air Force and the Evolution of Continental Air Defense, 1945–1960.* Office of Air Force History. Washington, DC: U.S. Government Printing Office, 1990.

North Atlantic Treaty Organization, History of (1948–1990)

Preliminary discussions surrounding an Atlantic treaty among the United States, Canada, and the Brussels Treaty Powers (Belgium, France, Luxembourg, the Netherlands, and Britain) began on July 6, 1948, in Washington, D.C. By the end of October, the framework for a mutual defense pact for the North Atlantic region was agreed upon. Drafting commenced in December 1948, and the final text was made public in March 1949. On March 15, 1949, the United States, Canada, and the Brussels Treaty Powers formally invited Denmark, Iceland, Italy, Norway, and Portugal to join the alliance. These nations all endorsed the North Atlantic Treaty on April 4, 1949, providing the legal basis for the North Atlantic Treaty Organization (NATO). On August 24, 1949, the treaty entered into force, and the first North Atlantic Council (NAC) meeting took place in Washington on September 17.

The first and primary task for the new organization was to put in place an effective and credible apparatus for collective defense. During NATO's first few years, efforts focused primarily on defense-related problems and their economic implications. The political process of cooperation, which was also a component of the alliance, remained largely undefined. In October 1949 President Harry S. Truman signed the Mutual Defense Assistance Act, setting the stage for U.S. involvement in NATO collective security arrangements. In January 1950 he approved plans for the integrated defense of the North Atlantic region and authorized the expenditure of a significant sum of money for military aid.

Other important tasks after NATO's founding were establishing its main organizations and bodies and making them operational. To this end, the NAC appointed U.S. general Dwight D. Eisenhower as the first Supreme Allied Commander Europe (SACEUR) on December 19, 1950. In April 1951, Supreme Headquarters Allied Powers Europe (SHAPE) became operational. Later that year, the NATO Defense College (NDC) was unveiled in Paris. In March 1952, British general Hastings Lionel Ismay was appointed NATO's first secretary-general. A month later, NATO opened its provisional headquarters in Paris and convened the first NAC meeting in permanent session. The first enlargement of the organization also took place in 1952, when Greece and Turkey were invited to join NATO.

Secretary of State Dean Acheson signing the North Atlantic Treaty on behalf of the United States on April 4, 1949. (NATO Photos)

On March 31, 1954, the Soviet Union requested membership in NATO but Britain, France, and the United States vetoed it. The Federal Republic of Germany (FRG, West Germany), on the other hand, was invited to join and became a member in 1955. By the mid-1950s, broad lines of intra-alliance cooperation on defense issues had been defined, and the main institutional bodies had been established. Strengthening the political consultation process and cooperation in non-military areas was identified as the new priority for NATO.

In 1961, NATO members reaffirmed their support of West Berlin, strongly condemning the building of the Berlin Wall, and approved the renewal of diplomatic contacts with the Soviet Union. In the 1962 Athens Guidelines, the circumstances involving the use of nuclear weapons were reviewed. Toward this end, the United States and Britain agreed to contribute and integrate part of their strategic nuclear forces to NATO. In a NATO military exercise (dubbed Operation Big Lift) in 1963, the United States ably demonstrated how quickly it could reinforce NATO forces in Europe in the event of a crisis.

In a move deeply troubling to other NATO states, French president Charles de Gaulle withdrew his nation from the integrated military structure of NATO in 1966. In 1967 the NAC approved the Harmel Report, aimed at reducing East–West tensions by proposing a new military strategy for NATO. NATO's old strategy had required a massive military response to any form of aggression. The new strategic concept of flexible response provided the alliance with myriad options to respond to many types of enemy aggression. In 1968, NATO issued the Declaration on Mutual and Balanced Force Reductions (MBFR), an initiative to work for disarmament and nuclear nonproliferation.

Because of the relentless growth in Warsaw Pact forces, in 1976 the NAC agreed to further strengthen NATO conventional defenses. Unfortunately, this decision interrupted the promising developments in the MBFR process. The 1979 Soviet invasion of Afghanistan also endangered the improvement in East–West relations. The controversial double-track decision made at a special ministerial meeting in 1979 announced the deployment of intermediate-range ballistic missiles (IRBMs) in Europe, to be paralleled by an arms control effort to obviate the need for such deployments.

The first deliveries of IRBM components to Britain in 1983 were the ultimate result of the double-track decision. Deployment of the missiles proved highly controversial and sparked a considerable nuclear freeze movement throughout Western Europe. In response, the Soviet Union suspended negotiations on intermediate nuclear forces reductions. In the mid-1980s, East–West relations began to thaw once again. In 1986 NATO called on the Soviet Union to help promote peace, security, and a productive East–West dialogue. A high-level task force on conventional arms control was established in 1986, and at the end of the year NATO foreign ministers issued the Brussels Declaration on Conventional Arms Control, calling for further negotiations on confidence-building measures and conventional stability. In 1987 the Intermediate-Range Nuclear Forces (INF) Treaty was signed, which eliminated American and Soviet land-based IRBMs.

The forward progress in East–West relations continued throughout 1988. NATO issued a statement on conventional arms control, calling for progress in eliminating conventional force disparities. In December, NATO foreign ministers welcomed Soviet reductions in conventional forces and outlined NATO proposals for negotiations on confidence-building measures and conventional stability.

In 1989 two new sets of negotiations were launched at the follow-up meeting in Vienna, the Conference on Security and Cooperation in Europe (CSCE) follow-up meeting in Vienna: talks on conventional armed forces in Europe (CFE) between NATO and the Warsaw Pact and negotiations on confidence-building and security measures among all 35 CSCE members. In December 1989 NATO celebrated its fortieth anniversary at a special summit meeting in Brussels. NATO set forth new goals and policies in recognition of the recent and sweeping changes in the waning Cold War and to further extend East–West cooperation. In July 1990 NATO issued the London Declaration, which provided a road map to guide the transition of the alliance from the era of Cold War confrontation to the age of post–Cold War cooperation and partnership. A joint declaration and commitment to nonaggression was signed in Paris in November 1990. The transformation of the alliance in the new security environment was clearly reflected in its new strategic concept unveiled in November 1991. Cooperation and partnership with Central and East European nations thus became a central and integral part of NATO policies.

Throughout the Cold War, NATO played an important deterrent role in checking Soviet expansion in Europe. It also provided the framework for consultation and coordination of policies among its member countries to diminish the risk of crisis and war.

Anna Boros-McGee

Further Reading

Kaplan, Lawrence S. *NATO and the United States: The Enduring Alliance.* Boston: Twayne, 1988.

Mastny, Vojtech, Sven Holtsmark, and Andreas Wenger, eds. *War Plans and Alliances in the Cold War: Threat Perceptions in the East and West.* New York: Routledge, 2006.

Schmidt, Gustav, ed. *A History of NATO: The First Fifty Years.* New York: Palgrave Macmillan, 2001.

Schneider, Peter. *The Evolution of NATO: The Alliance's Strategic Concept and Its Predecessors, 1945–2000.* München: Institut für Internationale Politik, Universität der Bundeswehr München, 2000.

Smith, Mark. *NATO Enlargement during the Cold War: Strategy and System in the Western Alliance.* New York: Palgrave Macmillan, 2000.

NSC-68, National Security Council Report

NSC-68 was a response by President Harry S. Truman's administration to the Soviets' first atomic explosion in late August 1949 as well as the October 1949 communist victory in the Chinese Civil War. The top secret report was released to the president on April 14, 1950. Its principal architect was Paul H. Nitze, director of the State Department's Policy Planning Staff.

The basic premise of NSC-68 was that because the Soviets had developed a workable atomic bomb, a hydrogen (thermonuclear) bomb would not be far behind. The drafters of NSC-68 estimated that by 1954, "the year of maximum danger," the Soviets would be capable of launching a crippling preemptive strike against the United States. According to NSC-68, the United States could not prevent such a blow without a massive increase in its military and economic capacities. Should the

report not be heeded, in case of Soviet aggression the United States would be forced into appeasement or nuclear war. Nitze and other policymakers believed, therefore, that the key to avoiding this dilemma and preserving free-world security lay in a vast conventional rearmament. NSC-68 also demanded greater foreign aid, along with expanded military assistance to the Western Allies, additional funding for information and propaganda campaigns, better intelligence gathering, and an expansion of nuclear weapons programs.

Alarmed by the report's recommendations and likely costs, President Truman initially shelved the plan. Only after the sudden outbreak of the Korean War in June 1950 did he agree to implement the NSC-68 rearmament program. Thanks in part to the Korean War, U.S. defense expenditures quadrupled, going from $13.5 billion before the war to more than $54 billion by the time Truman left office in January 1953. The lion's share of this massive rearmament program was not directed to the Korean War but instead went toward fulfilling America's long-term mobilization base as envisioned in NSC-68. Indeed, NSC-68 put muscle into Truman's containment policy.

Although subsequent administrations would tinker with the recommendations in NSC-68, the report nonetheless guided U.S. national security and military mobilization planning for almost a generation after its drafting. Fundamentally, NSC-68 was underpinned by the traditional Cold War mentality. Many of its critics have argued that the report overstated the nature and extent of the Soviet threat. Some, however, have maintained that NSC-68 was a wise and prudent response to a real and present Soviet danger. Still others have pointed out that although NSC-68 may have painted a somewhat distorted picture of the Soviet Union, this distortion results more from what is now known from newly opened Eastern bloc archives as opposed to what was known to officials at the time. Whatever the case, it is a truism that NSC-68 was a seminal and paradigmatic Cold War document.

Josh Ushay

Further Reading

Gaddis, John Lewis. *Strategies of Containment: A Critical Appraisal of Postwar American National Security.* New York: Oxford University Press, 1982.

Gaddis, John Lewis. *We Now Know: Rethinking Cold War History.* New York: Oxford University Press, 1997.

Leffler, Melvyn P. *A Preponderance of Power: National Security, the Truman Administration and the Cold War.* Stanford, CA: Stanford University Press, 1992.

May, Ernest R. *American Cold War Strategy: Interpreting NSC 68.* Boston: Bedford Books of St. Martin's, 1993.

Pierpaoli, Paul G., Jr. *Truman and Korea: The Political Culture of the Early Cold War.* Columbia: University of Missouri Press, 1999.

Nuclear Arms Race

The nuclear arms race is a general term for the undeclared Cold War contest in which the United States and the Soviet Union developed, tested, and deployed increasingly advanced nuclear weapons and delivery systems. The strategic motivation behind the arms race was each nation's drive to ensure that its adversary not gain any measurable advantage in nuclear-strike capability. Also at play was the evolving concept of nuclear deterrence, which held that a nation must retain adequate nuclear capabilities to deter the enemy from launching a preemptive nuclear attack. This concept became known as mutual assured destruction

(MAD) and held that any preemptive attack would result in an overwhelming and catastrophic retaliatory strike.

With its first test explosion in July 1945, the United States possessed an atomic monopoly. The Soviet Union feared the American nuclear threat, especially given the demonstrated ability of the United States to conduct long-range strategic bombing. Thus, the Soviets pursued their own atomic bomb with great vigor. Soviet spies who had infiltrated the Manhattan Project and a skilled scientific community allowed the Soviet Union to detonate its first nuclear weapon in September 1949.

The United States sought to retain its nuclear lead and, in an action-reaction cycle that would typify the arms race, pursued the next nuclear development—in this case, a thermonuclear (or hydrogen) bomb. America's success in developing the hydrogen bomb in 1952 was followed by Soviet success in 1955. The nuclear arms race now entered its most recognizable form, wherein the superpowers pursued weapons that were smaller in size, more powerful, and increasingly accurate. In the same vein, delivery systems became faster, more accurate, and more difficult to locate.

During the late 1940s and early 1950s, the primary delivery vehicle for nuclear weapons was strategic bombers. More advanced aircraft were needed to carry more than one nuclear weapon, and indeed, nuclear weapons needed to be smaller so that they could be carried by a variety of aircraft. The American B-29 was matched by the Soviet TU-4, but neither proved sufficient. Developments led ultimately to the B-52 and the TU-20, both intercontinental bombers capable of delivering large payloads to multiple targets.

The next step in the nuclear arms race was missile development. Advances in rocketry led to the development of ballistic missiles in

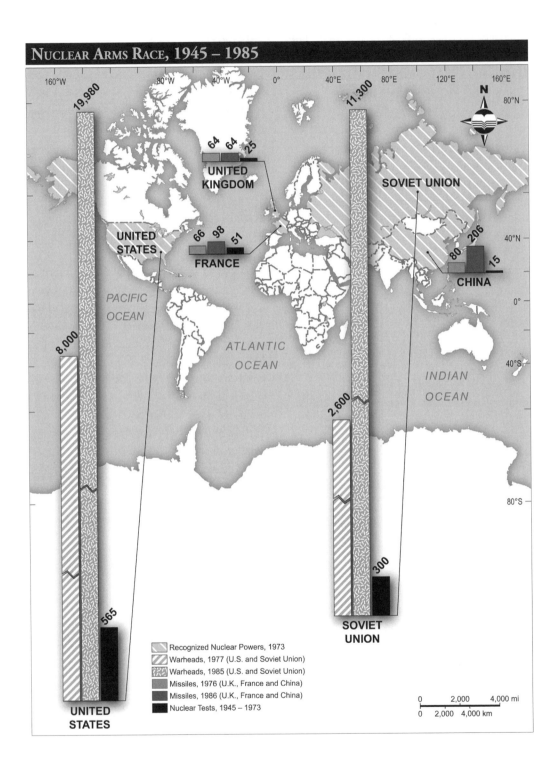

NUCLEAR ARMS RACE, 1945 – 1985

UNITED KINGDOM
64   64   25

FRANCE
66   98   51

SOVIET UNION

CHINA
80   206   15

UNITED STATES

PACIFIC OCEAN

ATLANTIC OCEAN

INDIAN OCEAN

19,980

11,300

8,000

2,600

565

300

UNITED STATES

SOVIET UNION

Recognized Nuclear Powers, 1973
Warheads, 1977 (U.S. and Soviet Union)
Warheads, 1985 (U.S. and Soviet Union)
Missiles, 1976 (U.K., France and China)
Missiles, 1986 (U.K., France and China)
Nuclear Tests, 1945 – 1973

0   2,000   4,000 mi
0   2,000   4,000 km

both the United States and the Soviet Union. The first U.S. intercontinental ballistic missile (ICBM), the Atlas D, was deployed on October 31, 1959. The Soviets followed suit with their own ICBM, the SS-6 Sapwood of North Atlantic Treaty Organization (NATO) designation, on January 20, 1960. ICBMs were a step up from their cousins, medium-range ballistic missiles (MRBMs) and intermediate-range ballistic missiles (IRBMs), and became the most popular delivery system because of their range and relative invulnerability to enemy air defenses. ICBMs had a maximum range of 10,000 miles and could be stationed on the other side of the world from their targets.

In the 1950s, both superpowers came to rely on nuclear weapons as the primary weapon for any major Cold War engagement.

The nuclear arms race created ever-larger arsenals and increasingly effective delivery systems. As a result, both sides became vulnerable to an enemy attack. It was this vulnerability that perpetuated the arms race during the decade and beyond. Neither side was willing to give up its weapons, and the newer weapons now meant that the nation that launched a first strike might be able to avoid a retaliatory strike if its nuclear advantage were enough to allow it to destroy most of the enemy's nuclear forces in the first blow. Any large gap in nuclear arms made one nation vulnerable, and nuclear stability could only be ensured by nuclear parity. As a result, scientific advances by one nation had to be matched by the other, or else a gap would result and one side would gain advantage.

Military parade through Red Square in Moscow, 1963. (Library of Congress)

This situation was aggravated in the 1960s with the evolution of the counterforce (or no cities) doctrine. Advocates of the doctrine suggested a general agreement between the superpowers to use nuclear weapons only against military installations, sparing population centers. Adopting this policy meant accepting the reality that in order to sustain the ability to launch an effective counterstrike, a nation must deploy enough weapons to ensure that the enemy could not destroy them all in a preemptive strike. Thus, more and better weapons were needed.

The alleged existence first of a bomber gap, then a missile gap, later an antiballistic missile gap, and later still a missile throw-weight gap kept arms manufacturers in perpetual development. In the United States, the military-industrial complex also contributed to the arms race as defense industries fought for lucrative military contracts by driving forward to the next level of weaponry and delivery systems. Changes in computer technology also advanced the nuclear arms race. In November 1960, the United States deployed the world's first nuclear-powered ballistic missile submarine (SSBN), the *George Washington*, capable of launching 16 Polaris missiles. The Soviets followed in 1968 with their own SSBN. These weapons increased the danger of the arms race and were potentially even more deadly than ICBMs, as they were capable of avoiding retaliatory strikes because of their ability to hide deep beneath the ocean.

Advances were made on both sides in ICBMs, bombers, and submarines, but the United States maintained strategic superiority. In the late 1960s and into the 1970s, however, the Soviet Union took the lead in ICBM production and in the development of antiballistic missile (ABM) technology. Soviet ABMs were designed primarily to protect major cities, such as Moscow, and were less effective against a full attack against

Soviet military installations. Multiple independently targeted reentry vehicles (MIRVs) complicated matters. MIRVs meant that each ICBM could deploy a dozen or more warheads, each programmed for a separate target. MIRVs promised to overcome any ABM system.

Arms control talks and treaties during the 1970s and arms reduction agreements during the 1980s slowed but did not stop the nuclear arms race. When the Cold War ended, so did the nuclear arms race in its original form.

Brian Madison Jones

Further Reading

Bottome, Edgar M. *The Balance of Terror: A Guide to the Arms Race.* Boston: Beacon, 1971.

Powaski, Ronald E. *March to Armageddon: The United States and the Nuclear Arms Race, 1939 to the Present.* New York: Oxford University Press, 1987.

Powaski, Ronald E. *Return to Armageddon: The United States and the Nuclear Arms Race, 1981–1999.* New York: Oxford University Press, 2000.

Nuclear Tests

Beginning with the first successful test of a nuclear weapon by the United States in July 1945, nuclear-armed nations have built and tested nuclear devices in a continuing effort to improve the design and increase the yield of fission (atomic bomb) and fusion (hydrogen bomb) weapons. Nuclear tests have been conducted in the atmosphere, underground, and underwater and have contributed to remarkable progress in nuclear weapons research. Nuclear tests serve both military and scientific purposes as well as diplomatic goals. Often, nations have used nuclear tests to convey a variety of diplomatic messages.

The first test of a fission weapon took place near Alamogordo, New Mexico, at 5:29 a.m. on July 16, 1945, under the auspices of the Manhattan Project, the top secret U.S. program aimed at building an atomic bomb. Named Trinity, the test successfully detonated and yielded the equivalent of 20,000 tons, or 20 kilotons (kt), of TNT.

In the years that followed the Trinity test, other nations pursued first fission weapons and later fusion, or thermonuclear, weapons. Successful tests were key markers of progress for these nations as they sought to be included in the elite "nuclear club." Indeed, until the advent of supercomputers in the late 1980s, nuclear tests were the only way of determining readiness of a nation's nuclear forces.

The United States conducted two additional nuclear tests after Trinity before the Soviet Union became the second nuclear nation, testing a fission bomb yielding 22 kt on August 29, 1949. The successful Soviet test convinced American policymakers to pursue the next level in nuclear weapons, the fusion bomb, which was first tested by the United States on October 3, 1952. That weapon yielded the equivalent of 10 million tons, or 10 megatons (mt), of TNT. The Soviets followed with their own thermonuclear test on November 22, 1955, with a device that yielded 1.6 mt. The Soviets claimed that an August 12, 1953, explosion was a thermonuclear test, but it was in fact a fission weapon boosted in yield by the use of tritium in the nuclear reaction. The United States had tested a similar device in 1951.

Three more nations—Britain, France, and the People's Republic of China (PRC)—all tested fission weapons during 1953–1964. Great Britain tested its first nuclear weapon on October 3, 1953, France on February 13, 1960, and China on October 16, 1964. These nations later successfully tested fusion

The mushroom cloud of an atomic explosion billows skywards as Communist China tests its first atomic bomb, on October 16, 1964. (AP/ Wide World Photos)

weapons. Great Britain was first among the three with a thermonuclear test on November 11, 1957, followed by China on June 17, 1967, and France on August 24, 1968. These five nations constituted the five declared nuclear nations. However, two other nations— India and Pakistan—have also tested nuclear weapons. India did so first on May 18, 1974, and then tested three more times in 1998 before Pakistan tested its first weapon on May 28, 1998, and its second on May 30, 1998. On October 9, 2006, the Democratic People's Republic of Korea (DPRK, North Korea) announced its first nuclear detonation. Western intelligence confirmed that a large underground explosion had occurred and it had emitted radioactivity, but it is believed that the detonation was a misfire because of its small yield (under one kiloton). North Korea admitted that the yield was less than expected but insisted that it was a full-fledged detonation. Scientists and scholars continue to debate the specifics of this test.

During 1945–1998, the five officially declared nuclear nations plus India and Pakistan conducted 2,051 nuclear weapons tests, 528 (26 percent) of which were atmospheric. The Soviet Union and the United States accounted for 1,745 (85 percent) of the total number of tests. The British tested 45 weapons and the French 210. The biggest year for nuclear tests was 1962, when 178 tests were conducted. Tests have been conducted in North America, Asia, Africa, and Australia. Israel is widely believed to have nuclear weapons, even though it has conducted no nuclear tests.

In the largest nuclear test ever recorded, the Soviet Union conducted an atmospheric test on October 30, 1961, that yielded 50 mt. The weapon was not suitable for deployment, however, as no delivery system had been constructed to carry such a large device. The largest underground test yielded 5 mt and was conducted by the United States on November 6, 1971. In the Soviet Union, 496 tests were in Kazakhstan. In the United States, Alaska, Mississippi, and Colorado have been hosts to nuclear tests, but 935 have been conducted in Nevada.

The goals of such tests vary but generally include a desire to improve the design, increase the yield, or shrink the size of nuclear weapons. Nations also utilized such tests to prepare for possible battlefield uses. After a test, troops would march into the area, simulating an actual engagement and testing their ability to operate in such an environment. Nuclear blasts were also detonated to test the survivability of various infrastructures, civilian homes, and even ships at sea.

During the Cold War, nuclear tests served as a means of communication between superpowers and regional powers, as in the case of India and Pakistan. The Soviet nuclear test of 1949 announced to the world that the American atomic monopoly had ended, a development that dramatically affected the course of the Cold War. Now possessing atomic weapons, the Soviets quickly regained a military advantage because the United States could never match the Soviet Red Army man-for-man.

An even better example might be the Soviet test in November 1961. Soviet Premier Nikita Khrushchev took every opportunity to test the new American president, John F. Kennedy. In Cuba, Laos, and Berlin, Khrushchev attempted to bully Kennedy. As part of this strategy, Khrushchev broke the three-year-long nuclear testing moratorium with a series of tests that concluded with the world's largest nuclear test, of 50 mt. This weapon was 3,000 times more powerful than the atomic bomb dropped on Hiroshima, and it forced Kennedy to resume nuclear testing in the United States. The Cold War grew increasingly tense in the months that followed.

In the United States, in particular, nuclear tests became a controversial political issue. Dangerous radioactive fallout resulted from every atmospheric test conducted, and those conducted in Nevada and New Mexico impacted those Americans living downwind of the nuclear fallout. Radioactive dust settled back to the earth, where it entered the food chain. Americans who lived close to the test sites suffered lasting and debilitating health effects. Increased cancer rates and genetic birth defects were just some of the deadly results of America's nuclear testing program.

In 1963, the United States and the Soviet Union signed the Partial Test Ban Treaty (PTBT), which halted nuclear testing in the atmosphere, underwater, and in space. With negotiations beginning in 1993, the Comprehensive Test Ban Treaty is a more inclusive treaty that would all but eliminate nuclear tests. Failure on the part of major nations to sign or ratify the treaty has hindered its utility. Neither India nor Pakistan has signed the treaty, and neither the United States nor China has ratified it.

Brian Madison Jones

Further Reading

Ball, Howard. *Justice Downwind: America's Atomic Testing Program in the 1950s.* New York: Oxford University Press, 1986.

Divine, Robert A. *Blowing on the Wind: The Nuclear Test Ban Debate, 1954–1960.* New York: Oxford University Press, 1978.

Miller, Richard L. *Under the Cloud: The Decades of Nuclear Testing.* New York: Free Press, 1986.

Norris, Robert S., and William Arkin. "Known Nuclear Tests Worldwide, 1945–1948." *Bulletin of the Atomic Scientists* 54, no. 6 (November/December 1998): 65–67.

Ostpolitik

Ostpolitik was a Federal Republic of Germany foreign policy initiative that sought rapprochement with the Soviet Union and the Warsaw Pact. During 1949–1963, West Germany, under the leadership of Chancellor Konrad Adenauer, pursued Westpolitik (Western Policy). Westpolitik involved, among other things, membership in the North Atlantic Treaty organization (NATO), the rearmament of West Germany, and participation in the European Coal and Steel Community (ECSC) and the European Common Market. Westpolitik also dictated a relatively uncompromising attitude toward the Soviet Union and its East European satellites, the German Democratic Republic (GDR, East Germany) in particular. Epitomizing this attitude were Bonn's refusal to open relations with the Soviets until forced to do so by Moscow's threat not to release thousands of German prisoners of war still held in captivity and the Hallstein Doctrine, which held that West Germany would not enter into relations with any country, the Soviet Union excepted, that recognized East Germany.

Beginning with Ludwig Erhard's chancellorship (1963–1966) and continuing with that of Kurt Kiesinger (1966–1969), West Germany's leadership began to modify its approach toward the Soviet bloc, sending trade missions to Poland, Hungary, and Romania in hopes that economic agreements would lead to political dialogue. This transformation served as a prelude to the more radical Ostpolitik (Eastern Policy) implemented by Chancellor Willy Brandt's government during 1969–1974.

Mayor of West Berlin during 1957–1966 and foreign minister in the Kiesinger government, Brandt became West Germany's first Social Democratic chancellor in October 1969, heading a coalition cabinet that included Walter Scheel, leader of the Free Democratic Party, as foreign minister. Seeking to reduce tensions in Central Europe, hoping to ameliorate conditions for Germans living in East Germany, and recognizing that a hard-line approach had brought German reunification no closer, Brandt as foreign minister had already set out to improve relations, via negotiations and diplomatic agreements, between West Germany and the Warsaw Pact. As chancellor, he and Scheel worked aggressively to expand this process.

Brandt's Ostpolitik encountered substantial obstacles, both internationally and domestically. President Richard M. Nixon's administration, itself seeking détente, proved reluctant to surrender the initiative in East–West relations to Bonn. At the same time, East Germany, led by Walter Ulbricht, made negotiations with West Germany dependent on Bonn's willingness to recognize East Germany diplomatically, a condition unacceptable to the Brandt cabinet. In addition, the Christian Democratic Union/Christian Socialist Union (CDU/CSU) opposition in the Bundestag made repeated attempts to stymie Brandt's initiatives.

Fortunately for Brandt, the Soviet Union had ample reason to embrace Ostpolitik. Concerned over growing hostilities with communist China, desirous of increasing economic ties with the West, and sensing an opportunity to possibly split NATO, the Kremlin welcomed Ostpolitik, agreeing to discuss relations with West Germany in early 1970. Talks between the Soviet Union and West Germany culminated in the Treaty of Moscow on August 12, 1970, whereby both sides renounced the use of force against each other and acknowledged existing European frontiers as inviolable. Moscow even added a supplemental declaration affirming Germany's right to reunify by peaceful means, thereby undercutting one of the CDU/CSU's chief criticisms of Ostpolitik. The Soviets agreed to discuss Berlin with the United States, Great Britain, and France, with the objective of redressing the divided city's status.

West Germany's willingness to recognize existing European frontiers paved the way for an agreement with Poland via the Treaty of Warsaw, signed on December 7, 1970. In so doing, Bonn acknowledged the disputed Oder-Neisse Line (although stipulating that it remained subject to change in a final peace settlement), and Warsaw agreed to allow Germans residing in Poland to relocate to either East or West Germany provided they conformed with Polish emigration laws. Moscow's decision to discuss Berlin's status led to the Quadripartite Agreement of September 3, 1971, which saw Britain, France, the United States, and the Soviet Union acknowledge that West Berlin was not part of West Germany, recognize West Germany's right to represent West Berlin internationally, and offer diplomatic protection to its citizens. Additionally, the agreement promised Soviet facilitation in the movement of traffic from West Germany to West Berlin and pledged the signatories to use negotiation to resolve any future problems concerning Berlin.

Eight months later, in May 1972, East Germany (now headed by Erich Honecker) and West Germany signed a transit agreement guaranteeing West Berliners access rights to East Germany—all but forbidden since the construction of the Berlin Wall in 1961—and granting East Germans the right to visit West Germany in cases of family emergency. This agreement set the stage for the West German–East German Basic Treaty, signed on December 21, 1972, in which the two Germanies renounced the use of force in their relations, agreed to recognize and respect each other's authority and independence, renounced any claim to represent the other internationally, agreed to respect human rights principles as enumerated in the United Nations (UN) Charter, and consented to an exchange of permanent missions (but not of ambassadors).

Brandt followed up the Basic Treaty by entering discussions with Czechoslovakia that led to a concrete agreement similar to the 1970 Treaty of Moscow in December 1973. That same month, West Germany exchanged ambassadors with both Hungary and Bulgaria, meaning that by the time Brandt left office in May 1974, West Germany enjoyed relations with every East European communist regime except Albania.

Ostpolitik greatly reduced Cold War tensions in Central Europe and thereby contributed to the success of détente in the 1970s. It essentially eliminated Berlin as a Cold War issue, opened the door for the entry of both Germanies into the UN in September 1973, and improved conditions for Berliners. It also marked West Germany's emergence as a state willing to act independently on the international stage. Finally, Ostpolitik earned Brandt acclaim both in Germany and abroad, symbolized by his selection as the winner of the 1971 Nobel Peace Prize.

Bruce J. DeHart

Further Reading

Brandt, Willy. *My Life in Politics*. London: Hamish Hamilton, 1992.

Marshall, Barbara. *Willy Brandt: A Political Biography*. New York: Palgrave Macmillan, 1997.

Sarotte, M. E. *Dealing with the Devil: East Germany, Detente, and Ostpolitik, 1969–1973*. Chapel Hill: University of North Carolina Press, 2001.

P

Partial Test Ban Treaty (August 5, 1963)

The Partial Test Ban Treaty (PTBT), also known as the Limited Test Ban Treaty (LTBT), was signed in Moscow on August 5, 1963, by representatives of Great Britain, the United States, and the Soviet Union and was entered into force on October 10, 1963, with unlimited duration. The PTBT was the result of five years of intense negotiations concerning the limiting of nuclear weapons tests. Some 125 nations have since signed the document, although France and the People's Republic of China (PRC) refused to sign, arguing that the test ban was a means of preserving the superiority of the three initial nuclear powers.

The PTBT was clearly an attempt to make nuclear weapons programs more difficult to sustain, thus limiting nuclear proliferation. The signatories to the treaty agreed that they would no longer carry out any nuclear test explosion in the atmosphere, underwater, in outer space, or in any other environment that would allow the spread of radioactive fallout beyond the territorial borders of the state conducting the test.

World public opinion was already attuned to the dangers of atmospheric nuclear testing as a result of the 1954 *Castle Bravo* incident, in which a thermonuclear weapons test at Bikini Island in the Pacific unwittingly exposed 28 Americans, 236 Marshall Islanders, and 23 crew members of the Japanese fishing boat *Lucky Dragon No. 5* to nuclear fallout. Public opinion was further inflamed by France's decision to conduct atmospheric tests in Polynesia in 1962.

Two more general developments were also influential in pushing forward a test ban. Considerable radioactive materials were being poured into the atmosphere as a result of atmospheric nuclear testing, and the world's nuclear states had advanced their nuclear technology to the point where a combination of underground tests and physical calculations gave them sufficient information to design and test their strategic weapons without the risk of radioactive fallout.

In the United States there was increasing support for a test ban throughout the summer of 1963. In early July of that year, 52 percent of Americans signaled unqualified support for a test ban. After the treaty had been signed, 81 percent of those polled approved the ban. In 1962, the newly established Eighteen-Nation Disarmament Committee (ENDC) within the United Nations (UN) became the principal forum for discussions concerning a test ban. After protracted negotiations, an agreement emerged on the use of seismic stations and on-site inspections for verification purposes, but there was still disagreement on the acceptable number of inspections continued

The PTBT seemed to offer hope for future disarmament agreements. Following the PTBT negotiations, worldwide concern over nuclear testing and the nuclear arms race in general declined dramatically. In 1968 the Nuclear Non-Proliferation Treaty (NPT) was signed, restricting the flow of weapons, technical knowledge, and fissile materials to states that did not already have nuclear weapons. The United States and the Soviet Union went a step further in 1974 when they signed the Threshold Test Ban Treaty (TTBT). It limited underground testing, which was allowed by the PTBT, to a maximum weapons yield of 150 kilotons, and only at declared testing sites. It also allowed on-site inspection by the other state for any test expected to exceed 35 kilotons. The TTBT did not enter into force until 1990. It had a duration of five years, with five-year extensions, and remains in force today. The Comprehensive Test Ban Treaty (CTBT) was called for in the preamble of the PTBT but was not signed until 1996. As of 2007, the United States had refused to ratify the CTBT, despite being one of the original signatories. Nonetheless, the United States, Great Britain, and Russia have observed unilateral nuclear testing moratoriums since 1992, and the last French test took place in 1995.

Jérôme Dorvidal and Jeffrey A. Larsen

Further Reading

Dean, Arthur H. *Test Ban and Disarmament: The Path of Negotiation*. New York: Harper and Row, 1966.

Seaborg, Glenn, with Benjamin S. Loeb. *Kennedy, Khrushchev, and the Test Ban*. Berkeley: University of California Press, 1981.

Sobel, Lester A. *Disarmament and Nuclear Tests, 1960–1963*. New York: Facts on File Series, Library of Congress, 1964.

Terchek, Ronald J. *The Making of the Test Ban Treaty*. The Hague: Martinus Nijhoff, 1970.

Peace Movements

The Cold War was perhaps unique with regard to the amount of dissent it created in both the East and West. During 1945–1990, three significant peace movements stand

out. The first was sparked by the 1954 U.S. testing of the hydrogen bomb on the South Pacific island of Bikini, leading to the rise of a large-scale international nuclear disarmament movement. In the second, the late 1960s and early 1970s saw a global rebellion against the Vietnam War. And in 1979, the North Atlantic Treaty Organization's (NATO) double-track decision to station intermediate-range ballistic missiles (IRBMs) in Western Europe led to large-scale antiwar and antinuclear protest demonstrations that culminated during 1982–1983.

Defined as autonomous, nongovernmental, generally nonpartisan, and nonviolent organizations, peace movements range from strict opposition to all wars (pacifism), to opposition against a specific type of weapon (such as nuclear bombs), to opposition against a particular conflict. After World War II, peace movements were overwhelmingly concerned with the banning of the production, testing, deployment, and use of nuclear weapons.

In the United States, uneasiness over the use of nuclear weapons was voiced only days after the atomic bombings of Hiroshima and Nagasaki in August 1945. Church groups were joined by scientists and politicians in promoting international controls over nuclear energy. As the Cold War intensified during the late 1940s, antinuclear activists—including prominent scientists Albert Einstein and Leo Szilard—were clearly fighting an uphill battle. At the time, the antinuclear movement found little support among an American public focused on combating the communist threat. During the early 1950s, McCarthyism further pushed peace activists onto the defensive.

On March 1, 1954, the U.S. testing of the most powerful hydrogen bomb to date on the Bikini Atoll in the South Pacific led to rising public concern over the long-term health effects of nuclear fallout. When 28 Americans, 236 Marshall Islanders, and 23 crew members of a Japanese fishing boat were contaminated by nuclear fallout from the blast, the Bikini tests made international headlines. This led to renewed demands for nuclear disarmament by international peace organizations such as the War Resisters' International (WRI), the International Fellowship of Reconciliation (IFR), and the Women's International League for Peace and Freedom (WILPF). Mainstream publications as well as period novels and films greatly alarmed the American public, while scientific studies on radioactivity further stirred pacifist sentiment.

By no means were these concerns limited to the United States, however. Japanese reaction to the Bikini tests had been furious, whereas in Britain as early as 1950 scientists had already urged their government not to develop the hydrogen bomb. In the Federal Republic of Germany (FRG, West Germany), the stationing of the first U.S. nuclear weapons in 1953 as well as the news of NATO military exercises that simulated the dropping of 335 atomic bombs gave overwhelming appeal to banning the bomb. There was rising concern in Scandinavia, Italy, and France as well. In the mid-1950s, polls all over Western Europe showed that between 80 and 90 percent of the population supported a test-ban treaty as well as a ban on nuclear weapons altogether.

Early on, scientists themselves played a prominent role in the struggle against the bomb. A key figure was British mathematician and philosopher Bertrand Russell, whose December 23, 1953, BBC radio address attracted considerable international attention and led to the creation of the Pugwash Movement, supported by a number of leading physicists on both sides of the Iron Curtain. Influenced by their Western colleagues, some Soviet physicists, most notably Andrei Sakharov, warned their government of the dangers of nuclear weapons.

When nuclear testing programs accelerated during the late 1950s, a first wave of mass protests to ban the bomb erupted. Britain took the lead with the formation of the Campaign for Nuclear Disarmament (CND). The first march from London to Aldermaston on Easter 1958 adopted the symbol that has become the emblem of peace movements ever since: a circle encompassing a broken cross. In West Germany, the CND was copied by the Easter March Movement, which originally grew out of opposition to NATO's decision to equip West German forces with nuclear weapons. Other countries such as Sweden and Switzerland followed suit, although French leftists were more concerned with the Algerian War than with antinuclear issues.

In the United States, the National Committee for a Sane Nuclear Policy (SANE) came into existence in 1957. Like the CND, it began by demanding a halt to nuclear testing but evolved into a broader nuclear disarmament movement. Unlike its European counterparts, however, SANE was unable to achieve the same kind of mass mobilization. At about the same time, European peace activists began to coordinate their efforts. In 1959, for example, British, Dutch, Swedish, Swiss, and West German nuclear disarmament organizations set up the European Federation Against Nuclear Arms.

Although the 1963 Partial Test Ban Treaty (PTBT) fell short of peace activists' demands, protesters could claim that they had helped pressure the Americans and Soviets to achieve a breakthrough at the negotiating table. Reaching its zenith in 1964 with the tally of Easter Marchers numbering 500,000 in 20 nations, the antinuclear campaign waned during the late 1960s as Cold War tensions eased. By politicizing a generation of young people, cooperating across national borders, and developing new forms of political action, however, it had set the stage for the coming protests against the Vietnam War.

By the mid-1960s, the Vietnam War had already replaced the antinuclear movement as the main focus of peace-related activities. In the United States, worries over the Vietnam War mounted even before President Lyndon Johnson began to dispatch large numbers of combat troops in 1965. In Britain, the CND staged large demonstrations against the war in 1966 and 1967. At its antiwar rally in February 1966, groups from West Germany, Austria, France, Sweden, Norway, Italy, and the Netherlands declared their solidarity with American student protesters. In October 1967, the march on the Pentagon was echoed by closely coordinated solidarity demonstrations against American military installations in West Berlin and by antiwar rallies in Amsterdam, London, Oslo, Paris, Rome, and Tokyo.

Throughout the world, Vietnam War protests stimulated the growth and expansion of student movements, which saw their culmination in 1968. In Britain and West Germany, student protests that had originally organized over issues of college discipline and curriculum were transformed into mass demonstrations with more than 100,000 participants in 1968. In France, student protests snowballed into mass demonstrations involving organized labor and other groups, nearly toppling the government of Charles de Gaulle. The greatest mobilization was in Japan, where Vietnam War protests rallied almost 800,000 people in 1970. There is much evidence from many other Western as well as developing countries that opposition to the American engagement in Vietnam led to the radicalization of students worldwide.

As with the antinuclear protests that preceded it, the Vietnam War protests witnessed the emergence of global networks of rebellion. The close ties among American and West German and other European protesters formed a striking parallel with their governments' Cold War cooperation. Important figures of the German New Left had become acquainted with their American counterparts as exchange students during the early 1960s. After their return to Germany, they helped organize protests against the American war in Vietnam using methods that they copied from the U.S. civil rights movements, such as mass sit-ins.

Whereas the nuclear disarmament activists of the 1950s had by and large accepted the established institutional framework, Vietnam War protests developed into a more systematic anti-imperialist and anti-capitalist ideological critique of Western democracy. European and American activists identified with developing-world revolutionaries such as Che Guevara, Ho Chi Minh, and Mao Zedong. However, their revolutionary rhetoric and violent methods often alienated even those middle-class voters who had been broadly sympathetic to the antinuclear cause.

Because of significant steps made toward nuclear arms control and superpower détente during the late 1960s and early 1970s and the focus on Vietnam, the antinuclear campaign had largely disintegrated. It returned, however, during the late 1970s and early 1980s, when NATO's 1979 double-track decision to deploy land-based cruise missiles and Pershing II missiles in Western Europe led to new fears of nuclear Armageddon. This second-wave antinuclear movement achieved an even larger protest mobilization than the first. Like its predecessor, it was transnational and was often built on the experiences of earlier protest efforts.

The antinuclear campaign of the early 1980s took place within the framework of renewed Cold War tensions and hostilities.

Soviet efforts to achieve military superiority in Europe and the 1979 invasion of Afghanistan as well as Ronald Reagan's election as president in 1980 ended the long phase of détente between the superpowers. Yet despite the Soviet military buildup, a majority of West Europeans did not fear an impending invasion. Because of growing public dissent to nuclear armaments in Eastern Europe as well, West European activists perceived themselves as part of a Pan-European movement battling against the dangers of the nuclear arms race.

President Jimmy Carter's Neutron Bomb Campaign had already raised antinuclear fears in Western Europe during 1977–1978. It was not until December 1979, however, when a NATO summit decided to deploy IRBMs if the Soviet Union did not withdraw its forward-basing of SS-20 missiles, that large-scale protests in several countries emerged. Campaigns achieved the most domestic support in Belgium and the Netherlands, where the peace movement was successful in coaxing the governments to delay the NATO deployment schedule. In Britain, where the CND was rejuvenated, nuclear weapons became an important political issue as well. In October 1980, 80,000 people marched to Trafalgar Square. In West Germany, protest demonstrations involved upward of 100,000 people in the same year. The high point occurred in December 1983, just before the deployment of the IRBMs began. As many as a million demonstrators protested throughout West Germany, in addition to 600,000 in Rome and 400,000 in London.

The transnational protest networks of the 1980s had their roots in the ecological and feminist movements that had sprung up during the 1970s. They also enjoyed the backing of a substantial number of churches and labor unions. Despite considerable support in Western Europe and among the media,

the peace movement of the early 1980s was unable to build on the same kind of nuclear anxiety that had lent the 1950s' movement such resonance. Because of its association with leftist and liberal causes, the 1980s' antinuclear campaign came to enjoy only limited support among mainstream political parties. This led to the founding of new political groups such as the West German Green Party.

The 1980s peace movement did not originate in the United States. Despite considerable support from American peace groups (such as the National Freeze Campaign), the European peace movement developed independently from American influences. The stationing of Pershing II and cruise missiles affected the balance of power in Europe. In addition, it had been European governments, above all West German chancellor Helmut Schmidt's government, that had taken the lead in pushing NATO toward the double-track decision. Finally, there was a strong sense of a European solidarity vis-à-vis the superpowers because East European antinuclear activists shared many concerns with their West European counterparts.

The Cold War–era peace movements did not produce immediate results in terms of disarmament or the lessening of tensions between East and West. Yet they had palpable effects on Western public opinion and to a lesser degree on East European governments. Beginning in the 1950s, they forced governments to address widespread fears of the destructive force of nuclear weapons. In addition, the Cold War, with its strong elite cooperation across national borders, provided a unique international framework for the unprecedented growth of transnational peace activity. Thus, antiwar activism during the 1945–1990 period paved the way for more recent peace, environmental, and anti-globalization movements.

Philipp Gassert

Further Reading

Carter, April. *Peace Movements: International Protests and World Politics since 1945.* London: Longman, 1992.

Kaltefleiter, Werner, and Robert L. Pfaltzgraff, eds. *The Peace Movements in Europe and the United States.* New York: St. Martin's, 1985.

Katz, Milton S. *Ban the Bomb: A History of SANE, the Committee for a Sane Nuclear Policy, 1957–1985.* New York: Greenwood, 1986.

Taylor, Richard. *Against the Bomb: The British Peace Movement, 1958–1965.* Oxford, UK: Clarendon, 1985.

Wittner, Lawrence S. *Rebels against War: The American Peace Movement, 1933–1983.* Philadelphia: Temple University Press, 1984.

Wittner, Lawrence S. *Resisting the Bomb: A History of the World Nuclear Disarmament Movement.* Stanford, CA: Stanford University Press, 1997.

Perestroika

Perestroika, meaning "restructuring" in Russian, was an important aspect of Soviet leader Mikhail Gorbachev's reform agenda, designed in conjunction with glasnost ("openness") and demokratizatsiia ("democratization") to renew socialism and end the political and economic stagnation that had plagued the Soviet state for nearly two decades. At the Twenty-Seventh Party Congress in 1986, Gorbachev first promoted his ideas of perestroika, which included reduced centralization and bureaucratization, a de-emphasis on state economic planning, and modest moves toward private ownership of commercial enterprises. In 1987, in an attempt to further promote his reform ideas, Gorbachev published *Perestroika: New Thinking for Our Country and the World.* In doing so, he propounded new economic con-

cepts, novel ideas on foreign policy, and his thoughts on socialist ethics.

Gorbachev's lack of detailed expertise on economic matters combined with great resistance among staunch Communist Party defenders of the status quo made significant changes in the Soviet Union exceedingly difficult to enact. In the end, his commitment to reforming communism rather than abolishing it meant that his reforms were too limited to satisfy those individuals and groups calling for more dramatic change. Although some parts of his reform agenda were successfully implemented, continued sociopolitical problems and a failed coup attempt in August 1991 led to the collapse of the Soviet Union and the simultaneous resignation of Gorbachev in December 1991. Perestroika may not have been successful domestically, but it was definitely influential on the international scene, allowing the Soviets and Americans to engage in revolutionary nuclear and conventional arms reduction agreements.

Melissa Jordine

Further Reading

Goldman, Marshall. *What Went Wrong with Perestroika.* New York: Norton, 1992.

Gorbachev, Mikhail. *Perestroika: New Thinking for Our Country and the World.* London: HarperCollins, 1987.

MacKenzie, David, and Michael W. Curran. *Russia and the USSR in the Twentieth Century.* 4th ed. New York: Wadsworth, 2002.

Prague Spring (1968)

The so-called Prague Spring was a brief period of unprecedented liberalization in communist-ruled Czechoslovakia, short-circuited by a Soviet-led Warsaw Pact invasion of the country. On January 5, 1968, the Communist

Party leadership of Czechoslovakia ousted Stalinist first secretary Antonín Novotný. Having been elevated to first secretary in March 1953 and thus enjoying one of the longest tenures among communist leaders in Soviet-dominated Eastern Europe, he fell victim to growing economic, political, and national discontents. Since the early 1960s, he had rejected reform while exhibiting a willingness to use repression against workers, intellectuals, and students who questioned the existing system.

Novotný's replacement as first secretary was 46-year-old Alexander Dubček, who as leader of the Slovak Communist Party since 1963 had championed reform in general and the cause of equality for Slovakia in particular. While committed to maintaining Czechoslovakia's relationship with Moscow, he advocated socialism with a human face, sponsoring reforms designed to transform the Czechoslovak system into one in which socialism coexisted with democracy,

individual rights, and moderate economic freedoms. The result was a brief era of political, cultural, and economic liberalization known as the Prague Spring.

While Dubček's accession to power brought an immediate change in the political climate in Czechoslovakia, the Prague Spring commenced in earnest on April 9, 1968, when the Czech Communist Party announced the so-called Action Program. This promised, among other things, reduced state economic planning and greater freedom for both industry and agriculture, a commitment to economic quality between Czechoslovakia and the Soviet Union, protection of civil liberties, and autonomy for Dubček's native Slovakia. The party would retain its leadership position, but the program stipulated that henceforth it would be more responsive to the desires of the people.

Over the course of the next several months, with the support of Ludvik Svoboda, who had replaced Novotný as Czechoslovak

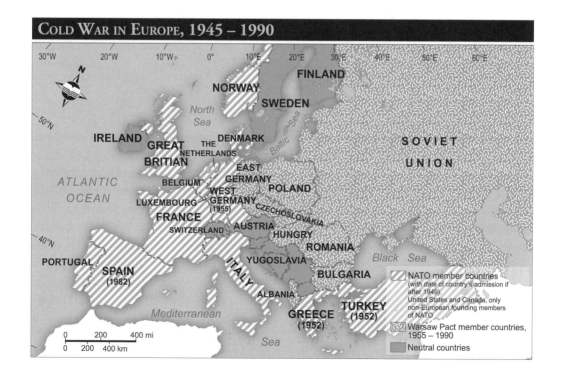

COLD WAR IN EUROPE, 1945 – 1990

Young Czechs holding a Czechoslovakian flag stand atop an overturned truck in Prague amid Soviet tanks in August 1968, while other youths surround the tanks. (AFP/Getty Images)

president in early April, Dubček fulfilled many of the program's promises. He abolished censorship, sanctioned the creation of workers' councils in factories, moved to increase trade with the West, allowed greater freedom to travel abroad, and supported the writing of a new party constitution designed to democratize the party. The Dubček regime even went so far as to enact a Rehabilitation Law in June that provided retrials for individuals previously convicted of political crimes by the communist regime.

The Czechoslovak population responded enthusiastically to the reforms, basking in a freedom it had not enjoyed since before the communist coup of February 1948. The press, radio, and television especially flourished, for the first time openly raising

questions about political purges, show trials, and concentration camps. By early summer, the public was pushing for further reforms to include the creation of independent political parties, the establishment of genuine political democracy, and more radical economic reforms.

As the Prague Spring unfolded, anxieties arose in Moscow. Soviet leader Leonid Brezhnev viewed the Czechoslovak reforms as a rejection of the Soviet political and economic model and worried that Prague might unilaterally withdraw from the Warsaw Pact. Similar anxieties took hold among German Democratic Republic (GDR, East Germany) and Polish conservative communist leaders who feared that the Czechoslovak reforms might destabilize their own countries.

On July 16, Soviet, East German, Polish, Hungarian, and Bulgarian leaders sent a joint letter to Prague demanding a halt to the reform movement. Blaming recent developments in Czechoslovakia on "reactionaries" supported by imperialism, the letter explained that the Czechoslovaks appeared headed off the socialist path and that the reforms threatened the entire socialist system. Dubček responded that his reforms should not be construed as anti-Soviet and that Czechoslovakia had no intention of leaving the Warsaw Pact. He also met twice with Brezhnev, in Prague on July 22 and in Cierna on July 29, apparently to prevent a Soviet military intervention.

Annoyed with Dubček's refusal to end the reforms, and unconvinced of his intentions, the Soviet Union and its Warsaw Pact partners, Romania excepted, decided to act. On the night of August 20–21, 1968, an estimated 500,000 Warsaw Pact troops (primarily Soviet Red Army but including units from East Germany, Poland, Hungary, and Bulgaria) invaded Czechoslovakia, meeting minimal resistance from a stunned population. Arrested and transported to Moscow on August 21, 1968, Dubček surrendered to Soviet demands to end the reforms. On August 27, he returned to Prague, tearfully informing the Czechoslovak population that the era of liberalization was over. Subsequently, the Prague Spring's most significant reforms were annulled as the old political and economic system was restored. Ultimately, in April 1969, Dubček was removed as the Communist Party of Czechoslovakia's first secretary. His replacement, Gustáv Husák, supported by Red Army troops, thereafter presided over one of the most repressive communist regimes in Eastern Europe.

Moscow justified its intervention by formulating what soon became known in the West as the Brezhnev Doctrine, which declared that no individual communist party had the right to make unilateral decisions that might be potentially damaging to socialism. It further stated that because a threat to the socialist system in any given country represented a threat to the socialist system as a whole, it was the duty of other socialist countries to intervene militarily to suppress any potential deviation from prescribed communist policies.

Although military intervention in Czechoslovakia headed off what Moscow perceived as a dangerous development, it exacerbated the Soviet Union's already precarious relations with the People's Republic of China (PRC), whose leaders publicly compared it to Nazi leader Adolf Hitler's aggression against Czechoslovakia in the 1930s. Equally significant, the intervention elicited public condemnation by the United States and led to the postponement of already-scheduled Strategic Arms Limitation Talks between President Lyndon Johnson and Brezhnev in Moscow.

Bruce J. DeHart

Further Reading

Kusin, Vladimir V. *The Intellectual Origins of the Prague Spring: The Development of Reformist Ideas in Czechoslovakia, 1956–1967.* Cambridge: Cambridge University Press, 2002.

Skilling, Gordon. *Czechoslovakia's Interrupted Revolution.* Princeton, NJ: Princeton University Press, 1976.

Williams, Kieran. *The Prague Spring and Its Aftermath: Czechoslovak Politics, 1968–1970.* Cambridge: Cambridge University Press, 1997.

R

Radio Free Europe and Radio Liberty

During the Cold War, the U.S. government-sponsored Radio Free Europe (RFE) and Radio Liberty (RL) broadcast uncensored news and information to audiences in the Soviet bloc in an attempt to weaken communist control over information and to foster internal opposition. RFE broadcast to Bulgaria, Czechoslovakia, Hungary, Poland, and Romania and, in the 1980s, to Estonia, Latvia, and Lithuania. RL transmitted in Russian and some 15 other national languages of the Soviet Union.

Unlike other Western broadcasters, RFE and RL concentrated on developments within and about their target countries not covered by state-controlled domestic media. They acted as surrogate home services, reporting on actions of the authorities and relaying views of dissidents and opposition movements. Notwithstanding repeated technical interference (jamming, for example), broadcasts generally reached their intended audiences. Evidence of the impact of the broadcasts on the eventual collapse of the communist regimes has been corroborated in the testimony of leaders such as Czech president Václav Havel after 1989.

RFE and RL were conceived in 1949 by George F. Kennan of the U.S. Department of State and Frank G. Wisner, head of the Central Intelligence Agency (CIA) Office of Policy Coordination, as instruments to utilize Soviet and East European émigrés in support of American foreign policy objectives. Founded as nonprofit corporations ostensibly supported with private funds, RFE and RL were in fact funded by the U.S. government through the CIA until 1972. The first official broadcast took place on July 4, 1950. RFE and RL initially adopted more confrontational editorial policies and used more aggressive language than other Western broadcasters. By the mid-1950s, however, as U.S. foreign policy toward the Soviet bloc became more conciliatory, the networks emphasized the need for liberalization and evolutionary system changes. In so doing, they broadcast news and information about domestic politics and economic issues as well as cultural and historical traditions normally suppressed by communist authorities. Over time, the networks evolved into saturation home services, seeking large audiences by broadcasting almost around the clock and by incorporating programs on Western music, religion, science, sports, youth, and labor issues.

The networks faced the considerable challenge of operating as surrogate home services in information-poor environments. They carefully monitored state-controlled print and electronic media and frequently interviewed travelers and defectors in field bureaus around the world. The networks cultivated ties with Western journalists and other visitors to communist countries and received information from regime opponents, often at great personal risk to the informants, within their target countries. This information was gathered to support broadcasts, but RFE and RL research reports also served many Western observers as their major source of information about the communist bloc.

RFE and RL programs were produced in Munich in the Federal Republic of Germany (FRG, West Germany) and were broadcast via shortwave transmitters operating on multiple frequencies and high power to overcome jamming and other frequency-disruption tactics. The networks enjoyed substantial operational autonomy and were highly decentralized in function. Émigré broadcast service directors with intimate knowledge of their audiences were responsible for most broadcast content, within broad policy guidelines and under American management oversight.

The communist authorities devoted major resources to countering RFE and RL broadcasts. In 1951, Soviet leader Josef Stalin personally ordered the establishment of local and long-distance jamming facilities to block Western broadcasts. Eastern bloc authorities also launched propaganda, diplomatic, and espionage campaigns intended to discredit the broadcasts. In addition, they jailed individuals providing information to either network. Ironically, the same authorities relied on secret transcripts of the broadcasts for information they could not obtain from local media that they themselves controlled.

After 1971, direct CIA involvement in the networks ended, and they were then openly funded by congressional appropriation through the Board for International Broadcasting. The network corporations were merged into a single entity, RFE/RL, Incorporated, in 1976.

The networks established intimate contact with their audiences during the 1970s and 1980s, when new waves of émigrés strengthened broadcast staffs and as dissidents and other regime opponents, emboldened by the Helsinki Final Act (1975), began to challenge the communist system. RFE and RL provided a "megaphone" through which independent figures, denied normal access to local media, could reach millions of their countrymen via uncensored writings. RFE and RL were able to document large audiences and acted as the leading international broadcaster in many target countries. After the Velvet Revolution of 1989, many East European and Russian leaders testified to the importance of RFE and RL broadcasts in ending the Cold War. Operating today from Prague in the Czech Republic, RFE/RL broadcasts to the southern Balkans, most of the former Soviet Union, Afghanistan, Iran, and Iraq in support of democratic institutions and a transition to democracy.

A. Ross Johnson

Further Reading

Mickelson, Sig. *America's Other Voice: The Story of Radio Free Europe & Radio Liberty*. New York: Praeger, 1983.

Puddington, Arch. *Broadcasting Freedom: The Cold War Triumph of Radio Free Europe and Radio Liberty*. Lexington: University Press of Kentucky, 2000.

Reagan, Ronald Wilson (1911–2004)

Born on February 11, 1911, in Tampico, Illinois, Ronald Reagan graduated from Eureka College in California, worked as a sports announcer, and in 1937 won a Hollywood contract with Warner Brothers, eventually appearing in 53 movies. As president of the Screen Actors Guild during the late 1940s and early 1950s, the once-liberal Reagan purged alleged communists and veered strongly to the Right. His politics grew increasingly conservative in the late 1950s and early 1960s.

In 1966 the genial Reagan won the first of two terms as the Republican governor of California. During his campaign he

Ronald Reagan was president of the United States during 1981–1989. A staunch anti-communist, he carried out the largest peacetime defense buildup in U.S. history and worked to reverse the liberal tradition that had dominated U.S. politics since the Great Depression. (Library of Congress)

supported U.S. intervention in Vietnam and condemned student antiwar protesters. He soon became one of the leading figures of the increasingly powerful Republican Right, supporting deep cuts in taxes and domestic expenditures, high defense budgets, and a strong anticommunist international posture, positions he affirmed while seeking the Republican presidential nomination in 1976 and 1980.

In 1980, when Reagan defeated Democratic incumbent president Jimmy Carter, the United States was suffering from spiraling inflation and high unemployment. In Iran, radical Muslims had overthrown Shah Mohammad Reza Pahlavi in 1979, sending

oil prices soaring, and for more than a year held U.S. diplomatic personnel hostage in Tehran. An almost simultaneous Soviet-backed coup in Afghanistan intensified a sense of American impotence, as did communist insurgencies in Central America and Africa. Reagan opposed compromise with communism. Believing firmly in the American way of life and convinced that an American victory in the Cold War was attainable, the ever-optimistic Reagan used blatantly triumphalist, anti-Soviet rhetoric, famously terming the Soviet Union an "evil empire."

Reagan purposefully engaged the Soviets in an arms race whereby he and his advisors hoped that American technological and economic superiority would strain the Soviet economy. In 1982 and 1983 the president issued directives intended to deny the Soviets Western credits, currency, trade, and technology and to embargo Soviet exports of oil and natural gas to the West. The Reagan administration hiked the defense budget from $171 billion to $376 billion between 1981 and 1986, hoping to force the Soviets into bankruptcy and to position the United States to better combat communism around the world. In 1983 Reagan announced that the United States would begin research on an expensive new ballistic missile defense system, the Strategic Defense Initiative (SDI), popularly known as Star Wars, to intercept and destroy incoming nuclear missiles. If successful, this program, which contravened several existing arms control treaties, would have provided the United States with substantial protection against a Soviet nuclear attack, thereby destabilizing the nuclear balance and quite possibly triggering a new arms race.

Breaking with Carter's policies, Reagan also deliberately de-emphasized human rights, consciously supporting dictatorships provided they were pro-American, while assailing human rights abuses within the Soviet sphere. Covert operations intensified as the United States offered support to anticommunist forces around the world, providing economic aid to the dissident Polish Solidarity trade union movement and military and economic assistance to antigovernment rebels in Angola, mujahideen guerrillas in Afghanistan, and the anti-Sandinista Contras in Nicaragua. Efforts to overthrow the existing Nicaraguan government included Central Intelligence Agency (CIA) mining of ports and harbors. When Congress responded by passing the Boland Amendment of 1984, forbidding funding for Nicaraguan covert actions, the Reagan administration embroiled itself in an ill-fated secret enterprise to sell arms to Iran—thereby evading its own embargo but, officials suggested, enhancing the political standing of Iranian moderate elements—and using the proceeds to aid the Nicaraguan Contras. Revelations of these illegal activities and his probable complicity in them embarrassed Reagan during his second term.

They did not, however, compromise Reagan's ability to reach unprecedented new understandings with the Soviet Union. Notwithstanding his bellicose rhetoric, in practice Reagan was surprisingly pragmatic and cautious. In potentially difficult guerrilla settings, his administration favored covert operations, preferably undertaken by surrogates such as the Afghan mujahideen or the Nicaraguan Contras, over outright military intervention. Wars were kept short and easily winnable, as in the small Caribbean island of Grenada in 1983 when American troops liberated the island from Marxist rule. When, almost simultaneously, radical pro-Syrian Druze Muslims bombed the Beirut barracks of an American peacekeeping force in Lebanon, killing 241 American soldiers, the United States quickly withdrew. In 1986, suspected Libyan involvement in

terrorist incidents provoked only retaliatory American surgical air strikes on Tripoli.

Despite campaign pledges to the contrary, Reagan did not shun the People's Republic of China (PRC) or restore American relations with the Republic of China (ROC, Taiwan). In 1982 the Reagan administration reached an understanding with China on Taiwan, after which the Chinese gave some support to the Afghan rebels. Sino-American trade increased, and Reagan made a 1984 state visit to Beijing. By 1984, domestic politics suggested that the president moderate his anti-Soviet line. He faced a reelection campaign against a liberal opponent, Walter Mondale, just as his nuclear buildup and the stalemating of inconclusive arms control talks had generated substantial public support in both America and Europe for a nuclear freeze. In September 1984, Reagan proposed combining all major ongoing nuclear weapons talks into one package, and Soviet leaders soon agreed.

Reagan's mellowing coincided with the culmination of long-standing Soviet economic problems. Empire imposed added burdens on the Soviets as military spending rose, diverting funds from domestic programs. Most countries in Eastern Europe still resented Soviet domination. In Poland, the Solidarity movement proved remarkably persistent, undercutting Soviet control. Assertive Soviet policies in Africa and Latin America carried a high price tag too, while the decade-long Afghan intervention embroiled Soviet troops in a costly and unwinnable guerrilla war.

In 1985 the young and energetic Mikhail Gorbachev became the general secretary of the Communist Party of the Soviet Union (CPSU). He immediately sought to address Russia's problems and reform the communist economic and social system, an uphill battle given the immense burdens of the Soviet military. In addition, the costly SDI program that Reagan had proposed was likely to demand massive further Soviet investment.

American and European leaders were initially wary of Gorbachev's overtures, but even so, he quickly won great popularity. After meeting Gorbachev, Margaret Thatcher, the hard-line British Conservative prime minister whom Reagan had long found to be a political soul mate, urged her colleague to work with the Soviet leader, and Reagan was more willing than many of his advisors to trust Gorbachev. Domestic economic factors may also have impelled Reagan toward rapprochement. Deep tax cuts meant that heavy government budget deficits financed the defense buildup in the 1980s, and in November 1987 an unexpected Wall Street stock market crash suggested that American economic fundamentals might be undesirably weak. Reagan had several summit meetings with Gorbachev, and in 1987 the superpowers signed the Intermediate-Range Nuclear Forces (INF) Treaty, eliminating all medium-range missiles in Europe and imposing strong verification procedures. This marked the beginning of a series of arms reduction agreements, continued under Reagan's successor George H. W. Bush, and of measures whereby the Soviet Union withdrew from its East European empire and, by 1991, allowed it to collapse. Although Bush's presidency saw the culmination of these developments, it was Reagan who first perceived their potential.

Reagan, the oldest U.S. president in history, left office in 1989. After a decade-long battle with Alzheimer's, he died of pneumonia at his home in Los Angeles, California, on June 5, 2004. Reagan's impressive state funeral in Washington, D.C., paid tribute to him as the American president whose policies effectively helped to end the Cold War on U.S. terms.

Priscilla Roberts

Further Reading

Cannon, Lou. *President Reagan: The Role of a Lifetime*. New York: Simon and Schuster, 1991.

Fischer, Beth A. *The Reagan Reversal: Foreign Policy and the End of the Cold War*. Columbia: University of Missouri Press, 1997.

Fitzgerald, Frances. *Way Out There in the Blue: Reagan, Star Wars, and the End of the Cold War*. New York: Simon and Schuster, 2000.

Matlock, Jack F., Jr. *Reagan and Gorbachev: How the Cold War Ended*. New York: Random House, 2004.

Mervin, David. *Ronald Reagan and the American Presidency*. New York: Longman, 1990.

Pemberton, William E. *Exit with Honor: The Life and Presidency of Ronald Reagan*. Armonk, NY: Sharpe, 1997.

Smith, Geoffrey. *Reagan and Thatcher*. New York: Norton, 1991.

Strober, Deborah Hart, and Gerald S. Strober. *The Reagan Presidency: An Oral History of the Era*. Washington, DC: Brassey's, 2003.

S

Sakharov, Andrei Dmitrievich (1921–1989)

Born on May 21, 1921, in Moscow, the son of a physics professor, Andrei Sakharov studied physics at Moscow University during 1939–1942 and at the Lebedev Institute of the Soviet Academy of Sciences during 1945–1947 under the eminent theoretical physicist Igor Tamm. Sakharov earned his doctorate in 1947 and joined the Soviet nuclear weapons program in 1948, working in a special group then headed by his mentor.

Spearheaded by Sakharov, Tamm's group produced the first Soviet hydrogen bomb, successfully tested in August 1953, a development that greatly intensified the nuclear arms race with the United States. For his contributions to the development of the hydrogen bomb, Sakharov received both the Lenin and Stalin Prizes and earned election as a full member of the Soviet Academy of Sciences in 1953.

Sakharov's participation in the Soviet nuclear weapons program lasted nearly 20 years. Initially, he believed that his work was of vital importance to the global balance of power. However, over time he grew uneasy with what he characterized as moral problems inherent in his work, and he became disillusioned with the Soviet system, specifically the absence of civil liberties and the secrecy surrounding science, culture, and technology.

Beginning in the late 1950s, Sakharov called on the Soviet regime to ban atmospheric testing of nuclear weapons. In the early to mid-1960s, he moved on to criticize the continuing influence of the erroneous theories of T. S. Lysenko on Soviet genetics and to protest Soviet leader Leonid Brezhnev's tentative first steps toward rehabilitating the legacy of Soviet dictator Josef Stalin. Sakharov ultimately crossed the Rubicon to full dissident in 1968, when his essay "Reflections on Progress, Peaceful Coexistence, and Intellectual Freedom" appeared in the Western press. This extended essay, also known as the Sakharov Memorandum, warned of the dangers, including thermonuclear annihilation, that threatened humanity. He also pushed for reconciliation between socialist and capitalist nations, advocated democratic freedoms in the Soviet Union, denounced collectivized agriculture, and called for a careful reexamination of the Stalin era. In response, the Brezhnev regime removed Sakharov from the Soviet nuclear weapons program and stripped him of all privileges to which he had been entitled as a member of the Soviet Nomenklatura.

In the summer of 1969, Sakharov became a senior researcher at the Lebedev Institute, but his primary concerns for the remainder of his life were human rights and the democratization of the Soviet Union. In 1970, he and fellow physicist Valeri Chalidze established the Moscow Human Rights Committee, which advocated freedom of speech and the full implementation of the Soviet constitution, and monitored violations of the law and the constitution including the arrests of dissidents by the Soviet regime. Sakharov's efforts in the name of human rights earned him the Nobel Peace Prize in 1975, making him the first Soviet citizen to garner the award,

Dissident Soviet physicist Andrei D. Sakharov, March 1974. (AP/Wide World Photos)

although he was not permitted to leave the Soviet Union to claim it.

Although the Soviet Komitet Gosudarstvennoi Bezopasnosti (KGB) harassed Sakharov and threatened him with prosecution, he remained a free man until 1980 when, in the wake of his criticisms of the 1979 invasion of Afghanistan and with the 1980 Moscow Olympics approaching, the Brezhnev regime exiled him to Gorky, a military-industrial city closed to foreigners. There Sakharov remained until December 1986, when Soviet leader Mikhail Gorbachev, as part of his policy of glasnost, freed him, allowing him and his wife Yelena Bonner to return to Moscow and resume his scientific endeavors.

In 1989, the Soviet Academy of Sciences selected Sakharov to serve as a deputy in the newly established Congress of People's Deputies, the first democratically elected national legislative body to sit in Russia since the Bolshevik Revolution. There Sakharov proved to be an outspoken critic of Gorbachev, constantly pushing him to carry his political and economic reforms further. Sakharov died of a heart attack in Moscow on December 14, 1989.

Bruce J. DeHart

Further Reading

Bailey, George. *Galileo's Children: Science, Sakharov and the Power of the State*. New York: Arcade Publishing, 1990.

Lourie, Richard. *Sakharov: A Biography*. Hanover, NH: University Press of New England, 2002.

Sakharov, Andrei. *Memoirs*. Translated by Richard Lourie. New York: Knopf, 1990.

Sino-Soviet Split (1956–1966)

The collapse of the Sino-Soviet alliance marked the transformation of the Cold War world from bipolarity to multi-polarity. Superficially an ideological partnership between the world's two largest communist countries, the Sino-Soviet alliance began on February 14, 1950, with the conclusion of the Sino-Soviet Treaty. From its inception, the seemingly monolithic union was fraught with constantly shifting expectations about its precise place in the socialist world, subjected to American attempts to split it, and afflicted by the progressively ideological radicalism of People's Republic of China (PRC) Chairman Mao Zedong. Although Sino-Soviet disagreements over Soviet leader Nikita Khrushchev's 1956 de-Stalinization campaign remained hidden for a time, the advanced state of the alliance's disintegration became known to the outside world by the early 1960s. Because Mao exploited ideological conflict for domestic purposes, the final breakdown of the Sino-Soviet partnership in mid-1966 coincided with the beginning of the Cultural Revolution (1966–1976), launched both to purge the Chinese Communist Party (CCP) of alleged ideological revisionists and to create a communist utopia.

Viewing any alliance with a great power solely as a temporary means to help restore past Chinese glory and power, the Chinese Communists by the late 1940s had decided to lean toward the Soviet Union. Surprised by Mao's request in late 1949 for an economic and military alliance, Soviet leader Josef Stalin first hesitated but then agreed for utilitarian reasons to conclude a Friendship and Alliance Treaty that provided the Soviet Union access to railroads, warm-water ports, and important raw materials deposits in Manchuria and Xinjiang in exchange for Soviet military and economic aid. Stalin's limited support of the PRC during the Korean War (1950–1953), however, revealed the limits of the military aspects of the alliance. After the dictator's 1953 death, the end of the Korean War, and Khrushchev's ascendancy to power, the focus of the Sino-Soviet relationship gradually shifted toward assistance in economic development and improved party relations.

Khrushchev's "secret speech" of February 25, 1956, charging Stalin with arbitrary and criminal rule, undermined Mao's growing personality cult in China but strengthened his hand in his relations with the Soviet leaders. After increasing his influence in the socialist world through diplomatic mediation during the 1956 Hungarian Revolution, Mao concluded that although he considered Khrushchev's criticism of Stalin unfair and imbalanced, it had nevertheless revealed the need to preempt internal dissent in China in order to prevent a crisis similar to the Hungarian Revolution. The PRC's Hundred Flowers campaign in the spring of 1957 was designed to allow party members and intellectuals to vent their pent-up frustrations in a highly controlled framework but threatened within only a few weeks to undermine the Chinese communist regime. While Beijing launched the Anti-Rightist campaign in the summer of 1957 to stamp out internal dissent, Khrushchev survived the so-called Anti-Party Incident, which the remaining Stalinists in the party leadership staged with the goal of reversing de-Stalinization. Both events proved to be crucial for the further development of the Sino-Soviet relationship, since they put the PRC and the Soviet Union on two conflicting political, ideological, and economic paths.

As modest liberalization continued in the Soviet Union in 1958, Mao, following the Anti-Rightist campaign, radicalized the domestic political discourse in the run-up to the Great Leap Forward, which was supposed to propel the PRC into full-fledged communism. These internal changes led to a more aggressive and anti-American foreign policy before and during the Second Taiwan Strait Crisis (August–September 1958). Mao's willingness, stated to Soviet foreign minister Andrey Gromyko in early September, to trigger a nuclear war over a series of small, disputed islands in the Taiwan Strait placed the first significant strains on the Sino-Soviet relationship.

Faced with widespread famine as a result of the misguided economic policies of the Great Leap Forward, the CCP leadership undertook internal discussions in mid-1959 about economic reforms aimed at averting further disaster. Fearing challenges to his leadership, Mao was able both to purge his opponents within the party and to relaunch an unreformed Great Leap Forward in late 1959 in order to save his vision of a communist utopia. The economic catastrophes resulting from the Great Leap Forward, however, shocked the Soviet Union. Furthermore, Mao's radical anti-American stance also clashed with Khrushchev's rapprochement policies.

People's Republic of China leader Mao Zedong confers with leader of the Soviet Union Nikita Khrushchev during the latter's 1958 visit to Beijing. (Library of Congress)

The unexpected April 1960 Chinese publication of the so-called Lenin Polemics—three articles released on the occasion of Vladimir I. Lenin's 90th birthday that promoted ideologically radical positions diametrically opposed to Soviet viewpoints—revealed the brewing Sino-Soviet tensions to the world. After ideological clashes between the Soviet and CCP delegations during the Third Romanian Party Congress in late June 1960, the Soviet Union decided to punish the PRC by withdrawing all of its advisors from the PRC in July 1960.

Although the Great Leap Forward had caused the complete collapse of China's economy and had brought Sino-Soviet trade to a virtual standstill, Beijing used the withdrawal to blame Moscow for its economic problems. Until the mid-1960s, the PRC

shifted much of its foreign trade away from the Soviet Union toward Japan and Western Europe. Because of China's pressing economic problems and the failure of Khrushchev's rapprochement with U.S. president Dwight D. Eisenhower after the May 1960 U-2 crisis, however, both sides realized the necessity of an ideological truce, which they formally reached at the Moscow Conference of the world's communist parties in late 1960.

Shunted aside from domestic decision making because of his close association with the failed Great Leap Forward, Mao used the 1961 Soviet–Albanian conflict as a tool to rebuild his political fortunes at home. Subsequent anti-Soviet propaganda in the PRC triggered conflicts between Soviet citizens and ethnic Central Asians living in Xinjiang on the one side and the local Chinese administration on the other. The mass flight of 67,000 people to Soviet Kyrgyzstan in the late spring of 1962 caused Beijing to abrogate its consular treaty with Moscow on the basis of alleged Soviet subversive activities in western China. Mao used these developments to restore his standing in the CCP leadership and to push for more anti-Soviet policies in the second half of 1962. Khrushchev's nuclear provocation and sudden retreat under U.S. pressure during the 1962 Cuban Missile Crisis provided Mao with an unexpected opportunity to attack the Soviet leadership publicly for ideological inconsistency and political unreliability.

The United States had been intent on splitting the Sino-Soviet alliance since 1950, but only in the aftermath of the Cuban Missile Crisis was it able to use the Soviet-British-American negotiations on the Partial Test Ban Treaty (PTBT) to deepen the Sino-Soviet rift. Aware of the problems between Beijing and Moscow, Washington played on Soviet fears about China's nuclear weapons program and Khrushchev's dissatisfaction with Mao's ideological warfare. Despite the fact that the PTBT (initialed on July 25, 1963) did not infringe on China's nuclear program, the signing of the treaty by almost all countries of the world within five months isolated the PRC internationally.

The period from mid-1963 to mid-1966 witnessed the final collapse of Sino-Soviet party and military relations. Convinced that the Sino-Soviet pact had fulfilled its usefulness, Mao fanned and exploited ideological conflict and territorial disputes with his Soviet comrades for domestic purposes. Because the launching of the Cultural Revolution required a prior break with what Mao termed Soviet "revisionists, traitors of Marxism-Leninism, and fascists," he eventually broke party relations in early 1966 by his

refusal to send a delegation to the Twenty-Third Soviet Party Congress. Simultaneously, his radical ideological stances precluded the invocation of Sino-Soviet Treaty obligations in support of the Democratic Republic of Vietnam (DRV, North Vietnam) during the Vietnam War (1964–1973). By the mid-1960s, the military alliance between Beijing and Moscow factually ceased to exist, although the treaty did not officially expire until February 14, 1980. Until the rapprochement initiated by Soviet president Mikhail Gorbachev in the late 1980s, for nearly 25 years Sino-Soviet relations consisted only of low-level cultural relations and limited trade links.

Lorenz M. Lüthi

Further Reading

Dittmer, Lowell. *Sino-Soviet Normalization and Its International Implications, 1945–1990.* Seattle: Washington University Press, 1992.

Hunt, Michael H. *The Genesis of Chinese Communist Foreign Policy.* New York: Columbia University Press, 1996.

Lüthi, Lorenz M. "The Sino-Soviet Split, 1956–1966." Unpublished doctoral diss., Yale University, 2003.

Robinson, Thomas W., and David Shambaugh, eds. *Chinese Foreign Policy: Theory and Practice.* Oxford, UK: Clarendon, 1998.

Westad, Odd Arne, ed. *Brothers in Arms: The Rise and the Fall of the Sino-Soviet Alliance, 1945–1953.* Washington, DC: Woodrow Wilson Center Press, 1998.

Solidarity Movement

The Solidarity Movement was a Polish independent labor union established in September 1980, credited with bringing democracy to Poland and helping to end the Cold War. On July 1, 1980, the Polish government, headed by Prime Minister Edward Babiuch and communist First Secretary Edward Gierek, announced across-the-board price increases. Immediately, factory workers throughout Poland staged protest strikes. These proliferated and soon reached the Baltic coast, affecting Poland's largest port cities of Gdańsk and Gdynia.

Workers at the Lenin Shipyards in Gdańsk went on strike at the beginning of August. The local strike committee, led by electrician Lech Wałęsa, was soon transformed into the Inter-Factory Strike Committee. It was unprecedented in both size and form, as it claimed to represent not just the shipyard workers but all Polish workers. The Strike Committee put forth a list of 21 demands to be met by the Polish Communist Party. These demands included the right to form independent labor unions, the right to strike, freedom of speech and press, the release of political prisoners, and other social and economic demands. On August 31, 1980, Wałęsa's committee signed an agreement in Gdańsk with Deputy Prime Minister Mieczysław Jagielski by which the government agreed to the workers' demands, including the formation of independent trade unions. Similar agreements were signed in Szczecin and Jastrzębie. Several days later, Gierek resigned his post.

As soon as the agreements were signed, workers began to organize themselves into union groups. Inter-Factory Strike Committees became Inter-Factory Founding Committees. Until this point, Polish labor unions had been an extension of the Communist Party and had no true independence.

On September 17, 1980, the Founding Committees decided to organize one umbrella labor union known as Solidarność (Solidarity). By this time, union membership was close to four million people, and the decision to form one central union was deeply troubling to Polish authorities. On November 10, 1980, following a series of difficult negotiations, Solidarity was officially registered as a union.

Moscow and Warsaw eyed Solidarity with great trepidation. The movement was large, and Soviet leaders especially viewed its antisocialist elements as particularly troubling. They also feared that it would set a precedent that might be followed in other communist bloc nations. Over the next 13 months, an uneasy relationship existed between the Communist Party and Solidarity. Solidarity was gradually realizing its demands through strikes or the threat of strikes. These demands were in most cases limited to working conditions, wages, and workers' rights. By the end of 1981, nearly 10 million members, some 80 percent of the national workforce, had joined the movement.

Polish authorities never fully accepted the legitimacy of Solidarity. In fact, they resorted to stalling tactics and harassment of union activists in the hope of weakening the movement. Meanwhile, the authorities were preparing plans to crush Solidarity, by military means if necessary. Tensions between Solidarity and the government peaked during the Solidarity Congress in September–October 1981. Solidarity's September 8, 1981, "Message to the Working People of Eastern Europe," which urged workers in other communist bloc nations to unite, brought applause among union members and near panic on the part of Polish and Soviet authorities. By then, it was clear that Solidarity had become a grave threat to communist rule. Moscow threatened Polish leaders with armed intervention unless Solidarity was shut down. For a time, the real threat of a Soviet military invasion loomed.

Then, on December 13, 1981, the Polish government, now headed by General Wojciech Jaruzelski, imposed martial law

Shipyard strikers hoist Lech Walesa on their shoulders after the official founding of the independent trade union *Solidarnosc* (Solidarity) in Warsaw, Poland, on September 24, 1980. (Alain Keler/Sygma/Corbis)

and declared Solidarity illegal. Almost 10,000 Solidarity members were detained. Wałęsa was among those arrested.

Pope John Paul II and the Catholic Church publicly supported the struggles of Solidarity and its imprisoned principals while clandestinely sending messages of encouragement to Wałęsa and others. Wałęsa credited the eventual triumph of Solidarity to the pope's intercession.

In April 1982, Solidarity activists who had avoided arrest formed the Solidarity Temporary Coordinating Committee to stage underground union activity. Four years later, in September 1986, Wałęsa initiated an open, albeit illegal, Solidarity Committee. The government refused to recognize this committee, and its members were closely watched by the secret police. Nevertheless, Wałęsa, who had won the 1983 Nobel Peace Prize, was now a prominent international figure. Silencing him was therefore exceedingly difficult for Polish authorities.

In August 1988, Polish authorities, together with the Catholic Church and the still-illegal Solidarity movement, commenced negotiations concerning the future of Poland. During February–April 1989, a roundtable brought together communists, opposition leaders, Solidarity members, and Catholic Church representatives. The talks brought an end to the government prohibition of Solidarity. In the elections that followed in June 1989, in which 35 percent of the seats were to be decided by election, Solidarity candidates won 161 of 161 seats in the Sejm and 99 of 100 in the Senate. In August 1989, Tadeusz Mazowiecki, one of Solidarity's founders, formed the first noncommunist post–World War II Polish

During a 1987 visit to Poland by Pope John Paul II, demonstrators march down a street carrying banners reading "Solidarnosc" ("Solidarity"), the name of the first Polish trade union, formed despite communist government opposition. (Peter Turnley/Corbis)

government. After 1989, Solidarity became a traditional political labor party.

Jakub Basista

Further Reading

Ash, Timothy Garton. *The Polish Revolution: Solidarity 1980–1982*. London: Jonathan Cape, 1983.

Biskupski, M. B. *The History of Poland*. Westport, CT: Greenwood, 2000.

Goodwyn, Lawrence. *Breaking the Barrier: The Rise of Solidarity in Poland*. New York: Oxford University Press, 1991.

Ost, David. *Solidarity and the Process of Anti-Politics: Opposition and Reform in Poland since 1968*. Philadelphia: Temple University Press, 1990.

Sputnik (October 4, 1957)

The world's first man-made, earth-orbiting satellite was launched by the Soviet Union on October 4, 1957. Although commonly used to describe the first satellite, *Sputnik*, meaning "fellow traveler," actually designates a series of satellites that were numbered sequentially. *Sputnik I* weighed 184 pounds, excluding the propulsion vehicle, and was placed into space as part of the 1957–1958 International Geophysical Year (IGY), which included the objective of launching artificial satellites for scientific research. *Sputnik I* was followed by the November 3, 1957, launch of *Sputnik II*, a 1,118-pound capsule with a dog named Laika as a passenger. These two stunning Soviet successes occurred before the failed launch attempt of *Vanguard*, the American contribution to the IGY scientific effort, on December 6, 1957.

The *Sputnik* launches, especially when contrasted with the American failure, were important symbols of Soviet technological prowess, which marked the beginning of the intense space competition with the United States that became known as the space race. The launch provided the Soviet Union with an important propaganda tool that was used to publicize the alleged advanced nature of Soviet society and the progress that was possible in a modern communist society.

The American public was shocked by the *Sputnik* success, and American domestic politics were soon dominated by discussions of the Soviets' technological superiority and of the implied threat to the United States. American political leaders quickly pushed for changes that would restore public confidence and retain technological superiority over the Soviets. The U.S. government responded to the challenge by passing the 1958 National Defense Education Act, which provided incentives to promote the study of science, mathematics, engineering, technical education, and other fields deemed necessary to national security. Additionally, the National Aeronautics and Space Act of 1958 created the National Aeronautics and Space Administration (NASA) to help centrally organize and coordinate American space efforts. However, military-oriented space

Passenger on the Soviet space craft *Sputnik 2*, Laika was the first life form in space. There were no plans for her to survive the journey. She probably died within hours of launch from heat and stress. (AP/Wide World Photos)

programs, such as reconnaissance satellites, remained outside NASA and were cloaked in secrecy.

Militarily speaking, the launch of a Soviet R-7 rocket, which propelled *Sputnik* into orbit, confirmed the Soviets' capability to field nuclear-armed intercontinental ballistic missiles (ICBMs). This created an impression of vulnerability in the United States and led to intensified American efforts to enhance early warning and defensive systems, expand the national civil defense program, and strengthen strategic nuclear forces. *Sputnik* directly contributed to the erroneous idea that a missile gap had developed between the Americans and Soviets, placing the United States at a comparative disadvantage. President Dwight D. Eisenhower knew that no such gap existed but was bound to maintain silence on the issue, as the information was highly classified. Ultimately, the missile gap became a hot-button issue in the 1960 presidential campaign.

For the Eisenhower administration, there was a beneficial side to *Sputnik*, however, as it removed concerns that the Soviet Union would raise national sovereignty issues in response to an orbital overflight by an American satellite. *Sputnik* established a precedent for satellites operating over sovereign territories and opened the legal window for reconnaissance satellite operations that were already being planned by the U.S. government. *Sputnik I* was an important scientific first, a clear public relations victory in the Cold War, and an important event that shaped the continuing international struggle between the United States and the Soviet Union.

Jerome V. Martin

Further Reading

Divine, Robert A. *The Sputnik Challenge*. New York: Oxford University Press, 1993.

Harford, James. *Korolev: How One Man Masterminded the Soviet Drive to Beat America to the Moon*. New York: Wiley, 1997.

Levine, Alan J. *The Missile and the Space Race*. Westport, CT: Praeger, 1994.

McDougall, Walter A. *The Heavens and the Earth: A Political History of the Space Age*. Baltimore: Johns Hopkins University Press, 1997.

Stalin, Josef (1879–1953)

More absolute a ruler than any Russian tsar, Josef Stalin (born Iosif Vissarionovich Dzhugashvili) was one of the most powerful and influential figures in history and certainly one of its most horrific. As many as 20 million people may have died as a direct result of his policies.

Much of Stalin's early life remains obscure, in part because he took pains to rewrite it. Born in the town of Gori, Georgia, in the Caucasus on December 21, 1879, he was the only child of his parents to survive infancy. His father was a cobbler and his mother a washerwoman and domestic. His father (who died in a barroom brawl) was an alcoholic and beat young Josef regularly.

Stalin's mother wanted Josef to become a priest, and he graduated from the four-year elementary ecclesiastical school in Gori in 1894 and then entered a theological seminary in Tiflis (Tblisi) on a scholarship. He grew up to be a small man, barely five feet in height, with a pockmarked face and a withered arm (or at least one of sufficient infirmity to keep him out of the Russian Army). He either quit the seminary or was expelled. In any case, he said it was there that he was introduced to Russian Marxism.

In 1901 Josef joined the Russian Social Democratic Labor Party. His activities to secure funds included robberies and counterfeiting operations. He was subsequently arrested, tried, and convicted. Exiled to Siberia in 1903, he escaped a year later. His enemies would later charge that he was also in the pay of the tsarist secret police.

One of Josef's aliases, the one by which he became best known, was that of Stalin (Man of Steel), given to him by his fellow revolutionaries for his strength and ruthlessness. Coarse and ill-mannered, Stalin was arrested and exiled six times and escaped five times. Freed during the March 1917 Revolution, he returned to Petrograd and became editor of the party newspaper *Pravda* (Truth). His role in the Bolshevik seizure of power that November is unclear, but he clearly did not take a leading part. Leon Trotsky, a rival for power later, remembered Stalin's role as "a gray blur."

Stalin was active in the Russian Civil War (1918–1921) and the Russo-Polish War (1920–1921), and from 1920 to 1923 he was commissar of nationalities. In 1923 he assumed the post of secretary-general of the Communist Party of the Soviet Union (CPSU), a position he used as a springboard to power. His political rise has been ascribed to his skill at infighting and playing one faction against another as well as his absolute ruthlessness, but he also put in long hours at his job and deserves considerable credit for his achievement.

By the late 1920s, Stalin had triumphed over his rivals, chief among them Trotsky, to wield absolute power in the Soviet Union. Stalin created the bureaucratic system and refined both the secret police and slave labor camps begun under his predecessor, Vladimir Lenin. Stalin abandoned Lenin's New Economic Policy (NEP) that permitted a degree of capitalism in Russia and initiated a series of five-year plans to modernize the economy, concentrating on heavy industry. Stalin's economic policies included the forced collectivization of agriculture that claimed an estimated 10–15 million lives.

Stalin was personally responsible for the Great Purge trials of the 1930s that consumed virtually all of the top party leadership. Also falling victim to the Great Purge were military leaders, including 60 percent of Red Army officers above the rank of major. In the so-called Deep Comb-Out that accompanied the show trials, hundreds of thousands of Soviet citizens simply vanished without benefit of judicial procedure.

Much of the blame for the dismal showing of the Red Army in the 1939–1940 war with Finland and at the outset of the German invasion of the Soviet Union in June 1941 must be attributed to Stalin's policies. He had also labeled repeated warnings of an impending German attack as "Western disinformation." He grew in stature as a military commander and strategist during the war, however. Learning the art of war and absorbing specialist military information, he made all important strategic decisions for the Red Army as well as taking many decisions on the tactical level.

In foreign affairs, Stalin seized opportunities that presented themselves in Eastern Europe and the Balkans. Knowing exactly what he wanted, he met with Western leaders in Moscow and at the Tehran, Yalta, and Potsdam conferences. In 1919, following World War I, the West had quarantined the new communist Russia with a series of new successor states, endeavoring to contain communism with a cordon sanitaire. Now, following World War II, Stalin sought the reverse, insisting at the very least on governments friendly to the Soviet Union in order to provide security for a badly wounded Soviet empire. Throughout his long reign, Stalin was intensely suspicious of foreigners and foreign, above all Western, influences. Thus, Soviets who had been in the West, including Red Army personnel captured during the war, were immediately suspect and treated as enemies. A great many people who had been in the West, voluntarily or involuntarily, were shipped off to the gulags. Many Soviet citizens had openly cooperated with the Germans during the war. Although Ukrainians were far too numerous to be uprooted, Stalin did make an example of the Crimean Tartars. He ordered some 300,000 of them sent to Uzbekistan in Central Asia.

Although there were fears in the West that Stalin's plans included the communization of Western Europe, the dictator's immediate motivation was simply that of securing the Soviet empire. Because of the Red Army presence on the ground, there was little that Western leaders could do to prevent this, short of war with the Soviet Union, which despite the U.S. nuclear monopoly was unimaginable to Washington in 1945. Stalin's regime emerged from the war with all of Eastern Europe and much of Central Europe under its control.

The Soviet Union had suffered grievously during the war, with perhaps 27 million people dead and widespread physical destruction. Stalin put the population to work rebuilding, although his people paid for this in retention of the 48-hour workweek and living standards well below those of 1940. In a new five-year plan, he continued his emphasis on building heavy industry, although some attention was paid to pressing housing needs.

To unite the Soviet people under his leadership, Stalin proclaimed the belief of a communist world threatened by encircling enemies. Everything was done to maintain the intense nationalist sentiments aroused by the ordeal of the long struggle against the Germans in World War II. Andrei Zhdanov, political boss of Leningrad, became the guiding spirit of this ideology, known as Zhdanovshchina. It championed Russian nationalism and attacked Western influence (now known as bourgeois cosmopolitanism), glorified communism, and above all trumpeted the accomplishments and inspiration of the Great Leader, Stalin, attributing to him all Soviet successes.

Once Stalin rejected a closer relationship with the West, the Cold War was launched in earnest. Stalin refused to allow the East European Soviet satellites to participate in the European Recovery Program (Marshall Plan), and following an impasse over German reunification on Soviet terms and impending Western currency reform in the Allies' zones of Germany, in the summer of 1948 Soviet troops cut off Western land access to the city of Berlin. This sparked a major East–West confrontation and led to the Berlin Airlift. Stalin's tactics and saber rattling resulted in the 1949 formation of the North Atlantic Treaty Organization (NATO) and prompted the movement toward West European unity.

Stalin pushed hard to develop an atomic bomb, a process greatly accelerated by Soviet espionage. Following the explosion of the Soviet Union's first nuclear device in late 1949, he adopted a less militant foreign policy, jettisoning the militant expansionism of the immediate postwar years in favor of one that was comparatively defensive in nature. While maintaining the traditionally truculent Soviet tone, he abandoned the further extension of his European empire. This move was accompanied by a massive propaganda effort, the great Stalinist Peace Campaign. Agitation against colonialism was increasingly used to weaken the Western hold on global military bases, while Soviet foreign policy also sought to sow discord between the United States and its allies.

Early in 1950, Stalin gave his blessing to plans by Democratic People's Republic of Korea (DPRK, North Korea) leader Kim Il Sung to invade the Republic of Korea (ROK, South Korea) and reunify the peninsula under communist rule. Stalin evidently believed Kim's contention that the United States would either do nothing or would not react in time to save South Korea. Later, when the war went badly for Kim and North Korea, Stalin sanctioned military intervention by the People's Republic of China (PRC).

The last act in the Stalinist drama was the so-called Doctors' Plot. Fed by Stalin's continuing paranoia, nine doctors, six of them Jewish, were accused of employing their medical skills to assassinate prominent individuals, among them Zhdanov, Stalin's heir apparent. Many in the Soviet Union believed that this heralded a return to the purges of the 1930s. But it may only have been a maneuver to strike out against the growing ascendancy of a leadership group headed by Georgy Malenkov and Lavrenty Beria or perhaps an effort to imbue the bureaucracy with renewed revolutionary zeal, much the way that Mao Zedong would do in the Cultural Revolution in China. Whatever the reasons, Stalin's death in Moscow on March 5, 1953, following a paralytic stroke, came as a relief to many in highly vulnerable Soviet leadership positions. His eventual successor, Nikita Khrushchev, began the slow process of de-Stalinization and denounced the many excesses of the Red Tsar.

Spencer C. Tucker

Further Reading

Bullock, Alan. *Hitler and Stalin: Parallel Lives*. New York: Knopf, 1992.

Conquest, Robert. *Stalin: Breaker of Nations*. London: Weidenfeld and Nicolson, 2000.

Deutscher, Isaac. *Stalin: A Political Biography*. New York: Oxford University Press, 1969.

McNeal, Robert H. *Stalin: Man and Ruler*. New York: New York University Press, 1988.

Todd, Allen. *The European Dictatorships: Hitler, Stalin, Mussolini*. Cambridge: Cambridge University Press, 2002.

Tucker, Robert C. *Stalin As Revolutionary, 1879–1929*. New York: Norton, 1973.

Tucker, Robert C. *Stalin in Power: The Revolution from Above, 1928–1941*. New York: Norton, 1990.

Ulam, Adam B. *Stalin: The Man and His Era*. Expanded ed. Boston: Beacon, 1989.

Volkogonov, Dimitrii. *Stalin: Triumph and Tragedy*. Translated and edited by Harold Shukman. New York: Grove Weidenfeld, 1991.

Strategic Air Command

The Strategic Air Command (SAC), a combat command of the U.S. Air Force, was responsible for long-range bombers and intercontinental ballistic missiles (ICBMs), two-thirds of the nation's strategic nuclear triad. SAC's main goal was to maintain a strong, credible strategic nuclear force that could swing into action within minutes, either to prevent a nuclear strike or to inflict one on an enemy nation.

SAC was formed in 1946, a year before the U.S. Air Force became a separate military service. Originally, SAC consisted of World War II B-17 and B-29 bombers. Its first commander was General George Kenney. On October 19, 1948, Lieutenant General Curtis LeMay took command and oversaw the move of SAC headquarters from Andrews Air Force Base in Maryland to Offutt Air Force Base outside Omaha, Nebraska. He quickly established stringent standards of performance, strict evaluation procedures, and incentive and retention programs. He also changed the way that personnel viewed the command.

During LeMay's tenure, SAC added B-50 and B-36 bombers. In its early years, the command had its own jet fighters for bomber protection and its own airlift. B-29 bombers were modified to be used as aerial tankers, with aerial refueling becoming an integral part of SAC and the nuclear war plan. In 1951, SAC began taking delivery of the all-jet B-47 bomber and the KC-97 tanker. These two aircraft were the mainstays of SAC forces into the early 1960s. In 1955, SAC received its first B-52 Stratofortress eight-engine bomber. SAC entered the missile age with the Snark subsonic intercontinental cruise missile and the Rascal, designed to be launched against ground targets from the B-47. The following year, the KC-135 Stratotanker, a four-engine jet air refueling aircraft, entered service.

At least one-third of all aircraft and almost all missiles were on alert at SAC bases 24 hours a day, 7 days a week. During the 1960s, B-52 bombers armed with nuclear weapons were on airborne alert, ready to strike targets from orbits outside the Soviet Union. The airborne alerts were terminated in late 1968.

In 1959, SAC employed 262,600 personnel, 3,207 aircraft, and 25 missiles, including the Snark, the first Atlas ICBMs, Thor intermediate-range ballistic missiles (IRBMs), and the Hound Dog, an air-launched cruise missile (ALCM) carried by the B-52. By 1959, SAC's bomber force was an all-jet force. In 1960, the Joint Strategic Target Planning Staff (JSTPS) was formed with SAC's commander as director and a vice admiral as deputy director. The JSTPS was established to provide centralized planning for the entire U.S. nuclear triad, SAC bombers and missiles as well as submarine-launched ballistic missiles (SLBMs), nuclear-armed tactical aircraft, and IRBMs. In the early 1960s, the Snark and Thor missiles were deactivated to make room for the new Atlas and Titan I ICBMs. B-47s and KC-97s were phased out, and the supersonic B-58 bomber was put into service. By 1962, the new Titan II and Minuteman I ICBMs came on-line. SAC reconnaissance aircraft included the U-2 and the SR-71, which was commissioned in the late 1960s. At its peak strength in 1962, SAC employed more than 282,000 personnel.

During the next 30 years, SAC's mission remained unchanged. Missile forces stabilized with a mix of 1,000 Minuteman II and III ICBMs (with 50 Peacekeeper ICBMs replacing 50 Minuteman IIIs in the late 1980s) and 54 Titan II ICBMs (phased out in the mid-1980s). SAC aircraft included, at various times, a mix of B-1, B-52, and FB-111 bombers armed with gravity weapons, short-range attack missiles, and ALCMs; a tanker force of KC-135s and KC-10s; and U-2 and SR-71 reconnaissance aircraft.

SAC B-52 bombers played a major role in the Vietnam War. The SAC airborne command post, dubbed "Looking Glass," with an airborne battle staff commanded by a general officer, was on alert with at least one EC-135 aircraft airborne at all times during 1961–1992. The number of people in the command remained near 200,000 until reductions in the bomber force caused a slow exodus. SAC had about 110,000 personnel when it was deactivated on June 1, 1992.

After the dissolution of the Soviet Union in 1991, the U.S. Air Force underwent a fundamental reorientation in structure and doctrine. Air force leadership acknowledged that SAC had accomplished its mission. It had maintained nuclear superiority—and peace—for 46 years. After it was deactivated, SAC's aircraft became part of new U.S. Air Force operational commands.

Charles G. Simpson

The Boeing B-52 Stratofortress strategic bomber first flew in 1954 and remains in active service. It is considered one of the greatest aircraft ever built. The B-52G Model shown here was photographed in 1984. (Department of Defense)

Further Reading

Anderton, David A. *Strategic Air Command: Two-Thirds of the Triad*. New York: Scribner, 1967.

Coard, Edna A. *U.S. Air Power: Key to Deterrence*. Maxwell Air Force Base, AL: Air University Press, 1976.

Freedman, Lawrence. *The Evolution of Nuclear Strategy*. 3rd ed. Houndmills, UK: Palgrave Macmillan, 2003.

Strategic Arms Limitation Talks and Treaties

Following the 1962 Cuban Missile Crisis, the United States and the Soviet Union began to move away from the abyss of nuclear war and toward the reduction of nuclear armaments. The two superpowers also sought cooperation on this issue because of the immense cost of the nuclear arms race. Continued production of nuclear weapons was becoming superfluous, as each side had more than enough capability to cripple the other even if only a small percentage of the weapons, should they be launched, actually struck their targets. The leadership of both nations was sufficiently motivated to seek an agreement on nuclear arms reduction. Adding to American motives were concerns that the Soviets might soon undermine U.S. superiority in nuclear arms and that the People's Republic of China (PRC) had acquired nuclear weapons beginning in 1964. Although the United States first approached the Soviet Union concerning strategic arms reduction talks in 1964, efforts to begin a dialogue failed repeatedly until the end of the decade.

Arms reduction talks between the two nations began in November 1969 and, after two and a half years of detailed negotiations, a two-part agreement was reached. The first major agreement to come out of the talks was the Anti-Ballistic Missile (ABM) Treaty, signed in Moscow on May 26, 1972. This treaty reflected a belief on the part of both nations that they should seek to limit the deployment of antiballistic missile systems.

ABMs were designed to destroy enemy missiles before they could strike their targets. The United States had sought an agreement with the Soviets since the late 1960s on ABMs, which the Soviets had begun to deploy, arguing that their continued deployment would lead the United States to develop larger nuclear weapons to defeat these defenses. Therefore, the development and deployment of ABMs would only intensify, not slash, the arms race. The Soviets finally accepted this line of reasoning. The preamble to the treaty reflected this understanding: "Effective measures to limit anti-ballistic missile systems would be a substantial factor in curbing the race in strategic offensive arms and would lead to a decrease in the risk of outbreak of war involving nuclear weapons."

The treaty had unlimited duration, with five-year reviews. The two sides created the Standing Consultative Commission to serve as the forum for discussing compliance issues or other problems with the treaty. The commission met in Geneva, Switzerland.

The ABM Treaty prohibited deployment of an ABM system for "the defense of the territory" or the provision of "a base for such defense." This effectively restricted the creation of a nationwide defensive system while permitting the Soviets and Americans to maintain two ABM sites, comprising no more than one hundred interceptor missiles at each location. Each country could position one ABM site to defend its capital, and the other could shield one group of land-based intercontinental ballistic missiles (ICBMs).

The agreement also prohibited transferring ABM sites to other nations.

Each side would verify compliance with the treaty through the use of national technical means. A 1974 Protocol to the treaty further limited each side to one ABM deployment site. The United States chose to place its system near the ICBM missile fields of Grand Forks, North Dakota, and the Soviet Union chose to defend Moscow.

The United States and Russia signed a series of agreements on September 27, 1997, that allowed Belarus, Kazakhstan, Russia, and Ukraine to succeed the Soviet Union as state parties to the treaty. These agreements also attempted to establish the demarcation between theater and national ballistic missile defense systems.

Ultimately, both sides realized that ABM systems lacked any real military value and were prohibitively expensive. The United States closed its sole ABM site in 1975. Russia's Galosh system surrounding Moscow is still operational. Citing national security concerns and a need to deploy a limited national missile defense system, the United States withdrew from the treaty on June 13, 2002.

Of greater importance was the wider-ranging arms control agreement that emerged from the Strategic Arms Limitation Talks (SALT). The Interim Agreement between the United States of America and the Union of Soviet Socialist Republics on Certain Measures with Respect to the Limitation of Strategic Offensive Arms, which came to be known as SALT I, was signed in Moscow by President Richard M. Nixon and Soviet Premier Leonid Brezhnev on May 26, 1972, along with the ABM treaty. The SALT I accord, which was scheduled to last for five years, required the two superpowers to maintain nuclear arsenals that were roughly equivalent to one another in terms of offensive land- and sea-launching platforms. The agreement froze the number of Soviet offensive ICBMs to 1,618 land-based missiles and 950 submarine-launched ballistic missiles (SLBMs). The American arsenal was restricted to 1,054 land-based missiles and 710 SLBMs. Mobile missile systems were not addressed. Though the Soviets seemed to have a numerical advantage in missile-launching capabilities, the United States continued to enjoy a substantial advantage in bombers (about 450 to 260 for the Soviets) and could also rely on the nuclear deterrents belonging to their European allies. The Americans also took advantage of their technological superiority to develop multiple independently targeted reentry vehicles (MIRVs). The Nixon administration refused to negotiate any limits in regard to this technological advance, and the Soviets would later take advantage of this.

In order to verify compliance with the terms of the treaty, both countries agreed to satellite photo reconnaissance of each other's territory. Even so, there were flaws in the agreement. The biggest problems were that the agreement failed to sufficiently regulate the upgrading of current missile systems. And it said nothing about the replacement of existing systems with new ones.

Each side took advantage of the loopholes in the treaty. The Soviets began to deploy a new missile system, the SS-19, that carried a warhead with six MIRVed warheads. This missile carried twice as many nuclear warheads as the mainstay of the U.S. intercontinental missile arsenal, the Minuteman. Eventually, the Soviet Union would develop the ability to launch missiles carrying 10 MIRVs. On the other hand, the United States began to work on the development of the cruise missile, arguing that such a system was not covered under the SALT I agreement. Further compromising the spirit of the treaty

were the new Soviet Backfire bomber, capable of reaching targets in the United States, and American plans to build the North American/Rockwell B-1 bomber and the Trident submarine. Another flaw in the treaty was that it permitted the replacement of so-called light missiles with heavy missiles, without adequately defining the term "heavy."

SALT I was designed to be an interim agreement, and the treaty contained a provision calling for continued talks aimed at creating a more detailed and comprehensive plan to regulate nuclear arms. Reaching agreement on what would become SALT II proved difficult, however. Progress was stalled by numerous factors, including President Nixon's resignation over the Watergate scandal in August 1974, American concerns with human rights violations in the Soviet Union, and a general deterioration in U.S.–Soviet relations during the 1970s. The broad numerical outlines of the eventual SALT II agreement were laid out in a summit meeting between Brezhnev and President Gerald Ford in Vladivostok in November 1974, but this did not lead to forward progress for many years.

Arms control talks continued between the two superpowers despite these obstacles. By 1979, both sides desired a new SALT agreement. Anxious to overcome numerous foreign policy setbacks, President Jimmy Carter's administration sought an arms deal to improve his chances for reelection in 1980. The Soviets sought an agreement chiefly for economic reasons, as the nation's rate of economic growth was quickly stagnating.

Concerned that the Soviets had an advantage in throw weight, or the size of the warhead that a missile could carry into space, Carter offered to cancel development of an experimental mobile ICBM that could carry 10 warheads (the MX missile) if the Soviets would cut their heavy ICBM force in half. The Soviets refused to consider an offer to prevent deployment of what was still an experimental system. Carter then backed away from this position, and the negotiations began to move toward an eventual agreement. As a result, Carter and Brezhnev affixed their signatures to the SALT II Treaty at the Vienna summit meeting on June 18, 1979.

By the terms of the treaty, both sides agreed to a limitation on the number of warheads that would be allowed on an ICBM and the total number of allowable strategic launchers. Strategic nuclear launch vehicles were limited to 2,250 on each side, and no more than 1,320 of these missiles could be outfitted with MIRVs. Within that total, a further subcategory limited MIRVed ballistic missiles to 1,200, of which only 820 could be ICBMs. New ICBMs were limited to carry no more than 10 warheads, and new SLBMs were limited to 14 warheads each. The treaty also prohibited space-based nuclear weapons, fractional orbital missiles, and rapid-reload missile launchers.

A protocol to the treaty was signed at the same time and remained in effect until December 31, 1981. The Soviets agreed not to utilize their Tupolev Tu-22M Backfire bomber, which had the ability to reach targets throughout most of the United States, as an intercontinental weapon, while the Americans consented to delay deployment of ground- and sea-launched cruise missiles for three years. In addition, MIRVed ground-launched cruise missiles (GLCMs) and submarine-launched cruise missiles (SLCMs) with a range of more than 600 kilometers could not be tested.

The SALT II treaty ran into considerable opposition in the United States, as some liberals expressed disappointment that the treaty had failed to halt the arms race, and con-

servatives complained that the Soviets had retained a significant edge in throw weight.

Soviet actions in 1979 added immeasurably to the problem of ratifying the treaty. Their support of the Vietnamese invasion of Cambodia, the Sandinista uprising in Nicaragua, and the Soviet invasion of Afghanistan in December 1979 all but torpedoed any prospects that SALT II would be ratified by the U.S. Senate. Knowing that the Senate would not ratify the SALT II treaty under such circumstances, Carter withdrew the treaty from Senate consideration on January 3, 1980. Although the treaty was never ratified by the United States, both sides nonetheless honored the agreement until May 1986, when President Ronald Reagan, citing Soviet violations, declared that the United States would no longer be bound by the limits of the SALT agreements.

Jeffrey A. Larsen and A. Gregory Moore

Further Reading

Carnesdale, Albert, and Richard N. Haass, eds. *Superpower Arms Control: Setting the Record Straight.* Cambridge, MA: Ballinger, 1987.

Donley, Michael B. *The SALT Handbook.* Washington, DC: Heritage Foundation, 1979.

Garthoff, Raymond L. *Détente and Confrontation: American-Soviet Relations from Nixon to Reagan.* Rev. ed. Washington, DC: Brookings Institution Press, 1994.

Morris, Charles R. *Iron Destinies, Lost Opportunities: The Arms Race between the U.S. and USSR, 1945–1987.* New York: Harper and Row, 1988.

Newhouse, John. *Cold Dawn: The Story of SALT.* New York: Holt, Rinehart and Winston, 1973.

Nixon, Richard. *RN: The Memoirs of Richard Nixon.* New York: Grosset and Dunlap, 1978.

Smith, Gerard. *Doubletalk: The Story of SALT I by the Chief American Negotiator.* New York: Doubleday, 1980.

Talbott, Strobe. *Endgame: The Inside Story of Salt II.* New York: HarperCollins, 1979.

Wolfe, Thomas W. *The SALT Experience.* Cambridge, MA: Ballinger, 1979.

Strategic Arms Reduction Talks and Treaties

In the early 1980s the United States launched an arms buildup that was part of an overall strategy to confront the Soviet Union. Reagan hoped to improve the American bargaining position vis-à-vis the Soviets by increasing the nation's military strength. He also hoped to force the Soviets to allocate more of their resources to the military in order to keep up. The most notable aspect of this renewed arms race was President Ronald Reagan's Strategic Defense Initiative (SDI), which was an attempt to create a space-based missile shield that would render offensive nuclear weapons impotent and obsolete. Critics viewed the SDI proposal as an expensive, unworkable, and possibly offensive weapons system that violated the 1972 Anti-Ballistic Missile (ABM) Treaty.

The North Atlantic Treaty Organization (NATO) began installing Pershing II and ground-launched cruise missiles in Europe in 1983 in response to the Soviets' refusal to downsize their arsenal of forward-deployed SS-20 theater-range missiles. This move caused the Soviets to walk out of arms control talks that had been ongoing in Geneva since 1982. Negotiations did not resume until March 1985.

In October 1986, Reagan abruptly reversed himself. During his first summit meeting with new Soviet leader Mikhail Gorbachev in Reykjavík, Iceland, the American president expressed his willingness to remove intermediate-range nuclear force (INF) weapons from Europe and to eliminate all strategic nuclear weapons. The initiative failed because Reagan was unwilling to include SDI in the proposal, and Gorbachev was unwilling to proceed unless SDI was part of the package.

Some two months later, the Soviets declared that they would negotiate according to the agenda laid out by the Americans, although initially focusing on the INF issue. The Soviets accepted the American proposal in February 1987, which called for the complete elimination of medium-range nuclear weapons from Europe. At the Washington Summit in December 1987, Gorbachev and Reagan signed the INF Treaty. This treaty established a double-zero solution, calling for the removal of two classes of intermediate-range missiles—those with a range of roughly 600–3,500 miles and those with a range of 300–600 miles. An extensive on-site verification process was established as well. By the end of 1988, the removal of the missiles was complete.

The Strategic Arms Reduction Talks (START) negotiations that had resumed in Geneva in 1985 bore fruit in 1991 with the signing of a treaty between the United States and the Union of Soviet Socialist Republics on the Reduction and Limitation of Strategic Offensive Arms, also known as the START I treaty. Under Presidents George H. W. Bush and Gorbachev, the two nations concluded the treaty on July 31, 1991, just months before the collapse of the Soviet Union. The complex document served to reduce strategic nuclear delivery systems to 1,600 on each side, with attributed nuclear warheads (a somewhat arbitrary but agreed-upon number associated with certain delivery systems) restricted to 6,000 each.

There were additional sublimits for attributed warheads: 4,900 on deployed ballistic missiles, of which no more than 1,100 could be on mobile launchers. The Soviet Union was also limited to 154 heavy ICBMs, each carrying 10 warheads. The treaty placed a limit on total nuclear throw weight, provided for verification processes, and also placed limitations on the types of vehicles that could carry nuclear warheads (including limits on the numbers of U.S. nuclear armed cruise missiles and Russian Backfire bombers).

On May 23, 1992, the Lisbon Protocol was signed, making START I a multilateral agreement among the United States, Russia, Belarus, Kazakhstan, and Ukraine. The treaty entered into force on December 5, 1994. The three new member states returned their residual Soviet-era nuclear arsenals to Russia prior to the implementation of the treaty and also joined the Nuclear Non-Proliferation Treaty (NPT) as nonnuclear weapons states.

The START I treaty had a duration of 15 years, with the option to extend it at five-year intervals. All parties officially reached their treaty limits on December 5, 2001. The parties created a Joint Compliance and Inspection Commission tasked with monitoring compliance with the treaty. The commission began meeting in Geneva, Switzerland, in 1991.

START I was followed by the signing of the Treaty between the United States and the Russian Federation on Further Reduction and Limitation of Strategic Offensive Arms, also known as START II, by Bush and Boris Yeltsin at the Moscow summit on January 3, 1993. START II relied heavily on START I for its definitions, procedures, and verification. The U.S. Senate ratified START II on January 26, 1996, and the Russian Duma ratified in on April 14, 2000.

This agreement called for a two-phase series of reductions. Phase one called for each side to reduce its deployed strategic forces to 3,800–4,250 attributed warheads within seven years of entry into force. There were sublimits for several categories within that total. Phase two, which was originally supposed to be completed by the year 2003, required each side to further reduce their deployed strategic forces to 3,000–3,500 attributed warheads. The following sublimits applied to phase two: 1,700–1,750 warheads on nuclear submarines, the elimination of multiple independently targeted reentry vehicles (MIRVs) on ballistic missiles, and the elimination of heavy ICBMs. America's B-2 bomber was left out of the START I treaty process since it was not scheduled to carry air-launched cruise missiles (ALCMs). In START II, however, the two parties agreed to include the B-2 as a strategic weapons delivery vehicle with a U.S. commitment not to hang ALCMs on its wings. This meant that it was accountable under the warhead limits and inspectable under the treaty's verification and compliance rules. The B-1 bomber was declared to have only a conventional mission. START II also significantly increased the level of on-site inspections necessary for implementation and compliance verification.

In March 1997, Yeltsin and President Bill Clinton met in Helsinki and agreed to extend the time period for START II implementation to December 31, 2007, as long as warheads were removed from the applicable systems by December 2003. Because of the delayed entry into force, phases one and two were to be completed simultaneously. The treaty parties created the Bilateral Implementation Commission, meeting in Geneva, Switzerland, to monitor the compliance regime.

Although eventually ratified by both sides, START II lost its relevance over the years, as the United States became more concerned with obtaining a modification to the ABM

Treaty in order to deploy a ballistic missile defense system, to which the Russians remained opposed. START II was supplanted by the 2002 Strategic Offensive Reductions Treaty (the Moscow Treaty), signed by Presidents Vladimir Putin and George W. Bush in May 2002. That agreement further reduces the number of nuclear warheads that can be deployed by each nation to 1,700–2,200 by the year 2012. Neither country any longer feels obliged to abide by the provisions of the START II treaty, but both are complying with START I.

The Start treaties were important to the history of the Cold War because unlike earlier arms control agreements that slowed or froze the rate of growth of strategic systems, they were the first treaties to actually reduce the number of warheads and delivery systems on both sides.

Jeffrey A. Larsen and A. Gregory Moore

Further Reading

Bunn, George. *Arms Control by Committee: Managing Negotiations with the Russians.* Stanford, CA: Stanford University Press, 1992.

Cimbala, Stephen J., ed. *Strategic Arms Control after SALT.* Wilmington, DE: Scholarly Resources, 1989.

Fitzgerald, Frances. *Way Out There in the Blue: Reagan, Star Wars, and the End of the Cold War.* New York: Simon and Schuster, 2000.

Graham, Thomas, Jr., and Damien J. LaVera. *Cornerstones of Security: Arms Control Treaties in the Nuclear Era.* Seattle: University of Washington Press, 2003.

Krepon, Michael. *Arms Control in the Reagan Administration.* Lanham, MD: University Press of America, 1989.

Mazarr, Michael J. *START and the Future of Deterrence.* London: Macmillan, 1990.

Talbott, Strobe. *Deadly Gambits: The Reagan Administration and the Stalemate in Nuclear Arms Control.* New York: Knopf, 1984.

Talbott, Strobe. *The Master of the Game: Paul Nitze and the Nuclear Peace.* New York: Knopf, 1988.

Strategic Defense Initiative

The Strategic Defense Initiative (SDI) was a space-based, antiballistic missile (ABM) system endorsed by U.S. president Ronald Reagan in 1983 as a way to neutralize the Soviet nuclear threat. Nicknamed "Star Wars" by its critics and the media, SDI foresaw the use of satellites, mirrors, and lasers that would detect, track, and destroy incoming nuclear missiles. Reagan believed that the SDI might force the Soviets to engage in nuclear arms reduction talks and serve as a partial solution to the threat posed by the nuclear arms race.

To counter the Soviet threat in the 1950s, the United States began work on an ABM system. Various incarnations emerged during the 1960s and early 1970s, until the United States and the Soviet Union signed the 1972 Anti-Ballistic Missile Treaty. This treaty limited the deployment of ABM systems to only two operational areas and stipulated that such a system could not protect the entire nation. Nevertheless, work continued in both nations to develop an effective means of nullifying an enemy nuclear attack.

Reagan had many motivations for pursuing the SDI. In principle, he disagreed with the concept of mutual assured destruction (MAD). MAD held that because of the catastrophic nature of thermonuclear war, any nation that initiated a nuclear exchange was guaranteed to suffer complete destruction in a counterstrike. Reagan believed that MAD was immoral and unacceptable. He was further motivated by the upcoming 1984 election and his desire not to be seen as a warmonger. Deploying a defensive system would demonstrate his desire to end the arms race.

Among those who supported the SDI were military contractors who stood to make money developing and deploying such a system. Other supporters included Robert McFarlane, Reagan's national security advisor during 1983–1985, who believed that the SDI could be used as a bargaining chip to motivate the Soviets to scale back their missile production. Opponents of the SDI, including some Reagan administration officials, mockingly nicknamed the plan "Star Wars" after the popular science fiction film series.

In a televised address on March 23, 1983, Reagan publicly announced his desire to pursue the SDI. The scientific task was difficult,

he admitted, but the rewards would be worth it: a United States whose citizens did not have to live in fear of nuclear destruction. The SDI would be costly, perhaps in the trillions of dollars. Reagan lobbied his friend and ally British prime minister Margaret Thatcher, who initially opposed the SDI but eventually came to see it as a good idea.

Unlike previous ABM systems, the SDI would provide missile defense from space. In fact, to intercept missiles in flight, space-based weapons were the best option, because land-based weapons could not overcome the problems presented by the curvature of the earth. Because Soviet long-range missiles took only 30 minutes to reach their targets, there was just enough time to detect, track, and intercept

Artist's rendering of one of the Strategic Defense Initiative designs from Los Alamos National Laboratory. It shows a space-based particle beam weapon attacking enemy intercontinental ballistic missiles. (U.S. Department of Energy)

the warheads before they reentered the atmosphere. As Reagan described it and as scientists conceived it, the SDI would employ a number of satellites and space-based radars to detect and track incoming missiles and land- or satellite-based lasers reflected off orbital mirrors to destroy a warhead in flight. Scientists planned lasers that would employ X-ray, infrared, ultraviolet, or microwave radiation. They also conceived of particle-beam weapons in which streams of charged atomic matter would be directed at incoming warheads.

From the perspective of some, particularly new Soviet leader Mikhail Gorbachev, the SDI was a great threat. When Reagan and Gorbachev first met in Geneva in 1985, the SDI proved the sticking point on any arms control agreements. Gorbachev fiercely objected to the SDI, arguing that such a system only made sense if the United States planned to launch a nuclear first-strike against the Soviet Union. Gorbachev also well understood that the Soviet Union lagged behind the United States in computer technology, an area crucial to such an advanced weapons system. For the Soviet Union to allow the SDI to move forward would be to admit defeat. Gorbachev therefore insisted that Reagan give up the SDI before agreements on limiting offensive weapons could be reached. Reagan refused, but he also told Gorbachev

that the SDI was necessary and that when it was finally completed, he would share the technology with the Soviets. Gorbachev did not believe Reagan. Reagan, in turn, could see no logical argument against the SDI. Because of the SDI, the two men departed Geneva without a deal on arms control.

The Reagan administration ultimately failed to develop and deploy the SDI. The technology proved too daunting, and the costs were too high. Still, the mere threat of the SDI put tremendous pressure on the Soviets. Some scholars attribute the Soviet Union's 1991 collapse to Reagan's vigorous pursuit of the SDI. Others, however, regard the SDI as a costly boondoggle that only escalated Cold War tensions and contributed to swollen defense allocations and mammoth budget deficits.

Brian Madison Jones

Further Reading

Duric, Mira. *The Strategic Defense Initiative: U.S. Policy and the Soviet Union.* Burlington, VT: Ashgate, 2003.

Fitzgerald, Frances. *Way Out There in the Blue: Reagan, Star Wars, and the End of the Cold War.* New York: Simon and Schuster, 2000.

Waller, Douglas C. *The Strategic Defense Initiative, Progress and Challenges: A Guide to Issues and References.* Claremont, CA: Regina Books, 1987.

T

Tiananmen Square (June 4, 1989)

A large public plaza in Beijing, capital of the People's Republic of China (PRC), Tiananmen Square, literally meaning "Gate of Heavenly Peace," has been the site of student movements since the 1919 May Fourth Movement. The Tiananmen Square protests of April 15–June 4, 1989 were of the utmost importance in both their domestic and international contexts. The protests began on April 15 when Beijing's students gathered in the square, mourning the death of Hu Yaobang, former secretary-general of the Chinese Communist Party (CCP) during 1980–1987. That Hu was ousted from office in January 1987 because of his sympathetic stance toward the prodemocracy student movement of 1986 helped transform mourning activities into a series of nationwide student demonstrations. Students renewed their calls for immediate democratization and demanded direct dialogues with senior leaders. The movement employed mass sit-ins, boycotts of classes, public forums, bicycle demonstrations, and hunger strikes.

On May 4, 1989, organized prodemocracy demonstrations occurred in 51 Chinese cities. Other sectors also expressed their discontent with the CCP. Coincident with the visit of Soviet leader Mikhail Gorbachev in mid-May, the protests received global media coverage.

The worldwide attention and escalation of the student movement irritated PRC leaders. The handling of students' demands renewed the factional struggles between the liberal reformers and the conservatives, whose origins dated to 1979, when the paramount leader Deng Xiaoping introduced a market economy and open-door policy to modernize China. This time, the struggle was personalized by the liberal reformist CCP secretary-general Zhao Ziyang and the conservative hard-liner Premier Li Peng. Zhao preferred a conciliatory stance, arguing that the protest was of a patriotic nature and that political reform should be accelerated to facilitate economic modernization. Li, by contrast, insisted on clear-cut coercive measures to disperse the demonstrators and restore stability.

Although away from the front line since the early 1980s, Deng remained highly influential as the chairman of the Central Military Commission. Fearing that his economic program would be jeopardized, he supported Zhao's soft-line, accommodating posture. The government's dialogues with students, however, proved fruitless. With no sign that the protests would soon end, Deng's patience was exhausted, and he decided to adopt Li's hard-line approach.

On May 20, 1989, Li declared martial law in Beijing, ordering the People's Liberation Army (PLA) to clear Tiananmen Square on the condition that no bloodshed occur. Owing to the students' blockade, the army stopped on the outskirts of Beijing city, resulting in a stalemate for the rest of the month. Meanwhile, the government was preoccupied with two issues: preparing a change in leadership to end the factional struggles and regaining Tiananmen Square to end the protests. On May 28, Zhao was placed under house arrest and was replaced by Jiang Zemin, the party secretary of the Shanghai Municipal

A Chinese man stands alone to block a line of tanks during a pro-democracy demonstration in Tiananmen Square in Beijing on June 5, 1989. The man, calling for an end to the recent violence and bloodshed against demonstrators, was pulled away by bystanders, and the tanks continued on their way. The Chinese government crushed a student-led demonstration for democratic reform and against government corruption, killing hundreds, or perhaps thousands of people. (AP/Wide World Photos)

Committee, whose decisive action in closing down a newspaper for reporting the Tiananmen Square protests drew the conservatives' attention.

After consulting retired elder statesmen such as Li Xiannian, Bo Yibo, and PRC president Yang Shangkun, Deng finally agreed on more forceful means to end the standoff, implying the clearance of the square at all costs. On June 2, Yang ordered a military crackdown on the student demonstrators and the clearance of Tiananmen Square on the grounds that an alleged counterrevolutionary riot was brewing and that continued instability would retard economic reform. On June 4 at midnight, the PLA marched into the square, and by dawn it had fulfilled its orders, thereby ending the seven-week-long protests. Because of a press blackout, the estimated deaths and injuries on that night vary from 240 to 10,000.

To prevent a recurrence, on June 9 the government ordered the arrest of all student leaders and activists. Some leaders, such as Wang Dan, were arrested and sentenced to long prison terms, whereas others, such as Chai Ling and Wuer Kaixi, fled abroad. On June 10, the PRC claimed that a total of 468 "troublemakers" had been arrested and that calm had been restored in Beijing.

The PRC's use of the PLA to suppress the student demonstrations stunned the world. Some contemporaries labeled the incident the Tiananmen Massacre. Foreign condemnations, including those from the Soviet bloc, flooded in, followed by a number of punitive sanctions, including the suspension of arms sale to China, the linking of human rights issues to the PRC's entry into the World Trade Organization (WTO), and economic embargoes. From a broader perspective, the legacy of the Tiananmen Square protests was twofold. In the PRC, the protests enabled the conservatives to gain the upper hand. In November 1989, Deng relinquished his remaining post to Jiang, passing the ruling power to the third generation, and his economic modernization was slowed down. In the Cold War context, there is a consensus that the Tiananmen Square protests in some ways inspired the liberation of Eastern Europe from Soviet control, precipitating the Cold War's end.

Law Yuk-fun

Further Reading

Blecher, Marc J. *China against the Tides: Restructuring through Revolution, Radicalism and Reform*. London: Continuum, 2003.

Evans, Richard. *Deng Xiaoping and the Making of Modern China*. Rev. ed. London: Penguin, 1997.

Nathan, Andrew J., and Perry Link, eds. *The Tiananmen Papers: The Chinese Leadership's Decision to Use Force against Their Own People—In Their Own Words*. New York: Public Affairs Press, 2001.

Tito, Josip Broz (1892–1980)

Born on May 7, 1892, into a peasant family in the village of Kumrovec in Croatia on the border with Slovenia (then part of Austria), Josip Broz was one of 15 children of a Croat blacksmith and a Slovene mother. Much of his early life remains obscure. With little formal education, he became a metalworker and machinist. Active in the Social-Democratic Party, he was drafted into the Austro-Hungarian Army in 1913. He fought in World War I and rose to the rank of sergeant, commanding a platoon in a Croatian regiment before being captured in 1915 on the Russian Front.

While in the camp, Broz became fluent in Russian. Released following the March 1917 Revolution, he made his way to Petrograd, where he joined the Bolsheviks but was imprisoned until the Bolsheviks took power in October 1917. He fought on the communist side in the Russian Civil War but returned to Croatia in 1920 and helped organize the Yugoslav Communist Party (YPJ). Rising rapidly in responsibility and position, he became a member of the YPJ Politburo and Central Committee. It was at this time that he took the pseudonym of "Tito" to conceal his identity. He was imprisoned from 1929 to 1934. In 1937 Stalin appointed Tito to head the YPJ as its secretary-general. Tito knew little of communist ideology, but Stalin was interested in loyalty.

Following the German invasion of Yugoslavia in April 1941, Tito took command of the communist partisan resistance movement with the twin goals of fighting the Axis occupiers and then seizing power in Yugoslavia once the Allies had won. Tito and the partisans did not hesitate to attack German garrisons, sparking retaliation and the execution of many more innocent hostages than Germans. Tito's partisans became archrivals of the Serb-dominated Četniks (Chetniks) led by General Draža Mihajlović, minister of war in the Yugoslav government-in-exile in London. The Četniks eschewed the types of attacks undertaken by the partisans, rightly fearing German reprisals. In a controversial decision that had far-reaching repercussions for the future of Yugoslavia, in 1943 the British government, which headed the Allied effort to assist the Yugoslav resistance, shifted all support to the partisans.

By the end of the war, the partisans had grown to a force of 800,000 people and had in fact liberated most of Yugoslavia themselves, placing Tito in a strong bargaining position with Stalin. Tito attempted to annex the southern provinces of Austria, moving Yugoslav forces into Carinthia, but was prevented in this design by the timely arrival of the British V Corps and was convinced to quit Austrian territory in mid-May 1945.

Tito extracted vengeance on the Croats, many of whom had been loyal to the Axis, as had many Slovenes. Perhaps 100,000 people who had sided with the Axis occupiers were executed by the partisans without trial within weeks of the war's end. The majority of German prisoners taken in the war also perished in the long March of Hate across Yugoslavia.

With the support of the Red Army, Tito formed the National Front and consolidated his power. Although superficially there appeared to be a coalition government in Yugoslavia, Tito dominated. In the November 1945 elections for a constituent assembly, the National Front headed by the Partisans won 96 percent of the vote. The assembly promptly deposed Peter II and proclaimed a republic. Yugoslavia's new constitution was modeled on that of the Soviet Union. Tito elaborated the twin ideas of national self-determination for Yugoslavia's nationalities and a strong, centralized communist party organization that would be the sole political expression of each national group's will. Under Tito, Yugoslavia became a federal republic, a beneficial change for a country that had suffered severely from rivalries among its various peoples. Tito also nationalized the economy and built it on the Soviet model.

Following the war, Tito had General Mihajlovi□ and some other leading □etniks put on trial under trumped-up charges of collaboration with the Germans. Despite vigorous Western protests, they were executed in July 1946. Equally destructive of European goodwill was the sentencing of Archbishop Aloysius Stepinac to life imprisonment for his anticommunist role during the war.

For 35 years, Tito held Yugoslavia together by ruling as a despot. In a departure from his past record of sharing hardships with his men, once in power he developed a taste for a luxurious lifestyle. He muzzled dissent, but repression and fear of outside powers, chiefly the Soviet Union, solidified his rule.

In 1948 Yugoslavia was expelled from the international communist movement. The break sprang in large part from Tito's desire to form under his leadership a Balkan confederation of Yugoslavia, Albania, and Bulgaria. There were also differences with Moscow over Yugoslav support for the communist side in the Greek Civil War, as Moscow lived up to its bargain with Winston Churchill during the war not to contest British control in Greece.

The break with Moscow and fears of a Russian invasion led Tito to build up a large military establishment. In this he was assisted by the West, chiefly the United States. By the time of Tito's death in 1980, the Yugoslav standing army and reserves totaled two million men. To protect his freedom of movement, Tito also joined Yugoslavia to the Non-Aligned Movement, and in the 1960s he became a leader of this group along with Gamal Abdel Nasser of Egypt and Jawaharlal Nehru of India.

Before the break, Tito was as doctrinaire as Stalin. After the schism, Tito became more flexible. He allowed peasants to withdraw from cooperative farms and halted the compulsory delivery of crops. He decentralized industry by permitting the establishment of workers' councils with a say in running the factories. He permitted citizens more rights in the courts and limited freedom of speech, and he opened cultural ties with the West and released Archbishop Stepinac (although he was not restored to authority). In 1949 Tito even wrote an article in the influential American journal *Foreign Affairs* titled "Different Paths to Socialism," giving birth to polycentralism.

By 1954, however, reform had ended. Tito reacted sharply to Milován Djilas's proposal to establish a more liberal socialist movement in the country that would in effect turn Yugoslavia into a two-party state. Djilas's book, *The New Class* (1957), charged that a new class of bureaucrats exploited the masses as much as or more than their predecessors. Djilas was condemned to prison. Meanwhile, financial problems multiplied. By the end of the 1970s, inflation was surging, Yugoslavia's foreign debt was up dramatically, its goods could not compete in the world marketplace, and there were dramatic economic differences between the prosperous North and impoverished South that threatened to break up the state.

As long as Tito lived, Yugoslavia held together. In 1974, Tito had set up a complicated collective leadership. The constitution of that year provided for an association of equals that helped to minimize the power of Serbia, diminish Yugoslavia's ethnic and religious hatreds and rivalries, and keep the lid on nationalism. There was a multiethnic, eight-man State Presidency representing the six republics and two autonomous regions. Each of the six republics had virtual veto power over federal decision making. Djilas claimed that Tito deliberately set things up so that after his death, no one would ever possess as much power as he did.

Tito died in Lubljana on May 4, 1980. With the collapse of the Soviet Union and Eastern Europe and the end of the threat of Soviet invasion, and with the discrediting of communism, the federal system that Tito had put together came apart in bloodshed and war.

Spencer C. Tucker

Further Reading

Djilas, Milován. *Tito*. New York: Harcourt Brace Jovanovich, 1980.

Pavlowitch, Steven K. *Tito, Yugoslavia's Great Dictator: A Reassessment*. Columbus: Ohio State University Press, 1992.

Roberts, Walter R. *Tito, Mihailović, and the Allies, 1941–1945*. New Brunswick, NJ: Rutgers University Press, 1973.

West, Richard. *Tito and the Rise and Fall of Yugoslavia*. New York: Carroll and Graf, 1994.

Wilson, Duncan. *Tito's Yugoslavia*. New York: Cambridge University Press, 1979.

Truman Doctrine (March 12, 1947)

On March 12, 1947, President Harry S. Truman addressed a joint session of Congress and stated: "I believe that it must be the policy of the United States to support free peoples who are resisting attempted subjugation by armed minorities or by outside pressures." He was of course referring to communist "pressures" and thereby committed the United States to uphold the containment policy, which pledged that all necessary measures would be taken to check the spread of communism and Soviet influence.

The catalyst for the Truman Doctrine had been Britain's February 1947 announcement that it could no longer afford to provide military or financial support to Greece and Turkey. This meant that these nations might fall to communism, especially Greece, whose pro-Western government was fighting a communist guerrilla insurgency in the northern part of the country.

The eastern basin of the Mediterranean, including the Middle East, had historically been under British influence since the 19th century. The area was still important to Britain after World War II, but it took on great importance in light of the developing Cold War. Soviet presence in the region would jeopardize the ability of the Western powers to launch strategic air strikes on the Soviet Union from bases in the area. The defense of the region had been a British preserve and rested on British military bases, the largest of which was in Egypt. British power was declining, however, while at the same time Soviet activity in the region seemed on the increase.

For planners in Washington, there seemed to be a power vacuum in the region. Britain was providing military aid to Turkey, but the U.S. Joint Chiefs of Staff (JCS) thought that because of its strategic importance and in order to increase its ability to meet Soviet aggression, the United States should increase its economic and military aid to Turkey. As long as the British furnished military assistance, however, the Truman administration would provide only economic aid.

American attitudes toward the situation in Turkey were linked to the situation in Greece. Like Turkey, Greece was considered a barrier between the Soviet Union and the Mediterranean. The struggle in Greece was not one inspired by the Soviet Union but rather resulted from conflict between rightists seeking to restore the monarchy, who were also failing to tackle the grave economic situation, and left-wing parties seeking to install a communist regime. Washington, however, chose to view the Greek Civil War through the lens of the Cold War. A loss in Greece to the communists would not only result in a victory for the Soviets but, it was argued, would also open the entire region to communist

subversion. Thus, the Americans could not tolerate the establishment of a communist regime in Athens whether or not it was inspired by Moscow. Despite the shortcomings of the anticommunist Greek government, the Truman administration now moved to provide assistance to it. The decisive turning point came with London's announcement in February 1947 that Britain would be unable to continue its support to Greece and Turkey. It was obvious to U.S. State Department officials that the United States had to fill the breach. While preparing the draft legislation for the 1947 Greco-Turkish aid package, however, Undersecretary of State Dean Acheson found it difficult to justify the assistance request for Turkey, as it was not under a direct threat from either the Kremlin or an indigenous communist insurgency. Acheson also knew that Congress was in no mood to approve a large foreign aid request without proper justification, as it was engaged in efforts to curtail spending and pay down the national debt accrued during World War II. Also, Moscow was issuing conciliatory messages, further reducing the incentive in Congress to take strong measures against the Soviet Union.

Truman and his advisors, determined to provide military and economic assistance to both Greece and Turkey, had to find a way to sell this foreign aid package to Congress. Just prior to Truman's speech, Acheson described to the congressional leadership in stark terms the implications of Soviet domination over the eastern Mediterranean and the worldwide geopolitical consequences of such a scenario. In response, Republican Senator Arthur H. Vandenberg, a formerly steadfast isolationist, informed Truman that if he were to present his request to Congress in the manner that had been used by Acheson, he and the majority of Congress would support the aid deal. As a result, Truman's request for a $400 million aid package earmarked for Turkey and Greece was presented in the Cold War terms of a struggle "between alternate ways of life," marking the emergence of the Truman Doctrine, which came to represent a concerted long-term effort to resist communist aggression around the world. Vandenberg kept his promise. The Greco-Turkish aid package was speedily approved.

David Tal

Further Reading

Kuniholm, Bruce R. *The Origins of the Cold War in the Near East.* Princeton, NJ: Princeton University Press, 1980.

Lafeber, Walter. *America, Russia and the Cold War, 1945–2002.* Updated 9th ed. New York: McGraw-Hill, 2004.

Leffler, Melvyn P. *A Preponderance of Power: National Security, the Truman Administration, and the Cold War.* Stanford, CA: Stanford University Press, 1992.

U

U-2 Incident (May 1960)

Because the closed nature of Soviet society made it difficult to determine that nation's military capabilities, in 1954 President Dwight Eisenhower secretly ordered the fabrication of a small number of special reconnaissance aircraft, built by Lockheed and dubbed the U-2, to secretly overfly the Soviet Union. The U-2 was an engineering marvel, essentially a glider outfitted with a jet engine and capable of flying at 70,000 feet and more than 4,000 miles without refueling.

Eisenhower feared that revelation of the flights could be considered a hostile action, but he believed that the need to obtain intelligence outweighed the potential risks of the U-2 program. On July 4, 1956, civilians under contract with the Central Intelligence Agency (CIA) began piloting U-2 aircraft on 24 missions over the Soviet Union, taking photographs and gathering other electronic data. The U-2 overflights showed that the Soviets had been exaggerating their bomber and missile capabilities.

Although initial studies suggested that the Soviet Union's defenses would be incapable of reliably tracking or attacking the U-2s at their normal flying altitude, the planes were nevertheless monitored closely and were frequently targeted by Soviet interceptors and surface-to-air missiles (SAMs). The Soviets lodged objections with the United States after the early flights but did not complain publicly, probably because of their reluctance to acknowledge their inability to destroy the planes.

In February and March 1960, having authorized only four overflights since 1958, Eisenhower approved two missions for the coming weeks. Although he was worried about harming East–West rapport on the eve of a summit among American, Soviet, British, and French leaders scheduled to begin on May 16 in Paris, he was convinced of the need to gather details about recent Soviet intercontinental ballistic missile (ICBM) developments before the meeting. Midway through the second of these flights, the U-2 jet piloted by Francis Gary Powers was shot down by Soviet air defenses, and he parachuted into Soviet hands. The Soviets also collected—largely intact—the camera and other remnants of the plane.

To Khrushchev, this overflight was a particular affront because it occurred on a communist holiday (May Day) and because he saw it as an intentional presummit provocation. Correctly assuming that the United States did not know that the Soviets had captured Powers and secured incriminating aircraft components, Khrushchev set out to embarrass the Eisenhower administration. After the United States announced that the downed plane was a weather research aircraft, the Soviet leader publicly revealed the damning evidence to the contrary and announced his intent to try Powers for espionage. The eventual confirmation of the Americans' activities and their attempts to cover them up created an international sensation and torpedoed the Paris summit.

Eisenhower tried to explain the overflights as regrettable infringements upon Soviet sovereignty that were nonetheless necessary to understand Soviet military capacity. Some of Eisenhower's advisors thought that the CIA had been ill-prepared for the possibility of a downed plane and failed to advise the president of the likelihood of an interception, especially given persistent Soviet efforts to achieve such a feat. Some aides proposed that Eisenhower avoid responsibility by claiming that the overflights occurred without his authorization, a suggestion the president rejected because it would improperly place blame on subordinates and would incorrectly suggest that underlings had the latitude to authorize such significant activity. Some officials, not privy to the details of what to do if captured, blamed Powers for allowing himself to be taken prisoner and too readily admitting to his activities.

While it is more difficult to assess Soviet reactions, many U.S. analysts believe that Khrushchev shared Eisenhower's quest for relaxed relations but faced resistance from hard-liners in the Kremlin. This forced Khrushchev to balance anger with interest in a rapprochement, although he did lash out against Pakistan and Norway, nations that he knew had facilitated some U-2 missions. When he arrived in Paris putatively for a preliminary meeting, Khrushchev made it clear that he would not assent to the formal convening of the summit without a public apology from Eisenhower. Although Eisenhower hoped that the summit would continue as planned and thus allow his presidential term to conclude on a high note by building on the improved relations that had resulted from Khrushchev's celebrated 1959 visit to the United States, he refused to apologize, although he renounced any further aircraft overflights. This stance was unacceptable to Khrushchev, who therefore refused to participate in the summit and canceled arrangements for Eisenhower's state visit to the Soviet Union.

Although global reaction varied as to which party was responsible for the meeting's failure (some believed that Khrushchev exaggerated his position for propaganda purposes), Eisenhower considered it a great loss. After an August 1960 show trial, Powers was sentenced to 10 years' imprisonment. In February 1962, however, he was traded for Colonel Rudolf Abel, a Soviet spy being held in U.S. custody. Subsequent investigations determined that Powers had acted properly during his mission and time in captivity. By the late summer of 1960, U.S. photographic intelligence of the Soviet Union began to rely on secret orbiting satellites that passed over Soviet territory. Because they traveled through space, international law did not consider them violations of sovereign airspace.

Christopher John Bright

Further Reading

Beschloss, Michael R. *Mayday: Eisenhower, Khrushchev, and the U-2 Affair.* New York: Harper and Row, 1986.

Pedlow, Gregory W., and Donald Welzenbach. *The CIA and the U-2 Program, 1954–1974.* Washington, DC: Central Intelligence Agency, 1998.

Powers, Francis Gary, with Curt Gentry. *Operation Overflight: A Memoir of the U-2 Incident.* Washington, DC: Brassey's, 2004.

United Nations

The United Nations (UN) was conceived as a multinational organization designed to promote four primary objectives: collective security, international economic and cultural cooperation, multilateral humanitarian assistance, and human rights. The UN's creation in 1945 represented an attempt by the World War II Allies to establish an international organization more effective than the interwar League of Nations, which had failed to mitigate the worldwide economic depression of the 1930s or prevent a second world war. UN architects were heavily influenced by the belief that during the 1930s, nationalist policies, economic and political rivalries, and the absence of international collaboration to help resolve outstanding disputes had contributed substantially to the outbreak of World War II.

Even before the United States officially joined the war effort, in the early months of World War II, U.S. secretary of state Cordell Hull established a departmental planning group for the purpose of creating the UN. At a meeting off the Newfoundland coast in August 1941, American president Franklin D. Roosevelt and British prime minister Winston Churchill included a broad proposal for an international security system in the Atlantic Charter, which was their declaration of overall war objectives.

On January 1, 1942, the governments of 26 nations fighting Germany, Italy, and Japan issued the Declaration by the United Nations affirming their alliance against the Axis powers and also stating their commitment to liberal war objectives, as set forth in the Atlantic Charter, and the restoration of the principles of international law. In 1943, both houses of the U.S. Congress also passed resolutions demanding the creation of a postwar international security organization in which, they implied, their own country should take the leading role that it had abdicated in the League of Nations. Meeting in Moscow in October 1943, foreign ministers of the four leading Allied powers—the United States, Great Britain, the Soviet Union, and China—signed the Declaration of Four Nations on General Security, committing their nations in general terms to the creation of a postwar international organization.

More specific proposals came out of the Dumbarton Oaks Conference held in Washington, D.C., from August to October 1944 in which 39 nations participated. These recommendations represented a compromise between the ideas of Roosevelt and other devotees of realpolitik—that agreement between the Big Four Allied powers, "the four policemen," must be the foundation of postwar international security—and more idealistic popular visions of a world in which all powers, great and small, enjoyed equal status and protection. The Dumbarton Oaks Conference agreed to create a bipartite UN modeled on the earlier League of Nations but reserving ultimate authority to the dominant Allied states. Any peace-loving state that was prepared to accept the terms of the UN Charter would be eligible to apply for membership. All member states would be represented in the UN General Assembly, which would debate, discuss, and vote on issues that came before it. Executive authority rested with the 11-member UN Security Council, which would have 5 permanent members: Britain, France, the United States, Russia, and China. The remaining Security Council representatives were drawn from other UN states, all of which would serve two-year terms in rotation. Besides providing an international security mechanism, the UN was also expected to promote international cooperation on economic, social, cultural, and humanitarian issues.

At the February 1945 Yalta Conference, the Allies—at Soviet insistence—agreed that each permanent Security Council member should enjoy veto power over all General Assembly decisions. The Soviet Union also obtained separate representation for Belorussia (Belarus) and Ukraine. The Yalta Conference further agreed on a UN trustee system to administer both former League of Nations mandatory territories—originally colonies taken from Germany and Turkey

Still keeping the UN General Assembly in New York in an uproar with his angry speeches, Soviet premier Nikita Khrushchev swings his clenched first as he pounds away at his topic, "American Imperialism," October 12, 1960. The October 12 session was adjourned abruptly in a scene of disorder after Khrushchev, among other things called the Philippines delegate a "jerk." (AP/Wide World Photos)

after World War I—and areas seized from the Axis powers when the current war ended.

The Yalta Conference formally invited all Allied and most neutral powers to attend a conference that would open in San Francisco on April 25, 1945, to establish the UN. Representatives of 51 nations attended this gathering, which ended on July 25, 1945, and hammered out the details of the UN Charter, which accorded smaller states slightly more authority than had the original Dumbarton Oaks proposals. The charter incorporated the International Labor Organization (ILO), established under the original 1919 League of Nations Covenant. To pursue its stated nonsecurity objectives, the charter also created the United Nations Economic, Social and Cultural Organization (UNESCO), together with an 18-member Economic and Social Council, a Trusteeship Council, an International Court of Justice, and the UN Secretariat, which administered the organization. By the end of 1945, all 51 states represented at San Francisco had ratified the UN Charter. In 1946 the body held its first session in London and in 1947 it moved permanently to the United States, where its headquarters was completed soon afterward in New York City.

So vast were the mandate and responsibilities of the UN that much regarding its future role remained open when it was founded in 1945. As is not uncommon with bureaucracies, additional agencies proliferated, and its structure gradually became more complex. As former colonies won independence and large states were sometimes partitioned into smaller units, by the end of the 20th century the membership had expanded from the original 51 member states to close to 200. As the number of members soared, the Security Council grew from 11 to 15 members, and the Economic and Social Council rose first to 27 members and eventually to 54. By the mid-1990s, the UN system embraced 15 specialized institutions, among them the ILO, the International Monetary Fund (IMF), the World Bank Group, UNESCO, and the World Health Organization (WHO); two semiautonomous affiliates, including the International Atomic Energy Authority (IAEA); 15 specific organizations established by and responsible to the General Assembly; 6 functional commissions; 5 regional commissions; and 75 special committees. By the mid-1990s, more than 29,000 international civil servants worked for the UN in its New York headquarters and its subsidiary offices in Geneva and Vienna.

The UN soon became an arena for Cold War contests and disputes in which the major powers tested their strength, while Third World nations came to see the UN as a forum where, given their growing numbers, the concerns of less-developed countries could be voiced and made effective, especially in the General Assembly, which was empowered to discuss all international questions of interest to members. In the Cold War context, the UN became a venue in which the Western and communist camps contended for power. Despite its stated security role, the organization proved remarkably unsuccessful in defusing the growing tensions. During the second half of the 1940s, the Western powers of Britain, France, and the United States were soon fiercely at odds with their former World War II ally the Soviet Union.

With UN endorsement, in 1948 the Republic of Korea (ROK, South Korea) established a pro-Western and noncommunist government, while the communist Democratic People's Republic of Korea (DPRK, North Korea) failed to win UN recognition. A much greater test of strength came after the communist takeover of Mainland China in October 1949, when the United States vetoed Soviet-backed efforts to transfer UN representation for China from the rejected Guomindang (GMD, Nationalist) government—which still controlled the island of Taiwan—to Mao Zedong's new People's Republic of China (PRC). In protest against the veto, the Soviet delegation withdrew from the UN, a boycott that was maintained for several months. Only in 1970 did the PRC win UN membership and China's Security Council seat.

When the UN was founded, it was anticipated that peacekeeping and the restoration of international security and order, if necessary by military means, would be among its major functions. Under Article 43 of the UN's charter, member states were originally expected to agree to make specified military forces available to the UN for deployment under the organization's control, for use on occasions when military intervention was required to maintain or reestablish international peace and security. In practice, no nation signed any such agreement relinquishing control of any military forces to UN authority.

The Soviet boycott permitted the United States in June 1950 to win UN endorsement for military intervention in Korea after North Korean forces invaded South Korea. Soviet attempts later that year to veto the continuation of UN intervention in Korea were blocked when the United States persuaded the General Assembly, where it possessed a majority, to pass the

Uniting for Peace Resolution, allowing the assembly to recommend measures to member states to implement the restoration of international peace and security. The Korean War was the only occasion until the 1990–1991 Persian Gulf War on which the UN itself intervened militarily to restore the status quo. In practice, the United States provided the bulk of troops involved, although other North Atlantic Treaty Organization (NATO) allies, most notably Britain and Canada, provided substantial forces, as did Australia and New Zealand. The fact that the stalemated Korean War lasted for approximately three years, despite all UN efforts at mediation, illustrated the limitations of the peacekeeping functions of the organization.

Between 1945 and 1988 the UN did, however, undertake 11 limited peacekeeping operations, deploying an Emergency Force of troops—usually from states such as Canada, Colombia, Sweden, Norway, and Pakistan that were not permanent members of the Security Council—at the request and on the territory of at least one nation involved in a conflict or crisis in efforts to maintain peace. The first such occasion was the Suez Crisis of October 1956, when British, French, and Israeli forces attacked Egypt. The UN responded to a request from Egypt's president Gamal Abdel Nasser by sending a contingent of 6,000 lightly armed personnel to oversee truce arrangements and the withdrawal of the invading forces. Although such arrangements were supposedly neutral, in practice the UN normally acted on the request of one party or the other in a dispute, and its forces often came to be identified with that side. When UN forces were dispatched to the Congo for several years in the early 1960s, they were soon perceived as working closely with Lieutenant General (and future president) Joseph Mobutu Sese Seko and against Prime Minister Moise Tshombe, a situation

that soon led to increased casualties among UN forces.

Apart from such peacekeeping efforts, the UN responded to most international crises, such as the successive Arab-Israeli wars, with calls for cease-fires and truces and offers of mediation. Often, the UN embargoed the shipment of military equipment to states at war, although the effectiveness of such sanctions varied according to the willingness of member states to enforce them. After the failure to implement the Geneva Accords of 1954, which mandated the unification of Vietnam after nationwide elections, the UN refused to admit either the northern or southern Vietnamese states as members. From the late 1950s to the early 1970s, successive UN secretary-generals nonetheless made repeated though unavailing efforts to negotiate a peace settlement in Vietnam. The UN verbally condemned the Soviet invasions of Hungary in 1956 and Czechoslovakia in 1968 and the imposition of martial rule in Poland in 1981. The UN generally encouraged all international efforts toward arms control and provided the arena for the negotiation of the 1968 Treaty on the Non-Proliferation of Nuclear Weapons, the 1972 Biological and Toxin Weapons Convention, and the 1992 Convention on the Prohibition of the Development, Production, Stockpiling, and Use of Chemical Weapons.

The UN General Assembly was the arena for some of the most significant pronouncements and dramatic confrontations of the Cold War. In 1953, President Dwight D. Eisenhower delivered his "Atoms for Peace" address before the assembly, calling for international cooperation to develop peaceful uses for nuclear energy. More tense occasions included those when the flamboyant Soviet leader Nikita Khrushchev openly defied the Western powers, and U.S. representative Adlai Stevenson's challenge to his Soviet counterpart in October 1962 to confirm the presence of Soviet missiles in Cuba. During the Cuban Missile Crisis, UN secretary-general U Thant offered to mediate a settlement, an offer that President John F. Kennedy might have accepted had his own efforts proved unsuccessful. More embarrassingly for the United States, during the American-backed Bay of Pigs invasion attempt against Cuba in April 1961, Stevenson initially denied that his country was involved, a statement that he was later forced to retract. The rapid increase in UN member-states during the 1950s and 1960s, largely the result of decolonization, brought growing numbers of African and Asian representatives to the General Assembly. In 1964, African, Asian, and Latin American nations formed the Group of Seventy-Seven, whose numbers eventually grew to 120 states from Third World or developing nations and who frequently voted as a bloc and constituted more than a two-thirds majority of the General Assembly. Cuba, the bête noire of successive American presidents, took a prominent role in this grouping. The group's concerns focused primarily on economic issues (including the global distribution of wealth, resources, and power), the Arab–Israeli conflict, and South Africa rather than the Cold War per se. These concerns nonetheless frequently put them at odds with the United States, whereas the Soviet Union endorsed most Group of Seventy-Seven positions. It was largely at the group's instigation, for example, that the UN in 1970 expelled the Republic of China (ROC, Taiwan), admitting the PRC in its place, and sought to impose international economic sanctions on countries such as Israel, Rhodesia (subsequently Zimbabwe), and South Africa that defied UN resolutions. Western moral authority within the UN was also affected by the revelation in the late 1970s that as a young man during World War II, the Austrian-born UN secretary-general Kurt Waldheim had belonged

not just to the Nazi party but also to a military unit that had committed atrocities in Yugoslavia. No secretary-general since Waldheim has been of European origin.

From the late 1960s onward the United States, faced with declining influence in the UN and from the mid-1960s finding itself on the winning side less than 50 percent of the time in General Assembly votes, became decidedly less enthusiastic toward the organization. In the mid-1970s, U.S. representative to the UN Daniel Patrick Moynihan chose to adopt more confrontational tactics, aggressively putting forward his country's position and its commitment to the values of liberty and democracy. For the rest of the 1970s his successor, Andrew Young, nominated by President Jimmy Carter, was more conciliatory, but under President Ronald Reagan UN ambassador Jeane Kirkpatrick once again adopted a confrontational stance, fiercely defending American values and the U.S. commitment to authoritarian but noncommunist regimes and assailing the communist position around the world. In Nicaragua, the United States not only supported the Contras who sought to undermine the left-wing Sandinista government but also defied the International Court of Justice by mining the harbor of Managua, the capital. In 1985, distaste for the organization's policies, outlook, and management led the United States to withdraw from UNESCO, an action that the United Kingdom and Singapore soon emulated. Even more significantly, citing financial mismanagement and inefficiency, in 1985 the United States, which normally contributed at least 25 percent of the UN's budget, declined to pay a substantial portion of its assessed contribution, a decision reversed only in the mid-1990s.

The announcement in 1988 by Soviet president Mikhail Gorbachev that his country intended to renounce the "use or threat of force" as an "instrument of foreign policy" and to make dramatic cuts in its military forces in Eastern Europe marked the beginning of a new era for the UN. Initially skeptical, U.S. leaders gradually came to credit Gorbachev's good faith. The Soviet Union and the United States were no longer at odds in the Security Council, and the Group of Seventy-Seven could no more rely automatically on Soviet, or subsequently Russian, support. Between 1988 and 1994, the Security Council undertook 20 peacekeeping operations, while the UN helped to bring about a settlement of the Iran–Iraq War and to facilitate Soviet withdrawal from its lengthy and fruitless intervention in Afghanistan. The UN also encouraged negotiation by the Soviet Union and the United States of wide-ranging arms control agreements that, by the mid-1990s, had massively reduced the numbers of nuclear weapons each side deployed on its own soil and elsewhere.

Although less controversial and publicized than its efforts to maintain peace and resolve international conflicts, at all times many of the UN's energies were devoted to economic, social, cultural, and humanitarian efforts, including the eradication and prevention of disease, environmental and climatic issues, human rights, women's and children's rights, immigration, education, the care of refugees, and measures to combat such transnational problems as international dealings in human beings and the narcotics trade. The UN was perhaps most successful in promoting joint international action on humanitarian, economic, social, and environmental issues that transcended national boundaries and demanded concerted international action, such as food and hunger, health, trade policies, social justice, women's rights, pollution, and other ecological concerns. The ending of the Cold War facilitated UN endeavors to promote such objectives by removing some of the East–West barriers to their successful implementation.

Although sometimes derided as ineffective and handicapped in international crises by its reliance on military forces contributed by member states, the UN often provided a valuable forum for the quiet exchange of views and the promotion of humanitarian and social goals. On occasion, it also conveniently furnished a useful alternative channel of communications among powers whose diplomatic relations were otherwise limited or even nonexistent. Though never as effective in terms of resolving international conflicts as its founders envisaged, the UN proved considerably more successful than its predecessor, the League of Nations, in attracting and retaining as members most of the world's major as well as minor states, whose continuing membership implicitly bestowed authority and legitimacy upon the organization's statements and actions. Although often hampered by Cold War antagonisms, during the 45 years from 1945 to 1990 the UN played a significant role in moderating Cold War tensions and defusing at least some international crises, providing an arena in which disputes could be nonviolently resolved.

Priscilla Roberts

Further Reading

Firestone, Bernard J. *The United Nations under U Thant, 1961–1971*. Lanham, MD: Scarecrow, 2001.

Gaglione, Anthony. *The United Nations under Trygve Lie, 1945–1953*. Lanham, MD: Scarecrow, 2001.

Heller, Peter B. *The United Nations under Dag Hammarskjöld, 1953–1961*. Lanham, MD: Scarecrow, 2001.

Hilderbrand, Robert C. *Dumbarton Oaks: The Origins of the United Nations and the*

Search for Postwar Security. Chapel Hill: University of North Carolina Press, 1990.

Lankevich, George J. *The United Nations under Javier Pérez de Cuéllar, 1982–1991*. Lanham, MD: Scarecrow, 2001.

Luard, Evan. *A History of the United Nations*. 2 vols. New York: St. Martin's, 1982–1989.

Meisler, Stanley. *The United Nations: The First Fifty Years*. New York: Atlantic Monthly Press, 1995.

Ostrower, Gary B. *The United Nations and the United States*. New York: Twayne, 1998.

Ryan, James Daniel. *The United Nations under Kurt Waldheim, 1972–1981*. Lanham, MD: Scarecrow, 2001.

Schlesinger, Stephen C. *Act of Creation: The Founding of the United Nations; A Story of Superpowers, Secret Agents, Wartime Allies and Enemies, and Their Quest for a Peaceful World*. Boulder, CO: Westview, 2003.

Simons, Jeff. *The United Nations: A Chronology of Conflict*. New York: St. Martin's, 1994.

Vietnam War (1957–1975)

The Vietnam War grew out of the Indochina War (1946–1954). The 1954 Geneva Conference, ending the Indochina War between France and the nationalist-communist Viet Minh, provided for the independence of Cambodia, Laos, and Vietnam. Agreements reached at Geneva temporally divided Vietnam at the 17th Parallel, pending national elections in 1956. In the meantime, Viet Minh military forces were to withdraw north of that line and the French forces south of it. The war left two competing entities, the northern Democratic Republic of Vietnam (DRV, North Vietnam) and the southern French-dominated State of Vietnam (SV), each claiming to be the legitimate government of a united Vietnam.

In June 1954, SV titular head Emperor Bao Dai appointed as premier the Roman Catholic Ngo Dinh Diem, whom Bao Dai believed had Washington's backing. Diem's base of support was narrow but had recently been strengthened by the addition of some 800,000 northern Catholics who relocated to southern Vietnam. In a subsequent power struggle between Bao Dai and Diem, in October 1955 Diem established the Republic of Vietnam (RVN, South Vietnam), with himself as president. The United States then extended aid to Diem, most of which went to the South Vietnamese military budget. Only minor sums went to education and social welfare programs. Thus, the aid seldom touched the lives of the preponderantly rural populace. As Diem consolidated his power, U.S. military advisors also reorganized the South Vietnamese armed forces. Known as the Army of the Republic of Vietnam (ARVN, South Vietnamese Army) and equipped with American weaponry, it was designed to fight a conventional invasion from North Vietnam rather than deal with insurgency warfare.

Fearing a loss, Diem refused to hold the scheduled 1956 elections. This jolted veteran communist North Vietnamese leader Ho Chi Minh. Ho had not been displeased with Diem's crushing of his internal opposition but was now ready to reunite the country under his sway and believed that he would win the elections. North Vietnam was more populous than South Vietnam, and the communists were well organized there. Fortified by the containment policy, the domino theory, and the belief that the communists, if they came to power, would never permit a democratic regime, U.S. president Dwight D. Eisenhower's administration backed Diem's defiance of the Geneva Agreements.

Diem's decision led to a renewal of fighting, which became the Vietnam War. Fighting resumed in 1957 when Diem moved against the 6,000–7,000 Viet Minh political cadres who had been allowed to remain in South Vietnam to prepare for the 1956 elections. The Viet Minh began the insurgency on their own initiative but were subsequently supported by the North Vietnamese government. The South Vietnamese communist insurgents came to be known as the Viet Cong (VC). In December 1960 they established the National Liberation Front (NLF) of South Vietnam. Supposedly independent, the NLF was controlled by Hanoi. The NLF program called for the overthrow of the

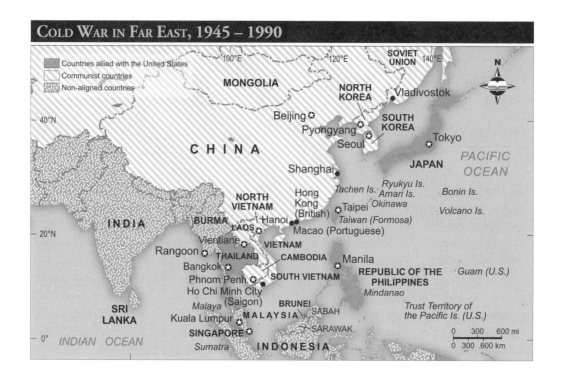

COLD WAR IN FAR EAST, 1945 – 1990

Countries allied with the United States
Communist countries
Non-aligned countries

100°E
120°E
140°E

N

SOVIET UNION

MONGOLIA

NORTH KOREA

Vladivostok

40°N

Beijing ✪

Pyongyang ✪

SOUTH KOREA

CHINA

Seoul ✪

Tokyo ✪

JAPAN

PACIFIC OCEAN

Shanghai ●

NORTH VIETNAM

Hong Kong (British)

Tachen Is.

Ryukyu Is.
Amari Is.

Bonin Is.

INDIA

BURMA

LAOS ✪

Hanoi ●

✪ Taipei

Okinawa

Volcano Is.

20°N

Vientiane ✪

VIETNAM

Macao (Portuguese)

Taiwan (Formosa)

Rangoon ✪

THAILAND

CAMBODIA

Manila

Bangkok ✪

Phnom Penh ●

SOUTH VIETNAM

REPUBLIC OF THE PHILIPPINES

Guam (U.S.)

Ho Chi Minh City (Saigon)

Mindanao

SRI LANKA

Malaya

BRUNEI

SABAH

Kuala Lumpur ✪

MALAYSIA

SARAWAK

Trust Territory of the Pacific Is. (U.S.)

0°

INDIAN OCEAN

SINGAPORE ✪

0   300   600 mi

0   300   600 km

Sumatra

INDONESIA

After a firefight, two soldiers of the U.S. 173rd Airborne Brigade wait for a helicopter to evacuate them and one of their fallen. (National Archives)

Saigon government, its replacement by a "broad national democratic coalition," and the "peaceful" reunification of Vietnam.

In September 1959, North Vietnamese defense minister Vo Nguyen Giap established Transportation Group 559 to send supplies and men south along what came to be known as the Ho Chi Minh Trail, much of which ran through supposedly neutral Laos. The first wave of infiltrators were native southerners and Viet Minh who had relocated to North Vietnam in 1954. Viet Cong sway expanded, spreading out from safe bases to one village after another. The insurgency was fed by the weaknesses of the central government, by the use of terror and assassination, and by Saigon's appalling ignorance of the movement. By the end of 1958, the insurgency had reached the status of conventional warfare in several provinces. In 1960, the communists carried out even more assassinations, and guerrilla units attacked ARVN regulars, overran district and provincial capitals, and ambushed convoys and reaction forces.

By mid-1961, the Saigon government had lost control over much of rural South Vietnam. Infiltration was as yet not significant, and most of the insurgents' weapons were either captured from ARVN forces or left over from the war with France. Diem rejected American calls for meaningful reform until the establishment of full security. He did not understand that the war was primarily a political problem and could be solved only through political means.

Diem, who practiced the divide and rule concept of leadership, increasingly delegated authority to his brother, Ngo Dinh Nhu, and his secret police. Isolated from his people and relying only on trusted family members and a few other advisors, Diem resisted U.S. demands that he promote his senior officials and officers on the basis of ability and pursue the war aggressively.

By now, U.S. president John F. Kennedy's administration was forced to reevaluate its position toward the war, but increased U.S. involvement was inevitable, given Washington's commitment to resisting communist expansion and the belief that all of Southeast Asia would become communist if South Vietnam fell. Domestic political considerations also influenced the decision.

In May 1961, Kennedy sent several fact-finding missions to Vietnam. These led to the Strategic Hamlet program as part of a general strategy emphasizing local militia defense and to the commitment of additional U.S. manpower. By the end of 1961, U.S. strength in Vietnam had grown to around 3,200 men, most in helicopter units or serving as advisors. In February 1962, the United States also established a military headquarters in Saigon, when the Military Assistance and Advisory Group (MAAG) was replaced by the Military Assistance Command, Vietnam (MACV), to direct the enlarged American commitment. The infusion of U.S. helicopters and additional support for the ARVN probably prevented a VC military victory in 1962. The VC soon learned to cope with the helicopters, however, and again the tide of battle turned.

Meanwhile, Nhu's crackdown on the Buddhists led to increased opposition to Diem's rule. South Vietnamese generals now planned a coup, and after Diem rejected reforms, the United States gave the plotters tacit support. On November 1, 1963, the generals overthrew Diem, murdering him and Nhu. Within three weeks Kennedy was also dead, succeeded by Lyndon B. Johnson.

The United States seemed unable to win the war either with or without Diem. A military junta now took power, but none of those who followed Diem had his prestige. Coups and countercoups occurred, and much of South Vietnam remained in turmoil. Not until General Nguyen Van Thieu became president in 1967 was there a degree of political stability.

Both sides steadily increased the stakes, apparently without foreseeing that the other might do the same. In 1964 Hanoi made three decisions. The first was to send to South Vietnam units of its regular army, the People's Army of Vietnam (PAVN), known to the Americans as the North Vietnamese Army (NVA). The second was to rearm its forces in South Vietnam with modern communist-bloc weapons, giving them a firepower advantage over the ARVN, which was still equipped largely with World War II–era U.S. infantry weapons. And the third was to order direct attacks on American installations, provoking a U.S. response.

On August 2, 1964, the Gulf of Tonkin Incident occurred when North Vietnamese torpedo boats attacked the U.S. destroyer *Maddox* in international waters in the Gulf of Tonkin. A second attack on the *Maddox* and another U.S. destroyer, the *Turner Joy*, reported two days later, probably never occurred, but Washington believed that it had, and this led the Johnson administration to order retaliatory air strikes against North Vietnamese naval bases and fuel depots. It also led to a near-unanimous vote in Congress for the Gulf of Tonkin Resolution authorizing the president to use whatever force he deemed necessary to protect U.S. interests in Southeast Asia.

Johnson would not break off U.S. involvement in Vietnam, evidently fearing possible impeachment if he did so. At the same time, he refused to make the tough decision of fully mobilizing the country and committing the resources necessary to win, concerned that this would destroy his cherished Great Society social programs. He also feared a widened war, possibly involving the People's Republic of China (PRC).

By 1965, Ho and his generals expected to win the war. Taking their cue from Johnson's own pronouncements to the American people, they mistakenly believed that Washington would not commit ground troops to the fight. Yet Johnson did just that. Faced with Hanoi's escalation, in March 1965 U.S. Marines arrived to protect the large American air base at Da Nang. A direct attack on U.S. advisors at Pleiku in February 1965 also led to a U.S. air campaign against North Vietnam.

Ultimately more than 2.5 million Americans served in Vietnam, and nearly 58,000 of them died there. At its height, Washington was spending $30 billion per year on the war. Although the conflict was the best-covered war in American history (it became known as the first television war), it was conversely the least understood by the American people.

Johnson hoped to win the war on the cheap, relying heavily on airpower. The air campaign, known as Operation Rolling Thunder, would be pursued in varying degrees of intensity over the next three and a half years. It was paralleled by Operation Barrel Roll, the secret bombing of Laos (which became the most heavily bombed country in the history of warfare). The goals of the air war were to force Hanoi to negotiate peace and to halt infiltration into South Vietnam. During the war, the United States dropped more bombs than in all of World War II, but the campaign failed in both its objectives.

In the air war, Johnson decided on graduated response rather than the massive strikes advocated by the military. Gradualism became the grand strategy employed by the United States in Vietnam. Haunted by the Korean War, at no time would Johnson consider an invasion of North Vietnam, fearful of provoking a Chinese reaction.

By May and June 1965, with PAVN forces regularly defeating ARVN units, MACV commander General William Westmoreland appealed for U.S. ground units, which Johnson committed. PAVN regiments appeared ready to launch an offensive in the rugged Central Highlands and then drive to the sea, splitting South Vietnam in two. Westmoreland mounted a spoiling attack with the recently arrived 1st Cavalry Division (Airmobile) formed around some 450 helicopters. During October–November 1965, the 1st Cavalry won one of the war's rare decisive encounters in the Battle of Ia Drang and may have derailed Hanoi's hopes of winning a decisive victory before full American might could be deployed.

Heavy personnel losses on the battlefield, though regrettable, were entirely acceptable to the North Vietnamese leadership. Ho remarked at one point that North Vietnam could absorb an unfavorable loss ratio of 10 to 1 and still win the war. Washington never did understand this and continued to view the war through its own lens of what would be unacceptable in terms of casualties. From 1966 on, Vietnam was an escalating military stalemate, as Westmoreland requested increasing numbers of men from Washington. By the end of 1966, 400,000 U.S. troops were in Vietnam. In 1968, U.S. strength was more than 500,000 men. Johnson also secured some 60,000 troops from other nations—most of them from the Republic of Korea (ROK, South Korea)—surpassing the 39,000-man international coalition of the Korean War.

Terrain was not judged important. The goals were to protect the population and kill the enemy, with success measured in terms of body counts that, in turn, led to abuses. During 1966, MACV mounted 18 major operations, each resulting in more than 500 supposedly verified VC/PAVN dead. Fifty thousand enemy combatants were supposedly killed in 1966. By the beginning of 1967,

the PAVN and VC had 300,000 men versus 625,000 ARVN and 400,000 Americans.

Hanoi, meanwhile, had reached a point of decision, with casualties exceeding available replacements. Instead of scaling back, North Vietnam prepared a major offensive that would employ all available troops to secure a quick victory. Hanoi believed that a major military defeat for the United States would end its political will to continue.

Giap now prepared a series of peripheral attacks, including a modified siege of some 6,000 U.S. Marines at Khe Sanh near the demilitarized zone (DMZ), beginning in January 1968. With U.S. attention riveted on Khe Sanh, Giap planned a massive offensive to occur over Tet, the lunar new year holidays, called the General Offensive–General Uprising. The North Vietnamese government believed that this massive offensive would lead people in South Vietnam to rise up and overthrow the South Vietnamese government, bringing an American withdrawal. The attacks were mounted against the cities. In a major intelligence failure, U.S. and South Vietnamese officials misread both the timing and strength of the attack, finding it inconceivable that the attack would come during Tet, sacrificing public goodwill.

The Tet Offensive began on January 31 and ended on February 24, 1968. Poor communication and coordination plagued Hanoi's plans. Attacks in one province occurred a day early, alerting the authorities. Hue, the former imperial capital, was especially hard hit. Fighting there destroyed half the city.

Hanoi's plan failed. ARVN forces generally fought well, and the people of South Vietnam did not support the attackers. In Hue, the communists executed 3,000 people, and news of this caused many South Vietnamese to rally to the South Vietnamese government. Half of the 85,000 VC and PAVN soldiers who took part in the offensive were killed or captured. It was the worst military setback for North Vietnam in the war.

Paradoxically, it was also its most resounding victory, in part because the Johnson administration and Westmoreland had trumpeted prior Allied successes, and the intensity of the fighting came as a profound shock to the American people. Despite the victory, they were disillusioned and turned against the war. At the end of March, Johnson announced a partial cessation of bombing and withdrew from the November presidential election.

Hanoi persisted, however. In the first six months of 1968, communist forces sustained more than 100,000 casualties, and the VC was virtually wiped out. In the same period, 20,000 Allied troops died. All sides now opted for talks in Paris in an effort to negotiate an end to the war.

American disillusionment with the war was a key factor in Republican Richard Nixon's razor-thin victory over Democrat Hubert Humphrey in the November 1968 presidential election. With no plan of his own, Nixon embraced Vietnamization, actually begun under Johnson. This turned over more of the war to the ARVN, and U.S. troop withdrawals began. Peak U.S. strength of 550,000 men occurred in early 1969. There were 475,000 men by the end of the year, 335,000 by the end of 1970, and 157,000 at the end of 1971. Massive amounts of equipment were turned over to the ARVN, including 1 million M-16 rifles and sufficient aircraft to make the South Vietnamese Air Force the world's fourth largest. Extensive retraining of the ARVN was begun, and training schools were established. The controversial counterinsurgency Phoenix Program also operated against the VC infrastructure, reducing the insurgency by 67,000 people between 1968 and 1971, but PAVN forces remained secure in sanctuaries in Laos and Cambodia.

Nixon's policy was to limit outside assistance to Hanoi and pressure the North Vietnamese government to end the war. For years, American and South Vietnamese military leaders had sought approval to attack the sanctuaries. In March 1970 a coup in Cambodia ousted Prince Norodom Sihanouk. General Lon Nol replaced him, and secret operations against the PAVN Cambodian sanctuaries soon began. Over a two-month span, there were 12 cross-border operations, known as the Cambodian Incursion. Despite widespread opposition in the United States to the widened war, the incursions raised the allies' morale, allowed U.S. withdrawals to continue on schedule, and purchased additional time for Vietnamization. PAVN forces now concentrated on bases in southern Laos and on enlarging the Ho Chi Minh Trail.

In the spring of 1971, ARVN forces mounted a major invasion into southern Laos, known as Operation Lam Son 719. There were no U.S. advisors, and ARVN units took heavy casualties. The operation set back Hanoi's plans to invade South Vietnam but took a great toll on the ARVN's younger officers and pointed out serious command weaknesses.

By 1972, PAVN forces had recovered and had been substantially strengthened with new weapons, including heavy artillery and tanks, from the Soviet Union. They now mounted a major conventional invasion of South Vietnam. Hanoi believed that the United States would not interfere. Giap had 15 divisions. He left only 1 in North Vietnam and 2 in Laos and committed the remaining 12 to the invasion.

The attack began on March 29, 1972. Known as the Spring or Easter Offensive, it began with a direct armor strike across the DMZ at the 17th Parallel and caught the best South Vietnamese troops facing Laos.

Allied intelligence misread its scale and precise timing. Giap risked catastrophic losses but hoped for a quick victory before ARVN forces could recover.

At first it appeared that the PAVN would be successful. Quang Tri fell, and rain limited the effectiveness of airpower. In May, President Nixon authorized B-52 bomber strikes on North Vietnam's principal port of Haiphong, and the mining of its harbor. This new air campaign was dubbed Linebacker I and involved the use of new precision-guided munitions (so-called smart bombs). The bombing cut off much of the supplies for the invading PAVN forces. Allied aircraft also destroyed large numbers of PAVN tanks. In June and July, the ARVN counterattacked. The invasion cost Hanoi half its force—some 100,000 men died—while ARVN losses were only 25,000.

With both Soviet and Chinese leaders anxious for better relations with the United States in order to obtain Western technology, Hanoi gave way and switched to negotiations. Finally, an agreement was hammered out in Paris that December, but President Thieu balked and refused to sign, whereupon Hanoi made the agreements public. A furious Nixon blamed Hanoi for the impasse, and in December he ordered a resumption of the bombing, dubbed Linebacker II, but also known as the December or Christmas Bombings. Although 15 B-52s were lost, Hanoi had fired away virtually its entire stock of surface-to-air missiles (SAMs) and now agreed to resume talks.

After a few cosmetic changes, an agreement was signed on January 23, 1973, with Nixon forcing Thieu to agree or risk the end of all U.S. aid. The United States recovered its prisoners of war and departed Vietnam. The Soviet Union and China continued to supply arms to North Vietnam, however, while Congress constricted U.S. supplies to South Vietnam. Tanks and planes were not replaced on the promised one-for-one basis as they were lost, and spare parts and fuel were both in short supply. All of this had a devastating effect on ARVN morale.

In South Vietnam, both sides violated the cease-fire, and fighting steadily increased in intensity. In January 1975, communist forces attacked and quickly seized Phuoc Long Province on the Cambodian border north of Saigon. Washington took no action. The communists next took Ban Me Thuot in the Central Highlands, then in mid-March President Thieu decided to abandon the northern part of his country. Confusion became disorder, then disaster, and six weeks later PAVN forces controlled all of South Vietnam. Saigon fell on April 30, 1975, to be renamed Ho Chi Minh City. Vietnam was now reunited, but under a communist government. An estimated 3 million Vietnamese, soldiers and civilians, had died in the struggle. Much of the country was devastated by the fighting, and Vietnam suffered from the effects of the widespread use of chemical defoliants.

The effects were also profound in the United States. The American military was shattered by the war and had to be rebuilt. Inflation was rampant from the failure to face up to the true costs of the war. Many questioned U.S. willingness to embark on such a crusade again, at least to go it alone. In this sense, the war forced Washington into a more realistic appraisal of U.S. power.

Spencer C. Tucker

Further Reading

Karnow, Stanley. *Vietnam: A History.* New York: Viking, 1983.

Maclear, Michael. *The Ten Thousand Day War: Vietnam, 1945–1975.* New York: St. Martin's, 1981.

O'Ballance, Edgar. *The Wars in Vietnam, 1954–1960.* New York: Hippocrene, 1981.

Palmer, General Bruce, Jr. *The 25-Year War: America's Military Role in Vietnam.* Lexington: University Press of Kentucky, 1984.

Tucker, Spencer C. *Vietnam.* Lexington: University Press of Kentucky, 1999.

Vladivostok Meeting (November 22–24, 1974)

The Vladivostok Summit Meeting between U.S. president Gerald Ford and Soviet general secretary Leonid Brezhnev took place November 22–24, 1974. It ended in a joint resolution that expressed mutual friendship and outlined future arms control measures between the United States and the Soviet Union. Vladivostok was a pivotal summit in that it not only set a working outline for the second Strategic Arms Limitation Treaty (SALT II) but also reinforced the spirit of détente that had been diminished following the 1973–1974 energy crisis and tensions in the Middle East.

Leaders from both nations and around the world initially hailed the summit at Vladivostok as a significant diplomatic success. The conference allowed Ford and Brezhnev the chance to discuss face-to-face concerns important to U.S.–Soviet relations including the situation in the Middle East, which both recognized as an intrinsically dangerous area. By far the most important issue at the Vladivostok Meeting, however, was the curtailment of the burgeoning nuclear arms race. By the end of the meeting, Ford and Brezhnev had arrived at a preliminary, nonbinding framework on which to base a future arms control agreement. The two leaders also reaffirmed their commitment to continued peaceful coexistence and détente.

The Vladivostok summit built on earlier arms control agreements, including the Anti-Ballistic Missile (ABM) Treaty and the Strategic Arms Limitation Treaty (SALT I) Interim Agreement, both signed in May 1972. The summit sought to redress inequalities in SALT I while promoting a new program to replace it when it expired in 1979. Fundamental to this was the difficult task of balancing the asymmetrical strategic forces of both sides. The draft produced at Vladivostok focused on a number of concrete issues. At the heart of the joint agreement was the overall ceiling of 2,400 placed on all nuclear delivery systems. An absolute and mutual limit of 313 heavy intercontinental ballistic missiles (ICBMs) was also part of the preliminary agreement. In addition, the talks included a ceiling on the number of multiple independently targeted reentry vehicles (MIRVs) as well as limits on the construction of new missile silos.

Although these preliminary agreements received an enthusiastic response in the Soviet Union, American critics from both sides of the political spectrum pointed to several perceived flaws. On the strategic side, they noted the unfair advantage the treaty would give to the Soviet Union by excluding its intercontinental Backfire bomber. Opponents also groused about the limited ability to monitor and enforce the agreements. Other critics attacked the framework for not placing sufficiently stringent limits on the development of new weapons systems, thus shifting the nuclear rivalry into a different but equally expensive and dangerous competition for better delivery technology.

Kurt Heinrich

Further Reading

Blechman, Barry M., ed. *Preventing Nuclear War: A Realistic Approach.* Bloomington: Indiana University Press, 1985.

Talbott, Strobe. *Endgame: The Inside Story of Salt II.* New York: HarperCollins, 1979.

Wolfe, Thomas W. *The SALT Experience.* Cambridge, MA: Ballinger, 1979.

W

Warsaw Pact

The multilateral Treaty of Friendship, Co-operation, and Mutual Assistance signed on May 14, 1955, in Warsaw, Poland, formally institutionalized the East European alliance system, the Warsaw Treaty Organization, known as the Warsaw Pact. The Warsaw Treaty was identical to bilateral treaties concluded during 1945–1949 between the Soviet Union and its East European client states to assure Moscow's continued military presence on their territory. The Soviet Union, Albania, Bulgaria, Romania, the German Democratic Republic (GDR, East Germany), Hungary, Poland, and Czechoslovakia pledged to defend each other if one or more of the members were attacked.

The Warsaw Pact was created as a political instrument for Soviet leader Nikita S. Khrushchev's Cold War policy in Europe. The immediate trigger was the admission of the Federal Republic of Germany (FRG, West Germany) into the North Atlantic Treaty Organization (NATO) on May 5, 1955, and the Austrian State Treaty of May 15, 1955, which provided for Austrian neutrality and the withdrawal of Soviet troops. The creation of the Warsaw Pact sent important signals to both Eastern Europe and the West. On the one hand, the Soviet Union made clear to its satellite states that Austria's neutral status would not likewise be granted to them. On the other hand, Khrushchev allured the West with a standing offer to disband the Warsaw Pact simultaneously with NATO, contingent upon East–West agreement on a new collective security system in Europe.

The Political Consultative Committee (PCC) was established as the alliance's highest governing body, consisting of the member states' party leaders. The PCC met almost annually in one of the capitals of the Warsaw Pact states. On the military side, a unified command and a joint staff were created to organize the actual defense of the Warsaw Treaty states. Soviet Marshal Ivan G. Konev was appointed as the first supreme commander of the Warsaw Pact's Joint Armed Forces.

In its early years, the Warsaw Pact served primarily as a Soviet propaganda tool in East–West diplomacy. Khrushchev used the PCC to publicize his disarmament, disengagement, and peace offensives and to accord them a multilateral umbrella. The first concrete military step taken was the admission of the East German Army into the unified command, but not until the Berlin Crisis (1958–1961) did a systematic militarization of the Warsaw Pact occur. The Soviet General Staff and the Warsaw Pact unified command prepared East European armies for a possible military conflict in Central Europe. In 1961, the Soviets replaced the old defensive strategy of Soviet leader Josef Stalin with an offensive strategy that provided for a deep thrust into Western Europe. In the early 1960s, the Warsaw Pact began to conduct joint military exercises to prepare for fighting a nuclear war in Europe. The new strategy remained in place until 1987. Despite détente, the militarization of the Warsaw Pact accelerated under Soviet leader Leonid Brezhnev in the 1970s.

Soviet mechanized troops on a tactical exercise in May 1984. (Department of Defense)

Behind the façade of unity, however, growing differences hounded the Eastern alliance. Following Khrushchev's campaign of de-Stalinization, Poles and Hungarians in the fall of 1956 demanded a reform of the Warsaw Pact to reduce overwhelming Soviet dominance within the alliance. Polish generals issued a memorandum that proposed modeling the Warsaw Pact more after NATO, while Hungary's new Communist Party leader, Imre Nagy, declared his country's neutrality and plans to leave the Warsaw Pact. In November 1956, the Soviet Army invaded Hungary and soon crushed all resistance.

In 1958, Romania demanded the withdrawal from its territory of all Soviet troops and military advisors. To cover Soviet embarrassment, Khrushchev termed this a unilateral troop reduction contributing to greater European security. At the height of the Berlin Crisis (1961), the Warsaw Pact's weakest and strategically least-important country, Albania, stopped supporting the pact and formally withdrew from the alliance in 1968.

The Warsaw Pact was left in ignorance when Khrushchev provoked the October 1962 Cuban Missile Crisis. Only after the crisis was ended did East European leaders learn in a secret meeting that a nuclear war had been narrowly avoided. In prompt reaction to Moscow's nonconsultation in such a serious matter, in 1963, the Romanian government gave secret assurances to the United States that it would remain neutral in the event of a confrontation between the superpowers. In the same year, Romanian and Polish opposition prevented Khrushchev from admitting Mongolia into the Warsaw Pact.

In the mid-1960s the Warsaw Pact, like NATO, underwent a major crisis. The 1965 PCC meeting, convened by East Germany, demonstrated profound disagreements among Warsaw Pact allies on matters such as the

German question, nuclear weapons' sharing, nuclear nonproliferation, and the Sino-Soviet split. In early 1966, Brezhnev proposed a Soviet plan to reform and institutionalize the Warsaw Pact. But resistance by Moscow's allies prevented the implementation of the scheme for more than three years.

In 1968, the Czechoslovak Crisis resulting from the Prague Spring seriously threatened the cohesion of the alliance. The Soviet Union tried to intimidate Alexander Dubček's liberal Czechoslovak government with purportedly multilateral Warsaw Pact military maneuvers, but the invading forces sent in on August 20, 1968 were mostly from the Soviet Union with token Polish, Hungarian, and East German contingents but no Romanian troops. Romania denounced the invasion as a violation of international law and demanded the withdrawal of all Soviet troops and military advisors from its territory. It also refused to allow additional Soviet forces to cross or conduct exercises on its territory.

The consolidation that resulted from the PCC session in Budapest in March 1969 transformed the Warsaw Pact into a more consultative organization. It established a committee of defense ministers, a military council, and a committee on technology. With these three new joint bodies, the Warsaw Pact finally became a genuine multilateral military alliance.

In 1976, previous informal gatherings of the Warsaw Pact foreign ministers were institutionalized into a committee of ministers of foreign affairs. In the 1970s, consultations within Warsaw Pact bodies primarily dealt with the Council on Security and Cooperation in Europe (CSCE) process. Despite détente, preparations for a deep offensive thrust into Western Europe accelerated and intensified during numerous military exercises. In 1979, a statute on the command of the alliance in wartime was finally accepted by all but Romania after a year-long controversy.

During 1980–1981, the Solidarity Crisis in Poland heralded the end of Moscow's domination of Eastern Europe. Yet it did not pose a serious threat to the Warsaw Pact's integrity. At first, Moscow was tempted to threaten the opposition with military exercises and, eventually, military intervention. To avoid the high political costs of such a move, however, Moscow in the end trusted that the loyal Polish military would suppress the opposition on its own. The imposition of martial law by General Wojciech Jaruzelski was a major success for Moscow, as it demonstrated that the Moscow-educated Polish generals were protecting the interests of the Warsaw Pact even against their own people.

During the renewed Cold War of the 1980s, internal disputes in the Warsaw Pact increased. Romania demanded cuts in nuclear and conventional forces as well as in national defense budgets. It also called for the dissolution of both Cold War alliances and for the withdrawal of both U.S. and Soviet forces from Europe.

The issue of an appropriate Warsaw Pact response to NATO's 1983 deployment of U.S. Pershing II and cruise missiles in Western Europe, matching Soviet SS-20 intermediate-range ballistic missiles (IRBMs) aimed at West European targets, proved to be most divisive for the Eastern alliance. In 1983, East Germany, Hungary, and Romania engaged in a damage control exercise to maintain their ties with the West, which they had established during the era of détente in the 1970s.

At the time of the Warsaw Pact's 30th anniversary in 1985, Mikhail Gorbachev became the new Soviet leader and improved the role of Warsaw Pact consultations on the desired nuclear and conventional cuts in the Eastern alliance. At the PCC meeting in Berlin in May 1987, he changed Warsaw Pact military doctrine from offensive to defensive. In the late 1980s, however, East

Germany, Bulgaria, and—in a reversal of its earlier opposition—even Romania proposed to strengthen the Warsaw Pact by improving its intrabloc political consultative functions.

After the fall of the Berlin Wall in 1989, East and West at first saw merit in keeping both Cold War alliances in place. In January and February 1991, however, Czechoslovakia, Hungary, Poland, and Bulgaria declared that they would withdraw all support by July 1 of that year. The Warsaw Pact thus came to an end on March 31, 1991, and was officially dissolved at a meeting in Prague on July 1, 1991.

Christian Nuenlist

Further Reading

Holden, Gerard. *The Warsaw Pact: The WTO and Soviet Security Policy.* Oxford, UK: Blackwell, 1989.

Jones, Christopher D. *Soviet Influence in Eastern Europe: Political Autonomy and the Warsaw Pact.* New York: Praeger, 1981.

Mastny, Vojtech, and Malcolm Byrne, eds. *A Cardboard Castle? An Inside History of the Warsaw Pact, 1955–1991.* Budapest: Central European Press, 2005.

Mastny, Vojtech, Sven Holtsmark, and Andreas Wenger, eds. *War Plans and Alliances in the Cold War: Threat Perceptions in the East and West.* New York: Routledge, 2006.

Washington Summit Meeting, Reagan and Gorbachev (December 7–10, 1987)

At a summit meeting between U.S. president Ronald Reagan and Soviet general secretary Mikhail Gorbachev in Washington, D.C., on December 7–10, 1987, the principal agenda item was nuclear arms reduction. The Washington Meeting showcased not only Gorbachev's new style of leadership but also the unprecedented thaw in the Cold War, which would by 1991 end with the dissolution of the Soviet Union. The conference marked the first superpower summit on U.S. soil in 14 years and endeavored to build on the November 1985 Geneva Meeting, during which Reagan and Gorbachev agreed to a 50 percent mutual reduction in strategic nuclear weapons, and the Reykjavík Meeting of October 1986, which ended on a negative note over disagreements concerning Reagan's Strategic Defense Initiative (SDI). The summit in Washington saw both sides agree to eliminate an entire class of nuclear weapons (land-based intermediate-range missiles), codified by the signing of the Intermediate-Range Nuclear Forces (INF) Treaty in Moscow during Reagan and Gorbachev's final meeting in May–June 1988.

In spite of the breakthrough in superpower relations, Reagan and Gorbachev still found themselves in disagreement on key issues during the 1987 negotiations. First, the 1972 Anti-Ballistic Missile (ABM) Treaty was interpreted differently by the Americans and the Soviets, which underscored the problems posed by SDI, colloquially referred to as "Star Wars." Gorbachev believed that SDI violated the ABM Treaty, while Reagan tried to legitimize SDI by arguing that it fell into a category of space-based testing and development that did not violate previous agreements. Neither leader even mentioned SDI during postconference speeches to their respective nations, which may explain why the conference was deemed a success. Further, Reagan and Gorbachev failed to come to terms on regional issues in American and Soviet spheres of influence. Reagan criticized Gorbachev for turning a blind eye to the human rights record of the People's Republic of China (PRC) and also for failing to establish a timetable for the withdrawal of Soviet troops from Afghanistan. Gorbachev, in a press conference held three hours after the departure ceremony, stated that a proposal for withdrawal would be instituted as soon as the United States agreed to halt arms shipments and financial aid to insurgent forces battling Soviet troops in Afghanistan. Gorbachev also criticized Reagan over the Iran-Contra scandal and argued that the time had not yet come for the United Nations (UN) Security Council to impose sanctions on Iran for refusing to accept an earlier UN resolution demanding a cease-fire in the Iran-Iraq War.

Even if deemed a marginal success, the 1987 Washington meeting should be considered a significant turning point in Cold War history. Americans were well aware of Gorbachev's internal reforms (glasnost and perestroika) and saw his visit as powerfully symbolic, perhaps even foreshadowing the end of the Cold War. People crowded the streets to get a glimpse of Gorbachev, and many scholars indeed argue that Reagan needed the Soviet leader's cooperation in order to improve the image of the United States. Reagan had little choice but to address Gorbachev's initiatives regarding nuclear disarmament as an opportunity to divert public attention from domestic issues, such as the Iran-Contra scandal, to those that involved a dynamic new approach to foreign policy.

Whatever the ramifications of the 1987 Washington Meeting, it must be remembered not as the culmination of a process but rather as the beginning of both a new route to nuclear arms reductions and, perhaps more importantly, the end of the Cold War.

John C. Horn

Further Reading

Fisher, Beth A. *The Reagan Reversal: Foreign Policy and the End of the Cold War*. Columbia: University of Missouri Press, 1997.

Garthoff, Raymond L. *Détente and Confrontation: American-Soviet Relations from Nixon to Reagan*. Rev. ed. Washington, DC: Brookings Institution Press, 1994.

Herrmann, Richard K. *Ending the Cold War: Interpretations, Causations, and the Study of International Relations*. New York: Palgrave Macmillan, 2004.

Lakhoff, Sanford, and Herbert F. York. *A Shield in Space? Technology, Politics, and the Strategic Defense Initiative*. Berkeley: University of California Press, 1989.

Matlock, Jack F. *Reagan and Gorbachev: How the Cold War Ended*. New York: Random House, 2004.

Y

Yeltsin, Boris (1931–2007)

Born on February 1, 1931, in Butka in the Sverdlovsk Oblast in the Ural Mountains, Boris Nikolayevich Yeltsin graduated from the Urals Polytechnical Institute in 1955 as a construction engineer. He joined the Communist Party of the Soviet Union (CPSU) in 1961 and worked on various construction projects in the Sverdlovsk area until 1968.

Yeltsin rose through the party ranks in the Sverdlovsk Oblast Party Committee. He was elected the region's industry secretary in 1975 and first secretary in 1976. During 1976–1985, he moved through the national ranks of the CPSU. He served as a deputy in the Council of the Union (1978–1989), a member of the Supreme Soviet Commission on Transport and Communication (1979–1984), a member of the Presidium of the Supreme Soviet (1984–1985), and chief of the Central Committee Department of Construction in 1985. The new CPSU general secretary, Mikhail Gorbachev, summoned Yeltsin to Moscow in April 1985 as part of a team of reform-minded party members.

Gorbachev asked Yeltsin to reform the Moscow City Committee. Yeltsin began to clear the city's Party Committee of corrupt officials, which endeared him to Muscovites. Eventually, he became dissatisfied with the slow pace of the perestroika reforms and openly criticized the CPSU officials. This was directed at the power base of Yegor Ligachev, who endorsed a moderate party–led reform. In 1987, Yeltsin resigned to force Gorbachev to take sides. Gorbachev needed Yeltsin to counterbalance Ligachev's growing skepticism and rejected his resignation, asking him to curb his critiques.

Yeltsin ignored Gorbachev's plea. Thus, Gorbachev allowed Ligachev to continue the campaign against Yeltsin, which finally led to Yeltsin's dismissal as first secretary of the Moscow Party Committee. In 1988 Yeltsin was also expelled from the Politburo, but he remained in Moscow as the first deputy chair of the State Committee for Construction.

Yeltsin went on to win a landslide victory in the newly established Congress of People's Deputies of the Russian Soviet Federated Socialistic Republic (RSFSR) in March 1989. In May 1990 he became chairman of the RSFSR. By June 12, 1990, the RSFSR, along with the other 14 Soviet republics, had declared its independence. Yeltsin was directly elected to the newly created office of president of the now-independent RSFSR on June 12, 1991. He then demanded Gorbachev's resignation. Gorbachev refused to step down, but he did agree to sign a new union treaty in late August 1991.

Hard-line conservative forces within the CPSU tried to prevent the signing of the treaty, which would lead to the dissolution of the Soviet Union. On August 19, 1991, the conservatives dispatched troops to key positions around Moscow and held Gorbachev under house arrest. Yeltsin climbed atop one of the tanks surrounding the parliament building, denounced the CPSU coup as illegal, and called for a general strike. He and his supporters remained in the parliament building as they rallied international support. For three days, thousands of people demonstrated in front of parliament, holding off an expected attack on the building.

The failed putsch and massive street demonstrations quickly destroyed the credibility of Gorbachev's perestroika and glasnost reforms. On December 24, 1991, the RSFSR and then later Russia took the Soviet Union's seat in the United Nation (UN) Security Council. The next day Gorbachev resigned, an act that officially dissolved the Soviet Union. Yeltsin, as president of Russia, immediately abolished the CPSU. In the meantime, he had negotiated with the leaders of Ukraine and Belarus to form the Commonwealth of Independent States as a federation of most of the former Soviet republics.

With a stagnating economy, a hostile legislature, and an attempted coup, Yeltsin was not expected to win reelection in 1996. However, he staged an amazing comeback. Despite becoming increasingly unpopular and suffering from ill health, he continued as president of Russia until December 31, 1999, when he named Vladimir Putin acting president. Yeltsin died in Moscow on April 23, 2007.

Frank Beyersdorf

Further Reading

Braithwaite, Rodric. *Across the Moscow River: The World Turned Upside-Down*. New Haven, CT: Yale University Press, 2002.

Breslauer, George W. *Gorbachev and Yeltsin As Leaders*. Cambridge: Cambridge University Press, 2002.

Yeltsin, Boris. *Against the Grain*. New York: Summit, 1999.

Yeltsin, Boris. *The Struggle for Russia*. New York: Random House, 1994.

Documents

Declaration on Liberated Europe: The Yalta Conference (February 1945)

The most controversial of the wartime summit meetings of the Big Three Allied leaders—Josef Stalin of the Soviet Union, British Prime Minister Winston Churchill, and U.S. president Franklin D. Roosevelt—was that held at Yalta in the Crimea in February 1945. With victory in both Europe and Asia looming ever closer on the horizon, the three men discussed numerous questions relating to the future government of many enemy or "liberated" states in both Europe and Asia. High on the agenda was the question of exactly who would control the new governments established in such countries. The Allied powers' wartime declarations had formally endorsed the principles of national self-determination, but in practice authority would ultimately rest with the state or states whose armed forces controlled a particular country. Apparently seeking to soothe the fears of his Western Allies that Soviet forces would exercise uncurbed and arbitrary power in those countries under their control, Stalin agreed to sign a declaration that promised all "liberated" European countries "democratic" governments chosen through "free elections" as soon as possible, in accordance with the principles stated earlier in the Atlantic Charter and the Declaration of the United Nations. In practice, this statement failed to define precisely what constituted "democratic" or "free" governments, a deliberate resort to vagueness that effectively permitted the occupying powers to make their own determination on the subject. Before long, East Europeans and U.S. Republican Party politicians alike would attack the Yalta agreements on the grounds that they effectively acquiesced in Soviet domination of Eastern Europe. Given Soviet military dominance of the area, however, Roosevelt and Churchill had few real alternatives to accepting Stalin's control there, no matter how harshly Russian rule might be implemented and exercised.

Protocol of Proceedings of Crimea Conference

The Crimea Conference of the heads of the Governments of the United States of America, the United Kingdom, and the Union of Soviet Socialist Republics, which took place from Feb. 4 to 11, came to the following conclusions:

[. . .]

II. Declaration of Liberated Europe

The following declaration has been approved:

The Premier of the Union of Soviet Socialist Republics, the Prime Minister of the United Kingdom and the President of the United States of America have consulted with each other in the common interests of the people of their countries and those of liberated Europe. They jointly declare their mutual agreement to concert during the temporary period of instability in liberated Europe the policies of their three Governments in assisting the peoples liberated from the domination of Nazi Germany and the peoples of the former Axis satellite states of Europe to solve by democratic means their pressing political and economic problems.

The establishment of order in Europe and the rebuilding of national economic life must be achieved by processes which will enable the liberated peoples to destroy the last vestiges of nazism and fascism and to create democratic institutions of their own choice. This is a principle of the Atlantic Charter—the right of all people to choose the form of government under which they will live—the restoration of sovereign rights and self-government to those peoples who have been forcibly deprived to them by the aggressor nations.

To foster the conditions in which the liberated people may exercise these rights, the three governments will jointly assist the people in any European liberated state or former Axis state in Europe where, in their judgment conditions require,

a. to establish conditions of internal peace;
b. to carry out emergency relief measures for the relief of distressed peoples;
c. to form interim governmental authorities broadly representative of all democratic elements in the population and pledged to the earliest possible establishment through free elections of Governments responsive to the will of the people; and
d. to facilitate where necessary the holding of such elections.

The three Governments will consult the other United Nations and provisional authorities or other Governments in Europe when matters of direct interest to them are under consideration.

When, in the opinion of the three Governments, conditions in any European liberated state or former Axis satellite in Europe make such action necessary, they will immediately consult together on the measure necessary to discharge the joint responsibilities set forth in this declaration.

By this declaration we reaffirm our faith in the principles of the Atlantic Charter, our pledge in the Declaration by the United Na-

tions and our determination to build in co-operation with other peace-loving nations world order, under law, dedicated to peace, security, freedom and general well-being of all mankind.

In issuing this declaration, the three powers express the hope that the Provisional Government of the French Republic may be associated with them in the procedure suggested.

[. . .]

Source: U.S. Department of State, *A Decade of American Foreign Policy: Basic Documents, 1941–1949* (Washington, DC: U.S. Government Printing Office, 1950), 24–25.

Ho Chi Minh: Telegrams to President Harry S. Truman (September 29, 1945, and February 28, 1946)

In 1941 Ho Chi Minh returned to Vietnam to fight against French occupation. Although he was the founder of the Vietnamese Communist Party, Ho downplayed orthodox communist ideology. Instead, he formed a broad nationalist alliance, the League for the Independence of Vietnam (Viet Minh), dedicated to anti-imperialism and land reform. In August 14, 1941, President Franklin Roosevelt and Prime Minister Winston Churchill announced the Atlantic Charter, which addressed the right of occupied peoples to choose their form of government. At his guerrilla base in northern Vietnam, Ho learned of the Atlantic Charter. He considered it a ringing endorsement for Vietnamese self-rule. Ho hoped that the United States would support Vietnamese independence from both the Japanese and the French. From an American perspective, there were two sticking points: France was an American ally in the war against the Axis powers; Ho was a well-known communist. In the early summer of 1944, the Viet Minh worked with American intelligence operatives, providing information about Japanese movements in

Vietnam and helping to rescue American airmen shot down over Indochina. On December 24, 1944, Ho ordered an attack against two small French outposts. From a communist viewpoint, this date marked the birth of the Vietnamese Army. From an American viewpoint, Ho's fight against the French marked a troubling attack against a key ally. Ho tried repeatedly to contact American political authorities regarding purported U.S. support for national self-determination. He warned that if the United States failed to support him he would turn to Russia for support. His final efforts came in 1945 when he sent numerous letters and telegrams to American ambassadors, generals, politicians, and President Harry S. Truman. He never received a reply. The fact that Ho wrote Truman remained an American state secret until it was declassified in 1972. His correspondence is stored at the National Archives.

Sept. 29, 1945

The President of the Provisional Government of the Republic of Viet-nam to The President of the United States of America.

. . .

Allow me to take this opportunity to assure you that the sentiments of friendship and of admiration which our people feel towards the American people and for its representatives here, and which have found enthusiastic expressions on various occasions, do come straight from the bottom of our hearts. That such friendly feelings have not only been shown to the American themselves but also to imposters wearing American uniforms is the evidence that America's fine stand for peace and international justice on all occasions is not only appreciated by our governing spheres but also by the whole Vietnamese nation.

In my personal name and in the name of my people I address here to you, Mr. President, and to the people of the U.S.A.,

the expression of our great admiration and respect.

Ho-Chi-Minh

Source: National Archives, Record Group 84, box 74, folder 800.

Hanoi February 28, 1946

Telegram

President Hochiminh Vietnam Democratic Republic Hanoi to the President of the United States of America Washington D.C.

On behalf of Vietnam government and people I beg to inform you that in course of conversations between Vietnam government and French representatives the latter require the secession of Cochinchina and the return of French troops in Hanoi. Meanwhile French population and troops are making active preparations for a coup de main in Hanoi and for military aggression. I therefore most earnestly appeal to you personally and to the American people to interfere urgently in support of our independence and help making the negotiations more in keeping with the principles of the Atlantic and san Francisco charters.

Respectfully

Ho-Chi-Minh

Source: National Archives, Record Group 226: Records of the Office of Strategic Services, 1919–2002.

Winston Churchill: "The Sinews of Peace" (Iron Curtain Speech) (March 5, 1946)

In a commencement address entitled "The Sinews of Peace" delivered at Westminster College in Fulton, Missouri, on March 5, 1946, former British prime minister Winston Churchill painted a picture of the post–World War II world and the emerging struggle between democracy and communism. Although Churchill was out of office, he spoke with all the prestige of "the greatest living Englishman," the charismatic

British leader who in 1940 had caught the world's imagination when he proclaimed his country's determination to stand alone against Adolf Hitler's German forces, which had already conquered Western Europe. President Harry S. Truman escorted Churchill when he gave this speech, which Truman had seen in advance and which—although Churchill was supposedly speaking as a private citizen—had also been quietly cleared with the British government. Describing the birth of the Cold War, Churchill proclaimed that an "iron curtain" had descended across Europe behind which the Soviet Union exercised unlimited control with no regard for basic human rights. He called upon the United States to join with Great Britain in preventing the further extension of Soviet power. Churchill's phrase caught the popular imagination, and the speech was widely publicized throughout the Western world. The iron curtain metaphor remained in prominent use throughout the Cold War.

[. . .]

From Stettin in the Baltic to Trieste in the Adriatic, an iron curtain has descended across the Continent. Behind that line lie all the capitals of the ancient states of Central and Eastern Europe. Warsaw, Berlin, Prague, Vienna, Budapest, Belgrade, Bucharest and Sofia, all these famous cities and the populations around them lie in what I must call the Soviet sphere, and all are subject in one form or another, not only to Soviet influence but to a very high and, in some cases, increasing measure of control from Moscow. Athens alone—Greece with its immortal glories—is free to decide its future at an election under British, American and French observation. The Russian-dominated Polish Government has been encouraged to make enormous and wrongful inroads upon Germany, and mass expulsions of millions of Germans on a scale grievous and undreamed-of are now

taking place. The Communist parties, which were very small in all these Eastern States of Europe, have been raised to pre-eminence and power far beyond their numbers and are seeking everywhere to obtain totalitarian control. Police governments are prevailing in nearly every case, and so far, except in Czechoslovakia, there is no true democracy.

[. . .]

In front of the iron curtain which lies across Europe are other causes for anxiety. In Italy the Communist Party is seriously hampered by having to support the Communist-trained Marshal Tito's claims to former Italian territory at the head of the Adriatic. Nevertheless the future of Italy hangs in the balance. Again one cannot imagine a regenerated Europe without a strong France. All my public life I have worked for a strong France and I never lost faith in her destiny, even in the darkest hours. I will not lose faith now. However, in a great number of countries, far from the Russian frontiers and throughout the world, Communist fifth columns are established and work in complete unity and absolute obedience to the directions they receive from the Communist centre. Except in the British Commonwealth and in the United States where Communism is in its infancy, the Communist parties or fifth columns constitute a growing challenge and peril to Christian civilisation. These are somber facts for anyone to have to recite on the morrow of a victory gained by so much splendid comradeship in arms and in the cause of freedom and democracy; but we should be most unwise not to face them squarely while time remains.

[. . .]

On the other hand I repulse the idea that a new war is inevitable; still more that it is imminent. It is because I am sure that our fortunes are still in our own hands and that we hold the power to save the future, that I feel the duty to speak out now that I have the occasion and the opportunity to do so. I do not believe that Soviet Russia desires war. What they desire is the fruits of war and the indefinite expansion of their power and doctrines. But what we have to consider here today while time remains, is the permanent prevention of war and the establishment of conditions of freedom and democracy as rapidly as possible in all countries. Our difficulties and dangers will not be removed by closing our eyes to them. They will not be removed by mere waiting to see what happens; nor will they be removed by a policy of appeasement. What is needed is a settlement, and the longer this is delayed, the more difficult it will be and the greater our dangers will become.

From what I have seen of our Russian friends and Allies during the war, I am convinced that there is nothing they admire so much as strength, and there is nothing for which they have less respect than for weakness, especially military weakness. For that reason the old doctrine of a balance of power is unsound. We cannot afford, if we can help it, to work on narrow margins, offering temptations to a trial of strength. If the Western Democracies stand together in strict adherence to the principles of the United Nations Charter, their influence for furthering those principles will be immense and no one is likely to molest them. If however they become divided or falter in their duty and if these all-important years are allowed to slip away then indeed catastrophe may overwhelm us all.

[. . .]

Source: Winston S. Churchill, *Sinews of Peace: Post-War Speeches by Winston S. Churchill*, edited by Randolph S. Churchill (Boston: Houghton Mifflin, 1949).

George C. Marshall: Remarks by the Secretary of State (Marshall Plan) (June 5, 1947)

By spring 1947, it was becoming clear that Western Europe was unlikely to recover from the devastation of World War II without a major infusion of outside funds. The harsh winter of 1946–1947 brought shortened working hours, power cuts, food and fuel shortages, and social unrest in France and Italy, enhancing the political position of domestic communist parties in the latter two countries. European leaders, spearheaded by the British, appealed to the United States for economic aid. State Department officials such as Undersecretary of State Will Clayton, who toured Europe in early 1947, returned convinced that without such assistance, the West European nations were likely to collapse, and communist regimes that looked to Moscow for guidance might well come to power there. On June 5, 1947, in a speech at the commencement ceremony of Harvard College in Cambridge, Massachusetts, U.S. secretary of state George C. Marshall proposed that the United States grant financial aid to countries in need to prevent them from succumbing to communism. U.S. president Harry S. Truman later dubbed the proposal the Marshall Plan, and it became one of the major U.S. initiatives of the early Cold War. American officials invited all European countries, including the communist satellite states in Eastern Europe, to participate in the plan, which envisaged a carefully coordinated scheme to revive the economies of all the European nations rather than a series of bilateral programs between the individual countries and the United States. To join the enterprise, each nation had to provide accurate and detailed economic information. Several East European states initially expressed interest in taking part but, on Soviet instructions, eventually withdrew. Congress debated the Marshall Plan throughout 1948 and eventually enacted a series of laws to implement the plan, officially known as the European Recovery Program and run by the Economic Cooperation

Administration. By 1953 the United States had provided approximately $13 billion in aid under the Marshall Plan, most of it directed to European nations but some to China, whose political allies in Congress demanded that China be included. The Marshall Plan gave a great boost to European economic recovery and helped to usher in two decades of prosperity in Western Europe. The plan also helped to intensify the Cold War. The inclusion of the Federal Republic of Germany (FRG, West Germany) in the Marshall Plan led Soviet leader Josef Stalin to fear that any German economic revival would eventually lead to a German military resurgence that would once more threaten the security of the Soviet state, and this was one reason for the Berlin Blockade of 1948–1949, a period when for almost a year East German and Soviet forces denied the Western powers land access to West Berlin. In 1948 Soviet-backed coups in Hungary and Czechoslovakia also ejected all noncommunist elements from the governments of those two states, tightening Soviet control. In response, in 1949 the Western powers established the North Atlantic Treaty Organization security pact in which the United States, Canada, and 10 West European states agreed to come to each other's assistance should any of them be attacked by another power.

I need not tell you gentlemen that the world situation is very serious. That must be apparent to all intelligent people. I think one difficulty is that the problem is one of such enormous complexity that the very mass of facts presented to the public by press and radio make it exceedingly difficult for the man in the street to reach a clear appraisement of the situation. Furthermore, the people of this country are distant from the troubled areas of the earth and it is hard for them to comprehend the plight and consequent reaction of the long-suffering peoples, and the effect of those reactions on their governments in connection with our efforts to promote peace in the world.

In considering the requirements for the rehabilitation of Europe the physical loss of life, the visible destruction of cities, factories, mines, and railroads was correctly estimated, but it has become obvious during recent months that this visible destruction was probably less serious than the dislocation of the entire fabric of the European economy. For the past 10 years conditions have been highly abnormal. The feverish maintenance of the war effort engulfed all aspects of national economies. Machinery has fallen into disrepair or is entirely obsolete. Under the arbitrary and destructive Nazi rule, virtually every possible enterprise was geared into the German war machine. Long-standing commercial ties, private institutions, banks, insurance companies and shipping companies disappeared, through the loss of capital, absorption through nationalization or by simple destruction. In many countries, confidence in the local currency has been severely shaken. The breakdown of the business structure of Europe during the war was complete. Recovery has been seriously retarded by the fact that 2 years after the close of hostilities a peace settlement with Germany and Austria has not been agreed upon. But even given a more prompt solution of these difficult problems, the rehabilitation of the economic structure of Europe quite evidently will require a much longer time and greater effort than had been foreseen.

There is a phase of this matter which is both interesting and serious. The farmer has always produced the foodstuffs to exchange with the city dweller for the other necessities of life. This division of labor is the basis of modern civilization. At the present time it is threatened with breakdown. The town and city industries are not producing adequate goods to exchange with the food-producing farmer. Raw materials and fuel are in short supply.

Machinery is lacking or worn out. The farmer or the peasant cannot find the goods for sale which he desires to purchase. So the sale of his farm produce for money which he cannot use seems to him an unprofitable transaction. He, therefore, has withdrawn many fields from crop cultivation and is using them for grazing. He feeds more grain to stock and finds for himself and his family an ample supply of food, however short he may be on clothing and the other ordinary gadgets of civilization. Meanwhile people in the cities are short of food and fuel. So the governments are forced to use their foreign money and credits to procure these necessities abroad. This process exhausts funds which are urgently needed for reconstruction. Thus a very serious situation is rapidly developing which bodes no good for the world. The modern system of the division of labor upon which the exchange of products is based is in danger of breaking down.

The truth of the matter is that Europe's requirements for the next 3 or 4 years of foreign food and other essential products—principally from America—are so much greater than her present ability to pay that she must have substantial additional help, or face economic, social, and political deterioration of a very grave character.

The remedy lies in breaking the vicious circle and restoring the confidence of the European people in the economic future of their own countries and of Europe as a whole. The manufacturer and the farmer throughout wide areas must be able and willing to exchange their products for currencies the continuing value of which is not open to question.

Aside from the demoralizing effect on the world at large and the possibilities of disturbances arising as a result of the desperation of the people concerned, the consequences to the economy of the United States should

be apparent to all. It is logical that the United States should do whatever it is able to do to assist in the return of normal economic health in the world, without which there can be no political stability and no assured peace. Our policy is directed not against any country or doctrine but against hunger, poverty, desperation, and chaos. Its purpose should be the revival of a working economy in the world so as to permit the emergence of political and social conditions in which free institutions can exist. Such assistance, I am convinced, must not be on a piecemeal basis as various crises develop. Any assistance that this Government may render in the future should provide a cure rather than a mere palliative. Any government that is willing to assist in the task of recovery will find full cooperation, I am sure, on the part of the United States Government. Any government which maneuvers to block the recovery of other countries cannot expect help from us. Furthermore, governments, political parties, or groups which seek to perpetuate human misery in order to profit therefrom politically or otherwise will encounter the opposition of the United States.

It is already evident that, before the United States Government can proceed much further in its efforts to alleviate the situation and help start the European world on its way to recovery, there must be some agreement among the countries of Europe as to the requirements of the situation and the part those countries themselves will take in order to give proper effect to whatever action might be undertaken by this Government. It would be neither fitting nor efficacious for this Government to undertake to draw up unilaterally a program designed to place Europe on its feet economically. This is the business of the Europeans. The initiative, I think, must come from Europe. The role of this country should consist of friendly aid in the drafting of a European program and of later support of such a program so far as it may be practical for us to do so. The program should be a joint one, agreed to by a number, if not all European nations.

An essential part of any successful action on the part of the United States is an understanding on the part of the people of America of the character of the problem and the remedies to be applied. Political passion and prejudice should have no part. With foresight, and a willingness on the part of our people to face up to the vast responsibilities which history has clearly placed upon our country, the difficulties I have outlined can and will be overcome.

Source: George C. Marshall, "European Initiative Essential to Economic Recovery," *Department of State Bulletin* 16, no. 415 (1947): 1159–60.

North Atlantic Treaty (1949)

Signed on April 4, 1949, the North Atlantic Treaty created the North Atlantic Treaty Organization (NATO), a mutual defense alliance of nations from Europe and North America. NATO was organized to defend member nations from the possible aggression of the Soviet Union and the nations of Eastern Europe, which formed the Warsaw Treaty Organization six years later. Originally NATO comprised the United States, Canada, and 10 West European nations, including Great Britain, France, Italy, Belgium, the Netherlands, Luxembourg, Iceland, Denmark, Norway, and Portugal. In 1955 the Federal Republic of Germany (FRG, West Germany) became a member, a move that reawakened bitter Soviet memories of past German attacks on Russia and impelled Soviet leaders to respond by establishing the Warsaw Pact. Greece and Turkey both joined NATO in 1952, and Spain joined in 1982 after dictator Francisco Franco's death brought the restoration of democracy in that country. NATO was intended as a purely defensive alliance whose very existence would deter any Soviet attack

on any of the signatory nations, since all of them were bound to come to the assistance of any member that came under attack from an outside power. The alliance did not cover attacks on or uprisings within the colonies of the various European signatories. Perhaps one of the greatest successes of NATO was that no signatory ever found it necessary to invoke the alliance during the Cold War, a fact that was either a tribute to its deterrent effect or, perhaps, evidence that the Soviet Union never had any intention of attacking any of its signatories. NATO was the first permanent military alliance ever concluded by the United States, a development that marked a new departure in American foreign policy. Although it was initially intended that NATO military forces in Europe should be small and the United States only committed two divisions there, the outbreak of the Korean War in 1950 soon brought the dispatch of an additional four divisions to Western Europe. One unspoken purpose of the alliance was to counter any potential future military resurgence on the part of Germany, whose belligerent record since the mid-nineteenth century prompted fears on the part of other NATO members, especially France, that German leaders might once again seek to dominate Europe by force of arms. Despite differences among members and the withdrawal of France in the mid-1960s, NATO endured even the end of the Cold War. As East–West tensions eased, former Soviet satellites—including the Czech Republic, Hungary, and Poland in 1999 and Bulgaria, Estonia, Latvia, Lithuania, Romania, Slovakia, and Slovenia in 2004—joined the alliance, perceiving it in part as a guarantee of their own security should Russia once again seek to dominate them. The Warsaw Pact, by contrast, collapsed. NATO also sought to redefine its role, participating in the 1991 Persian Gulf War and seeking to maintain peace in former Yugoslavia during the 1990s. The NATO alliance was formally invoked for the first time in September 2001 when, after Muslim al-Qaeda extremists mounted suicide aircraft attacks on the World Trade Center in New York City and the Pentagon building in Washington, D.C., NATO forces took part in the subsequent war against Afghanistan.

Treaty Establishing the North Atlantic Treaty Organization

The Parties to this Treaty reaffirm their faith in the purposes and principles of the Charter of the United Nations and their desire to live in peace with all peoples and all governments.

They are determined to safeguard the freedom, common heritage and civilization of their peoples, founded on the principles of democracy, individual liberty and the rule of law.

They seek to promote stability and well-being in the North Atlantic area.

They are resolved to unite their efforts for collective defense and for the preservation of peace and security.

They therefore agree to this North Atlantic Treaty:

Article 1

The Parties undertake, as set forth in the Charter of the United Nations, to settle any international dispute in which they may be involved by peaceful means in such a manner that international peace and security and justice are not endangered, and to refrain in their international relations from the threat or use of force in any manner inconsistent with the purposes of the United Nations.

Article 2

The Parties will contribute toward the further development of peaceful and friendly international relations by strengthening their free institutions, by bringing about a better understanding of the principles upon which these institutions are founded, and by promoting conditions of stability and well-being. They will seek to eliminate conflict in their international economic policies and will encourage economic collaboration between any or all of them.

Article 3

In order more effectively to achieve the objectives of this Treaty, the Parties, separately and jointly, by means of continuous and effective self-help and mutual aid, will maintain and develop their individual and collective capacity to resist armed attack.

Article 4

The Parties will consult together whenever, in the opinion of any of them, the territorial integrity, political independence or security of any of the Parties is threatened.

Article 5

The Parties agree that an armed attack against one or more of them in Europe or North America shall be considered an attack against them all, and consequently they agree that, if such an armed attack occurs, each of them, in exercise of the right of individual or collective self-defense recognized by Article 51 of the Charter of the United Nations, will assist the Party or Parties so attacked by taking forthwith, individually, and in concert with the other Parties, such action as it deems necessary, including the use of armed force, to restore and maintain the security of the North Atlantic area.

Any such armed attack and all measures taken as a result thereof shall immediately be reported to the [United Nations] Security Council. Such measures shall be terminated when the Security Council has taken the measures necessary to restore and maintain international peace and security.

Article 6

For the purpose of Article 5, an armed attack on one or more of the Parties is deemed to include an armed attack:

a. on the territory of any of the Parties in Europe or North America, on the Algerian Departments of France, on the territory of Turkey or on the islands under the jurisdiction of any of the Parties in the North Atlantic area north of the Tropic of Cancer;

b. on the forces, vessels, or aircraft of any of the Parties, when in or over these territories or any area in Europe in which occupation forces of any of the Parties were stationed on the date when the Treaty entered into force or the Mediterranean Sea or the North Atlantic area north of the Tropic of Cancer.

Article 7

The Treaty does not affect, and shall not be interpreted as affecting, in any way the rights and obligations under the Charter of the Parties which are members of the United Nations, or the primary responsibility of the Security Council for the maintenance of international peace and security.

Article 8

Each Party declares that none of the international engagements now in force between it and any other of the Parties or any third State is in conflict with the provisions of this Treaty, and undertakes not to enter into any international engagement in conflict with this Treaty.

Article 9

The Parties hereby establish a Council, on which each of them shall be represented to consider matters concerning the implementation of this Treaty. The Council shall be so organized as to be able to meet promptly at any time. The Council shall set up such subsidiary bodies as may be necessary; in particular it shall establish immediately a defense committee which shall recommend measures for the implementation of Articles 3 and 5.

Article 10

The Parties may, by unanimous agreement, invite any other European State in a position to further the principles of this Treaty and to contribute to the security of the North Atlantic area to accede to this Treaty. Any State so invited may become a party to the Treaty by depositing its instrument of accession with the Government of the United States of America. The Government of the United States of America will inform each of the Parties of the deposit of each such instrument of accession.

[. . .]

Source: North Atlantic Treaty Organisation, "The North Atlantic Treaty," Online Library, NATO Basic Texts. http://www.nato.int/docu/basictxt/treaty.htm.

Harry S. Truman: First U.S. Acknowledgment of Soviet Atomic Bomb Detonation (September 23, 1949)

From July 1945 to August 1949, the United States and Britain enjoyed a nuclear monopoly that the Soviet Union was determined to break. On learning of the success of the first U.S. atomic test, Soviet leader Josef Stalin immediately launched a crash program to build a Soviet bomb. Due in part to the help of spies within the Anglo-American Manhattan Project laboratories at Los Alamos, New Mexico, four years later, on August 29, 1949, the Soviet Union successfully tested an atomic device. Three days later, specially equipped U.S. radar airplanes detected atmospheric debris from the test. The newly established Central Intelligence Agency (CIA) had predicted that Soviet scientists would eventually develop a bomb but had not expected this to occur for several more years. Soviet success in doing so led to a rapid reevaluation of the U.S. national security position. In late September, President Harry S. Truman tersely informed the American people that the Soviet Union now possessed atomic weapons, stating that this reinforced the need to bring nuclear power under "truly effective enforceable international control." In practice, neither the United States nor the Soviet Union was prepared to relinquish direction of its own atomic weapons to an outside body. At that juncture, American scientists and government officials were debating whether to mount an expensive program to develop thermonuclear weapons in the form of the immensely more powerful hydrogen bomb. On January 31, 1950, Truman authorized this project and ordered that it be implemented as expeditiously as possible. Soviet scientists likewise began work on such weapons, which both sides developed in the mid-1950s, bringing a mutual escalation of the nuclear arms race that eventually helped to generate growing popular and official support for arms control negotiations. In early 1950 the president also instructed the State Department Policy Planning Staff and the National Security Council (NSC) to undertake a major review of U.S. national security policies, which resulted in the April 1950 paper NSC-68, a document that urged major increases in U.S. defense spending and overseas commitments and bases and envisaged the quadrupling of military budgets. Truman initially rejected these conclusions on the grounds that they were too expensive, but with the outbreak of the Korean War in late June 1950, most of NSC-68's recommendations were eventually implemented. Russian possession of atomic weapons contributed to a new sense of U.S. vulnerability, one reason that the domestic anticommunism of Senator Joseph McCarthy and other Truman administration critics appealed to so many Americans in the early 1950s.

President Harry S. Truman
September 23, 1949.

I believe the American people, to the fullest extent consistent with national security, are entitled to be informed of all developments in the field of atomic energy. That is my reason for making public the following information.

We have evidence that within recent weeks an atomic explosion occurred in the U.S.S.R.

Ever since atomic energy was first released by man, the eventual development of this new force by other nations was to be expected. This probability has always been taken into account by us.

Nearly 4 years ago I pointed out that "scientific opinion appears to be practically unanimous that the essential theoretical knowledge upon which the discovery is based is already widely known. There is also substantial agreement that foreign research can come abreast of our present theoretical knowledge in time." And, in the Three-Nation Declaration of the President of the United States and the Prime Ministers of the United Kingdom and of Canada, dated November 15, 1945, it was emphasized that no single nation could in fact have a monopoly of atomic weapons.

This recent development emphasizes once again, if indeed such emphasis were needed, the necessity for that truly effective enforceable international control of atomic energy which this Government and the large majority of the members of the United Nations support.

Source: Harry S. Truman, *Public Papers of the Presidents of the United States: Harry S. Truman, 1949* (Washington, DC: U.S. Government Printing Office, 1964), 485.

Joseph McCarthy: Speech on Spread of Communism (February 20, 1950)

In February 1950 Senator Joseph McCarthy of Wisconsin spoke before the Women's Club of

Wheeling, West Virginia, claiming that he had a list of 205 known communists working in the U.S. State Department. McCarthy, whose Senate record was decidedly mediocre, was apparently looking for an issue that would help him win reelection in 1952. His allegations came a few months after the Chinese Communist Party had won the four-year Chinese Civil War and established the People's Republic of China. Also in 1949, the Soviet Union successfully tested an atomic bomb, an event that made the United States feel more vulnerable to sudden and devastating external attack than ever before. It soon became public that some Canadian, American, and British scientists working in the American-financed nuclear program had passed information to the Soviets, accelerating the development of Russian atomic weapons. Alger Hiss, a former State Department official accused of passing secret government information to the Soviet Union during the 1930s and 1940s, had also been tried and convicted for perjury in 1949, though his former associate, Secretary of State Dean Acheson, publicly refused to condemn him.

McCarthy's accusations therefore came at a psychologically fertile moment. They quickly made him into the foremost leader of the eponymous McCarthyism, the movement in the early 1950s to weed out communists and communist sympathizers in the U.S. government and American society in general. McCarthy was not inhibited by any considerations of accuracy or even probability, accusing such leading Cold Warriors as Acheson and former secretary of state George Marshall of being communist sympathizers or dupes, if not outright agents. McCarthy's charges touched off a hailstorm of controversy that led to loyalty investigations of numerous diplomats, especially those concerned with China policy, and other government officials. As chairman of the Senate Permanent Investigating Subcommittee of the Government Operations Committee, McCarthy held well-broadcast public hearings to determine the political ideologies of political figures and public personalities, including movie stars. McCarthy was taking advantage of a climate of increasing suspicion of leftist dissent, exemplified by the anti-radical activities of the House Un-American Activities Committee from the 1930s onward, and later by President Harry S. Truman's Executive Order 9835, issued in March 1947, establishing a loyalty-security program for federal employees.

McCarthy later submitted his speech to Congress so that it could be recorded in the Congressional Record, but he changed the number of known communists to 57. For several years, few Americans dared to challenge McCarthy, fearing that they themselves would be attacked as communist agents. McCarthy also appealed to the populist resentment many ordinary Americans harbored toward the internationally oriented East Coast elite, whose members tended to dominate the U.S. diplomatic and national security apparatus. In the long run, his inaccuracies and a general disregard of facts led to McCarthy's downfall, but he ruined the reputations of several prominent people in the process, and generated a climate of fear that discouraged dissent from or even honest criticism of American foreign policies.

Senator Joseph McCarthy
February 20, 1950

Five years after a world war has been won, men's hearts should anticipate a long peace, and men's minds should be free from the heavy weight that comes from war. But this is not such a period—for this is not a period of peace. This is a time of the "cold war." This is a time when all the world is split into two vast, increasingly hostile armed camps. . . .

The reason why we find ourselves in a position of impotency is not because our only powerful potential enemy has sent men to invade our shores, but rather because of the traitorous actions of those who have been treated so well by this Nation. It has not been the less fortunate or members of minority groups who have been selling this Nation out, but rather those who have had all the benefits that the wealthiest nation on earth has to offer—the finest homes, the finest college education, and the finest jobs in Government.

This is glaringly true in the State Department. There the bright young men who are born with silver spoons in their mouths are the ones who have been the worst. . . . In my opinion, the State Department, which is one of the most important government departments, is thoroughly infested with Communists.

I have in my hand 205 cases of individuals who would appear to be either card carrying members or certainly loyal to the Communist Party, but who nevertheless are still helping to shape our foreign policy. . . .

As you know, very recently the Secretary of State proclaimed his loyalty to a man guilty of what has always been considered as the most abominable of all crimes—of being a traitor to the people who gave him a position of great trust. The Secretary of State in attempting to justify his continued devotion to the man who sold out the Christian world to the atheistic world, referred to Christ's Sermon on the Mount as a justification and reason therefor, and the reaction of the American people to this would have made the heart of Abraham Lincoln happy.

When this pompous diplomat in striped pants, with a phony British accent, proclaimed to the American people that Christ on the Mount endorsed communism, high treason, and a betrayal of a sacred trust, the blasphemy was so great that it awakened the dormant indignation of the American people.

He has lighted the spark which is resulting in a moral uprising and will end only when the whole sorry mess of twisted, warped thinkers are swept from the national scene so that we may have a new birth of national honesty and decency in government.

Source: U.S. Congress, Congressional Record, 81st Cong., 2nd sess., 1954–1957.

Harry S. Truman: Declaration of a National Emergency (December 16, 1950)

Until late November 1950, when it became apparent that communist Chinese forces had intervened in large numbers in the Korean War, the Democratic administration of President Harry S. Truman assumed that by the end of 1950 the conflict would be over and would have ended in a sweeping United Nations (UN) victory, uniting all Korea under a pro-Western government. Chinese intervention ensured that the fighting would be protracted and would eventually end in a stalemate, a compromise that completely satisfied none of the combatants. It also meant that the United States would have to make far greater efforts than originally expected to attain even these limited goals. As the forces under General Douglas MacArthur's command retreated in a near rout throughout December, Truman proclaimed a national state of emergency, urging the American people to make all necessary sacrifices to ensure their country's ultimate triumph over communism. In apocalyptic terms, Truman warned that unless they did so, they faced a communist threat to their way of life, which would mean that Americans would lose the freedoms of religion, speech, thought, education, and political and economic activity that they currently enjoyed. The draft was reinstated for young men of military age, and rationing and price controls were imposed. The United States also launched a massive military buildup, implementing the permanent expansion of its armed forces and American overseas bases and commitments envisaged the previous year in the policy planning paper NSC-68.

By the President of the United States of America a Proclamation

WHEREAS recent events in Korea and elsewhere constitute a grave threat to the peace of the world and imperil the efforts of this country and those of the United Nations to prevent aggression and armed conflict; and

WHEREAS world conquest by communist imperialism is the goal of the forces of aggression that have been loosed upon the world; and

WHEREAS, if the goal of communist imperialism were to be achieved, the people of this country would no longer enjoy the full and rich life they have with God's help built for themselves and their children; they would no longer enjoy the blessings of the freedom of worshipping as they severally choose, the freedom of reading and listening to what they choose, the right of free speech including the right to criticize their Government, the right to choose those who conduct their Government, the right to engage freely in collective bargaining, the right to engage freely in their own business enterprises, and the many other freedoms and rights which are a part of our way of life; and

WHEREAS the increasing menace of the forces of communist aggression requires that the national defense of the United States be strengthened as speedily as possible:

Now, THEREFORE, I, HARRY S. TRUMAN, President of the United States of America, do proclaim the existence of a national emergency, which requires that the military, naval, air, and civilian defenses of this country be strengthened as speedily as possible to the end that we may be able to repel any and all threats against our national security and to fulfill our responsibilities in the efforts being made through the United Nations and otherwise to bring about lasting peace.

I summon all citizens to make a united effort for the security and well-being of our beloved country and to place its needs foremost in thought and action that the full moral and material strength of the Nation may be readied for the dangers which threaten us.

I summon our farmers, our workers in industry, and our businessmen to make a mighty production effort to meet the defense requirements of the Nation and to this end to eliminate all waste and inefficiency and to subordinate all lesser interests to the common good.

I summon every person and every community to make, with a spirit of neighborliness, whatever sacrifices are necessary for the welfare of the Nation.

I summon all State and local leaders and officials to cooperate fully with the military and civilian defense agencies of the United States in the national defense program.

I summon all citizens to be loyal to the principles upon which our Nation is founded, to keep faith with our friends and allies, and to be firm in our devotion to the peaceful purposes for which the United Nations was founded.

I am confident that we will meet the dangers that confront us with courage and determination, strong in the faith that we can thereby "secure the Blessings of Liberty to ourselves and our Posterity."

[. . .]

Source: Harry S. Truman, *Public Papers of the Presidents of the United States: Harry S. Truman, 1950* (Washington, DC: U.S. Government Printing Office, 1965), 746–47.

Douglas MacArthur: Post-Recall Speech to Congress (April 19, 1951)

U.S. general Douglas MacArthur, Allied commander of United Nation forces during the Korean War, was an able general but also a controversial figure, whom top American officials in Washington feared might readily use nuclear weapons to ignite World War III. MacArthur, commander of U.S. military forces in the Pacific during World War II, headed the postwar Allied forces that occupied Japan. In early July 1950, shortly after the onset of the Korean War, MacArthur was appointed commander of the United Nations forces that were to be deployed to Korea. MacArthur, a fierce anticommunist, also had close ties to Jiang Jieshi (Chiang Kai-shek), the Chinese Nationalist or Guomindang leader who fled to Taiwan in 1949 with the remnants of his forces as the Chinese Communist Party conquered mainland China. In defiance of Secretary of State Dean Acheson's policies, by June 1950 MacArthur already favored a continuing American commitment to Taiwan, and hoped that U.S. forces would ultimately attack and overthrow the new People's Republic of China. As United Nations commander, in September 1950 MacArthur reversed the initial North Korean advances in the war by taking the enemy from behind after a daring amphibious landing at Inchon. The original remit of the United Nations resolution authorizing military intervention in Korea had been merely to drive North Korean troops out of the South, but MacArthur's UN forces quickly drove the enemy back well beyond the earlier Thirty-Eighth Parallel border that had previously divided the Koreas. MacArthur ignored Chinese warnings that, should non-Korean troops cross this boundary and try to unite Korea under a noncommunist government, the PRC would in its turn intervene. In November 1950 hundreds of thousands of Chinese "People's Volunteer" troops came to the assistance of North Korea, once more driving the United Nations army back well beyond the Thirty-Eighth Parallel boundary. Ignoring repeated instructions from President Harry Truman that he would not authorize the use of nuclear weapons against the PRC, a move that Truman feared might provoke Soviet intervention, in early 1951 MacArthur publicly advocated the employment of atomic bombs to devastate the northeastern Manchurian provinces, the Chinese industrial heartland bordering on North Korea, and 30–50 Chinese cities. Whereas Truman wished to wage a limited war, MacArthur favored total war, even at the risk of provoking World War III. MacArthur's bellicose rhetoric was intended to undercut moves by Truman to open peace negotiations with the North Koreans and Chinese. It deeply alarmed the European allies of the United States, most of whom were contributing military contingents to the United Nations army,

but who feared that the Korean conflict might escalate into a full-scale great power confrontation. Infuriated by the arrogant general's constant insubordination, President Harry Truman relieved MacArthur of his office on April 11, 1951. Eight days later, on April 19, the still charismatic MacArthur used masterly rhetoric to deliver a farewell address to Congress, offering a defense of his actions in Korea. His speech was interrupted by 30 ovations. MacArthur's public popularity soared and that of Truman declined but, although he harbored political ambitions, MacArthur never served again in any significant public office. His criticisms of Truman's policies did, however, give additional ammunition to Senator Joseph McCarthy and others who repeatedly attacked Truman administration officials, alleging that they were overly soft on communism and that such figures as Secretary of State Dean Acheson and Secretary of Defense George Marshall were communist agents or at least gullible fellow travelers. During the Truman administration's final two years in office, such allegations helped to make both the Korean War and many of Truman's top officials extremely unpopular.

April 19, 1951

Mr. President, Mr. Speaker and distinguished members of the Congress:

I stand on this rostrum with a sense of deep humility and great pride—humility in the wake of those great American architects of our history who have stood here before me, pride in the reflection that this forum of legislative debate represents human liberty in the purest form yet devised.

Here are centered the hopes and aspirations and faith of the entire human race. I do not stand here as advocate for any partisan cause, for the issues are fundamental and reach quite beyond the realm of partisan consideration. They must be resolved on the highest plane of national interest if our course is to prove sound and our future protected.

I trust, therefore, that you will do me the justice of receiving that which I have to say as solely expressing the considered viewpoint of a fellow American.

I address you with neither rancor nor bitterness in the fading twilight of life with but one purpose in mind: to serve my country.

The issues are global and so interlocked that to consider the problems of one sector, oblivious to those of another, is but to court disaster for the whole.

While Asia is commonly referred to as the gateway to Europe, it is no less true that Europe is the gateway to Asia, and the broad influence of the one cannot fail to have its impact upon the other. There are those who claim our strength is inadequate to protect on both fronts, that we can not divide our effort. I can think of no greater expression of defeatism.

If a potential enemy can divide his strength on two fronts, it is for us to counter his effort. The Communist threat is a global one. Its successful advance in one sector threatens the destruction of every other sector. You cannot appease or otherwise surrender to Communism in Asia without simultaneously undermining our efforts to halt its advance in Europe.

Beyond pointing out these general truisms, I shall confine my discussion to the general areas of Asia. Before one may objectively assess the situation now existing there, he must comprehend something of Asia's past and the revolutionary changes which have marked her course up to the present.

Long exploited by the so-called colonial powers, with little opportunity to achieve any degree of social justice, individual dignity, or a higher standard of life such as guided our own noble administration of the Philippines, the peoples of Asia found their opportunity in the war just past to throw off the shackles of colonialism, and now see the dawn of new opportunity, a heretofore unfelt dignity, and the self-respect of political freedom.

Mustering half of the earth's population and 60 per cent of its natural resources, these peoples are rapidly consolidating a new force, both moral and material, with which to raise the living standard and erect adaptations of the design of modern progress to their own distinct cultural environments.

Whether one adheres to the concept of colonization or not, this is the direction of Asian progress and it may not be stopped. It is a corollary to the shift of the world economic frontiers, as the whole epicenter of world affairs rotates back toward the area whence it started.

In this situation it becomes vital that our own country orient its policies in consonance with this basic evolutionary condition rather than pursue a course blind to the reality that the colonial era is now passed and the Asian peoples covet the fight to shape their own free destiny. What they seek now is friendly guidance, understanding and support, not imperious direction; the dignity of equality and not the shame of subjugation. Their prewar standard of life, pitifully low, is infinitely lower now in the devastation left in war's wake.

World ideologies play little part in Asian thinking and are little understood. What the people strive for is the opportunity for a little more food in their stomachs, a little better clothing on their backs, and a little firmer roof over their heads, and the realization of the normal nationalist urge for political freedom.

These political-social conditions have but an indirect bearing upon our own national security but do form a backdrop to contemporary planning which must be thoughtfully considered if we are to avoid the pitfalls of unrealism.

Of more direct and immediate beating upon our national security are the changes wrought in the strategic potential of the Pacific Ocean in the course of the past war. Prior thereto, the western strategic frontier of the United States lay on the littoral line of the Americas with an exposed island salient extending out through Hawaii, Midway and Guam to the Philippines.

That salient proved not an outpost of strength but an avenue of weakness along which the enemy could and did attack. The Pacific was a potential area of advance for any predatory force intent upon striking at the bordering land areas.

All this was changed by our Pacific victory. Our strategic frontier then shifted to embrace the entire Pacific Ocean, which became a vast moat to protect us as long as we held it.

Indeed, it acts as a protective shield for all of the Americas and all free lands of the Pacific Ocean area. We control it to the shores of Asia by a chain of islands extending in an arc from the Aleutians to the Marianas held by us and our free allies.

From this island chain we can dominate with sea and air power every Asiatic port from Vladivostok to Singapore—with sea and air power, as I said, every port from Vladivostok to Singapore—and prevent any hostile movement into the Pacific. Any predatory attack from Asia must be an amphibious effort. No amphibious force can be successful without control of the sea lanes and the air over those lanes in its avenue of advance.

With naval and air supremacy and modest ground elements to defend bases, any major attack from continental Asia toward us or our friends in the Pacific would be doomed to failure. Under such conditions the Pacific no longer represents menacing avenues of approach for a prospective invader. It assumes instead the friendly aspect of a peaceful lake.

Our line of defense is a natural one and can be maintained with a minimum of military effort and expense. It envisions no attack against anyone, nor does it provide the bastions essential for offensive operations, but properly maintained would be an invincible defense against aggression.

The holding of this littoral defense in line in the Western Pacific is entirely dependent upon holding all segments thereof. For any major breach of this line by an unfriendly power would render vulnerable to determined attack every other major segment.

This is a military estimate as to which I have yet to find a military leader who will take exception.

For that reason I have strongly recommended in the past as a matter of military urgency that under no circumstances must Formosa fall under Communist control.

Such an eventuality would at once threaten the freedom of the Philippines and the loss of Japan, and might well force our western frontier back to the coast of California, Oregon and Washington.

To understand the changes which now appear upon the Chinese mainland, one must understand the changes in Chinese character and culture over the past 50 years. China, up to 50 years ago, was completely nonhomogeneous, being compartmented into groups divided against each other. The warmaking tendency was almost nonexistent, as they still follow the tenets of the Confucian ideal of pacifist culture. At the turn of the century, under the regime of Chang Tso-lin, efforts toward greater homogeneity produced the start of a nationalist urge. This was further and more successfully developed under the leadership of Chiang Kai-shek but has been brought to its greatest fruition under the present regime to the point that it has now taken on the character of a united nationalism, of increasingly dominant aggressive tendencies.

Through these past 50 years the Chinese people have thus become militarized in their concepts and in their ideals. They now constitute excellent soldiers with competent staffs and commanders. This has produced a new and dominant power in Asia which, for its own purposes, is allied with Soviet Russia, but which in its own concepts and methods has become aggressively imperialistic, with a lust for expansion and increased power normal to this type of imperialism. There is little of the ideological concept either one way or another in the Chinese makeup. The standard of living is so low and the capital accumulation has been so thoroughly dissipated by war that the masses are desperate, unable to follow any leadership which seemed to promise an alleviation of local stringencies.

I have from the beginning believed that the Chinese Communist support of the North Koreans was the dominant one. Their interests are at present parallel to those of the Soviet, but I believe that the aggressiveness recently displayed not only in Korea but also in Indo-China and Tibet and pointing potentially toward the south reflects predominantly the same lust for the expansion of power which has animated every would-be conqueror since the beginning of time.

The Japanese people, since the war, have undergone the greatest reformation recorded in modern history. With a commendable will, eagerness to learn, and marked capacity to understand, they have, from the ashes left in war's wake erected in Japan an edifice dedicated to the primacy of individual liberty and personal dignity, and in the ensuing process there has been created a truly representative Government committed to the advance of political mo-rality, freedom of economic enterprise, and social justice.

Politically, economically and socially, Japan is now abreast of many free nations of the earth and will not again fail the universal trust. That it may be counted upon to wield a profoundly beneficial influence over the course of events in Asia is attested by the magnificent manner in which the Japanese people have met the recent challenge of war, unrest and confusion surrounding them from the outside, and checked Communism within their own frontiers without the slightest slackening in their forward progress.

I sent all four of our occupation divisions to the Korean battlefront without the slightest qualms as to the effect of the resulting power vacuum upon Japan. The results fully justified my faith. I know of no nation more serene, orderly and industrious nor in which higher hopes can be entertained for future constructive service in the advance of the human race.

Of our former ward, the Philippines, we can look forward in confidence that the existing unrest will be corrected and a strong and healthy nation will grow in the longer aftermath of war's terrible destructiveness. We must be patient and understanding and never fail them as in our hour of need they did not fail us.

A Christian nation, the Philippines stands as a mighty bulwark of Christianity in the Far East, and its capacity for high moral leadership in Asia is unlimited.

On Formosa, the Government of the Republic of China has had the opportunity to refute by action much of the malicious gossip which so undermined the strength of its leadership on the Chinese mainland.

The Formosan people are receiving a just and enlightened administration with majority representation on the organs of government; and politically, economically and socially appear to be advancing along sound and constructive lines.

With this brief insight into the surrounding areas, I now turn to the Korean conflict.

While I was not consulted prior to the President's decision to intervene in support of the Republic of Korea, that decision, from a military standpoint, proved a sound one. As I say, it proved a sound one, as we hurled back the invader and decimated his forces. Our victory was complete and our objectives within reach when Red China intervened with numerically superior ground forces.

This created a new war and an entirely new situation, a situation not contemplated when our forces were committed against the North Korean invaders, a situation which called for new decisions in the diplomatic sphere to permit the realistic adjustment of military strategy.

Such decisions have not been forthcoming.

While no man in his right mind would advocate sending our ground forces into continental China, and such was never given a thought, the new situation did urgently demand a drastic revision of strategic planning if our political aim was to defeat this new enemy as we had defeated the old.

Apart from the military need, as I saw it, to neutralize the sanctuary protection given the enemy north of Yalu, I felt that military necessity in the conduct of the war made necessary, first, the intensification of our economic blockade against China; second, the imposition of a naval blockade against the China coast; third, removal of restrictions on air reconnaissance of China's coastal areas and of Manchuria; fourth, removal of restrictions on the forces of the Republic of China on Formosa with logistical support to contribute to their effective operations against the Chinese mainland.

For entertaining these views, all professionally designed to support our forces committed to Korea and bring hostilities to an end with the least possible delay at a saving of countless American and Allied lives, I have been severely criticized in lay circles, principally abroad, despite my understanding that from a military standpoint the above views have been fully shared in the past by practically every military leader concerned with the Korean campaign, including our own Joint Chiefs of Staff.

I called for reinforcements, but was informed that reinforcements were not available. I made clear that, if not permitted to destroy the enemy-built-up bases north of the Yalu, if not permitted to utilize the friendly Chinese force of some 600,000 men on Formosa, if not permitted to blockade the China coast to prevent the Chinese Reds from getting succor from without, and if there were to be no hope of major reinforcements, the position of the command from the military standpoint forbade victory.

We could hold in Korea by constant maneuver, and at an approximate area where our supply-line advantages were in balance with the supply-line disadvantages of the enemy. But we could hope at best for only an indecisive campaign with its terrible and constant attrition upon our forces if the enemy utilized his full military potential.

I have constantly called for the new political decisions essential to a solution. Efforts have been made to distort my position. It has been said in effect that I was a warmonger. Nothing could be further from the truth.

I know war as few other men now living know it, and nothing, to me, is more revolting. I have long advocated its complete abolition, as its very destructiveness on both friend and foe has rendered it useless as a means of settling international disputes. Indeed, on the second day of September, 1945, just following the surrender of the Japanese nation on the battleship *Missouri,* I formally cautioned as follows:

"Men, since the beginning of time, have sought peace. Various methods, through the ages, have been attempted to devise an international process to prevent or settle disputes between nations. From the very start, workable methods were found insofar as individual citizens were concerned, but the mechanics of an instrumentality of larger international scope have never been successful. Military alliances, balances of power, leagues of nations, all in turn failed, leaving the only path to be by way of the crucible of war."

The utter destructiveness of war now blots out this alternative. We have had our last chance. If we will not devise some greater and more equitable system, Armageddon will be at our door.

The problem basically is still logical and involves a spiritual recrudescence and improvement of human character that will synchronize with our almost matchless advances in science, art, literature, and all material and cultural developments of the past 2,000 years. It must be of the spirit if we are to save the flesh.

But once war is forced upon us, there is no other alternative than to apply every available means to bring it to a swift end. War's very object is victory, not prolonged indecision.

In war there is no substitute for victory. There are some who, for varying reasons, would appease Red China. They are blind to history's clear lesson, for history teaches, with unmistakable emphasis, that appeasement but begets new and bloodier war. It points to no single instance where this end has justified that means, where appeasement has led to more than a sham peace. Like blackmail, it lays the basis for new and successively greater demands until, as in blackmail, violence becomes the only other alternative. Why, my soldiers asked of me, surrender military advantages to an enemy in the field? I could not answer.

Source: U.S. Congress. Congressional Record. 82nd Cong., 1st sess., 1951. Vol. 97, pp. 4124–25.

Korean Armistice Agreement (1953)

By the spring of 1951 the Korean War was effectively stalemated, with neither side able to attain full victory. Hostilities continued until June 1953, although armistice negotiations intended to end actual fighting in the Korean War opened in July 1951 and continued, with intermissions, for two years. One major stumbling block was the repatriation of North Korean and Chinese prisoners of war who did not wish to return to their home countries, an issue eventually resolved by permitting those who wished to return to do so and handing over the remainder to a neutral commission, leaving their ultimate disposition undetermined or at least unstated. South Korean president Syngman Rhee hoped that hostilities would continue until, with American assistance, he had unified his country, but U.S. president Dwight D. Eisenhower, who took office in January 1953, was determined to end the unpopular war as soon as possible. In exchange for Rhee's acquiescence in the armistice, the following November the United States signed a bilateral security treaty with the Republic of Korea (ROK, South Korea). The death of Soviet leader Josef Stalin in March 1953 was another factor facilitating an armistice. Whereas Stalin apparently welcomed the entanglement of both communist China, a potential rival, and the United States, his major opponent, in the costly and protracted war, his successors were more inclined to end the stalemated conflict, which placed some aid burdens upon the Soviet Union. On July 27, 1953, representatives from the United Nations, which included delegates from both the United States and South Korea, met with top communist officials from China and the Democratic

People's Republic of Korea (DPRK, North Korea) to sign an armistice ending the Korean War, which had raged on the Korean peninsula since June 1950. The signatories intended that a formal peace treaty, to be negotiated at a conference to be held in Geneva the following summer, would follow the armistice, but when the Geneva Conference took place, it proved impossible for the interested parties to agree on any such permanent settlement. The supposedly temporary armistice therefore remained in force into the 21st century, with the demilitarized zone separating the two opposed Korean states flanked by massive defenses on each side. Numerous minor violations of the cease-fire became almost routine occurrences, but in the half century following the armistice, the war was not resumed.

AGREEMENT BETWEEN THE COMMANDER-IN-CHIEF, UNITED NATIONS COMMAND, ON THE ONE HAND, AND THE SUPREME COMMANDER OF THE KOREAN PEOPLE'S ARMY AND THE COMMANDER OF THE CHINESE PEOPLE'S VOLUNTEERS, ON THE OTHER HAND, CONCERNING A MILITARY ARMISTICE IN KOREA.

Preamble

The undersigned, the Commander-in-Chief, United Nations Command, on the one hand, and the Supreme Commander of the Korean People's Army and the Commander of the Chinese People's Volunteers, on the other hand, in the interest of stopping the Korean conflict, with its great toll of suffering and bloodshed on both sides, and with the objective of establishing an armistice which will insure a complete cessation of hostilities and of all acts of armed force in Korea until a final peaceful settlement is achieved, do individually, collectively, and mutually agree to accept and to be bound and governed by the conditions and terms of armistice set forth in the following Articles and Paragraphs, which said conditions and terms are intended to be purely military in character and to pertain solely to the belligerents in Korea.

Article I: Military Demarcation Line and Demilitarized Zone

1. A Military Demarcation Line shall be fixed and both sides shall withdraw two (2) kilometers from this line so as to establish a Demilitarized Zone between opposing forces. A Demilitarized Zone shall be established as a buffer zone to prevent the occurrence of incidents which might lead to a resumption of hostilities.

2. The Military Demarcation Line is located as indicated on the attached map.

3. The Demilitarized Zone is defined by a northern and a southern boundary as indicated on the attached map.

4. The Military Demarcation Line shall be plainly marked as directed by the Military Armistice Commission hereinafter established. The Commanders of the opposing sides shall have suitable markers erected along the boundary between the Demilitarized Zone and their respective areas. The Military Armistice Commission shall supervise the erection of all markers placed along the Military Demarcation Line and along the boundaries of the Demilitarized Zone.

5. The waters of the Han River Estuary shall be open to civil shipping of both sides wherever one bank is controlled by one side and the other bank is controlled by the other side. The Military Armistice Commission shall prescribe rules for the shipping in that part of the Han River Estuary indicated on the attached map. Civil shipping of each side

shall have unrestricted access to land under the military control of that side.

6. Neither side shall execute any hostile act within, from, or against the Demilitarized Zone.

7. No person, military or civilian, shall be permitted to cross the Military Demarcation Line unless specifically authorized to do so by the Military Armistice Commission.

8. No person, military or civilian, in the Demilitarized Zone shall be permitted to enter the territory under the military control of either side unless specifically authorized to do so by the Commander into whose territory entry is sought.

9. No person, military or civilian, shall be permitted to enter the Demilitarized Zone except persons concerned with the conduct of civil administration and relief and persons specifically authorized to enter by the Military Armistice Commission.

10. Civil administration and relief in that part of the Demilitarized Zone which is south of the Military Demarcation Line shall be the responsibility of the Commander-in-Chief, United Nations Command; and civil administration and relief in that part of the Demilitarized Zone which is north of the Military Demarcation Line shall be the joint responsibility of the Supreme Commander of the Korean People's Army and the Commander of the Chinese People's Volunteers. The number of persons, military or civilian, from each side who are permitted to enter the Demilitarized Zone for the conduct of civil administration and relief shall be as determined by the respective Commanders, but in no case shall the total number authorized by either side exceed one thousand (1,000) persons at any one time. The number of

civil police and the arms to be carried by them shall be as prescribed by the Military Armistice Commission. Other personnel shall not carry arms unless specifically authorized to do so by the Military Armistice Commission.

11. Nothing contained in this Article shall be construed to prevent the complete freedom of movement to, from, and within the Demilitarized Zone by the Military Armistice Commission, its assistants, its Joint Observer Teams with their assistants, the Neutral Nations Supervisory Commission hereinafter established, its assistants, and of any other persons, materials, and equipment specifically authorized to enter the Demilitarized Zone by the Military Armistice Commission. Convenience of movement shall be permitted through the territory under the military control of either side over any route necessary to move between points within the Demilitarized Zone where such points are not connected by roads lying completely within the Demilitarized Zone.

[. . .]

Article III: Arrangements Relating to Prisoners of War

51. The release and repatriation of all prisoners of war held in the custody of each side at the time this Armistice Agreement becomes effective shall be effected in conformity with the following provisions agreed upon by both sides prior to the signing of this Armistice Agreement.

a. Within sixty (60) days after this Armistice Agreement becomes effective, each side shall, without offering any hindrance, directly repatriate and hand over in groups all those prisoners of war in its custody who insist on repatriation to the side to which they belonged at the time of capture. Repatriation shall be accomplished in accordance with the related provisions of this Article. In order to expedite the repatriation process of such personnel, each side shall, prior to the signing of the Armistice Agreement, exchange the total numbers, by nationalities, of personnel to be directly repatriated. Each group of prisoners of war delivered to the other side shall be accompanied by rosters, prepared by nationality, to include name, rank (if any) and internment or military serial number.

b. Each side shall release all those remaining prisoners of war, who are not directly repatriated, from its military control and from its custody and hand them over to the Neutral Nations Repatriation Commission for disposition in accordance with the provisions in the Annex hereto: "Terms of Reference for Neutral Nations Repatriation Commission".

c. So that there may be no misunderstanding owing to the equal use of three languages, the act of delivery of a prisoner of war by one side to the other side shall, for the purposes of this Armistice Agreement, be called "repatriation" in English, "[Korean characters]" (SONG HWAN) in Korean, and "[Chinese characters]" (CH'IEN FAN) in Chinese, notwithstanding the nationality or place of residence of such prisoner of war.

52. Each side insures that it will not employ in acts of war in the Korean conflict any prisoner of war released and repatriated

incident to the coming into effect of this Armistice Agreement.

53. All the sick and injured prisoners of war who insist upon repatriation shall be repatriated with priority. Insofar as possible, there shall be captured medical personnel repatriated concurrently with the sick and injured prisoners of war, so as to provide medical care and attendance en route.

54. The repatriation of all prisoners of war required by Sub-paragraph 51a hereof shall be completed within a time limit of sixty (60) days after this Armistice Agreement becomes effective. Within this time limit each side undertakes to complete the repatriation of the above-mentioned prisoners of war in its custody at the earliest practicable time.

55. PANMUNJOM is designated as the place where prisoners of war will be delivered and received by both sides. Additional place(s) of delivery and reception of prisoners of war in Demilitarized Zone may be designated, if necessary, by the Committee for Repatriation of Prisoners of War.

[. . .]

Source: "Text of the Korean War Armistice Agreement," U.S. Department of State, http://www.state.gov/t/ac/rls/or/2004/31006.htm.

Dwight D. Eisenhower: "The Row of Dominoes," Presidential Press Conference (April 7, 1954)

From summer 1945 onward, France sought to restore colonial rule in French Indochina but faced increasingly effective opposition from the nationalist and communist Viet Minh forces led by Ho Chi Minh, who had declared Vietnam's independence in September 1945. Despite substantial U.S. financial support, by early 1954 French efforts to defeat Ho's forces in the Democratic Republic of Vietnam (DRV, North Vietnam) had stalled. In mid-March that year, the French Army found itself encircled by Viet Minh forces at the mountain fortress of Dien Bien Phu. France urged the United States to intervene militarily, but President Dwight D. Eisenhower, on finding that Britain was not prepared to join in any such effort, refused to commit American forces to Indochina. The beleaguered French Army surrendered in early May, a humiliating defeat for France that marked the end of almost a decade of French efforts to maintain its colonial position in Indochina. Despite his decision against intervention, Eisenhower clearly disliked the prospect of a communist Indochina. At a press conference held while the French garrison at Dien Bien Phu was still besieged and the United States had made no formal decision, the president set out the domino theory that would become so influential as a justification for subsequent American assistance to Vietnam: that if one nation went communist its neighbors would inevitably be affected, and eventually the communist infection would spread from state to state throughout Asia and beyond.

Q. Robert Richards, Copley Press: Mr. President, would you mind commenting on the strategic importance of Indochina for the free world? I think there has been, across the country, some lack of understanding on just what it means to us.

The President. You have, of course, both the specific and the general when you talk about such things.

First of all, you have the specific value of a locality in its production of materials that the world needs.

Then you have the possibility that many human beings pass under a dictatorship that is inimical to the free world.

Finally, you have broader considerations that might follow what you would call the "falling domino" principle. You have a row of dominoes set up, you knock over the first one, and what will happen to the last one is the certainty that it will go over very quickly. So you could have a beginning of a disintegration that would have the most profound influences.

Now, with respect to the first one, two of the items from this particular area that the world uses are tin and tungsten. They are very important. There are others, of course, the rubber plantations and so on.

Then with respect to more people passing under this domination, Asia, after all, has already lost some 450 million of its peoples to the Communist dictatorship, and we simply can't afford greater losses.

But when we come to the possible sequence of events, the loss of Indochina, of Burma, of Thailand, of the Peninsula, and Indonesia following, now you begin to talk about areas that not only multiply the disadvantages that you would suffer through the loss of materials, sources of materials, but now you are talking really about millions and millions and millions of people.

Finally, the geographical position achieved thereby does many things. It turns the so-called island defensive chain of Japan, Formosa, of the Philippines and to the southward; it moves in to threaten Australia and New Zealand.

It takes away, in its economic aspects, that region that Japan must have as a trading area or Japan, in turn, will have only one place in the world to go—that is, toward the Communist areas in order to live.

So, the possible consequences of the loss are just incalculable to the free world. . . .

Q. Raymond Brandt, St. Louis Post-Dispatch: Mr. President, what response has Secretary Dulles and the administration got [from Great Britain] to the request for united action in Indochina?

The President. So far as I know, there are no positive reactions as yet, because the time element would almost forbid.

Q. Robert G. Spivack, New York Post: Mr. President, do you agree with Senator [John F.] Kennedy that independence must be guaranteed the people of Indochina in order to justify an allout effort there?

The President. Well, I don't know, of course, exactly in what way a Senator was talking about this thing.

I will say this: for many years, in talking to different countries, different governments, I have tried to insist on this principle: no outside country can come in and be really helpful unless it is doing something that the local people want.

Now, let me call your attention to this independence theory. Senator Lodge, on my instructions, stood up in the United Nations and offered one country independence if they would just simply pass a resolution saying they wanted it, or at least said, "I would work for it." They didn't accept it. So I can't say that the associated states want independence in the sense that the United States is independent. I do not know what they want.

I do say this: the aspirations of those people must be met, otherwise there is in the long run no final answer to the problem.

Q. Joseph Dear, Capital Times: Do you favor bringing this Indochina situation before the United Nations?

The President. I really can't say. I wouldn't want to comment at too great a length at this moment, but I do believe

this: this is the kind of thing that must not be handled by one nation trying to act alone. We must have a concert of opinion, and a concert of readiness to react in whatever way is necessary.

Of course, the hope is always that it is peaceful conciliation and accommodation of these problems.

Source: Dwight D. Eisenhower, *Public Papers of the Presidents of the United States: Dwight D. Eisenhower, 1954* (Washington, DC: U.S. Government Printing Office, 1960), 382–85.

Warsaw Security Pact (1955)

Signed on May 14, 1955, the Warsaw Security Pact established a mutual defense alliance between the countries of Eastern Europe, all of which were under Soviet control. Besides the Soviet Union, member states were Bulgaria, Czechoslovakia, the German Democratic Republic (GDR, East Germany), Hungary, Poland, and Romania. The pact was intended to function as a counterbalance to the North Atlantic Treaty Organization (NATO), established by the countries of Western Europe and the United States in 1949. The immediate impetus for the formation of the Warsaw Pact was NATO's acceptance of the Federal Republic of Germany (FRG, West Germany) into its alliance, a move that aroused bitter memories of past German eastward military attacks and fears of their recurrence. The Soviet Union directed Warsaw Pact policies and operations, and the organization had no independent headquarters of its own. In practice, another major function of the Warsaw Pact was to maintain Soviet control of Eastern Europe, as Poland and Hungary proved recalcitrant in 1956, Czechoslovakia in 1968, and Poland during the early 1980s. Hungary's announcement in October 1956 of its intention to withdraw from the Warsaw Pact triggered a Soviet invasion. The Warsaw Pact remained in effect until the collapse of communism in Eastern Europe in 1989 and 1990 but then collapsed as the East

European states all withdrew, in several cases entering NATO soon afterward.

Treaty of friendship, cooperation and mutual assistance between the People's Republic of Albania, the People's Republic of Bulgaria, the Hungarian People's Republic, the German Democratic Republic, the Polish People's Republic, the Rumanian People's Republic, the Union of Soviet Socialist Republics, and the Czechoslovak Republic, May 1, 1955

The contracting parties, Reaffirming their desire for the organization of a system of collective security in Europe, with the participation of all the European states, irrespective of their social and state systems, which would make it possible to combine their efforts in the interests of securing peace in Europe,

Taking into consideration at the same time the situation obtaining in Europe as the result of ratification of the Paris agreements, which provide for the formation of a new military grouping in the shape of the "Western European Union" together with a remilitarised Western Germany, and for the integration of Western Germany in the North Atlantic bloc, which increases the threat of another war and creates a menace to the national security of the peaceloving states,

Convinced that, under these circumstances, the peaceloving states of Europe should take the necessary measures for safeguarding their security, and in the interests of maintaining peace in Europe,

Guided by the purposes and principles of the United Nations Charter,

In the interests of further strengthening and promoting friendship, co-operation and mutual assistance, in accordance with the principles of respect for the independence and sovereignty of states, and also with the principle of noninterference in their internal affairs,

Have resolved to conclude this Treaty of Friendship, Co-operation and Mutual Assistance.

Article 1

The contracting parties undertake, in accordance with the Charter of the United Nations Organization, to refrain in their international relations from the threat or use of force, and to settle their international disputes by peaceful means so as not to endanger international peace and security.

Article 2

The contracting parties declare their readiness to take part, in the spirit of sincere co-operation, in all international undertakings intended to safeguard international peace and security and they shall use all their energies for the realization of these aims.

Moreover, the contracting parties shall work for the adoption, in agreement with other states desiring to co-operate in this matter, of effective measures towards a general reduction of armaments and prohibition of atomic, hydrogen and other weapons of mass destruction.

Article 3

The contracting parties shall take council among themselves on all important international questions relating to their common interests, guided by the interests of strengthening international peace and security.

They shall take council among themselves immediately, whenever, in the opinion of any of them, there has arisen the threat of an armed attack on one or several states that are signatories of the treaty, in the interests of organizing their joint defense and of upholding peace and security.

Article 4

In the event of an armed attack in Europe on one or several states that are signatories of the treaty by any state or group of states, each state that is a party to this treaty shall, in the exercise of the right to individual or collective self-defense in accordance with Article 51 of the Charter of the United Nations Organization, render the state or states so attacked immediate assistance, individually and in agreement with other states that are parties to this treaty, by all the means it may consider necessary, including the use of armed force. The states that are parties to this treaty shall immediately take council among themselves concerning the necessary joint measures to be adopted for the purpose of restoring and upholding international peace and security.

In accordance with the principles of the Charter of the United Nations Organization, the Security Council shall be advised of the measures taken on the basis of the present article. These measures shall be stopped as soon as the Security Council has taken the necessary measures for restoring and upholding international peace and security.

Article 5

The contracting parties have agreed on the establishment of a joint command for their armed forces, which shall be placed, by agreement among these parties, under this command, which shall function on the basis of jointly defined principles. They shall also take other concerted measures necessary for strengthening their defense capacity, in order to safeguard the peaceful labour of their peoples, to guarantee the inviolability of their frontiers and territories and to provide safeguards against possible aggression.

Article 6

For the purpose of holding the consultations provided for in the present treaty among the states that are parties to the treaty, and for the purpose of considering problems arising in connection with the implementation of this treaty, a political consultative committee shall be formed in which each state that is a party to this treaty shall be represented by a member of the government, or any other specially appointed representative.

The committee may form the auxiliary organs for which the need may arise.

Article 7

The contracting parties undertake not to participate in any coalitions and alliances, and not to conclude any agreements the purposes of which would be at variance with those of the present treaty.

The contracting parties declare that their obligations under existing international treaties are not at variance with the provisions of this treaty.

Article 8

The contracting parties declare that they will act in the spirit of friendship and cooperation with the object of furthering the development of, and strengthening the economic and cultural relations between them, adhering to the principles of mutual respect for their independence and sovereignty, and of non-interference in their internal affairs.

Article 9

The present treaty is open to be acceded to by other states—irrespective of their social and state systems—which may express their readiness to assist, through participation in the present treaty, in combining the efforts of the peaceloving states for the purpose of safeguarding the peace and security of nations. This act of acceding to the treaty shall become effective, with the consent of the states that are parties to this treaty, after the instrument of accedence has been deposited with the government of the Polish People's Republic.

Article 10

The present treaty is subject to ratification, and the instruments of ratification shall be deposited with the government of the Polish People's Republic.

The treaty shall take effect on the date on which the last ratification instrument is deposited. The government of the Polish People's Republic shall advise the other states that are parties to the treaty of each ratification instrument deposited with it.

Article 11

The present treaty shall remain in force for 20 years. For the contracting parties which will not have submitted to the government of the Polish People's Republic a statement denouncing the treaty a year before the expiration of its term, it shall remain in force throughout the following ten years.

In the event of the organization of a system of collective security in Europe and the conclusion of a general European treaty of collective security to that end, which the contracting parties shall unceasingly seek to bring about, the present treaty shall cease to be effective on the date the general European treaty comes into force.

[. . .]

Source: "Treaty of Friendship, Co-operation and Mutual Assistance. Albania, Bulgaria, Hungary, German Democratic Republic, Poland, Romania, Union of Soviet Socialist Republics and Czechoslovakia," May 14, 1955. *United Nations Treaty Series* 2962.

Mao Zedong: "U.S. Imperialism Is a Paper Tiger" (July 14, 1956)

For international communist revolutionaries during the Cold War, the United States represented the head and front of the capitalist forces raised against them. Chinese Communist Party (CCP) chairman Mao Zedong regarded the United States as the foremost enemy that China would ultimately have to confront and overcome. A leader who favored dramatic and grandiloquent rhetoric, Mao nonetheless urged his countrymen and leftists around the world not to fear the United States, characterizing it as a "paper tiger" that was far less formidable than it appeared. Strong though the United States was in military and economic terms, its power could, he proclaimed, be destroyed piecemeal and incrementally, although this would take time. In the mid-1950s Mao called on all the oppressed peoples of the world to launch armed struggle against the United States and its allies, and China provided training and military aid to a wider variety of international revolutionary movements. His approach differed from that of the new Soviet premier Nikita Khrushchev, who now sought peaceful coexistence with the West, and contributed to growing divisions between Soviet Russia and Communist China that culminated in an outright split by the end of the decade. Soviet leaders thought Mao's policies likely to destabilize the international system and perhaps provoke nuclear war. Ironically, in practice Mao was far more cautious than his rhetoric implied in challenging the United States, suggesting that he himself may have been something of a paper tiger. After intervening in 1950 against UN forces in the lengthy, expensive, and wearing Korean War, which ended in stalemate, Mao was careful in successive international crises over Taiwan and Vietnam to avoid provoking outright war between China and the United States (UN). Eventually, moreover, when Sino-Soviet hostility led to outright fighting on the joint border in 1969, Mao even initiated a rapprochement with the United States, for two decades supposedly China's greatest enemy, as a means of countering the potential Soviet menace.

The United States is flaunting the anti-communist banner everywhere in order to perpetrate aggression against other countries.

The United States owes debts everywhere. It owes debts not only to the countries of Latin America, Asia and Africa, but also to the countries of Europe and Oceania. The whole world, Britain included, dislikes the United States. The masses of the people dislike it. Japan dislikes the United States because it oppresses her. None of the countries in the East is free from U.S. aggression. The United States has invaded our Taiwan Province. Japan, Korea, the Philippines, Viet Nam and Pakistan all suffer from U.S. aggression, although some of them are allies of the United States. The people are dissatisfied and in some countries so are the authorities.

All oppressed nations want independence.

Everything is subject to change. The big decadent forces will give way to the small new-born forces. The small forces will change into big forces because the majority of the people demand this change. The U.S. imperialist forces will change from big to small because the American people, too, are dissatisfied with their government.

In my own lifetime I myself have witnessed such changes. Some of us present were born in the Ching Dynasty and others after the 1911 Revolution.

The Ching Dynasty was overthrown long ago. By whom? By the party led by Sun Yat-sen, together with the people. Sun Yat-sen's forces were so small that the Ching officials didn't take him seriously. He led many uprisings which failed each time. In the end, however, it was Sun Yat-sen who brought down the Ching Dynasty. Bigness is nothing to be afraid of. The big will be overthrown by the small. The small will become big. After overthrowing the Ching Dynasty, Sun Yat-sen met with defeat. For he failed to satisfy the demands of the people, such as their demands for land and for opposition to imperialism. Nor did he understand the necessity of suppressing the counter-revolutionaries who were then moving about freely. Later, he suffered defeat at the hands of Yuan Shih-kai, the chieftain of the Northern warlords. Yuan Shih-kai's forces were larger than Sun Yat-sen's. But here again this law operated: small forces linked with the people become strong, while big forces opposed to the people become weak. Subsequently Sun Yat-sen's bourgeois-democratic revolutionaries co-operated with us Communists and together we defeated the warlord set-up left behind by Yuan Shih-kai.

Chiang Kai-shek's rule in China was recognized by the governments of all countries and lasted twenty-two years, and his forces were the biggest. Our forces were small, fifty thousand Party members at first but only a few thousand after counter-revolutionary suppressions. The enemy made trouble everywhere. Again this law operated: the big and strong end up in defeat because they are divorced from the people, whereas the small and weak emerge victorious because they are linked with the people and work in their interest. That's how things turned out in the end.

During the anti-Japanese war, Japan was very powerful, the Kuomintang troops were driven to the hinterland, and the armed forces led by the Communist Party could only conduct guerrilla warfare in the rural areas behind the enemy lines. Japan occupied large Chinese cities such as Peking, Tientsin, Shanghai, Nanking, Wuhan and Canton. Nevertheless, like Germany's Hitler the Japanese militarists collapsed in a few years, in accordance with the same law.

We underwent innumerable difficulties and were driven from the south to the north, while our forces fell from several hundred thousand strong to a few tens of thousands.

At the end of the 25,000-*li* Long March we had only 25,000 men left.

[. . .]

During the War of Resistance, our troops grew and became 900,000 strong through fighting against Japan. Then came the War of Liberation. Our arms were inferior to those of the Kuomintang. The Kuomintang troops then numbered four million, but in three years of fighting we wiped out eight million of them all told. The Kuomintang, though aided by U.S. imperialism, could not defeat us. The big and strong cannot win, it is always the small and weak who win out.

Now U.S. imperialism is quite powerful, but in reality it isn't. It is very weak politically because it is divorced from the masses of the people and is disliked by everybody and by the American people too. In appearance it is very powerful but in reality it is nothing to be afraid of, it is a paper tiger. Outwardly a tiger, it is made of paper, unable to withstand the wind and the rain. I believe the United States is nothing but a paper tiger.

History as a whole, the history of class society for thousands of years, has proved this point: the strong must give way to the weak. This holds true for the Americas as well.

Only when imperialism is eliminated can peace prevail. The day will come when the paper tigers will be wiped out. But they won't become extinct of their own accord, they need to be battered by the wind and the rain.

When we say U.S. imperialism is a paper tiger, we are speaking in terms of strategy. Regarding it as a whole, we must despise it. But regarding each part, we must take it seriously. It has claws and fangs. We have to destroy it piecemeal. For instance, if it has ten fangs, knock off one the first time, and there will be nine left; knock off another, and there will be eight left. When all the fangs are gone, it will still have claws. If we deal with it step by step and in earnest, we will certainly succeed in the end.

Strategically, we must utterly despise U.S. imperialism. Tactically, we must take it seriously. In struggling against it, we must take each battle, each encounter, seriously. At present, the United States is powerful, but when looked at in a broader perspective, as a whole and from a long-term viewpoint, it has no popular support, its policies are disliked by the people, because it oppresses and exploits them. For this reason, the tiger is doomed. Therefore, it is nothing to be afraid of and can be despised. But today the United States still has strength, turning out more than 100 million tons of steel a year and hitting out everywhere. That is why we must continue to wage struggles against it, fight it with all our might and wrest one position after another from it. And that takes time.

It seems that the countries of the Americas, Asia and Africa will have to go on quarrelling with the United States till the very end, till the paper tiger is destroyed by the wind and the rain.

To oppose U.S. imperialism, people of European origin in the Latin-American countries should unite with the indigenous Indians. Perhaps the white immigrants from Europe can be divided into two groups, one composed of rulers and the other of ruled. This should make it easier for the group of oppressed white people to get close to the local people, for their position is the same.

Our friends in Latin America, Asia and Africa are in the same position as we and are doing the same kind of work, doing something for the people to lessen their oppression by imperialism. If we do a good job, we can root out imperialist oppression. In this we are comrades.

We are of the same nature as you in our opposition to imperialist oppression, differing only in geographical position, nationality and language. But we are different in nature from imperialism, and the very sight of it makes us sick.

What use is imperialism? The Chinese people will have none of it, nor will the people in the rest of the world. There is no reason for the existence of imperialism.

Source: Mao Tse-tung, *Selected Works of Mao Tse-Tung*, Vol. 5 (Peking: Foreign Languages Press, 1975), 308–11.

Imre Nagy: Final Message to the Hungarian People (1956)

Imre Nagy served as prime minister of Hungary from 1953 to 1955 before falling from Soviet favor and losing office. He proved a sympathetic supporter of the Hungarian Revolution of 1956, during which students and reformers attempted to undermine Soviet control of Hungary and revise the communist system in a democratic and multiparty direction. On October 23, 1956, as demonstrations against Soviet rule expanded almost uncontrollably, Nagy was reappointed as prime minister. Fearing Soviet intervention, he sought to bring events under control, introducing reforms and offering amnesty to demonstrators while placating the Soviets and seeking to negotiate the peaceable withdrawal of Soviet troops from Hungary. When Nagy realized that his efforts had failed to persuade the Soviets to eschew military intervention, he finally announced Hungary's withdrawal from the Warsaw Pact, the Soviet-run military alliance of its East European satellite states. On November 4, 1956, Soviet troops invaded Hungary, capturing Nagy and numerous other Hungarian leaders. As Soviet troops surrounded the capital city of Budapest, Nagy delivered his final message to the Hungarian people, appealing for support from other countries. His hopes of assistance from the Western powers or the United Nations (UN) were illusory, since—despite their proclaimed wish to roll back communism in Eastern Europe— U.S. president Dwight D. Eisenhower and his

secretary of state John Foster Dulles were not prepared to risk nuclear war over an area that they knew the Soviet Union considered essential to its own national security. In 1958 the Soviets executed Nagy for his involvement in the revolution. After the Soviets relinquished control of Eastern Europe in 1989, Nagy was posthumously rehabilitated.

This fight is the fight for freedom by the Hungarian people against the Russian intervention, and it is possible that I shall only be able to stay at my post for one or two hours. The whole world will see how the Russian armed forces, contrary to all treaties and conventions, are crushing the resistance of the Hungarian people. They will also see how they are kidnapping the Prime Minister of a country which is a Member of the United Nations, taking him from the capital, and therefore it cannot be doubted at all that this is the most brutal form of intervention. I should like in these last moments to ask the leaders of the revolution, if they can, to leave the country. I ask that all that I have said in my broadcast, and what we have agreed on with the revolutionary leaders during meetings in Parliament, should be put in a memorandum, and the leaders should turn to all the peoples of the world for help and explain that today it is Hungary and tomorrow, or the day after tomorrow, it will be the turn of other countries because the imperialism of Moscow does not know borders, and is only trying to play for time.

Source: Department of State Bulletin, November 12, 1956, pp. 746–47.

Soviet Announcement of *Sputnik* (October 5, 1957)

The International Council of Scientific Unions declared the period from July 1957 to December 1958 the International Geophysical Year

(IGY). American scientists worked throughout the mid-1950s to construct a successful science satellite for the IGY. The project confronted numerous technical obstacles and was proceeding poorly. Then, on the evening of October 4, 1957, came the shocking news that the Soviet Union had successfully launched the first-ever artificial satellite into Earth orbit. Named _Sputnik_, the basketball-sized satellite weighed 184 pounds. The launch announcement, first issued in a terse, English-language radio broadcast from Tass and then published the next day in the Soviet official news organ _Pravda_, surprised American scientists. Although they knew their Soviet counterparts were working on a science satellite for the IGY, they had no idea that the Soviets had made such tremendous progress. On November 3, 1957, the Soviets launched _Sputnik 2_, a 1,118-pound capsule with a dog as a passenger. These two stunning Soviet successes preceded the attempted American contribution to the IGY. On December 6, 1957, the U.S. launch attempt of its own satellite failed. _Sputnik_'s launch, which came at a time of escalating Cold War tensions, shattered American confidence in its technical and scientific superiority. _Sputnik_ also had frightening military implications. The American public realized that the Soviets were acquiring the capability to launch long-range nuclear missiles against the United States. The U.S. government responded to _Sputnik_ by passing the 1958 National Defense Education Act, which promoted space science and other scientific and technical fields deemed necessary to national security. The government also created the National Aeronautics and Space Administration (NASA) to administer American space programs.

For several years scientific research and experimental design work have been conducted in the Soviet Union on the creation of artificial satellites of the earth.

As already reported in the press, the first launching of the satellites in the USSR were planned for realization in accordance with the scientific research program of the International Geophysical Year.

As a result of very intensive work by scientific research institutes and design bureaus the first artificial satellite in the world has been created. On October 4, 1957, this first satellite was successfully launched in the USSR. According to preliminary data, the carrier rocket has imparted to the satellite the required orbital velocity of about 8000 meters per second. At the present time the satellite is describing elliptical trajectories around the earth, and its flight can be observed in the rays of the rising and setting sun with the aid of very simple optical instruments (binoculars, telescopes, etc.).

According to calculations which now are being supplemented by direct observations, the satellite will travel at altitudes up to 900 kilometers above the surface of the earth; the time for a complete revolution of the satellite will be one hour and thirty-five minutes; the angle of inclination of its orbit to the equatorial plane is 65 degrees. On October 5 the satellite will pass over the Moscow area twice—at 1:46 a.m. and at 6:42 a.m. Moscow time. Reports about the subsequent movement of the first artificial satellite launched in the USSR on October 4 will be issued regularly by broadcasting stations.

The satellite has a spherical shape 58 centimeters in diameter and weighs 83.6 kilograms. It is equipped with two radio transmitters continuously emitting signals at frequencies of 20.005 and 40.002 megacycles per second (wave lengths of about 15 and 7.5 meters, respectively). The power of the transmitters ensures reliable reception of the signals by a broad range of radio amateurs. The signals have the form of telegraph pulses of about 0.3 second's duration with a pause of the same duration. The signal of one frequency is sent during the pause in the signal of the other frequency.

Scientific stations located at various points in the Soviet Union are tracking the satellite and determining the elements of its trajectory. Since the density of the rarified upper layers of the atmosphere is not accurately known, there are no data at present for the precise determination of the satellite's lifetime and of the point of its entry into the dense layers of the atmosphere. Calculations have shown that owing to the tremendous velocity of the satellite, at the end of its existence it will burn up on reaching the dense layers of the atmosphere at an altitude of several tens of kilometers.

As early as the end of the nineteenth century the possibility of realizing cosmic flights by means of rockets was first scientifically substantiated in Russia by the works of the outstanding Russian scientist K[onstatin] E. Tsiolkovskii [Tsiolkovskiy].

The successful launching of the first man-made earth satellite makes a most important contribution to the treasure-house of world science and culture. The scientific experiment accomplished at such a great height is of tremendous importance for learning the properties of cosmic space and for studying the earth as a planet of our solar system.

During the International Geophysical Year the Soviet Union proposes launching several more artificial earth satellites. These subsequent satellites will be larger and heavier and they will be used to carry out programs of scientific research.

Artificial earth satellites will pave the way to interplanetary travel and, apparently our contemporaries will witness how the freed and conscientious labor of the people of the new socialist society makes the most daring dreams of mankind a reality.

Source: "Announcement of the First Satellite," from *Pravda*, October 5, 1957; in F. J. Krieger, *Behind*

the Sputniks (Washington, DC: Public Affairs Press, 1958), 311–12. Made available by the Historical Reference Collection, NASA History Division, NASA Headquarters, Washington, D.C. http://history.nasa.gov/sputnik/14.html.

John F. Kennedy: Inaugural Address (January 20, 1961)

The young Democrat John F. Kennedy became president of the United States in January 1961, the youngest man ever elected to that office, succeeding the Republican Dwight D. Eisenhower, the oldest man until that time to be president. Kennedy subscribed almost unthinkingly to orthodox Cold War ideology and proclaimed the need for the United States to fight Soviet communism more energetically than in the past. Despite serious health problems of which the American people were largely unaware, Kennedy projected an image of youthful dynamism and vigor, and his administration made almost a cult of physical fitness. Young, handsome, and a master of appealing rhetoric, through his style Kennedy caught the imagination not just of Americans but of young people around the world. He appealed to Americans to be prepared to make sacrifices for their country and to wage the Cold War until victory was attained, pledging that the United States would help its allies whatever the price. Breaking with Eisenhower's New Look strategy, which was heavily reliant on the threat of nuclear weapons, Kennedy sought to make American military forces better able to fight conventional and guerrilla wars. Seeking to win the loyalties of decolonizing and relatively poor states, he also urged ordinary Americans to work closely with their counterparts in developing countries, sharing their living standards and cooperating on projects designed to benefit those nations, an appeal that led to the establishment of the Peace Corps. Despite promising to build up American military forces and to stand firm in the Cold War, he also sought to open serious arms control negotiations with the Soviet Union, evidence of his recognition that neither power could afford an outright nuclear war. In Kennedy's inaugural address, therefore, one can discern the seeds of many of his subsequent policies, including his 1961 decision to support West Berlin, his moves to increase the American commitment to the Republic of Vietnam (RVN, South Vietnam), his demand that the Soviet Union withdraw its missiles from nearby Cuba in 1962, and his support for serious disarmament negotiations and the Atmospheric Nuclear Test Ban Treaty in 1963.

We observe today not a victory of party but a celebration of freedom—symbolizing an end as well as a beginning—signifying renewal as well as change. For I have sworn before you and Almighty God the same solemn oath our forebears prescribed nearly a century and three quarters ago.

The world is very different now. For man holds in his mortal hands the power to abolish all forms of human poverty and all forms of human life. And yet the same revolutionary beliefs for which our forebears fought are still at issue around the globe—the belief that the rights of man come not from the generosity of the state but from the hand of God.

We dare not forget today that we are the heirs of that first revolution. Let the word go forth from this time and place, to friend and foe alike, that the torch has been passed to a new generation of Americans—born in this century, tempered by war, disciplined by a hard and bitter peace, proud of our ancient heritage—and unwilling to witness or permit the slow undoing of those human rights to which this Nation has always been committed, and to which we are committed today at home and around the world.

Let every nation know, whether it wishes us well or ill, that we shall pay any price, bear any burden, meet any hardship, support any friend, oppose any foe to assure the survival and the success of liberty.

This much we pledge—and more.

To those old allies whose cultural and spiritual origins we share, we pledge the loyalty of faithful friends. United, there is little we cannot do in a host of cooperative ventures. Divided, there is little we can do—for we dare not meet a powerful challenge at odds and split asunder.

To those new states whom we welcome to the ranks of the free, we pledge our word that one form of colonial control shall not have passed away merely to be replaced by a far more iron tyranny. We shall not always expect to find them supporting our view. But we shall always hope to find them strongly supporting their own freedom—and to remember that, in the past, those who foolishly sought power by riding the back of the tiger ended up inside.

To those people in the huts and villages of half the globe struggling to break the bonds of mass misery, we pledge our best efforts to help them help themselves, for whatever period is required—not because the Communists may be doing it, not because we seek their votes, but because it is right. If a free society cannot help the many who are poor, it cannot save the few who are rich.

To our sister republics south of our border, we offer a special pledge—to convert our good words into good deeds—in a new alliance for progress—to assist free men and free governments in casting off the chains of poverty. But this peaceful revolution of hope cannot become the prey of hostile powers. Let all our neighbors know that we shall join with them to oppose aggression or subversion anywhere in the Americas. And let every other power know that this hemisphere intends to remain the master of its own house.

To that world assembly of sovereign states, the United Nations, our last best hope in an age where the instruments of war have far outpaced the instruments of peace, we renew our pledge of support—to prevent it from becoming merely a forum for invective—to strengthen its shield of the new and the weak—and to enlarge the area in which its writ may run.

Finally, to those nations who would make themselves our adversary, we offer not a pledge but a request: that both sides begin anew the quest for peace, before the dark powers of destruction unleashed by science engulf all humanity in planned or accidental self-destruction.

We dare not tempt them with weakness. For only when our arms are sufficient beyond doubt can we be certain beyond doubt that they will never be employed.

But neither can two great and powerful groups of nations take comfort from our present course—both sides overburdened by the cost of modern weapons, both rightly alarmed by the steady spread of the deadly atom, yet both racing to alter that uncertain balance of terror that stays the hand of mankind's final war.

So let us begin anew—remembering on both sides that civility is not a sign of weakness, and sincerity is always subject to proof. Let us never negotiate out of fear. But let us never fear to negotiate.

Let both sides explore what problems unite us instead of belaboring those problems which divide us.

Let both sides, for the first time, formulate serious and precise proposals for the inspection and control of arms—and bring the absolute power to destroy other nations under the absolute control of all nations.

Let both sides seek to invoke the wonders of science instead of its terrors. Together let us explore the stars, conquer the deserts, eradicate disease, tap the ocean depths, and encourage the arts and commerce.

Let both sides unite to heed in all corners of the earth the command of Isaiah—to "undo the heavy burdens. . .[and] let the oppressed go free."

And if a beachhead of cooperation may push back the jungle of suspicion, let both sides join in creating a new endeavor, not a new balance of power, but a new world of law, where the strong are just and the weak secure and the peace preserved.

All this will not be finished in the first one hundred days. Nor will it be finished in the first one thousand days, nor in the life of this administration, nor even perhaps in our lifetime on this planet. But let us begin.

In your hands, my fellow citizens, more than mine, will rest the final success or failure of our course. Since this country was founded each generation of Americans has been summoned to give testimony to its national loyalty. The graves of young Americans who answered the call to service surround the globe.

Now the trumpet summons us again—not as a call to bear arms, though arms we need—not as a call to battle, though embattled we are—but a call to bear the burden of a long twilight struggle, year in and year out, "rejoicing in hope, patient in tribulation"—a struggle against the common enemies of man: tyranny, poverty, disease, and war itself.

Can we forge against these enemies a grand and global alliance, North and South, East and West, that can assure a more fruitful life for all mankind? Will you join in that historic effort?

In the long history of the world, only a few generations have been granted the role of defending freedom in its hour of maximum danger. I do not shrink from this responsibility—I welcome it. I do not believe that any of us would exchange places with any other people or any other generation. The energy, the faith, the devotion which we bring to this endeavor will light our country and all who serve it—and the glow from that fire can truly light the world.

And so, my fellow Americans: ask not what your country can do for you—ask what you can do for your country.

My fellow citizens of the world: ask not what America will do for you, but what together we can do for the freedom of man.

Finally, whether you are citizens of America or citizens of the world, ask of us here the same high standards of strength and sacrifice which we ask of you. With a good conscience our only sure reward, with history the final judge of our deeds, let us go forth to lead the land we love, asking His blessing and His help, but knowing that here on earth God's work must truly be our own.

Source: John F. Kennedy, *Public Papers of the Presidents of the United States: John F. Kennedy, 1961* (Washington, DC: U.S. Government Printing Office, 1962), 1–3.

Vadim Orlov: Account of the B-59 Incident (1962)

As part of the U.S. naval blockade of Cuba, U.S. ships forced to the surface three Soviet submarines. Neither American political nor military leaders knew that the Soviet submarines were nuclear armed. Nor did the Americans understand that conditions aboard the Soviet submarines were so physically difficult and unstable that commanding officers considered arming nuclear-tipped torpedoes in response to intense American naval harassment. Moreover, the effort to force the submarine B-59 to the surface on October 27, 1962, occurred on one of the most dangerous days of the missile crisis. Only hours earlier, the Soviets had downed an American U-2 spy plane over Cuba. Vadim Orlov, who served as a communications intelligence officer on B-59, recounted the tense and stressful situation on October 27 when U.S. destroyers lobbed small depth charges at B-59. According to Orlov, B-59's "totally exhausted" captain

ordered a nuclear torpedo to be assembled for battle readiness. A subordinate calmed down the captain and they made the decision to surface the submarine. Historians are uncertain if Orlov's account is completely accurate. They noted that like their American counterparts, Soviet submarine commanders were highly disciplined and unlikely to use nuclear weapons by design. However, the unstable conditions on board B-59 raised the specter of an accident. Indeed, military historians and Orlov himself have concluded that the real danger was not from the unauthorized use of a nuclear weapon, but rather from an accident caused by the interaction of men and machines under the highly stressful circumstances. If the Soviets had accidentally or intentionally used nuclear torpedoes, the United States would have made a nuclear counter-response. Instead, the two great Cold War rivals narrowly averted open conflict due to a combination of military professionalism and some degree of luck.

In the beginning, the Norwegian hydroplanes were searching for us, then at the Farer line—the British "Shackletons." Then it was the turn of the American "Neptunes." But judging by the events, they had not succeeded in discovering us. In any case, not until we reached the Sargasso Sea. There they got us. A naval forward searching aircraft carrier group headed by the aircraft carrier "Randolph" confronted submarine B-59. According to our hydro-acoustic specialists, 14 surface units were following our boat. Together with the navigator, we did parallel plotting [on the map]—he did the route of B-59, as he was assigned, I recalled my first naval specialization—and plotted the movements of the American ships. For some time we were able to avoid them quite successfully. However the Americans were not dilettantes either—following all the canons of the military art, they surrounded us and started to tighten the circle, practicing attacks and dropping depth charges. They exploded right next to the hull. It felt like you were sitting in a metal barrel, which somebody is constantly blasting with a sledgehammer. The situation was quite unusual, if not to say shocking—for the crew.

The accumulators on B-59 were discharged to the state of water, only emergency light was functioning. The temperature in the compartments was 45–50 C, up to 60 C in the engine compartment. It was unbearably stuffy. The level of CO2 in the air reached a critical practically deadly for people mark. One of the duty officers fainted and fell down. Then another one followed, then the third one . . . They were falling like dominoes. But we were still holding on, trying to escape. We were suffering like this for about four hours. The Americans hit us with something stronger than the grenades [depth charges]—apparently with a practical depth bomb. We thought—that's it—the end. After this attack, the totally exhausted Savitsky, who in addition to everything, was not able to establish connection with the General Staff, became furious. He summoned the officer who was assigned to the nuclear torpedo, and ordered him to assemble it to battle readiness. "Maybe the war has already started up there, while we are doing somersaults here—screamed emotional Valentin Grigorievich, trying to justify his order. "We're going to blast them now! We will die, but we will sink them all—we will not disgrace our Navy!" But we did not fire the nuclear torpedo—Savitsky was able to rein in his wrath. After consulting with Second Captain Casili Alexandrovich Arkhipov [deceased] and Deputy political officer Ivan Semenovich Maslennikov, he made the decision to come to the surface. We gave an echo locator signal, which in international navigation rules means that "the submarine is coming to the surface." Our pursuers slowed down.

Source: Excerpt from Recollections of Vadim Orlov (USSR Submarine B-59). "We Will Sink Them All, But We Will Not Disgrace Our Navy." Alexander Mozgovoi, The Cuban Samba of the Quartet of Foxtrots: Soviet Submarines in the Caribbean Crisis of 1962, Military Parade, Moscow, 2002. Translated by Svetlana Savranskaya, The National Security Archive. http://www.gwu.edu/~nsarchiv/NSAEBB/NSAEBB75.

John F. Kennedy: Commencement Address Announcing Cooperation with Soviets (June 10, 1963)

From the 1950s onward, American, Soviet, and European leaders alike, conscious of the dangers that full-scale nuclear warfare posed to their countries, showed considerable interest in disarmament proposals. But there was little concrete advancement until the summer of 1963, when the Soviet Union and United States signed a treaty banning atmospheric nuclear testing, a practice that had previously been responsible for the release of substantial amounts of radioactive fallout. Somewhat sobered by the Cuban Missile Crisis the previous year, the originally somewhat brash President John F. Kennedy mounted a major lobbying effort to secure the ratification of this treaty by the U.S. Senate. Around the same time, he also announced his intention to mount a major initiative for peace and disarmament, and to open serious discussions with the Soviet Union for this purpose. Kennedy expressed his understanding of Soviet suffering during World War II, which he believed predisposed Russian leaders to wish to avoid future destructive conflicts. Declaring that "both the United States and its allies, and Soviet Union and its allies, have a mutually deep interest in a just and genuine peace and in halting the arms race," Kennedy expressed his willingness to tolerate diverse political systems while hoping that the Soviet bloc would eventually change. While affirming American commitments to the various U.S. allies, he pledged the United States to work with the Soviet Union for peace and disarmament. He also announced that the two great powers were establishing a direct telephone hot line, to facilitate communication in times of crisis and thereby prevent "dangerous delays, misunderstandings, and misreadings of the other's actions." Kennedy's assassination the following November, and the subsequent U.S. preoccupation with the escalating Vietnam War, meant that not until in the early 1970s, under President Richard Nixon, did the United States and the Soviet Union sign major arms limitation agreements. Kennedy's address nonetheless indicated a sharpened awareness by American leaders in the wake of the Cuban missile crisis that both great powers had a shared stake in avoiding nuclear war and in preventing an unrestrained arms race.

President John F. Kennedy
Commencement Address at American University in Washington
June 10, 1963

President Anderson, members of the faculty, Board of Trustees, distinguished guests, my old colleague, Senator Bob Byrd, who has earned his degree through many years of attending night law school, while I am earning mine in the next 30 minutes, ladies and gentlemen:

It is with great pride that I participate in this ceremony of the American University, sponsored by the Methodist Church, founded by Bishop John Fletcher Hurst, and first opened by President Woodrow Wilson in 1914. This is a young and growing university, but it has already fulfilled Bishop Hurst's enlightened hope for the study of history and public affairs in a city devoted to the making of history and to the conduct of the public's business. By sponsoring this institution of higher learning for all who wish to learn whatever their color or their creed, the Methodists of this area and the nation deserve the nation's thanks, and I commend all those who are today graduating.

Professor Woodrow Wilson once said that every man sent out from a university should be a man of his nation as well as a man of his time, and I am confident that the men and women who carry the honor of graduating from this institution will continue to give from their lives, from their talents, a high measure of public service and public support.

"There are few earthly things more beautiful than a University," wrote John Masefield, in his tribute to the English Universities—and his words are equally true here. He did not refer to spires and towers, to campus greens and ivied walls. He admired the splendid beauty of the University, he said, because it was "a place where those who hate ignorance may strive to know, where those who perceive truth may strive to make others see."

I have, therefore, chose this time and this place to discuss a topic on which ignorance too often abounds and the truth is too rarely perceived—yet it is the most important topic on earth: world peace.

What kind of peace do I mean? What kind of peace do we seek? Not a Pax Americana enforced on the world by American weapons of war. Not the peace of the grave or the security of the slave. I am talking about genuine peace, the kind of peace that makes life on earth worth living, the kind that enables man and nations to grow and to hope and to build a better life for their children—not merely peace for Americans but peace for all men and women—not merely peace in our time but peace for all time.

I speak of peace because of the new face of war. Total war makes no sense in an age when great powers can maintain large and relatively invulnerable nuclear forces and refuse to surrender without resort to those forces. It makes no sense in an age when a single nuclear weapon contains almost ten times the explosive force delivered by all of the allied air forces in the Second World War. It makes no sense in an age when the deadly poisons produced by a nuclear exchange would be carried by the wind and water and soil and seed to the far corners of the globe and to generations unborn.

Today the expenditure of billions of dollars every year on weapons acquired for the purpose of making sure we never need to use them is essential to keeping the peace. But surely the acquisition of such idle stockpiles—which can only destroy and never create—is not the only, much less the most efficient, means of assuring peace.

I speak of peace, therefore, as the necessary rational end of rational men. I realize that the pursuit of peace is not as dramatic as the pursuit of war—and frequently the words of the pursuer fall on deaf ears. But we have no more urgent task.

Some say that it is useless to speak of world peace or world law or world disarmament—and that it will be useless until the leaders of the Soviet Union adopt a more enlightened attitude. I hope they do. I believe we can help them do it. But I also believe that we must reexamine our own attitude—as individuals and as a Nation—for our attitude is as essential as theirs. And every graduate of this school, every thoughtful citizen who despairs of war and wishes to bring peace, should begin by looking inward—by examining his own attitude toward the possibilities of peace, toward the Soviet Union, toward the course of the Cold War and toward freedom and peace here at home.

First: Let us examine our attitude toward peace itself. Too many of us think it is impossible. Too many of us think it is unreal. But that is dangerous, defeatist belief. It leads to the conclusion that war is inevitable—that mankind is doomed—that we are gripped by forces we cannot control.

We need not accept that view. Our problems are manmade—therefore, they can be solved by man. And man can be as big as he wants. No problem of human destiny is beyond human beings. Man's reason and spirit have often solved the seemingly unsolvable—and we believe they can do it again.

I am not referring to the absolute, infinite concept of universal peace and good will of which some fantasies and fanatics dream. I do not deny the values of hopes and dreams but we merely invite discouragement and incredulity by making that our only and immediate goal.

Let us focus instead on a more practical, more attainable peace—based not on a sudden revolution in human nature but on a gradual evolution in human institutions—on a series of concrete actions and effective agreements which are in the interest of all concerned. There is no single, simple key to this peace—no grand or magic formula to be adopted by one or two powers. Genuine peace must be the product of many nations, the sum of many acts. It must be dynamic, not static, changing to meet the challenge of each new generation. For peace is a process—a way of solving problems.

With such a peace, there will still be quarrels and conflicting interests, as there are within families and nations. World peace, like community peace, does not require that each man love his neighbor—it requires only that they live together in mutual tolerance, submitting their disputes to a just and peaceful settlement. And history teaches us that enmities between nations, as between individuals, do not last forever. However fixed our likes and dislikes may seem the tide of time and events will often bring surprising changes in the relations between nations and neighbors.

So let us persevere. Peace need not be impracticable, and war need not be inevitable. By defining our goal more clearly, by making it seem more manageable and less remote, we can help all peoples to see it, to draw hope from it, and to move irresistibly toward it.

Second: Let us reexamine our attitude toward the Soviet Union. It is discouraging to think that their leaders may actually believe what their propagandists write. It is discouraging to read a recent authoritative Soviet text on *Military Strategy* and find, on page after page, wholly baseless and incredible claims—such as the allegation that " American imperialist circles are preparing to unleash different types of wars . . . that there is a very real threat of a preventive war being unleashed by American imperialists against the Soviet Union . . . (and that) the political aims of the American imperialists are to enslave economically and politically the European and other capitalist countries . . . (and) to achieve world domination . . . by means of aggressive wars."

Truly, as it was written long ago: "The wicked flee when no man pursueth." Yet it is sad to read these Soviet statements—to realize the extent of the gulf between us. But it is also a warning—a warning to the American people not to fall into the same trap as the Soviets, not to see only a distorted and desperate view of the other side, not to see conflict as inevitable, accommodations as impossible and communication as nothing more than an exchange of threats.

No government or social system is so evil that its people must be considered as lacking in virtue. As Americans, we find communism profoundly repugnant as a negation of personal freedom and dignity. But we can still hail the Russian people for their many achievements—in science and space, in economic and industrial growth, in culture and in acts of courage.

Among the many traits the peoples of our two countries have in common, none is stronger than our mutual abhorrence of war. Almost unique, among the major world powers, we have never been at war with each other. And no nation in the history of battle ever suffered more than the Soviet Union suffered in the course of the Second World War. At least 20 million lost their lives. Countless millions of homes and farms were burned or sacked. A third of the nation's territory, including nearly two thirds of its industrial base, was turned into a wasteland—a loss equivalent to the devastation of this country east of Chicago.

Today, should total war ever break out again—no matter how—our two countries would become the primary targets. It is an ironic but accurate fact that the two strongest powers are the two in the most danger of devastation. All we have built, all we have worked for, would be destroyed in the first 24 hours. And even in the cold war, which brings burdens and dangers to so many countries, including this Nation's closest allies—our two countries bear the heaviest burdens. For we are both devoting massive sums of money to weapons that could be better devoted to combating ignorance, poverty and disease. We are both caught up in a vicious and dangerous cycle in which suspicion on one side breeds suspicion on the other, and new weapons beget counterweapons.

In short, both the United States and its allies, and the Soviet Union and its allies, have a mutually deep interest in a just and genuine peace and in halting the arms race. Agreements to this end are in the interests of the Soviet Union as well as ours—and even the most hostile nations can be relied upon to accept and keep those treaty obligations, and only those treaty obligations, which are in their own interest.

So, let us not be blind to our differences—but let us also direct attention to our common interests and to means by which those differences can be resolved. And if we cannot end now our differences, at least we can help make the world safe for diversity. For, in the final analysis, our most basic common link is that we all inhabit this planet. We all breathe the same air. We all cherish our children's future. And we are all mortal.

Third: Let us re-examine our attitude toward the cold war, remembering that we are not engaged in a debate, seeking to pile up debating points. We are not here distributing blame or pointing the finger of judgment. We must deal with the world as it is, and not as it might have been had history of the last eighteen years been different.

We must, therefore, persevere in the search for peace in the hope that constructive changes within the Communist bloc might bring within reach solutions which now seem beyond us. We must conduct our affairs in such a way that it becomes in the Communists' interest to agree on a genuine peace. Above all, while defending our vital interest, nuclear powers must avert those confrontations which bring an adversary to a choice of either a humiliating retreat or a nuclear war. To adopt that kind of course in the nuclear age would be evidence only of the bankruptcy of our policy—or of a collective death-wish for the world.

To secure these ends, America's weapons are nonprovocative, carefully controlled, designed to deter, and capable of selective use. Our military forces are committed to peace and disciplined in self-restraint. Our diplomats are instructed to avoid unnecessary irritants and purely rhetorical hostility.

For we can seek a relaxation of tensions without relaxing our guard. And, for our part, we do not need to use threats to prove that we are resolute. We do not need to jam foreign broadcasts out of fear our faith will be eroded. We are unwilling to impose our system on any unwilling people—but we are willing and able to engage in peaceful competition with any people on earth.

Meanwhile, we seek to strengthen the United Nations, to help solve its financial problems, to make it a more effective instrument for peace, to develop it into a genuine world security system—a system capable of resolving disputes on the basis of law, of insuring the security of the large and the small, and of creating conditions under which arms can finally be abolished.

At the same time we seek to keep peace inside the non-Communist world, where many nations, all of them our friends, are divided over issues which weaken Western unity, which invite Communist intervention or which threaten to erupt into war. Our efforts in West New Guinea, in the Congo, in the Middle East and in the Indian subcontinent, have been persistent and patient despite criticism from both sides. We have also tried to set an example for others—by seeking to adjust small but significant differences with our own closest neighbors in Mexico and in Canada.

Speaking of other nations, I wish to make one point clear. We are bound to many nations by alliances. These alliances exist because our concern and theirs substantially overlap. Our commitment to defend Western Europe and West Berlin, for example, stands undiminished because of the identity of our vital interests. The United States will make no deal with the Soviet Union at the expense of other nations and other peoples, not merely because they are our partners, but also because their interests and ours converge.

Our interests converge, however, not only in defending the frontiers of freedom, but in pursuing the paths of peace. It is our hope—and the purpose of allied policies—to convince the Soviet Union that she, too, should let each nation choose its own future, so long as that choice does not interfere with the choices of others. The communist drive to impose their political and economic system on others is the primary cause of world tension today. For there can be no doubt that if all nations could refrain from interfering in the self-determination of others, then peace would be much more assured.

This will require a new effort to achieve world law—a new context for world discussions. It will require increased understanding between the Soviets and ourselves. And increased understanding will require increased contact and communications. One step in this direction is the proposed arrangement for a direct line between Moscow and Washington, to avoid on each side the dangerous delays, misunderstandings, and misreadings of the other's actions which might occur at a time of crisis.

We have also been talking in Geneva about other first-step measures of arms control, designed to limit the intensity of the arms race and to reduce the risks of accidental war. Our primary long-range interest in Geneva, however, is general and complete disarmament—designed to take place by stages, permitting parallel political developments to build the new institutions of peace which would take the place of arms. The pursuit of disarmament has been an effort of this Government since the 1920's. It has been urgently sought by the past three administrations. And however dim the prospects may be today, we intend to continue this effort—to continue it in order that all countries, including our own, can better grasp what the problems and possibilities of disarmament are.

The one major area of these negotiations where the end is in sight, yet where a fresh start is badly needed, is in a treaty to outlaw nuclear tests. The conclusion of such a treaty, so near and yet so far, would check the spiraling arms race in one of its most dangerous areas. It would place the nuclear powers in a position to deal more effectively with one of the greatest hazards which man faces in 1963, the further spread of nuclear arms. It would increase our security—it would decrease the prospects of war. Surely this goal is sufficiently important to require our steady pursuit, yielding neither to the temptation to give up the whole effort nor the temptation to give up our insistence on vital and responsible safeguards.

I am taking this opportunity, therefore, to announce two important decisions in this regard.

First: Chairman Khrushchev, Prime Minister Macmillan, and I have agreed that high-level discussions will shortly begin in Moscow looking toward early agreement on a comprehensive test ban treaty. Our hopes must be tempered with the caution of history—but with our hopes go the hopes of all mankind.

Second: To make clear our good faith and solemn convictions on the matter, I now declare that the United States does not propose to conduct nuclear tests in the atmosphere so long as other states do not do so. We will not be the first to resume. Such a declaration is no substitute for a formal binding treaty, but I hope it will help us achieve one. Nor would such a treaty be a substitute for disarmament, but I hope it will help us achieve it.

Finally, my fellow Americans, let us examine our attitude toward peace and freedom here at home. The quality and spirit of our own society must justify and support our efforts abroad. We must show it in the dedication of our own lives—as many of you who are graduating today will have a unique opportunity to do, by serving without pay in the Peace Corps abroad or in the proposed National Service Corps here at home.

But wherever we are, we must all, in our daily lives, live up to the age-old faith that peace and freedom walk together. In too many of our duties today, the peace is not secure because freedom is incomplete.

It is the responsibility of the executive branch at all levels of government—local, State and National—to provide and protect that freedom for all of our citizens by all means within their authority. It is the responsibility of the legislative branch at all levels, wherever that authority is not now adequate, to make it adequate. And it is the responsibility of all citizens in all sections of this country to respect the rights of all others and to respect the law of the land.

All this is not unrelated to world peace. "When a man's ways please the Lord," the Scriptures tell us, "he maketh even his enemies to be at peace with him." And is not peace, in the last analysis, basically a matter human rights—the right to live out our lives without fear of devastation—the right to breathe air as nature provided it—the right of future generations to a healthy existence?

While we proceed to safeguard our national interests, let us also safeguard human interests. And the elimination of war and arms is clearly in the interest of both. No treaty, however much it may be to the advantage of all, however tightly it may be worded, can provide absolute security against the risks of deception and evasion. But it can—if it is sufficiently effective in its enforcement and if it is sufficiently in the interests of its signers—offer far more security and far fewer risks than an unabated, uncontrolled, unpredictable arms race.

The United States, as the world knows, will never start a war. We do not want a war.

We do not now expect a war. This generation of Americans has already had enough— more than enough—of war and hate and oppression. We shall be prepared if others wish it. We shall be alert to try to stop it. But we shall also do our part to build a world of peace where the weak are safe and the strong are just. We are not helpless before that task or hopeless of its success. Confident and unafraid, we labor on—not toward a strategy of annihilation but toward a strategy of peace.

Source: John F. Kennedy, *Public Papers of the Presidents of the United States: John F. Kennedy, 1963.* (Washington, DC: U.S. Government Printing Office, 1964), 459–64.

Nuclear Test Ban Treaty (1963)

By the mid-1950s it had become apparent that tests of nuclear weapons contaminated the atmosphere with radioactive fallout, which could be highly detrimental to both human health and the environment. In March 1954 the *Lucky Dragon*, a Japanese fishing boat with a crew of 23, was exposed to fallout from the Bikini Island hydrogen bomb test. The fishermen suffered from radiation sickness, and one of them died, leading to an international furor in Japan. Scientists also demonstrated that radioactive fallout was carried around the world by the wind and that no area was immune to it, leading to fears of cumulative genetic damage to humans and others. Negotiations among nuclear powers to ban atmospheric and underwater testing of nuclear weapons began in 1955 but foundered over issues of verification. The Cuban Missile Crisis of October 1962 gave renewed impetus to negotiations for a test ban treaty, and representatives from the Soviet Union, the United States, and Great Britain signed an agreement at Moscow on August 5, 1963. The Nuclear Test Ban Treaty was intended to be the first step toward total nuclear disarmament. It prohibited any of the signatory countries from testing nuclear weapons in outer space, the Earth's atmosphere, or underwater, although underground testing was not banned. During the two months before the treaty went into effect on October 10, more than one hundred countries around the world added their names to the treaty. Notable exceptions were France and China, two powers that regarded the treaty as an example of collusive Soviet–American ambitions to dominate the rest of the world and reserved the right to test nuclear weapons as they saw fit.

TREATY BANNING NUCLEAR WEAPON TESTS IN THE ATMOSPHERE, IN OUTER SPACE AND UNDER WATER

The governments of the United States of America, the United Kingdom of Great Britain and Northern Ireland, and the Union of Soviet Socialist Republics, hereinafter referred to as the "Original Parties",

Proclaiming as their principal aim the speediest possible achievement of an agreement on general and complete disarmament under strict international control in accordance with the objectives of the United Nations which would put an end to the armaments race and eliminate the incentive to the production and testing of all kinds of weapons, including nuclear weapons,

Seeking to achieve the discontinuance of all test explosions of nuclear weapons for all time, determined to continue negotiations to this end, and desiring to put an end to the contamination of man's environment by radioactive substances,

Have agreed as follows:

Article 1

1. Each of the Parties to this Treaty undertakes to prohibit, to prevent, and not to carry out any nuclear weapon test explosion, or any other nuclear explosion, at any place under its jurisdiction or control:

    a. in the atmosphere; beyond its limits, including outer space; or under water, including territorial waters or high seas; or

    b. in any other environment if such explosion causes radioactive debris to be present outside the territorial limits of the State under whose jurisdiction or control such explosion is conducted. It is understood in this connection that the provisions of this subparagraph are without prejudice to the conclusion of a treaty resulting in the permanent banning of all nuclear test explosions, including all such explosions underground, the conclusion of which, as the Parties have stated in the Preamble to this Treaty, they seek to achieve.

2. Each of the Parties to this Treaty undertakes furthermore to refrain from causing, encouraging, or in any way participating in, the carrying out of any nuclear weapon test explosion, or any other nuclear explosion, anywhere which would take place in any of the environments described, or have the effect referred to, in paragraph 1 of this Article.

Article 2

1. Any Party may propose amendments to this Treaty. The text of any proposed amendment shall be submitted to the Depositary Governments which shall circulate it to all Parties to this Treaty. Thereafter, if requested to do so by one-third or more of the Parties, the Depositary Governments shall convene a conference, to which they shall invite all the Parties, to consider such amendment.

2. Any amendment to this Treaty must be approved by a majority of the votes of

all the Parties to this Treaty, including the votes of all of the Original Parties. The amendment shall enter into force for all Parties upon the deposit of instruments of ratification by a majority of all the Parties, including the instruments of ratification of all of the Original Parties.

Article 3

1. This Treaty shall be open to all States for signature. Any State which does not sign this Treaty before its entry into force in accordance with paragraph 3 of this Article may accede to it at any time.

[. . .]

Article 4

This Treaty shall be of unlimited duration.

Each Party shall in exercising its national sovereignty have the right to withdraw from the Treaty if it decides that extraordinary events, related to the subject matter of this Treaty, have jeopardized the supreme interests of its country. It shall give notice of such withdrawal to all other Parties to the Treaty three months in advance.

[. . .]

Source: "Treaty Banning Nuclear Weapon Tests in the Atmosphere, in Outer Space and Under Water," August 5, 1963, U.S. Department of State, http://www.state.gov/t/ac/trt/4797.htm.

Tonkin Gulf Resolution (August 7, 1964)

Passed by the U.S. Congress in August 1964, the Tonkin Gulf Resolution permitted President Lyndon B. Johnson to take whatever measures he considered appropriate to deal with the growing crisis in Vietnam. As the military situation in Vietnam deteriorated in early 1964, Johnson and his advisors decided that

only with heavy support from the United States could the government of the Republic of Vietnam (RVN, South Vietnam) survive. Johnson, running for reelection against hard-line Republican Senator Barry Goldwater, feared that a major escalation might jeopardize his campaign, so he relied extensively on covert operations, including DeSoto intelligence-gathering missions undertaken by American destroyers to test North Vietnamese radar efficiency or land South Vietnamese forces on North Vietnamese territory. On the morning of August 2, three North Vietnamese patrol boats attacked the destroyer USS *Maddox* as it undertook one such mission in the Tonkin Gulf, beyond the three-mile Vietnamese territorial limits that the United States recognized but within the 12-mile zone that the Democratic Republic of Vietnam (DRV, North Vietnam) claimed. Aircraft from the nearby USS *Ticonderoga* came to its assistance, sinking one patrol boat and disabling the others, and Johnson ordered the *Maddox* to continue patrolling farther offshore in the Gulf, accompanied by a fellow destroyer, the *C. Turner Joy.* On the night of August 4, both vessels reported hostile attacks, although it was later suggested that nervous radar and sonar operators or malfunctioning equipment probably triggered false alarms. North Vietnam subsequently claimed that none of its patrol boats were responsible, alleging that the U.S. government deliberately fabricated the incident as a pretext to escalate the war. Johnson, nettled by Goldwater's repeated criticisms that his Vietnam policy was irresolute and ineffective, made no attempt to verify or question the reports. Without mentioning their involvement in covert operations, Johnson announced that American ships had encountered an unprovoked "deliberate attack," and he ordered retaliatory American bombing raids on an oil depot and North Vietnamese patrol boat bases. He also submitted to Congress a draft resolution authorizing him to "take all necessary measures" to "repel any armed attack" on U.S. forces, "prevent further aggression," and give any aid necessary, "including the use of armed force," to help any country that requested assistance through the Southeast Asian Treaty

Organization (SEATO), to which South Vietnam belonged. The Tonkin Gulf Resolution, passed unanimously by the House and with only two dissenting Senate votes, provided the legal basis for the conflict's future expansion, including massive bombing raids on North Vietnam, which began in February 1965, and two months later a major deployment of American ground troops and the drastic expansion of such forces' operational activities within Vietnam. Only on December 30, 1970, after the Cambodian incursion authorized by President Richard Nixon that spring, did an increasingly restive Congress repeal the Tonkin Gulf Resolution. Skeptical congressional reluctance to ever again give a president a similar blank check was a major factor in the passage of the 1973 War Powers Resolution, drastically limiting the chief executive's future ability to deploy U.S. troops in combat situations.

[H.J. Res. 1145]

To promote the maintenance of international peace and security in southeast Asia.

Whereas naval units of the Communist regime in Vietnam, in violation of the principles of the Charter of the United Nations and of international law, have deliberately and repeatedly attacked United States naval vessels lawfully present in international waters, and have thereby created a serious threat to international peace; and

Whereas these attacks are part of a deliberate and systematic campaign of aggression that the Communist regime in North Vietnam has been waging against its neighbors and the nations joined with them in the collective defense of their freedom; and

Whereas the United States is assisting the peoples of southeast Asia to protect their freedom and has no territorial, military or political ambitions in that area, but desires only that these peoples should be left in peace to work out their own destinies in their own way: Now, therefore, be it

Resolved by the Senate and House of Representatives of the United States of America in Congress assembled, That the Congress approves and supports the determination of the President, as Commander in Chief, to take all necessary measures to repel any armed attack against the forces of the United States and to prevent further aggression.

SEC. 2. The United States regards as vital to its national interest and to world peace the maintenance of international peace and security in southeast Asia. Consonant with the Constitution of the United States and the Charter of the United Nations and in accordance with its obligations under the Southeast Asia Collective Defense Treaty, the United States is, therefore, prepared, as the President determines, to take all necessary steps, including the use of armed force, to assist any member or protocol state of the Southeast Asia Collective Defense Treaty requesting assistance in defense of its freedom.

SEC. 3. This resolution shall expire when the President shall determine that the peace and security of the area is reasonably assured by international conditions created by action of the United Nations or otherwise, except that it may be terminated earlier by concurrent resolution of the Congress.

Source: "Text of Joint Resolution, August 7," *Department of State Bulletin* 51, no. 1313 (1964): 268.

Chinese Announcement of Nuclear Test (October 16, 1964)

In 1945 the United States possessed a nuclear monopoly. The Soviet Union rushed to develop its own nuclear weapons and the so-called nuclear arms race began. The Soviet Union detonated its first nuclear device in September 1949. In 1951 the People's Republic of China (PRC) signed a secret agreement with the Soviet Union by which China provided uranium ores in exchange for Soviet assistance in the nuclear field. Thereafter, Chinese scientists worked clandestinely to develop nuclear weapons. Chinese leaders made a formal decision to develop an independent strategic nuclear force sometime around early 1956. During the 1950s, the Soviets provided vital technical and material assistance including an experimental nuclear reactor, facilities for processing uranium, a cyclotron, and gaseous diffusion equipment. The cooling of Sino-Soviet relations in the late 1950s and early 1960s ended Soviet help and convinced Chinese leaders to continue their nation's nuclear development program on their own. Chinese leaders wanted to break the nuclear monopoly held by the other superpowers, ensure security against Soviet and U.S. threats, and enhance Chinese prestige and power. To develop an atomic bomb, China had to choose between producing Pu239 from a reactor or developing the method of producing U235 through isotope separation. Although technically more challenging, Chinese scientists chose to separate physically U235 and U238 isotopes. To the surprise of western observers, Chinese scientists made remarkable progress in pursuing this path. The first Chinese nuclear test was conducted at Lop Nor on October 16, 1964, using uranium 235 as the nuclear fuel. China was the fifth nation to develop a nuclear weapon. Henceforth, nuclear tensions associated with the Cold War would play out in a more complex world. China launched its first nuclear missile on October 25, 1966, and detonated its first hydrogen bomb on June 14, 1967. For the remainder of the Cold War, Chinese nuclear capacity constrained American decision makers, particularly during the Vietnam War.

The Atomic Bomb, *Statement of the Government of the People's Republic of China, October 16, 1964*

China exploded an atomic bomb at 15:00 hours on October 16, 1964, thereby successfully carrying out its first nuclear test. This is a major achievement of the Chinese people in their struggle to strengthen their national

defence and oppose the U.S. imperialist policy of nuclear blackmail and nuclear threats.

To defend oneself is the inalienable right of every sovereign state. To safeguard world peace is the common task of all peace-loving countries. China cannot remain idle in the face of the ever increasing nuclear threats from the United States. China is conducting nuclear tests and developing nuclear weapons under compulsion.

The Chinese Government has consistently advocated the complete prohibition and thorough destruction of nuclear weapons. If this had been achieved, China need not have developed nuclear weapons. But our proposal has met with stubborn resistance from the U.S. imperialists. The Chinese Government pointed out long ago that the treaty on the partial halting of nuclear tests signed in Moscow in July 1963 by the United States, Britain and the Soviet Union was a big fraud to fool the people of the world, that it was an attempt to consolidate the nuclear monopoly of the three nuclear powers and tie the hands of all peace-loving countries, and that it had increased, and not decreased, the nuclear threat of U.S. imperialism against the people of China and of the whole world. . . .

The atomic bomb is a paper tiger. This famous statement by Chairman Mao Tse-tung is known to all. This was our view in the past and this is still our view at present. China is developing nuclear weapons not because it believes in their omnipotence nor because it plans to use them. On the contrary, in developing nuclear weapons, China's aim is to break the nuclear monopoly of the nuclear powers and to eliminate nuclear weapons.

The Chinese Government is loyal to Marxism-Leninism and proletarian internationalism. We believe in the people. It is the people, and not any weapons, that decide the outcome of a war. The destiny of China is decided by the Chinese people, while the destiny of the world is decided by the people of the world, and not by nuclear weapons. China is developing nuclear weapons for defence and for protecting the Chinese people from U.S. threats to launch a nuclear war.

The Chinese Government hereby solemnly declares that China will never at any time or under any circumstances be the first to use nuclear weapons. . . .

The Chinese Government will, as always, exert every effort to promote, through international consultations, the realization of the lofty aim of complete prohibition and thorough destruction of nuclear weapons. Until that day comes, the Chinese Government and people will firmly and unswervingly follow their own path to strengthen their national defence, defend their motherland and safeguard world peace.

We are convinced that man, who creates nuclear weapons, will certainly be able to eliminate them.

Source: Break the Nuclear Monopoly, Eliminate Nuclear Weapons (Peking: Foreign Languages Press, 1965), 1–5. http://www.fordham.edu/halsall/mod/1964china-bomb.html.

Nuclear Nonproliferation Treaty (1968)

By the early 1960s, the United States, Britain, the Soviet Union, the People's Republic of China (PRC), and France had all developed nuclear weapons. Although wedded to maintaining their own nuclear forces, the first three of these powers were all keen to keep the "nuclear club" exclusive and to prevent the further spread of such weapons to smaller and weaker nations. One fear was that weak governments might not be able to maintain adequate security over their nuclear programs. For much of the 1960s, negotiations on the subject continued at the United Nations (UN). The goal of the Nuclear Nonproliferation Treaty was to prevent the spread and development of nuclear weaponry. The treaty was signed by 130 nations in 1968 and went into effect on March 5, 1970. Signatory powers who possessed nuclear weapons bound themselves not to transfer such technology to nonnuclear powers, while those who did not possess nuclear weapons pledged not to develop them. Neither France nor China agreed to sign the treaty until 1992, and despite widespread international condemnation, both countries continued to develop their nuclear arsenals and on occasion to provide assistance that enabled other states to develop nuclear weapons. It was widely believed, though never confirmed, that Israel possessed a nuclear deterrent. By the late 20th century, several states had disregarded the treaty's provisions. India tested a nuclear device in 1974, and both Pakistan and India detonated nuclear devices in May 1998. In the early 21st century, Iran and the Democratic People's Republic of Korea (DPRK, North Korea) also mounted programs apparently intended to develop nuclear weapons, causing much alarm to the United States and West European powers, as the number of nuclear-armed states seemed likely to increase appreciably over the next decades.

[. . .]

Article I

Each nuclear-weapon State Party to the Treaty undertakes not to transfer to any recipient whatsoever nuclear weapons or other nuclear explosive devices or control over such weapons or explosive devices directly, or indirectly; and not in any way to assist, encourage, or induce any non-nuclear weapon State to manufacture or otherwise acquire nuclear weapons or other nuclear explosive devices, or control over such weapons or explosive devices.

Article II

Each non-nuclear-weapon State Party to the Treaty undertakes not to receive the transfer from any transferor whatsoever of nuclear weapons or other nuclear explosive devices or of control over such weapons or explosive devices directly, or indirectly; not to manufacture or otherwise acquire nuclear weapons or other nuclear explosive devices; and not to seek or receive any assistance in the manufacture of nuclear weapons or other nuclear explosive devices.

Article III

1. Each non-nuclear-weapon State Party to the Treaty undertakes to accept safeguards, as set forth in an agreement to be negotiated and concluded with the International Atomic Energy Agency in accordance with the Statute of the International Atomic Energy Agency and the Agency's safeguards system, for the exclusive purpose of verification of the fulfillment of its obligations assumed under this Treaty with a view to preventing diversion of nuclear energy from peaceful uses to nuclear weapons or other nuclear explosive devices. Procedures for the safeguards required by this article shall be followed with respect to source or special fissionable material whether it is being produced, processed or used in any principal nuclear facility or is outside any such facility. The safeguards required by this article shall be applied to all source or special fissionable material in all peaceful nuclear activities within the territory of such State, under its jurisdiction, or carried out under its control anywhere.

2. Each State Party to the Treaty undertakes not to provide: (a) source or special fissionable material, or (b) equipment or material especially designed or prepared for the processing, use or production of special fissionable material, to any non-nuclear-weapon State for peaceful purposes, unless the source or special fissionable material shall be subject to the safeguards required by this article.

3. The safeguards required by this article shall be implemented in a manner designed to comply with article IV of this Treaty, and to avoid hampering the economic or technological development of the Parties or international cooperation in the field of peaceful nuclear activities, including the international exchange of nuclear material and equipment for the processing, use or production of nuclear material for peaceful purposes in accordance with the provisions of this article and the principle of safeguarding set forth in the Preamble of the Treaty.

4. Non-nuclear-weapon States Party to the Treaty shall conclude agreements with the International Atomic Energy Agency to meet the requirements of this article either individually or together with other States in accordance with the Statute of the International Atomic Energy Agency. Negotiation of such agreements shall commence within 180 days from the original entry into force of this Treaty. For States depositing their instruments of ratification or accession after the 180-day period, negotiation of such agreements shall commence not later than the date of such deposit. Such agreements shall enter into force not later than eighteen months after the date of initiation of negotiations.

Article IV

1. Nothing in this Treaty shall be interpreted as affecting the inalienable right of all the Parties to the Treaty to develop research, production and use of nuclear energy for peaceful purposes without discrimination and in conformity with articles I and II of this Treaty.

2. All the Parties to the Treaty undertake to facilitate, and have the right to participate in, the fullest possible exchange of equipment, materials and scientific and technological information for the peaceful uses of nuclear energy. Parties to the Treaty in a position to do so shall also cooperate in contributing alone or together with other States or international organizations to the further development of the applications of nuclear energy for peaceful purposes, especially in the territories of non-nuclear-weapon States Party to the Treaty, with due consideration for the needs of the developing areas of the world.

Article V

Each party to the Treaty undertakes to take appropriate measures to ensure that, in accordance with this Treaty, under appropriate international observation and through appropriate international procedures, potential benefits from any peaceful applications of nuclear explosions will be made available to non-nuclear-weapon States Party to the Treaty on a nondiscriminatory basis and that the charge to such Parties for the explosive devices used will be as low as possible and exclude any charge for research and development. Non-nuclear-weapon States Party to the Treaty shall be able to obtain such benefits, pursuant to a special international agreement or agreements, through an appropriate international

body with adequate representation of non-nuclear-weapon States. Negotiations on this subject shall commence as soon as possible after the Treaty enters into force. Non-nuclear-weapon States Party to the Treaty so desiring may also obtain such benefits pursuant to bilateral agreements.

Article VI

Each of the Parties to the Treaty undertakes to pursue negotiations in good faith on effective measures relating to cessation of the nuclear arms race at an early date and to nuclear disarmament, and on a Treaty on general and complete disarmament under strict and effective international control.

Article VII

Nothing in this Treaty affects the right of any group of States to conclude regional treaties in order to assure the total absence of nuclear weapons in their respective territories.

[. . .]

Article IX

1. This Treaty shall be open to all States for signature. Any State which does not sign the Treaty before its entry into force in accordance with paragraph 3 of this article may accede to it at any time.

[. . .]

Article X

1. Each Party shall in exercising its national sovereignty have the right to withdraw from the Treaty if it decides that extraordinary events, related to the subject matter of this Treaty, have jeopardized the supreme interests of its country. It shall give notice of such withdrawal to all other Parties to the Treaty and to the

United Nations Security Council three months in advance. Such notice shall include a statement of the extraordinary events it regards as having jeopardized its supreme interests.

2. Twenty-five years after the entry into force of the Treaty, a conference shall be convened to decide whether the Treaty shall continue in force indefinitely, or shall be extended for an additional fixed period or periods. This decision shall be taken by a majority of the Parties to the Treaty.

[. . .]

Source: "Treaty on the Non-Proliferation of Nuclear Weapons," July 1, 1968, *United States Treaties and Other International Agreements* 2.1, pt. 484.

Strategic Arms Limitation Treaty I (May 26, 1972)

One major objective of President Richard Nixon and Secretary of State Henry Kissinger in seeking détente with the Soviet Union was to conclude agreements limiting the further growth of nuclear weapons and antiballistic missile (ABM) systems. At a May 1972 summit meeting in Moscow, Nixon and Soviet leader Leonid Brezhnev signed two strategic arms limitation treaties, jointly known as SALT I, which took effect the following October. The ABM Treaty limited antiballistic missile defense sites in each country to two, neither hosting more than 100 ABMs. The Interim Agreement froze for five years the number of nuclear warheads each side possessed, giving the Soviets numerical superiority (2,328 to the American 1,710) in exchange for accepting the American lead in multiple independent reentry vehicles (MIRVs), the delivery system. SALT I allowed its signatories to upgrade their nuclear weaponry provided they observed these limits. Although American conservatives regarded them with suspicion, these treaties were widely viewed as a diplomatic triumph for Nixon and were the first major arms control agreements concluded since the beginning of the Cold War. Further warming in Soviet–American relations was anticipated. Several Soviet–American commercial agreements followed the disarmament accords, providing for Soviet purchases of $750 million of American grain, largely financed by American credits; various business contracts; maritime understandings; and comprehensive trade agreements settling outstanding Soviet debts to the United States and promising the Soviets most-favored trading nation status. At a second Nixon–Brezhnev summit, held in Washington in June 1973, the two leaders signed the Agreement on Prevention of Nuclear War, binding them to consult whenever international crises that might precipitate nuclear war between them or with other states arose and to act "in such a manner as to help prevent the development of situations capable of causing a dangerous exacerbation of their relations." They also concluded four executive agreements on oceanography, transport, agricultural research, and cultural exchange and issued a declaration of principles intended to accelerate talks at Geneva designed to produce a second and permanent nuclear arms limitation agreement (SALT II). Airline services were expanded, and trade missions were established. The SALT agreements seemed a triumph for Nixon–Kissinger triangular diplomacy, promising further progress in the direction of Soviet–American détente, but in practice they marked its high tide.

The United States of America and the Union of Soviet Socialist Republics, hereinafter referred to as the Parties,

Convinced that the Treaty on the Limitation of Anti-Ballistic Missile Systems and this Interim Agreement on Certain Measures with Respect to the Limitation of Strategic Offensive Arms will contribute to the creation of more favorable conditions for active negotiations on limiting strategic arms as well as to the relaxation of international tension and the strengthening of trust between States,

Taking into account the relationship between strategic offensive and defensive arms,

Mindful of their obligations under Article VI of the Treaty on the Non-Proliferation of Nuclear Weapons,

Have agreed as follows:

Article I

The Parties undertake not to start construction of additional fixed land-based intercontinental ballistic missile (ICBM) launchers after July 1, 1972.

Article II

The Parties undertake not to convert land-based launchers for light ICBMs, or for ICBMs of older types deployed prior to 1964, into land-based launchers for heavy ICBMs of types deployed after that time.

Article III

The Parties undertake to limit submarine-launched ballistic missile (SLBM) launchers and modern ballistic missile submarines to the numbers operational and under construction on the date of signature of this Interim Agreement, and in addition to launchers and submarines constructed under procedures established by the Parties as replacements for an equal number of ICBM launchers of older types deployed prior to 1964 or for launchers on older submarines.

Article IV

Subject to the provisions of this Interim Agreement, modernization and replacement of strategic offensive ballistic missiles and launchers covered by this Interim Agreement may be undertaken.

Article V

1. For the purpose of providing assurance of compliance with the provisions of this Interim Agreement, each Party shall use national technical means of verification at its disposal in a manner consistent with generally recognized principles of international law.
2. Each Party undertakes not to interfere with the national technical means of verification of the other Party operating in accordance with paragraph 1 of this Article.
3. Each Party undertakes not to use deliberate concealment measures which impede verification by national technical means of compliance with the provisions of this Interim Agreement. This obligation shall not require changes in current construction, assembly, conversion, or overhaul practices.

Article VI

To promote the objectives and implementation of the provisions of this Interim Agreement, the Parties shall use the Standing Consultative Commission established under Article XIII of the Treaty on the Limitation of Anti-Ballistic Missile Systems in accordance with the provisions of that Article.

Article VII

The Parties undertake to continue active negotiations for limitations on strategic offensive arms. The obligations provided for in this Interim Agreement shall not prejudice the scope or terms of the limitations on strategic offensive arms which may be worked out in the course of further negotiations.

Article VIII

1. This Interim Agreement shall enter into force upon exchange of written notices

of acceptance by each Party, which exchange shall take place simultaneously with the exchange of instruments of ratification of the Treaty on the Limitation of Anti-Ballistic Missile Systems.

2. This Interim Agreement shall remain in force for a period of five years unless replaced earlier by an agreement on more complete measures limiting strategic offensive arms. It is the objective of the Parties to conduct active follow-on negotiations with the aim of concluding such an agreement as soon as possible.

3. Each Party shall, in exercising its national sovereignty, have the right to withdraw from this Interim Agreement if it decides that extraordinary events related to the subject matter of this Interim Agreement have jeopardized its supreme interests. It shall give notice of its decision to the other Party six months prior to withdrawal from this Interim Agreement. Such notice shall include a statement of the extraordinary events the notifying Party regards as having jeopardized its supreme interests.

[. . .]

Source: "Interim Agreement between the United States of America and the Union of Soviet Socialist Republics on Certain Measures with Respect to the Limitation of Strategic Offensive Arms," May 26, 1972, U.S. State Department, http://www.state.gov/t/ac/trt/4795.htm.

U.S. War Powers Act (November 7, 1973)

In the aftermath of the Vietnam War, many American senators and congressmen resented the way in which President Lyndon B. Johnson, after the passage of the August 1964 Tonkin Gulf Resolution authorizing him to take such measures as he considered appropriate to deal with the situation in Vietnam, had sought no further congressional authorization before committing more than 500,000 military personnel to that country. Congress also resented the way in which Johnson's successor, Richard Nixon, had felt free to expand the war beyond Vietnam, launching heavy bombing raids on both Laos and Cambodia and even sending American forces to invade the latter country for two months in May and June 1970. In November 1973 Congress passed a joint resolution, the terms of which required the president to consult with Congress before beginning hostilities with another country and at regular intervals during the course of such hostilities. Unless Congress voted either to declare war or to approve the use of U.S. forces in a hostile situation, the president was required to withdraw all military personnel within 60 days, with at most an additional 30 days should circumstances make such an extension unavoidable. President Nixon vetoed the resolution, but Congress found the two-thirds majority necessary to pass it. Successive presidents stated that they considered it unconstitutional but nonetheless observed its provisions, and by the early 21st century, presidents had submitted 118 reports to Congress in connection with the War Powers Act. The occasions on which it was invoked included U.S. participation in United Nations (UN) peacekeeping missions as well as before the interventions in Grenada and Panama and prior to the Persian Gulf War of 1991.

Concerning the War Powers of Congress and the President.

Resolved by the Senate and the House of Representatives of the United States of America in Congress assembled, Short Title Section 1. This joint resolution may be cited as the "War Powers Resolution".

Purpose and Policy

Sec. 2. (a) It is the purpose of this joint resolution to fulfill the intent of the framers of the Constitution of the United States and insure that the collective judgement of both the

Congress and the President will apply to the introduction of United States Armed Forces into hostilities, or into situations where imminent involvement in hostilities is clearly indicated by the circumstances, and to the continued use of such forces in hostilities or in such situations.

(b) Under article I, section 8, of the Constitution, it is specifically provided that the Congress shall have the power to make all laws necessary and proper for carrying into execution, not only its own powers but also all other powers vested by the Constitution in the Government of the United States, or in any department or officer thereof.

(c) The constitutional powers of the President as Commander-in-Chief to introduce United States Armed Forces into hostilities, or into situations where imminent involvement in hostilities is clearly indicated by the circumstances, are exercised only pursuant to (1) a declaration of war, (2) specific statutory authorization, or (3) a national emergency created by attack upon the United States, its territories or possessions, or its armed forces.

Consultation

Sec. 3. The President in every possible instance shall consult with Congress before introducing United States Armed Forces into hostilities or into situations where imminent involvement in hostilities is clearly indicated by the circumstances, and after every such introduction shall consult regularly with the Congress until United States Armed Forces are no longer engaged in hostilities or have been removed from such situations.

Reporting

Sec. 4. (a) In the absence of a declaration of war, in any case in which United States Armed Forces are introduced—

(1) into hostilities or into situations where imminent involvement in hostilities is clearly indicated by the circumstances;

(2) into the territory, airspace or waters of a foreign nation, while equipped for combat, except for deployments which relate solely to supply, replacement, repair, or training of such forces; or

(3) in numbers which substantially enlarge United States Armed Forces equipped for combat already located in a foreign nation; the president shall submit within 48 hours to the Speaker of the House of Representatives and to the President pro tempore of the Senate a report, in writing, setting forth—

(A) the circumstances necessitating the introduction of United States Armed Forces;

(B) the constitutional and legislative authority under which such introduction took place; and

(C) the estimated scope and duration of the hostilities or involvement.

(b) The President shall provide such other information as the Congress may request in the fulfillment of its constitutional responsibilities with respect to committing the Nation to war and to the use of United States Armed Forces abroad.

(c) Whenever United States Armed Forces are introduced into hostilities or into any situation described in subsection (a) of this section, the President shall, so long as such armed forces continue to be engaged in such hostilities or situation, report to the Congress periodically on the status of such hostilities or situation as well as on the scope and duration of such hostilities or situation, but in no event shall he report to the Congress less often than once every six months.

Congressional Action

Sec. 5. (a) Each report submitted pursuant to section 4(a)(1) shall be transmitted to the Speaker of the House of Representatives and to the President pro tempore of the Senate on the same calendar day. Each report so transmitted shall be referred to the Committee on Foreign Affairs of the House of Representatives and to the Committee on Foreign Relations of the Senate for appropriate action. If, when the report is transmitted, the Congress has adjourned sine die or has adjourned for any period in excess of three calendar days, the Speaker of the House of Representatives and the President pro tempore of the Senate, if they deem it advisable (or if petitioned by at least 30 percent of the membership of their respective Houses) shall jointly request the President to convene Congress in order that it may consider the report and take appropriate action pursuant to this section.

(b) Within sixty calendar days after a report is submitted or is required to be submitted pursuant to section 4(a)(1), whichever is earlier, the President shall terminate any use of United States Armed Forces with respect to which such report was submitted (or required to be submitted), unless the Congress (1) has declared war or has enacted a specific authorization for such use of United States Armed Forces, (2) has extended by law such sixty-day period, or (3) is physically unable to meet as a result of an armed attack upon the United States. Such sixty-day period shall be extended for not more than an additional thirty days if the President determines and certifies to the Congress in writing that unavoidable military necessity respecting the safety of United States Armed Forces requires the continued use of such armed forces in the course of bringing about a prompt removal of such forces.

(c) Notwithstanding subsection (b), at any time that United States Armed Forces are engaged in hostilities outside the territory of the United States, its possessions and territories without a declaration of war or specific statutory authorization, such forces shall be removed by the President if the Congress so directs by concurrent resolution.

[. . .]

Source: War Powers Resolution, Public Law 93–148, 93rd Cong., 1st sess. (November 7, 1973).

Yuri Andropov: Memorandum to Brezhnev on Afghanistan (December 1979)

In April 1978 the Marxist People's Democratic Party of Afghanistan (PDP) overthrew the government of Prime Minister Mohammad Daoud Khan, executing Daoud and his family and seizing power itself. PDP secretary-general Nur Muhammad Taraki became prime minister, and in December 1978 he signed a bilateral treaty of friendship and cooperation with the Soviet Union under whose terms substantial Soviet aid and several hundred military advisers were dispatched to Kabul, the capital. Taraki was himself overthrown and killed in a palace coup in September 1979 that placed his deputy prime minister, Hafizullah Amin, in power. Facing a guerrilla insurgency supported by the United States, Amin likewise relied heavily on Soviet military equipment and advisers, but on December 28, 1979, his Russian patrons, considering him too unreliable, organized a coup in which Soviet forces stormed the presidential palace and killed Amin. Former deputy prime minister Babrak Karmal, at that time ambassador to Czechoslovakia, succeeded him. Moscow apparently hoped that removing Amin would restore some kind of stability in Afghanistan. Yuri Andropov, then head of the KGB, warned that

Amin was unable to maintain order and was likely to shift to the West, follow neutralist policies, and move against his Soviet advisers. Initially, Soviet leader Leonid Brezhnev rejected no fewer than 18 requests for assistance from Babrak and other Afghan communists outside the country, but it seems that eventually warnings that Amin was moving against "suspect persons" and might take action against the Soviet military advisers already present in the country tipped the balance. Soviet ground forces and paratroopers entered the country on December 27, 1979, and remained there for almost a decade. Anticommunist Afghan guerrillas (mujahideen), many of them wedded to fundamentalist Islamic principles, proved as intransigent toward the Babrak government as they had been to Amin's. The coup marked the beginning of a lengthy stalemated war in which more than 15,000 Soviet troops and almost one million Afghans died in a guerrilla conflict often compared, in its effect upon the Soviet Union, to the entanglement of the United States in Vietnam in the 1960s and 1970s.

Soviet Intervention in Afghanistan
Personal memorandum from Andropov to Brezhnev
December 1979

1. After the coup and the murder of Taraki in September of this year, the situation in Afghanistan began to undertake an undesirable turn for us. The situation in the party, the army and the government apparatus has become more acute, as they were essentially destroyed as a result of the mass repressions carried out by Amin. At the same time, alarming information started to arrive about Amin's secret activities, forewarning of a possible political shift to the West. [These included:] Contacts with an American agent about issues which are kept secret from us. Promises to tribal leaders to shift away from USSR and to adopt a "policy of neutrality." Closed meetings in which attacks were made against Soviet policy and the activities of our specialists. The practical removal of our headquarters in Kabul, etc. The diplomatic circles in Kabul are widely talking of Amin's differences with Moscow and his possible anti-Soviet steps.

All this has created, on the one hand, the danger of losing the gains made by the April [1978] revolution (the scale of insurgent attacks will increase by spring) within the country, while on the other hand—the threat to our positions in Afghanistan (right now there is no guarantee that Amin, in order to protect his personal power, will not shift to the West), [There has been] a growth of anti-Soviet sentiments within the population.

2. Recently we were contacted by group of Afghan communists abroad. In the course of our contact with Babrak [Karmal] and [Asadullah] Sarwari, it became clear (and they informed us of this) that they have worked out a plan for opposing Amin and creating new party and state organs. But Amin, as a preventive measure, has begun mass arrests of 'suspect persons' (300 people have been shot).

In these conditions, Babrak and Sarwari, without changing their plans of opposition, have raised the question of possible assistance, in case of need, including military. We have two battalions stationed in Kabul and there is the capability of rendering such assistance. It appears that this is entirely sufficient for a successful operation. But, as a precautionary measure in the event of unforeseen complications, it would be wise to have a military group close to the border. In case of the deployment of military forces we could at the same time decide various questions pertaining to the liquidation of gangs.

The implementation of the given operation would allow us to decide the question of defending the gains of the April revolution, establishing Leninist principles in the party and state leadership of Afghanistan, and securing our positions in this country.

Source: "Personal Memorandum Andropov to Brezhnev, 12/01/1979, APRF, from notes taken by A. F. Dobrynin and provided to Norwegian Nobel Institute." Published in translation in Cold War International History Project Virtual Archive. http://cwihp.org.

Civil Defense Instructions for Home Fallout Shelters (1980)

During the Cold War, the U.S. government devoted enormous energy to preparations designed to enable Americans to survive a nuclear war. Top federal government officials were expected to take refuge in huge shelters hollowed out in the Catoctin Mountains near Washington, D.C. Businesses, government agencies, and other organizations were encouraged to include nuclear shelters when constructing new buildings or to adapt existing structures to include them. The Federal Emergency Management Agency (FEMA) also urged individual families to add their own personal fallout shelters to their homes. To assist in such undertakings, FEMA published a range of pamphlets giving detailed plans for a variety of shelters designed to suit every family's and house's particular circumstances. The majority were intended to take advantage of existing basements: individuals could choose between two models of Modified Ceiling Shelter, the Concrete Block Shelter, the Tilt-Up Storage Unit Shelter, and the Lean-To Shelter. Families without a basement were not forgotten. They could opt for the aboveground home shelter, which could double "as a tool shed or workshop," or the outside concrete shelter, whose "roof . . . can be used as an attractive patio." Each pamphlet was an illustrated manual giving detailed plans for the appropriate shelter's construction, listing the materials that would be needed, describing the topographical situations that a particular shelter was most advantageously designed to meet, and even mentioning suppliers of suitable ventilators and plumbing. Further manuals gave advice as to what supplies should be stored in a given shelter for particular family sizes. The home shelter program was intended to allay public fears and convince Americans that nuclear war was survivable but may well have simply contributed to a lurking sense of Cold War insecurity and vulnerability.

Aboveground Home Shelter
General information

This family shelter is intended for persons who prefer an aboveground shelter or, for some reason such as a high water table, cannot have a belowground shelter. In general, belowground shelter is superior and more economical than an aboveground shelter.

The shelter is designed to meet the standard of protection against fallout radiation that has been established by the Federal Emergency Management Agency for public fallout shelters. It can also be constructed to provide significant protection from the blast and fire effects of a nuclear explosion. It has sufficient space to shelter six adults.

The shelter can be built of two rows of concrete blocks, one 12″ and one 8″, filled with sand or grout, or of poured reinforced concrete. Windows have been omitted; therefore, electric lights are recommended for day to day use.

The details and construction methods are considered typical. If materials other than shown are selected—for example, concrete block faced with brick—care should be taken to provide at least the same weight of materials per square foot: 200 lb. per sq. ft. in the walls and 100 lb. per sq. ft. in the roof. The wood frame roof over the reinforced concrete ceiling probably would be blown off by extremely high winds such as caused by a blast wave or tornado. However the wood frame roof is intended primarily for appearance; the concrete ceiling provides the protection. When using the shelter for protection against high winds, DO NOT place the concrete blocks in the doorway or windows.

This structure has been designed for areas where frost does not penetrate the ground more than 20 inches. If 20 inches is not a sufficient depth for footings, one or two additional courses of concrete blocks may be used to lower the footings. Average soil bearing pressure is 1,500 lb. per sq. ft. Most soils can be assumed to support this pressure without special testing or investigation.

The baffle wall outside the entrance to the shelter is extended out 7´4˝ to allow storage of lawn equipment such as wheel-barrows and lawn mowers. If additional space is desired, extend this dimension.

Before starting to build the shelter, make certain that the plan conforms to the local building code. Obtain a building permit if required. If the shelter is to be built by a contractor, engage a reliable firm that offers protection from liability or other claims arising from its construction.

FIRST ALTERNATIVE indicates windows in the workshop area. Solid blocks, equal to a thickness of 12 inches, should be available to fill these openings to provide adequate fallout protection. Window sizes should be kept small. When using the shelter for protection against high winds, do not place the concrete blocks in the doorway or windows.

SECOND ALTERNATIVE shows the cement block faced with bricks. Use one course 4-inch brick and two courses of 8-inch cement block to obtain the required weight per unit area.

THIRD ALTERNATIVE is to attach the tool shed or workshop to the house, with a covered area between. In this case, the facing materials should match the house.

FOURTH ALTERNATIVE is to install built-up roofing of asphalt or tar, or other wearing surface, on top of the concrete deck.

Source: Federal Emergency Management Agency, Aboveground Home Shelter, Pamphlet H-12–2 (Washington, DC: U.S. Government Printing Office, 1980).

U.S. Government: Disappearances and Human Rights, Three Document Excerpts (1980–1996)

In 1979 a U.S. congressional committee took up the issue of postwar disappearances into the Soviet Union. The most prominent of these was the disappearance of Swedish diplomat Raoul Wallenberg while in Soviet hands. In 1944 Wallenberg—acting on the request of the American War Refugee Board—had risked his life to rescue thousands of Hungarian Jews from the Nazis. He was apparently abducted and taken from Hungary by the Soviets in 1945 and his fate remains unknown despite continuing efforts by the Swedish government and human rights advocates. Soviet authorities first denied knowledge of Wallenberg's fate, but then claimed that he died in a Soviet prison in 1947. Following reports by former prisoners that they had seen Wallenberg alive, in 1980 Congress passed a joint resolution (presented here) decrying Wallenberg's disappearance as a violation of human rights principles stated in the 1975 Helsinki Final Act. A number of Americans believe that the Soviets and their allies also retained more than 20,000 U.S. prisoners of war after World War II, the Korean War, and the Vietnam War and incarcerated them in the Soviet Union. In order to investigate these allegations, the United States and a post–Cold War Russia formed the Joint Commission on POW/MIAs in 1992. In addition, Congress established a Select Committee on POW/MIA Affairs. The following excerpts from the Senate's 1993 report and the Commission's 1996 report state that no evidence exists to back up the claim that the Soviets incarcerated thousands of American servicemen. However, investigations continued into several reports that appeared to have substance regarding postwar disappearances of American servicemen.

House Concurrent Resolution 404 (August 20, 1980)

Human Rights in Eastern Europe and the Soviet Union
Hearing and Markup before the Committee on Foreign Affairs and its Subcommittee on International Organizations.
House of Representatives, Ninety-Sixth Congress, Second Session on H. Con. Res. 434.
September 16 and 24, 1980.
U.S. Government Printing Office, Washington: 1980.

H. Con. Res. 404
Expressing the sense of the Congress that the President should convey to the Soviet Government the deep concern of the Congress and the American people for the fate of Raoul Wallenberg and that the United States delegation to the Madrid Conference on Security and Cooperation in Europe should urge consideration of the case of Raoul Wallenberg at that meeting by the signatories to the Helsinki Final Act.

In the House of Representatives
August 20, 1980
Mr. Dodd (for himself, Ms. Holtzman, Mr. Maguire, Mr. Wolfe, Mr. Lehman, Mr. Scheuer, Mr. Stark, Mr. Ford of Tennessee, Mr. Matsul, Mr. AuCoin, Mr. Bungham, Mr. Conyers, Mr. Ambro, Mr. Blanchard, Mr. Oberstar, Mr. Pepper, Mr. Drinan, Mr. Garcia, Mr. Roe, Mr. Beilenson, Mr. Portee, Mr. Fazio, Mr. Cleveland, Mr. Whitehurst, Mr. Corman, Mr. Rodino, Mr. Yates, Mr. Waxman, Mr. Edwards of California, Mr. Horton, Mr. Evans of the Virgin Islands, Ms. Mikulski, Mr. Ottinger, Mr. Richmond, Mr. Gray, and Mr. Dougherty), submitted the following concurrent resolution; which was referred to the Committee on Foreign Affairs.

Concurrent Resolution

Expressing the sense of the Congress that the President should convey to the Soviet Government the deep concern of the Congress and the American people for the fate of Raoul Wallenberg and that the United States delegation to the Madrid Conference on Security and Cooperation in Europe should urge consideration of the case of Raoul Wallenberg at that meeting by the signatories to the Helsinki Final Act.

Whereas in July 1944, at the request of the American War Refugee Board and the Swedish Government, Swedish Diplomat Raoul Wallenberg undertook a mission of mercy to Bedapest, Hungary, as a result of which thousands of Hungarian Jews were saved;

Whereas considerable evidence exists that Raoul Wallenberg was abducted by Soviet forces in Hungary in 1945, in violation of international standards of diplomatic immunity;

Whereas Soviet officials originally denied having custody of Wallenberg, but subsequently stated that a prisoner named "Walenberg" died in a Soviet prison in 1947;

Whereas reports from former Soviet prisoners indicate that Wallenberg may not have died in 1947 but may still be alive in a Soviet prison;

Whereas significance of Wallenberg's heroic and humanitarian actions has been obscured by the wall of silence that surrounds his fate;

Whereas the continued internment of Wallenberg, if indeed he is still alive, is in direct contravention of the Final Act of the Helsinki Conference on Security and Cooperation in Europe, which states: "The participating states will respect human rights and fundamental freedoms . . . and fulfill in good faith their obligations under international law. . ."; and

Whereas the purpose of the Madrid Conference on Security and Cooperation in Europe to be held in November, as stated at the Belgrade Conference held in 1978, is to "continue the multilateral process initiated by the CSCE" to review compliance with the Helsinki Final Act: Now, therefore, be it

1 Resolved by the House of Representatives (the Senate

2 concurring), That it is the sense of the Congress that the

3 President should express to the Soviet Government the deep

4 concern of the Congress and the American people for the fate

5 of Raoul Wallenberg, and should urge the Soviet Govern-

6 ment to cooperate fully in ascertaining his fate.

7 Sec. 2. It is further the sense of the Congress that the

8 United States delegation to the review meeting of the Con-

9 ference on Security and Cooperation in Europe which will be

10 held in Madrid in November 1980 should urge that the case

11 of Raoul Wallenberg be considered at that meeting by the

12 signatory countries to the Final Act of the Helsinki Confer-

13 ence on Security and Cooperation in Europe.

Source: House Concurrent Resolution 404 (August 20, 1980).

Excerpt: Senate Report 103–1, Report of the Select Committee on POW / MIA Affairs (January 13, 1993)

Senate Report 103-1

POW / MIA'S

REPORT

OF THE

SELECT COMMITTEE ON POW / MIA
AFFAIRS
UNITED STATES SENATE
January 13, 1993
EXECUTIVE SUMMARY
DEDICATION

To POWs

This report begins with three tributes, the first to those Americans who have been imprisoned in any war. Each person who has worn the uniform and fought the battle understands the nature of sacrifice. And there is a sense in which anyone caught in a firefight, flying through flak, patrolling the jungle while sensing ambush or working desperately to perform triage in a makeshift hospital, is a prisoner of war. But we owe a special debt of respect and gratitude to those who were captured and yet still kept faith, even while deprived of their freedom, victimized by brutal tortures, and forced to battle not only their captors, but the temptation to yield to self-pity and despair.

In the words of former POW, Admiral James Stockdale:

Young Americans in Hanoi learned fast. They made no deals. (In the end) the prisoner learns he can't be hurt and he can't be had as long as he tells the truth and clings to that forgiving hand of the brothers who are becoming his country, his family . . .

What does it all come down to? It does not come down to coping or supplication or hatred or strength beyond the grasp of any normal person. It comes down to comradeship, and it comes down to pride, dignity, an enduring sense of self-worth and to that enigmatic mixture of conscience and egoism called personal honor.[1]

To the families

America's POWs and servicemen have met the test of personal honor, and so have the families of those still missing from past American wars. For these families, the wounds of conflict have been especially slow to heal. For them, there have been no joyous reunions, nor even the solace of certainty ratified by a flagdraped casket and the solemn sound of taps. There has been no grave to visit and often no peace from gnawing doubt. For them, there has been only the search for answers through years when they did not have active and visible support from their own government to the present day when our ability to get real answers has finally been enhanced. Their search for answers is truly understandable because to them, POW/MIA is not merely an issue or a symbolic figure on a black and white flag, it is a brother, a husband, a father or a son. These families, too, deserve our nation's gratitude and to them, as to their loved ones, we pay tribute.

To those who remembered

We salute, as well, the veterans and responsible activist groups who have never stopped pushing for answers. These are the people who fought against the forgetting; who persisted in their questioning; and whose concerns led directly to the creation of the Select Committee. The Committee's investigation has validated their efforts, for they had good reason to argue that the full story was not being told, to suggest that there was more to learn and to insist that a renewed focus on the issue would produce greater pressure and yield new results.

It is to these Americans, therefore, to the POWs who returned and to all those who did not, to the families and veterans who kept the memory alive, that we pay tribute, and to whom we have dedicated the work of this Committee, including this final report.

The Committee's Purpose

The most basic principle of personal honor in America's armed forces is never willingly to leave a fellow serviceman behind. The black granite wall on the Mall in Washington is filled with the names of those who died in the effort to save their comrades in arms. That bond of loyalty and obligation which spurred so many soldiers to sacrifice themselves is mirrored by the obligation owed to every soldier by our nation, in whose name those sacrifices were made.

Amidst the uncertainties of war, every soldier is entitled to one certainty—that he will not be forgotten. As former POW Eugene "Red" McDaniel put it, as an American asked to serve:

> I was prepared to fight, to be wounded, to be captured, and even prepared to die, but I was not prepared to be abandoned.

The Senate Select Committee on POW/MIA Affairs was created to ensure that our nation meets its obligation to the missing and to the families of those still listed as unaccounted for from the war in Southeast Asia or prior conflicts. As past years have shown, that obligation cannot fully be paid with sympathy, monuments, medals, benefits or flags. It is an obligation—a solemn duty—that can be met only with the best and most complete answers that are within our power to provide.

Tragically, and for reasons found both at home and abroad, those answers have been slow in coming. Our nation has been haunted by the possibility that some of the missing may have survived and that, somewhere in Southeast Asia, brave men remain in captivity.

Although we know that the circumstances of war make it impossible for us to learn what happened to all the missing, we have been haunted, as well, by our knowledge that there are some answers from Southeast Asia we could have had long ago, but have been denied. Because our wartime adversaries in Vietnam and Laos have been so slow to provide the answers, the American people turned to the U.S. Government for help, but events over the past 20 years have undermined the public's trust. The Indochina war, itself, was partly a secret war and records were falsified at the time to maintain that secrecy. The Paris Peace Accords promised answers to POW/MIA families, but the war between North and South Vietnam did not stop, and for the families of many, the answers did not come. Ever-changing Defense Department policies confused families and others about the official status of the missing and obscured even the number of men who might possibly have remained alive. The official penchant for secrecy left many families, activists and even Members of Congress unable to share fully in their own government's knowledge about the fate of fellow citizens and loved ones and this, more than anything, contributed to the atmosphere of suspicion and doubt.

Underpinning all this, the POW/MIA issue is alive today because of a fundamental conflict between the laws of probability and the dictates of human nature. On a subject as personal and emotional as the survival of a family member, there is nothing more difficult than to be asked to accept the probability of death when the possibility of life remains. Since Operation Homecoming, the U.S. Government has sought to avoid raising the hopes of POW/ MIA families; it has talked about the need to maintain perspective and about the lack of convincing evidence that Americans remain alive. But

U.S. officials cannot produce evidence that all of the missing are dead; and because they have been so careful not to raise false hopes, they have left themselves open to the charge that they have given up hope. This, too, has contributed to public and family mistrust.

Many of the factors that led to controversy surrounding the fates of Vietnam-era POW/MIAs are present, as well, with respect to the missing from World War II, Korea and the Cold War. Here, too, there have been barriers to gaining information from foreign governments; excessive secrecy on the part of our own government; and provocative reports—official and unofficial—about what might have happened to those left behind.

The Select Committee was created because of the need to reestablish trust between our government and our people on this most painful and emotional of issues. It was created to investigate and tell publicly the complete story about what our government knows and has known, and what it is doing and has done on behalf of our POW/MIAs. It was created to examine the possibility that unaccounted for Americans might have survived in captivity after POW repatriations at Odessa in World War II, after Operation Big Switch in Korea in 1953, after Cold War incidents, and particularly after Operation Homecoming in Vietnam in 1973. It was created to ensure that accounting for missing Americans will be a matter of highest national priority, not only in word but in practice. It was created to encourage real cooperation from foreign governments. It was created, in short, to pursue the truth, at home and overseas.

Whether the Committee has succeeded in its assigned tasks will be a matter for the public and for history to judge. Clearly, we cannot claim, nor could we have hoped, to have learned everything. We had neither the authority nor the resources to make case

by case determinations with respect to the status of the missing. The job of negotiating, conducting interviews, visiting prisons, excavating crash sites, investigating live-sighting reports and evaluating archival materials can only be completed by the Executive branch. This job, long frustrated by the intransigence of foreign governments, will take time to complete notwithstanding the recent improvements in cooperation, especially from Vietnam. The Committee takes considerable pride, however, in its contribution, through oversight, to improvements in the accountability process, and in the record of information and accomplishment it leaves behind.

That record includes the most rapid and extensive declassification of public files and documents on a single issue in American history. It includes a set of hearings and Committee files in which virtually every part of the POW/MIA controversy has been examined. It includes disclosure after disclosure about aspects of U.S. policy and actions that have never before been made public. It includes a rigorous, public examination of relevant U.S. intelligence information. It includes an exposure of the activities of some private groups who have sought inexcusably to exploit the anguish of POW/MIA families for their own gain. It includes a contribution to changed policies that is reflected on the ground in Vietnam in the form of unprecedented access to prisons, military bases, government buildings, documents, photographs, archives and material objects that bear on the fate of our missing servicemen. And it includes encouraging the Executive branch to establish a process of live-sighting response, investigation and evaluation that is more extensive and professional than ever before.

How then, one might ask, does this issue get brought to a close? There is no simple answer to that question. Clearly, the desire for closure cannot override the obligation to pursue promising leads. Just as clearly, our future expectations must be confined within the borders of what the chaotic circumstances of war, the passage of time, the evidence of survival and the logic of human motivation allow.

We want to make clear that this report is not intended to close the door on this issue. It is meant to open it. We knew at the outset that we could never answer all the questions that exist. In fact, some questions may never be answered or are more properly answered by other branches of government.

What we set out to accomplish, however, was to guarantee that the doors and windows of government were opened so that Americans would know where to go for information, so that the information would, to the greatest degree possible, be available, so that an unparalleled record would exist on which to base judgments, and so that a process of accountability would be in place to provide answers over time. We have accomplished our goal.

The Committee believes that a process is now in place that, over time, will provide additional answers. Americans can have confidence that our current efforts can ultimately resolve this painful issue. As this Committee's investigation of World War II and Korea shows, new information can come unexpectedly, years after the fact. That is why our goal must not be to put the issue to rest, but to press the search for answers and, in this case, to go to the source for those answers in Southeast Asia and elsewhere.

We must build on recent progress to guarantee that we reach the limits of what is knowable through an accounting process that is professional, open, genuine and unrestricted. We must constantly measure whether the promises and commitments of foreign governments are being fulfilled. We must maintain the momentum that has built at the highest levels within our own country to continue the search for new information. And we must ensure that as long as there is good reason to hope for more answers, our national obligation to pursue those answers continues, as a matter of honor, and as a duty to all those who have or who someday will put their lives at risk in service to our country.

The Committee's Methods and Approach

The POW/MIA issue has proven almost as emotional and controversial as the Vietnam War itself. As mentioned above, vigorous disagreements have caused some to be accused of conspiracy and betrayal; and others to be accused of allowing their hopes to obscure their reason. The Committee has sought to transform this troubled atmosphere by encouraging all participants in the debate to join forces in an objective search for the truth.

Because the overriding hope and objective of the Committee was to identify information that would lead to the rescue or release of one or more live U.S. POWs, the Committee gave first priority to investigation of issues related to our most recent war, the conflict in Vietnam. Nevertheless, substantial resources were devoted to seeking and reviewing information concerning Americans missing from World War II, the Korean War and the Cold War.

To ensure credibility, the Committee has operated on a nonpartisan basis, with a nonpartisan staff, directed by Members equally divided between the two parties.

To ensure perspective, the Committee sought the guidance of family members, activists, veterans' organizations and many others about how to conduct the investigation, where to focus, whom to consult and what issues to address. Every single individual or group that has claimed to have information on the issue has been invited—and in a few cases repeatedly invited—to provide it. Former U.S. POWs from the Indochina War were contacted and asked to share their knowledge and all previous inquiries and investigations on the subject were reviewed.

To ensure thoroughness, the Committee requested, and received, access to the records of a wide range of U.S. Government agencies, including intelligence agencies and the White House. Unlike previous investigators, we refused to accept "national security" as grounds for denying information and obtained assurances from the highest levels of government that no relevant information would be withheld.[2] We traveled overseas to Moscow, Pyongyang, and several times to Southeast Asia for face to face talks with foreign officials and gained access to long-secret archives and facilities in Russia, Vietnam and North Korea. And we solicited the sworn testimonies of virtually every living U.S. military and civilian official or former official who has played a major role in POW/MIA affairs over the past 20 years.

To ensure openness, the Committee's hearings were held almost entirely in public session. Among these were first-ever public hearings on POW-related signal and photographic intelligence and thorough discussions of live-sighting reports. Also, the Committee has worked with the Executive branch to declassify and make public more than one million pages of Committee, Defense Department, State Department, intelligence community and White House documents, including Committee depositions, related to POW/MIA matters. The Committee believes that this process must—and will—continue until all relevant documents are declassified.[3]

We believe that the Select Committee's hearing and investigatory process provide grounds for pride on the part of every American. The Committee's very existence was a testament to the effectiveness of public action. And although offensive to a few and painful to some, the rigorous examination of current and former high government officials and some private citizens on a matter of public interest is what democratic accountability is all about. Members of the Committee asked difficult and probing questions in order to ensure the fullest possible exploration of the issue. And, indeed, the Committee's own work has been subject to rigorous public questioning and that, too, has been healthy and appropriate.

Summary of Findings and Recommendations
Americans "last known alive" in Southeast Asia

Information available to our negotiators and government officials responsible for the repatriation of prisoners indicated that a group of approximately 100 American civilians and servicemen expected to return at Operation Homecoming did not.[4] Some of these men were known to have been taken captive; some were known only to have survived their incidents; others were thought likely to have survived. The White House expected that these individuals would be accounted for by our adversaries, either as alive or dead, when the war came to an end. Because they were not accounted for then, despite our protests, nor in the period immediately following when the trail was freshest and the evidence strongest, twenty years of agony over this issue began. This was the moment when the POW/MIA controversy was born.

The failure of our Vietnam war adversaries to account for these "last known alive"

Americans meant that families who had had good reason to expect the return of their loved ones instead had cause for renewed grief. Amidst their sorrow, the nation hailed the war's end; the President said that all our POWs are "on the way home";[5] and the Defense Department, following standard procedures, began declaring missing men dead. Still, the governments in Southeast Asia did not cooperate, and the answers that these families deserved did not come. In 1976, the Montgomery Committee concluded that because there was no evidence that missing Americans had survived, they must be dead.[6] In 1977, a Defense Department official said that the distinction between Americans still listed as "POW" and those listed as "missing" had become "academic".[7] Nixon, Ford and Carter Administration officials all dismissed the possibility that American POWs had survived in Southeast Asia after Operation Homecoming.[8]

This Committee has uncovered evidence that precludes it from taking the same view. We acknowledge that there is no proof that U.S. POWs survived, but neither is there proof that all of those who did not return had died. There is evidence, moreover, that indicates the possibility of survival, at least for a small number, after Operation Homecoming:

First, there are the Americans known or thought possibly to have been alive in captivity who did not come back; we cannot dismiss the chance that some of these known prisoners remained captive past Operation Homecoming.

Second, leaders of the Pathet Lao claimed throughout the war that they were holding American prisoners in Laos. Those claims were believed—and, up to a point, validated—at the time; they cannot be dismissed summarily today.

Third, U.S. defense and intelligence officials hoped that forty or forty-one prisoners captured in Laos would be released at Operation Homecoming, instead of the twelve who were actually repatriated. These reports were taken seriously enough at the time to prompt recommendations by some officials for military action aimed at gaining the release of the additional prisoners thought to be held.

Fourth, information collected by U.S. intelligence agencies during the last 19 years, in the form of live-sighting, hearsay, and other intelligence reports, raises questions about the possibility that a small number of unidentified U.S. POWs who did not return may have survived in captivity.

Finally, even after Operation Homecoming and returnee debriefs, more than 70 Americans were officially listed as POWs based on information gathered prior to the signing of the peace agreement; while the remains of many of these Americans have been repatriated, the fates of some continue unknown to this day.

Given the Committee's findings, the question arises as to whether it is fair to say that American POWs were knowingly abandoned in Southeast Asia after the war. The answer to that question is clearly no. American officials did not have certain knowledge that any specific prisoner or prisoners were being left behind. But there remains the troubling question of whether the Americans who were expected to return but did not were, as a group, shunted aside and discounted by government and population alike. The answer to that question is essentially yes.

Inevitably the question wfll be asked: who is responsible for that? The answer goes beyond any one agency, Administration or faction. By the time the peace agreement was signed, a decade of division, demonstrations and debate had left our entire nation weary of killing and tired of involvement in an inconclusive and morally complex war. The psychology of the times, from rural kitchens to the Halls of Congress to the Oval Office, was to move on; to put the war out of mind; and to focus again on other things. The President said, and our nation wanted to believe, that all of our American POWs were on the way home.[9] Watergate loomed; other crises seized our attention. Amidst it all, the question of POW/MIA accountability faded. In a sense, it, too, became a casualty of war.

The record does indicate that efforts to gain accountability were made. Dr. Henry Kissinger personally raised the issue and lodged protests with Le Duc Tho and leaders of the Pathet Lao. Defense and State Department spokesmen told Congress of their continuing dissatisfaction with the accounting process; stressed their view that the POW/MIA lists received were not complete, and referred to the cases of Americans last known alive as the "most agonizing and frustrating of all."[10]

However, compared to the high-level, high-visibility protests about prisoners made public during the war, post-Homecoming Administration efforts and efforts to inform the American public were primarily low-level and low-key.

Before the peace agreement was signed, those "last known alive," were referred to as "POWs;" afterward, they were publicly, although not technically, lumped together with all of the others called "missing."

Before the agreement, Secretary of Defense Melvin Laird and other Administration officials had berated the North Vietnamese for their failure to disclose the status of these "last known alive" cases, while citing

their dramatic case histories and distributing photographs to the press. After Homecoming, Administration criticisms were less vociferous and names and case histories cited only rarely and, even then, not publicly by cabinet officials, but by their assistants and their assistants' assistants."[11]

When the war shut down, so, too, did much of the POW/MIA related intelligence operations. Bureaucratic priorities shifted rapidly and, before long, the POW/MIA accounting operation had become more of a bureaucratic backwater than an operations center for matters of life and death.

From the fall of Saigon in 1975 through the early 1980's, efforts to gain answers from the Government of Vietnam and the other communist governments of Southeast Asia bore little fruit. In 1982, President Reagan wisely raised the issue of accounting for our missing to a "matter of highest national priority." In 1987, a Special Presidential Emissary to Vietnam was named and serious discussions resumed. More recently, the disintegration of the Soviet empire has opened new doors and created compelling new incentives for foreign cooperation—almost 20 years after the last American soldier was withdrawn. Today, the U.S. spends at least $100 million each year on POW/MIA efforts.

Still, the families wait for answers and, still, the question haunts, is there anyone left alive? The search for a definitive answer to that question prompted the creation of this Committee.

As much as we would hope that no American has had to endure twenty years of captivity, if one or more were in fact doing so, there is nothing the Members of the Committee would have liked more than to be able to prove this fact. We would have recommended the use of all available resources to respond to such evidence if it had been found, for nothing would have been more rewarding than to have been able to re-unite a long-captive American with family and country.

Unfortunately, our hopes have not been realized. This disappointment does not reflect a failure of the investigation, but rather a confrontation with reality. While the Committee has some evidence suggesting the possibility a POW may have survived to the present, and while some information remains yet to be investigated, there is, at this time, no compelling evidence that proves that any American remains alive in captivity in Southeast Asia.

The Committee cannot prove a negative, nor have we entirely given up hope that one or more U.S. POWs may have survived. As mentioned above, some reports remain to be investigated and new information could be forthcoming. But neither live-sighting reports nor other sources of intelligence have provided grounds for encouragement,[12] particularly over the past decade. The live-sighting reports that have been resolved have not checked out; alleged pictures of POWs have proven false; purported leads have come up empty; and photographic intelligence has been inconclusive, at best.

In addition to the lack of compelling evidence proving that Americans are alive, the majority of Committee Members believes there is also the question of motive. These Members assert that it is one thing to believe that the Pathet Lao or North Vietnamese might have seen reason to hold back American prisoners in 1973 or for a short period thereafter; it is quite another to discern a motive for holding prisoners alive in captivity for another 19 years. The Vietnamese and Lao have been given a multitude of opportunities to demand money in exchange for the prisoners some allege they hold but our investigation has uncovered no credible evidence that they have ever done so.

Yes, it is possible even as these countries become more and more open that a prisoner or prisoners could be held deep within a jungle or behind some locked door under conditions of the greatest security. That possibility argues for a live-sighting followup capability that is alert, aggressive and predicated on the assumption that a U.S. prisoner or prisoners continue to be held. But, sadly, the Committee cannot provide compelling evidence to support that possibility today.

Finally, there is the question of numbers. Part of the pain caused by this issue has resulted from rumors about hundreds or thousands of Americans languishing in camps or bamboo cages. The circumstances surrounding the losses of missing Americans render these reports arithmetically impossible. In order for Americans to judge for themselves, we will append to this report a summary of the facts surrounding each known discrepancy case.[13]

An analysis of these incidents will show that:

Only in a few cases did the U.S. Government know for certain that someone was captured;

In many of the cases, there is only an indication of the potential of capture; and

In a large number of the cases, there is a strong indication that the individual was killed.

The Committee emphasizes that simply because someone was listed as missing in action does not mean that there was any evidence, such as a radio contact, an open parachute or a sighting on the ground, of survival. We may make a presumption that an individual could have survived, and that is the right basis upon which to operate. But a presumption is very different from knowledge or fact, and cannot lead us—in the absence of evidence—to conclude that someone is alive. Even some of the cases about which we know the most and which show the strongest indication that someone was a prisoner of war leave us with certain doubts as to what the circumstances were. The bottom line is that there remain only a few cases where we know an unreturned POW was alive in captivity and we do not have evidence that the individual also died while in captivity.

There is at least one aspect of the POW/MIA controversy that should be laid to rest conclusively with this investigation and that is the issue of conspiracy. Allegations have been made in the past that our government has had a "mindset to debunk" reports that American prisoners have been sighted in Southeast Asia. Our Committee found reason to take those allegations seriously. But we also found in some quarters a "mindset to accuse" that has given birth to vast and implausible theories of conspiracy and conscious betrayal. Those theories are without foundation.

Yes, there have been failures of policy, priority and process. Over the years, until this investigation, the Executive branch's penchant for secrecy and classification contributed greatly to perceptions of conspiracy. In retrospect, a more open Policy would have been better. But America's government too closely reflects America's people to have permitted the knowing and willful abandonment of U.S. POWs and a subsequent coverup spanning almost 20 years and involving literally thousands of people.

The POW/MIA issue is too important and too personal for us to allow it to be driven by theory; it must be driven by fact. Witness after witness was asked by our Committee if they believed in, or had evidence of, a conspiracy either to leave POWs behind or to conceal knowledge of their fates—and

no evidence was produced. The isolated bits of information out of which some have constructed whole labyrinths of intrigue and deception have not withstood the tests of objective investigation; and the vast archives of secret U.S. documents that some felt contained incriminating evidence have been thoroughly examined by the Committee only to fmd that the conspiracy cupboard is bare.

The quest for the fullest possible accounting of our Vietnam-era POW/MIAs must continue, but if our efforts are to be effective and fair to families, they must go forward within the context of reality, not fiction.

Investigation of issues related to Paris Peace Accords

Most of the questions and controversies that still surround the POW/MIA issue can be traced back to the Paris Peace Accords and their immediate aftermath. If that agreement had been implemented in good faith by North Vietnam and with necessary cooperation from Cambodia and Laos, the fullest possible accounting of missing Americans would have been achieved long ago.

During negotiations, the American team, headed by Dr. Henry Kissinger, had sought an agreement that would provide explicitly for the release of American prisoners and an accounting for missing American servicemen throughout Indochina. The U.S. negotiators said, when the agreement was signed, that they had "unconditional guarantees" that these goals would be achieved.

The great accomplishment of the peace agreement was that it resulted in the release of 591 American POWs, of whom 566 were military and 25 civilian. It also established a framework for cooperation in resolving POW/MIA related questions that remains of value today. Unfortunately, efforts to implement the agreement failed, for a number of reasons, to resolve the POW/MIA issue.

Obstacles faced by U.S. negotiators

During its investigation, the Committee identified several factors that handicapped U.S. officials during the negotiation of the peace agreement, and during the critical first months of implementation.

The first and most obvious obstacle to a fully effective agreement was the approach taken to the POW/MIA issue by North Vietnam (DRV) and its allies. During the war, the DRV violated its obligations under the Geneva Convention by refusing to provide complete lists of prisoners, and by prohibiting or severely restricting the right of prisoners to exchange mail or receive visits from international humanitarian agencies.

During negotiations, the DRV insisted that the release of prisoners could not be completed prior to the withdrawal of all U.S. forces, and consistently linked cooperation on the POW/MIA issue to other issues, including a demand for reconstruction aid from the United States. Once the agreement was signed, the DRV was slow to provide a list of prisoners captured in Laos. Following Operation Homecoming, the North Vietnamese refused to cooperate in providing an accounting for missing Americans, including some who were known to have been held captive at one time within the DRV prison system. Perhaps most important of all, the DRV's continued pursuit of a military conquest of South Vietnam dissipated prospects for cooperation on POW/MIA issues.

A second factor inhibiting the achievement of U.S. objectives was the limited leverage enjoyed by U.S. negotiators. It was U.S. policy, fully known to the North Vietnamese, that the U.S. sought to disengage from the war. President Nixon was elected on a platform calling for an end to U.S. involvement; support was building rapidly within the Congress for measures that would have mandated a withdrawal conditioned on the return of prisoners; and the American public had become increasingly divided and war-weary as the conflict continued. These same factors, along with the debilitating effects of the Watergate scandal on the Nixon Presidency, weakened the U.S. hand in responding to DRV violations after the peace agreement was signed.

A third factor limiting the success of the agreement was the absence of Lao and Cambodian representatives from the peace table. Although the U.S..negotiators pressed the DRV for commitments concerning the release of prisoners and an accounting for the missing throughout Indochina, the peace accords technically apply only to Vietnam. Although the DRV, in a side understanding, assured Dr. Kissinger that it would cooperate in obtaining the release of U.S. prisoners in Laos, the fact is that the prisoners captured in Laos who were actually released had long since been transferred to Hanoi. No Americans held captive in Laos for a significant period of time have ever been returned. Neither the peace agreement, nor the assurances provided by North Vietnam to Dr. Kissinger, established procedures to account for missing Americans in Cambodia or Laos.

American protests

The Paris Peace Accords provided for the exchange of prisoner lists on the day the agreement was signed and for the return of all prisoners of war within 60 days. It also required the parties to assist each other in obtaining information about those missing in action and to determine the location of graves for the purpose of recovering and repatriating remains.

U.S. officials, especially in the Department of Defense, were disappointed that more live American prisoners were not included on the lists exchanged when the peace agreement was signed or—with respect to prisoners captured in Laos—four days after the agreement was signed. The record uncovered by the Committee's investigation indicates that high level Defense Department and Defense Intelligence Agency officials were especially concerned about the incompleteness of the list of prisoners captured in Laos.

This concern was based on intelligence that some Americans had been held captive by the Pathet Lao, on repeated Pathet Lao claims that prisoners were being held, and on the large number of American pilots who were listed as missing in action in Laos compared to the number being proposed for return. Top military and intelligence officials expressed the hope, at the time the peace agreement was signed, that as many as 41 servicemen lost in Laos would be returned. However, only ten men (7 U.S. military, 2 U.S. civilian and a Canadian) were on the list of prisoners captured in Laos that was turned over by the DRV.

During the first 60 days, while the American troop withdrawal was underway, the Nixon Administration contacted North Vietnamese officials repeatedly to express concern about the incomplete nature of the prisoner lists that had been received. In early February, President Nixon sent a message to the DRV Prime Minister saying, with respect to the list of only ten POWs from Laos, that:

> U.S. records show there are 317 American military men unaccounted for in Laos and it is inconceivable that only ten of these men would be held prisoner in Laos.[14]

Soon thereafter, Dr. Kissinger presented DRV officials with 19 case folders of Americans who should have been accounted for, but who were not. The U.S. protests continued[15] and in mid-March, the U.S. threatened briefly to halt the withdrawal of American troops if information about the nine American prisoners on the DRV/Laos list and about prisoners actually held by the Pathet Lao were not provided.[16] By the end of the month, top Defense Department officials were recommending a series of diplomatic and military options aimed at achieving an accounting for U.S. prisoners thought to be held in Laos.

Ultimately, the Nixon Administration proceeded with the withdrawal of troops in return for the release of prisoners on the lists provided by the North Vietnamese and Viet Cong.

Post-homecoming

The public statements made by President Nixon and by high Defense Department officials following the end of Operation Homecoming did not fully reflect the Administration's prior concern that live U.S. prisoners may have been kept behind. Administration officials did, however, continue to stress publicly the need for Vietnam to meet its obligations under the peace agreement, and U.S. diplomats pressed both the North Vietnamese and the Pathet Lao for information concerning missing Americans. Unfortunately, due to the intransigence of our adversaries, those efforts were largely unavailing.

During the Committee's hearings, it was contended by Dr. Kissinger and some Members of the Committee that Congressional attitudes would have precluded any Administration effort to respond forcefully to the DRV's failure to provide an accounting for missing American servicemen. These Members of the Committee contend that their view is supported by the Senate's rejection on May 31, 1973 of an amendment offered by U.S. Sen. Robert Dole that would have permitted the continued bombing of Laos and Cambodia if the President certified that North Vietnam "is not making an accounting, to the best of its ability, of all missing in action personnel in Southeast Asia.[17]

Conclusions

The Committee believes that its investigation contributed significantly to the public record of the negotiating history of the POW/MIA provisions of the Paris Peace Accords, and of the complications that arose during efforts to implement those provisions both before and after the completion of Operation Homecoming. That record indicates that there existed a higher degree of concern within the Administration about the possibility that prisoners were being left behind in Laos than had been known previously, and that various options for responding to that concern were discussed at the highest levels of government.

The Committee notes that some Administration statements at the time the agreement was signed expressed greater certainty about the completeness of the POW return than they should have and that other statements may have understated the problems that would arise during implementation and that—taken together, these statements may have raised public and family expectations too high. The Committee further notes that statements made after the agreement was signed may have understated U.S. concerns about the possibility that live prisoners remained, thereby contributing in subsequent years to public suspicion and distrust. However, the Committee concludes that the phrasing of these statements was designed to avoid raising what were believed to be false hopes among POW/MIA families, rather than to mislead the American people.

Investigation of the accounting process

The Committee investigation included a comprehensive review of the procedures used by the U.S. Government to account for American prisoners and missing from the beginning of the war in Southeast Asia until the present day. The purposes were:

To determine accurately the number of Americans who served in Southeast Asia during the war who did not return, either alive or dead;

To evaluate the accuracy of the U.S. Government's own past and current process for determining the likely status and fate of missing Americans;

To learn what the casualty data and intelligence information have to tell us about the number of Americans whose fates are truly "unaccounted for" from the war in Vietnam; and

To consider whether efforts to obtain the fullest possible accounting of our POW/MIAs was treated, as claimed, as a matter of "highest national priority" by the Executive branch;

To assess the extent to which Defense Department and DIA accounting policies and practices contributed to the confusion, suspicion and distrust that has characterized the POW/MIA issue for the past 20 years; and

To determine what changes need to be made to policies and procedures in order to instill public confidence in the government's POW/MIA accounting process with respect to past and future conflicts.

Although 2,264 Americans currently are listed as "unaccounted for" from the war in Indochina, the number of Americans whose fate is truly unknown is far smaller. Even during the war, the U.S. Government knew and the families involved knew that, in many of these cases, there was certainty that the soldier or airman was killed at the time of the incident. These are generally cases involving individuals who were killed when their airplanes crashed into the sea and no parachutes were sighted, or where others witnessed the death of a serviceman in combat but were unable to recover the body.

Of the 2,264 Americans now listed as unaccounted for, 1,095 fall into this category. These individuals were listed as "killed in action/body not recovered" (KIA/BNR) and were not included on the lists of POW/MIAs that were released publicly by the Defense and State Departments during the war or for several years thereafter. It was not until the late 1970's that KIA/BNRs were added to the official lists of "missing" Americans.

The next largest group of Americans now on the list of 2,264 originally was listed by the military services or by DIA as "missing in action." These are individuals who became missing either in combat or in noncombat circumstances, but who were not known for certain either to have been killed or to have been taken into captivity. In most, but not all, of these cases, the circumstances of disappearance coupled with the lack of evidence of survival make it highly probable that the individual died at the time the incident occurred.

Approximately 1,172 of the still unaccounted for Americans were originally listed either as MIA or as POW. Of these, 333 were lost in Laos, 348 in North Vietnam, 450 in South Vietnam, 37 in Cambodia and 4 in China. Since before the war ended, the POW/MIA accounting effort has focused, for good reason, on a relatively small number of these 1,172 Americans, that is, those who were either known to have been taken captive, or who were lost in circumstances under which survival was deemed likely or at least reasonably possible. These cases, in addition to others in which intelligence indicates a Southeast Asian Government may have known the fate of the missing men, are currently referred to as "discrepancy cases."

In 1987, Gen. John W. Vessey, Jr. (USA-Ret.) was appointed Presidential Emissary to Vietnam on POW/MIA matters. Gen. Vessey subsequently persuaded Vietnam to allow in-country investigations by the U.S. Government of high-priority discrepancy cases. The DIA and DOD's Joint Task Force-Full Accounting (JTF-FA) have identified a total of 305 discrepancy cases, of which 196 are in Vietnam, 90 are in Laos, and 19 are in Cambodia.[18]

In 61 of the cases in Vietnam, the fate of the individual has been determined through investigation, and the Committee finds that Gen. Vessey correctly states that the evidence JTF-FA has gathered in each of these cases indicates that the individuals had died prior to Operation Homecoming. The first round of investigation of the 135 remaining cases in Vietnam is expected to be completed by January 18, 1993. A second round of investigation, which will proceed geographically on a district by district basis, will commence in February, 1993.

None of the discrepancy cases in Laos and Cambodia has been resolved. Because many of the Americans lost in those countries disappeared in areas that were under the control of North Vietnamese forces at the time, resolution of the majority of Laos/Cambodia cases will depend on a process of tripartite cooperation that has barely begun. The Committee further finds that, in addition to the past reluctance of the Vietnamese and Lao to agree to a series of tripartite talks with the United States, both the Department of State and the Department of

Defense have been slow to push such a process forward.

As mentioned above, the Committee will append a case-by-case description of the circumstances of loss of each unresolved discrepancy case to this report. Those descriptions demonstrate that the U.S. Government has knowledge in only a small number of cases that the individuals involved were held captive and strong indications in only a small number more.

However, that is not to say that the Governments of Vietnam and Laos do not have knowledge pertaining to these or other MIA cases which may indicate survival. Answers to these troublesome questions will best be obtained through an accounting process that enjoys full cooperation from those governments.

The findings of this phase of the Committee's investigation include:

By far the greatest obstacle to a successful accounting effort over the past twenty years has been the refusal of the foreign governments involved, until recently, to allow the U.S. access to key files or to carry out in-country, on-site investigations.

The U.S. Government's process for accounting for Americans missing in Southeast Asia has been flawed by a lack of resources, organizational clarity, coordination and consistency. These problems had their roots during the war and worsened after the war as frustration about the ability to gain access and answers from Southeast Asian Governments increased. Through the mid-1980's, accounting for our POW/MIAs was viewed officially more as a bureaucratic exercise than as a matter of "highest national priority."

The accounting process has improved dramatically in recent years as a result of the high priority attached to it by Presidents Reagan and Bush; because of the success of Gen. Vessey and the JTF-FA in gaining permission for the U.S. to conduct investigations on the ground in Southeast Asia; because of an increase in resources; and because of the Committee's own efforts, in association with the Executive branch, to gain greater cooperation from the Governments of Vietnam, Laos and Cambodia.

After an exhaustive review of official and unofficial lists Of captive and missing Americans from wartime years to the present, the Committee uncovered numerous errors in data entry and numerous discrepancies between DIA records and those of other military offices. The errors that have been identified, however, have since been corrected. As a result, the Committee fmds no grounds to question the accuracy of the current, official list of those unaccounted for from the war in Southeast Asia. This list includes 2,222 missing servicemen except deserters and 42 missing civilians who were lost while performing services for the United States Government. The Committee has found no evidence to support the existence of rumored "secret lists" of additional missing Americans.

The decision by the U.S. Government to falsify "location of loss" data for American casualties in Cambodia and Laos during much of the war contributed significantly both to public distrust and to the difficulties experienced by the DIA and others in trying to establish what happened to the individuals involved.

The failure of the Executive branch to establish and maintain a consistent, sustainable set of categories and criteria governing the status of missing Americans during and after the war in

Southeast Asia contributed substantially to public confusion and mistrust. During the war, a number of individuals listed as "prisoner" by DIA were listed as "missing in action" by the military services.

After the war, the legal process for settling status determinations was plagued by interference from the Secretary of Defense, undermined by financial and other considerations affecting some POW/MIA families and challenged in court. Later, the question of how many Americans remain truly "unaccounted for" was muddied by the Defense Department's decision to include "KIA/BNR's"—those known to have been killed, but with bodies not recovered—in their listings. This created the anomalous situation of having more Americans considered unaccounted for today than we had immediately after the war.

The Committee's recommendations for this phase of its investigation include:

Accounting for missing Americans from the war in Southeast Asia should continue to be treated as a "matter of highest national priority" by our diplomats, by those participating in the accounting process, by all elements of our intelligence community and by the nation, as a whole.

Continued, best efforts should be made to investigate the remaining, unresolved discrepancy cases in Vietnam, Laos and Cambodia.

The United States should make a continuing effort, at a high level, to arrange regular tripartite meetings with the Governments of Laos and Vietnam to seek information on the possible control and movement of unaccounted for U.S. personnel by Pathet Lao and North Vietnamese forces in Laos during the Southeast Asia war.

The President and Secretary of Defense should order regular, independent reviews of the efficiency and professionalism of the DOD's POW/MIA accounting process for Americans still listed as missing from the war in Southeast Asia.

A clear hierarchy of responsibility for handling POW/MIA related issues that may regretably arise as a result of future conflicts must be established. This requires full and rapid coordination between and among the intelligence agencies involved and the military services. It requires the integration of missing civilians and suspected deserters into the overall accounting process. It requires a clear liaison between those responsible for the accounting (and related intelligence) and those responsible for negotiating with our adversaries about the terms for peace. It requires procedures for the full, honest and prompt disclosure of information to next of kin, at the time of incident and as other information becomes available. And it requires, above all, the designation within the Executive branch of an individual who is clearly responsible and fully accountable for making certain that the process works as it should.

In the future, clear categories should be established and consistently maintained in accounting for Americans missing during time of war. At one end of the listings should be Americans known with certainty to have been taken prisoner; at the other should be Americans known dead with bodies not recovered. The categories should be carefully separated in official summaries and discussions of the accounting process and should be applied consistently and uniformly.

Present law needs to be reviewed to minimize distortions in the status determination process that may result from the financial considerations of the families involved.

Wartime search and rescue (SAR) missions have an urgent operational value, but they are also crucial for the purposes of accounting for POW/MIAs. The records concerning many Vietnam era SAR missions have been lost or destroyed. In the future, all information obtained during any unsuccessful or partially successful military search and rescue mission should be shared with the agency responsible for accounting for POW/MIAs from that conflict and should be retained by that agency.

Investigation of POW/MIA-related intelligence activities

The Committee undertook an investigation of U.S. intelligence agency activities in relation to POW/MIA issues. This included a review of the DIA's primary role in investigating and evaluating reports that Americans missing from the Vietnam war were or are being held against their will since the end of the war in Southeast Asia. The investigation also included a review of signals intelligence (SIGINT) obtained by the National Security Agency (NSA), a review of imagery intelligence (IMINT) obtained by aerial photography and a review of covert U.S. Government activities associated with POW/MIA concerns.

In the area of intelligence, more than any other, the Committee and the Executive branch had to balance concerns about the public's right to know with a legitimate national need to maintain secrecy about intelligence sources and methods. The Committee insisted, however, that the fullest possible accounting of government activities in the intelligence field be made public and that no substantive information bearing directly on the question of whether there are live American POWs in Southeast Asia be withheld.

As a result of Executive branch cooperation, especially from CIA Director Robert Gates and National Security Adviser Brent Scowcroft, the Committee gained unprecedented access to closely-held government documents, including access to relevant operational files, the President's Daily briefs, the Executive Registry and the debriefs of returning POWs. Unfortunately, the limited number of individuals affiliated with the Committee who were given access to these materials prevented as thorough a review as the Committee would have preferred.

At the Committee's insistence, and despite the reservations of the Executive branch, public hearings were held for the first time on the products of satellite imagery related to the POW/MIA issue. Two former employees of the National Security Agency testified in public about information they gathered while working as specialists in the field of signal intelligence. And two days of hearings culminated an exhaustive Committee investigation of reports that American captives had been seen in Southeast Asia during the postwar period. In addition, thousands of pages of live-sighting reports have been declassified and made available to the public.

The Committee understands that the process of analyzing intelligence information is complicated and subjective. In most instances, the quality and source of information is such that it can be interpreted in more than one way and isolated bits of information may easily be misinterpreted. As a result, the Committee believes in the importance of taking all sources of information and intelligence into account when judging the validity of a report or category of data.

Overall intelligence community support

During the Committee's investigation, all DIA directors since the late 1970's testified that the POW effort lacked national level Intelligence Community support in terms of establishing a high priority for collection, in funding, in the allocation of personnel and in high-level attention. None of the former directors recalled attending national-level management meetings to discuss the POW/MIA issue prior to the mid-1980's, and only one national intelligence estimate was produced on this issue during the first 17 years after the end of the war.

Senior CIA officials told the Committee that there was no written collection requirement on POWs, but that everyone understood that POW information was important when obtained. CIA officials also asserted that this issue was the near exclusive preserve of the Department of Defense and that the CIA played only a supporting role.

Former NSA Director, Admiral Bobby Inman, testified that the NSA signals intelligence collection efforts in Southeast Asia were dismantled after the war and was not resumed until at least 1978.

Over the past decade, the Reagan and Bush Administrations have raised the priority of POW/MIA intelligence collection, have increased resources and improved policy level management. The basic structure of responsibilities, however, has not changed.

The role of the Defense Intelligence Agency

The DIA has had a central, two-pronged, role in U.S efforts to account for our POW/MIAs. First, the DIA is responsible for investigating and analyzing reports of live-sightings or other evidence that American prisoners may still be held. Second, the Department of Defense relies heavily on DIA's analysis to reach conclusions about the fate of missing servicemen.

In addition to these responsibilities, the DIA's prominent role in the POW/MIA issue over the years has caused it to become a focal point for family, Congressional, press and public questions on the subject.

Criticisms of DIA Operations. The Committee identified and arranged for the declassification of a series of internal reviews of the DIA'S POW/MIA operations that were conducted during the mid-1980's. A principal concern raised by these reviews were the agency's procedures for evaluating and responding to reports that U.S. POWs had been seen alive after the conclusion of the war.[19]

The Committee agrees that the DIA'S POW/MIA Office has historically been:

Plagued by a lack of resources;
Guilty of over-classification;
Defensive toward criticism;
Handicapped by poor coordination with other elements of the intelligence community;
Slow to follow-up on live-sighting and other reports; and
Frequently distracted from its basic mission by the need to respond to outside pressures and requests.

In addition, several of those who reviewed the workings of DIA during this period also faulted DIA's analytical process and referred to a "mindset to debunk" live-sighting reports.

Several Committee Members express concern and disappointment that, on occasion, individuals within DIA have been evasive, unresponsive and disturbingly incorrect and cavalier. Several Members of the Committee also note that other individuals within DIA have performed their work with great professionalism and under extraordinarily difficult circumstances both at home and abroad.

The Committee recommends that the Secretary of Defense ensure the regular review and evaluation of the DIA's POW/MIA office to ensure that intelligence information is acted upon quickly and that information is shared with families promptly.

The Committee also believes that a central coordinating mechanism for pooling and acting upon POW/MIA-related intelligence information should be created as one of the Intelligence Community's Interagency Coordination Centers.

The Committee notes that the focus of the POW/MIA accounting process is in Southeast Asia. As a result, DIA analysts are spending more and more of their time traveling back and forth between Washington and the region or to Hawaii. The Committee believes that this would be an opportune time to move the DIA's POW/MIA office to Hawaii where it could be closer to JTF-FA and CINCPAC, which it supports. A number of tasks now sometimes performed by the office involving public and family relations can be handled, and handled more capably and appropriately, by the office of the Deputy Assistant Secretary of Defense for POW/MIA Affairs.

Live-sighting Reports. For the past 20 years, there has been nothing more tantalizing for POW/MIA families than reports that Americans have been seen alive in Southeast Asia and nothing more frustrating than the failure of these reports to become manifest in the form of a returning American—with the single exception of Marine Private Robert Garwood in 1979.

A live-sighting report is just that—a report that an American has been seen alive in Southeast Asia in circumstances which are not readily explained. The report could come from a refugee, boat person, traveler or anyone else in a position to make such an observation. The information could be first-hand or hearsay; it could involve one American or many; it could be detailed or vague; it could be recent or as far back as the end of the war.

The sheer number of first-hand live sighting reports, almost 1600 since the end of the war, has convinced many Americans that U.S. POWs must have been kept behind and may still be alive. Other Americans have concluded sadly that our failure, after repeated efforts, to locate any of these alleged POWs means the reports are probably not true. It is the Committee's view that every livesighting report is important as a potential source of information about the fate of our POW/MIAs.

Accordingly, the review and analysis of live-sighting reports consumed more time and staff resources than any other single issue. The Committee investigation used a method of analysis that was based on the content of a carefully screened set of reports that dealt only with men allegedly seen in captivity after Operation Homecoming. The Committee took into account past criticisms and assessed current procedures while examining and testing DIA's methodology for evaluating live-sighting reports. In so doing, Committee investigators examined more than 2000 hearsay and first-hand live-sighting files while compiling a list of 928 reports for "content" analysis. These reports were plotted on a map and grouped into geographic "clusters". During briefings and public hearings, the Committee reviewed the most significant "clusters" for the purpose of determining whether they would, taken together, constitute evidence of the presence of U.S. POWs in certain locations after Operation Homecoming.

DIA Assessment. It is DIA's position that the live-sighting reports evaluated to date do not constitute evidence that currently unaccounted for U.S. POWs remained behind in Southeast Asia after the end of the war. Of the 1638 first-hand reports received since 1975, DIA considers 1,553 to be resolved.[20]

Committee View. The Committee notes that 40 first-hand live-sighting reports remain under active investigation and that the nature of the analytical process precludes certainty that all past DIA evaluations are correct. Accordingly, the Committee recommends a strong emphasis on the rapid and thorough follow-up and evaluation of current unresolved and future live-sighting reports. The DIA is urged to make a continued and conscious effort to maintain an attitude among analysts that presumes the possible survival of U.S. POWs. The Executive branch is also urged to continue working with the governments of Southeast Asia to expand our ability to conduct on the ground, on-site investigation and inspections throughout the region.

The role of the National Security Agency (signals intelligence)

The responsibility for monitoring and collecting,signals (including communications) intelligence rests with the National Security Agency (NSA). During the Vietnam War, the NSA monitored all available sources of signals intelligence bearing on the loss, capture or condition of American personnel. Such information would sometimes provide a basis for concluding whether or not a missing American had survived his incident and, if so, possibly been taken prisoner.

During its investigation, the Committee was disturbed to learn that the NSA and its Vietnam branch were never asked to provide an overall assessment of the status of POW/MIA personnel prior to Operation Homecoming. The Committee believes that this information would have been useful both for the U.S. negotiating team and for those preparing for the repatriation of American POWs. The Committee also found that neither DIA nor any other agency within the Intelligence Community placed a formal requirement for collection with NSA concerning POW/MIA related information. In fact, the Committee found that NSA end product reports were not used regularly to evaluate the POW/MIA situation until 1977. It was not until 1984 that the collection of information on POW/ MIAs was formally established as a matter of highest priority for SIGINT.

After the fall of Saigon, the National Security Agency and the military service components that support it largely dismantled their collection efforts in Southeast Asia. The elaborate collection capabilities that supported the war essentially ceased or were relocated to other trouble spots around the world. The analytical organizations that monitored signals intelligence in the region were also disbanded or sharply reduced as personnel were transferred to other assignments.

U.S. collection capabilities were further diminished during this period as Vietnam and Laos developed secure landline communications to replace the radio networks used during time of war. If officials in either country were communicating about live U.S. POWs, the likelihood that these communications would be detected by the U.S. had become remote. However, during this period, the NSA did receive third party intercepts concerning the reported presence of American POWs in Laos.[21]

In conducting its review of NSA files, the Committee examined more than 3,000 postwar reports and 90 boxes of wartime files. The Committee discovered that previous surveys of NSA files for POW/MIA related information had been limited to the agency's automated data base. Hundreds of thousands of hard copy documents, memoranda, raw reports, operational messages and possibly tapes from both the wartime and post-war periods remain unreviewed in various archives and storage facilities. Most troubling, NSA failed to locate for investigators any wartime analyst files related specifically to tracking POWs, despite the fact that tracking POWs was a known priority at the time. This failure made it impossible for the Committee to confirm some information on downed pilots that was provided by NSA employee Jerry Mooney.

At the Committee's request, the NSA and DIA are conducting a review of past SIGINT reports that appear relevant to the POW/ MIA issue for the purpose of adding to the all-source database used in the accounting process. Thousands of such reports have been identified. Although it is not clear that the reports will succeed in resolving questions about missing American servicemen, they have raised questions about an individual's status in several cases and will, at a minimum, add to the context in which other POW/MIA information is considered.

The Committee benefitted from the insights of a retired NSA SIGINT analyst, Senior Master Sergeant Jerry Mooney (USAF-retired). During the war, SMSgt. Mooney maintained detailed personal files concerning losses of aircraft and downed airmen. Unfortunately, those personal files did not become part of the archived files maintained by the NSA and have been lost. Although SmSgt. Mooney has sought to reconstruct some of that information from personal memory, the loss of the files makes it impossible to check those recollections against the contemporaneous information.

The Committee found no evidence to substantiate claims that signals intelligence gathered during the war constitute evidence that U.S. POWs were transferred to the Soviet Union from Vietnam.

Pilot distress symbols

The Committee's investigation of pilot distress symbols as a possible source of evidence of live POWs after 1973 was the first such investigation conducted by anybody of Congress.

During the war, the military services gave many pilots who flew combat missions individual authenticator numbers to identify themselves by radio or other means in the event their airplanes were shot down or crashed. During their pre-flight training, pilots were also given Escape and Evasion (E&E) signals to employ either as an evader or POW to facilitate their eventual recovery. Most pilots received training in methods of constructing these E&E symbols in survival courses, prior to assignment to Vietnam. Both E&E symbols and authenticator numbers were classified.

It was expected that these symbols would be used to attract rescuers and would be deployed in ways which would avoid ground detection and yet be visible to overhead collecting sources. Consequently, intelligence analysts have been encumbered with the difficult task of searching for signals which could be extremely faint, or a clever blend of natural and man-made features.

The Committee became interested in this area while looking into intelligence concerning the reported presence of POWs at a camp near Nhom Marrott, Laos, in 1980. This intelligence included the discovery of what appeared to be a "52" possibly followed by a "K" in the prison garden. It was learned that "K" was a pilot distress signal used during the war.

The Committee discovered that the intelligence community had other overhead photographs, taken by both airborne and satellite collection platforms, showing what appeared to be symbols or unexplained markings.

The earliest example was a four digit set of numbers followed by what appeared to be the letters "TH" found on a May, 1973 photograph of an area in central Laos. According to the Joint Service SERE Agency (JSSA),[22] the four digit number could be an authenticator number followed by the primary and back-up distress symbols of a downed pilot. Another example was a 1975 photograph of a prison facility in Vietnam, in which the CIA noted unusual markings on the roof of one of the buildings. Although the CIA analysts assessed as remote the possibility that this represented a signal from a POW, they noted that the markings might be transposed to the letter "K" in Morse code. The Committee also learned of a 1988 photograph of a valley near Sam Neua, Laos, showing what clearly was a "USA" dug into a rice paddy. Beneath the "USA", DIA also noted a possible "K" created by "ground scarring.

During its investigation, the Committee was surprised by statements from DIA and CIA imagery analysts directly involved in POW/MIA work that they were not very knowledgeable about the military's E&E signals or, in some cases, even aware of the program. These analysts were not even tasked to look for such information prior to April, 1992. The Committee concluded that there had not been a purposeful effort to search for distress signals, or a written formal requirement for symbols, after the end of the war. The Committee is confident, however, that if a symbol appeared clearly on imagery, it would be identified by imagery analysts, as was the case with the 1988 "USA" symbol.

The Committee recommends that the search for possible POW distress symbols

in Southeast Asia be a written intelligence requirement and that imagery analysts be educated fully about JSSA training. This is because a prisoner under detention is not likely to have the opportunity to construct distress signals that are blatant or elaborate; they are, in fact, trained to use discreet methods to avoid detection. The more familiar imagery analysts are with JSSA training, the more likely it is that they will be able to detect such a discreet signal. Also, given the possibility that past signals could have been missed, the Committee recommends that past photography of suspect detention sites be reviewed to the extent that resources permit.[23]

The Committee notes that JSSA officials had not been consulted previously with respect to the suspected symbols, except for the 1973 "TH" photograph, which was shown to them in the mid-1980's. Accordingly, the Committee asked JSSA to evaluate a number of possible symbols and markings to see if they were consistent with JSSA training methods and distress symbols used during the war. JSSA concluded that the "USA, possible K", the "52 possible K", the "TH", the roof top markings and one other symbol were consistent with the methods taught to pilots downed in Laos.[24] JSSA analysis of the "USA possible K" concluded that this should be considered a valid distress symbol until proven otherwise. It should be emphasized, however, that JSSA officials are not trained in photo analysis, and are not qualified to determine whether, in fact, symbols that may seem to appear in imagery actually exist.

The Committee notes that imagery anomalies are caused by regularly occurring natural phenomena and that JSSA originally identified 150 such numbers during its review of photography, of which 19 appeared to match the four-digit authenticator numbers of U.S. airmen. It was later demonstrated to the satisfaction of all parties that none of these numbers were man-made, and all were naturally occurring phenomena such as shadows, ridges, or trees, with the exception of one additional symbol identified by one consultant in an altogether different location.

The DIA does not dispute that two of the possible symbols, the "USA" in 1988, and the 1973 "TH" are intentionally-constructed man-made symbols. In a message to the Committee received in January, 1993, however, the agency stated that the " 'USA' symbol was not a distress symbol and had nothing to do with missing Americans." This finding was based on a December, 1992 on-site investigation which "determined that the symbol was made by Hmong tribe members." In the same message, the DIA raised the possibility that the 1973 "TH" symbol may have been made by a Hmong tribesman whose name started with the English letters "TH" and who was a passenger on an aircraft piloted by the American Emmet Kay which went down in May, 1973, "a few kilometers" away from where the symbol appeared.

DIA now contends that the "52", possible "K" seen at Nhom Marrott is the result of shadowing and in no way represents a pilot distress symbol. The Committee notes, however, that DIA had earlier discounted the possibility that the symbol was caused by shadowing because of the constant shape of the figures over a period of days and at different times of the day. In fact, the intelligence community had concluded in 1980 that this symbol had been dug into the ground intentionally.

Due to the complexity of interpreting symbols obtained through imagery, the Committee decided to hire two independent imagery consultants. Each consultant was given access to the necessary equipment and each submitted independently a report to the Committee. The consultants' reports, which differed on only the one symbol referred to earlier, were subsequently provided to the intelligence community for its comments and evaluation.

A joint task group of DIA, CIA and NPIC imagery analysts found that an unresolved symbol found by one consultant was "probably not manmade." This consultant had detected, with "100 percent confidence" a faint "GX 2527" in a photograph of a prison facility in Vietnam taken in June, 1992. This number correlates to the primary and back-up distress symbols and authenticator number of a pilot lost in Laos in 1969. The joint agency team agreed that there were visible markings that could be interpreted as letters and numbers, but concluded that the marking "appeared" too "haphazard and ill-defined" to be man-made distress symbols.

Disagreement arose within the Committee about the interpretation of some of the possible symbols, including the question of whether there is reason to believe that the "GX 2527" symbol is man-made, rather than the result of natural phenomena. However, the Committee agrees that the benefit of the doubt should go to the individual in this case, because the apparent number corresponds to a particular authenticator number and because it was identified by one analyst with 100 percent confidence. Accordingly, the Committee urges the appropriate officials in the Executive branch to request information about the serviceman involved from the Government of Vietnam.

Although the Committee cannot rule out the possibility that U.S. POWs have attempted to signal their status to aerial observers, the Committee cannot conclude, based on its own investigation and the guidance of imagery experts, that this has definitely happened. Although there is now an adequate collection process in place, the Committee investigators found unacceptable lapses in time between the point of collection and evaluation; and between evaluation and follow-up. The Committee recommends better integration among the various intelligence agencies, including improved training and a better system for collecting and acting on information gathered through imagery.

Covert operations

The Committee investigated whether the United States Government may have undertaken or supported covert operations in order to confirm the presence of U.S. POWs in Southeast Asia after Operation Homecoming and, if so, to review the intelligence information upon which those operations were based.

The Committee has identified only one operation of this type mounted after 1973. Although operational details remain classified, the fact that the operation took place has been reported publicly. The operation was prompted by a combination of human, photographic and signals intelligence concerning the possible presence of as many as 30 American POWs at a detention camp near the village of Nhom Marrot in Laos from 1979 until early 1981. The intelligence resulted in extensive and highest level efforts by the U.S. Government to confirm the information. Unfortunately, the results of the covert operation were inconclusive and subsequent efforts were rendered impossible by press leaks.[25]

Intelligence support in Laos during the Vietnam war

During the Vietnam war, intelligence support for the U.S. effort in Laos was handicapped because Administration policy, at the insistence of the State Department, excluded the significant use of military intelligence assets. This was true despite the fact that accounting for missing military personnel in Laos was the responsibility of the respective military services, and despite strenuous efforts made by Secretary of Defense Melvin Laird to gain support for an improved POW/MIA related military intelligence effort. The Committee believes that an expanded wartime military intelligence effort in Laos might have increased significantly our ability to account for the Americans lost in that country.

Cooperation from governments in Southeast Asia

It is not possible to account for the Americans who are missing from the war in Southeast Asia without cooperation from the governments of the region, especially Vietnam. The U.S. has requested this cooperation in four forms. First, we have requested information concerning live American prisoners, former prisoners or deserters. Second, we have asked for the return of any recovered or recoverable remains of missing American servicemen. Third, we have sought accesss to files, records, documents and other materials that are relevant to the fate of missing Americans. Finally, we have asked for permission to visit certain locations within these countries for the purpose of investigating live-sighting reports and searching actual or suspected airplane crash sites.

The Committee has done everything it could to complement the diplomatic and political initiatives of the Executive branch in seeking to encourage a greater degree of cooperation on POW/MIA issues from the governments of Southeast Asia.

Vietnam

The U.S. has long suspected that the North Vietnamese have been withholding a considerable amount of information bearing on the fate of missing Americans. The North Vietnamese maintained detailed records of U.S. servicemen who came within their prison system during the war, including many lost in North Vietnamese-controlled areas of South Vietnam, Cambodia and Laos. U.S. intelligence agencies are convinced, moreover, that the Government of Vietnam recovered and stored an unknown quantity of remains of American servicemen for release at politically strategic points ill time.

The level of U.S.-Vietnamese cooperation in accounting for missing Americans has varied over the years depending on bilateral and global political conditions and on the degree of emphasis placed on the issue by officials of the United States. At the time the Select Committee was created, there was considerable progress being made in the investigation of discrepancy cases. In addition, an agreement had been reached with Vietnam to allow an official Defense Department investigating presence to be established in Hanoi. These steps were directly attributable to the work of Gen. John Vessey, the President's Special Emissary to Vietnam on POW/MIA issues.

The impetus for Vietnam's cooperation has come from several directions. Gen. Vessey has provided the Vietnamese with a respected and influential source of contact within our government. Bush Administration policies have established a clear linkage between different levels of Vietnamese cooperation and American response. The disintegration of the Soviet empire has deprived Vietnam of many external sources of economic assistance and political comfort. The rapid economic growth of other Southeast Asian nations has given younger Vietnamese leaders a strong incentive to establish their own contacts with the west. And the creation of the Select Committee

has demonstrated anew the high priority attached to the POW/MIA issue by the American people and government. Obviously, the Committee does not know precisely how all of these matters have been factored into the calculations of the Vietnamese Government, but clearly the overall trends are hopeful.

Over the past year, Committee Members have visited Vietnam on four occasions to press for further information. Committee delegations met with a wide range of high-level Vietnamese officials, including those in charge of administering the wartime prisoner of war system. The Committee visits, coupled with ongoing efforts from the Executive branch, have yielded substantial results.

These results include:

Permission for U.S. investigators to carry out short-notice investigations of many live-sighting reports;

ermission for U.S. investigators to use U.S.-owned, maintained and operated helicopters in the course of investigations within Vietnam;

Grants of access to certain highly-secure prison and defense ministry buildings for the purpose of investigating live sighting reports;

Guarantees of full access for JTF-FA investigators to political and military archives containing POW/MIA related information;

Access to certain key archival documents and personnel that had been long-requested, and long-denied by Vietnam;

The provision of thousands of photographs of American war-time casualties;

Access to Vietnam's military museum, including hundreds of material objects once owned by American servicemen that might contain clues about the fate of missing Americans;

Declaration of an amnesty for any Vietnamese citizens illegally holding American remains to come forward with them without fear of punishment;

A commitment to cooperate in the conduct of an "oral history" program that would seek to record information from Vietnamese military officials, soldiers and civilians who might have information about the fate of missing Americans;

Promises of full cooperation from Vietnam in working with Laos and Cambodia to investigate discrepancy cases involving servicemen lost in parts of those countries controlled by North Vietnamese forces during the war; and

Permission for POW/MIA families, if they so desire, to come to Vietnam and evaluate the investigation process.

The Committee welcomes the very substantial strides towards full cooperation on the POW/MIA issue that the Government of Vietnam has made in recent months. The Committee looks forward to the implementation of those steps in the hope that they will yield significant additional information concerning missing Americans and encourages the Executive branch to do all it can to see that the promises and commitments made by Vietnam are fulfilled.

In noting recent progress, the Committee does not wish to understate the fact that the progress is coming very late—almost 20 years after the signing of the peace agreement, and after two decades of noncooperation, stalling and deception on the part of Vietnam's leaders. The Committee also recognizes that the recent changes in policy appear to be the result primarily of Vietnam's desire for economic contacts with the west. The closed and nondemocratic nature of the government in Vietnam argues for caution in accepting Vietnamese promises, for pledges given by a government unwilling to be open with its own people can hardly be taken at face value. Nonetheless, the Committee remains hopeful that recent improvements in POW/MIA cooperation are symptomatic of a trend in Vietnam that will lead ultimately to dramatic improvements in human rights, and political, economic and religious freedoms.

United States policy towards Vietnam should reflect the importance of freedoms that are central to American society and which have been central to our investigation. Without a free press or representative government, the American people would not have learned the full extent of our own government's knowledge about our POW/MIAs. Our policy towards Vietnam, as towards the other nations of Southeast Asia, should be predicated on a vision of the same freedoms for the people of that region that we enjoy here at home.

Laos

More than 500 Americans are still listed as unaccounted for in Laos, including 335 who were originally considered either POW or MIA. Accordingly, the Committee has attached a high priority to gaining greater cooperation from the Lao Government. The current leaders of Laos, who are successors to the Pathet Lao forces that contended for power during the war, almost certainly have some information concerning missing Americans that they have not yet shared. At a minimum, they should be able to provide specific information about the fates of a small number of U.S. POWs known to have been held by the Pathet Lao during the early stages of the war. Unfortunately, Lao leaders have been significantly less cooperative than those in Vietnam. The Lao have denied any knowledge of U.S. POWs; they have refused access to some requested sources of information; and they have been even more reluctant than the Vietnamese to grant U.S. access to their territory for conducting live-sighting investigations and inspecting crash sights. The atmosphere has improved to some extent in recent months, however. As a result, some discrepancy case investigations are underway and negotiations are ongoing for the establishment of a permanent POW/MIA investigation office in Vientiane.

Cambodia

The present government of war-ravaged Cambodia cannot be expected to possess documentary information relevant to the fate of missing American servicemen. Nonetheless, the Committee met with Cambodian President Hun Sen, who expressed his government's full cooperation with the U.S. in efforts to resolve discrepancy cases. Unfortunately, the Cambodian Government is unable to guarantee security in areas controlled by the brutal and lawless Khmer Rouge. The Committee is grateful to President Hun Sen for his help on this issue, given the scope and urgency of the other perils faced by his government and his country.

Government policies and actions
Declassification

The Committee believes that much of the controversy surrounding the U.S. Government's handling of the POW/MIA issue could have been avoided if relevant documents had been declassified and made available to the public long ago. Unnecessary secrecy breeds the suspicion that important information is being withheld, while fueling speculation about what that information may be.

From its inception, the Committee has urged the Executive branch to identify and declassify all documents and other materi-als within its possession that are related to POW/MIA issues, with the single exception of information bearing directly on intelligence sources and methods.

A Task Force of the Select Committee, led by Senators Charles Robb and Chuck Grassley, formulated specific requests and recommendations upon which the Committee acted. For example, the President was asked, and agreed, to order the expeditious declassification of POW/MIA records from the Vietnam War, and the U.S. Senate unanimously approved a resolution calling for the declassification of POW/MIA materials. A series of letters sent, requests made and meetings held resulted in a high degree of cooperation and understanding between the Committee and the Executive branch on this issue.

The result of the Committee's efforts has been the most rapid and comprehensive declassification of materials on a single subject in American history. More than one million pages have already been declassified and the Committee is confident that remaining documents will be made available. The Committee believes that President Bush and National Security Adviser Brent Scowcroft should be congratulated for their cooperation on this issue.

Although the Committee was generally very satisfied with the degree of understanding and help it received from the Executive branch, its request for the release of relevant CIA operational files has, to date, been denied. The Committee recommends that the process of declassification of current POW/MIA related materials go forward rapidly until completion and that the relevant CIA operations files be included.

The Committee also recommends that policies be put in place to assure the rapid declassification of POW/MIA related information from possible future conflicts. It should be enshrined in both attitude and law that the right of a POW/MIA family to know what the government knows about its loved one is as inalienable a right as any spelled out in the Constitution.

Finally, the Committee's records will be sent to the National Archives, with specific instructions that they be made available for public review. We caution, however, that these records include staff materials, memoranda of conversation, notes and other documents that may reflect raw opinion, incorrect data, discredited theories, or bits of fact that may mislead unless placed within a proper context. The Committee emphasizes that judgments reached by the Committee, after consideration of all available evidence, are reflected in this report. Other information and judgments should not be accorded credibility simply because of tneir presence in the Committee's working files.

Inter-agency group

Since January, 1980, Executive branch policy-making has been coordinated by the Interagency Group on POW/MIA Affairs (IAG). Agencies and organizations represented on the IAG include the Departments of State and Defense, the Joint Chiefs of Staff, the National Security Council and the National League of POW/MIA Families (the League). In recent years, IAG meetings have occurred every two to three weeks on the average. Meetings are characterized by informal discussions of policy options; decisions are reached by consensus; and no formal minutes of the meetings are maintained.

The scope of IAG discussion covers a broad spectrum of POW/ MIA related matters including intelligence collection, communications with families, diplomatic initiatives and public awareness activities. A major focus of attention over the past two years has been U.S. policy towards Vietnam.

The presence of league President Ann Mills Griffiths on the IAG is controversial. During Committee hearings, Members of the IAG said Griffiths was a highly constructive and energetic member of the group who has contributed significantly to improvements in U.S. policy. It is, however, extremely unusual for a private citizen to serve on a high-level panel such as the IAG, and to have access to sensitive intelligence information without the kind of accountability and official responsibility demanded of government representatives on that group.

During the summer of 1991, for example, Griffiths actively discouraged the Defense Department from granting access to classified POW/MIA materials to Senate staff investigators with appropriate clearances. The Committee finds it anomalous that a private citizen representing POW/MIA families would be in a position to try to deny Senate investigators the same right to review sensitive materials that she herself has been granted.

The Committee believes that an interagency coordinating body for POW/MIA policies is needed and that the IAG ably fulfills this role. However, the Committee is disturbed by the lack of formality in IAG record-keeping and believes that, at a minimum, that the minutes of discussions at such meetings should be maintained.

Second, although the IAG should consult regularly with the League and other POW/MIA family organizations, the Committee believes that the role of the IAG and issues of membership on it should be reviewed by the new Administration.

Government-to-government offers

The Committee investigated the possibility that Vietnam or Laos had approached U.S. officials at any time since the end of the war in Southeast Asia with a proposal that live U.S. POWs be returned in exchange for money or some other consideration. The Committee found no convincing evidence of any such offer being made. There were, however, two incidents which require further explanation.

The Committee received information that the Reagan Administration may have received an offer from Vietnam in 1981, transmitted through a third country, to exchange live POWs for $4.5 billion. The source of the information was a Secret Service agent who reported that he had overheard a discussion in the White House concerning this subject. The Committee deposed one of the individuals, former National Security Adviser Richard Allen, said to have been involved in the discussion, and several individuals who were said to have been in the area of the discussion. The Secret Service agent was not willing to provide testimony to the Committee voluntarily, and the Committee voted 7-4 not to subpoena that testimony. A complete description of the investigation and the subpoena issue is contained in Chapter 6 of this report.

The Committee also received a report concerning a possible approach by Vietnam in 1984, through officials in an ASEAN nation, concerning the exchange of American remains and possibly live POWs. According to the report, the Vietnamese had indicated that they would welcome an offer from the U.S. on the subject. U.S. officials traveled to Vietnam late in 1984, but were reportedly told by Vietnamese officials that there were no live POWs and that the only issue that could be discussed involved remains. Select Committee investigators traveled to the ASEAN nation to interview officials in an effort to determine whether an approach from Vietnam concerning live U.S. POWs had, in fact, been made. The results were inconclusive. Two secondary sources disagreed about whether an exchange involving live POWs had been discussed. The individual who had initially discussed the subject with Vietnamese officials later told the State Department that the issue of live American POWs had not been raised. This investigation is also described in greater detail in chapter 6.

Review of private activities

A major part of the Committee's investigation entailed the review of private activities related to the POW/MIA issue. This review focused on efforts by such organizations to educate the public about the issue, to influence government policy, to raise funds and to recover information concerning possible American POWs.

In its review, the Committee asked more than 50 POW/MIA-related organizations to provide information, on a voluntary basis, concerning their activities. Committee staff also interviewed or took formal testimony from organization officials and from the family members of some POW/MIAs.

The Committee found that the vast majority of POW/MIA related organizations are modest, local groups of volunteers operating on small budgets and dedicated to public education, grassroots lobbying, mutual assistance and remembrance activities. These organizations, and those who support them, have performed an important service for the nation in maintaining a strong national spotlight on the need for the fullest possible accounting of our POW/MIAS.

The Committee investigated several privately-organized operations aimed at physically rescuing or recovering information concerning possible American POWs. These included: (1) the Team Falcon operation in 1991-1992; (2) a 1988 effort to locate prisoners in Laos; (3) Operation Skyhook II, an early 1980's initiative also aimed at finding prisoners in Laos; and (4) the efforts of retired Army Lt. Col. Bo Gritz. None of these operations have been successful in rescuing prisoners or in uncovering evidence that prisoners are being held.

The Committee also investigated a number of photographs of individuals purported to be of U.S. POWs. In the cases investigated, we found that such photographs are sometimes used by private organizations as a means of attracting financial support for "rescue" or "reconnaissance" operations. The Committee concluded, based on investigative work done by the DIA, that photographs circulated in 1991 allegedly depicting missing Americans Donald Carr, Daniel V. Borah, John L. Robertson, Larry J. Stevens and Albro Lundy are fraudulent. (The Committee respects the fact that the Robertson, Stevens and Lundy families have not accepted the DIA analysis). In contrast to the large number of small, voluntary POW/MIA organizations, there are a few private POW organizations that are relatively large, have paid staff and use professional fundraisers to prepare and distribute solicitation materials to millions of actual or potential contributors. These solicitations have yielded tens of millions of dollars in contributions since the end of the war. The Committee was concerned about a number of issues, including the extent to which some groups have diverted funds for purposes other than those advertised, the possibility that misleading or false information has been included in solicitations, the failure of fund-raisers to disclose information to potential donors and the impact that these solicitations may have had on the emotions and expectations of POW/MIA families.

The Committee's principal findings are:

The vast majority of private organizations engaged in POW/MIA related activities reflect the highest standards of voluntary, public service and deserve the nation's gratitude and praise.

Private initiatives aimed at the "rescue" of U.S. prisoners have failed in the past and are problematic for several reasons. In general, such operations are dependent on sources of information in Southeast Asia that have a very poor record of reliability and, in some cases, a consistent track record of fraud. Second, it is unrealistic to believe that such efforts will have a better chance of success than official efforts. Third, the possibility exists that such operations might jeopardize ongoing U.S. diplomatic and intelligence activities. Fourth, such activities sometimes involve the violation of U.S. and/or foreign law.

The manufacture of fraudulent POW/MIA related materials, including photographs, dog tags and other purported evidence of live Americans has become a cottage industry in certain parts of Southeast Asia, and particularly Thailand. Sadly, these activities have been spurred by well-intentioned private offers of large rewards for information leading to the return of live U.S. POWs. The Committee is angered and repulsed by activities that exploit the anguish of POW/MIA families for private gain.

The Committee's examination of POW/MIA-related fundraising activities has created serious reason for concern. In some instances, an excessive percentage of funds raised has been retained by the fundraising organization. In others, the fundraising solicitations have over stated to the point of distortion the weight of evidence indicating that live U.S. POWs continue to be held in Southeast Asia.

Information from Russia and Eastern Europe

Although the Committee's investigation focused primarily on efforts to account for Americans missing from the war in Southeast Asia, the principle of accounting for lost American servicemen is the same, whether the war occurred 20 years ago or 50 years ago. Accordingly, the Committee undertook a review of information and allegations concerning Americans missing from earlier conflicts and hired a full time investigator to work in Moscow on this and related issues.

The Committee's effort was facilitated greatly by the lifting of the Iron Curtain and by the policies of openness and cooperation advocated by Russian President Boris Yeltsin. In February, 1992, the Committee's Chairman, Sen. John Kerry, and Vicechairman, Sen. Bob Smith, met with Russian officials and veterans in Moscow to discuss cooperation on the POW/MIA issue. This visit laid the groundwork for the creation of the U.S.-Russia Joint Commission (Commission) on POW/MIA Affairs under the leadership of Col. Gen. Dimitri Volkogonov and Malcolm Toon, former U.S. Ambassador to the Soviet Union.[26] The objectives of the Commission are (1) to gain access to people and documents in Russia that could shed light on the fate of missing Americans; (2) to pursue reports that current or former U.S. POWs may be alive within the borders of the former Soviet Union; and (3) to establish a means by which remains identified as American may be repatriated. Investigative work by the U.S. side to the Joint Commission is carried out by the Defense Department's Task Force Russia (TFR), under the leadership of Gen. Bernard Loeffke.

The Committee's investigation was conducted, in large part, through the staff investigator assigned to work with the Commission in Moscow. In Washington, the Committee reviewed documents obtained from the National Archives and from private researchers. We also conducted interviews with former officials of the Eisenhower Administration and others possessing information on the subject.

In June, 1992, the Committee hosted a meeting of the Commission with Gen. Volkogonov following Russian President Yeltsin's public statements on the POW/MIA issue. In November, 1992, two days of public hearings were held during which both U.S. investigators and Gen. Volkogonov testified. Finally, in December, 1992, Committee investigators participated in fact-finding trips to Czechoslovakia and Ukraine, and attended a formal meeting of the Commission in Moscow.

The Committee emphasizes that firm or precise judgments about the number and circumstances under which American military and civilian personnel may have found themselves detained within the former Soviet Union in the past cannot yet be made. Large quantities of records, both in Moscow and elsewhere, remain to be reviewed. There are also many well-informed former military and intelligence officers and diplomatic personnel who have not yet been interviewed. It is possible that evidence will be uncovered indicating greater involvement of former Soviet officials in the interrogation, transportation or detention of U.S. POWs from the Vietnam War and prior conflicts. Thus, the findings below, which are based on work to date, must be considered as preliminary in nature:

Gen. Volkogonov's assessment

Gen. Volkogonov contends that, to his knowledge, no Americans are currently being held against their will within the borders of the former Soviet Union.[27] Although the Committee has found evidence that some U.S. POWs were held in the former Soviet Union after WW II, the Korean War and Cold War incidents, we have found no proof that would contradict Gen. Volkogonov's contention with respect to the present. However, the Committee cannot, based on its investigation to date, rule out the possibility that one or more U.S. POWs from past wars or incidents are still being held somewhere within the borders of the former Soviet Union.

World War II

The Committee found that the Russians have been particularly successful in producing World War II archival documents, and is pleased to report that the fate of some American military and civilian personnel from the World War II era has been determined through recent investigations in Russia. Moreover, archival doeu ments provided by Russia indicate that several hundred U.S. POWs were held against their will on Soviet territory at the end of World War II. In almost all cases, these were individuals who had been born in, or who had previously lived in, the Soviet Union, and who could, therefore, be considered Soviet citizens by the Soviet Government. Many of these individuals served in the Armed Forces of Germany, fought against the Soviet Army and were captured in combat. Some U.S. civilians from this era survived terms in concentration camps and are still alive today, living freely either in one of the former Soviet Republics or in the United States.

Cold war

There is evidence, some of which has been confirmed to the Committee by President Yeltsin, that some U.S. personnel, still unaccounted for from the Cold War, were taken captive and held within the former Soviet Union. This information involves several incidents stretching across the former Soviet Union from the Baltic Sea to the Sea of Japan.

The Committee is pleased to report that Task Force Russia has been actively investigating these cases and is keeping surviving family members fully apprised of its progress to date. The Committee notes, however, that progress is, in large part, dependent on cooperation from Russian authorities. In the Committee's November, 1992 hearings, our investigator in Moscow testified that the U.S. was "intentionally being stonewalled" by the Russians on the subject of Cold War incidents, despite pledges of cooperation from President Yeltsin and Gen. Volkogonov. The Committee, therefore, urges the Joint Commission to place special attention and focus on obtaining further information on the fate of those U.S. personnel who are believed to have been taken captive during the Cold War.

Korean conflict

There is strong evidence, both from archived U.S. intelligence reports and from recent interviews in Russia, that Soviet military and intelligence officials were involved in the interrogation of American POWs during the Korean Conflict, notwithstanding recent official statements from the Russian side that this did not happen. Additionally, the Committee has reviewed information and heard testimony which we believe constitutes strong evidence that some unaccounted for American POWs from the Korean Conflict were transferred to the former Soviet Union in the early 1950's. While the identity of these POWs has not yet been determined, the Committee notes that Task Force Russia concurs in our assessment concerning the transfers. We are pleased that this subject was raised by the U.S. side in December, 1992 at the plenary session of the Joint Commission in Moscow.

The Committee further believes it is possible that one or more POWs from the Korean Conflict could still be alive on the territory of the former Soviet Union. The most notable case in this regard concerns a USAF pilot named David "Markham" or "Markin", who was reportedly shot down during the Korean Conflict. According to several sources, this pilot was reportedly alive in detention facilities in Russia as late as 1991. Although Task Force Russia has thus far been unable to confirm these reports, we note that the investigation is continuing.

Vietnam war

The Committee is aware of several reports that U.S. POWs may have been transferred to the Soviet Union during the Vietnam War. Information about this possibility that was provided by a former employee of the National Security Agency (NSA), Mr. Jerry Mooney, was thoroughly investigated and could not be substantiated. The Committee notes that Mr. Mooney testified that he personally believed prisoners were transferred to the Soviet Union but that he had "no direct information" that this took place.[28] Other reports concerning the possibility that U.S. POWs were transferred from Vietnam to the former Soviet Union deserve further investigation and followup.

With respect to interrogations, the Committee has confirmed that one KGB officer participated directly in the questioning of an American POW during the Vietnam Conflict. More generally, Soviet military officers have told the Committee that they received intelligence from North Vietnamese interrogations of American POWs and that the Soviets "participated" in interroga-tions through the preparation of questions and through their presence during some of the interrogations. It is possible that American POWs would not have been aware of the presence of Soviet officers during these interrogations. The Committee has also received information that Soviet personnel operated certain SAM sites in Vietnam which shot down American aircraft during the war.

The Committee notes that the cooperation received to date from Russia on POW/MIA matters has been due largely to the leadership of President Boris Yeltsin. During a visit to Washington last summer, President Yeltsin declared that "each and every document in each and every archive will be examined to investigate the fate of every American unaccounted for." Although there is still much work to be done, Russian officials deserve credit for providing access to archival material, for cooperating in efforts to solicit testimony from Russian veterans and other citizens and for their willingness to disclose certain previously undisclosed aspects of the historical record. The ultimate success of the Joint Commission will be judged, however, on whether the U.S. side is able to obtain full support for its interview program and archival research from all levels of power and authority throughout the former Soviet Union.

President Yeltsin has made a heroic effort to demonstrate his own commitment to full cooperation and Gen. Volkogonov has done a great deal, with limited resources, to meet this standard. Unfortunately, the level of cooperation from within the Russian military and intelligence bureaucracy has been less extensive and has, at times, seemed intentionally obstructive. This may well be due to the uncertainty of the current political situationin Russia. It is vital, therefore, that U.S. officials, both in Congress and the Executive branch, continue to demonstrate to Russian authorities that America attaches a high priority to cooperation on this issue and to ensure that any problems. that might develop are raised with the Russians promptly and at a senior level.

The Committee also recommends strongly that the U.S.-Russia Joint Commission be continued and that efforts be made to gain the full cooperation, as needed and appropriate, of the other Republics of the former Soviet Union.

Notes

1. "Perot's Veep: From Hanoi to the Debate", Wall Street Journal, Oct. 13, 1992.

2. There were a few instances where the Executive branch denied the Committee access to specific intelligence sources. The Committee has been assured, however, that the information that could have been provided by those sources has not been withheld. Also, access to the debriefings of returned POWs was granted only to the Chairman and Vice-Chairman.

3. Subject only to the deletion of specific information that, if made public, would compromise intelligence sources and methods.

4. On January 29, 1973, at a meeting of the Washington Special Action Group, a DOD representative told Dr. Henry Kisssinger that "We have only six known prisoners in Laos, although we hope there may be forty or forty-one." On February 1, 1973, DIA statistics listed 80 Americans as POWs who were not accounted for on the lists provided by the North Vietnamese or Viet Cong.

5. Richard M. Nixon, Address of the President to the nation, March 29, 1973.

6. Final Report of the House Committee on Missing Persons in Southeast Asia, 12/13/76.

7. Dr. Roger Shields, head of the Defense Department's POW/MIA Task Force, briefmg of the Woodcock Commission, February, 1977.

8. This discussion refers to U.S. POWs who were captured prior to Operation Homecoming. One civilian pilot, Emmet Kay, was known to have been taken captive after Operation Homecoming and was held prisoner from May, 1973 until his release in September,

1974. In addition, a small number of other Americans, including Private Robert Garwood, USMC, are known to have remained in Southeast Asia after the end of the war.

9. In an address to the nation on March 29, 1973, President Nixon said: "For the first time in 12 years, no American military forces are in Vietnam. All of our American POWs are on their way home . . . There are still some problem areas. The provisions of the agreement requiring an accounting for all missing in action in Indochina, the provisions with regard to Laos and Cambodia, the provisions concerning infiltration from North Vietnam into South Vietnam have not been complied with . . . "

10. Testimony of Dr. Roger Shields, head of the DOD Task Force on POW/MIA, before the House Committee on Foreign Affairs, May 31, 1973.

11. Sen. Brown wishes to stress his view that, based on testimony received by the Committee, when the Administration discussed those missing in action, they were referring to prisoners of war and those last known alive; and that significant efforts were made to raise these issues as a matter of public concern.

12. Senators Smith and Grassley dissent from this statement because they believe that live-sighting reports and other sources of intelligence are evidence that POWs may have survived to the present.

13. The Defense Intelligence Agency defines a "discrepancy case" as including three categories of missing Americans: "individuals who were carried as POWs by their respective services during the war but did not return during Operation Homecoming; "individuals who were known or suspected to have survived their loss incidents and might have been taken prisoner"; and "other cases in which intelligence indicates the Indochinese government may know the fate of a missing man."

14. Cable from President Nixon to Pham Van Dong, February 2, 1973.

15. For example, Dr. Kissinger sent a cable to Le Due Tho on March 20, 1973 saying, in part: "The. U.S. side has become increasingly disturbed about the question of American prisoners held or missing in Laos . . . the U.S.

side has made clear on many occasions that the list of only nine American prisoners presented belatedly by the Pathet Lao is clearly incomplete."

16. Some Members of the Select Committee believe that the U.S. threat to halt troop withdrawals referred only to the prisoners on the DRV/Laos list, and have cited testimony by some former Nixon Administration officials and some contemporary press accounts to support that view.

17. Other Committee Members believe that this second degree amendment to an amendment offered by Sen. Mark Hatfield was aimed far more at authorizing President Nixon to continue prosecuting the war in Southeast Asia than to gain an accounting for missing Americans.

18. Gen. Vessey's responsibilities are limited to Vietnam. The investigation of discrepancy cases in Laos and Cambodia is the responsibility of the Joint Task Force-Full Accounting, established January 23, 1992, as a successor to the Joint Casualty Resolution Center.

19. The reviews included Inspector General reports in 1983 and 1984/5; a 1985 interagency review; a September, 1985 review by Rear Admiral Thomas Brooks (USN-Ret.); and Task Force reports conducted in 1986 by Gen. Eugene Tighe (USAF-Ret.) and Col. Kimball Gaines (USAF-Ret.)

20. According to DIA, 1111 (68%) firsthand live-sighting reports correlate to Americans who are accounted for (returned POWs, missionaries, civilians jailed for reasons unrelated to the war etc); 45 (3%) of the reports were correlated to wartime sightings of military personnel or pre-1975 sightings of civilians who remain unaccounted for; and 397 (24%) of the reports were found to be fabrications. Of the 85 reports that remain under investigation, 54 pertain to Americans allegedly seen in a captive environment.

21. A description of these intercepts is contained in Chapter 4 of the Committee's fmal report.

22. The JSSA is the service proponent agency for pilot distress symbols, code of conduct, survival training and POW resistance training.

23. Some members note DIA's contention that many DIA analysts are well aware of E&E signals and have worked with the agency's analysts for years, searching for E&E signals. The DIA also points out that the two alleged E&E signals given most prominence in this report were discovered by U.S. government imagery analysts.

24. Some members note DIA's contention that the symbols in question are consistent with expected actions only because they are symbols; they do not relate to any evader signal in use during the Vietnam War.

25. Some members note DIA's contention that U.S. intelligence has interviewed former Royal Laotian officials held at Nhom Marrott for a number of years, including the time period in question. These individuals stated that no Americans were held at Nhom Marrott.

26. Senators Kerry and Smith were appointed to serve as the Senate's representatives on the joint commission.

27. Gen. Volkogonov did not mean to include in this contention any Americans who might legitimately be under arrest for recent violations of civil or criminal law. For example, at the time of the Select Committee hearing, one American was under arrest for dealing in contraband religious icons.

28. Committee hearing, Jan. 22, 1992.

Source: Excerpt: Senate Report 103-1, Report of the Select Committee on POW/MIA Affairs (January 13, 1993).

Excerpt: Comprehensive Report of the U.S. Side of the U.S.-Russia Joint Commission on POW/MIAS (June 17, 1996)

Doc 27C: 1992–1996 Findings of the WWII Working Group

Despite these efforts, allegations that there were 15,597 American POWs being held in late May 1945 by the Soviets in Austria persist.

If there had been 15,000 US POWs in Austria in late May 1945, whence had they come? Allied intelligence estimated in February 1945 that there were only 4,000 American prisoners in Austria, most in Stalag XVII-B, the largest camp in Austria. But the Germans evacuated that camp and moved the POWs westward, away from Marshal Tolbukhin's advancing forces. On 3 May 1945, US troops liberated 3,000 American POWs at Branau, on the Austrian-German border, who had been evacuated and marched westward from XVII-B. By late May, clearly there were few American POWs remaining in Austria and certainly not 15,000 to be held by the Red Army or anyone else.

For it to be true (as Brown, Sanders, and Waley allege) that the Soviets liberated but never repatriated 23,000 US prisoners of war, all of the following, among other unlikely possibilities, also had to be true:

1. A substantial part of the historical documentary record from World War II not only is completely inaccurate, but has been deliberatsssely falsified.
2. Discrepancies in the numbers of American POWs liberated and not recovered simultaneously and identically appear in US, Soviet, German, and British data.
3. The Soviets had almost twice as many US POWs that they claimed or than Allied and German records indicated, and these 23,000 were transferred and imprisoned in the Soviet Union without a trace.
4. The families of the 23,000 allegedly left behind participated in the cover up, because these was no public outcry from these people regarding the status of their missing relatives.

There is no documentary evidence that could lead to a conclusion that significant numbers of American prisoners of war disappeared into Soviet prisons after World War II.

The historical record in that regard is neither inaccurate, nor has it been deliberately falsified. In the contemporary debriefings, interrogations, and similar documentation, and in the postwar POW memoir literature, there are no verifiable accounts that claim the Soviets held back 23,000 or any other substantial number of US prisoners. Such numbers, furthermore, are not consistent with the final postwar casualty resolution and accounting.

Conclusions and Further Directions

It remains to be determined whether any American prisoners of war liberater in 1945 by Soviet forces were not returned to US military control but were held in Soviet prisons. There were individuals known to have been POWs of the Germans who did not return to US military control after VE Day. Military authorities expended considerable effort, including inquiries to the Soviets, in determining what might have happened to these men.

On 27 July 1945, the Provost Marshal General of the European Theater sent a list of 492 names identified as "unrecovered American prisoners of war" to the POW Information Bureau in Washington. Not all of the POWs on this or subsequent lists of discrepancy cases would necessarily have been in Soviet hands. Most on the ETO list eventually were accounted for and otherwise identified; others had died during the harsh conditions early in 1945, especially on the marches westward when the Germans evacuated the POW camps in the east. In December 1945 the Machine Records Branch of the Adjutant General's Office produced a somewhat refined listing, which included 207 names of "Unaccounted for American Prisoners of War Held by the German Government (CFN 74)." A further refinement produced on 14 March 1946, by the POW

Information Bureau of the Provost Marshal General's Office, included 31 unrecovered prisoners known to have been held by the Japanese and 77 held by the Germans.

At an early date in its research into World War II questions, the Joint Commission Support Directorate (JCSD) of the Department of Defense POW/MIA Office identified the "207 List" as a significant "find" and as a possible source for names of American POWs who might have been in Soviet custody at the end of the war. JCSD compared the names on this list against a variety of other documentary sources; the process has further accounted for and reduced to 87 the number of unresolved cases on this "207 List." Cases were resolved by identifying individuals who did return to military controls, or who had died in captivity, or who were killed in action, or who were not actually POWs. We are continuing to pursue leads to resolve the fate of the 87 from the "207 List" and other World War II discrepancy cases.

We developed files on all of the individual cases examined; a description of several of the more significant cases is included in our report. The discrepancy cases we pursued, in which an individual POW or MIA was identifiable, all led to a conclusion that the person dies or had been returned to military control, not that they had been incarcerated in a Soviet prison. Our conclusions, in effect, are consistent with the original findings of death issued by the War Department nearly fifty years ago and with the other earlier efforts at casualty resolution. Evidence supporting our conclusions comes from several sources including official personnel files, deceased personnel files, reports of the casualty resolution boards, from other American military records, and from Soviet-era documents.

The evidence in the case studies we pursued does not indicate that liberated American POWs were held against their will by the Soviet Government after VE Day. We uncovered no evidence from Russian or American archives that conclusively demonstrates such a finding, although research on several cases is still underway that could indicate otherwise. There is certainly no evidence that the Soviets held thousands of American POWs in the GULAG, or that the US Government participated in a cover-up of such an operation. We located ample evidence that contradicts such contentions and that demonstrated the "good faith effort" of military authorities following the war to resolve individual casualty status, including that of MIAs.

Ongoing Issues

The work of the World War II Working Group is complicated by a number of factors:

1. The lack of an activist constituency. There are very few immediate family members still living who lost loved ones in World War II. There are no parents, wives, or children of former World War II POWs asking us the whereabouts of their loved ones. Any leads or issues that were developed have been done so primarily from information contained in archival documents;

2. Lack of living eyewitnesses. It is becoming increasingly more difficult to locate actual participants in the events, both Russian and American;

3. The vast volume of information to review and the lack of access. World War II is the most extensively documented twentieth century conflict. There are still literally tons of documents that should be reviewed for POW informa-

tion. The same is true in the former Soviet Union. The issue is compounded in Russia by the lack of access to this material by JCSD analysts. Presently we rely heavily on Russian archivists to search for information. Not only is there a lack of Russian manpower dedicated to this project, but Russian archivists are not always aware of the types of documents that would aid our project and do not always provide us with archival citations in case a promising holding is found. Full access to unclassified archives is paramount.

We would like to propose an archival research exchange program to the Joint Commission. Under this program, JCSD analysts would be allowed to do active, long-term research in unclassified holdings in the former Soviet Union, and Russian researchers would have the same rights in the United States archives. Experience has shown that key documents are found in the most unlikely places. Presently, members of Task Force Russia, the Moscow-based branch of the Joint Commission Support Directorate, have been allowed some limited access to some Russian archives, but have never been allowed to devote the time or obtain the access required to perform team research.

There are a number of ongoing issues of concern to the US side of the Joint Commission. These deal primarily with servicemen, whose names have either appeared in Russian archival documents, in documents generated by the wartime US Military Mission to Moscow in various publications, or are amount the 87 on "The 207 List" that we have not yet resolved. From our Russian colleagues, we have requested information or documents relating to a number of cases. We will continue to pursue these requests.

As other names or issues arise, they will be addressed through Commission channels.

Source: Excerpt: Comprehensive Report of the U.S. Side of the U.S.-Russia Joint Commission on POW/MIA (June 17, 1996).

Ronald Reagan: The "Evil Empire" (March 8, 1983)

In 1981 the former Hollywood actor and governor of California Ronald Reagan, a staunch conservative from the right wing of the Republican Party, became president. Unlike his more pragmatic predecessors, he was a fierce anticommunist who felt a deep ideological antipathy toward the Soviet Union and did not hesitate to express this antagonism. Alarmed that during the late 1970s the Soviet Union had become more assertive in Latin America, Africa, and the Middle East, Reagan launched a major defense buildup, improving on the increases in military spending already projected by his predecessor, Jimmy Carter. Reagan consciously sought to restore the national confidence of the United States after the demoralizing 1970s. He repeatedly proclaimed the superiority of capitalism, democracy, and free institutions over the Soviet Union and sought to encourage free enterprise, reduce the role of government, and cut taxes by curtailing spending on welfare and other social programs. Excessive intervention by the government, he proclaimed, was the problem, not the solution. One of Reagan's closest international allies was Margaret Thatcher, the equally conservative and ideologically driven prime minister of Great Britain, who shared his anticommunist and free market outlook. Reagan did not hesitate to use undiplomatic language to describe the Soviet Union. In June 1982 he made a state visit to Britain. Speaking in the British House of Commons, he relegated Soviet totalitarianism to the "ash heap of history." He deliberately drew on memories of Winston Churchill, the towering British politician who had sounded the alarm against Adolf Hitler's Germany during the 1930s, served as an inspiring prime minister during World War II, and warned in 1946 that the Soviet Union had drawn an "iron curtain" across Europe. In the original draft of this speech, Reagan referred to the Soviet Union as "the focus of evil in the modern world" and a "militaristic empire," passages that were later cut as too provocative. Reagan did, however, proclaim his mission to "preserve freedom as well as peace" and described the conflict between totalitarianism and democracy as a battle between good and evil, optimistically stating that good would prevail. Nine months later, he recycled his uncompromising "evil empire" description of the Soviet Union when addressing the National Association of Evangelicals, a forum in which he also emphasized the antireligious aspects of communism. On this occasion, Reagan was particularly concerned to counter growing pressures in both the United States and Europe for a nuclear freeze agreement that would have halted deployments of additional short- and intermediate-range missiles in Western Europe.

[. . .]

Especially in this century, America has kept alight the torch of freedom, but not just for ourselves but for millions of others around the world.

And this brings me to my final point today. During my first press conference as President, in answer to a direct question, I pointed out that, as good Marxist-Leninists, the Soviet leaders have openly and publicly declared that the only morality they recognize is that which will further their cause, which is world revolution. I think I should point out I was only quoting Lenin, their guiding spirit, who said in 1920 that they repudiate all morality that proceeds from supernatural ideas—that's their name for religion—or ideas that are outside class conceptions. Morality is entirely subordinate to the interests of class war. And everything is moral that is necessary for the annihilation

of the old, exploiting social order and for uniting the proletariat.

Well, I think the refusal of many influential people to accept this elementary fact of Soviet doctrine illustrates an historical reluctance to see totalitarian powers for what they are. We saw this phenomenon in the 1930's. We see it too often today.

This doesn't mean we should isolate ourselves and refuse to seek an understanding with them. I intend to do everything I can to persuade them of our peaceful intent, to remind them that it was the West that refused to use its nuclear monopoly in the forties and fifties for territorial gain and which now proposes 50-percent cut in strategic ballistic missiles and the elimination of an entire class of land-based, intermediate-range nuclear missiles.

At the same time, however, they must be made to understand we will never compromise our principles and standards. We will never give away our freedom. We will never abandon our belief in God. And we will never stop searching for a genuine peace. But we can assure none of these things America stands for through the so-called nuclear freeze solutions proposed by some.

The truth is that a freeze now would be a very dangerous fraud, for that is merely the illusion of peace. The reality is that we must find peace through strength.

I would agree to a freeze if only we could freeze the Soviets' global desires. A freeze at current levels of weapons would remove any incentive for the Soviets to negotiate seriously in Geneva and virtually end our chances to achieve the major arms reductions which we have proposed. Instead, they would achieve their objectives through the freeze.

A freeze would reward the Soviet Union for its enormous and unparalleled military buildup. It would prevent the essential and long overdue modernization of United

States and allied defenses and would leave our aging forces increasingly vulnerable. And an honest freeze would require extensive prior negotiations on the systems and numbers to be limited and on the measures to ensure effective verification and compliance. And the kind of a freeze that has been suggested would be virtually impossible to verify. Such a major effort would divert us completely from our current negotiations on achieving substantial reductions.

A number of years ago, I heard a young father, a very prominent young man in the entertainment world, addressing a tremendous gathering in California. It was during the time of the cold war, and communism and our own way of life were very much on people's minds. And he was speaking to that subject. And suddenly, though, I heard him saying, "I love my little girls more than anything "And I said to myself, "Oh, no, don't. You can't—don't say that." But I had underestimated him. He went on: "I would rather see my little girls die now, still believing in God, than have them grow up under communism and one day die no longer believing in God."

There were thousands of young people in that audience. They came to their feet with shouts of joy. They had instantly recognized the profound truth in what he had said, with regard to the physical and the soul and what was truly important.

Yes, let us pray for the salvation of all of those who live in that totalitarian darkness—pray they will discover the joy of knowing God. But until they do, let us be aware that while they preach the supremacy of the state, declare its omnipotence over individual man, and predict its eventual domination of all peoples on the Earth, they are the focus of evil in the modern world.

It was C. S. Lewis who, in his unforgettable "Screwtape Letters," wrote: "The greatest evil is not done now in those sordid 'dens of crime' that Dickens loved to paint. It is not even done in concentration camps and labor camps. In those we see its final result. But it is conceived and ordered (moved, seconded, carried and minuted) in clear, carpeted, warmed, and well-lighted offices, by quiet men with white collars and cut fingernails and smooth-shaven cheeks who do not need to raise their voice."

Well, because these "quiet men" do not "raise their voices," because they sometimes speak in soothing tones of brotherhood and peace, because, like other dictators before them, they're always making "their final territorial demand," some would have us accept them at their word and accommodate ourselves to their aggressive impulses. But if history teaches anything, it teaches that simple-minded appeasement or wishful thinking about our adversaries is folly. It means the betrayal of our past, the squandering of our freedom.

So, I urge you to speak out against those who would place the United States in a position of military and moral inferiority. You know, I've always believed that old Screwtape reserved his best efforts for those of you in the church. So, in your discussions of the nuclear freeze proposals, I urge you to beware the temptation of pride—the temptation of blithely declaring yourselves above it all and label both sides equally at fault, to ignore the facts of history and the aggressive impulses of an evil empire, to simply call the arms race a giant misunderstanding and thereby remove yourself from the struggle between right and wrong and good and evil.

I ask you to resist the attempts of those who would have you withhold your support for our efforts, this administration's efforts, to keep America strong and free, while we negotiate real and verifiable reductions in the world's nuclear arsenals and one day, with God's help, their total elimination.

While America's military strength is important, let me add here that I've always maintained that the struggle now going on for the world will never be decided by bombs or rockets, by armies or military might. The real crisis we face today is a spiritual one; at root, it is a test of moral will and faith.

Whittaker Chambers, the man whose own religious conversion made him a witness to one of the terrible traumas of our time, the Hiss-Chambers case, wrote that the crisis of the Western World exists to the degree in which the West is indifferent to God, the degree to which it collaborates in communism's attempt to make man stand alone without God. And then he said, for Marxism-Leninism is actually the second oldest faith, first proclaimed in the Garden of Eden with the words of temptation, "Ye shall be as gods."

The Western World can answer this challenge, he wrote, "but only provided that its faith in God and the freedom He enjoins is as great as communism's faith in Man."

I believe we shall rise to the challenge. I believe that communism is another sad, bizarre chapter in human history whose last pages even now are being written. I believe this because the source of our strength in the quest for human freedom is not material, but spiritual. And because it knows no limitation, it must terrify and ultimately triumph over those who would enslave their fellow man. For in the words of Isaiah: "He giveth power to the faint; and to them that have no might He increased strength. . . . But they that wait upon the Lord shall renew their strength; they shall mount up with wings as eagles; they shall run, and not be weary. . . ."

Yes, change your world. One of our Founding Fathers, Thomas Paine, said, "We have it within our power to begin the world over again." We can do it, doing together what no one church could do by itself.

Source: Ronald Reagan, *Public Papers of the Presidents of the United States: Ronald Reagan, 1983*, Bk. 1 (Washington, DC: U.S. Government Printing Office, 1984), 359–64.

Ronald Reagan: "Tear Down This Wall" Speech (June 12, 1987)

After Mikhail Gorbachev became general secretary of the Soviet Communist Party in 1985, Soviet relations with the West gradually improved. Gorbachev initially sought to reform rather than destroy communism in the Soviet Union, through policies of economic restructuring (*perestroika*) and openness (*glasnost*). Gorbachev also began to rein back Soviet military spending and overseas interventions, and made serious overtures for cuts in nuclear and conventional forces. While responding to such overtures with growing enthusiasm, U.S. president Ronald Reagan remained a staunch anticommunist, and was unwilling as ever to appear to countenance Soviet domination of Eastern Europe. Speaking at the Brandenburg Gate in 1987, the symbolic heart of Berlin, Reagan urged Gorbachev to "tear down this wall" and allow the people of East Germany to choose their own destiny. Less than three years later, in November 1989, Reagan's hopes were fulfilled, as Gorbachev relaxed Soviet control of Eastern Europe and the people of Berlin demolished the Berlin Wall themselves.

President Ronald Reagan

Remarks on the East-West Relations at the Brandenburg Gate in West Berlin

June 12, 1987

Thank you very much. Chancellor Kohl, Governing Mayor Diepgen, ladies and gentlemen: Twenty-four years ago, President John F. Kennedy visited Berlin, speaking to the people of this city and the world at the City Hall. Well, since then two other presidents have come, each in his turn, to Berlin. And today I, myself, make my second visit to your city.

We come to Berlin, we American Presidents, because it's our duty to speak, in this place, of freedom. But I must confess, we're drawn here by other things as well: by the feeling of history in this city, more than 500 years older than our own nation; by the beauty of the Grunewald and the Tiergarten; most of all, by your courage and determination. Perhaps the composer Paul Lincke understood something about American presidents. You see, like so many Presidents before me, I come here today because wherever I go, whatever I do: Ich hab noch einen Koffer in Berlin. [I still have a suitcase in Berlin.]

Our gathering today is being broadcast throughout Western Europe and North America. I understand that it is being seen and heard as well in the East. To those listening throughout Eastern Europe, a special word: Although I cannot be with you, I address my remarks to you just as surely as to those standing here before me. For I join you, as I join your fellow countrymen in the West, in this firm, this unalterable belief: Es gibt nur ein Berlin. [There is only one Berlin.]

Behind me stands a wall that encircles the free sectors of this city, part of a vast system of barriers that divides the entire continent of Europe. From the Baltic, south, those barriers cut across Germany in a gash of barbed wire, concrete, dog runs, and guard towers. Farther south, there may be no visible, no obvious wall. But there remain armed guards and checkpoints all the same—still a restriction on the right to travel, still an instrument to impose upon ordinary men and women the will of a totalitarian state. Yet it is here in Berlin where the wall emerges most clearly; here, cutting across your city, where the news photo and the television screen have imprinted this brutal division of a continent upon the mind of the world. Standing before the Brandenburg Gate, every man is a German, separated from his fellow men. Every man is a Berliner, forced to look upon a scar.

President von Weizsacker has said, "The German question is open as long as the Brandenburg Gate is closed." Today I say: As long as the gate is closed, as long as this scar of a wall is permitted to stand, it is not the German question alone that remains open, but the question of freedom for all mankind. Yet I do not come here to lament. For I find in Berlin a message of hope, even in the shadow of this wall, a message of triumph.

In this season of spring in 1945, the people of Berlin emerged from their air-raid shelters to find devastation. Thousands of miles away, the people of the United States reached out to help. And in 1947 Secretary of State—as you've been told—George Marshall announced the creation of what would become known as the Marshall plan. Speaking precisely 40 years ago this month, he said: "Our policy is directed not against any country or doctrine, but against hunger, poverty, desperation, and chaos."

In the Reichstag a few moments ago, I saw a display commemorating this 40th anniversary of the Marshall plan. I was struck by the sign on a burnt-out, gutted structure that was being rebuilt. I understand that Berliners of my own generation can remember seeing signs like it dotted throughout the Western sectors of the city. The sign read simply: "The Marshall plan is helping here to strengthen the free world." A strong, free world in the West, that dream became real. Japan rose from ruin to become an economic giant. Italy, France, Belgium—virtually every nation in Western Europe saw political and economic rebirth; the European Community was founded.

In West Germany and here in Berlin, there took place an economic miracle, the

Wirtschaftswunder. Adenauer, Erhard, Reuter, and other leaders understood the practical importance of liberty—that just as truth can flourish only when the journalist is given freedom of speech, so prosperity can come about only when the farmer and businessman enjoy economic freedom. The German leaders reduced tariffs, expanded free trade, lowered taxes. From 1950 to 1960 alone, the standard of living in West Germany and Berlin doubled.

Where four decades ago there was rubble, today in West Berlin there is the greatest industrial output of any city in Germany—busy office blocks, fine homes and apartments, proud avenues, and the spreading lawns of park land. Where a city's culture seemed to have been destroyed, today there are two great universities, orchestras and an opera, countless theaters, and museums. Where there was want, today there's abundance—food, clothing, automobiles—the wonderful goods of the Ku'damm. From devastation, from utter ruin, you Berliners have, in freedom, rebuilt a city that once again ranks as one of the greatest on earth. The Soviets may have had other plans. But my friends, there were a few things the Soviets didn't count on—Berliner Herz, Berliner Humor, ja, und Berliner Schnauze. [Berliner heart, Berliner humor, yes, and a Berliner Schnauze.]

In the 1950s, Khrushchev predicted: "We will bury you." But in the West today, we see a free world that has achieved a level of prosperity and well-being unprecedented in all human history. In the Communist world, we see failure, technological backwardness, declining standards of health, even want of the most basic kind—too little food. Even today, the Soviet Union still cannot feed itself. After these four decades, then, there stands before the entire world one great and inescapable conclusion: Freedom leads to prosperity. Freedom replaces the ancient hatreds among the nations with comity and peace. Freedom is the victor.

And now the Soviets themselves may, in a limited way, be coming to understand the importance of freedom. We hear much from Moscow about a new policy of reform and openness. Some political prisoners have been released. Certain foreign news broadcasts are no longer being jammed. Some economic enterprises have been permitted to operate with greater freedom from state control. Are these the beginnings of profound changes in the Soviet state? Or are they token gestures, intended to raise false hopes in the West, or to strengthen the Soviet system without changing it? We welcome change and openness; for we believe that freedom and security go together, that the advance of human liberty can only strengthen the cause of world peace.

There is one sign the Soviets can make that would be unmistakable, that would advance dramatically the cause of freedom and peace. General Secretary Gorbachev, if you seek peace, if you seek prosperity for the Soviet Union and Eastern Europe, if you seek liberalization: Come here to this gate! Mr. Gorbachev, open this gate! Mr. Gorbachev, tear down this wall!

I understand the fear of war and the pain of division that afflict this continent—and I pledge to you my country's efforts to help overcome these burdens. To be sure, we in the West must resist Soviet expansion. So we must maintain defenses of unassailable strength. Yet we seek peace; so we must strive to reduce arms on both sides. Beginning 10 years ago, the Soviets challenged the Western alliance with a grave new threat, hundreds of new and more deadly SS-20 nuclear missiles, capable of striking every capital in Europe. The Western alliance responded by committing itself to a counter-deployment unless the Soviets agreed to negotiate a better solution; namely, the elimination of such weapons on both sides. For many months, the Soviets refused to bargain in earnestness. As the alliance, in turn, prepared to go forward with its counter-deployment, there were difficult days—days of protests like those during my 1982 visit to this city—and the Soviets later walked away from the table.

But through it all, the alliance held firm. And I invite those who protested then—I invite those who protest today—to mark this fact: Because we remained strong, the Soviets came back to the table. And because we remained strong, today we have within reach the possibility, not merely of limiting the growth of arms, but of eliminating, for the first time, an entire class of nuclear weapons from the face of the earth. As I speak, NATO ministers are meeting in Iceland to review the progress of our proposals for eliminating these weapons. At the talks in Geneva, we have also proposed deep cuts in strategic offensive weapons. And the Western allies have likewise made far-reaching proposals to reduce the danger of conventional war and to place a total ban on chemical weapons.

While we pursue these arms reductions, I pledge to you that we will maintain the capacity to deter Soviet aggression at any level at which it might occur. And in cooperation with many of our allies, the United States is pursuing the Strategic Defense Initiative—research to base deterrence not on the threat of offensive retaliation, but on defenses that truly defend; on systems, in short, that will not target populations, but shield them. By these means we seek to increase the safety of Europe and all the world. But we must remember a crucial fact: East and West do not mistrust each other because we are armed; we are armed because we mistrust each

other. And our differences are not about weapons but about liberty. When President Kennedy spoke at the City Hall those 24 years ago, freedom was encircled, Berlin was under siege. And today, despite all the pressures upon this city, Berlin stands secure in its liberty. And freedom itself is transforming the globe.

In the Philippines, in South and Central America, democracy has been given a rebirth. Throughout the Pacific, free markets are working miracle after miracle of economic growth. In the industrialized nations, a technological revolution is taking place—a revolution marked by rapid, dramatic advances in computers and telecommunications.

In Europe, only one nation and those it controls refuse to join the community of freedom. Yet in this age of redoubled economic growth, of information and innovation, the Soviet Union faces a choice: It must make fundamental changes, or it will become obsolete. Today thus represents a moment of hope. We in the West stand ready to cooperate with the East to promote true openness, to break down barriers that separate people, to create a safe, freer world.

And surely there is no better place than Berlin, the meeting place of East and West, to make a start. Free people of Berlin: Today, as in the past, the United States stands for the strict observance and full implementation of all parts of the Four Power Agreement of 1971. Let us use this occasion, the 750th anniversary of this city, to usher in a new era, to seek a still fuller, richer life for the Berlin of the future. Together, let us maintain and develop the ties between the Federal Republic and the Western sectors of Berlin, which is permitted by the 1971 agreement.

And I invite Mr. Gorbachev: Let us work to bring the Eastern and Western parts of the city closer together, so that all the inhabitants of all Berlin can enjoy the benefits that come with life in one of the great cities of the world. To open Berlin still further to all Europe, East and West, let us expand the vital air access to this city, finding ways of making commercial air service to Berlin more convenient, more comfortable, and more economical. We look to the day when West Berlin can become one of the chief aviation hubs in all central Europe.

With our French and British partners, the United States is prepared to help bring international meetings to Berlin. It would be only fitting for Berlin to serve as the site of United Nations meetings, or world conferences on human rights and arms control or other issues that call for international cooperation. There is no better way to establish hope for the future than to enlighten young minds, and we would be honored to sponsor summer youth exchanges, cultural events, and other programs for young Berliners from the East. Our French and British friends, I'm certain, will do the same. And it's my hope that an authority can be found in East Berlin to sponsor visits from young people of the Western sectors.

One final proposal, one close to my heart: Sport represents a source of enjoyment and ennoblement, and you may have noted that the Republic of Korea—South Korea—has offered to permit certain events of the 1988 Olympics to take place in the North. International sports competitions of all kinds could take place in both parts of this city. And what better way to demonstrate to the world the openness of this city than to offer in some future year to hold the Olympic games here in Berlin, East and West?

In these four decades, as I have said, you Berliners have built a great city. You've done so in spite of threats—the Soviet attempts to impose the East-mark, the blockade. Today the city thrives in spite of the challenges implicit in the very presence of this wall. What keeps you here? Certainly there's a great deal to be said for your fortitude, for your defiant courage. But I believe there's something deeper, something that involves Berlin's whole look and feel and way of life—not mere sentiment. No one could live long in Berlin without being completely disabused of illusions. Something instead, that has seen the difficulties of life in Berlin but chose to accept them, that continues to build this good and proud city in contrast to a surrounding totalitarian presence that refuses to release human energies or aspirations. Something that speaks with a powerful voice of affirmation, that says yes to this city, yes to the future, yes to freedom. In a word, I would submit that what keeps you in Berlin is love—love both profound and abiding.

Perhaps this gets to the root of the matter, to the most fundamental distinction of all between East and West. The totalitarian world produces backwardness because it does such violence to the spirit, thwarting the human impulse to create, to enjoy, to worship. The totalitarian world finds even symbols of love and of worship an affront. Years ago, before the East Germans began rebuilding their churches, they erected a secular structure: the television tower at Alexander Platz. Virtually ever since, the authorities have been working to correct what they view as the tower's one major flaw, treating the glass sphere at the top with paints and chemicals of every kind. Yet even today when the sun strikes that sphere—that sphere that towers over all Berlin—the light makes the sign of the cross. There in Berlin, like the city itself, symbols of love, symbols of worship, cannot be suppressed.

As I looked out a moment ago from the Reichstag, that embodiment of German unity, I noticed words crudely spray-painted upon the wall, perhaps by a young Berliner: "This wall will fall. Beliefs become reality." Yes, across Europe, this wall will fall. For it cannot withstand faith; it cannot withstand truth. The wall cannot withstand freedom.

And I would like, before I close, to say one word. I have read, and I have been questioned since I've been here about certain demonstrations against my coming. And I would like to say just one thing, and to those who demonstrate so. I wonder if they have ever asked themselves that if they should have the kind of government they apparently seek, no one would ever be able to do what they're doing again.

Thank you and God bless you all.

Source: Ronald Reagan, *Public Papers of the Presidents of the United States: Ronald Reagan, 1987,* Bk. 1 (Washington, DC: U.S. Government Printing Office, 1989), 634–38.

The Minsk Declarations (Dissolution of the Soviet Union) (December 8, 1991)

By 1990 the readiness of Soviet president Mikhail Gorbachev to allow the former Soviet satellites in Eastern Europe to reject communism and leave the Warsaw Pact had strengthened separatist forces within the Soviet Union itself. The Baltic republics, Estonia, Latvia, and Lithuania, which had only been incorporated in the Soviet Union during World War II, were particularly outspoken in demanding autonomy or independence, but nationalist forces were also developing in various Soviet republics, including Azerbaijan, Armenia, Georgia, and Ukraine. In January 1991 unrest in Lithuania, whose government had declared that the Soviet constitution was no longer valid there, led Gorbachev to order the Soviet military to replace the republic's government. At least 14 people were killed and another 600 injured, provoking protests from many Western states. Seeking to defuse the growing internal crisis, Gorbachev and his advisors proceeded to draw up a treaty of union that would have made the Soviet Union into a voluntary democratic federation whose members enjoyed economic free trade with each other. In August 1991 nationalist hard-liners within the Soviet leadership, who feared that this arrangement would lead to the breakup of the Soviet Union, mounted a coup against Gorbachev, then on holiday in the Crimea. Although Gorbachev's government survived, largely due to the intervention of Boris Yeltsin, elected two months earlier as president of the Russian Republic, Gorbachev's authority was fatally weakened. Yeltsin, who sought to implement sweeping economic reforms within Russia, regarded the Soviet Union as expendable, and during the fall the Russian Republic gradually took over the Soviet ministries based in Moscow. After confidential negotiations, in early December 1991 Yeltsin met with the leaders of the republics of Ukraine and Belarus, and the three declared the dissolution of the Soviet Union and its replacement by a voluntary Commonwealth of Independent States. Membership in this organization was open to all former Soviet republics, and by the end of the month 11 states—Armenia, Azerbaijan, Belarus, Kazakhstan, Kyrgystan, Moldova, the Russian Federation, Tajikistan, Turkmenistan, Ukraine, and Uzbekistan—had joined. On December 30 the signatories agreed to coordinate their military policies and to observe the arms control agreements concluded by the former Soviet Union. Gorbachev objected strongly but unavailingly to the dismantling of the Soviet Union, which he had hoped to preserve. On December 24, 1991, the Russian Federation took over the Soviet seat in the United Nations (UN). The following day, Gorbachev finally resigned his position as the last Soviet president, leaving Yeltsin in undisputed control as president of the Russian Federation, an outcome that had probably been one major underlying reason behind Yeltsin's move to break up the Soviet Union.

The Minsk Agreement signed by the heads of state of Belarus, the Russian Federation, and Ukraine on December 8, 1991

Preamble

We, the Republic of Belarus, the Russian Federation and the Republic of Ukraine, as founder states of the Union of Soviet Socialist Republics (USSR), which signed the 1922 Union Treaty, further described as the high contracting parties, conclude that the USSR has ceased to exist as a subject of international law and a geopolitical reality.

[. . .]

Article 1

The high contracting parties form the Commonwealth of Independent States.

Article 2

The high contracting parties guarantee their citizens equal rights and freedoms regardless of nationality or other distinctions. Each of the high contracting parties guarantees the citizens of the other parties, and also persons without citizenship that live on its territory, civil, political, social, economic and cultural rights and freedoms in accordance with generally recognized international norms of human rights, regardless of national allegiance or other distinctions.

Article 3

The high contracting parties, desiring to promote the expression, preservation and development of the ethnic, cultural, linguistic and religious individuality of the national minorities resident on their territories, and

that of the unique ethno-cultural regions that have come into being, take them under their protection.

Article 4

The high contracting parties will develop the equal and mutually beneficial co-operation of their peoples and states in the spheres of politics, the economy, culture, education, public health, protection of the environment, science and trade and in the humanitarian and other spheres, will promote the broad exchange of information and will conscientiously and unconditionally observe reciprocal obligations.

The parties consider it a necessity to conclude agreements on co-operation in the above spheres.

Article 5

The high contracting parties recognize and respect one another's territorial integrity and the inviolability of existing borders within the Commonwealth.

They guarantee openness of borders, freedom of movement for citizens and of transmission of information within the Commonwealth.

Article 6

The member-states of the Commonwealth will co-operate in safeguarding international peace and security and in implementing effective measures for reducing weapons and military spending. They seek the elimination of all nuclear weapons and universal total disarmament under strict international control.

The parties will respect one another's aspiration to attain the status of a non-nuclear zone and a neutral state.

The member-states of the community will preserve and maintain under united command a common military-strategic space, including unified control over nuclear weapons, the procedure for implementing which is regulated by a special agreement.

They also jointly guarantee the necessary conditions for the stationing and functioning of and for material and social provision for the strategic armed forces. The parties contract to pursue a harmonized policy on questions of social protection and pension provision for members of the services and their families.

Article 7

The high contracting parties recognize that within the sphere of their activities, implemented on the equal basis through the common coordinating institutions of the Commonwealth, will be the following:

—co-operation in the sphere of foreign policy;
—co-operation in forming and developing the united economic area, the common European and Eurasian markets, in the area of customs policy;
—co-operation in developing transport and communication systems;
—co-operation in preservation of the environment, and participation in creating a comprehensive international system of ecological safety;
—migration policy issues;
—and fighting organized crime.

Article 8

The parties realize the planetary character of the Chernobyl catastrophe and pledge themselves to unite and co-ordinate their efforts in minimizing and overcoming its consequences.

To these ends they have decided to conclude a special agreement which will take

consider [sic] the gravity of the consequences of this catastrophe.

Article 9

The disputes regarding interpretation and application of the norms of this agreement are to be solved by way of negotiations between the appropriate bodies, and when necessary, at the level of heads of the governments and states.

Article 10

Each of the high contracting parties reserved the right to suspend the validity of the present agreement or individual articles thereof, after informing the parties to the agreement of this a year in advance.

The clauses of the present agreement may be addended to or amended with the common consent of the high contracting parties.

Article 11

From the moment that the present agreement is signed, the norms of third states, including the former USSR, are not permitted to be implemented on the territories of the signatory states.

Article 12

The high contracting parties guarantee the fulfillment of the international obligations binding upon them from the treaties and agreements of the former USSR.

Article 13

The present agreement does not affect the obligations of the high contracting parties in regard to third states.

The present agreement is open for all member-states of the former USSR to join, and also for other states which share the goals and principles of the present agreement.

Article 14

The city of Minsk is the official location of the coordinating bodies of the Commonwealth.

The activities of bodies of the former USSR are discontinued on the territories of the member-states of the Commonwealth.

Agreement on Strategic Forces

Concluded between the 11 members of the Commonwealth of Independent States on December 30, 1991.

Preamble

Guided by the necessity for a coordinated and organized solution to issues in the sphere of the control of the strategic forces and the single control over nuclear weapons, the Republic of Armenia, the Republic of Azerbaijan, the Republic of Belarus, the Republic of Kazakhstan, the Republic of Kyrgyzstan, the Republic of Moldova, the Russian Federation, the Republic of Tajikistan, the Republic of Turkmenistan, the Republic of Ukraine and the Republic of Uzbekistan, subsequently referred to as 'the member-states of the Commonwealth,' have agreed on the following:

Article 1

The term 'strategic forces' means: groupings, formations, units, institutions, the military training institutes for the strategic missile troops, for the air force, for the navy and for the air defenses; the directorates of the Space Command and of the airborne troops, and of strategic and operational intelligence, and the nuclear technical units and also the forces, equipment and other military facilities designed for the control and maintenance of the strategic forces of the former USSR (the schedule is to be determined for each state participating in the Commonwealth in a separate protocol).

Article 2

The member-states of the Commonwealth undertake to observe the international treaties of the former USSR, to pursue a coordinated policy in the area of international security, disarmament and arms control, and to participate in the preparation and implementation of programs for reductions in arms and armed forces. The member-states of the Commonwealth are immediately entering into negotiations with one another and also with other states which were formerly part of the USSR, but which have not joined the commonwealth, with the aim of ensuring guarantees and developing mechanisms for implementing the aforementioned treaties.

Article 3

The member-states of the Commonwealth recognize the need for joint command of strategic forces and for maintaining unified control of nuclear weapons, and other types of weapons of mass destruction, of the armed forces of the former USSR.

Article 4

Until the complete elimination of nuclear weapons, the decision on the need for their use is taken by the president of the Russian Federation in agreement with the heads of the Republic of Belarus, the Republic of Kazakhstan and the Republic of Ukraine, and in consultation with the heads of the other member-states of the Commonwealth.

Until their destruction in full, nuclear weapons located on the territory of the Republic of Ukraine shall be under the control of the Combined Strategic Forces Command, with the aim that they not be used and be dismantled by the end of 1994, including tactical nuclear weapons by 1 July 1992.

The process of destruction of nuclear weapons located on the territory of the Republic of Belarus and the Republic of Ukraine shall take place with the participation of the Republic of Belarus, the Russian Federation and the Republic of Ukraine under the joint control of the Commonwealth states.

Article 5

The status of strategic forces and the procedure for service in them shall be defined in a special agreement.

Article 6

This agreement shall enter into force from the moment of its signing and shall be terminated by decision of the signatory states or the Council of Heads of State of the Commonwealth.

This agreement shall cease to apply to a signatory state from whose territory strategic forces or nuclear weapons are withdrawn.

Source: "The Minsk Agreement," The Library of Congress Country Studies, http://lcweb2.loc.gov/frd/cs/belarus/by_appnb.html. "Agreement on Strategic Forces," Berlin Information-Center for Transatlantic Security, http://www.bits.de/NRANEU/START/documents/strategicforces91.htm.

Competition Spurs Technology

How Did Tensions between Global Superpowers Fuel Technological Advancements during the Cold War?

Motivated by the urgency of national security, and possibly even survival, the United States and Soviet Union poured money, resources, and talent into decades of scientific research. A number of events serve as important milestones in this decades-long competition. For instance, American development of the hydrogen bomb dramatically increased tension with the Soviets, who responded by focusing more on their evolving technology programs. These efforts paid off in 1957 with the launch of Sputnik 1, the first artificial satellite. The United States' sense of technological preeminence was shattered, and the space race had begun.

In the following Defining Moments, Dr. Larry Simpson analyzes the role of these two events—the detonation of the first hydrogen bomb and the launch of Sputnik—on Cold War relations and the technological arms race. In the first, he explores the dramatic deterioration of U.S.–Soviet relations in the first few years after World War II and the U.S. drive to create ever more powerful weapons. Both sides' keen interest in producing new weapons was both caused by and a product of this breakdown. In the second Defining Moment, Dr. Simpson demonstrates how the Soviet triumph of Sputnik altered

the balance of power between the two enemies. With the launch of that small satellite, outer space became a potential battlefield for the next war. Americans were stunned by the Soviet success but would soon counter it with their own space program, which would eventually come to eclipse that of the Soviet Union.

Defining Moment 1: Development of the Hydrogen Bomb

On November 1, 1952, the United States tested its first hydrogen device on Eniwetok Atoll in the Marshall Islands in the South Pacific. The thermonuclear explosion—the equivalent of 10 million tons, or 10 megatons, of TNT—created a three-mile-wide fireball that instantly obliterated the tiny land mass. The blast propelled the Cold War into another more potentially lethal stage. Its power was so unnerving that it took the Harry S. Truman administration two weeks to reveal what had happened to the world.

"Mike," the codename of the operation, was largely the product of the work of two individuals: the so-called father of the H-bomb, Edward Teller, and the lesser-known Stanislaw Ulam. Teller was a Hungarian Jew and a brilliant physicist who had come to the United States in 1935 fleeing totalitarianism in Europe. Ulam was an equally gifted Polish mathematician who had also come to the United States in the mid-1930s. During World War II, Teller became a leader of one of the research teams at Los Alamos, New Mexico, working on the Manhattan Project, which was responsible for creating the atomic bomb. That weapon had been detonated by atomic fission, but Teller's research led him to suggest making a much more powerful device using nuclear fusion as a triggering mechanism. Many influential scientists, however, opposed Teller's proposal. Chief among these was J. Robert Oppenheimer, who had been the lead scientist on the Manhattan Project. Oppenheimer had been appalled by the devastation wrought at both Hiroshima and Nagasaki and, as an adviser to the Atomic Energy Commission, which administered nuclear policy, he counseled against producing an even more destructive device than the atomic bomb. Moreover, as the United States then held a monopoly on the possession of atomic weapons, there was little incentive to develop more advanced ones. Ulam also demonstrated that some of the initial calculations behind Teller's model were incorrect. Hence, there was little progress in the development of the new weapon.

The dramatic deterioration of relations between the United States and the Soviet Union in the period following World War II had a profound influence on the American decision to produce a thermonuclear device. In August 1949, the Soviets stunned the world when they tested their first atomic bomb. Then, on January 27, 1950, the German-born nuclear physicist Klaus Fuchs confessed to authorities at the War Office in London that he was a communist spy who had relayed top-secret information to the Soviets. President Truman worried what would happen if Josef Stalin possessed thermonuclear weapons and the United States did not. Thus, just four days after Fuchs's revelations to the British, the American president ordered the accelerated development of the new weapon.

Within a year, Ulam had solved some of the problems with the original conception for the hydrogen bomb with the idea of compressing liquid deuterium, and he and Teller collaborated to produce a new theoretical version of the device. Nonetheless, officials at Los Alamos did not allow Teller to head the H-bomb project, so he left the team to continue teaching at the University of California, Berkeley, and to pursue his dream of creating a thermonuclear research institution at the Livermore Laboratory in California. He played no part in the test and learned of it by watching a seismograph in a Berkeley basement.

Whatever advantages the United States may have had in the technological race for more powerful weapons soon evaporated in a scant nine months with the detonation of a Soviet thermonuclear device on August 12, 1953. By the end of 1955, both sides had produced the first operational bombs and, by the 1980s, they had 40,000 thermonuclear weapons in their arsenals—and thus had the capability of inflicting cataclysmic destruction on each other.

Larry Simpson

Defining Moment 2: Sputnik *and the Beginning of the Space Race*

The Soviet launch into space of the 83.6-kilogram aluminum sphere called *Sputnik*, or "little traveler" in Russian, on October 4, 1957, was the first time man had successfully placed an artificial object into Earth's orbit. In just over an hour and a half, as it accomplished its first revolution, the basketball-sized satellite had inaugurated a new chapter in the Cold War with the start of the space race between the United States and the Soviet Union. For the next two weeks, *Sputnik*'s four antennas broadcast beeping radio signals and, all told, the satellite remained in space for 92 days and completed 1,440 orbits before plunging back into the atmosphere and incinerating on January 4, 1958.

Meanwhile, a month after the first launch, the Soviets sent a second, much larger satellite (1,110 pounds, or 508.3 kilograms) into orbit on which the dog, Laika, became the first living creature ever to be shot into space.

Americans and the world were stunned by the news, even as Soviet leader Nikita Khrushchev trumpeted the dramatic achievement of socialist science. The remarkable news resulted in deep soul-searching and self-questioning on the part of many in the United States. America had its own space program, led by Wernher von Braun, and President Dwight D. Eisenhower had already announced in mid-1955 that the United States would launch an object into orbit sometime during the International Geophysical Year (July 1957 through December 1958), a period when solar activity was to be at a high-point. The United States successfully sent the satellite *Explorer* into orbit at the end of the following January, but only after an embarrassing, nationally televised failure nearly two months earlier. In addition, the Americans could not launch payloads nearly as large as those launched by the Soviets. The Russian Ministry of Defense, which was responsible for *Sputnik*, clearly had a more advanced rocket propulsion program than did the United States. Such technology also had the potential of delivering nuclear weapons, and Americans feared that they were losing the Cold War to the communists. The U.S. Senate, with Majority Leader Lyndon B. Johnson taking the lead, held hearings to dramatize the alleged failure of the Eisenhower administration.

The Soviets would once more beat the Americans in the space race when cosmonaut Yuri Gagarin became the first man to orbit the earth on April 12, 1961. But the United States was already on its way to catching up with the Soviets with the passage of the National Defense Education Act in September 1958 and the creation of the National Aeronautics and Space Administration (NASA) the following month. The former emphasized funding for mathematics and the sciences, while NASA became the instrument for overtaking the Soviets in space exploration. John F. Kennedy would set the terms of the international contest when, in 1961, he declared America's intent to put a man on the moon. By the time Neil Armstrong walked on the lunar surface on July 20, 1969, the Americans and Soviets had successfully launched more than 5,000 objects into space and the United States had taken the lead in the space race.

Larry Simpson

Print Resources

Ball, Howard. *Justice Downwind: America's Atomic Testing Program in the 1950s.* New York: Oxford University Press, 1986.

Breuer, William B. *Race to the Moon: America's Duel with the Soviets.* Westport, CT: Praeger, 1993.

Divine, Robert A. *Blowing on the Wind: The Nuclear Test Ban Debate, 1954–1960.* New York: Oxford University Press, 1978.

Fursenko, Aleksandr. *Khrushchev's Cold War: The Inside Story of an American Adversary.* New York: W. W. Norton, 2007.

Gaddis, John Lewis. *The Cold War: A New History.* New York: Penguin, 2006.

Kennedy, Robert F. *Thirteen Days: A Memoir of the Cuban Missile Crisis.* New York: W. W. Norton, 1999.

Launius, Roger D. *Frontiers of Space Exploration.* Westport, CT: Greenwood Press, 1998.

Miller, Richard L. *Under the Cloud: The Decades of Nuclear Testing.* New York: The Free Press, 1986.

Norris, Robert S., and William Arkin. "Known Nuclear Tests Worldwide, 1945–1948." *Bulletin of Atomic Scientists* (November–December 1998): 65–67.

Schefter, James L. *The Race.* New York: Doubleday, 1999.

Evolving East–West Relations

How Did U.S. Diplomatic Relations with Communist Nations Vary during the Cold War?

Relations between nations will vary over time, from friendly to cool to tense, depending on a number of factors, including internal and external issues relevant to each power and the ascendancy of new leaders and new policies. This was certainly the case during the Cold War. Although the capitalist West (in particular, the United States) and the communist East (in particular, the Soviet Union and China) were generally at odds with one another, there were a number of both high and low points. Such diplomatic crises as the Berlin Blockade and the Taiwan Straits Crisis were counterbalanced by triumphs such as détente and arms reduction treaties. Such ups and downs, however, help to underscore the uncertainty of the era.

In the following Defining Moments, Dr. Larry Simpson explores two key moments in the Cold War and analyzes how each impacted East–West relations. In the first, he examines the Cuban Missile Crisis of October 1962. The Cuban Missile Crisis was, to that point in history, the closest the world had ever come to nuclear war. American–Soviet relations were, for a short period of time in 1962, at their nadir, and only a combination of public maneuvers and secret deals resolved the crisis peacefully. The

second Defining Moment jumps ahead a decade to highlight Richard Nixon's 1972 visit to China and the subsequent rapprochement between the two countries. This development changed the global balance of power by introducing another major player to the table. Thus, both the Cuban Missile Crisis and the thawing of Sino-American relations significantly changed the landscape of the Cold War.

Defining Moment 1: Cuban Missile Crisis

For 13 days in October 1962, Washington and Moscow came closer to an armed conflict than at any other time during the Cold War. Considering that each side then possessed an arsenal of nuclear weapons, the possibility of a clash between the superpowers had profound global ramifications.

The crisis followed the attempted introduction of ballistic missiles into Cuba by Nikita Khrushchev, premier of the Soviet Union. The Caribbean island, which lies just 70 miles from the United States, was under the leadership of Fidel Castro and aligned with the Soviet bloc. Castro sought and obtained massive military support from the Soviet Union, particularly in the wake of the Bay of Pigs invasion in 1961, during which the Central Intelligence Agency (CIA) had supported a failed attempt by Cuban exiles to invade the island and overthrow its communist government. For his part, Khrushchev decided to up the ante and secretly introduced medium-range and intermediate-range ballistic missiles as well as nuclear warheads into Cuba, thereby greatly enhancing his strategic capability against the United States. It was a high-risk gambit mainly done to save Castro's communist outpost in the Western Hemisphere. While Soviet officials assured their American counterparts that the weapons were strictly of a defensive nature, some in Washington became alarmed with the introduction of surface-to-air missiles (SAMs) with the capability of downing U.S. reconnaissance aircraft. Suspecting that the communists were trying to hide the introduction of offensive weapons, the Americans decided to conduct photoreconnaissance missions over Cuba. On October 15, 1962, analyses of pictures taken by a U-2 spy plane the previous day revealed that the Soviets were in the process of placing surface-to-surface missiles (SSMs) on the island.

The most dangerous confrontation of the Cold War now unfolded. When President John F. Kennedy saw the photographs on October 16, he responded to the threat by organizing a special committee of high-ranking officials to advise him through the crisis. Kennedy's advisers intensely debated whether Washington should respond militarily or diplomatically. Meanwhile, Soviet foreign minister Andrei Gromyko, who was unaware of what the president knew, continued to assert in a White House visit that his country was supplying Cuba with defensive weapons only. An angry Kennedy weighed two options: conducting an air strike to remove the missiles or initiating a blockade of the island while seeking a compromise. One week after the U.S. discovery of the missile sites, Kennedy appeared on television and revealed the information to a stunned public.

He called for the immediate withdrawal or elimination of the missiles and imposed a "quarantine," as he termed the blockade, of Cuban waters. Elsewhere, American ambassador to the United Nations (UN) Adlai Stevenson confronted the Soviet representative on the floor of the Security Council. On October 26, Khrushchev sent a letter demanding an American pledge not to invade Cuba. The Russian leader sent another message the following day that demanded that the United States remove Jupiter medium-range missiles that had recently been deployed in Turkey. When a Soviet antiaircraft unit exceeded its orders and shot down a U-2 over Cuba and killed its pilot that same day, it appeared the situation might get out of control.

The moment of truth had arrived. Kennedy chose to publicly accept the Soviet leader's condition that he should not invade Cuba while privately giving reassurances that the Jupiters would be withdrawn. The Soviet Union also suffered from a 17:1 disadvantage in strategic weaponry should any conflict escalate, and knew that fighting a conventional war at America's doorstep, where the United States had a preponderance of force, was a foolhardy undertaking. Hence, Khrushchev decided to compromise by not challenging the blockade and agreeing to remove the missiles on October 28. Nonetheless, tensions remained high over the next few weeks as the United States verified that the Soviets were actually removing their weapons, over Castro's vehement protests. When, on November 20, 1962, Kennedy halted the blockade, the confrontation officially came to an end.

Larry Simpson

Defining Moment 2: Rapprochement with China

When Richard Nixon began an eight-day visit to the People's Republic of China

(PRC) on February 21, 1972, he completed a diplomatic revolution. The historic opening to America's erstwhile enemy, termed the "Nixon Shock," followed more than two decades during which the United States had no relations with communist China. The visit consequently had profound geopolitical and economic ramifications. On the final day of his stay, the president issued the joint Shanghai Communiqué recognizing the PRC as the legitimate government of China and pledging to seek normalized relations with Beijing. Playing the so-called China Card gave Nixon the potential of gaining leverage over both Moscow and Beijing, while at the same time it increased the ability for U.S. diplomatic maneuvering. The new relationship with communist China thereby contributed in the short-term to the end of the Vietnam War and helped ease global tensions in the long run. Another lasting effect of the foreign policy initiative was that it allowed for the development of trade between the world's richest nation and its most populous one. Critics assert, however, that the initiative came at the cost of ignoring China's dreadful human rights record and abandoning the Nationalist Chinese, who had relocated to Taiwan after losing the Chinese Civil War in 1949. Ultimately, some detractors would question who had influence over who.

The change of course in Sino-American relations began in 1969. Chinese leader Mao Zedong was uneasy following the 1968 Warsaw Pact invasion of Czechoslovakia and, heeding the advice of some top Chinese marshals, sent signals that he might be willing to consider a less antagonistic relationship with the United States. Having come to office only a month before, Nixon responded cautiously to Mao's initiative and charged his national security adviser, Henry Kissinger, with undertaking a thorough review of America's China policy. Kissinger saw a possibility of exploiting the bitter rift that had arisen between the Chinese and the Soviets over ideological issues, foreign policy, and territorial disputes. Despite some of the harsh rhetoric that Beijing continued to direct publicly at the United States, Kissinger thought that Mao might be willing to accept rapprochement with the United States as a counterweight to the threat from Moscow.

A series of clashes along the Sino-Soviet border that began in March 1969 gave the United States the unique opportunity to test the diplomatic waters. In April, Secretary of State William Rogers announced the possibility of the United States adopting a new "two China" policy whereby Washington would recognize both the PRC and the Nationalist Chinese on Taiwan. During the summer, the State Department eased travel and trade restrictions directed against the PRC, and Nixon sent signals that the United States sought an improvement in its dealings with the Chinese. When, in September, it appeared that the Soviets were poised to attack their neighbor preemptively, Nixon warned Leonid Brezhnev that he would not sit by and allow China's defeat. Finally, in December, Nixon sent word via the American ambassador in Poland that he was interested in opening direct talks with the Chinese.

The next two years saw further steps between the two sides to improve their relations, although U.S. involvement in the conflict in Southeast Asia complicated diplomatic overtures. The Americans indicated a willingness to back off of their support of Taiwan, ended travel restrictions to China, and eased restraints on trade. In April 1971, after receiving a Chinese invitation, the U.S. table-tennis team became the first Americans allowed into the PRC since the communists came to power in 1949. In July, during a secret visit by Kissinger (part of the so-called ping-pong diplomacy), Nixon's national security adviser made concessions on Taiwan in exchange for an invitation for the president to visit China. Shortly thereafter, the Nixon administration removed its opposition to China becoming a member of the United Nations (UN) and, in October, the United States allowed the PRC's admission to the international body and Nationalist China's expulsion by the General Assembly. The way was thus set for Nixon's historic trip to China the following February.

Larry Simpson

Print Resources

Ausland, John C. *Kennedy, Khrushchev, and the Berlin-Cuba Crisis 1961–1964*. Oslo, Norway: Scandinavian University Press, 1996.

Beschloss, Michael R. *Mayday: Eisenhower, Khrushchev, and the U-2 Affair*. New York: Harper and Row, 1988.

Cooper, Chester L. *In the Shadows of History: 50 Years Behind the Scenes of Cold War Diplomacy*. Amherst, NY: Prometheus Book, 2005.

Fursenko, Aleksandr, and Timothy Naftali. *One Hell of a Gamble: Khrushchev, Castro, and Kennedy, 1958–1964*. New York: W. W. Norton, 1997.

Gaddis, John Lewis. *We Now Know: Rethinking Cold War History*. New York: Oxford University Press, 1997.

Kennedy, Robert F. *Thirteen Days: A Memoir of the Cuban Missile Crisis*. New York: W. W. Norton, 1999.

Nalebuff, Barry. *Brinkmanship and Nuclear Deterrence: The Neutrality of Escalation*. Princeton, NJ: Princeton University Press, 1987.

Salisbury, Harrison E. *The New Emperors: China in the Era of Mao and Deng*. Boston: Little, Brown, 1992.

Schelling, Thomas C. *The Strategy of Conflict*. New York: Oxford University Press, 1965.

Spence, Jonathan. *The Search for Modern China*. New York: W. W. Norton, 1990.

Proxy Wars and Military Aid

How Did the Larger Context of the Cold War Influence the Nature of Military Conflict during That Period?

There were a number of "hot" conflicts during the Cold War. None, however, directly involved both of the world's two nuclear superpowers at the time—the United States and the Soviet Union. This does not mean, however, that these superpowers were removed from these smaller wars. In fact, nearly all military conflicts between 1945 and 1991 were shaped by the larger tensions that fueled the Cold War. Rather than fighting one another on the battlefield (which could have quickly escalated to include the use of nuclear weapons), the United States and the Soviet Union used proxy states to do battle. They supplied these nations, most of which were in the developing world, with arms, technologies, and training. This allowed each to fulfill what it saw as its geopolitical, economic, and ideological imperatives without having to go head-to-head with the other superpower. Even when one of the superpowers did become militarily engaged, the other found alternative methods of supporting its side without open military action.

In the Defining Moments that follow, Dr. Larry Simpson explores two of the most important military conflicts during the Cold War in order to illustrate the nature of warfare during that period. In the first, he examines U.S. involvement in the Korean War, which erupted in 1950 when communist North Korea attacked South Korea. In the second Defining Moment, Dr. Simpson discusses the Soviet invasion of Afghanistan in late 1979, and the subsequent Soviet occupation of that country, which dragged on until 1988. Although these wars occurred in different parts of the globe and were separated from each other by more than two decades, they share many similarities. Both occurred in developing nations caught between the opposing forces of East and West. In each case, one of the two superpowers directly intervened in accordance with its interests. In contrast, the other superpower found a more indirect way to try to achieve its own aims during the conflict.

Defining Moment 1: The Korean War

To understand the Korean War (1950–1953), some background information is necessary. Korea had been part of the Japanese Empire from 1910, but at the end of World War II, Soviet troops moved in to occupy the north while American soldiers took over the south, with the peninsula divided at the 38th parallel of latitude. In 1948, the United Nations (UN) held elections to determine the future of Korea, with the South participating but the North boycotting. Thus, Syngman Rhee, a Princeton PhD who fled Korea in 1912 and led a government-in-exile for 20 years, came to power with American support in what became the Republic of Korea. For its part, the Soviet Union backed the Democratic People's Republic of Korea led by a Russian-trained officer named Kim Il Sung. Despite the fact that the two men were bitter rivals and that each aspired to reunify the Korean nation under his personal leadership, both the Soviet Union and the United States withdrew their forces from Korea by mid-1949. Yet, that development did not signal a movement toward peace. In October, Mao Zedong and the Chinese Communist Party took over mainland China and an opportunistic Soviet leader, Josef Stalin, saw a chance to do in East Asia what he could not accomplish in Western Europe. Stalin thus began a massive military build-up of North Korea and supported Kim's "liberation" of South Korea, which began when the Communists crossed the frontier in force on June 25, 1950.

The conflict quickly involved not just the Koreans but also the United Nations. While the South Korean army crumbled beneath the Communist onslaught, Harry Truman acted decisively to enlist the international body in supporting a "police action" to resist the invasion. Ironically, the Soviet Union was boycotting the UN Security Council at the time, so it could not veto this unprecedented use of collective force. Nonetheless, the actual fighting continued to go against South Korea and its American-led UN allies until the latter were confined to the southeast portion of the peninsula around the vital port of Pusan. Then, on September 15, General Douglas MacArthur, commander of UN forces, made a bold and daring move and landed American troops behind North Korean lines at Inchon, on the western coast of the peninsula near Seoul. Cutting the North Koreans' supply lines as well as their route of retreat, MacArthur soon turned the tables on

the Communists and defeated the invading troops in the South. MacArthur next moved north and, with Truman's permission, drove deep into North Korea. Disregarding warnings that something was afoot, MacArthur was taken by surprise in mid-November when seven divisions of Chinese "volunteers" crossed the Yalu River into Korea and overran his unprepared forces. Mao had hesitated before sending the soldiers against the Americans, but pressure from Stalin and the prospect of having Yankee imperialists along his border forced the Chinese leader's hand. By year's end, Communist troops were again south of the 38th parallel.

The war now moved to another stage. MacArthur's subordinate, General Matthew Ridgway, played a pivotal role in deploying the beleaguered allied forces to halt the Chinese offensive. A frustrated MacArthur appealed to Truman to allow him to fight without restraint and approve the bombing of Chinese industrial areas as well as a blockade of the coast. When MacArthur took his case to the American public and sided with Republican critics of Truman's policies, Truman dismissed the still-popular commander for insubordination and replaced him with Ridgway. Ridgway managed to advance again roughly to the 38th parallel before the conflict stalemated by mid-1951. Protracted and bitter negotiations ensued, complicated by the issue of repatriating prisoners–of war and Stalin's unwillingness to compromise. The Soviet strongman's death in March 1953 paved the way for an armistice on July 27, although no peace treaty concluded the war. The number of those who died in the fighting is uncertain, but estimates are that among the four principal belligerents, the United States suffered more than 33,000 combat deaths, South Korea at least 103,000, North Korea as many as 316,000, and the Chinese perhaps 422,000.

Larry Simpson

Defining Moment 2: The Soviet Invasion of Afghanistan

On Christmas Eve 1979, Afghanistan reached a turning point. Just three months earlier, division within the ruling People's Democratic Party had culminated in the overthrow of Hafizullah Amin and murder of Nur Muhammad Taraki, who had himself only taken power the prior December with Soviet help in a bloody coup. Revolts throughout the countryside had followed the political repression that accompanied the pro-Soviet government's implementation of land "reform" along with other Marxist-inspired attempts to modernize the traditional, Muslim country. Violence spread from the provinces to Afghanistan's cities, and even a massive influx of aid from the Soviet Union could not stem the collapse of the Afghan army and the continued impotence of the Afghani government in Kabul. A desperate Amin turned to Pakistan for help and even approached Washington. Then, on December 12, hardline members of the Politburo met with and persuaded the ailing and aged Soviet leader, Leonid Brezhnev, to send in troops to suppress the Afghan unrest and ensure that the Central Asian country not slip into the Western orbit.

What followed was disastrous for both Afghanistan and the Soviet Union. Amin, whom the Russian leaders claimed had invited the airlift of Soviet troops into Kabul, fell to bullets in just days in a coup led by Babrak Karmal, the Afghan ambassador to Czechoslovakia, and Moscow's handpicked man. When the last Soviet soldier left Russia's "Vietnam" in February 1989, he would leave behind him more than 14,000 dead companions and many times that number wounded in a conflict that had cost the Soviet Union a million rubles per day. Yet, the price the Afghanis paid was even more staggering. Out of a population of 15 million,

1.5 million Afghanis died and another 3 million became refugees. The Afghan rebels styled themselves mujahideen, or holy warriors, and received arms and aid from other countries in the Muslim world as well as the United States. The brutal Soviet invasion led President Jimmy Carter to boycott the Moscow Olympics in 1980 and ensured that the U.S. Senate would not approve the SALT II treaty whereby Carter had sought to contain the strategic arms race with the USSR. Having warned the Soviet Union against attempting to move beyond Afghanistan and capture the Persian Gulf in his 1980 State of the Union Address, the Carter Doctrine, the American president created the Rapid Deployment Force to back his new foreign policy initiative. Carter's successor, Ronald Reagan, would transform that military unit into the Central Command. Reagan would likewise funnel money and modern arms through the Central Intelligence Agency and Pakistani intelligence to aid the mujahideen, whom he referred to as "freedom fighters." Probably the most important weapons that the Americans sent to the rebels were Stinger surface-to-air missiles, which the fighters used effectively to shoot down Russian aircraft and thus remove an important advantage the Soviets had heretofore enjoyed.

The involvement of the Western superpower had consequences that went beyond what Washington intended. Continued stalemate in the vicious mountain war led the Russians to replace Karmal with Muhammad Najibullah, who had served as head of the Afghan secret police. Nonetheless, Najibullah was no more successful than his predecessor. In April 1988, Soviet leader Mikhail Gorbachev accepted a negotiated settlement at Geneva, Switzerland, that resulted in the final withdrawal of Soviet troops from Afghanistan. Yet, it would not be until after the fall of the Soviet Union that the mujahideen would oust Najibullah. Moreover, the rebels soon would fight among themselves in a devastating civil war, creating a power vacuum that only would be filled by the radical Islamist group, the Taliban, in the late-1990s.

Larry Simpson

Print Resources

Ambrose, Stephen E. *The Cold War: A Military History*. New York: Random House, 2006.

Bogle, Lori. *The Cold War*. Vol. 3: *Hot Wars of the Cold Wars*. Oxford: Routledge, 2001.

Burgen, Michael. *Hot Conflicts*. Cold War series. Orlando, FL: Steck-Vaughn, 2001.

DeMarco, Neil. *Hot War–Cold War*. London: Hodder Murray, 2001.

Kinsella, David, and Herbert K. Tillema. "Arms and Aggression in the Middle East: Overt Military Interventions, 1948–1991." *The Journal of Conflict Resolution* 39, no. 2 (June 1995): 306–29.

Layton, Mike. *Easy Blood: Ronald Reagan's Proxy Wars in Central America*. N.p.: Dragonred Pub., 1997.

Sayegh, Fayez. "Arab Nationalism and Soviet-American Relations." *Annals of the American Academy of Political and Social Science* 324 (July 1959): 103–10.

Stone, David. *Wars of the Cold War: Campaigns and Conflicts, 1945–1990*. London: Brassey's, 2004.

Wallensteen, Peter, and Karin Axell. "Armed Conflict at the End of the Cold War, 1989–92." *Journal of Peace Research* 30, no. 3 (August 1993): 331–46.

Westad, Odd Arne. *The Global Cold War: Third World Interventions and the Making of Our Times*. Cambridge, MA: Cambridge University Press, 2005.

Ronald Reagan and the Cold War

Was Ronald Reagan Responsible for the Collapse of the Soviet Union and the End of the Cold War?

A definitive answer as to why and how the Cold War ended when it did has proven to be elusive. Many historians are in disagreement as to what set of events and decisions was critical, and who, if anyone, was responsible. Since the collapse of the Soviet Union in 1991, a clear political divide has emerged in the argument. Generally, more liberal historians have seen the collapse as inevitable, while conservative voices see Ronald Reagan's administration as the vital factor. Despite the sometimes politicized nature of the debate concerning this dilemma, most historians have recognized that no one single factor was responsible, but rather it has become a matter of ranking factors in the importance of their impact. As is almost always the case with an historical event, there are numerous causes that contributed to the outcome.

Writers from both perspectives readily admit that there were several factors that contributed to the demise of the Soviet Union, but their opinions differ as to what were the most critical reasons. In the first essay, Dr. Spencer C. Tucker takes the position that accumulating internal problems in the Soviet Union were the deciding factors in bringing about an end to the USSR and the Cold War. He argues that the Soviets sowed the seeds of their own destruction. In the second essay, Dr. Lee W. Eysturlid asserts that though other factors may have played a role in the dissolution of the Soviet Union, it was President Reagan's policies, applied evenly over eight years, that ended the Cold War on American terms.

Perspective 1: The Soviet Collapse Was Inevitable

Though the massive defense buildup of Ronald Reagan's administration undoubtedly had an influence, it was not the principal reason for the 1991 collapse of the Soviet Union and its empire, and thus, the end of the Cold War. Indeed, the Soviet Union had been tottering toward collapse for some time, although U.S. officials and the military had failed to recognize the signs.

One factor was certainly the vast corruption and inefficiency of the Soviet economy. The Soviet Union was a command economy, in which the government bureaucracy determined exactly what and how much of it would be produced. The West, on the other hand, had a demand economy, driven by consumers. The latter produced far better goods. If its leadership threw considerable resources at a problem, the Soviet Union could produce spectacular successes, as with some of its military hardware or in the 1957 *Sputnik*, the first satellite placed in Earth's orbit; but even in the space race the Soviets were soon far outdistanced by the United States. Most of what the Soviets produced in their state-run factories, particularly in the area of consumer goods, was shoddy. Health care was declining, and the average life span was actually decreasing, not increasing as in the West (the Soviet Union was the only developing nation where this was occurring). Despite government efforts to keep the truth from the Soviet people, the average citizen knew that life was far better in the West.

Far from a classless society, the Soviet Union was as riven by economic division as under the czars. The elite lived very well, while the average citizen found it difficult to get by. Corruption was rampant and bribes were a way of life. The judiciary was not independent; it was an arm of the government charged with carrying out its policies. The lack of free flow of ideas and information was part of the problem. The Soviet leadership was afraid of the truth and sought to control this area, and yet it impacted every aspect of national life, including the economy. Cybernetics had become vital yet, in 1985, the Soviet Union had an estimated 50,000 personal computers, whereas the United States had 40 million.

Another factor was the failure of the Soviet Union to create a unified nation. Despite the claim of a classless society free of discrimination, ethnic Russians predominated and controlled key government and military posts. There was rampant discrimination against minorities, who had been drifting back into their national republics. These minorities, especially in Central Asia, had higher birth rates than the Russians, who were about to become a minority within the union. Sociologists were pointing out these democratic trends decades before the end of the Cold War.

Another factor was certainly the restlessness of the Soviet Empire. On several important occasions—East Germany in 1953, Hungary in 1956, Czechoslovakia in 1968, and Poland in 1981—the Eastern and Central European states had demonstrated their desire for full independence. Perhaps only Bulgaria really desired close ties with the Soviet Union at the end of World War II. The rest of the empire would bolt, given the opportunity.

Finally, there was, above all, Mikhail Gorbachev, the leader of the Soviet Union from 1985 to 1991. Today, many Russians blame him for the dramatic loss of national power. That is unfair, for it was inevitable. Thanks to Gorbachev, the dissolution of Soviet power was a peaceful process. True, he would have to worry about keeping the Soviet Union strong militarily (and not incidentally, keep an eye on the powerful military establishment should it seek to take power), but much more important was the need to modernize the economy and make communism actually work. Gorbachev was one of the few who truly believed in the communist ideal. Gorbachev was also fully aware of the need to reform his nation economically. This was not only because he genuinely wanted to improve the lot of the Soviet people but because he knew that the Soviet Union could not continue to fall farther and farther behind the West and hope to compete. He was undoubtedly the best-informed leader in the history of the Soviet Union.

Gorbachev at first tried to impose discipline on his people in an effort to make the system really work for the benefit of the people as it was supposed to. When that failed, he introduced perestroika in order to make the Soviet bureaucracy accountable and modernize the economy. When the Soviet bureaucrats, virtually all of whom had a vested interest in maintaining the status quo, balked at Gorbachev's reforms, he responded with glasnost. This meant open criticism and democratization, but this also led to full revelations that the Soviet Union was really the "emperor with no clothes." And once the Soviet people were allowed full freedom of expression, many turned their backs on failed communism. Gorbachev, in essence, had failed. The hole he opened became a massive breach, and he could not control the ensuing rushing torrent.

Gorbachev's foreign policy was also revolutionary, for he sought a new international era based on cooperation, rather than competition, with the West. If the cost of keeping up with the Americans militarily was a burden, so too was the bleeding wound of the senseless war in Afghanistan. What had begun in 1979 as an effort to maintain a communist regime became a quagmire that threatened to endure indefinitely with no resolution. The economic and human costs of this effort were heavy. Gorbachev withdrew Soviet forces in 1989, and he also determined that the Soviet Union could not afford to prop up communist regimes elsewhere in the world, from Vietnam, to Cuba, and Eastern Europe. The natural consequence of the withdrawal of Soviet aid, coupled with Gorbachev's reluctance to use force to maintain communism, was the inevitable collapse of communism in Eastern and Central Europe. By November 1989, the Berlin Wall had been toppled.

Without Gorbachev, the Soviet Union would not have collapsed in 1990. If the members of the Politburo had chosen a communist hard-liner or if the August 1991 coup against Gorbachev had succeeded, there is little doubt that, regardless of increased defense spending, communism would have continued for at least another decade or so until the same factors of economic inefficiency and demographics simply overwhelmed it. Probably the end would have come violently in a breakup of the member republics. Thanks to Mikhail Gorbachev, what was inevitable occurred earlier and was peaceful.

Spencer C. Tucker

Perspective 2: Reagan's Policies Hastened the Soviet Collapse

U.S. president Ronald Reagan's policies and tough stance were key factors in causing the Soviet Union—through its spending and adoption of *glasnost*—to hasten its own collapse. In 1981, President Reagan, addressing an audience at Notre Dame University, stated: "The West won't contain communism. It will transcend communism. It will dismiss it as some bizarre chapter in human history whose last pages are even now being written." This prophetic assertion was dismissed at the time as wishful at best, and many felt that Reagan was undermining the current status quo of a stagnant, détente-oriented world. But within 10 years, the Soviet Union, which in 1981 appeared to be winning the Cold War, was dissolved, and the United States was about to enter into a decade of peace and prosperity.

When Reagan became president, he inherited a significantly compromised situation. The old notion of parity between the Soviet Union and the United States had been slowly collapsing under pressure from without and from within. The Brezhnev Doctrine, the idea that once a state entered into the Soviet sphere it would remain there, even if by force, had seen Ethiopia, Kampuchea, Angola, Mozambique, Yemen, Grenada, Nicaragua, and Afghanistan fall to communist insurgencies between 1974 and 1980. Soviet military spending had exceeded 20 percent of gross domestic product (GDP), and the Russians and the Warsaw Pact countries had moved ahead of the West in both conventional and nuclear weapons. Internally, America was suffering from what historian

Paul Johnson has labeled a serious effort at "national suicide." The U.S. economy, suffering from "stagflation," or the double burden of high unemployment and soaring inflation, had stalled. The administration of President Jimmy Carter talked of a shaken American self-confidence and the need for citizens to expect less in the future.

Much to the shock of liberals, conservatives, and the Soviet leadership, Reagan immediately charted a separate course. He made it clear that he felt the policy of détente was finished, and that the U.S. would reassert itself with a substantial arms buildup, both in conventional and in cutting-edge nuclear weapons. At the same time, he also managed to gain substantial tax cuts and deregulation that, following a brief recession, saw the revival of the U.S. economy. To make the buildup possible, Reagan initiated a $1.5 trillion military spending program, the largest ever in American peacetime history. His intention was clearly to draw the Soviets into an arms race that he was certain they could not match, let alone win. This paved the way for the advent of a high-tech weapons arsenal still in use today, which included the M-1 tank, stealth fighters, and laser-guided bombs.

Concerning nuclear arms, Reagan found allies in the European leadership of the United Kingdom (Margaret Thatcher) and West Germany (Helmut Kohl) that allowed him to offer a new generation of nuclear weapons for forward deployment. Reagan got approval for the placement of 108 Pershing II and 404 Tomahawk cruise missiles in Europe to counter Soviet medium-range SS-20s. At the same time, Reagan dropped the moribund Strategic Arms Limitation Talks (SALT) idea for a new "zero option" Strategic Arms Reduction Treaty (START). Combined with his March 1983 announcement of a new antimissile program called the Strategic Defense Initiative (SDI), the idea of reducing nuclear weapons became an option for the first time.

Reagan also made it clear to the Soviet leaders, who were now facing an economic crisis that originated from a failed economic system and overextended military spending, that the U.S. policy of coexistence was over. The Reagan Doctrine, as it came to be called, asserted that the United States would support anticommunist movements worldwide with money and weapons. He also worked with the Vatican and the international branch of the AFL-CIO to support the Polish trade union Solidarity as it struggled to survive. Finally, Reagan ordered the surprise invasion of Grenada in October 1983, where the democratically elected government had been overthrown by communist insurgents aided by Cuba. This military operation, a successful assertion of U.S. willingness to use force, started the decline of communist guerrilla movements that was to continue throughout the 1980s.

That the Soviets saw what they were up against is clear. Experienced diplomat Andrei Gromyko stated that "behind all of this [military build-up] lies the clear calculation that the USSR will exhaust its material resources and therefore will be forced to surrender." Yuri Andropov, general secretary when SDI was announced, stated that the program was intended as "a bid to disarm the Soviet Union." By 1985, the normally ultraconservative Soviet leadership, unable to sustain the economy and an arms buildup, chose a relative unknown to lead, Mikhail Gorbachev. It was clear to Reagan that this shift in leadership gave him someone that he could deal with, and the two entered into a series of meetings that culminated in agreements for serious reductions in nuclear weapons. It can be asserted that this was only possible because the Soviets understood they could no longer count on weak Western leadership. Gorbachev, fighting a losing, Vietnam-style war in Afghanistan and faced with a failed economy and demand for reform, had little choice but to cooperate. These reforms, given the general title of glasnost, would lead, in 1989 and 1991, to the collapse of the Soviet Union, Gorbachev's removal from power, the end of the Soviet domination of Eastern Europe, and the end of the Cold War.

Certainly, Reagan's policies were not the only reason for the demise of the Soviet Union and the end of the Cold War. Further, the successes came at the cost of soaring federal deficits and intense bitterness between liberals and conservatives. Yet it is also clear that Reagan's leadership played an absolutely key role in resurrecting U.S. confidence and power while fatally undermining the Soviet Union.

Lee W. Eysturlid

Print Resources

Ball, S. J. *The Cold War: An International History, 1947–1991.* London: Hodder, 1997.

Blum, William. *Rogue State: A Guide to the World's Only Superpower.* Monroe, ME: Common Courage Press, 2005.

Brzezinski, Zbigniew K. *The Grand Failure: The Birth and Death of Communism in the Twentieth Century.* New York: Macmillan, 1989.

Brzezinski, Zbigniew K. *Ideology and Power in Soviet Politics.* Westport, CT: Greenwood, 1976.

Fischer, Beth A. *The Reagan Reversal: Foreign Policy and the End of the Cold War.* Columbia: University of Missouri Press, 1997

Fitzgerald, Francis. *Way Out There in the Blue: Reagan, Star Wars, and the End of the Cold War.* New York: Simon and Schuster, 2000.

Gaddis, John Lewis. *The United States and the End of the Cold War.* Oxford, UK: Oxford University Press, 1992.

Gaddis, John Lewis. *What We Now Know: Rethinking the Cold War.* Oxford University Press, 1997.

Kowalski, Ronald. *European Communism: 1848–1991.* New York: Macmillan, 2006.

Kyvig, David E. ed. *Reagan and the World.* Westport, CT: Greenwood, 1990.

Lafeber, Walter. *America, Russia, and the Cold War, 1945–2006.* New York: McGraw Hill, 2006.

Reagan, Ronald. *An American Life: The Autobiography.* New York: Simon & Schuster, 1990.

Ulam, Bruno Adam. *Understanding the Cold War: A Historian's Personal Reflections.* Piscataway, NJ: Transaction Publishers, 2002.

Cold War Chronology

1945 **February 4–12:** Yalta Conference—Big Three (United States, United Kingdom, Soviet Union) represented by Franklin Roosevelt, Winston Churchill, and Josef Stalin

May 8: V-E Day (end of World War II in Europe)

June 26: United Nations (UN) founding conference ends with the promulgation of the UN Charter

July 17–August 2: Potsdam Conference—Big Three represented by Harry Truman, Winston Churchill (replaced by Clement Attlee during the conference), and Josef Stalin

August 14: V-J Day (end of World War II in the Pacific)—17 U.S. and Soviet officials agree on 38th Parallel as the boundary line between their occupation forces in Korea

September 2: Ho Chi Minh proclaims in Hanoi the Democratic Republic of Vietnam (DRV, North Vietnam)

November 17: Nationalist leader Sukarno declares the Netherlands East Indies (Indonesia) independent

November 27: U.S. General of the Army George C. Marshall begins his mission to China to try to mediate between the Guomindang (GMD, Nationalist) and Communist Party of China (CCP)

1946 **January 10:** UN General Assembly holds its first meeting; Trygve Lie of Norway becomes first UN secretary general

January 19: Iran complains to the UN Security Council that the Soviet Union is meddling in internal Iranian affairs

January 31: An agreement is reached in China on a new governmental structure for the country

February 9: Speech by Josef Stalin stating that capitalism and communism are "incompatible"

February 22: George Kennan issues the "Long Telegram," the basis for the containment policy of the United States

February 25: Chinese Nationalists and Communists agree on a program to integrate their armed forces

March 5: British statesman Winston Churchill delivers his "Sinews of Peace" speech (also known as the "Iron Curtain" speech) at Westminster College in Fulton, Missouri

March 25: Under pressure from the West, the Soviet Union announces that it will withdraw its troops from northern Iran

April 18: Chinese Nationalist and Communist forces clash in Manchuria

April 22: Merger of communist and socialist parties in Germany, creating the Socialist Unity Party (SED), in effect the new communist party

July 12: The U.S. House of Representatives approves $3.75 billion loan to Great Britain

July 29: Opening of conference in Paris to conclude peace treaties with World War II cobelligerents—Bulgaria, Finland, Hungary, Italy, and Romania—of Germany

August: The Nationalist and Communist negotiations in China collapse

September: The Greek Civil War between the royalist British-backed government and Greek communist guerrillas begins

September 6: In an important speech in Stuttgart, U.S. secretary of state James F. Byrnes declares the U.S. intention to restore the German economy and vows that U.S. forces will remain in Europe as long as other powers retain occupying forces there

September 17: In Zurich, Winston Churchill calls for the creation of a "United States of Europe"

November 25: President Harry S. Truman establishes the Loyalty Commission (Presidential Temporary Commission on Employee Loyalty)

December 3: The Greek government complains to the UN Security Council that the neighboring communist states are providing military support to the communist insurgency

December 19: Viet Minh forces attack the French in Tonkin (northern Vietnam), beginning the Indochina War

1947   **January 8:** Marshall, having failed to bridge the wide gulf between the Nationalists and Communists, leaves China

February 10: Peace treaties signed with German cobelligerents of World War II: Bulgaria, Finland, Hungary, Italy, and Romania

February 21: British diplomats in Washington inform the U.S. State Department that Britain, hard-pressed financially, can no longer provide aid to Greece and Turkey

March 12: In a speech to Congress, President Truman asks for $400 million in aid for Greece and Turkey and outlines the policy that later comes to be known as the Truman Doctrine

March 21: Truman issues Executive Order 9835 calling for an investigation into the loyalty of all federal employees

May 8: In a speech to the Delta Cotton Council in Mississippi that is in effect a trial balloon for the later Marshall Plan, U.S. undersecretary of state Dean Acheson discusses the economic plight of Europe and the U.S. stake in Europe's well-being

June 5: In a speech at Harvard University, Marshall, now secretary of state, proposes an economic aid program for Europe that will later be known as the Marshall Plan

July: "Sources of Soviet Conduct" by "X" (George Kennan) is published in *Foreign Affairs*

July 2: The Soviet Union rejects U.S. assistance under the Marshall Plan given the conditions attached, forcing its European satellites to follow suit

July 20: Fighting erupts in Indonesia between Dutch and nationalist forces, beginning a two-year war

July 26: Truman signs the National Security Act, which establishes the Department of Defense, the Central Intelligence Agency (CIA), the National Security Council (NSC), and the Joint Chiefs of Staff (JCS)

September 2: Western Hemisphere states sign the Treaty of Rio, designed to establish inter-American solidarity against aggression

September 22–23: Communist delegates meeting in Poland establish the Communist Information Bureau (Cominform)

October 18: The House Un-American Activities Committee (HUAC) begins an investigation of communism and the movie industry in Hollywood

December: The Chinese Civil War between the Nationalists and the Communists intensifies

1948

February 25: Communist coup in Czechoslovakia—after the collapse of a coalition government, President Edvard Beneš is pressured into appointing a government dominated by the communists

March 10: Czechoslovak government authorities announce the death, allegedly by suicide, of Czechoslovak foreign minister Jan Masaryk (a 2004 Czech Republic government investigation concludes that he had been murdered)

March 17: Treaty of Brussels is signed by France, Britain, Belgium, the Netherlands, and Luxembourg—forerunner to the North Atlantic Treaty Organization (NATO)

March 20: Soviet representatives walk out of the four-power Allied Control Council for Germany

April 1: Soviet authorities in Germany impose restrictions on road and rail traffic from the Western zones of Germany into Berlin

April 2: The U.S. Congress establishes the Economic Cooperation Administration to oversee the Economic Recovery Program (Marshall Plan)

April 30: In Bogatá, Colombia, the United States and Latin American countries establish the Organization of American States (OAS)

June 13: The U.S. Senate adopts the Vandenberg Resolution endorsing U.S. participation in regional defense organizations

June 18: The Western occupying powers introduce a new currency in their zones of Germany and Berlin

June 24: The Berlin Blockade begins when the Soviet Union halts all land and water traffic between the Western zones of Germany and West Berlin

June 26: The Berlin Airlift begins

June 28: Yugoslavia is expelled from the Cominform

August 3: Whittaker Chambers testifies to HUAC that former State Department official Alger Hiss was a communist in the 1930s

November 2: In one of the most stunning upsets in U.S. political history, Truman wins reelection as president over the favored Republican Party challenger Thomas E. Dewey

December 10: The UN General Assembly adopts the Universal Declaration of Human Rights

1949

January 22: Communist forces capture Beijing in China

January 25: The Soviet Union announces the creation of the Council of Mutual Economic Assistance (Comecon), the Soviet counterpart to the Marshal Plan, for its satellites of Eastern Europe

January 28: The UN Security Council orders the Netherlands to end military operations in Indonesia and grant it independence

February 26: The government of the Netherlands agrees to grant independence to Indonesia

March 25: Chinese communist leader Mao Zedong proclaims Beijing to be the capital of China

April 4: NATO is established by 12 nations, including the United States

April 22: Nationalist forces in China abandon their capital of Nanjing (Nanking)

May 5: Ten Western European states form the Council of Europe at Strasbourg, France

May 8: The Western German parliament approves the Basic Law, in effect the constitution of the Federal Republic of Germany (FRG, West Germany)

May 12: The Soviet Union ends the Berlin Blockade

May 23: West Germany is established

May 25: Chinese communist forces occupy Shanghai

August 24: The North Atlantic Treaty goes into effect following its ratification by France

August 29: The Soviet Union tests its first atomic bomb

October 1: Mao proclaims the establishment of the People's Republic of China (PRC)

October 7: The German Democratic Republic (GDR, East Germany) is established

1950 **January 21:** Hiss is convicted of perjury

January 31: Truman announces that the United States will proceed with the development of nuclear fusion (the hydrogen bomb)

February 9: In a speech in Wheeling, West Virginia, U.S. senator Joseph R. McCarthy claims to have a list of 205 communist sympathizers working in the State Department

February 14: The Sino-Soviet Treaty of Friendship, Alliance, and Mutual Assistance is signed in Moscow

April 7: The National Security Council produces NSC-68, which calls for a massive military buildup

April 25: Truman approves NSC-68

May 9: French foreign minister Robert Schuman proposes creation of a European coal and steel community

June 25: North Korean forces invade the Republic of Korea (ROK, South Korea), beginning the Korean War

June 27: The UN Security Council passes a resolution sponsored by the United States calling for the defense of Korea

June 30: Truman approves the dispatch of U.S. ground forces to Korea

August 11: In the course of a speech to the European Assembly in Strasbourg, Winston Churchill, still a private citizen, calls for the establishment of a European army, with West German participation

September 15: Successful amphibious landing by American forces at Inchon, South Korea

October 7: UN forces cross the 38th Parallel into the Democratic People's Republic of Korea (DPRK, North Korea)

October 28: Chinese communist forces launch a major intervention in the Korean War

November 25–26: Chinese communist forces carry out a massive offensive against UN forces in the Korean War

December 15: Truman proclaims a state of national emergency

December 31: Chinese communist forces cross the 38th Parallel, invading South Korea

1951 **January 4:** Chinese communist forces capture Seoul

March 15: UN forces recapture Seoul and Inchon

March 29: Julius and Ethel Rosenberg are convicted of passing nuclear secrets to the Soviet Union and on April 5 they receive the death sentence

April 11: Truman dismisses General Douglas MacArthur as commander of UN forces in Korea, replacing him with General Matthew Ridgway

April 18: Delegates of West European states, meeting in Paris, establish the European Coal and Steel Community (ECSC)

May 23: The PRC takes control of Tibet

May 25: Guy Burgess and Donald Maclean, British Foreign Office officials, leave Britain—later it is revealed that they had spied for the Soviet Union

June 23: Soviet UN delegate Jacob Malik proposes a cease-fire in Korea and the reestablishment of the status quo antebellum

July 10: Armistice talks begin at Kaesong in Korea

September 8: The Treaty of San Francisco is signed between the Allied powers, associated nations (49 in all), and Japan and goes into effect on April 28, 1952

September 27: Iran takes control of the Anglo-Iranian oil refinery at Abadan

1952

February 23: NATO authorities announces a plan to create an army of 50 divisions within a year's time

March 10: Stalin proposes a reunified and neutral Germany

July 21: Egyptian military officers overthrow King Farouk

October 3: In waters off Australia, Britain detonates its first atomic bomb

November 1: The United States tests the world's first thermonuclear device (hydrogen bomb)

1953

March 5: Stalin dies

March 6: Georgy Malenkov becomes Soviet premier and first secretary of the Communist Party of the Soviet Union (CPSU)

March 14: Malenkov is forced to relinquish leadership of the CPSU to Nikita Khrushchev

June 17: Workers in East Berlin strike and riot against increases in work quotas and shortages of basic goods—the riots spread across East Germany and have to be put down by Soviet troops

June 19: Julius and Ethel Rosenberg are executed despite widespread protests against their sentence

July 27: The United States and North Korea sign an armistice, ending the fighting in Korea

August 19: A CIA-sponsored coup overthrows the government of nationalist premier Mohammed Mossadegh in Iran

1954

January 12: U.S. secretary of state John Foster Dulles enunciates the defense doctrine that will become known as massive retaliation

January 21: The United States launches the *Nautilus*, the world's first nuclear-powered submarine

March 1: The United States explodes its first deliverable thermonuclear bomb on Bikini Atoll in the Pacific

March 13: The Battle of Dien Bien Phu opens in Indochina

April 22: Opening of the Army-McCarthy Hearings in Washington, D.C.

April 26: Beginning of the Geneva Conference on Korea and on the war in Indochina

May 7: Viet Minh forces defeat the French at Dien Bien Phu following a furious two-month siege

June 27: A CIA-sponsored coup overthrows President Jacobo Arbenz of Guatemala

July 21: The Indochina War ends with the signing of agreements in Geneva, although in order to comply with a deadline imposed by French premier Mendès-France, the document is dated July 20

August 30: The French National Assembly rejects the European Defense Community (EDC) treaty

September 3: The shelling of offshore Chinese islands in the Taiwan Strait until May 1, 1955 is initiated by the PRC

September 8: Establishment of the Southeast Asia Treaty Organization (SEATO) with signing of documents in Manila

October 3: In London, the Western Allies sign an agreement that will allow the rearmament of West Germany within NATO

December 2: The U.S. Senate votes to censure Senator McCarthy

The United States and the Republic of China (Taiwan) sign a mutual defense treaty

1955

February 8: Malenkov resigns as premier of the Soviet Union and is replaced by Nikolai Bulganin, while Khrushchev emerges as the leader of the Soviet Union

February 24: Turkey and Iraq sign the Baghdad Pact

April 5: Britain, Turkey, and Iraq sign the Baghdad Pact, and Iran and Pakistan join later in the year (after Iraq leaves in 1959, the name is changed to the Central Treaty Organization, or CENTO)

May 5: West Germany regains full sovereignty and joins NATO as a full member on May 8

May 14: The Soviet Union and its satellites form the Warsaw Treaty Organization to counter NATO

May 15: The Western Allies and the Soviet Union sign the Austrian State Treaty, ending the occupation of Austria

June 18: Summit meeting involving Khrushchev, Dwight Eisenhower, Anthony Eden, and Edgar Faure at Geneva

August 4: The U-2 spy plane makes its first overflight of the Soviet Union

December 1: The Western Allies declare that despite Soviet contentions to the contrary, Berlin remains an occupied city

December 9: The West German government announces the Hallstein Doctrine, indicating that West Germany will no longer maintain diplomatic relations with those states that recognize the East German government

1956

February 25: Khrushchev gives his so-called secret speech to the Twentieth Party Congress of the Soviet Communist Party in which he denounces the "cult of personality built by Stalin," thus beginning a campaign of de-Stalinization

June 28: Workers riot in Poznań, Poland, against poor economic conditions and communist rule

July 26: Gamal Abdel Nasser, president of Egypt, nationalizes the Suez Canal

October 21: The Soviet Union accepts Władysław Gomułka as the new leader of Poland

October 23: The Hungarian Revolution begins

October 26: Representatives of 70 nations sign a document creating the International Atomic Energy Agency (IAEA)

October 29: The Suez Crisis begins, during which Israel, backed by Britain and France, attacks Egypt

November 1: Imre Nagy announces that Hungary is leaving the Warsaw Treaty Organization

November 4: Soviet tanks enter Budapest to crush the Hungarian Revolution

December 2: Fidel Castro and his followers land in Cuba and begin the Cuban Revolution

1957

January 5: President Eisenhower announces a new policy, later known as the Eisenhower Doctrine, that promises U.S. military aid to victims of aggression in the Middle East

March 9: Eisenhower signs into law congressional legislation authorizing U.S. forces to come to the aid of Middle Eastern states

July 3: Khrushchev defeats opposition to his rule and solidifies his position as leader of the Soviet Union

July 14: Coup in Iraq during which King Faisal and others are slain

October 4: The Soviet Union launches *Sputnik I*, the world's first orbiting satellite

1958

January 1: The European Common Market and Atomic Energy Commission are established

January 13: British government announces that a Soviet attack on the West, regardless of the weapons employed, will evoke a British hydrogen bomb response

January 31: U.S. Army launches *Explorer I*, the first American artificial satellite

May: Mao's disastrous Great Leap Forward (1958–1961), an attempt at rural industrialization and increased agricultural production that results in a massive famine and the deaths of perhaps as many as 30 million people, begins

July–October: The United States sends troops under the Eisenhower Doctrine to protect Lebanon's pro-Western government

July 29: Establishment of the National Aeronautics and Space Administration (NASA)

August 23: Renewed shelling of Jinmen and Mazu (part of the Republic of China) in the Taiwan Strait by the PRC

October 4: Establishment of the French Fifth Republic

December 14: The Western Allies reject the Soviet demand that they withdraw their soldiers from West Berlin

1959   **January 1:** Castro takes power in Cuba

March 30: Release of earlier congressional testimony by U.S. Chief of Naval Operations Admiral Arleigh Burke in which he announces the beginning of a shift in U.S. defense posture with a renewed emphasis on conventional forces to build up a capability to wage limited war

April 4: The NATO Council announces its determination to maintain the status quo in West Berlin and the rights of all occupying powers to be there

July 24: Vice President Richard Nixon and Khrushchev have the "Kitchen Debate" at a U.S. exhibition in Moscow

September 15–27: Khrushchev becomes the first Soviet leader to visit the United States

December 1: Signing of the agreement on the peaceful use of Antarctica, the first major postwar arms-control agreement

1960   **March 17:** Eisenhower approves a CIA plan calling for Cuban exiles to invade Cuba and overthrow Castro's regime

May 5: Khrushchev announces that the Soviet Union shot down a U-2 spy plane on May 1 and captured the pilot, Francis Gary Powers

May 7: The U.S. government admits that the U-2 shot down over the Soviet Union had been on a surveillance mission

May 16: Eisenhower refuses to apologize for the U-2 flights, resulting in Khrushchev's departure from Paris and the collapse of the scheduled summit there

July: Civil war breaks out in the Republic of the Congo, which had recently received independence from Belgium

September–October: Khrushchev attends the UN General Assembly session, and Eisenhower does not offer to meet him

October 19: The United States bans most trade with Cuba

December 20: Establishment of the National Liberation Front (NLF) in the Republic of Vietnam (RVN, South Vietnam) by Vietnamese communists

1961   **January 1:** The United States breaks diplomatic relations with Cuba

April 12: Major Yuri Gagarin of the Soviet Union becomes the first human to orbit Earth in space

April 17: Cuban exiles invade Cuba at the Bay of Pigs

May 5: Commander Alan Shepard becomes the first American in space

May 15: U.S. president John F. Kennedy declares in a speech to Congress that the United States should achieve a manned flight to the moon before the end of the decade

June 3–4: Kennedy and Khrushchev hold a summit meeting in Vienna

July 24: Kennedy warns the Soviet Union not to interfere with Western access to West Berlin

August 13: East German authorities close their border with the West and begin construction of the Berlin Wall

October 26–27: Confrontation in Berlin between U.S. and Soviet tanks ends peacefully

1962 **February 7:** The United States embargoes trade with Cuba

February 10: The United States swaps Soviet spy Colonel Rudolf Abel for U-2 pilot Powers

February 20: Lieutenant Colonel John H. Glenn Jr. becomes the first American to orbit Earth in space

July 1: French rule ends in Algeria following a vote in that country in favor of independence

July 23: The neutrality of Laos is guaranteed by accords signed in Geneva

October 14: Beginning of the Cuban Missile Crisis with the discovery in a U-2 reconnaissance flight of the construction of Soviet missile bases in Cuba

October 22: In a speech to the American people, Kennedy announces the presence of the Soviet missile bases in Cuba and declares a quarantine on the shipment to Cuba of offensive weapons

October 28: Khrushchev agrees to withdraw missiles from Cuba in return for a U.S. guarantee not to invade the island

November 20: Kennedy announces an end to the U.S. blockade of Cuba

1963 **June 20:** A hotline between the White House and the Kremlin is established

June 26: Kennedy's speech at the Berlin Wall affirming support for Berlin

August 5: The United States, Britain, and the Soviet Union sign a partial nuclear test-ban treaty

1964 **August 2:** Attack by North Vietnamese torpedo boats against the U.S. destroyer *Maddox* in international waters in the Gulf of Tonkin

August 7: The U.S. Congress passes the Gulf of Tonkin Resolution

October 15: Leonid Brezhnev becomes first secretary of the CPSU, replacing Khrushchev

October 16: The PRC tests its first atomic bomb

1965 **February 7:** Communist forces in South Vietnam attack U.S. military installation at Pleiku

March 8–9: U.S. Marines arrive in South Vietnam, the first U.S.

combat troops sent there, charged with protecting U.S. bases

April 28: U.S. president Lyndon B. Johnson sends Marines to the Dominican Republic

September 30–October 1: A communist coup is crushed by the Indonesian Army

1966 March 9: France withdraws from NATO's military command but remains part of the alliance

1967 June 6: The Six-Day War begins between Israel and Egypt, to include Syria and Jordan

June 23: Johnson meets with Premier Alexei Kosygin in Glassboro, New Jersey

October 21: March on the Pentagon to protest the Vietnam War

1968 January 5: Alexander Dubček becomes leader of the Czechoslovakian Communist Party (CPCz), and the Prague Spring begins two months later, in March

January 30: The Tet Offensive begins in South Vietnam

May 10–13: The United States and North Vietnam begin peace talks in Paris

July 1: The United States, the Soviet Union, and Britain sign the Nuclear Non-Proliferation Treaty (NPT)

August 20–21: Warsaw Pact troops end the Prague Spring by invading Czechoslovakia

November 12: Brezhnev announces the Brezhnev Doctrine in which socialist states are obligated to aid a socialist state threatened by counterrevolutionary forces

1969 March 2: Clashes erupt between the Soviet Union and the PRC along the Ussuri River

June 8: The Nixon Doctrine proclaims that Asian nations will have to defend themselves with their own soldiers in the future

November 17: U.S. and Soviet negotiators begin the Strategic Arms Limitation Talks (SALT)

1970 April 30: Incursion by the United States and South Vietnam into Cambodia

August 12: West Germany signs a nonaggression pact with the Soviet Union

December 7: West German–Polish Treaty recognizes the Oder-Neisse border

1971 June 13: *The New York Times* begins publishing the Pentagon Papers

July 15: Nixon announces that he will visit the PRC in 1972

1972 February 21: Nixon begins his visit to the PRC

May 26: Nixon and Kosygin sign the SALT I treaty and the Anti-Ballistic Missile (ABM) Treaty

June 3: A four-power agreement between the United States, the Soviet Union, Britain, and France resolves the Berlin issue

December 21: The Basic Treaty establishes mutual relations between West Germany and East Germany

1973 **January 27:** A Vietnam peace
agreement is signed

July 3: The Helsinki Conference
on European security begins

October 6: Egyptian forces
strike across the Suez Canal,
beginning what is known as the
October, Yom Kippur, or Rama-
dan War between Egyptian and
Syrian forces against Israel

November 7: Congress overrides
Nixon's veto of the War Powers
Act

1974 **June 27:** Summit meeting between Nixon and Brezhnev

November 23–24: President
Gerald Ford and Brezhnev agree
on a draft for a SALT II treaty

1975 **April 17:** Cambodia falls to the
Khmer Rouge, and a genocidal
campaign soon begins

April 30: Fall of Saigon and end
of the Vietnam War

August 1: Leaders of 35 nations
sign the Helsinki Accords

1976 **July 2:** North and South Vietnam
are officially united

1977 **March 17:** President Jimmy
Carter announces that human
rights will be a major focus of
U.S. foreign policy

1978 **December 25:** Vietnam invades
Cambodia

1979 **January 1:** The United States
and the PRC open diplomatic relations

June 18: Carter and Brezhnev
sign the SALT II treaty (never
ratified)

July 17: Marxist Sandinista
guerrillas seize control in Nicaragua

November 4: Radical Iranian
students seize the U.S. embassy
in Tehran, taking 70 Americans
hostage

December 12: European members of NATO agree to deploy
U.S. Pershing II and cruise missiles in Western Europe

December 27: Soviet forces invade Kabul and kill Afghan president Hafizullah Amin, thereby
beginning a long occupation and
war

1980 **January 3:** Carter withdraws the
SALT II treaty from consider-
ation by the Senate in response to
the Soviet invasion of Afghanistan

January 23: Carter, in a statement that later becomes known
as the Carter Doctrine—a reaf-
firmation of the Truman and
Eisenhower Doctrines and a
partial repudiation of the Nixon
Doctrine—announces that the
United States will regard any
Soviet aggression directed at the
Persian Gulf as a threat to its
vital interests

April 7: The United States
breaks off diplomatic relations
with Iran

May 4: President Josip Broz
Tito of Yugoslavia, in power
since 1945, dies

August 31: Solidarity, led by
Lech Wałęsa, signs an agreement

with the Polish government that allows the establishment of the trade union movement

1981 **January 20:** American hostages held in Iran are freed

April 1: The United States suspends aid to the Sandinista regime in Nicaragua

October 6: President Anwar Sadat of Egypt assassinated by Muslim fundamentalist military officers

December 13: The Polish government declares martial law and arrests the leaders of Solidarity

1982 **June 6:** Israeli forces invade southern Lebanon in an attempt to end the terrorist activities of the Palestine Liberation Organization (PLO)

November 10: Brezhnev dies

1983 **March 9:** President Ronald Reagan calls the Soviet Union an "evil empire"

March 23: Reagan announces support for the Strategic Defense Initiative (SDI), popularly known as Star Wars

April18: Arab terrorists set off a bomb at the U.S. embassy in Beirut, killing 63 people

September 1: Soviet aircraft shoot down Korean passenger jet KAL 007 in Soviet airspace

October 5: Wałęsa wins the Nobel Peace Prize for his work with Solidarity

October 23: Arab terrorists drive a truck full of explosives into a U.S. barracks in Lebanon, killing 241 Marines

October 25: Invasion of Grenada by U.S. and Caribbean contingents

November 23: The Soviet Union responds to the U.S. deployment of Pershing II missiles in Western Europe by walking out of the intermediate-range nuclear forces reduction talks in Geneva

1984 **May 24:** Congress bans further aid to the Contras in their struggle against the Sandinista regime in Nicaragua

September 26: The PRC and Britain sign an agreement on the transfer of Hong Kong to the PRC in 1997

1985 **February 6:** Reagan announces U.S. support for all anticommunist rebels (freedom fighters) in a policy that later becomes known as the Reagan Doctrine

March 11: Mikhail Gorbachev becomes general secretary of the CPSU

May 20: Federal Bureau of Investigation (FBI) agents arrest naval officer John Anthony Walker Jr. as a Soviet spy

November 19–21: First summit meeting between Reagan and Gorbachev is held in Geneva

1986 **April 26:** A major nuclear accident occurs at the Chernobyl nuclear power plant near Kiev in the Soviet Union

October 11–12: Gorbachev and Reagan meet at Reykjavík, Iceland, for a second summit but fail to reach agreement on arms control

1987

May 5: Congress begins hearings on the Iran-Contra Affair

June 14: Pope John Paul II makes his third papal visit to his native Poland and strongly endorses Solidarity

December 8–10: Gorbachev and Reagan hold a summit in Washington, D.C., and sign the Intermediate-Range Nuclear Forces (INF) Treaty, which bans all intermediate-range nuclear missiles from Europe

1988

May 29–June 2: Reagan and Gorbachev hold a summit meeting in Moscow

December 7: Gorbachev announces unilateral reductions in troop (100,000) and tank (10,000) strength in Europe in a speech to the UN General Assembly

1989

January 11: Hungary introduces political reforms

February 15: Soviet troops leave Afghanistan

March 26: The Soviet Union holds the first partially free elections in its history for the Congress of People's Deputies

May 2: Hungary begins removing the barbed-wire fence along its border with Austria

June 3–4: Chinese troops kill and injure thousands of pro-democracy demonstrators in Beijing's Tiananmen Square

June 4–18: Solidarity is victorious in Poland's first free election under communist rule

June 16: Imre Nagy, executed for his role in the 1956 Hungar-

ian Revolution, is reburied with honors

August 24: Poland gets its first noncommunist premier since World War II

October 9: Demonstrations in Leipzig begin an expanding series of protests against the East German government

October 18: Egon Krenz replaces Erich Honecker as head of the East German Communist Party

October 25: Gorbachev publicly rejects the Brezhnev Doctrine

November 9: East Germany inadvertently opens the Berlin Wall

November 20: More than 200,000 people demonstrate in Prague against the Czechoslovak communist regime

November 24: Czechoslovak communist leader Miloš Jakeš and his entire politburo resign

December 2–3: President George H. W. Bush meets with Gorbachev at sea near Malta

December 25: A military tribunal tries and executes Romanian dictator Nicolae Ceauşescu and his wife Elena

December 29: Václav Havel becomes Czechoslovakia's first noncommunist president since 1948

1990

March 11: Lithuania declares its independence from the Soviet Union

13 The Congress of People's Deputies repeals Article 6 of the Soviet constitution, depriving the

CPSU of its legal monopoly on political power, and the CPSU's Central Committee agrees to the change two days later

May 30–June 3: Bush and Gorbachev hold a summit meeting in Washington, D.C.

July 16: Meeting between Helmut Kohl, chancellor of West Germany, and Gorbachev leads to an agreement allowing German unification

October 3: Germany is officially united

October 15: Gorbachev is awarded the Nobel Peace Prize

November 21: The 34 members of the Conference on Security and Cooperation in Europe sign

1991

the Charter of Paris, formally ending the Cold War

July 1: The Warsaw Pact formally disbands

July 31: Bush and Gorbachev, meeting in Moscow, sign the Strategic Arms Reduction Treaty (START I)

August 19–21: Unsuccessful coup in Moscow by Soviet Communist Party hard-liners

December 25: Gorbachev resigns as leader of the Soviet Union

December 31: The Soviet Union is officially dissolved

Michael D. Richards
and Spencer C. Tucker

Bibliography

Acheson, Dean. *Present at the Creation: My Years at the State Department.* New York: Norton, 1969.

Aldrich, Richard J. *The Hidden Hand: Britain, America, and Cold War Secret Intelligence.* Woodstock, NY: Overlook Press, 2002.

Ali, S. Mahmud. *Cold War in the High Himalayas: The USA, China, and South Asia in the 1950s.* New York: St. Martin's, 1999.

Allen, Debra J. *The Oder-Neisse Line: The United States, Poland, and Germany in the Cold War.* Westport, CT: Praeger, 2003.

Allin, Dana H. *Cold War Illusions: America, Europe, and Soviet Power, 1969–1989.* New York: St. Martin's, 1995.

Allison, Graham, and Philip Zelikow. *Essence of Decision: Explaining the Cuban Missile Crisis.* 2nd ed. New York: Longman, 1999.

Allison, Roy. *The Soviet Union and the Strategy of Non-Alignment in the Third World.* Cambridge: Cambridge University Press, 1988.

Ambrose, Stephen E. *Eisenhower: The President.* 2 vols. New York: Simon and Schuster, 1984.

Ambrose, Stephen E. *The Cold War: A Military History.* New York: Random House, 2006.

Ambrose, Stephen E., and Richard H. Immerman. *Ike's Spies: Eisenhower and the Espionage Establishment.* Garden City, NY: Doubleday, 1981.

Anderson, Terry H. *The United States, Great Britain, and the Cold War, 1944–1947.* Columbia: University of Missouri Press, 1981.

Anderton, David A. *Strategic Air Command: Two-Thirds of the Triad.* New York: Scribner, 1967.

Applebaum, Anne. *Gulag: A History.* New York: Broadway Books, 2003.

Appy, Christian G. *Cold War Constructions: The Political Culture of United States Imperialism, 1945–1966.* Amherst: University of Massachusetts Press, 2000.

Arnold, James R. *The First Domino: Eisenhower, the Military, and America's Intervention in Vietnam.* New York: William Morrow, 1991.

Ash, Timothy Garton. *The Polish Revolution: Solidarity 1980–1982.* London: Jonathan Cape, 1983.

Ausland, John C. *Kennedy, Khrushchev, and the Berlin-Cuba Crisis 1961–1964.* Oslo, Norway: Scandinavian University Press, 1996.

Bacon, Edwin, and Mark Sandle. *Brezhnev Reconsidered.* Basingstoke, UK: Palgrave Macmillan, 2002.

Bailey, George. *Galileo's Children: Science, Sakharov and the Power of the State.* New York: Arcade Publishing, 1990.

Ball, Howard. *Justice Downwind: America's Atomic Testing Program in the 1950s.* New York: Oxford University Press, 1986.

Ball, Simon J. *The Cold War: An International History, 1947–1991.* New York: St. Martin's, 1998.

Bamford, James. *Body of Secrets: Anatomy of the Ultra-Secret National Security Agency.* New York: Anchor, 2002.

Bamford, James. *The Puzzle Palace: A Report on America's Most Secret Agency.* New York: Penguin, 1983.

Bearden, Milt, and James Risen. *The Main Enemy: The Inside Story of the CIA's Final Showdown with the KGB.* New York: Random House, 2003.

Bell, Jonathan. *The Liberal State on Trial: The Cold War and American Politics in the Truman Years.* New York: Columbia University Press, 2004.

Bender, Gerald, James Coleman, and Richard Sklar, eds. *African Crisis Areas and United States Foreign Policy.* Berkeley: University of California Press, 1985.

Berman, Larry. *Planning a Tragedy: The Americanization of the War in Vietnam.* New York: Norton, 1982.

Bernhard, Nancy E. *U.S. Television News and Cold War Propaganda, 1947–1960.* New York: Cambridge University Press, 1999.

Beschloss, Michael R. *Mayday: Eisenhower, Khrushchev, and the U-2 Affair.* New York: Harper and Row, 1986.

Beschloss, Michael R. *The Crisis Years: Kennedy and Khrushchev, 1960–1963.* New York: HarperCollins, 1991.

Beschloss, Michael R., and Strobe Talbott. *At the Highest Levels: The Inside Story of the End of the Cold War.* Boston: Little, Brown, 1993.

Beschloss, Michael, ed. *Taking Charge: The Johnson White House Tapes, 1963–1964.* New York: Simon and Schuster, 1997.

Bessel, Richard, and Ralph Jessen, eds. *Die Grenzen der Diktatur: Staat und Gesellschaft in der DDR.* Göttingen: Vanderhoeck and Ruprecht, 1996.

Bills, Scott L. *Empire and Cold War: The Roots of US-Third World Antagonism, 1945–47.* New York: St. Martin's, 1990.

Biskupski, M. B. *The History of Poland.* Westport, CT: Greenwood, 2000.

Black, Jan Knippers. *The Dominican Republic: Politics and Development in an Unsovereign State.* Boston: Allen and Unwin, 1986.

Blair, Clay. *The Forgotten War: America in Korea, 1950–1953.* New York: Times Books, 1987.

Blecher, Marc J. *China against the Tides: Restructuring through Revolution, Radicalism and Reform.* London: Continuum, 2003.

Blechman, Barry M., ed. *Preventing Nuclear War: A Realistic Approach.* Bloomington: Indiana University Press, 1985.

Blight, James, and David Welch, eds. *Intelligence and the Cuban Missile Crisis.* London: Frank Cass, 1998.

Blight, James, and David Welch, eds. *On the Brink: Americans and Soviets Reexamine the Cuban Missile Crisis.* New York: Hill and Wang, 1989.

Blum, William. *Rogue State: A Guide to the World's Only Superpower.* Monroe, ME: Common Courage Press, 2005.

Bogle, Lori. *The Cold War.* Vol. 3: *Hot Wars of the Cold Wars.* Oxford: Routledge, 2001.

Borstelmann, Thomas. *Apartheid's Reluctant Uncle: The United States and Southern Africa in the Early Cold War.* New York: Oxford University Press. 1993.

Borstelmann, Thomas. *The Cold War and the Color Line: American Race Relations in the Global Arena.* Cambridge: Harvard University Press, 2001.

Botti, Timothy J. *Ace in the Hole: Why the United States Did Not Use Nuclear Weapons in the Cold War, 1945 to 1965.* Westport, CT: Greenwood, 1996.

Bottome, Edgar M. *The Balance of Terror: A Guide to the Arms Race.* Boston: Beacon, 1971.

Bowie, Robert R., and Richard H. Immerman. *Waging Peace: How Eisenhower Shaped an Enduring Cold War Strategy.* New York: Oxford University Press, 1998.

Bowker, Mike. *Russian Foreign Policy and the End of the Cold War.* Brookfield, VT: Dartmouth Publishing, 1997.

Bowker, Mike, and Robin Brown. *From Cold War to Collapse: Theory and World Politics in the 1980s.* New York: Cambridge University Press, 1993.

Boyer, Paul S. *Fallout: A Historian Reflects on America's Half-Century Encounter with Nuclear Weapons.* Columbus: Ohio State University Press, 1998.

Boyle, Peter G., ed. *The Churchill-Eisenhower Correspondence, 1953–1955.* Chapel

Hill: University of North Carolina Press, 1990.

Bradlee, Benjamin C. *Conversations with Kennedy*. New York: Norton, 1975.

Braithwaite, Rodric. *Across the Moscow River: The World Turned Upside-Down*. New Haven, CT: Yale University Press, 2002.

Brands, H. W., *Cold Warriors: Eisenhower's Generation and American Foreign Policy*. New York: Columbia University Press, 1988.

Brands, H. W. *Inside the Cold War: Loy Henderson and the Rise of the American Empire, 1918–1961*. New York: Oxford University Press, 1991.

Brands, H. W. *The Devil We Knew: Americans and the Cold War*. New York: Oxford University Press, 1993.

Brands, H. W. *The Specter of Neutralism: The United States and the Emergence of the Third World, 1947–1960*. New York: Columbia University Press, 1989.

Brands, H. W. *The Wages of Globalism: Lyndon Johnson and the Limits of American Power*. New York: Oxford University Press, 1995.

Brandt, Willy. *My Life in Politics*. London: Hamish Hamilton, 1992.

Breslauer, George W. *Gorbachev and Yeltsin As Leaders*. Cambridge: Cambridge University Press, 2002.

Breuer, William B. *Race to the Moon: America's Duel with the Soviets*. Westport, CT: Praeger, 1993.

Brinkley, Douglas. *Dean Acheson: The Cold War Years, 1953–71*. New Haven, CT: Yale University Press, 1992.

Brogi, Alessandro. *A Question of Self-Esteem: The United States and Cold War Choices in France and Italy, 1944–1958*. Westport, CT: Praeger, 2002.

Brown, Archibald Haworth. *The Gorbachev Factor*. Oxford: Oxford University Press, 1996.

Brown, Edward J. *Russian Literature since the Revolution*. New York: Collier-Macmillan, 1963.

Brune, Lester H. *The Cuba-Caribbean Missile Crisis of October 1962: A Review of Issues and References*. Claremont, CA: Regina Books, 1996.

Brzezinski, Zbigniew K. *Ideology and Power in Soviet Politics*. Westport, CT: Greenwood, 1976.

Brzezinski, Zbigniew K. *The Grand Failure: The Birth and Death of Communism in the Twentieth Century*. New York: MacMillian, 1989.

Buckley, William F. *The Fall of the Berlin Wall*. New York: Wiley, 2004.

Bucklin, Steven J. *Realism and American Foreign Policy: Wilsonians and the Kennan-Morgenthau Thesis*. Westport, CT: Praeger, 2001.

Bullock, Alan. *Hitler and Stalin: Parallel Lives*. New York: Knopf, 1992.

Bundy, William. *A Tangled Web: The Making of Foreign Policy in the Nixon Presidency*. New York: Hill and Wang, 1998.

Bunn, George. *Arms Control by Committee: Managing Negotiations with the Russians*. Stanford, CA: Stanford University Press, 1992.

Burgen, Michael. *Hot Conflicts*. Cold War series. Orlando, FL: Steck-Vaughn, 2001.

Burr, Willliam, ed. *The Kissinger Transcripts: The Top-Secret Talks with Beijing & Moscow*. New York: New Press, 1998.

Burrows, William E. *By Any Means Necessary: America's Secret Air War in the Cold War*. New York: Farrar, Straus and Giroux, 2001.

Cahn, Anne Hessing. *Killing Detente: The Right Attacks the CIA*. University Park: Pennsylvania State University Press, 1998.

Callahan, David. *Dangerous Capabilities: Paul Nitze and the Cold War*. New York: HarperCollins, 1990.

Cannon, Lou. *President Reagan: The Role of a Lifetime*. New York: Simon and Schuster, 1991.

Carlton, David, and Herbert M. Levine, eds. *The Cold War Debated*. New York: McGraw-Hill, 1988.

Carmichael, Virginia. *Framing History: The Rosenberg Story and the Cold War*. Minneapolis: University of Minnesota Press, 1993.

Carnesdale, Albert, and Richard N. Haass, eds. *Superpower Arms Control: Setting the Record Straight*. Cambridge, MA: Ballinger, 1987.

Caro, Robert. *Master of the Senate: The Years of Lyndon Johnson*. New York: Knopf, 2002.

Carter, April. *Peace Movements: International Protests and World Politics since 1945*. London: Longman, 1992.

Castle, Timothy N. *At War in the Shadow of Vietnam: U.S. Military Aid to the Royal Lao Government, 1955–1975*. New York: Columbia University Press, 1993.

Chace, James. *Acheson: The Secretary of State Who Created the American World*. New York: Simon and Schuster, 1998.

Chafer, Tony, and Brian Jenkins. *France: From the Cold War to the New World Order*. New York: St. Martin's, 1996.

Chaliand, Gérard, ed. *Guerrilla Strategies*. Berkeley: University of California Press, 1982.

Chandler, Alfred D., Jr., and Louis Galambos, eds. *The Papers of Dwight D. Eisenhower*. 21 vols. to date. Baltimore: Johns Hopkins University Press, 1970–.

Chang Jung and Jon Halliday. *Mao: The Unknown Story*. New York: Knopf, 2005.

Chen, Jian. *Mao's China and the Cold War*. Chapel Hill: University of North Carolina Press, 2001.

Cimbala, Stephen J., ed. *Strategic Arms Control after SALT*. Wilmington, DE: Scholarly Resources, 1989.

Clarfield, Gerard H. *Dwight D. Eisenhower and the Shaping of the American Military Establishment*. Westport, CT: Praeger, 1999.

Clay, Lucius D. *Decision in Germany*. Garden City, NY: Doubleday, 1950.

Clemens, Walter C. *The Superpowers and Arms Control: From Cold War to Interdependence*. Lexington, MA: Lexington Books, 1973.

Clogg, Richard. *A Concise History of Greece*. 2nd ed. Cambridge: Cambridge University Press, 2002.

Close, David H. *The Greek Civil War, 1943–1950: Studies of Polarization*. London: Routledge, 1993.

Close, David H. *The Origins of the Greek Civil War*. New York: Longman, 1995.

Clough, Michael. *Free at Last? U.S. Policy toward Africa and the End of the Cold War*. New York: Council on Foreign Relations Press, 1992.

Coard, Edna A. *U.S. Air Power: Key to Deterrence*. Maxwell Air Force Base, AL: Air University Press, 1976.

Colby, William, with Peter Forbath. *Honorable Men: My Life in the CIA*. New York: Simon and Schuster, 1978.

Collins, Alan. *The Security Dilemma and the End of the Cold War*. New York: St. Martin's, 1997.

Collins, John M. *U.S.-Soviet Military Balance: Concepts and Capabilities, 1960–1980*. New York: McGraw-Hill, 1980.

Collins, Richard. *Bridge across the Sky: The Berlin Blockade and Airlift, 1948–1949*. New York: Pan Macmillan, 1978.

Conquest, Robert. *Stalin: Breaker of Nations*. London: Weidenfeld and Nicolson, 2000.

Cooper, Chester L. *In the Shadows of History: 50 Years Behind the Scenes of Cold War Diplomacy*. Amherst, NY: Prometheus Book, 2005.

Copson, Raymond. *Africa's War and Prospects for Peace*. Armonk, NY: Sharpe, 1994.

Craig, Campbell. *Destroying the Village: Eisenhower and Thermonuclear War*. New York: Columbia University Press, 1998.

Crane, Conrad C. *American Airpower Strategy in Korea, 1950–1953*. Lawrence: University Press of Kansas, 2000.

Craven, John P. *The Silent War: The Cold War Battle beneath the Sea*. New York: Simon and Schuster, 2001.

Crockatt, Richard. *The Fifty Years' War: The United States and the Soviet Union in World Politics, 1941–1991*. New York: Routledge, 1995.

Crocker, Chester A. *High Noon in Southern Africa: Making Peace in a Rough Neighborhood*. New York: Norton, 1992.

Cronin, James E. *The World the Cold War Made: Order, Chaos and the Return of History*. New York: Routledge, 1996.

Currey, Cecil B. *Victory at Any Cost: The Genius of Viet Nam's Gen. Vo Nguyen Giap.* Washington, DC: Brassey's, 1997.

D'Agostino, Anthony. *Gorbachev's Revolution.* New York: New York University Press, 1998.

Dallas, Gregor. *1945: The War That Never Ended.* New Haven, CT: Yale University Press, 2005.

Dallek, Robert. *An Unfinished Life: John F. Kennedy, 1917–1963.* Boston: Little, Brown, 2003.

Dallek, Robert. *Flawed Giant.* New York: Oxford University Press, 2003.

Dalloz, Jacques. *The War in Indo-China, 1945–54.* Translated by Josephine Bacon. New York: Barnes and Noble, 1990.

Dark, Ken R., and A. L. Harris. *The New World and the New World Order: US Relative Decline, Domestic Instability in the Americas, and the End of the Cold War.* New York: St. Martin's, 1996.

Davis, Lynn E. *The Cold War Begins: Soviet-American Conflict over Eastern Europe.* Princeton, NJ: Princeton University Press, 1974.

Dawisha, Adeed. *Arab Nationalism in the 20th Century.* Princeton, NJ: Princeton University Press, 2003.

Dean, Arthur H. *Test Ban and Disarmament: The Path of Negotiation.* New York: Harper and Row, 1966.

Defty, Andrew. *Britain, America, and Anti-Communist Propaganda, 1945–53: The Information Research Department.* New York: Routledge, 2004.

Deighton, Anne. *The Impossible Peace: Britain, the Division of Germany and the Origins of the Cold War.* New York: Oxford University Press, 1990.

DeLoach, Cartha D. *"Deke." Hoover's FBI: The Inside Story by Hoover's Trusted Lieutenant.* Washington, DC: Regnery, 1995.

DeMarco, Neil. *Hot War–Cold War.* London: Hodder Murray, 2001.

Denitch, Bogdan Denis. *The End of the Cold War: European Unity, Socialism, and the Shift in Global Power.* Minneapolis: University of Minnesota Press, 1990.

Deutscher, Isaac. *Stalin: A Political Biography.* New York: Oxford University Press, 1969.

Devillers, Philippe, and Jean Lacouture. *End of a War: Indochina, 1954.* Translated by Alexander Liven and Adam Roberts. New York: Praeger, 1969.

Dittmer, Lowell. *Sino-Soviet Normalization and Its International Implications, 1945–1990.* Seattle: Washington University Press, 1992.

Divine, Robert A. *Blowing on the Wind: The Nuclear Test Ban Debate, 1954–1960.* New York: Oxford University Press, 1978.

Divine, Robert A. *The Sputnik Challenge.* New York: Oxford University Press, 1993.

Djilas, Milován. *Tito.* New York: Harcourt Brace Jovanovich, 1980.

Dockrill, Saki. *Eisenhower's New Look: National Security Policy, 1953–1961.* New York: St. Martin's, 1996.

Doherty, Thomas Patrick. *Cold War, Cool Medium: Television, McCarthyism, and American Culture.* New York: Columbia University Press, 2003.

Dominguez, Jorge I. *To Make a World Safe for Revolution: Cuba's Foreign Policy.* Cambridge: Harvard University Press, 1989.

Donley, Michael B. *The SALT Handbook.* Washington, DC: Heritage Foundation, 1979.

Donnelly, Jack. *International Human Rights.* Boulder, CO: Westview, 1993.

Dudley, William. *The Cold War: Opposing Viewpoints.* San Diego, CA: Greenhaven, 1992.

Dudziak, Mary L. *Cold War Civil Rights: Race and the Image of American Democracy.* Princeton, NJ: Princeton University Press, 2000.

Duggan, Christopher, and C. Wagstaff, eds. *Italy in the Cold War: Politics, Culture and Society, 1948–1958.* Oxford, UK; Berg, 1995.

Duiker, William J. *Ho Chi Minh: A Life.* New York: Hyperion, 2000.

Duiker, William J. *The Rise of Nationalism in Vietnam, 1900–1941.* Ithaca, NY: Cornell University Press, 1976.

Dumbrell, John. *President Lyndon Johnson and Soviet Communism*. Manchester, UK: Manchester University Press, 2004.

Dunbabin, J. P. D. *International Relations since 1945: A History in Two Volumes*. New York: Longman, 1994.

Duric, Mira. *The Strategic Defense Initiative: U.S. Policy and the Soviet Union*. Burlington, VT: Ashgate, 2003.

Eckstein, Susan, ed. *Power and Popular Protest: Latin American Social Movements*. Berkeley: University of California Press, 2001.

Ent, Uzal. *Fighting on the Brink: Defense of the Pusan Perimeter*. Paducah, KY: Turner Publishing, 1996.

Evangelista, Matthew. *Unarmed Forces: The Transnational Movement to End the Cold War*. Ithaca, NY: Cornell University Press, 1999.

Evans, Grant. *A Short History of Laos: The Land in Between*. Crows Nest, Australia: Allen and Unwin, 2002.

Evans, Richard. *Deng Xiaoping and the Making of Modern China*. Rev. ed. London: Penguin, 1997.

Falk, Barbara J. *The Dilemmas of Dissidence in East-Central Europe: Citizen Intellectuals and Philosopher Kings*. Budapest: Central European University Press, 2003.

Falk, Richard. *Human Rights and State Sovereignty*. New York: Holmes and Meier, 1981.

Fall, Bernard B. *Hell in a Very Small Place: The Siege of Dienbienphu*. Philadelphia: Lippincott, 1966.

Fatton, Robert. "The Reagan Foreign Policy toward South Africa: The Ideology of the New Cold War." *African Studies Review* 27, no. 1 (1984): 57–82.

Feldman, Burton. *The Nobel Prize: A History of Genius, Controversy, and Prestige*. New York: Arcade Publishing, 2000.

Field, James A. *History of United States Naval Operations: Korea*. Washington, DC: Naval History Division, 1962.

Firestone, Bernard J. *The United Nations under U Thant, 1961–1971*. Lanham, MD: Scarecrow, 2001.

Fischer, Beth A. *The Reagan Reversal: Foreign Policy and the End of the Cold War*. Columbia: University of Missouri Press, 1997.

FitzGerald, Frances. *Fire in the Lake: The Vietnamese and the Americans in Vietnam*. Boston: Little, Brown, 1972.

FitzGerald, Frances. *Way Out There in the Blue: Reagan, Star Wars, and the End of the Cold War*. New York: Simon and Schuster, 2000.

Flapan, Simha. *The Birth of Israel: Myths and Realities*. New York: Pantheon, 1987.

Fordham, Benjamin O. *Building the Cold War Consensus: The Political Economy of U.S. National Security Policy, 1949–51*. Ann Arbor: University of Michigan Press, 1998.

Forsythe, David P. *Human Rights and World Politics*. Lincoln: University of Nebraska Press, 1983.

Frankel, Max. *High Noon in the Cold War: Kennedy, Khrushchev, and the Cuban Missile Crisis*. New York: Ballantine, 2004.

Freedman, Lawrence. *Europe Transformed: Documents on the End of the Cold War*. New York: St. Martin's, 1990.

Freedman, Lawrence. *Kennedy's Wars: Berlin, Cuba, Laos, and Vietnam*. New York: Oxford University Press, 2000.

Freedman, Lawrence. *The Evolution of Nuclear Strategy*. 3rd ed. Houndmills, UK: Palgrave Macmillan, 2003.

Freedman, Lawrence, and John Keegan. *The Cold War: A Military History*. London: Cassell, 2001.

Fried, Richard M. *Nightmare in Red: The McCarthy Era in Perspective*. New York: Oxford University Press, 1990.

Friedman, Norman. *The Fifty Year War: Conflict and Strategy in the Cold War*. Annapolis, MD: Naval Institute Press, 2000.

Fulbrook, Mary. *Anatomy of a Dictatorship: Inside the GDR, 1949–1989*. Oxford: Oxford University Press, 1995.

Fursenko, Aleksandr. *Khrushchev's Cold War: The Inside Story of an American Adversary*. New York: W. W. Norton, 2007.

Fursenko, Aleksandr, and Timothy Naftali. *"One Hell of a Gamble": Khrushchev,*

Castro, & Kennedy, 1958–1964. New York: Norton, 1997.

Gaddis, John Lewis. *Cold War Statesmen Confront the Bomb: Nuclear Diplomacy since 1945*. New York: Oxford University Press, 1999.

Gaddis, John Lewis. *Strategies of Containment: A Critical Appraisal of Postwar American National Security*. New York: Oxford University Press, 1982.

Gaddis, John Lewis. *The Cold War: A New History*. New York: Penguin, 2005.

Gaddis, John Lewis. *The United States and the End of the Cold War: Implications, Reconsiderations, Provocations*. New York: Oxford University Press, 1992.

Gaddis, John Lewis. *The United States and the Origins of the Cold War, 1941–1947*. New York: Columbia University Press, 1972.

Gaddis, John Lewis. *We Now Know: Rethinking Cold War History*. New York: Oxford University Press, 1997.

Gaglione, Anthony. *The United Nations under Trygve Lie, 1945–1953*. Lanham, MD: Scarecrow, 2001.

Gambone, Michael D. *Eisenhower, Somoza, and the Cold War in Nicaragua, 1953–1961*. Westport, CT: Praeger, 1997.

Garber, Marjorie B., and Rebecca L. Walkowitz. *Secret Agents: The Rosenberg Case, McCarthyism, and Fifties' America*. New York: Routledge, 1995.

Gardner, Lloyd. *Pay Any Price: Lyndon Johnson and the Wars for Vietnam*. Chicago: Ivan R. Dee, 1995.

Gardner, Lloyd C., Arthur M. Schlesinger, and Hans Joachim Morgenthau. *The Origins of the Cold War*. Waltham, MA: Ginn-Blaisdell, 1970.

Garthoff, Raymond L. *A Journey through the Cold War: A Memoir of Containment and Coexistence*. Washington, DC: Brookings Institution Press, 2001.

Garthoff, Raymond L. *Détente and Confrontation: American-Soviet Relations from Nixon to Reagan*. Rev. ed. Washington, DC: Brookings Institution Press, 1994.

Garthoff, Raymond L. *The Great Transition: American-Soviet Relations and the End of the Cold War*. Washington, DC: Brookings Institution Press, 1994.

Garver, John W. *The Sino-American Alliance: Nationalist China and American Cold War Strategy in Asia*. Armonk, NY: Sharpe, 1997.

Gavin, Francis J. *The Cold War*. Chicago: Fitzroy Dearborn, 2001.

Gellman, Barton D. *Contending with Kennan: Toward a Philosophy of American Power*. New York: Praeger, 1984.

Gentry, Curt. *J. Edgar Hoover: The Man and the Secrets*. New York: Norton, 1991.

George, Alice L. *Awaiting Armageddon: How Americans Faced the Cuban Missile Crisis*. Chapel Hill: University of North Carolina Press, 2003.

Gerolymatos, Andre. *Red Acropolis, Black Terror: The Greek Civil War and the Origins of Soviet-American Rivalry*. New York: Basic Books, 2004.

Gerson, Mark. *The Neoconservative Vision: From the Cold War to the Culture Wars*. Lanham, MD: Madison Books, 1996.

Gibson, James N. *Nuclear Weapons of the United States: An Illustrated History*. Atglen, PA: Schiffer, 1996.

Gilbert, Martin S. *Winston S. Churchill*. 8 vols. New York: Random House, 1966–1988.

Gimbel, John. *The Origins of the Marshall Plan*. Stanford, CA: Stanford University Press, 1976.

Ginzburg, Evgeniia. *Journey into the Whirlwind*. Translated by Paul Stevenson and Max Hayward. New York: Harcourt Brace and World, 1967.

Glaser, Charles L. *Analyzing Strategic Nuclear Policy*. Princeton, NJ: Princeton University Press, 1990.

Gleason, Abbott. *Totalitarianism: The Inner History of the Cold War*. New York: Oxford University Press, 1995.

Gleijeses, Piero. *Conflicting Missions: Havana, Washington, and Africa, 1959–1976*. Chapel Hill: University of North Carolina Press, 2002.

Gleijeses, Piero. *The Dominican Crisis: The 1965 Constitutionalist Revolt and American Intervention*. Baltimore: Johns Hopkins University Press, 1978.

Glynn, Patrick. *Closing Pandora's Box: Arms Races, Arms Control, and the History of the Cold War*. New York: Basic Books, 1992.

Goldman, Marshall. *What Went Wrong with Perestroika*. New York: Norton, 1992.

Goodwin, Doris Kearns. *Lyndon Johnson and the American Dream*. New York: St. Martin's, 1976.

Goodwyn, Lawrence. *Breaking the Barrier: The Rise of Solidarity in Poland*. New York: Oxford University Press, 1991.

Gorbachev, Mikhail. *Memoirs*. Translated by Georges Peronansky and Tatjana Varsavsky. New York: Doubleday, 1996.

Gorbachev, Mikhail. *Perestroika: New Thinking for Our Country and the World*. London: HarperCollins, 1987.

Gormly, James L. *From Potsdam to the Cold War: Big Three Diplomacy, 1945–1947*. Wilmington, DE: Scholarly Resources, 1990.

Gouré, Leon. *War Survival in Soviet Strategy: USSR Civil Defense*. 1976. Reprint, Westport, CT: Greenwood, 1986.

Graham, Thomas, Jr., and Damien J. LaVera. *Cornerstones of Security: Arms Control Treaties in the Nuclear Era*. Seattle: University of Washington Press, 2003.

Gras, Yves. *Histoire de la guerre d'Indochine*. Paris: Editions Denoël, 1992.

Greene, John Robert. *The Limits of Power: The Nixon and Ford Administrations*. Bloomington: Indiana University Press, 1992.

Gregory, Ross. *Cold War America, 1946 to 1990*. New York: Facts on File, 2003.

Grogin, Robert C. *Natural Enemies: The United States and the Soviet Union in the Cold War, 1917–1991*. Lanham, MD: Lexington Books, 2001.

Gromyko, Anatoli. *Andrey Gromyko: In the Kremlin's Labyrinth*. Moscow: Avtor, 1997.

Gromyko, Anatoli. *Memories*. New York: Arrow Books, 1989.

Grose, Peter. *Operation Rollback: America's Secret War behind the Iron Curtain*. Boston: Houghton Mifflin, 2000.

Grossman, Andrew D. *Neither Dead nor Red: Civilian Defense and American Political Development during the Early Cold War*. New York: Routledge, 2001.

Guhin, Michael A. *John Foster Dulles: A Statesman and His Times*. New York: Columbia University Press, 1972.

Hahn, Peter L. *The United States, Great Britain, and Egypt, 1945–1956: Strategy and Diplomacy in the Early Cold War*. Chapel Hill: University of North Carolina Press, 1991.

Halberstam, David. *The Best and the Brightest*. New York: Random House, 1972.

Hamilton-Merritt, Jane. *Tragic Mountains: The Hmong, the Americans, and the Secret Wars for Laos, 1942–1992*. Bloomington: Indiana University Press, 1993.

Hammer, Ellen J. *The Struggle for Indochina*. Stanford, CA: Stanford University Press, 1954.

Hanhimaki, Jussi. "'They Can Write it in Swahili': Kissinger, The Soviets, and the Helsinki Accords, 1973–1975." *Journal of Transatlantic Studies* 1, no. 1 (2003): 37–58.

Hanhimäki, Jussi. *The Flawed Architect: Henry Kissinger and American Foreign Policy*. New York: Oxford University Press, 2004.

Harbutt, Fraser J. *The Cold War Era*. Malden, MA: Blackwell, 2002.

Harbutt, Fraser J. *The Iron Curtain: Churchill, America, and the Origins of the Cold War*. New York: Oxford University Press, 1986.

Harford, James. *Korolev: How One Man Masterminded the Soviet Drive to Beat America to the Moon*. New York: Wiley, 1997.

Harper, T. N. *The End of Empire and the Making of Malaya*. Cambridge: Cambridge University Press, 1999.

Harrison, Hope M. *Driving the Soviets up the Wall: Soviet–East German Relations, 1953–1961*. Princeton, NJ: Princeton University Press, 2003.

Hastings, Max. *The Korean War*. New York: Simon and Schuster, 1987.

Hauner, Milan. *The Soviet War in Afghanistan: Patterns of Russian Imperialism*. Lanham, MD: University Press of America, 1991.

Haydock, Michael D. *City under Siege: The Berlin Blockade and Airlift, 1948–1949.* London: Brassey's, 1999.

Heller, Peter B. *The United Nations under Dag Hammarskjöld, 1953–1961.* Lanham, MD: Scarecrow, 2001.

Henriksen, Margot A. *Dr. Strangelove's America: Society and Culture in the Atomic Age.* Berkeley: University of California Press, 1997.

Herring, George C. *America's Longest War: The United States and Vietnam, 1950–1975.* 4th ed. New York: McGraw-Hill, 2001.

Herrmann, Richard K. *Ending the Cold War: Interpretations, Causations, and the Study of International Relations.* New York: Palgrave Macmillan, 2004.

Hersh, Seymour. *The Price of Power: Kissinger in the Nixon White House.* New York: Simon and Schuster, 1983.

Hershberg, James G. *James B. Conant: Harvard to Hiroshima and the Making of the Nuclear Age.* New York: Knopf, 1993.

Hess, Gary R. *Presidential Decisions for War: Korea, Vietnam, and the Persian Gulf.* Baltimore: Johns Hopkins University Press, 2001.

Hewison, Robert. *In Anger: British Culture in the Cold War, 1945–60.* New York: Oxford University Press, 1981.

Higgins, Trumbull. *The Perfect Failure: Kennedy, Eisenhower, and the CIA at the Bay of Pigs.* New York: Norton, 1989.

Hilderbrand, Robert C. *Dumbarton Oaks: The Origins of the United Nations and the Search for Postwar Security.* Chapel Hill: University of North Carolina Press, 1990.

Hill, Kenneth L. *Cold War Chronology: Soviet-American Relations, 1945–1991.* Washington, DC: Congressional Quarterly, 1993.

Hilsman, Roger. *The Cuban Missile Crisis: The Struggle over Policy.* Westport, CT: Praeger, 1996.

Hinds, Lynn Boyd, and Theodore Windt. *The Cold War As Rhetoric: The Beginnings, 1945–1950.* New York: Praeger, 1991.

Hixson, Walter L. *George F. Kennan: Cold War Iconoclast.* New York: Columbia University Press, 1989.

Hixson, Walter L. *Parting the Curtain: Propaganda, Culture, and the Cold War, 1945–1961.* New York: St. Martin's, 1997.

Ho Chi Minh. *Ho Chi Minh on Revolution: Selected Writings, 1920–1966.* New York: Signet, 1967.

Hoff, Joan. *Nixon Reconsidered.* New York: Basic Books, 1994.

Hoffmann, Stanley, and Charles Maier, eds. *The Marshall Plan: A Retrospective.* Boulder, CO: Westview, 1984.

Hogan, Michael J. *A Cross of Iron: Harry S. Truman and the Origins of the National Security State, 1945–1954.* New York: Cambridge University Press, 1998.

Hogan, Michael J. *The End of the Cold War: Its Meaning and Implications.* New York: Cambridge University Press, 1992.

Hogan, Michael J. *The Marshall Plan: America, Britain, and the Reconstruction of Western Europe, 1948–1952.* New York: Cambridge University Press, 1987.

Holden, Gerard. *The Warsaw Pact: The WTO and Soviet Security Policy.* Oxford, UK: Blackwell, 1989.

Hoopes, Townsend. *The Devil and John Foster Dulles.* Boston: Little, Brown, 1973.

Horowitz, David. *Containment and Revolution.* Boston: Beacon, 1967.

Hourani, Albert. *A History of the Arab Peoples.* Cambridge: Harvard University Press, 1991.

Howe, Herbert. *Military Forces in African States: Ambiguous Order.* Boulder, CO: Lynne Rienner, 2001.

Hunt, Michael H. *The Genesis of Chinest Communist Foreign Policy.* New York: Columbia University Press, 1996.

Hunter, Allen. *Rethinking the Cold War.* Philadelphia: Temple University Press, 1998.

Iatrides, John O. *Greece in the 1940s: A Nation in Crisis.* Hanover, NH: University Press of New England, 1981.

Immerman, Richard H. *John Foster Dulles: Piety, Pragmatism, and Power in U.S.*

Foreign Policy. Wilmington, DE: Scholarly Resources, 1999.

Isaacson, Walter. *Kissinger: A Biography*. New York: Simon and Schuster, 1992.

Ivanova, Galina Mikhailovna, with Donald J. Raleigh. *Labor Camp Socialism: The Gulag in the Soviet Totalitarian System*. Translated from the Russian by Carol Fath. Armonk, NY: Sharpe, 2000.

Jeffreys-Jones, Rhodri. *The CIA and American Democracy*. 2nd ed. New Haven, CT: Yale University Press, 1998.

Jenkins, Philip. *The Cold War at Home: The Red Scare in Pennsylvania, 1945–1960*. Chapel Hill: University of North Carolina Press, 1999.

Jenkins, Roy. *Churchill*. London: Macmillan, 2001.

Jensen, Kenneth M., ed. *Origins of the Cold War: The Novikov, Kennan, and Roberts "Long Telegrams" of 1946; With Three New Commentaries*. Rev. ed. Washington, DC: United States Institute of Peace Press, 1993.

Jockel, Joseph T. *No Boundaries Upstairs: Canada, the United States, and the Origins of North American Air Defense, 1945–1958*. Vancouver: University of British Columbia Press, 1987.

Jockel, Joseph T., and Joel J. Sokolsky, eds. *Fifty Years of Canada-United States Defense Cooperation: The Road from Ogdensburg*. Lewiston, NY: Edwin Mellen, 1992.

Johnson, Chalmers. *The Sorrows of Empire: Militarism, Secrecy, and the End of the Republic*. New York: Metropolitan Books, 2004.

Johnson, Lyndon B. *The Vantage Point: Perspectives of the Presidency 1963–1969*. New York: Holt, Rinehart and Winston, 1971.

Jones, Christopher D. *Soviet Influence in Eastern Europe: Political Autonomy and the Warsaw Pact*. Brooklyn, NY: Praeger, 1981.

Judge, Edward, and John W. Langdon, eds. *The Cold War: A History through Documents*. Upper Saddle River, NJ: Prentice Hall, 1999.

Judt, Tony. *Postwar: A History of Europe since 1945*. London: Penguin, 2005.

Kaiser, David E. *American Tragedy: Kennedy, Johnson, and the Origins of the Vietnam War*. Cambridge: Belknap Press of Harvard University Press, 2000.

Kaledin, Eugenia. *Mothers and More: American Women in the 1950s*. Boston: Twayne, 1984.

Kaltefleiter, Werner, and Robert L. Pfaltzgraff, eds. *The Peace Movements in Europe & the United States*. New York: St. Martin's, 1985.

Kanet, Roger E., and Edward A. Kolodziej. *The Cold War As Cooperation*. Baltimore: Johns Hopkins University Press, 1991.

Kaplan, Fred. *The Wizards of Armageddon: Strategists of the Nuclear Age*. New York: Simon and Schuster, 1983.

Kaplan, Lawrence S. *NATO and the United States: The Enduring Alliance*. Boston: Twayne, 1988.

Kaplan, Lawrence S. *The Long Entanglement: NATO's First Fifty Years*. Westport, CT: Praeger, 1999.

Karabell, Zachary. *Architects of Intervention: The United States, the Third World, and the Cold War, 1946–1962*. Baton Rouge: Louisiana State University Press, 1999.

Karnow, Stanley. *Mao and China: A Legacy of Turmoil*. New York: Penguin, 1990.

Karnow, Stanley. *Vietnam: A History*. New York: Viking, 1983.

Katz, Milton S. *Ban the Bomb: A History of SANE, the Committee for a Sane Nuclear Policy, 1957–1985*. New York: Greenwood, 1986.

Kaufman, Burton I. *The Korean War: Challenges in Crisis, Credibility, and Command*. Philadelphia: Temple University Press, 1986.

Kelly, George A. *Lost Soldiers: The French Army and Empire in Crisis, 1947–1962*. Cambridge, MA: MIT Press, 1965.

Kennan, George F. *Around the Cragged Hill: A Personal and Political Philosophy*. New York: Norton, 1994.

Kennan, George F. *Sketches from a Life*. New York: Pantheon, 1990.

Kennedy, Robert F. *Thirteen Days: A Memoir of the Cuban Missile Crisis*. New York: Norton, 1999.

Kent, John. *British Imperial Strategy and the Origins of the Cold War, 1944–49*. Leicester, UK: Leicester University Press, 1993.

Khevniuk, Oleg. *History of the Gulag*. New Haven, CT: Yale University Press, 2003.

Khrushchev, Nikita S. *Khrushchev Remembers*. Introduction and commentary by Edward Crankshaw. Translated by Strobe Talbott. Boston: Little, Brown 1970.

Khrushchev, Nikita S. *Khrushchev Remembers: The Glasnost Tapes*. Translated and edited by Jerrold L. Schecter with Vyacheslav V. Luchkov. Boston: Little, Brown, 1990.

Khrushchev, Nikita S. *Khrushchev Remembers: The Last Testament*. Translated and edited by Strobe Talbott. Boston: Little, Brown, 1974.

Khrushchev, Nikita S. *Memoirs of Nikita Khrushchev*. Edited by Sergei Khrushchev and translated by George Shriver. University Park: Pennsylvania State University Press, 2004.

Kim, Young Hum. *Twenty Years of Crises: The Cold War Era*. Englewood Cliffs, NJ: Prentice Hall, 1968.

Kimball, Jeffrey. *Nixon's Vietnam War*. Lawrence: University Press of Kansas, 1998.

Kimball, Warren F., ed. *Churchill and Roosevelt: The Complete Correspondence*. Princeton, NJ: Princeton University Press, 1984.

Kinsella, David, and Herbert K. Tillema. "Arms and Aggression in the Middle East: Overt Military Interventions, 1948–1991." *The Journal of Conflict Resolution* 39, no. 2 (June 1995): 306–29.

Kissinger, Henry A. *The White House Years*. Boston: Little, Brown, 1979.

Kissinger, Henry A. *Years of Renewal*. New York: Simon and Schuster, 1999.

Kissinger, Henry A. *Years of Upheaval*. Boston: Little, Brown, 1982.

Kleinman, Mark L. *A World of Hope, a World of Fear: Henry A. Wallace, Reinhold Niebuhr, and American Liberalism*. Columbus: Ohio State University Press, 2000.

Kofsky, Frank. *Harry S. Truman and the War Scare of 1948: A Successful Campaign to Deceive the Nation*. New York: St. Martin's, 1993.

Korea Institute of Military History. *The Korean War*. 3 vols. Seoul: Korea Institute of Military History, 1997.

Kornbluh, Peter. *Bay of Pigs Declassified: The Secret CIA Report on the Invasion of Cuba*. New York: New Press, 1998.

Kowalski, Ronald. *European Communism: 1848–1991*. New York: Macmillan, 2006.

Kozlov, V. A., and Elaine McClarnand Mackinnon. *Mass Uprisings in the USSR: Urban Unrest under Khrushchev and Brezhnev, 1953–82*. Armonk, NY: Sharpe, 2002.

Kramer, Hilton. *The Twilight of the Intellectuals: Culture and Politics in the Era of the Cold War*. Chicago: Ivan R. Dee, 1999.

Krepon, Michael. *Arms Control in the Reagan Administration*. Lanham, MD: University Press of America, 1989.

Kuhns, Woodrow J. *Assessing the Soviet Threat: The Early Cold War Years*. Center for the Study of Intelligence, Central Intelligence Agency. Library of Congress Photo Duplication Service. Springfield, VA, 1997.

Kumar, Satish. "Nonalignment: International Goals and National Interests." *Asian Survey* 23, no. 4 (April 1983): 445–62.

Kuniholm, Bruce R. *The Origins of the Cold War in the Near East*. Princeton, NJ: Princeton University Press, 1980.

Kusin, Vladimir V. *The Intellectual Origins of the Prague Spring: The Development of Reformist Ideas in Czechoslovakia, 1956–1967*. Cambridge: Cambridge University Press, 2002.

Kuznick, Peter J., and James Burkhart Gilbert. *Rethinking Cold War Culture*. Washington, DC: Smithsonian Institution Press, 2001.

Kyvig, David E. ed. *Reagan and the World*. Westport, CT: Greenwood, 1990.

Lacouture, Jean. *Ho Chi Minh: A Political Biography*. New York: Random House, 1968.

Ladd, Brian. *The Ghosts of Berlin: Confronting German History in the Urban Land-

scape. Chicago: University of Chicago Press, 1997.

Lafeber, Walter. *America, Russia, and the Cold War, 1945–2006*. New York: McGraw Hill, 2006.

Lake, Anthony. *The "Tar Baby" Option: American Policy towards Southern Rhodesia*. New York: Columbia University Press, 1976.

Lakhoff, Sanford, and Herbert F. York. *A Shield in Space? Technology, Politics, and the Strategic Defense Initiative*. Berkeley: University of California Press, 1989.

Lambakis, Steven James. *Winston Churchill, Architect of Peace: A Study of Statesmanship and the Cold War*. Westport, CT: Greenwood, 1993.

Lankevich, George J. *The United Nations under Javier Pérez de Cuéllar, 1982–1991*. Lanham, MD: Scarecrow, 2001.

Large, David Clay. *Berlin: A Modern History*. New York: Basic Books, 2000.

Larres, Klaus. *Churchill's Cold War: The Politics of Personal Diplomacy*. New Haven, CT: Yale University Press, 2002.

Larson, Deborah Welch. *Anatomy of Mistrust: U.S.-Soviet Relations during the Cold War*. Ithaca, NY: Cornell University Press, 1997.

Latham, Robert. *The Liberal Moment: Modernity, Security, and the Making of Postwar International Order*. New York: Columbia University Press, 1997.

Launius, Roger D. *Frontiers of Space Exploration*. Westport, CT: Greenwood Press, 1998.

Layton, Mike. *Easy Blood: Ronald Reagan's Proxy Wars in Central America*. N.p.: Dragonred Pub., 1997.

Lebow, Richard Ned, and Janice G. Stein. *We All Lost the Cold War*. Princeton, NJ: Princeton University Press, 1994.

Lebow, Richard Ned, and Thomas Risse-Kappen. *International Relations Theory and the End of the Cold War*. New York: Columbia University Press, 1995.

Ledeen, Michael Arthur. *Freedom Betrayed: How America Led a Global Democratic Revolution, Won the Cold War, and Walked Away*. Washington, DC: AEI Press, 1996.

Leebaert, Derek. *The Fifty-Year Wound: The True Price of America's Cold War Victory*. Boston: Little, Brown, 2002.

Lees, Lorraine M. *Keeping Tito Afloat: The United States, Yugoslavia, and the Cold War*. University Park: Pennsylvania State University Press, 1997.

Leffler, Melvyn P. *A Preponderance of Power: National Security, the Truman Administration, and the Cold War*. Stanford, CA: Stanford University Press, 1992.

Leffler, Melvyn P. *The Specter of Communism: The United States and the Origins of the Cold War, 1917–1953*. New York: Hill and Wang, 1994.

Leffler, Melvyn P., and David S. Painter. *Origins of the Cold War: An International History*. New York: Routledge, 1994.

Levering, Ralph B. *Debating the Origins of the Cold War: American and Russian Perspectives*. Lanham, MD: Rowman and Littlefield, 2002.

Levi, Barbara G., et al., eds. *The Future of Land Based Ballistic Missiles*. New York: American Institute of Physics, 1989.

Levine, Alan J. *The Missile and the Space Race*. Westport, CT: Praeger, 1994.

Liang-Fenton, Debra, ed. *Implementing U.S. Human Rights Policy: Agendas, Policies, and Practices*. Washington, DC: United States Institute of Peace Press, 2004.

Linden, Carl. *Khrushchev and the Soviet Leadership, 1957–1964*. Baltimore: Johns Hopkins University Press, 1966.

Lippmann, Walter. *The Cold War: A Study in U.S. Foreign Policy*. New York: Harper and Row, 1972.

Lipschutz, Ronnie D. *Cold War Fantasies: Film, Fiction, and Foreign Policy*. New York: Rowman and Littlefield, 2001.

Litwak, Robert S. *Détente and the Nixon Doctrine: American Foreign Policy and the Pursuit of Stability, 1969–1976*. Cambridge: Cambridge University Press, 1984.

Loth, Wilfried. *Overcoming the Cold War: A History of Détente, 1950–1991*. Translated by Robert F. Hogg. New York: Palgrave, 2002.

Lourie, Richard. *Sakharov: A Biography*. Hanover, NH: University Press of New England, 2002.

Lowe, Peter. *Containing the Cold War in East Asia: British Policies towards Japan, China and Korea, 1948–1953*. Manchester: Manchester University Press, 1997.

Lowenthal, John. "Venona and Alger Hiss." *Intelligence and National Security* 15, no. 3 (2000): 98–130.

Luard, Evan. *A History of the United Nations*. 2 vols. New York: St. Martin's, 1982–1989.

Lucas, Scott. *Freedom's War: The American Crusade against the Soviet Union*. New York: New York University Press, 1999.

Lukacs, John. *Churchill: Visionary, Statesman, Historian*. New Haven, CT: Yale University Press, 2002.

Lüthi, Lorenz M. "The Sino-Soviet Split, 1956–1966." Unpublished doctoral diss., Yale University, 2003.

Lykins, Daniel L. *From Total War to Total Diplomacy: The Advertising Council and the Construction of the Cold War Consensus*. Westport, CT: Praeger, 2003.

Lyman, Princeton. *Partner to History: The U.S. Role in South Africa's Transition to Democracy*. Washington, DC: United States Institute of Peace Press, 2002.

Lynch, Allen. *The Cold War Is Over—Again*. Boulder, CO: Westview, 1992.

Lynch, Michael J. *Mao*. London: Routledge, 2004.

Lyons, Thomas P. *Economic Integration and Planning in Maoist China*. New York: Columbia University Press, 1987.

Macdonald, Douglas J. *Adventures in Chaos: American Intervention for Reform in the Third World*. Cambridge: Harvard University Press, 1992.

MacKenzie, David. *From Messianism to Collapse: Soviet Foreign Policy, 1917–1991*. Fort Worth, TX: Harcourt Brace, 1994.

MacKenzie, David, and Michael W. Curran. *Russia and the USSR in the Twentieth Century*. 4th ed. New York: Wadsworth, 2002.

Maclear, Michael. *The Ten Thousand Day War: Vietnam, 1945–1975*. New York: St. Martin's, 1981.

MacShane, Denis. *International Labour and the Origins of the Cold War*. New York: Oxford University Press, 1992.

Maddox, Robert James. *The New Left and the Origins of the Cold War*. Princeton, NJ: Princeton University Press, 1973.

Maier, Charles S. *The Cold War in Europe: Era of a Divided Continent*. 3rd ed. Princeton, NJ: Markus Wiener, 1996.

Maier, Charles S. *The Origins of the Cold War and Contemporary Europe*. New York: New Viewpoints, 1978.

Mamdani, Mahmood. *Good Muslim, Bad Muslim: America, the Cold War, and the Roots of Terror*. New York: Pantheon, 2004.

Mandelbaum, Michael. *The Ideas That Conquered the World: Peace, Democracy, and Free Markets in the Twenty-First Century*. New York: Public Affairs, 2002.

Mao Zedong. "On Protracted War." In *Selected Military Writings*, 187–267. Beijing: Foreign Languages Press, 1967.

Mao Zedong. *Selected Works of Mao Zedong*. Beijing: Foreign Languages Press, 1966–1977.

Maresca, John J. *To Helsinki: The Conference on Security and Cooperation in Europe, 1973–1975*. Durham, NC: Duke University Press, 1985.

Marks, Frederick W., III. *Power and Peace: The Diplomacy of John Foster Dulles*. Westport, CT: Praeger, 1993.

Markusen, Ann, et al. *The Rise of the Gunbelt: The Military Remapping of Industrial America*. New York: Oxford University Press, 1991.

Marr, David G. *Vietnam 1945: The Quest for Power*. Berkeley: University of California Press, 1995.

Marr, David G. *Vietnamese Anti-Colonialism*. Berkeley: University of California Press, 1971.

Marshall, Barbara. *Willy Brandt: A Political Biography*. New York: Palgrave Macmillan, 1997.

Marte, Fred. *Political Cycles in International Relations: The Cold War and Africa, 1945–1990*. Amsterdam: VU University Press, 1994.

Marullo, Sam. *Ending the Cold War at Home: From Militarism to a More Peaceful World Order*. New York: Lexington Books, 1993.

Mastny, Vojtech, and Malcolm Byrne, eds. *A Cardboard Castle? An Inside History of the Warsaw Pact, 1955–1991*. Budapest/New York: Central European Press, 2005.

Mastny, Vojtech, Sven Holtsmark, and Andreas Wenger, eds. *War Plans and Alliances in the Cold War: Threat Perceptions in the East and West*. New York: Routledge, 2006.

Matlock, Jack F., Jr. *Reagan and Gorbachev: How the Cold War Ended*. New York: Random House, 2004.

Matthias, Willard C. *America's Strategic Blunders: Intelligence Analysis and National Security Policy, 1936–1991*. University Park: Pennsylvania State University Press, 2001.

May, Elaine Tyler. *Homeward Bound: American Families in the Cold War Era*. New York: Basic Books, 1988.

May, Ernest R. *American Cold War Strategy: Interpreting NSC 68*. Boston: Bedford Books of St. Martin's, 1993.

May, Ernest R., and Philip D. Zelikow, eds. *The Kennedy Tapes: Inside the White House during the Cuban Missile Crisis*. Cambridge: Harvard University Press, 1997.

Mayers, David. *George Kennan and the Dilemmas of US Foreign Policy*. New York: Oxford University Press, 1988.

Mayne, Richard. *The Recovery of Europe: From Devastation to Unity*. London: Weidenfeld and Nicolson, 1970.

Mazarr, Michael J. *START and the Future of Deterrence*. London: Macmillan, 1990.

McCalla, Robert B. *Uncertain Perceptions: U.S. Cold War Crisis Decision Making*. Ann Arbor: University of Michigan Press, 1992.

McClintock, Cynthia. *Revolutionary Movements in Latin America*. Washington, DC:

United States Institute of Peace Press, 1998.

McDougall, Walter A. *The Heavens and the Earth: A Political History of the Space Age*. Baltimore: Johns Hopkins University Press, 1997.

McEnaney, Laura. *Civil Defense Begins at Home: Militarization Meets Everyday Life in the Fifties*. Princeton, NJ: Princeton University Press.

McGinnis, Michael D., and John T. Williams. *Compound Dilemmas: Democracy, Collective Action, and Superpower Rivalry*. Ann Arbor: University of Michigan Press, 2001.

McMahon, Robert J. *The Cold War on the Periphery*. New York: Columbia University Press, 1996.

McMahon, Robert J. *The Limits of Empire: The United States and Southeast Asia since World War II*. New York: Columbia University Press, 1999.

McNair, Brian. *Images of the Enemy: Reporting the New Cold War*. New York: Routledge, 1988.

McNamara, Robert S. *Out of the Cold: New Thinking for American Foreign and Defense Policy in the 21st Century*. New York: Simon and Schuster, 1989.

McNay, John T. *Acheson and Empire: The British Accent in American Foreign Policy*. Columbia: University of Missouri Press, 2001.

McNeal, Robert H. *Stalin: Man and Ruler*. New York: New York University Press, 1988.

Medhurst, Martin J. *Cold War Rhetoric: Strategy, Metaphor, and Ideology*. New York: Greenwood, 1990.

Medhurst, Martin J., and H. W. Brands. *Critical Reflections on the Cold War: Linking Rhetoric and History*. College Station: Texas A&M University Press, 2000.

Meditz, Sandra, and Tim Merrill. *Zaire: A Country Study*. Washington, DC: Federal Research Division, Library of Congress, 1994.

Medvedev, Roi A. *Khrushchev*. Translated by Brian Pearce. Oxford, UK: Blackwell, 1982.

Meisler, Stanley. *The United Nations: The First Fifty Years*. New York: Atlantic Monthly Press, 1995.

Mervin, David. *Ronald Reagan and the American Presidency*. New York: Longman, 1990.

Meyer, Karl E., and Tad Szulc. *The Cuban Invasion: The Chronicle of a Disaster*. New York: Praeger, 1968.

Meyerowitz, Joanne, ed. *Not June Cleaver: Women and Gender in Postwar America*. Philadelphia: Temple University Press, 1994.

Mickelson, Sig. *America's Other Voice: The Story of Radio Free Europe & Radio Liberty*. New York: Praeger, 1983.

Miller, David. *The Cold War: A Military History*. New York: St. Martin's, 1999.

Miller, Lynn H., and Ronald W. Pruessen, eds. *Reflections on the Cold War: A Quarter Century of American Foreign Policy*. Philadelphia: Temple University Press, 1974.

Miller, Richard L. *Under the Cloud: The Decades of Nuclear Testing*. New York: Free Press, 1986.

Millett, Allan R., and Peter Maslowski. *For the Common Defense: A Military History of the United States of America*. New York: Free Press, 1994.

Milward, Alan S. *The Reconstruction of Western Europe, 1945–51*. Berkeley: University of California Press, 1984.

Miscamble, Wilson D. *George F. Kennan and the Making of American Foreign Policy, 1947–1950*. Princeton, NJ: Princeton University Press, 1992.

Mitrovich, Gregory. *Undermining the Kremlin: America's Strategy to Subvert the Soviet Bloc, 1947–1956*. Ithaca, NY: Cornell University Press, 2000.

Moreno, José. *Barrios in Arms: Revolution in Santo Domingo*. Pittsburgh, PA: University of Pittsburgh Press, 1970.

Morris, Charles R. *Iron Destinies, Lost Opportunities: The Arms Race between the U.S. and USSR, 1945–1987*. New York: Harper and Row, 1988.

Morris, Eric. *Blockade: Berlin and the Cold War*. New York: Stein and Day, 1973.

Moulton, Harland B. *From Superiority to Parity: The United States and the Strategic Arms Race, 1961–1971*. Westport, CT: Greenwood, 1973.

Müllerson, Rein. *Human Rights Diplomacy*. New York: Routledge, 1997.

Murphy, David E., Sergei A. Kondrashev, and George Bailey. *Battleground Berlin: CIA vs. KGB in the Cold War*. New Haven, CT: Yale University Press, 1997.

Nagai, Yonosuke, and Akira Iriye. *The Origins of the Cold War in Asia*. New York: Columbia University Press, 1977.

Nalebuff, Barry. *Brinkmanship and Nuclear Deterrence: The Neutrality of Escalation*. Princeton, NJ: Princeton University Press, 1987.

Nathan, Andrew J., and Perry Link, eds. *The Tiananmen Papers: The Chinese Leadership's Decision to Use Force against Their Own People—In Their Own Words*. New York: Public Affairs Press, 2001.

Nathan, James A. *Anatomy of the Cuban Missile Crisis*. Westport, CT: Greenwood, 2001.

Navazelskis, Ina L. *Leonid Brezhnev*. Langhorne, PA: Chelsea House, 1987.

Naylor, Thomas H. *The Cold War Legacy*. Lexington, MA: Lexington Books, 1991.

Nelson, Deborah. *Pursuing Privacy in Cold War America*. New York: Columbia University Press, 2002.

Neufeld, Jacob. *The Development of Ballistic Missiles in the United States Air Force, 1945–1960*. Washington, DC: Office of Air Force History, 1989.

Neville, John F. *The Press, the Rosenbergs, and the Cold War*. Westport, CT: Praeger, 1995.

Newhouse, John. *Cold Dawn: The Story of SALT*. New York: Holt, Rinehart and Winston, 1973.

Nichols, Thomas M. *Winning the World: Lessons for America's Future from the Cold War*. Westport, CT: Praeger, 2002.

Nincic, Miroslav. *Anatomy of Hostility: The U.S.-Soviet Rivalry in Perspective*. San Diego: Harcourt Brace Jovanovich, 1989.

Nixon, Richard. *RN: The Memoirs of Richard Nixon*. New York: Grosset and Dunlap, 1978.

Norris, Robert S., and William Arkin. "Known Nuclear Tests Worldwide, 1945–1948." *Bulletin of the Atomic Scientists* 54, no. 6 (November/December 1998): 65–67.

O'Ballance, Edgar. *The Wars in Vietnam, 1954–1960*. New York: Hippocrene, 1981.

O'Neill, Bard E. "Insurgency: A Framework for Analysis." In *Insurgency in the Modern World*, edited by Bard E. O'Neill, William R. Heaton, and Donald J. Alberts, 1–42. Boulder, CO: Westview, 1980.

O'Neill, William L. *American High: The Years of Confidence, 1945–1960*. New York: Free Press, 1986.

Oakes, Guy. *The Imaginary War: Civil Defense and American Cold War Culture*. New York: Oxford University Press, 1994.

Oberdorfer, Don. *From the Cold War to a New Era: The United States and the Soviet Union, 1983–1991*. Baltimore: Johns Hopkins University Press, 1998.

Offner, Arnold A. *Another Such Victory: President Truman and the Cold War, 1945–1953*. Stanford, CA: Stanford University Press, 2002.

Oren, Michael. *The Six Day War*. Novato, CA: Presidio, 2002.

Ost, David. *Solidarity and the Process of Anti-Politics: Opposition and Reform in Poland since 1968*. Philadelphia: Temple University Press, 1990.

Ostrower, Gary B. *The United Nations and the United States*. New York: Twayne, 1998.

Ovendale, Ritchie. *The English-Speaking Alliance: Britain, the United States, the Dominions, and the Cold War, 1945–1951*. Boston: Allen and Unwin, 1985.

Painter, David S. *The Cold War: An International History*. New York: Routledge, 1999.

Palmer, General Bruce, Jr. *The 25-Year War: America's Military Role in Vietnam*. Lexington: University Press of Kentucky, 1984.

Parkinson, F. *Latin America, the Cold War & the World Powers, 1945–1973: A Study in Diplomatic History*. Beverly Hills, CA: Sage, 1974.

Parry-Giles, Shawn J. *The Rhetorical Presidency, Propaganda, and the Cold War, 1945–1955*. Westport, CT: Praeger, 2002.

Partos, Gabriel. *The World That Came in from the Cold: Perspectives from East and West on the Cold War*. London: Royal Institute of International Affairs, BBC World Service, 1993.

Pastor, Robert. *The Carter Administration and Latin America*. Occasional Paper Series, Vol. 2, No. 3. Atlanta, GA: Carter Center of Emory University, 1992.

Paterson, Thomas G. *On Every Front: The Making and Unmaking of the Cold War*. New York: Norton, 1992.

Paterson, Thomas G. *Soviet-American Confrontation: Postwar Reconstruction and the Origins of the Cold War*. Baltimore: Johns Hopkins University Press, 1973.

Pavlowitch, Steven K. *Tito, Yugoslavia's Great Dictator: A Reassessment*. Columbus: Ohio State University Press, 1992.

Payne, Keith B. *The Fallacies of Cold War Deterrence and a New Direction*. Lexington: University Press of Kentucky, 2001.

Pedlow, Gregory W., and Donald Welzenbach. *The CIA and the U-2 Program, 1954–1974*. Washington, DC: Central Intelligence Agency, 1998.

Peebles, Curtis. *Shadow Flights: America's Secret War against the Soviet Union: A Cold War History*. Novato, CA: Presidio, 2001.

Pemberton, William E. *Exit with Honor: The Life and Presidency of Ronald Reagan*. Armonk, NY: Sharpe, 1997.

Peng, Chin. *Alias Chin Peng: My Side of History*. Singapore: Media Masters, 2003.

Perret, Geoffrey. *Eisenhower*. New York: Random House, 1999.

Pessen, Edward. *Losing Our Souls: The American Experience in the Cold War*. Chicago: Ivan R. Dee, 1993.

Pierpaoli, Paul G., Jr. *Truman and Korea: The Political Culture of the Early Cold War*.

Columbia: University of Missouri Press, 1999.

Pollard, Robert A. *Economic Security and the Origins of the Cold War*. New York: Columbia University Press, 1985.

Powaski, Ronald E. *March to Armageddon: The United States and the Nuclear Arms Race, 1939 to the Present*. New York: Oxford University Press, 1987.

Powaski, Ronald E. *Return to Armageddon: The United States and the Nuclear Arms Race, 1981–1999*. New York: Oxford University Press, 2000.

Powaski, Ronald E. *The Cold War: The United States and the Soviet Union, 1917–1991*. New York: Oxford University Press, 1998.

Powers, Francis Gary, with Curt Gentry. *Operation Overflight: A Memoir of the U-2 Incident*. Washington, DC: Brassey's, 2004.

Powers, Richard Gid. *Secrecy and Power: The Life of J. Edgar Hoover*. New York: Free Press, 1988.

Prados, John. *Presidents' Secret Wars: CIA and Pentagon Covert Operations from World War II through the Persian Gulf*. Chicago. IL: Ivan R. Dee, 1996.

Puddington, Arch. *Broadcasting Freedom: The Cold War Triumph of Radio Free Europe and Radio Liberty*. Lexington: University Press of Kentucky, 2000.

Pulzer, Peter G.J. *German Politics, 1945–1995*. Oxford: Oxford University Press, 1995.

Quandt, William B. *Peace Process: American Diplomacy and the Arab-Israeli Conflict since 1967*. Washington, DC: Brookings Institution and University of California Press, 1993.

Ramakrishna, Kumar. *Emergency Propaganda: The Winning of Malayan Hearts and Minds, 1948–1958*. London: Curzon, 2002.

Ramsden, John. *Man of the Century: Churchill and His Legend since 1945*. New York: Columbia University Press, 2002.

Randle, Robert F. *Geneva 1954: The Settlement of the Indochinese War*. Princeton, NJ: Princeton University Press, 1969.

Ranelagh, John. *The Agency: The Rise and Decline of the CIA, from Wild Bill Donovan to William Casey*. New York: Simon and Schuster, 1986.

Reagan, Ronald. *An American Life: The Autobiography*. New York: Simon & Schuster, 1990.

Reed, Thomas. *At the Abyss: An Insider's History of the Cold War*. New York: Presidio/Ballantine, 2004.

Reeves, Thomas C. *The Life and Times of Joe McCarthy*. 1980. Reprint. Lanham, MD: Madison Books, 1997.

Reynolds, David. *From World War to Cold War: Churchill, Roosevelt, and the International History of the 1940s*. Oxford: Oxford University Press, 2006.

Reynolds, David, ed. *The Origins of the Cold War in Europe: International Perspectives*. New Haven, CT: Yale University Press, 1994.

Rhodes, Richard. *Dark Sun: The Making of the Hydrogen Bomb*. New York: Simon and Schuster, 1995.

Roberts, Geoffrey. *The Soviet Union in World Politics: Coexistence, Revolution, and Cold War, 1945–1991*. New York: Routledge, 1999.

Roberts, Walter R. *Tito, Mihailovi□, and the Allies, 1941–1945*. New Brunswick, NJ: Rutgers University Press, 1973.

Robin, Ron Theodore. *The Making of the Cold War Enemy: Culture and Politics in the Military-Intellectual Complex*. Princeton, NJ: Princeton University Press, 2001.

Robinson, Thomas W., and David Shambaugh, eds. *Chinese Foreign Policy: Theory and Practice*. Oxford, UK: Clarendon, 1998.

Rodman, Peter W. *More Precious Than Peace: The Cold War and the Struggle for the Third World*. New York: Scribner, 1994.

Rose, Kenneth. *One Nation Underground: The Fallout Shelter in American Culture*. New York: New York University Press, 2001.

Rose, Lisle Abbott. *The Cold War Comes to Main Street: America in 1950*. Lawrence: University Press of Kansas, 1999.

Ross, Robert S., and Changbin Jiang, eds. *Re-examining the Cold War: U.S.-China Diplomacy, 1954–1973*. Cambridge: Harvard University Press, 2001.

Rothwell, Victor. *Britain and the Cold War, 1941–1947*. London: Cape, 1982.

Roy, Jules. *The Battle of Dienbienphu*. New York: Harper and Row, 1965.

Rusk, Dean. *As I Saw It*. New York: Norton, 1990.

Russian General Staff. *The Soviet-Afghan War: How a Superpower Fought and Lost*. Lawrence: University of Kansas Press, 2002.

Ryan, Henry Butterfield. *The Vision of Anglo-America: The US-UK Alliance and the Emerging Cold War, 1943–1946*. New York: Cambridge University Press, 1987.

Ryan, James Daniel. *The United Nations under Kurt Waldheim, 1972–1981*. Lanham, MD: Scarecrow, 2001.

Sachar, Abram L. *The Redemption of the Unwanted: From the Liberation of the Death Camps to the Founding of Israel*. New York: St. Martin's, 1983.

Sachar, Howard M. *A History of Israel: From the Rise of Zionism to Our Time*. New York: Knopf, 1976.

Sainteny, Jean. *Ho Chi Minh and His Vietnam: A Personal Memoir*. Chicago: Cowles, 1972.

Sakharov, Andrei. *Memoirs*. Translated by Richard Lourie. New York: Knopf, 1990.

Salisbury, Harrison E. *The New Emperors: China in the Era of Mao and Deng*. Boston: Little, Brown, 1992.

Samuel, Wolfgang W.E. *I Always Wanted to Fly: America's Cold War Airmen*. Jackson: University Press of Mississippi, 2001.

Sanders, Jerry Wayne. *Peddlers of Crisis: The Committee on the Present Danger and the Politics of Containment*. Boston: South End Press, 1983.

Sarotte, M.E. *Dealing with the Devil: East Germany, Detente, and Ostpolitik, 1969–1973*. Chapel Hill: University of North Carolina Press, 2001.

Saunders, Frances Stonor. *The Cultural Cold War: The CIA and the World of Arts and Letters*. New York: New Press/Norton, 2000.

Sayegh, Fayez. "Arab Nationalism and Soviet-American Relations." *Annals of the American Academy of Political and Social Science* 324, Resolving the Russian-American Deadlock (July 1959): 103–10.

Schaffel, Kenneth. *The Emerging Shield: The Air Force and the Evolution of Continental Air Defense, 1945–1960*. Office of Air Force History. Washington, DC: U.S. Government Printing Office, 1990.

Schaub, Thomas Hill. *American Fiction in the Cold War*. Madison: University of Wisconsin Press, 1991.

Schefter, James L. *The Race*. New York: Doubleday, 1999.

Schelling, Thomas C. *The Strategy of Conflict*. New York: Oxford University Press USA, 1965.

Schlain, Avi. *The United States and the Berlin Blockade, 1948–1949: A Study in Decision-Making*. Berkeley: University of California Press, 1983.

Schlesinger, Arthur M. *A Thousand Days: John F. Kennedy in the White House*. New York: Houghton Mifflin, 1965.

Schlesinger, Stephen C. *Act of Creation: The Founding of the United Nations; A Story of Superpowers, Secret Agents, Wartime Allies and Enemies, and Their Quest for a Peaceful World*. Boulder, CO: Westview, 2003.

Schmidt, Gustave, ed. *A History of NATO: The First Fifty Years*. 3 vols. New York: Palgrave Macmillan, 2001.

Schneider, Peter. *The Evolution of NATO: The Alliance's Strategic Concept and Its Predecessors, 1945–2000*. München: Institut für Internationale Politik, Universität der Bundeswehr München, 2000.

Schoenbaum, David. *The United States and the State of Israel*. New York: Oxford University Press, 1993.

Schraeder, Peter. *African Politics and Society: A Mosaic in Transformation*. New York: St. Martin's, 2000.

Schraeder, Peter J. *United States Foreign Policy toward Africa: Incrementalism, Cri-

sis and Change. Cambridge: Cambridge University Press, 1994.

Schrecker, Ellen, ed. *Cold War Triumphalism: The Misuse of History after the Fall of Communism*. New York: New Press, 2004.

Schrecker, Ellen. *Many Are the Crimes: McCarthyism in America*. Princeton, NJ: Princeton University Press, 1998.

Schulzinger, Robert D. *A Time for War: The United States and Vietnam, 1941–1975*. New York: Oxford University Press, 1997.

Schulzinger, Robert D. *Henry Kissinger: Doctor of Diplomacy*. New York: Columbia University Press, 1989.

Schweizer, Peter. *Reagan's War: The Epic Story of His Forty Year Struggle and Final Triumph over Communism*. New York: Doubleday, 2002.

Schweizer, Peter. *The Fall of the Berlin Wall: Reassessing the Causes and Consequences of the End of the Cold War*. Stanford, CA: Hoover Institution Press, 2000.

Schweizer, Peter. *Victory: The Reagan Administration's Secret Strategy That Hastened the Collapse of the Soviet Union*. New York: Atlantic Monthly Press, 1994.

Seaborg, Glenn, with Benjamin S. Loeb. *Kennedy, Khrushchev, and the Test Ban*. Berkeley: University of California Press, 1981.

Seldon, Anthony. *Churchill's Indian Summer: The Conservative Government, 1951–55*. London: Hodder and Stoughton, 1981.

Senarclens, Pierre de. *From Yalta to the Iron Curtain: The Great Powers and the Origins of the Cold War*. Washington, DC: Berg, 1995.

Shannon, Christopher. *A World Made Safe for Differences: Cold War Intellectuals and the Politics of Identity*. Lanham, MD: Rowman and Littlefield, 2001.

Sheehan, Neil. *The Pentagon Papers As Published by the New York Times*. New York: Quadrangle, 1971.

Sibley, Katherine A. S. *The Cold War*. Westport, CT: Greenwood, 1998.

Sidey, Hugh. *John F. Kennedy, President*. New York: Atheneum, 1964.

Siebers, Tobin. *Cold War Criticism and the Politics of Skepticism*. New York: Oxford University Press, 1993.

Simons, Jeff. *The United Nations: A Chronology of Conflict*. New York: St. Martin's, 1994.

Simons, Thomas W. *The End of the Cold War?* New York: St. Martin's, 1990.

Singham, A. W., and Shirley Hune. *Non-Alignment in an Age of Alignments*. Westport, CT: Lawrence Hill, 1986.

Skilling, Gordon. *Czechoslovakia's Interrupted Revolution*. Princeton, NJ: Princeton University Press, 1976.

Smith, Denis. *Diplomacy of Fear: Canada and the Cold War, 1941–1948*. Toronto: University of Toronto Press, 1988.

Smith, Geoffrey. *Reagan and Thatcher*. New York: Norton, 1991.

Smith, Gerard. *Doubletalk: The Story of SALT I by the Chief American Negotiator*. New York: Doubleday, 1980.

Smith, Mark. *NATO Enlargement during the Cold War: Strategy and System in the Western Alliance*. New York: Palgrave Macmillan, 2000.

Smith, Wayne. *The Closest of Enemies: A Personal and Diplomatic History of the Castro Years*. New York: Norton, 1987.

Smyser, W. R. *From Yalta to Berlin: The Cold War Struggle over Germany*. New York: St. Martin's, 1999.

Snead, David L. *The Gaither Committee, Eisenhower, and the Cold War*. Columbus: Ohio State University Press, 1999.

Snyder, Alvin A. *Warriors of Disinformation: American Propaganda, Soviet Lies, and the Winning of the Cold War; An Insider's Account*. New York: Arcade, 1995.

Sobel, Lester A. *Disarmament and Nuclear Tests, 1960–1963*. New York: Facts on File Series, Library of Congress, 1964.

Solberg, Carl. *Riding High: America in the Cold War*. New York: Mason and Lipscomb, 1973.

Solzhenitsyn, Aleksandr. *The Gulag Archipelago, 1918–1956: An Experiment in*

Literary Investigation. 3 vols. New York: Harper and Row, 1974–1978.

Spector, Ronald H. *United States Army in Vietnam: Advice and Support; The Early Years, 1941–1960.* Washington, DC: Center of Military History, U.S. Army, 1985.

Spence, Jonathan. *The Search for Modern China.* New York: W.W. Norton, 1990.

Stafford, David. *Spies beneath Berlin.* Woodstock, NY: Overlook Press, 2003.

Stafran, Nadav. *Israel, The Embattled Ally.* Cambridge: Harvard University Press, 1978.

Stebbins, Richard B., and Elaine P. Adams, eds. *American Foreign Relations 1972: A Documentary Record.* New York: New York University Press, 1976.

Stephanson, Anders. *Kennan and the Art of Foreign Policy.* Cambridge: Harvard University Press, 1989.

Stern, Sheldon. *Averting "The Final Failure": John F. Kennedy and the Secret Cuban Missile Crisis Meetings.* Stanford, CA: Stanford University Press, 2003.

Stevenson, Richard William. *The Rise and Fall of Détente: Relaxations of Tensions in US-Soviet Relations, 1953–1984.* Urbana: University of Illinois Press, 1985.

Stone, David. *Wars of the Cold War: Campaigns and Conflicts, 1945–1990.* London: Brassey's, 2004.

Strober, Deborah Hart, and Gerald S. Strober. *The Reagan Presidency: An Oral History of the Era.* Washington, DC: Brassey's, 2003.

Stuart-Fox, Martin. *A History of Laos.* Cambridge: Cambridge University Press, 1997.

Summy, Ralph, and Michael E. Salla. *Why the Cold War Ended: A Range of Interpretations.* Westport, CT: Greenwood, 1995.

Talbott, Strobe. *Deadly Gambits: The Reagan Administration and the Stalemate in Nuclear Arms Control.* New York: Knopf, 1984.

Talbott, Strobe. *Endgame: The Inside Story of Salt II.* New York: HarperCollins, 1979.

Talbott, Strobe. *The Master of the Game: Paul Nitze and the Nuclear Peace.* New York: Knopf, 1988.

Tanham, George K. *Communist Revolutionary Warfare: The Vietminh in Indochina.* Santa Monica, CA: RAND Corporation, 1961.

Tarling, Nicholas. *Britain, Southeast Asia and the Onset of the Cold War, 1945–1950.* Cambridge and New York: Cambridge University Press, 1998.

Taubman, Philip. *Secret Empire: Eisenhower, the CIA, and the Hidden Story of America's Space Espionage.* New York: Simon and Schuster, 2003.

Taubman, William S. *Khrushchev: The Man and His Era.* New York: Norton, 2003.

Taylor, Richard. *Against the Bomb: The British Peace Movement, 1958–1965.* Oxford, UK: Clarendon, 1985.

Terchek, Ronald J. *The Making of the Test Ban Treaty.* The Hague: Martinus Nijhoff, 1970.

Theoharis, Athan G. *Chasing Spies: How the FBI Failed in Counterintelligence but Promoted the Politics of McCarthyism in the Cold War Years.* Chicago: Ivan R. Dee, 2002.

Theoharis, Athan G., and John Stuart Cox. *The Boss: J. Edgar Hoover and the Great American Inquisition.* Philadelphia: Temple University Press, 1988.

Thompson, Robert. *Defeating Communist Insurgency: The Lessons of Malaya and Vietnam.* New York: Praeger, 1966.

Thompson, Robert. *Revolutionary War in World Strategy.* London: Secker and Warburg, 1970.

Thompson, Robert Smith. *The Missiles of October: The Declassified Story of John F. Kennedy and the Cuban Missile Crisis.* New York: Simon and Schuster, 1992.

Todd, Allen. *The European Dictatorships: Hitler, Stalin, Mussolini.* Cambridge: Cambridge University Press, 2002.

Toulouse, Mark G. *The Transformation of John Foster Dulles: From Prophet of Realism to Priest of Nationalism.* Macon, GA: Mercer University Press, 1985.

Tucker, Aviezer. *The Philosophy and Politics of Czech Dissidence from Patočka to Havel.* Pittsburgh, PA: Pittsburgh University Press, 2000.

Tucker, Robert C. *Stalin As Revolutionary, 1879–1929.* New York: Norton, 1973.

Tucker, Robert C. *Stalin in Power: The Revolution from Above, 1928–1941.* New York: Norton, 1990.

Tucker, Spencer C. *Vietnam.* Lexington: University Press of Kentucky, 1999.

Tusa, Ann. *The Last Division: A History of Berlin, 1945–1989.* Reading, MA: Addison-Wesley, 1997.

Tyroler, Charles, II. *Alerting America: The Papers of the Committee on the Present Danger.* Washington, DC: Pergamon-Brassey's, 1984.

Ulam, Adam B. *Stalin: The Man and His Era.* Expanded ed. Boston: Beacon, 1989.

Ulam, Bruno Adam. *Understanding the Cold War: A Historian's Personal Reflections.* Piscataway, NJ: Transaction Publishers, 2002.

U.S. Department of State. *Foreign Relations of the United States, 1945–1950: Emergence of the Intelligence Establishment.* Washington, DC: U.S. Government Printing Office, 1996.

Vale, Lawrence J. *The Limits of Civil Defense in the USA: Switzerland, Britain, and the Soviet Union; The Evolution of Policies since 1945.* New York: St. Martin's, 1987.

VanDeMark, Brian. *Into the Quagmire: Lyndon Johnson and the Escalation of the Vietnam War.* New York: Oxford University Press, 1991.

Vo Nguyen Giap. *Dien Bien Phu.* Hanoi: Gioi, 1994.

Vo Nguyen Giap. *People's War, People's Army.* New York: Praeger, 1962.

Vogele, William B. *Stepping Back: Nuclear Arms Control and the End of the Cold War.* Westport, CT: Praeger, 1994.

Volkogonov, Dimitrii. *Stalin: Triumph and Tragedy.* Translated and edited by Harold Shukman. New York: Grove Weidenfeld, 1991.

Walker, Martin. *The Cold War: A History.* New York: Holt, 1994.

Wallensteen, Peter, and Karin Axell. "Armed Conflict at the End of the Cold War, 1989–92." *Journal of Peace Research* 30, no. 3 (August 1993): 331–46.

Waller, Douglas C. *The Strategic Defense Initiative, Progress and Challenges: A Guide to Issues and References.* Claremont, CA: Regina Books, 1987.

Weiler, Peter. *British Labour and the Cold War.* Stanford, CA: Stanford University Press, 1988.

Weinstein, Allen. *Perjury: The Hiss-Chambers Case.* New York: Knopf, 1978.

West, Richard. *Tito and the Rise and Fall of Yugoslavia.* New York: Carroll and Graf, 1994.

Westad, Odd Arne, ed. *Brothers in Arms: The Rise and the Fall of the Sino-Soviet Alliance, 1945–1953.* Washington, DC: Woodrow Wilson Center Press, 1998.

Westad, Odd Arne. *Reviewing the Cold War: Approaches, Interpretations, and Theory.* Portland, OR: Frank Cass, 2000.

Westad, Odd Arne. *The Global Cold War: Third World Interventions and the Making of Our Times.* Cambridge: Cambridge University Press, 2005.

Whitaker, Reg, and Greg Marcuse. *Cold War Canada: The Making of a National Insecurity State, 1945–1957.* Toronto: University of Toronto Press, 1996.

Whitcomb, Roger S. *The Cold War in Retrospect: The Formative Years.* Westport, CT: Praeger, 1998.

White, G. Edward. *Alger Hiss's Looking-Glass Wars: The Covert Life of a Soviet Spy.* Oxford: Oxford University Press, 2004.

White, Mark J. *The Kennedys and Cuba: The Declassified Documentary History.* Chicago: Ivan R. Dee, 1999.

Whitfield, Stephen J. *The Culture of the Cold War.* 2nd ed. Baltimore: Johns Hopkins University Press, 1996.

Willetts, Peter. *The Non-Aligned Movement: The Origins of a Third World Alliance.* New York: Nichols, 1978.

Williams, Kieran. *The Prague Spring and Its Aftermath: Czechoslovak Politics, 1968–1970.* Cambridge: Cambridge University Press, 1997.

Wilson, Duncan. *Tito's Yugoslavia.* New York: Cambridge University Press, 1979.

Winik, Jay. *On the Brink: The Dramatic, Behind-the-Scenes Saga of the Reagan Era and the Men and Women Who Won the Cold War*. New York: Simon and Schuster, 1996.

Winkler, David F. *Cold War at Sea: High-Seas Confrontation between the United States and the Soviet Union*. Annapolis, MD: Naval Institute Press, 2000.

Wittner, Lawrence S. *Rebels against War: The American Peace Movement, 1933–1983*. Philadelphia: Temple University Press, 1984.

Wittner, Lawrence S. *Resisting the Bomb: A History of the World Nuclear Disarmament Movement*. Stanford, CA: Stanford University Press, 1997.

Wohlforth, William Curti. *The Elusive Balance: Power and Perceptions during the Cold War*. Ithaca, NY: Cornell University Press, 1993.

Wolfe, Thomas W. *The SALT Experience*. Cambridge, MA: Ballinger, 1979.

Woods, Randall Bennett, and Howard Jones. *Dawning of the Cold War: The United States' Quest for Order*. Athens: University of Georgia Press, 1991.

Woodward, Bob. *Veil: The Secret Wars of the CIA, 1981–1987*. New York: Simon and Schuster, 1987.

Wyden, Peter. *The Bay of Pigs: The Untold Story*. New York: Vintage/Ebury, 1979.

Yegorov, Pavel Timofaevich. *Civil Defense: A Soviet View*. Honolulu: University Press of the Pacific, 2002.

Yeltsin, Boris. *Against the Grain*. New York: Summit, 1999.

Yeltsin, Boris. *The Struggle for Russia*. New York: Random House, 1994.

Yergin, Daniel H. *Shattered Peace: The Origins of the Cold War*. New York: Penguin, 1990.

Yohannes, Okbazghi. *The United States and the Horn of Africa: An Analytical Study of Pattern and Process*. Boulder, CO: Westview, 1997.

Young, John W. *Cold War Europe, 1945–1991: A Political History*. 2nd ed. New York: St. Martin's, 1996.

Young, John W. *France, the Cold War, and the Western Alliance, 1944–49: French Foreign Policy and Post-War Europe*. New York: St. Martin's, 1990.

Young, John W. *The Longman Companion to Cold War and Detente, 1941–91*. New York: Longman, 1993.

Young, John W. *Winston Churchill's Last Campaign: Britain and the Cold War, 1951–5*. New York: Clarendon, 1996.

Zubok, Vladislav, and Constantine Pieshakov. *Inside the Kremlin's Cold War: From Stalin to Khrushchev*. Cambridge: Harvard University Press, 1996.

Editors and Contributors

Editors

James R. Arnold
Independent Scholar

Roberta Wiener
Independent Scholar

Contributors

Dr. Valerie Adams
Embry-Riddle Aeronautical University

Dr. Dewi I. Ball
Independent Scholar

Lacie A. Ballinger
Independent Scholar

Dr. Jakub Basista
Institute of History
Jagiellonian University
Poland

Robert G. Berschinski
Independent Scholar

Frank Beyersdorf
University of Heidelberg
Germany

Anna Boros-McGee
Independent Scholar

Christopher John Bright
Independent Scholar

Colonel George M. Brooke III (retired)
Virginia Military Institute

Barry Carr
Department of History
La Trobe University
Australia

Phillip Deery
Victoria University
Australia

Dr. Bruce J. DeHart
Department of History
University of North Carolina at Pembroke

Dr. Jérôme Dorvidal
University of La Reunion
Réunion

Dr. Timothy C. Dowling
Associate Professor of History
Virginia Military Institute

Jaroslav Dvorak
Klaipeda University
Lithuania

Dr. Lee W. Eysturlid
Department of History
Illinois Mathematics and Science Academy

Dr. Richard M. Filipink Jr.
Associate Professor
Western Illinois University

Dr. Philipp Gassert
DAAD Visiting Professor of History
University of Pennsylvania

Beatrice de Graaf
Institute for History
University of Utrecht
Netherlands

Magarditsch Hatschikjan
Department of East European History
University of Cologne
Germany

Kurt Heinrich
Independent Scholar

James J. Hentz
Professor and Chair, Department
of International Studies
Virginia Military Insitute

John C. Horn
Department of History
University of Victoria

Dr. Donna R. Jackson
Wolfson College, Cambridge

A. Ross Johnson
Research Fellow
Hoover Institution

Brian Madison Jones
University of North Carolina at Charlotte

Dr. Melissa Jordine
California State University, Fresno

Robert S. Kiely
Independent Scholar

Dr. Arne Kislenko
Ryerson University
Canada

Jonathan H. L'Hommedieu
University of Turku
Finland

Dr. Jeffrey A. Larsen
Science Applications International
Corporation

Daniel Lewis
Department of History
California Polytechnic State University

Arturo Lopez-Levy
Independent Scholar

Dr. Lorenz M. Lüthi
Assistant Professor
McGill University
Canada

Dr. Jerome V. Martin
Command Historian
U.S. Strategic Command

Dr. James I. Matray
Professor and Chair of History
Department of History
California State University, Chico

A. Gregory Moore
Department of History
Notre Dame College

Caryn E. Neumann
Miami University of Ohio

Dr. Christian Nuenlist
University of Zurich
Switzerland

Dr. Vernon L. Pedersen
University of Great Falls

Allene Phy-Olsen
Languages/Literature Department
Austin Peay State University

Dr. Paul G. Pierpaoli Jr.
Fellow
Military History, ABC-CLIO, Inc.

Dr. Michael Richards
Department of History
Sweet Briar College

Dr. Priscilla Roberts
Associate Professor of History, School of Humanities
Honorary Director, Centre of American Studies
University of Hong Kong

Bevan Sewell
De Montfort University
United Kingdom

Colonel Charles G. Simpson (retired)
Executive Director
Association of Air Force Missileers

Dr. Larry Simpson
Department of History
High Point University

Sarah B. Snyder
Cassius Marcellus Clay Fellow
Yale University

Dr. Daniel E. Spector
Independent Scholar

Dr. David Tal
Emroy University

Dr. Aviezer Tucker
Queens University
Northern Ireland

Dr. Spencer C. Tucker
Senior Fellow
Military History, ABC-CLIO, Inc.

Josh Ushay
Independent Scholar

Joseph Robert White
Department of History
University of Pittsburgh

Dr. James H. Willbanks
Director
Department of Military History
U.S. Army Command and General Staff College, Fort Leavenworth

Law Yuk-fun
Shue Yan University
China

Index

About the Editors

James R. Arnold is a military historian and the author of more than 20 books, including *Grant Wins the War: Decision at Vicksburg* and *Jungle of Snakes: A Century of Counterinsurgency Warfare from the Philippines to Iraq*. His most recent book, *The Moro War: How America Battled a Muslim Insurgency in the Philippine Jungle, 1902–1913*, was published in 2011.

Roberta Wiener is managing editor of the *Journal of Military History* and a contributor to several ABC-CLIO encyclopedias, including *The Encyclopedia of North American Colonial Conflicts to 1775: A Political, Social, and Military History*.